PHILOSOPHY
FOR ADULTS

Thomas O. Buford
Furman University

My thanks to those delightful people who having worked all day came to Furman University at night to study philosophy. Their suggestions have saved this text from serious errors. But more, their enthusiasm for this approach to philosophical study has been encouraging. My thanks to Louis Phillips, Director of Continuing Education at Furman, for first suggesting to me that philosophy would be a valuable study for adults. John Crabtree, Academic Dean, and Frank Bonner, Vice President and Provost, along with the Research and Professional Growth Committee of the Faculty have given me invaluable assistance. Peter Bertocci and Ed Casey gave me valuable suggestions and even more valuable encouragement to venture into an unexplored area. Sylvia Livingston in typing the manuscript worked beyond reward. Finally, Dee has always known what it meant.

Furman University
Greenville, South Carolina
December 12, 1979

TABLE OF CONTENTS

vi

PREFACE

The thesis of this text is that philosophy is an important resource for adults as they attempt to develop life structures conducive to happy lives. Stated somewhat differently, philosophy is a valuable resource for persons facing the developmental tasks of adults. While philosophy can be variously defined, the concept employed here is that it is at least a method by which assumptions about what is true, real and valuable are articulated, clarified and evaluated. As adults work through the tasks they face as they move through the stages of adult life, they do so on the basis of assumptions that may be quite different from those of the pre-adult. Decisions made at one stage influence decisions made at later stages, and decisions are significantly influenced by assumptions. Thus it is important to examine constructively as well as critically the assumptions underlying decisions adults make. While other resources are available to adults such as religion and psychiatry, philosophy is uniquely suited to give assumptions the type of examination they need so that adults can fashion satisfying lives.

Philosophy as viewed here is primarily an adult activity. Young people are other directed, undergoing many varied experiences, attempting to establish their own identity, learning for the future, and concerned with physiological and mental maturation. As they begin to create life structures of their own they begin to enter the adult world. When they do they make decisions for themselves that have consequences for their lives—these decisions are made on the basis of assumptions. To live in the adult world then is to create a uniquely self conscious life for oneself. To do this well requires the discipline of philosophy. So that an adult can know he is making the best decisions he needs to examine the evidence which persuades him and the assumption underlying the decisions. Indeed autonomy requires the freedom which comes from controlling one's assumptions rather than being controlled by them. While young people can engage in philosophical studies, the adult seeking full autonomy is in the best position to utilize the full resources of philosophy. Also, the adult in creating life structures as he faces developmental tasks utilizes his experiences, both past and present. Adults have lived through many situations, events, crises, good times, and they call on this background to help them face the tasks of changing adulthood. Also, new developmental tasks produce a readiness to learn. He wants to learn not only new facts and new skills but also about himself. Indeed it is important to understand oneself when approaching a new challenge in adult life. And this means articulating, clarifying and evaluating assumptions being carried into the new challenge. Because of the wealth of experiences the adult brings to the new learning situation, he is in an excellent situation to evaluate carefully his beliefs and values. Finally, the adult going through a transition from one life structure to another is not interested in learning for the future. Philosophy is valuable to him not because it is a method designed for examining possible future assumptions and life structures that could be built on them (although that is possible) but because it is a way of examining assumptions held now. As the adult faces the difficulties of creating endlessly his life he needs resources to help him now. Philosophy, as a way of articulating, clarifying and evaluating assumptions, must be employed by the adult to act autonomously when facing present developmental tasks. A failure to do so could lead to acting with prejudice or to creating unintentionally unproductive life structures. So, philosophy is a valuable resource for adults who are working through the problems of creating satisfying patterns of living.

The text is designed to teach adults how to work through basic life-like cases in the hope that they can learn philosophical skills and apply them to their own lives. The method employed is the case method. At the beginning of each section is a case. Each case is a situation drawn either from my own experience or from that of people I know. They are also similar enough to those of the readers of this book that they should provoke the response, "Yes, I know what you are talking about," or "I understand; I've been there too." To work through the issues of the cases it would be helpful to have a great deal more information. But, no case could be described in such detail that additional information would not be needed. All that a problematic situation can do is to raise a problem which will suggest one or more possible solutions. In each case a <u>claim</u> is made about what is true, real or good. That claim is based on <u>presuppositions</u>. These presuppositions are believed to be correct. To decide that, however, sound philosophical procedures are required. The methods discussed and used by Socrates will be helpful in thinking through the presuppositions. Following each case are essays included to guide one through an examination of the presuppositions uncovered in the cases. These essays will provide not only clarifying definitions and distinctions but also arguments useful in evaluating the presupposition. As a result of working through the presuppositions evidenced in the cases and addressed in the essays the student will have examined some important dimensions of his own life and will be able to carry the approach beyond the confines of this text.

INTRODUCTION

Every adult is a philosopher. In the changing patterns and stages of their lives, adults face problems which drive them to examine again and again those beliefs and values which form the basis of their life styles. Most of us may not think of ourselves as philosophers, but when we attempt to think through our presuppositions about what is real and what is valuable we are engaged in philosophical work. The purpose of this book is to help adults to become better philosophers by discussing both how philosophers go about their work and some of the major problems adults face. Also adults are asked to sharpen their philosophical tools by doing some philosophical thinking on their own.

Philosophical thinking takes place in the context of life, and for the adult this means that they do their philosophical thinking when crises and periods of transition focus their attention on those fundamental assumptions around which their patterns of life are developed. The old myth that only young people go through stages as they grow to adulthood has been rejected, and such writers as Erik Erikson and Gail Sheehy have fully discussed the types of changes adults are likely to face.[1] Changes in life continue to occur until death; what may be a satisfactory pattern for a person in his twenties may not be satisfactory for that person in his forties. The transitional periods and subsequent stages are often accompanied by emotional upheavals, interpersonal problems, changes in economic status, or a questioning of meaning of life. To deal with these problems people turn to psychiatrists, friends, business associates, and ministers. Yet, basic to these transitional periods are issues which are fundamentally philosophical in character. If these issues are to be thought through carefully then a person needs to develop his philosophical skills as fully as possible. Dealing creatively with life's problems emerging in the changing patterns of adult life requires more than an awareness, an acceptance, and control of feelings and interpersonal relationships; disciplined philosophical thought is a must. If adults are to become better philosophers, it is important to understand the nature of philosophy, the main periods of adult life, and some of the philosophical problems adults face in the changing patterns of their lives.

The attempt to define philosophy has been one of the thorniest problems philosophers have faced since the beginning of their inquiry. It should be no surprise that those who spend their lives attempting to understand the assumptions underlying the thoughts and actions of men should turn their critical gaze on themselves. This spirit of critical inquiry, which is deeply rooted in the philosophical tradition of the West, suggests the following definition: Philosophy is the attempt to interpret rationally the totality of man's experience. As it stands, this statement provides little understanding of the meaning of philosophy as a critically reflective discipline. However, each word is packed with meaning, and through an analysis or "unpacking" of each term the view of philosophy couched therein can be clarified.

The word "attempt" points to the searching character of the philosophical enterprise. It may seem strange to those who are entering the study of philosophy that final answers are rarely if ever given to the questions philosophers raise. It is not in finding so called "final answers" that the vitality of philosophy is based. Rather it is the search, the creative attempt to understand, that invigorates philosophers to continue their work. In a society in which security is a primary concern, particularly economic and political security, it is noteworthy that some people find their security neither in final answers nor in an economic or political system. Rather, security for them is found in searching, in seeking defensible answers to ultimate questions. To what end should men live? What is the nature of man? What method should one use in the search for philosophical understanding? In this anthology, for example, no attempt is made to guide the reader to accept a set of preconceived "final answers" to the questions raised. On the contrary, the search motif is present in setting up the problems adults face in contemporary American society, in outlining the major philosophical issues those problems raise, and in helping adults to do a better job grappling with philosophical issues in their own lives. Part of the search is present in the attempt to outline the problems and issues.

The philosophical search for understanding is carried on in a rational manner. The history of Western philosophy has been conducted on the belief that man through his rational powers is able to understand whatever he considers important to understand. Although some philosophers, such as the skeptic Sextus Empiricus, questioned whether man could know either through sense or through reason, most philosophers remain confident in the capacity of reason to know. Since the beginning of the modern period of philosophy, the nature of reason has been a topic of philosophical investigation. The apex of this philosophical study was achieved by Immanuel Kant in his works, The Critique of Pure Reason, The Critique of Practical Reason, and The Critique of Judgement. Even though "reason" has come under the critical investigation of men such as Kant, it has been through a belief in the capacity of reason to know that those conducting the investigations were confident that they could articulate questions and search for defensible answers. This belief also pervades this anthology.

The attempt to understand in a rational manner is to go about the philosophical search in a particular way. Feelings, intuitions, insights, although important as data for reason in its search, do not guide the search. One could follow their lead if one wanted to do so, but there is nothing in them that is self-corrective, that would allow one to determine the best or the correct answer. To allow reason to guide the search is to proceed in an analytic and a synoptic manner. Reason proceeding analytically divides the data under investigation into parts. But reason does not rest with the data broken into discrete units. It then seeks to put the pieces back together again, to interrelate them, to establish some kind of connectedness within experience. This attempt to view the data of experience from the point of view of the whole is reason operating synoptically. Furthermore, to follow reason in the search is to apply standards of consistency to determine the adequacy of one's analytic and synoptic understanding. In the chapters to follow, the attempt is made to divide the issues adults face into areas, to examine the issues carefully, and to establish interconnections among them.

When the philosophical search is conducted in a rational manner, an attempt is made to achieve self understanding through interpreting a dimension of our living. To interpret an aspect of living is to uncover the assumptions[2] which underlie and guide it, to evaluate critically the assumptions, and to promulgate new ones or retread the old ones. For example, in Section IV the question is asked, "What is the nature of persons?" All of us conduct our lives within the framework of some assumed belief about what personhood means, but few of us attempt to become critically self-conscious about our assumption and to evaluate them. To interpret 'person' is to articulate the beliefs which are assumed or presupposed about persons, to clarify and evaluate the beliefs, and to attempt to advance a defensible theory of person. Philosophers since Plato have investigated the nature of persons and have developed theories which to them were acceptable. Through such investigatory activities an understanding may be gained of areas of experience which are the most direct and immediate experiences persons have. What is learned about these experiences are the assumptions which underlie them and the physical, social, and cultural forces which have contributed to their development. Such achievement of critical self-awareness is a liberating experience. Once one is aware of his assumptions and has critically evaluated them, he is then able to exert some control over his decisions or, at least, to understand the forces influencing him.

Finally, the philosophical search is to be conducted in every area of experience. Nothing is sacrosanct to the critical evaluation of the philosopher's roving eye whether it is personhood, values, existence, or death. Philosophy has as its province for investigation all of man's life and asks ultimate questions about every aspect of human existence. Of course, the areas of human experience under investigation here are limited to those which are dominant in adult life. Within this parameter, however, every aspect of experience is liable to critical study. Without a willingness to examine all relevant data how else could an adequate understanding be achieved?

A final comment about philosophy must be made. The rational search for understanding every dimension of human experience is a paradoxical endeavor. On the one hand, philosophy is the most concrete, "down to earth," personal study one can pursue. Indeed, what is more immediate to us than existing, valuing, dying? On the other hand, philosophy is one of the most abstract studies in which one can become involved. To think about existence, dying, and valuing is to deal with a subject matter which seems distant, obscure, and strange. To become involved in the philosophical quest is to ask questions which drive to the core of the personal dimensions of life, to learn that we often do not really understand ourselves, and to discover that the attempt to understand philosophically is a difficult but liberating task. How philosophy is integrally related to adult life is amplified by examining the stages of adulthood and how philosophical problems arise in those stages.[3]

One way of thinking about the stages people
go through is that developed by Erik Erikson in
Childhood and Society. [4] The first four stages of
psychosocial development are those ranging from
birth to 11 years of age and need not interest us
here except to note that Erikson believes that success in later stages is dependent on success in
earlier stages. The fifth stage of development is
during the teen years, 12 to 18 years. The young
person is faced with the alternatives of identity
and role confusion. During this period he is
working through his own identity. He is seeking
to integrate all that he knows about himself and
the ways people react to him. He is seeking some
sense of where he has been, who he is, and where
he is going. When this understanding is not
achieved he experiences role confusion. The
sixth stage occurs during young adulthood. The
young adult is faced with intimacy vs. isolation.
This stage runs from courtship through early family life. In this stage the person is usually
engaged in productive work and has achieved some
sense of personal identity. He now enters into a
new dimension of interpersonal relationships. By
intimacy Erikson means ability to care about another person and share with that person without
losing one's own sense of personal self. If intimacy is not established with friends or a marriage partner then isolation occurs. Isolation
means to be alone without anyone to care about
and to share with. Generativity vs. self-absorption is the seventh stage in the psychosocial
development of person. Generativity means being
concerned with others beyond the immediate confines of family and close friends. A person is
concerned with the welfare of other people such
as young people and with making this world a better place to live and work. If a person fails to
establish a sense of generativity, he falls into
a state of being overly concerned with himself
and his welfare and cares little for the people
about him. The last stage is integrity vs. despair. In this stage a person is entering old
age. His major efforts to live life have come
almost to a conclusion, and there is time for

reflection. A sense of integrity means that one
can accept one's life with satisfaction. His
life makes sense and can be defended. Feeling
that it is too late to make up for missed opportunities leads to a sense of despair. Thus,
Erikson believes that adults go through stages,
that their lives have a social and a psychological
dimension, that what they did not achieve at earlier stages can be rectified at later stages, and
that while these stages come at different times
for different people much depends on their social
circumstances. While Erikson's analysis may have
its critics, he does force us to recognize that
adult life is constantly changing and possesses
enormous complexity replete with opportunities
for developing meaning.

   Erikson's description of the stages of adult
life can be enriched by noting that at each stage
adults attempt to fashion a way of living within
the framework of a satisfactory life structure.[5]
The life structure is not static. Rather it
changes as adults move through different developmental stages. At each new stage the developmental tasks facing them are those of creating a
life structure satisfactory for that time of their
lives. This life structure, the "fabric of one's
life," is created when a person chooses to become
engaged with some aspects of his world and not
with others. He lives out his life on the basis
of his choices, the relationships he establishes
with his world. Each choice is made on the basis
of beliefs about what is true and false, good and
evil, real and unreal, right and wrong. These
beliefs governing choice are presuppositions, and
they can be called philosophical because they
form the foundation within which a meaningful
life can be created. For example, a young person
in his late teens who believes that a person is
an economic creature whose sole function is to
compete in the market place to satisfy his own
self interests will likely solve the developmental task of establishing his own identity and
create a life structure differently than a person
who believes that a person is made in the image of

God, whose sole function is to love God and love his fellow persons. Furthermore, the identity a person achieves and the corresponding life structure he develops has implications for the way he handles issues later in his life. A belief held in one stage may become a presupposition at a later stage. For example, the individual who solves his identity crisis by seeing himself as motivated solely by economic self-interest could hold that belief as a presupposition when he works through the next developmental stage: intimacy vs. isolation. He could have a great deal of difficulty achieving a sense of intimacy with friends or a marriage partner if the guiding beliefs of previous stages steer him toward isolation. Again, an individual who is primarily concerned about his own self-interests and has never established intimacy with another person will likely become increasingly absorbed with his own interests in the middle of his life. He will probably see little reason to work for the well being of the society to which he is heavily indebted. Not until he has examined critically the conception of human nature he believes to be true will he have any chance of developing a genuine caring attitude about persons other than himself. When he enters the last part of his life and has not understood the conception of man dominating his life it is possible that he will spend his last years despairing over what might have been. Of course, if he has carefully investigated his deepest philosophical beliefs and has freely adopted a viewpoint of unbridled self interest he may be able to defend his actions or he may believe that he was wrong. Yet, at least he freely chose his life and is in a better position to live with the consequences of his choices. Thus, presuppositions, while possibly thickly layered, are at bottom highly influential on the life structures a person creates for himself. Thus, the way a person works through the everyday problems of his life is deeply influenced by his philosophical presuppositions.

While a specific philosophical issue cannot

be limited to specific stages in human development, the experiences of a particular stage tend
to call attention to some issues more than others.
In the search for a sense of identity in the teen
years, how a young person views personhood will influence the way he works through this crisis and
the stages that follow. Young adults concern
themselves with developing intimate relations with
other people and with the responsibilities of establishing a family. While these relations have
their emotional dimensions they also have philosophical dimensions. He approaches this period
with beliefs regarding such topics as life style,
sexual relations, women's liberation, and the
rights of children. In their middle years most
adults broaden their horizons and think about
their relation to the larger world and how to
make it a better place to live in for themselves,
their families, and their children. Their beliefs play a crucial part in their attitudes regarding areas such as the free enterprise system,
the use of wealth, education, and health care.
The end of life is a time for reflection of what
it all means. Attitudes toward death become important to persons living in their final years.
The way they work through this stage is greatly
influenced by belief previously developed in
their lives about personhood and the meaning of
life. The same issues raised in the identity
crisis of youth are raised anew, fresh from the
perspective of old age and long experience.
Achieving integrity or falling into despair is
influenced by the presuppositions a person holds
as he moves into this stage. Obviously these
issues can arise for different people at different times, yet at each stage in his life a person
has basic beliefs which significantly influence
his behavior. Not until these are carefully
thought through and evaluated can a person possess
that level of wholeness or integrity that gives
life its highest meaning.

Achieving integrity in life is not simply a
matter of gaining control of one's feelings and
emotions. It also has a deeply intellectual

dimension, a philosophical dimension. This
achievement depends on knowing oneself, knowing
one's presuppositions about what is true, real,
and good so that he can control them rather than
their controlling him. The failure to state,
clarify, and evaluate presuppositions could result in falling into the negative dimensions of
any one stage and in creating difficulties for
achieving the positive dimensions in later stages.
Any serious attempt to gain this kind of knowledge
of oneself involves the discipline of philosophy.
This means that getting one's life together will
be achieved in the fullest sense when attempting
to work out a philosophy of life. Looked at from
this viewpoint philosophy provides an important
resource for adults who seek meaning and intelli-
gibility in their lives.

Notes

[1]Erik H. Erikson, <u>Childhood and Society</u>, (2nd
ed., rev.; New York: W. W. Norton and Co., 1963)
and Gail Sheehy, <u>Passages</u> (New York: E. P. Dut-
ton, 1976).
[2]In this book 'assumption' and 'presupposition' are being used interchangeably.
[3]This view of philosophy is adopted with
slight revisions from Thomas O. Buford (ed.),
<u>Toward a Philosophy of Education</u> (New York: Holt,
Rinehart and Winston, 1969), pp. 2-4.
[4]Erikson, <u>Childhood and Society</u>, pp. 247-269.
[5]Daniel J. Levinson (et al), <u>The Seasons of a
Man's Life</u> (New York: Ballentine Books, 1978),
pp. 43-44.

I

THE ADULT AND PHILOSOPHY

Introduction

The most important problem for any serious minded adult is living a good life. In recent years adults have begun to recognize that their lives will probably last until they are in their 60's or 70's. Many years are ahead of them, and they want their lives to be satisfying and significant. But with the plethora of alternative life-styles and ways of understanding what a good life is, adults are faced with difficult problems regarding what is a good life, in all its ramifications, and how it is to be achieved. Central to these important issues then are two additional questions: what is an adult so that one can do a good job living that kind of life, and how to go about doing it? While there are important psychological, religious, and social dimensions to these questions, it is important to realize that they are fundamentally philosophical questions and require the resource of philosophy to deal with them. Philosophy can shed some light on what living well means and on what an adult means. In this chapter it is important (1) to explore the way at least one person did philosophy who was an adult and who talked primarily to adults about adult problems and (2) to focus attention on a problem that pervades this book, what is an adult?

Socrates lived in Athens during the golden age of Greek culture. He knew the problems of forging a good life in the midst of the vicissitudes of 5th century A.D. Athenian life: of plenty and poverty, political stability and

1

instability, and peace and war. Throughout his life he was deeply concerned with the art of living. Socrates was beset by the general disillusionment of many regarding traditional Greek religious, moral and educational beliefs and values and the specific moral relativism of the sophists who claimed not only that they could teach a person to live effectively in society but also that gaining status and honor was the only important goal for any man. The sophists believed that once a person knew his interests then he could be taught how to fulfill them. The good life was fulfilling one's own interests. Faced with these challenges, Socrates set about to discover the art of living so that he could realize it in his own life and teach it to others. The art of living, he believed, was basically a matter of achieving virtue in one's life. Thus, Socrates' problem settled to what is virtue and how it is achieved. Virtue for Socrates was not a matter of simply fulfilling one's own interests, desires or needs. It was clear to him that interests vary and some could be self-destructive, while others could be self-fulfilling. He wanted to determine what is in a person's best interest. Finding out what is in one's best interest is not a matter of luck. Rather, becoming virtuous requires intelligence, understanding, and wisdom. It is only on the basis of wisdom and knowledge that one can determine what is and what is not in one's best interest. Reason plays a critical role in the good life. Without reason we could never know the difference between good and evil and hence the difference between those interests that are good and those that are evil. A virtuous person is one who is good at determining what is truly in his best interest and who has the skill to achieve it. Anyone who possesses virtue, arete, has mastered the art of living. The art of living is analogous to the art of making shoes. The craftsman of a pair of shoes picks the kind of leather for the top of the shoes, the type of material he wants for the soles, the kind of stitching he needs, and the design of the shoes. Skillfully he integrates these into a pair of shoes. Yet that which deter-

2

mines his choices at each stage, the selection of
the materials and the design, is the function for
which the shoes are made. The shoes may be used
for hiking or for dress. The use to which the
shoes are put or the function for which the shoes
are made is crucial to the whole enterprise of the
craftsman. That for the sake of which the shoes
are made must be known by the craftsman before he
begins making the shoes. Once the shoes are made
they must function correctly to be called good
shoes. They must do the job they were designed to
do. Analogously, the good craftsman of his own
life picks the "materials" of his life and the
"design" he wants. These decisions are made in
light of the function which he wants his life to
fulfill. Obviously some functions are better than
others. So, the person who is attempting to get
his life together must know to what ends he ought
to live if he is to live well. The kinds of behavior and style of one's life must be selected in
light of the function they are to fulfill, and
they must harmonize with the end; there must be
an integration (integrity) of ends and means. For
Socrates a person who lives well is one who possesses that kind of integrity in his life which
results from a symphony of deeds and words, actions
and knowledge. The artisan of life must not only
possess knowledge of those ends which are best for
him to achieve but also he must habitually act consistently with those ends. It is through habitually acting consistently with justified ends that
a way of life is established. And this way is
one's character. For Socrates a man of virtue is
one who through the mastery of the art of living
has established a good character.

This picture of the art of living raises some
difficult questions. First, what is the content
of the artfully lived life? Supposedly it would
be good and evil. Also, since life is multidi-
mensional it seems that many goods would be appropriate for it. If there are many possible goods,
are they equally good or are some better than
others? These are difficult to answer. Their
force becomes stronger when we recognize the

bewildering number of possible life-styles or ways in which people have seemingly found to live their lives. It seems very difficult to master the art of living in the midst of a plethora of alternatives many of which seem to be equally good. Nevertheless, Socrates is contending that the art of living is a kind of craftsmanship which demands knowledge of that which is best for us to achieve. Living well is not a matter of luck, or acting only on the needs and desires a person might have, or accepting unthinkingly a way of life offered by the society of which one is a part. If living well demands knowledge of good and evil, how is that knowledge to be attained?

When Socrates talked about knowledge he meant knowledge about living life well. He did not spend much time considering the nature of the physical world around him. Rather he was interested in man and the good life. Rather than inquire into nature and its structure, he inquired into man, his behavior, and living well. Socrates believed that we ought to lead lives that can be shown by reason to be good. A person's behavior can be shown to be good if he knows why he did it, that is, the end for the sake of which he behaved the way he did. Furthermore, he must not only be able to state what that end is but also be able to say what is the nature of that end. Only then will he know for sure that what he was doing was right or wrong. Most people act out of habit. Few grasp the assumptions which form the foundation of their life structure well enough to be able to defend their actions. But that is exactly what Socrates believed anyone ought to know. A person's beliefs are usually submerged in his life; yet they are the main influences on behavior. Since these submerged beliefs and values or presuppositions play a crucial role in a person's life, it is important to articulate them, clarify them, and evaluate them. Once this has taken place anyone can then develop a satisfactory defense of his behavior. Socrates' procedure for doing this is called the dialectic. What the dialectic is can be illustrated with an encounter Socrates had with a young

4

man, Euthyphro.

Euthyphro was on his way to charge his father with murder, and he was making the charge on religious grounds. What his father had done was considered by the young man to be impious. Euthyphro was acting on a belief and a value he held; he thought persons ought not to act impiously, and he believed he understood the nature of piety. Socrates began to converse with Euthyphro about the nature of piety. His contention was that if Euthyphro was to do such a drastic thing as take his father to court on charge of murder Euthyphro surely must know precisely the nature of piety. Through a series of questions and answers Socrates sought to help Euthyphro articulate, define, and evaluate the concept of piety, that for the sake of which Euthyphro was charging his father with murder. Socrates wanted Euthyphro to tell him that characteristic which all instances of pious actions have in common. If that characteristic can be specified then the definition of piety would be secured. The problem is to come up with a definition that includes everything that should be included and exludes everything that ought to be excluded. Euthyphro tried to give Socrates a defensible definition, but in each case the definition was shown to be defective. The result of the dialogue between the two men was simple: Euthyphro thought he understood what piety is, but it was clear from the conversation that he did not. Socrates seemed to be hoping that Euthyphro would recognize that he did not know what he thought he knew and would seek to learn the true nature of piety. Even recognizing that he did not know would be a step in the right direction. Unfortunately the young man neither learned the nature of piety nor did he come to see that he did not know. What is important about the encounter is that we see Socrates in action seeking understanding and seeking to help others to understand. We see a way to move in the examination of our deepest presuppositions about what is true, real, and valuable.

Socrates was a man who believed that philosophical understanding was important to anyone who seeks to live life well. He was committed to rationality; only on that basis can anyone save himself from error and find the truth. He was also an adult who talked with other adults about their own lives. He wanted the people he engaged to make sense out of their lives and do it in a careful, precise, orderly, consistent manner. His discussions with them ranged over most of the fundamental aspects of their lives: piety, courage, justice, love, education, art. Those who strive to get integrity, meaning, satisfaction into their lives will find that the Socratic way of philosophy can help them by directing their attention to their presuppositions, by showing them a process by which they can consider critically and constructively those presuppositions. Hopefully they can then be in control of their lives rather than be unthinkingly controlled by beliefs and values held uncritically. Socratic philosophy is a good paradigm to follow in the pursuit of understanding how to live well as adults. With the Socratic method in mind it is time to return to the initial problem of living well as an adult. What it means to live well as an adult is discussed throughout this book. But what is an adult?

Jordan contends that adulthood is a creation of the twentieth century. Only in the last twenty years has the adult received much attention by psychologists and educators. Most studies conducted in the areas of human development and in human learning are investigations of childhood and adolescence. With the work of Erikson and lately of Levinson, adulthood, its changing character and stages, has become an important topic of conversation. People can expect to live forty to fifty years beyond adolescence, and they want to live those years meaningfully and satisfactorily. Once the aspirations are recognized, however, the problem of clarifying the nature of an adult must be faced. What is an adult?

Numerous answers have been given to this question. An adult has been variously defined in terms of age, financial independence, have a job, moral

self-determination, giving oneself permission, a
developed ethical sense, possessing distinctive
types of problems, and legal position. The issue,
however, runs deeper than these social, cultural
considerations. Since every adult would be considered a person, the question arises, what is a
person and what kind of person is an adult person?
It is persons who live well. If living well always
involves ends, that for the sake of which life is
lived, and if being a person is intimately related
to those ends, then understanding the nature of a
person, particularly an adult person, is crucial
to living well as an adult. What is an adult person and how ought he or she live who lives well?
These are questions which are at the base of all
the materials in this book. In this chapter, however, Jordan and Erikson provide some information
and parameters within which the issue of adult
personhood can be approached.

    Learning how to live well as an adult requires
the best information and procedures available to
use. Psychology, sociology, psychotherapy, religion provide useful insights. Yet, many of the
basic issues are philosophical in characher. We
can learn from Socrates how to approach the vast
array of issues with which we grapple, particularly
what is an adult person. We may never settle this
problem because in a fundamental sense it is part
of being persons that we are problems unto ourselves. Yet, some light is available in the passage through adulthood and we must use it to the
best advantage. Our lives depend on it.

Philosophy: The Socratic Way

The Apology*
  Plato

Characters

Socrates

Meletus

Scene—The Court of Justice

Socrates. I do not know what impression my
accusers have made upon you, Athenians. But I do
know that they nearly made me forget who I was, so
persuasive were they. And yet they have scarcely
spoken one single word of truth. Of all their many
falsehoods, the one which astonished me most was
their saying that I was a clever speaker, and that
you must be careful not to let me deceive you. I
thought that it was most shameless of them not to
be ashamed to talk in that way. For as soon as I
open my mouth they will be refuted, and I shall
prove that I am not a clever speaker in any way
at all—unless, indeed, by a clever speaker they
mean someone who speaks the truth. If that is
their meaning, I agree with them that I am an
orator not to be compared with them. My accusers,
I repeat, have said little or nothing that is true,
but from me you shall hear the whole truth. Certainly you will not hear a speech, Athenians,
dressed up, like theirs, with fancy words and
phrases. I will say to you what I have to say,
without artifice, and I shall use the first words
which come to mind, for I believe that what I have

*Reprinted by permission of The Bobbs-Merrill
Company, Inc. from Euthyphro, Apology, and Crito
by Plato and translated by F. J. Church. Copyright © 1956 by The Bobbs-Merrill Company, Inc.

8

to say is just; so let none of you expect anything else. Indeed, my friends, it would hardly be right for me, at my age, to come before you like a schoolboy with his concocted phrases. But there is one thing, Athenians, which I do most earnestly beg and entreat of you. Do not be surprised and do not interrupt with shouts if in my defense I speak in the same way that I am accustomed to speak in the market place, at the tables of the money-changers, where many of you have heard me, and elsewhere. The truth is this: I am more than seventy, and this is the first time that I have ever come before a law court; thus your manner of speech here is quite strange to me. If I had really been a stranger, you would have forgiven me for speaking in the language and the manner of my native country. And so now I ask you to grant me what I think I have a right to claim. Never mind the manner of my speech - it may be superior or it may be inferior to the usual manner. Give your whole attention to the question, whether what I say is just or not? That is what is required of a good judge, as speaking the truth is required of a good orator.

I have to defend myself, Athenians, first against the older false accusations of my old accusers, and then against the more recent ones of my present accusers. For many men have been accusing me to you, and for very many years, who have not spoken a word of truth; and I fear them more than I fear Anytus[1] and his associates, formidable as they are. But, my friends, the others are still more formidable, since they got hold of most of you when you were children and have been more persistent in accusing me untruthfully, persuading you that there is a certain Socrates, a wise man, who speculates about the heavens, who investigates things that are beneath the earth, and who can make the worse argument appear the stronger. These men, Athenians, who spread abroad this report are the accusers whom I fear; for their hearers think that persons who pursue such inquiries never believe in the gods. Besides they are many, their attacks have been going on for a long time, and they spoke to you when you were most ready to believe them, since you were all young, and some of you were children. And there was no one to answer them when they attacked me. The most preposterous thing of all is that I do not even know their names: I cannot tell you who they are except when one happens to be a comic poet. But all the rest who have persuaded you, from motives of resentment and prejudice, and sometimes, it may be, from conviction, are hardest to cope with. For I cannot call any one of them forward in court to cross-examine him. I have, as it were, simply to spar with shadows in my defense, and to put questions which there is no one to answer. I ask you, therefore, to believe that, as I say, I have been attacked by two kinds of accusers—first, by Meletus[2] and his associates, and, then, by those older ones of whom I have spoken. And, with your leave, I will defend myself first against my old accusers, since you heard their accusations first, and they were much more compelling than my present accusers are.

Well, I must make my defense, Athenians, and try in the short time allowed me to remove the prejudice which you have been so long a time acquiring. I hope that I may manage to do this, if it be best for you and for me, and that my defense may be successful; but I am quite aware of the nature of my task, and I know that it is a difficult one. Be the outcome, however, as is pleasing to god, I must obey the law and make my defense.

Let us begin from the beginning, then, and ask what is the accusation that has given rise to the prejudice against me, on which Meletus relied when he brought his indictment. What is the prejudice which my enemies have been spreading about me? I must assume that they are formally accusing me, and read their indictment. It would run somewhat in this fashion: "Socrates is guilty of engaging in inquiries into things beneath the earth and in the heavens, of making the weaker argument appear the stronger, and of teaching others these same things." That is what they say. And in the comedy of Aristophanes[3] you yourselves saw a man called Socrates swinging around in a basket and

saying that he walked on air, and sputtering a
great deal of nonsense about matters of which I
understand nothing at all. I do not mean to dis-
parage that kind of knowledge if there is anyone
who is wise about these matters. I trust Meletus
may never be able to prosecute me for that. But
the truth is, Athenians, I have nothing to do with
these matters, and almost all of you are yourselves
my winesses of this. I beg all of you who have
ever heard me discussing, and they are many, to
inform your neighbors and tell them if any of you
have ever heard me discussing such matters at all.
That will show you that the other common statements
about me are as false as this one.

    But the fact is that not one of these is true.
And if you have heard that I undertake to educate
men, and make money by so doing, that is not true
either, though I think that it would be a fine
thing to be able to educate men, as Gorgias of
Leontini, and Prodicus of Ceos, and Hippias of
Elis do. For each of them, my friends, can go
into any city, and persuade the young men to leave
the society of their fellow citizens, with any of
whom they might associate for nothing, and to be
only too glad to be allowed to pay money for the
privilege of associating with themselves. And I
believe that there is another wise man from Paros
residing in Athens at this moment. I happened to
meet Callias, the son of Hipponicus, a man who has
spent more money on sophists than everyone else
put together. So I said to him (he has two sons),
"Callias, if your two sons had been foals or calves,
we could have hired a trainer for them who would
have trained them to excel in doing what they are
naturally capable of. He would have been either
a groom or a farmer. But whom do you intend to
take to train them, seeing that they are men? Who
understands the excellence which a man and citizen
is capable of attaining? I suppose that you must
have thought of this, because you have sons. Is
there such a person or not?" "Certainly there is,"
he replied. "Who is he," said I, "and where does
he come from, and what is his fee?" "Evenus,
Socrates," he replied, "from Paros, five minae."

Then I thought that Evenus was a fortunate person if he really understood this art and could teach so cleverly. If I had possessed knowledge of that kind, I should have been conceited and disdainful. But, Athenians, the truth is that I do not possess it.

Perhaps some of you may reply: "But, Socrates, what is the trouble with you? What has given rise to these prejudices against you? You must have been doing something different from other men. So tell us what it is, that we may not give our verdict arbitrarily." I think that that is a fair question, and I will try to explain to you what it is that has raised these prejudices against me and given me this reputation. Listen, then. Some of you, perhaps, will think that I am joking, but I assure you that I will tell you the whole truth. I have gained this reputation, Athenians, simply by reason of a certain wisdom. But by what kind of wisdom? It is by just that wisdom which is perhaps human wisdom. In that, it may be, I am really wise. But the men of whom I was speaking just now must be wise in a wisdom which is greater than human wisdom, or else I cannot describe it, for certainly I know nothing of it myself, and if any man says that I do, he lies and speaks to arouse prejudice against me. Do not interrupt me with shouts, Athenians, even if you think that I am boasting. What I am going to say is not my own statement. I will bring the god of Delphi to be the witness of my wisdom, if it is wisdom at all, and of its nature. You remember Chaerephon. From youth upwards he was my comrade; and also a partisan of your democracy, sharing your recent exile[4] and returning with you. You remember, too, Chaerephon's character—how impulsive he was in carrying through whatever he took in hand. Once he went to Delphi and ventured to put this question to the oracle—I entreat you again, my friends, not to interrupt me with your shouts—he asked if there was anyone who was wiser than I. The priestess answered that there was no one. Chaerephon himself is dead, but his brother here will witness to what I say.

Now see why I tell you this. I am going to explain to you how the prejudice against me has arisen. When I heard of the oracle I began to reflect: What can the god mean by this riddle? I know very well that I am not wise, even in the smallest degree. Then what can he mean by saying that I am the wisest of men? It cannot be that he is speaking falsely, for he is a god and cannot lie. For a long time I was at a loss to understand his meaning. Then, very reluctantly, I turned to investigate it in this manner: I went to a man who was reputed to be wise, thinking that there, if anywhere, I should prove the answer wrong, and meaning to point out to the oracle its mistake, and to say, "You said that I was the wisest of men, but this man is wiser than I am." So I examined the man—I need not tell you his name, he was a politician—but this was the result, Athenians. When I conversed with him I came to see that, though a great many persons, and most of all he himself, thought that he was wise, yet he was not wise. Then I tried to prove to him that he was not wise, though he fancied that he was. By so doing I made him indignant, and many of the by-standers. So when I went away, I thought to myself, "I am wiser than this man: neither of us knows anything that is really worth knowing, but he thinks that he has knowledge when he has not, while I, having no knowledge, do not think that I have. I seem at any rate, to be a little wiser than he is on this point: I do not think that I know what I do not know." Next I went to another man who was reputed to be still wiser than the last, with exactly the same result. And there again I made him and many other men, indignant.

Then I went on to one man after another, realizing that I was arousing indignation every day, which caused me much pain and anxiety. Still I thought that I must set the god's command above everything. So I had to go to every man who seemed to possess any knowledge, and investigate the meaning of the oracle. Athenians, I must tell you the truth; I swear, this was the result of the investigation which I made at the god's command: I found that the men whose reputation for wisdom stood highest were nearly the most lacking in it, while others who were looked down on as common people were much more intelligent. Now I must describe to you the wanderings which I undertook, like Herculean labors, to prove the oracle irrefutable. After the politicians, I went to the poets, tragic, dithyrambic, and others, thinking that there I should find myself manifestly more ignorant than they. So I took up the poems on which I thought that they had spent most pains, and asked them what they meant, hoping at the same time to learn something from them. I am ashamed to tell you the truth, my friends, but I must say it. Almost any one of the bystanders could have talked about the works of these poets better than the poets themselves. So I soon found that it is not by wisdom that the poets create their works, but by a certain instinctive inspiration, like soothsayers and prophets, who say many fine things, but understand nothing of what they say. The poets seemed to me to be in a similar situation. And at the same time I perceived that, because of their poetry, they thought that they were the wisest of men in other matters too, which they were not. So I went away again, thinking that I had the same advantage over the poets that I had over the politicians.

Finally, I went to the artisans, for I knew very well that I possessed no knowledge at all worth speaking of, and I was sure that I should find that they knew many fine things. And in that I was not mistaken. They knew what I did not know, and so far they were wiser than I. But, Athenians, it seemed to me that the skilled artisans had the same failing as the poets. Each of them believed himself to be extremely wise in matters of the greatest importance because he was skillful in his own art: and this presumption of theirs obscured their real wisdom. So I asked myself, on behalf of the oracle, whether I would choose to remain as I was, without either their wisdom or their ignorance, or to possess both, as they did. And I answered to myself and to the oracle that it was better for me to remain as I was.

From this examination, Athenians, has arisen much fierce and bitter indignation, and as a result a great many prejudices about me. People say that I am "a wise man." For the bystanders always think that I am wise myself in any matter wherein I refute another. But, gentlemen, I believe that the god is really wise, and that by this oracle he meant that human wisdom is worth little or nothing. I do not think that he meant that Socrates was wise. He only made use of my name, and took me as an example, as though he would say to men, "He among you is the wisest who, like Socrates, knows that his wisdom is really worth nothing at all." Therefore I still go about testing and examining every man whom I think wise, whether he be a citizen or a stranger, as the god has commanded me. Whenever I find that he is not wise, I point out to him on the god's behalf, that he is not wise. I am so busy in this pursuit that I have never had leisure to take any part worth mentioning in public matters or to look after my private affairs. I am in great poverty as the result of my service to the god.

Besides this, the young men who follow me about, who are the sons of wealthy persons and have the most leisure, take pleasure in hearing men cross-examined. They often imitate me among themselves; then they try their hands at cross-examining other people. And, I imagine, they find plenty of men who think that they know a great deal when in fact they know little or nothing. Then the persons who are cross-examined get angry with me instead of with themselves, and say that Socrates is an abomination and corrupts the young. When they are asked, "Why, what does he do? What does he teach?" they do not know what to say. Not to seem at a loss, they repeat the stock charges against all philosophers, and allege that he investigates things in the air and under the earth, and that he teaches people to disbelieve in the gods, and to make the worse argument appear the stronger. For, I suppose, they would not like to confess the truth, which is that they are shown up as ignorant pretenders to knowledge that they do not possess. So they have been filling your ears with their bitter prejudices for a long time, for they are ambitious, energetic, and numerous; and they speak vigorously and persuasively against me. Relying on this, Meletus, Anytus, and Lycon have attacked me. Meletus is indignant with me on behalf of the poets, Anytus on behalf of the artisans and politicians, and Lycon on behalf of the orators. And so, as I said at the beginning, I shall be surprised if I am able, in the short time allowed me for my defense, to remove from your minds this prejudice which has grown so strong. What I have told you, Athenians, is the truth: I neither conceal nor do I suppress anything, trivial or important. Yet I know that it is just this outspokenness which rouses indignation. But that is only a proof that my words are true, and that the prejudice against me, and the causes of it, are what I have said. And whether you investigate them now or hereafter, you will find that they are so.

What I have said must suffice as my defense against the charges of my first accusers. I will try next to defend myself against Meletus, that "good patriot," as he calls himself, and my later accusers. Let us assume that they are a new set of accusers, and read their indictment, as we did in the case of the others. It runs thus: Socrates is guilty of corrupting the youth, and of believing not in the gods whom the state believes in, but in other new divinities. Such is the accusation. Let us examine each point in it separately. Meletus says that I am guilty of corrupting the youth. But I say, Athenians, that he is guilty of playing a solemn joke by casually bringing men to trial, and pretending to have a solemn interest in matters to which he has never given a moment's thought. Now I will try to prove to you that this is so.

Come here, Meletus. Is it not a fact that you think it very important that the young should be as good as possible?

Meletus. It is.

Socrates. Come, then, tell the judges who improves them. You care so much,[5] you must know. You are accusing me, and bringing me to trial, because, as you say, you have discovered that I am the corrupter of the youth. Come now, reveal to the gentlemen who improves them. You see, Meletus, you have nothing to say; you are silent. But don't you think that this is shameful? Is not your silence a conclusive proof of what I say—that you have never cared? Come, tell us, my good man, who makes the young better?

Mel. The laws.

Socr. That, my friend, is not my question. What man improves the young, who begins by knowing the laws?

Mel. The judges here, Socrates.

Socr. What do you mean, Meletus? Can they educate the young and improve them?

Mel. Certainly.

Socr. All of them? Or only some of them?

Mel. All of them.

Socr. By Hera, that is good news! Such a large supply of benefactors! And do the members of the audience here improve them, or not?

Mel. They do.

Socr. And do the councilors?

Mel. Yes.

Socr. Well, then, Meletus, do the members of the assembly corrupt the young or do they again all improve them?

Mel. They, too, improve them.

<u>Socr</u>. Then all the Athenians, apparently, make the young into good men except me, and I alone corrupt them. Is that your meaning?

<u>Mel</u>. Certainly, that is my meaning.

<u>Socr</u>. You have discovered me to be most unfortunate. Now tell me: do you think that the same holds good in the case of horses? Does one man do them harm and everyone else improve them? On the contrary, is it not one man only, or a very few—namely, those who are skilled with horses—who can improve them, while the majority of men harm them if they use them and have anything to do with them? Is it not so, Meletus, both with horses and with every other animal? Of course it is, whether you and Anytus say yes or no. The young would certainly be very fortunate if only one man corrupted them, and everyone else did them good. The truth is, Meletus, you prove conclusively that you have never thought about the young in your life. You exhibit your carelessness in not caring for the very matters about which you are prosecuting me.

Now be so good as to tell us, Meletus, is it better to live among good citizens or bad ones? Answer, my friend. I am not asking you at all a difficult question. Do not the bad harm their associates and the good do them good?

<u>Mel</u>. Yes.

<u>Socr</u>. Is there anyone who would rather be injured than benefited by his companions? Answer, my good man; you are obliged by the law to answer. Does anyone like to be injured?

<u>Mel</u>. Certainly not.

<u>Socr</u>. Well, then, are you prosecuting me for corrupting the young and making them worse, voluntarily or involuntarily?

<u>Mel</u>. For doing it voluntarily.

18

Socr. What, Meletus? Do you mean to say that you, who are so much younger than I, are yet so much wiser than I that you know that bad citizens always do evil, and that good citizens do good, to those with whom they come in contact, while I am so extraordinarily ignorant as not to know that, if I make any of my companions evil, he will probably injure me in some way? And you allege that I do this voluntarily? You will not make me believe that, nor anyone else either, I should think. Either I do not corrupt the young at all or, if I do, I do so involuntarily, so that you are lying in either case. And if I corrupt them involuntarily, the law does not call upon you to prosecute me for an error which is involuntary, but to take me aside privately and reprove and educate me. For, of course, I shall cease from doing wrong involuntarily, as soon as I know that I have been doing wrong. But you avoided associating with me and educating me; instead you bring me up before the court, where the law sends persons, not for education, but for punishment.

The truth is, Athenians, as I said, it is quite clear that Meletus has never cared at all about these matters. However, now tell us, Meletus, how do you say that I corrupt the young? Clearly, according to your indictment, by teaching them not to believe in the gods the state believes in, but other new divinities instead. You mean that I corrupt the young by that teaching, do you not?

Mel. Yes, most certainly I mean that.

Socr. Then in the name of these gods of whom we are speaking, explain yourself a little more clearly to me and to these gentlemen here. I cannot understand what you mean. Do you mean that I teach the young to believe in some gods, but not in the gods of the state? Do you accuse me of teaching them to believe in strange gods? If that is your meaning, I myself believe in some gods, and my crime is not that of complete atheism. Or do you mean that I do not believe in the gods at

all myself, and that I teach other people not to
believe in them either?

Mel. I mean that you do not believe in the
gods in any way whatever.

Socr. You amaze me, Meletus! Why do you say
that? Do you mean that I believe neither the sun
nor the moon to be gods, like other men?

Mel. I swear he does not, judge. He says
that the sun is a stone, and the moon earth.

Socr. My dear Meletus, do you think that you
are prosecuting Anaxagoras? You must have a very
poor opinion of these men, and think them illiter-
ate, if you imagine that they do not know that the
works of Anaxagoras of Clazomenae are full of these
doctrines. And so young men learn these things
from me, when they can often buy them in the theater for a drachma at most, and laugh at Socrates
were he to pretend that these doctrines, which are
very peculiar doctrines, too were his own. But
please tell me, do you really think that I do not
believe in the gods at all?

Mel. Most certainly I do. You are a complete
atheist.

Socr. No one believes that, Meletus, not
even you yourself. It seems to me, Athenians, that
Meletus is very insolent and reckless, and that he
is prosecuting me simply out of insolence, recklessness, and youthful bravado. For he seems to be
testing me, by asking me a riddle that has no answer. "Will this wise Socrates," he says to himself, "see that I am joking and contradicting myself? Or shall I deceive him and everyone else
who hears me?" Meletus seems to me to contradict
himself in his indictment: it is as if he were to
say, "Socrates is guilty of not believing in the
gods, but believes in the gods." This is joking.

Now, my friends, let us see why I think that
this is his meaning. You must answer me, Meletus,

20

and you, Athenians, must remember the request which
I made to you at the start, and not interrupt me
with shouts if I talk in my usual manner.

Is there any man, Meletus, who believes in the
existence of things pertaining to men and not in
the existence of men? Make him answer the question, gentlemen, without these interruptions. Is
there any man who believes in the existence of
horsemanship and not in the existence of horses?
Or in flute playing and not in flute players? There
is not, my friend. If you will not answer, I will
tell both you and the judges. But you must answer
my next question. Is there any man who believes in
the existence of divine things and not in the existence of divinities?

Mel. There is not.

Socr. I am very glad that these gentlemen
have managed to extract an answer from you. Well
then, you say that I believe in divine things,
whether they be old or new, and that I teach others
to believe in them. At any rate, according to your
statement, I believe in divine things. That you
have sworn in your indictment. But if I believe
in divine things, I suppose it follows necessarily
that I believe in divinities. Is it not so? It
is. I assume that you grant that, as you do not
answer. But do we not believe that divinities are
either gods themselves or the children of the gods?
Do you admit that?

Mel. I do.

Socr. Then you admit that I believe in divinities. Now, if these divinities are gods, then, as
I say, you are joking and asking a riddle, and asserting that I do not believe in the gods, and at
the same time that I do, since I believe in divinities. But if these divinities are the illegitimate children of the gods, either by the nymphs or
by other mothers, as they are said to be, then, I
ask, what man could believe in the existence of the
children of the gods, and not in the existence of

the gods? That would be as absurd as believing in the existence of the offspring of horses and asses, and not in the existence of horses and asses. You must have indicted me in this manner, Meletus, either to test me or because you could not find any act of injustice that you could accuse me of with truth. But you will never contrive to persuade any man with any sense at all that a belief in divine things and things of the gods does not necessarily involve a belief in divinities, and in the gods.

But in truth, Athenians, I do not think that I need say very much to prove that I have not committed the act of injustice for which Meletus is prosecuting me. What I have said is enough to prove that. But be assured it is certainly true, as I have already told you, that I have aroused much indignation. That is what will cause my condemnation if I am condemned; not Meletus nor Anytus either, but that prejudice and resentment of the multitude which have been the destruction of many good men before me, and I think will be so again. There is no prospect that I shall be the last victim.

Perhaps someone will say: "Are you not ashamed, Socrates, of leading a life which is very likely now to cause your death?" I should answer him with justice, and say: "My friend, if you think that a man of any worth at all ought to reckon the chances of life and death when he acts, or that he ought to think of anything but whether he is acting justly or unjustly, and as a good or a bad man would act, you are mistaken. According to you, the demigods who died at Troy would be foolish, and among them Achilles, who thought nothing of danger when the alternative was disgrace. For when his mother—and she was a goddess—addressed him, when he was resolved to slay Hector, in this fashion, 'My son, if you avenge the death of your comrade Patroclus and slay Hector, you will die yourself, for fate awaits you next after Hector.' When he heard this, he scorned danger and death; he feared much more to live a coward and not to avenge his friend. 'Let me punish the evildoer and afterwards die,' he said, 'that I may not remain here by the beaked ships jeered at, encumbering the earth.'"[6] Do you suppose that he thought of danger or of death? For this, Athenians, I believe to be the truth. Wherever a man's station is, whether he has chosen it of his own will, or whether he has been placed at it by his commander, there it is his duty to remain and face the danger without thinking of death or of any other thing except disgrace.

When the generals whom you chose to command me, Athenians, assigned me my station during the battles of Potidaea, Amphipolis, and Delium, I remained where they stationed me and ran the risk of death, like other men. It would be very strange conduct on my part if I were to desert my station now from fear of death or of any other thing when the god has commanded me—as I am persuaded that he has done—to spend my life in searching for wisdom, and in examining myself and others. That would indeed be a very strange thing. Then certainly I might with justice be brought to trial for not believing in the gods, for I should be disobeying the oracle, and fearing death and thinking myself wise when I was not wise. For to fear death, my friends, is only to think ourselves wise without really being wise, for it is to think that we know what we do not know. For no one knows whether death may not be the greatest good that can happen to man. But men fear it as if they knew quite well that it was the greatest of evils. And what is this but that shameful ignorance of thinking that we know what we do not know? In this matter, too, my friends, perhaps I am different from the multitude. And if I were to claim to be at all wiser than others, it would be because, not knowing very much about the other world, I do not think I know. But I do know very well that it is evil and disgraceful to do an unjust act, and to disobey my superior, whether man or god. I will never do what I know to be evil, and shrink in fear from what I do not know to be good or evil. Even if you acquit me now, and do not listen to Anytus' argument that, if I am to be acquitted, I ought never to have been brought to trial at all, and that, as it is, you are bound to put me to death because, as he said, if I escape, all your sons will be utterly corrupted by practicing what Socrates teaches. If you were therefore to say to me, "Socrates, this time we will not listen to Anytus. We will let you go, but on the condition that you give up this investigation of yours, and philosophy. If you are found following these pursuits again, you shall die." I say, if you offered to let me go on these terms, I should reply: Athenians, I hold you in the highest regard and affection, but I will be persuaded by the god rather than you. As long as I have breath and strength I will not give up philosophy and exhorting you and declaring the truth to every one of you whom I meet, saying, as I am accustomed, 'My good friend, you are a citizen of Athens, a city which is very great and very famous for its wisdom and power—are you not ashamed of caring so much for the making of money and for fame and prestige, when you neither think nor care about wisdom and truth and the improvement of your soul?'" If he disputes my words and says that he does care about these things, I shall not at once release him and go away: I shall question him and cross-examine him and test him. If I think that he has not attained excellence, though he says that he has, I shall reproach him for undervaluing the most valuable things, and overvaluing those that are less valuable. This I shall do to everyone whom I meet, young or old, citizen or stranger, but especially to citizens, since they are more closely related to me. This, you must recognize, the god has commanded me to do. And I think that no greater good has ever befallen you in the state than my service to the god. For I spend my whole life in going about and persuading you all to give your first and greatest care to the improvement of your souls, and not till you have done that to think of your bodies or your wealth. And I tell you that wealth does not bring excellence, but that wealth, and every other good thing which men have, whether in public or in private, comes from excellence. If then I corrupt the youth by this teaching, these things must be harmful.

24

But if any man says that I teach anything else, there is nothing in what he says. And therefore, Athenians, I say, whether you are persuaded by Anytus or not, whether you acquit me or not, I shall not change my way of life; no, not if I have to die for it many times.

Do not interrupt me, Athenians, with your shouts. Remember the request which I made to you, and do not interrupt my words. I think that it will profit you to hear them. I am going to say something more to you, at which you may be inclined to protest, but do not do that. Be sure that if you put me to death, I who am what I have told you that I am, you will do yourselves more harm than me. Meletus and Anytus can do me no harm: that is impossible, for I am sure it is not allowed that a good man be injured by a worse. He may indeed kill me, or drive me into exile, or deprive me of my civil rights. Perhaps Meletus and others think those things great evils. But I do not think so. I think it is a much greater evil to do what he is doing now, and to try to put a man to death unjustly. And now, Athenians, I am not arguing in my own defense at all, as you might expect me to do, but rather in yours in order you may not make a mistake about the gift of the god to you by condemning me. For if you put me to death, you will not easily find another who, if I may use a ludicrous comparison, clings to the state as a sort of gadfly to a horse that is large and well-bred but rather sluggish because of its size, so that it needs to be aroused. It seems to me that the god has attached me like that to the state, for I am constantly alighting upon you at every point to arouse, persuade, and reproach each of you all day long. You will not easily find anyone else, my friends, to fill my place; and if you are persuaded by me, you will spare my life. You are indignant, as drowsy persons are when they are awakened, and, of course, if you are persuaded by Anytus, you could easily kill me with a single blow, and then sleep on undisturbed for the rest of your lives, unless the god in his care for you sends another to arouse you. And you may easily see that it is the god who has given me to your city; for it is not human, the way in which I have neglected all my own interests and allowed my private affairs to be neglected for so many years, while occupying myself unceasingly in your interests, going to each of you privately, like a father or an elder brother, trying to persuade him to care for human excellence. There would have been a reason for it, if I had gained any advantage by this, or if I had been paid for my exhortations; but you see yourselves that my accusers, though they accuse me of everything else without shame, have not had the shamelessness to say that I ever either exacted or demanded payment. To that they have no witness. And I think that I have sufficient witness to the truth of what I say—my poverty.

Perhaps it may seem strange to you that, though I go about giving this advice privately and meddling in others' affairs, yet I do not venture to come forward in the assembly and advise the state. You have often heard me speak of my reason for this, and in many places: it is that I have a certain divine guide, which is what Meletus has caricatured in his indictment. I have had it from childhood. It is a kind of voice which, whenever I hear it, always turns me back from something which I was going to do, but never urges me to act. It is this which forbids me to take part in politics. And I think it does well to forbid me. For, Athenians, it is quite certain that, if I had attempted to take part in politics, I should have perished at once and long ago without doing any good either to you or to myself. And do not be indignant with me for telling the truth. There is no man who will preserve his life for long, either in Athens or elsewhere, if he firmly opposes the multitude, and tries to prevent the commission of much injustice and illegality in the state. He who would really fight for justice must do so as a private citizen, not as a political figure, if he is to preserve his life, even for a short time.

I will prove to you that this is so by very strong evidence, not by mere words, but by what you value more—actions. Listen, the, to what has happened to me, that you may know that there is no

26

man who could make me consent to commit an unjust act from the fear of death, but that I would perish at once rather than give way. What I am going to tell you may be commonplace in the law court; nevertheless, it is true. The only office that I ever held in the state, Athenians, was that of councilor. When you wished to try the ten admirals who did not rescue their men after the battle of Arginusae as a group, which was illegal, as you all came to think afterwards, the executive committee was composed of members of the tribe Antiochis, to which I belong.[7] On that occasion I alone of the committee members opposed your illegal action and gave my vote against you. The orators were ready to impeach me and arrest me; and you were clamoring and urging them on with your shouts. But I thought that I ought to face the danger, with law and justice on my side, rather than join with you in your unjust proposal, from fear of imprisonment or death. That was when the state was democratic. When the oligarchy came in, The Thirty sent for me, with four others, to the council-chamber, and ordered us to bring Leon the Salaminian from Salamis, that they might put him to death. They were in the habit of frequently giving similar orders to many others, wishing to implicate as many as possible in their crimes. But then I again proved, not by mere words, but by my actions, that, if I may speak bluntly, I do not care a straw for death; but that I do care very much indeed about not doing anything unjust or impious. That government with all its power did not terrify me into doing anything unjust. When we left the council-chamber, the other four went over to Salamis and brought Leon across to Athens; I went home. And if the rule of The Thirty had not been overthrown soon afterwards, I should very likely have been put to death for what I did then. Many of you will be my witnesses in this matter.[8]

Now do you think that I could have remained alive all these years if I had taken part in public affairs, and had always maintained the cause of justice like a good man, and had held it a paramount duty, as it is, to do so? Certainly not,

Athenians, nor could any other man. But throughout my whole life, both in private and in public, whenever I have had to take part in public affairs, you will find I have always been the same and have never yielded unjustly to anyone; no, not to those whom my enemies falsely assert to have been my pupils. But I was never anyone's teacher. I have never withheld myself from anyone, young or old, who was anxious to hear me converse while I was making my investigation; neither do I converse for payment, and refuse to converse without payment. I am ready to ask questions of rich and poor alike, and if any man wishes to answer me, and then listen to what I have to say, he may. And I cannot justly be charged with causing these men to turn out good or bad, for I never either taught or professed to teach any of them any knowledge whatever. And if any man asserts that he ever learned or heard anything from me in private which everyone else did not hear as well as he, be sure that he does not speak the truth.

Why is it, then, that people delight in spending so much time in my company? You have heard why, Athenians. I told you the whole truth when I said that they delight in hearing me examine persons who think that they are wise when they are not wise. It is certainly very amusing to listen to. And, as I have said, the god has commanded me to examine men, in oracles and in dreams and in every way in which the divine will was ever declared to man. This is the truth, Athenians, and if it were not the truth, it would be easily refuted. For if it were really the case that I have already corrupted some of the young men, and am now corrupting others, surely some of them, finding as they grew older that I had given them bad advice in their youth, would have come forward today to accuse me and take their revenge. Or if they were unwilling to do so themselves, surely their relatives, their fathers or brothers, or others, would, if I had done them any harm, have remembered it and taken their revenge. Certainly I see many of them in court. Here is Crito, of my own district and of my own age, the father of Critobulus; here is Lysanias of Sphettus, the father of Aeschines; here is also Antiphon of Cephisus, the father of Epigenes. Then here are others whose brothers have spent their time in my compnay—Nicostratus, the son of Theozotides and brother of Theodotus—and Theodotus is dead, so he at least cannot entreat his brother to be silent; here is Paralus, the son of Demodocus and the brother of Theages; here is Adeimantus, the son of Ariston, whose brother is Plato here; and Aeantodorus, whose brother is Aristodorus. And I can name many others to you, some of whom Meletus ought to have called as witnesses in the course of his own speech; but if he forgot to call them then, let him call them now—I will yield the floor to him—and tell us if he has any such evidence. No, on the contrary, my friends, you will find all these men ready to support me, the corrupter who has injured their relatives, as Meletus and Anytus call me. Those of them who have been already corrupted might perhaps have some reason for supporting me, but what reason can their relatives have who are grown up, and who are uncorrupted, except the reason of truth and justice—that they know very well that Meletus is lying, and that I am speaking the truth?

Well, my friends, this, and perhaps more like this, is pretty much all I have to offer in my defense. There may be some one among you who will be indignant when he remembers how, even in a less important trail than this, he begged and entreated the judges, with many tears, to acquit him, and brought forward his children and many of his friends and relatives in court in order to appeal to your feelings; and then finds that I shall do none of these things, though I am in what he would think the supreme danger. Perhaps he will harden himself against me when he notices this; it may make him angry, and he may cast his vote in anger. If it is so with any of you—I do not suppose that it is, but in case it should be so—I think that I should answer him reasonably if I said: "My friends, I have relatives, too, for, in the words of Homer, I am 'not born of an oak or a rock'[9] but of flesh and blood." And so, Athenians, I have relatives, and I have three sons, one of them nearly grown up, and

the other two still children. Yet I will not bring
any of them forward before you and implore you to
acquit me. And why will I do none of these things?
It is not from arrogance, Athenians, nor because I
lack respect for you—whether or not I can face
death bravely is another question—but for my own
good name, and for your good name, and for the good
name of the whole state. I do not think it right,
at my age and with my reputation, to do anything of
that kind. Rightly or wrongly, men have made up
their minds that in some way Socrates is different
from the multitude of men. And it will be shameful if those of you who are thought to excel in
wisdom, or in bravery, or in any other excellence,
are going to act in this fashion. I have often
seen men of reputation behaving in an extraordinary
way at their trial, as if they thought it a terrible
fate to be killed, and as though they expected to
live for ever if you did not put them to death.
Such men seem to me to bring shame upon the state,
for any stranger would suppose that the best and
most eminent Athenians, who are selected by their
fellow citizens to hold office, and for other honors, are no better than women. Those of you,
Athenians, who have any reputation at all ought
not to do these things, and you ought not to allow
us to do them. You should show that you will be
much more ready to condemn men who make the state
ridiculous by these pathetic performances than men
who remain quiet.

But apart from the question of reputation, my
friends, I do not think that it is right to entreat
the judge to acquit us, or to escape condemnation
in that way. It is our duty to teach and persuade
him. He does not sit to give away justice as a
favor, but to pronounce judgment; and he has sworn,
not to favor any man whom he would like to favor,
but to judge according to law. And, therefore, we
ought not to encourage you in the habit of breaking your oaths; and you ought not to allow yourselves to fall into this habit, for then neither
you nor we would be acting piously. Therefore,
Athenians, do not require me to do these things,
for I believe them to be neither good nor just nor

pious; especially, do not ask me to do them today when Meletus is prosecuting me for impiety. For were I to be successful and persuade you by my entreaties to break your oaths, I should be clearly teaching you to believe that there are no gods, and I should be simply accusing myself by my defense of not believing in them. But, Athenians, that is very far from the truth. I do believe in the gods as no one of my accusers believes in them; and to you and to the god I commit my cause to be decided as is best for you and for me.

(He is found guilty by 281 votes to 220.)

I am not indignant at the verdict which you have given, Athenians, for many reasons. I expected that you would find me guilty; and I am not so much surprised at that as at the numbers of the votes. I certainly never thought that the majority against me would have been so narrow. But now it seems that if only thirty votes had changed sides, I should have escaped. So I think that I have escaped Meletus, as it is; and not only have I escaped him, for it is perfectly clear that if Anytus and Lycon had not come forward to accuse me, too, he would not have obtained the fifth part of the votes, and would have had to pay a fine of a thousand drachmae.

So he proposes death as the penalty. Be it so. And what alternative penalty shall I propose to you, Athenians?[10] What I deserve, of course, must I not? What then do I deserve to pay or to suffer for having determined not to spend my life in ease? I neglected the things which most men value, such as wealth, and family interests, and military commands, and public oratory, and all the civic appointments, and social clubs, and political factions, that there are in Athens; for I thought that I was really too honest a man to preserve my life if I engaged in these affairs. So I did not go where I should have done no good either to you or to myself. I went, instead, to each one of you privately to do him, as I say, the greatest of benefits, and tried to persuade him not to think

31

of his affairs until he had thought of himself and
tried to make himself as good and wise as possible,
nor to think of the affairs of Athens until he had
thought of Athens herself; and to care for other
things in the same manner. Then what do I deserve
for such a life? Something good, Athenians, if I
am really to propose what I deserve; and something
good which it would be suitable for me to receive.
Then what is a suitable reward to be given to a
poor benefactor who requires leisure to exhort you?
There is no reward, Athenians, so suitable for him
as receiving free meals in the prytaneum. It is a
much more suitable reward for him than for any of
you who has won a victory at the Olympic games with
his horse or his chariots. Such a man only makes
you seem happy, but I make you really happy; he is
not in want, and I am. So if I am to propose the
penalty which I really deserve, I propose this—
free meals in the prytaneum.

Perhaps you think me stubborn and arrogant in
what I am saying now, as in what I said about the
entreaties and tears. It is not so, Athenians. It
is rather that I am convinced that I never wronged
any man voluntarily, though I cannot persuade you
of that, since we have conversed together only a
little time. If there were a law at Athens, as
there is elsewhere, not to finish a trial of life
and death in a single day, I think that I could
have persuaded you; but now it is not easy in so
short a time to clear myself of great prejudices.
But when I am persuaded that I have never wronged
any man, I shall certainly not wrong myself, or
admit that I deserve to suffer any evil, or propose any evil for myself as a penalty. Why should
I? Lest I should suffer the penalty which Meletus
proposes when I say that I do not know whether it
is a good or an evil? Shall I choose instead of it
something which I know to be an evil, and propose
that as a penalty? Shall I propose imprisonment?
And why should I pass the rest of my days in prison,
the slave of successive officials? Or shall I propose a fine, with imprisonment until it is paid? I
have told you why I will not do that. I should
have to remain in prison, for I have no money to

pay a fine with. Shall I then propose exile? Perhaps you would agree to that. Life would indeed be very dear to me if I were unreasonable enough to expect that strangers would cheerfully tolerate my discussions and arguments when you who are my fellow citizens cannot endure them, and have found them so irksome and odious to you that you are seeking now to be relieved of them. No, indeed, Athenians, that is not likely. A fine life I should lead for an old man if I were to withdraw from Athens and pass the rest of my days in wandering from city to city, and continually being expelled. For I know very well that the young men will listen to me wherever I go, as they do here. If I drive them away, they will persuade their elders to expel me; if I do not drive them away, their fathers and other relatives will expel me for their sakes.

Perhaps someone will say, "Why cannot you withdraw from Athens, Socrates, and hold your peace?" It is the most difficult thing in the world to make you understand why I cannot do that. If I say that I cannot hold my peace because that would be to disobey the god, you will think that I am not in earnest and will not believe me. And if I tell you that no greater good can happen to a man than to discuss human excellence every day and the other matters about which you have heard me arguing and examining myself and others, and that an unexamined life is not worth living, then you will believe me still less. But that is so, my friends, though it is not easy to persuade you. And, what is more, I am not accustomed to think that I deserve anything evil. If I had been rich, I would have proposed as large a fine as I could pay: that would have done me no harm. But I am not rich enough to pay a fine unless you are willing to fix it at a sum within my means. Perhaps I could pay you a mina, so I propose that. Plato here, Athenians, and Crito, and Critobulus, and Apollodorus bid me propose thirty minae, and they guarantee its payment. So I propose thirty minae. Their security will be sufficient to you for the money.

(He is condemned to death.)

You have not gained very much time, Athenians, and at the price of the slurs of those who wish to revile the state. And they will say that you put Socrates, a wise man, to death. For they will certainly call me wise, whether I am wise or not, when they want to reproach you. If you had waited for a little while, your wishes would have been fulfilled in the course of nature; for you see that I am an old man, far advanced in years, and near to death. I am saying this not to all of you, only to those who have voted for my death. And to them I have something else to say. Perhaps, my friends, you think that I have been convicted because I was wanting in the arguments by which I could have persuaded you to acquit me, if I had thought it right to do or to say anything to escape punishment. It is not so. I have been convicted because I was wanting, not in arguments, but in impudence and shamelessness—because I would not plead before you as you would have liked to hear me plead, or appeal to you with weeping and wailing, or say and do many other things which I maintain are unworthy of me, but which you have been accustomed to from other men. But when I was defending myself, I thought that I ought not to do anything unworthy of a free man because of the danger which I ran, and I have not changed my mind now. I would very much rather defend myself as I did, and die, than as you would have had me do, and live. Both in a lawsuit and in war, there are some things which neither I nor any other man may do in order to escape from death. In battle, a man often sees that he may at least escape from death by throwing down his arms and falling on his knees before the pursuer to beg for his life. And there are many other ways of avoiding death in every danger if a man is willing to say and to do anything. But, my friends, I think that it is a much harder thing to escape from wickedness than from death, for wickedness is swifter than death. And now I, who am old and slow, have been overtaken by the slower pursuer: and my accusers, who are clever and swift, have been overtaken by the swifter pursuer—wickedness. And now

34

I shall go away, sentenced by you to death; they will go away, sentenced by truth to wickedness and injustice. And I abide by this award as well as they. Perhaps it was right for these things to be so. I think that they are fairly balanced.

And now I wish to prophesy to you, Athenians, who have condemned me. For I am going to die, and that is the time when men have most prophetic power. And I prophesy to you who have sentenced me to death that a far more severe punishment than you have inflicted on me will surely overtake you as soon as I am dead. You have done this thing, thinking that you will be relieved from having to give an account of your lives. But I say that the result will be very different. There will be more men who will call you to account, whom I have held back, though you did not recognize it. And they will be harsher toward you than I have been, for they will be younger, and you will be more indignant with them. For if you think that you will restrain men from reproaching you for not living as you should, by putting them to death, you are very much mistaken. That way of escape is neither possible nor honorable. It is much more honorable and much easier not to suppress others, but to make yourselves as good as you can. This is my parting prophecy to you who have condemned me.

With you who have acquitted me I should like to discuss this thing that has happened, while the authorities are busy, and before I go to the place where I have to die. So, remain with me until I go: there is no reason why we should not talk with each other while it is possible. I wish to explain to you, as my friends, the meaning of what has happened to me. An amazing thing has happened to me, judges—for I am right in calling you judges.[11] The prophetic guide has been constantly with me all through my life till now, opposing me even in trivial matters if I were not going to act rightly. And now you yourselves see what has happened to me—a thing which might be thought, and which is sometimes actually reckoned, the supreme evil. But the divine guide did not oppose me when I was leaving my house in the morning, nor when I was coming up here to the court, nor at any point in my speech when I was going to say anything; though at other times it has often stopped me in the very act of speaking. But now, in this matter, it has never once opposed me, either in my words or my actions. I will tell you what I believe to be the reason. This thing that has come upon me must be a good; and those of us who think that death is an evil must needs be mistaken. I have a clear proof that that is so; for my accustomed guide would certainly have opposed me if I had not been going to meet with something good.

And if we reflect in another way, we shall see that we may well hope that death is a good. For the state of death is one of two things: either the dead man wholly ceases to be and loses all consciousness or, as we are told, it is a change and a migration of the soul to another place. And if death is the absence of all consciousness, and like the sleep of one whose slumbers are unbroken by any dreams, it will be a wonderful gain. For if a man had to select that night in which he slept so soundly that he did not even dream, and had to compare with it all the other nights and days of his life, and then had to say how many days and nights in his life he had spent better and more pleasantly than this night, I think that a private person, nay, even the Great King of Persia himself, would find them easy to count, compared with the others. If that is the nature of death, I for one count it a gain. For then it appears that all time is nothing more than a single night. But if death is a journey to another place, and what we are told is true—that all who have died are there—what good could be greater than this, my judges? Would a journey not be worth taking, at the end of which, in the other world, we should be delivered from the pretended judges here and should find the true judges who are said to sit in judgment below, such as Minos and Rhadamanthus and Aeacus and Triptolemus, and the other demigods who were just in their own lives? Or what would you not give to converse with Orpheus and Musaeus and Hesiod and

Homer? I am willing to die many times if this be
true. And for my own part I should find it wonderful to meet there Palamedes, and Ajax the son of
Telamon, and the other men of old who have died
through an unjust judgment, and to compare my experiences with theirs. That I think would be no
small pleasure. And, above all, I could spend my
time in examining those who are there, as I examine men here, and in finding out which of them is
wise, and which of them thinks himself wise when
he is not wise. What would we not give, my judges,
to be able to examine the leader of the great expe-
dition against Troy, or Odysseus, or Sisyphus, or
countless other men and women whom we could name?
It would be an inexpressible happiness to converse
with them and to live with them and to examine
them. Assuredly there they do not put men to death
for doing that. For besides the other ways in
which they are happier than we are, they are immortal, at least if what we are told is true.

    And you too, judges, must face death hopefully,
and believe this one truth, that no evil can happen
to a good man, either in life or after death. His
affairs are not neglected by the gods; and what has
happened to me today has not happened by chance. I
am persuaded that it was better for me to die now,
and to be released from trouble; and that was the
reason why the guide never turned me back. And so
I am not at all angry with my accusers or with those
who have condemned me to die. Yet it was not with
this in mind that they accused me and condemned me,
but meaning to do me an injury. So far I may blame
them.

    Yet I have one request to make of them. When
my sons grow up, punish them, my friends, and har-
ass them in the same way that I have harassed you,
if they seem to you to care for riches or for any
other thing more than excellence; and if they think
that they are something when they are really nothing,
reproach them, as I have reproached you, for not
caring for what they should, and for thinking that
they are something when really they are nothing.
And if you will do this, I myself and my sons will

have received justice from you.

But now the time has come, and we must go away—I to die, and you to live. Which is better is known to the god alone.

Notes

[1]Anytus is singled out as politically the most influential member of the prosecution. He had played a prominent part in the restoration of the democratic regime at Athens.—Ed.

[2]Apparently in order to obscure the political implications of the trial, the role of chief prosecutor was assigned to Meletus, a minor poet with fervent religious convictions. Anytus was evidently ready to make political use of Meletus' convictions without entirely sharing his fervor, for in the same year as this trial Meletus also prosecuted Andocides for impiety, but Anytus came to Andocides' defense.—Ed.

[3]The Clouds. The basket was satirically assumed to facilitate Socrates' inquiries into things in the heavens.—Ed.

[4]During the totalitarian regime of The Thirty which remained in power for eight months (404 B.C.), five years before the trial.—Ed.

[5]Throughout the following passage Socrates plays on the etymology of the name "Meletus" as meaning "the man who cares."—Ed.

[6]Homer, Iliad, xviii, 96,98.—Ed.

[7]The Council was the administrative body in Athens. Actual administrative functions were performed by an executive committee of the Council, and the members of this committee were recruited from each tribe in turn. The case Socrates is alluding to was that of the admirals who were accused of having failed to rescue the crews of ships which sank during the battle of Arginusae. The six admirals who were actually put on trial were condemned as a group and executed.—Ed.

[8]There is evidence that Meletus was one of the four who turned in Leon. Socrates' recalling this

earlier lapse from legal procedure is probably also
a thrust at Anytus. The Thirty successfully implicated so many Athenians in their crimes that an amnesty
was declared, which Anytus strongly favored,
in order to enlist wider support for the restored
democracy. Thus those who were really implicated
could now no longer be prosecuted legally, but
Socrates is himself being illegally prosecuted (as
he now goes on to suggest) because he was guilty of
having associated with such "pupils" as Critias, who
was leader of The Thirty.—Ed.

[9]Homer, _Odyssey_, xix, 163.

[10]For certain crimes no penalty was fixed by
Athenian law. Having reached a verdict of guilty,
the court had still to decide between the alternative penalties proposed by the prosecution and
the defense.—Ed.

[11]The form of address hitherto has always been
"Athenians," or "my friends." The "Judges" in an
Athenian court were simply the members of the
jury.—Ed.

Euthyphro*
Plato

Characters

Socrates

Euthyphro

Scene—The Hall of the King

Euthyphro. What in the world are you doing here in the king's hall,[1] Socrates? Why have you left your haunts in the Lyceum? You surely cannot have a suit before him, as I have.

Socrates. The Athenians, Euthyphro, call it an indictment, not a suit.

Euth. What? Do you mean that someone is prosecuting you? I cannot believe that you are prosecuting anyone yourself.

Socr. Certainly I am not.

Euth. Then is someone prosecuting you?

*Reprinted by permission of The Bobbs-Merrill Company, Inc. from Euthyphro, Apology, and Crito by Plato and translated by F. J. Church. Copyright © 1956 by The Bobbs-Merrill Company, Inc.

Socr. Yes.

Euth. Who is He?

Socr. I scarcely know him myself, Euthyphro; I think he must be some unknown young man. His name, however, is Meletus, and his district Pitthis, if you can call to mind any Meletus of that district—a hook-nosed man with lanky hair and rather a scanty beard.

Euth. I don't know him, Socrates. But tell me, what is he prosecuting you for?

Socr. What For? Not on trivial grounds, I think. It is no small thing for so young a man to have formed an opinion on such an important matter. For he, he says, knows how the young are corrupted, and who are their corrupters. He must be a wise man who, observing my ignorance, is going to accuse me to the state, as his mother, of corrupting his friends. I think that he is the only one who begins at the right point in his political reforms; for his first care is to make the young men as good as possible, just as a good farmer will take care of his young plants first, and, after he has done that, of the others. And so Meletus, I suppose, is first clearing us away who, as he says, corrupt the young men growing up; and then, when he has done that, of course he will turn his attention to the older men, and so become a very great public benefactor. Indeed, that is only what you would expect when he goes to work in this way.

Euth. I hope it may be so, Socrates, but I fear the opposite. It seems to me that in trying to injure you, he is really setting to work by striking a blow at the foundation of the state. But how, tell me, does he say that you corrupt the youth?

Socr. In a way which sounds absurd at first, my friend. He says that I am a maker of gods; and so he is prosecuting me, he says, for inventing new gods and for not believing in the old ones.

41

<u>Euth</u>. I understand, Socrates. It is because you say that you always have a divine guide. So he is prosecuting you for introducing religious reforms; and he is going into court to arouse prejudice against you, knowing that the multitude are easily prejudiced about such matters. Why, they laugh even at me, as if I were out of my mind, when I talk about divine things in the assembly and tell them what is going to happen; and yet I have never foretold anything which has not come true. But they are resentful of all people like us. We must not worry about them; we must meet them boldly.

<u>Socr</u>. My dear Euthyphro, their ridicule is not a very serious matter. The Athenians, it seems to me, may think a man to be clever without paying him much attention, so long as they do not think that he teaches his wisdom to others. But as soon as they think that he makes other people clever, they get angry, whether it be from resentment, as you say, or for some other reason.

<u>Euth</u>. I am not very anxious to test their attitude toward me in this matter.

<u>Socr</u>. No, perhaps they think that you are reserved, and that you are not anxious to teach your wisdom to others. But I fear that they may think that I am; for my love of man makes me talk to everyone whom I meet quite freely and unreservedly, and without payment. Indeed, if I could I would gladly pay people myself to listen to me. If then, as I said just now, they were only going to laugh at me, as you say they do at you, it would not be at all an unpleasant way of spending the day—to spend it in court, joking and laughing. But if they are going to be in earnest, then only prophets like you can tell where the matter will end.

<u>Euth</u>. Well, Socrates, I dare say that nothing will come of it. Very likely you will be successful in your trial, and I think that I shall be in mine.

Socr. And what is this suit of yours, Euthyphro? Are you suing, or being sued?

Euth. I am suing.

Socr. Whom?

Euth. A man whom people think I must be mad to prosecute.

Socr. What? Has he wings to fly away with?

Euth. He is far enough from flying; he is a very old man.

Socr. Who is he?

Euth. He is my father.

Socr. Your father, my good man?

Euth. He is indeed.

Socr. What are you prosecuting him for? What is the accusation?

Euth. Murder, Socrates.

Socr. Good heavens, Euthyphro! Surely the multitude are ignorant of what is right. I take it that it is not everyone who could rightly do what you are doing; only a man who was already well advanced in wisdom.

Euth. That is quite true, Socrates.

Socr. Was the man whom your father killed a relative of yours? But, of course, he was. You would never have prosecuted your father for the murder of a stranger?

Euth. You amuse me, Socrates. What difference does it make whether the murdered man were a relative or a stranger? The only question that you have to ask is, did the murderer kill justly or not?

43

If justly, you must let him alone; if unjustly, you must indict him for murder, even though he share your hearth and sit at your table. The pollution is the same if you associate with such a man, knowing what he has done, without purifying yourself, and him too, by bringing him to justice. In the case the murdered man was a poor laborer of mine, who worked for us on our farm in Naxos. While drunk he got angry with one of our slaves and killed him. My father therefore bound the man hand and foot and threw him into a ditch, while he sent to Athens to ask the priest what he should do. While the messenger was gone, he entirely neglected the man, thinking that he was a murderer, and that it would be no great matter, even if he were to die. And that was exactly what happened; hunger and cold and his bonds killed him before the messenger returned. And now my father and the rest of my family are indignant with me because I am prosecuting my father for the murder of this murderer. They assert that he did not kill the man at all; and they say that, even if he had killed him over and over again, the man himelf was a murderer, and that I ought not to concern myself about such a person because it is impious for a son to prosecute his father for murder. So little, Socrates, do they know the divine law of piety and impiety.

Socr. And do you mean to say, Euthyphro, that you think that you understand divine things and piety and impiety so accurately that, in such a case as you have stated, you can bring your father to justice without fear that you yourself may be doing something impious?

Euth. If I did not understand all these matters accurately, Socrates, I should not be worth much—Euthyphro would not be any better than other men.

Socr. Then, my dear Euthyphro, I cannot do better than become your pupil and challenge Meletus on this very point before the trial begins. I should say that I had always thought it very important to have knowledge about divine things; and that now, when he says that I offend by speaking carelessly about them, and by introducing reforms, I have become your pupil. And I shoud say, "Meletus, if you acknowledge Euthyphro to be wise in these matters and to hold the correct belief, then think the same of me and do not put me on trial; but if you do not, then bring a suit, not against me, but against my master, for corrupting his elders—namely, myself whom he corrupts by his teaching, and his own father whom he corrupts by admonishing and punishing him." And if I did not succeed in persuading him to release me from the suit or to indict you in my place, then I could repeat my challenge in court.

Euth. Yes, by Zeus! Socrates, I think I should find out his weak points if he were to try to indict me. I should have a good deal to say about him in court long before I spoke about myself.

Socr. Yes, my dear friend, and knowing this I am anxious to become your pupil. I see that Meletus here, and others too, seem not to notice you at all, but he sees through me without difficulty and at once prosecutes me for impiety. Now, therefore, please explain to me what you were so confident just now that you knew. Tell me what are righteousness and sacrilege with respect to murder and everything else. I suppose that piety is the same in all actions, and that impiety is always the opposite of piety, and retains its identity, and that, as impiety, it always has the same character, which will be found in whatever is impious.

Euth. Certainly, Socrates, I suppose so.

Socr. Tell me, then, what is piety and what is impiety?

Euth. Well, then, I say that piety means prosecuting the unjust individual who has committed murder or sacrilege, or any other such crime, as I am doing now, whether he is your father or your mother or whoever he is; and I say that

45

impiety means not prosecuting him. And observe, Socrates, I will give you a clear proof, which I have already given to others, that it is so, and that doing right means not letting off unpunished the sacrilegious man, whosoever he may be. Men hold Zeus to be the best and the most just of the gods; and they admit that Zeus bound his own father, Cronos, for wrongfully devouring his children; and that Cronos, in his turn, castrated his father for similar reasons. And yet these same men are incensed with me because I proceed against my father for doing wrong. So, you see, they say one thing in the case of the gods and quite another in mine.

Socr. Is not that why I am being prosecuted, Euthyphro? I mean, because I find it hard to accept such stories people tell about the gods? I expect that I shall be found at fault because I doubt those stories. Now if you who understand all these matters so well agree in holding all those tales true, then I suppose that I must yield to your authority. What could I say when I admit myself that I know nothing about them? But tell me, in the name of friendship, do you really believe that these things have actually happened?

Euth. Yes, and more amazing things, too, Socrates, which the multitude do not know of.

Socr. Then you really believe that there is war among the gods, and bitter hatreds, and battles, such as the poets tell of, and which the great painters have depicted in our temples, notably in the pictures which cover the robe that is carried up to the Acropolis at the great Panathenaic festival? Are we to say that these things are true, Euthyphro?

Euth. Yes, Socrates, and more besides. As I was saying, I will report to you many other stories about divine matters, if you like, which I am sure will astonish you when you hear them.

Socr. I dare say. You shall report them to

me at your leisure another time. At present please try to give a more definite answer to the question which I asked you just now. What I asked you, my friend, was, What is piety? and you have not explained it to me to my satisfaction. You only tell me that what you are doing now, namely, prosecuting your father for murder, is a pious act.

Euth. Well, that is true, Socrates.

Socr. Very likely. But many other actions are pious, are they not, Euthyphro?

Euth. Certainly.

Socr. Remember, then, I did not ask you to tell me one or two of all the many pious actions that there are; I want to know what is characteristic of piety which makes all pious actions pious. You said, I think, that there is one characteristic which makes all pious actions pious, and another characteristic which makes all impious actions impious. Do you not remember?

Euth. I do.

Socr. Well, then, explain to me what is this characteristic, that I may have it to turn to, and to use as a standard whereby to judge your actions and those of other men, and be able to say that whatever action resembles it is pious, and whatever does not, is not pious.

Euth. Yes, I will tell you that if you wish, Socrates.

Socr. Certainly I do.

Euth. Well, then, what is pleasing to the gods is pious, and what is not pleasing to them is impious.

Socr. Fine, Euthyphro. Now you have given me the answer that I wanted. Whether what you say is true, I do not know yet. But, of course, you

47

will go on to prove that it is true.

Euth. Certainly.

Socr. Come, then, let us examine our statement. The things and the men that are pleasing to the gods are pious, and the things and the men that are displeasing to the gods are impious. But piety and impiety are not the same; they are as opposite as possible—was not that what we said?

Euth. Certainly.

Socr. And it seems the appropriate statement?

Euth. Yes, Socrates, certainly.

Socr. Have we not also said, Euthyphro, that there are quarrels and disagreements and hatreds among the gods?

Euth. We have.

Socr. But what kind of disagreement, my friend, causes hatred and anger? Let us look at the matter thus. If you and I were to disagree as to whether one number were more than another, would that make us angry and enemies? Should we not settle such a dispute at once by counting?

Euth. Of course.

Socr. And if we were to disagree as to the relative size of two things, we should measure them and put an end to the disagreement at once, should we not?

Euth. Yes.

Socr. And should we not settle a question about the relative weight of two things by weighing them?

Euth. Of course.

Socr. Then what is the question which would
make us angry and enemies if we disagreed about it,
and could not come to a settlement? Perhaps you
have not an answer ready; but listen to mine. Is
it not the question of the just and unjust, of the
honorable and the dishonorable, of the good and
the bad? Is it not questions about these matters
which make you and me and everyone else quarrel,
when we do quarrel, if we differ about them and
can reach no satisfactory agreement?

Euth. Yes, Socrates, it is disagreements
about these matters.

Socr. Well, Euthyphro, the gods will quarrel
over these things if they quarrel at all, will they
not?

Euth. Necessarily.

Socr. Then, my good Euthyphro, you say that
some of the gods think one thing just, the others
another; and that what some of them hold to be
honorable or good, others hold to be dishonorable
or evil. For there would not have been quarrels
among them if they had not disagreed on these
points, would there?

Euth. You are right.

Socr. And each of them loves what he thinks
honorable, and good, and just; and hates the opposite, does he not?

Euth. Certainly.

Scor. But you say that the same action is
held by some of them to be just, and by others to
be unjust; and that then they dispute about it,
and so quarrel and fight among themselves. Is it
not so?

Euth. Yes.

Socr. Then the same thing is hated by the

49

gods and loved by them; and the same thing will be displeasing and pleasing to them.

Euth. Apparently.

Socr. Then, according to your account, the same thing will be pious and impious.

Euth. So it seems.

Socr. Then, my good friend, you have not answered my question. I did not ask you to tell me what action is both pious and impious; but it seems that whatever is pleasing to the gods is also displeasing to them. And so, Euthyphro, I should not be surprised if what you are doing now in punishing your father is an action well pleasing to Zeus, but hateful to Cronos and Uranus, and acceptable to Hephaestus, but hateful to Hera; and if any of the other gods disagree about it, pleasing to some of them and displeasing to others.

Euth. But on this point, Socrates, I think that there is no difference of opinion among the gods: they all hold that if one man kills another unjustly, he must be punished.

Socr. What, Euthyphro? Among mankind, have you never heard disputes whether a man ought to be punished for killing another man unjustly, or for doing some other unjust deed?

Euth. Indeed, they never cease from these disputes, especially in courts of justice. They do all manner of unjust things; and then there is nothing which they will not do and say to avoid punishment.

Socr. Do they admit that they have done something unjust, and at the same time deny that they ought to be punished, Euthyphro?

Euth. No, indeed, that they do not.

Socr. Then it is not the case that there is nothing which they will not do and say. I take it, they do not dare to say or argue that they must not be punished if they have done something unjust. What they say is that they have not done anything unjust, is it not so?

<u>Euth</u>. That is true.

<u>Socr</u>. Then they do not disagree over the question that the unjust individual must be punished. They disagree over the question, who is unjust, and what was done and when, do they not?

<u>Euth</u>. That is true.

<u>Socr</u>. Well, is not exactly the same thing true of the gods if they quarrel about justice and injustice, as you say they do? Do not some of them say that the others are doing something unjust, while the others deny it? No one, I suppose, my dear friend, whether god or man, dares to say that a person who has done something unjust must not be punished.

<u>Euth</u>. No, Socrates, that is true, by and large.

<u>Socr</u>. I take it, Euthyphro, that the disputants, whether men or gods, if the gods do disagree, disagree over each separate act. When they quarrel about any act, some of them say that it was just, and others that it was unjust. Is it not so?

<u>Euth</u>. Yes.

<u>Socr</u>. Come, then, my dear Euthyphro, please enlighten me on this point. What proof have you that all the gods think that a laborer who has been imprisoned for murder by the master of the man whom he has murdered, and who dies from his imprisonment before the master has had time to learn from the religious authorities what he should do, dies unjustly? How do you know that it is just for a son to indict his father and to prosecute him for the murder of such a man? Come, see if you can make it clear to me that the gods necessarily agree in thinking that this action of yours is just; and if you satisfy me, I will never cease singing your praises for wisdom.

51

Euth. I could make that clear enough to you, Socrates; but I am afraid that it would be a long business.

Socr. I see you think that I am duller than the judges. To them, of course, you will make it clear that your father has committed an unjust action, and that all the gods agree in hating such actions.

Euth. I will indeed, Socrates, if they will only listen to me.

Socr. They will listen if they think that you are a good speaker. But while you were talking, it occurred to me to ask myself this question: suppose that Euthyphro were to prove to me as clearly as possible that all the gods think such a death unjust, how has he brought me any nearer to understanding what piety and impiety are? This particular act, perhaps, may be displeasing to the gods, but then we have just seen that piety and impiety cannot be defined in that way; for we have seen that what is displeasing to the gods is also pleasing to them. So I will let you off on this point, Euthyphro; and all the gods shall agree in thinking your father's action wrong and in hating it, if you like. But shall we correct our definition and say that whatever all the gods hate is impious, and whatever they all love is pious; while whatever some of them love, and others hate, is either both or neither? Do you wish us now to define piety and impiety in this manner?

Euth. Why not, Socrates?

Socr. There is no reason why I should not, Euthyphro. It is for you to consider whether that definition will help you to teach me what you promised.

Euth. Well, I should say that piety is what all the gods love, and that impiety is what they all hate.

52

<u>Socr</u>. Are we to examine this definition, Euthyphro, and see if it is a good one? Or are we to be content to accept the bare statements of other men or of ourselves without asking any questions? Or must we examine the statements?

<u>Euth</u>. We must examine them. But for my part I think that the definition is right this time.

<u>Socr</u>. We shall know that better in a little while, my good friend. Now consider this question. Do the gods love piety because it is pious, or is it pious because they love it?

<u>Euth</u>. I do not understand you, Socrates.

<u>Socr</u>. I will try to explain myself: we speak of a thing being carried and carrying, and being led and leading, and being seen and seeing; and you understand that all such expressions mean different things, and what the difference is.

<u>Euth</u>. Yes, I think I understand.

<u>Socr</u>. And we talk of a thing being loved, of a thing loving, and the two are different?

<u>Euth</u>. Of course.

<u>Socr</u>. Now tell me, is a thing which is being carried in a state of being carried because it is carried, or for some other reason?

<u>Euth</u>. No, because it is carried.

<u>Socr</u>. And a thing is in a state of being led because it is led, and of being seen because it is seen?

<u>Euth</u>. Certainly.

<u>Socr</u>. Then a thing is not seen because it is in a state of being seen: it is in a state of being seen because it is seen; and a thing is not led because it is in a state of being led: it is

in a state of being led because it is led; and a
thing is not carried because it is in a state of
being carried: it is in a state of being carried
because it is carried. Is my meaning clear now,
Euthyphro? I mean this: if anything becomes or
is affected, it does not become because it is in
a state of becoming: it is in a state of becoming
because it becomes; and it is not affected because
it is in a state of being affected: it is in a
state of being affected because it is affected.
Do you not agree?

Euth. I do.

Socr. Is not that which is being loved in a
state either of becoming or of being affected in
some way by something?

Euth. Certainly.

Socr. Then the same is true here as in the
former cases. A thing is not loved by those who
love it because it is in a state of being loved;
it is in a state of being loved because they love
it.

Euth. Necessarily.

Socr. Well, then, Euthyphro, what do we say
about piety? Is it not loved by all the gods,
according to your definition?

Euth. Yes.

Socr. Because it is pious, or for some other
reason?

Euth. No, because it is pious.

Socr. Then it is loved by the gods because it
is pious; it is not pious because it is loved by
them?

Euth. It seems so.

Socr. But, then, what is pleasing to the gods is pleasing to them, and is in a state of being loved by them, because they love it?

Euth. Of course.

Socr. Then piety is not what is pleasing to the gods, and what is pleasing to the gods is not pious, as you say, Euthyphro. They are different things.

Euth. And why, Socrates?

Socr. Because we are agreed that the gods love piety because it is pious, and that it is not pious because they love it. Is not this so?

Euth. Yes.

Socr. And that what is pleasing to the gods because they love it, is pleasing to them by reason of this same love, and that they do not love it because it is pleasing to them.

Euth. True.

Socr. Then, my dear Euthyphro, piety and what is pleasing to the gods are different things. If the gods had loved piety because it is pious, they would also have loved what is pleasing to them because it is pleasing to them; but if what is pleasing to them had been pleasing to them because they loved it, then piety, too, would have been piety because they loved it. But now you see that they are opposite things, and wholly different from each other. For the one is of a sort to be loved because it is loved, while the other is loved because it is of a sort to be loved. My question, Euthyphro, was, What is piety? But it turns out that you have not explained to me the essential character of piety; you have been content to mention an effect which belongs to it—namely, that all the gods love it. You have not yet told me what its essential character is. Do not, if you please, keep from me what piety is; begin again and tell me that. Never mind whether the gods love it, or whether it has other effects: we shall not differ on that point. Do your best to make clear to me what is piety and what is impiety.

Euth. But, Socrates, I really don't know how to explain to you what is in my mind. Whatever statement we put forward always somehow moves round in a circle, and will not stay where we put it.

Socr. I think that your statements, Euthyphro, are worthy of my ancestor Daedalus.[2] If they had been mine and I had set them down, I dare say you would have made fun of me, and said that it was the consequence of my descent from Daedalus that the statements which I construct run away, as his statues used to, and will not stay where they are put. But, as it is, the statements are yours, and the joke would have no point. You yourself see that they will not stay still.

Euth. Nay, Socrates, I think that the joke is very much in point. It is not my fault that the statement moves round in a circle and will not stay still. But you are the Daedalus, I think; as far as I am concerned, my statements would have stayed put.

Socr. Then, my friend, I must be a more skillful artist than Daedalus; he only used to make his own works move, while I, you see, can make other people's works move, too. And the beauty of it is that I am wise against my will. I would rather that our statements had remained firm and immovable than have all the wisdom of Daedalus and all the riches of Tantalus to boot. But enough of this. I will do my best to help you to explain to me what piety is, for I think that you are lazy. Don't give in yet. Tell me, do you not think that all piety must be just?

Euth. I do.

Socr. Well, then, is all justice pious, too?

Or, while all piety is just, is a part only of justice pious, and the rest of it something else?

Euth. I do not follow you, Socrates.

Socr. Yet you have the advantage over me in your youth no less than your wisdom. But, as I say, the wealth of your wisdom makes you complacent. Exert yourself, my good friend: I am not asking you a difficult question. I mean the opposite of what the poet [3] said, when he wrote:

"You shall not name Zeus the creator, who made all things: for where there is fear there also is reverence."

Now I disagree with the poet. Shall I tell you why?

Euth. Yes.

Socr. I do not think it true to say that where there is fear, there also is reverence. Many people who fear sickness and poverty and other such evils seem to me to have fear, but no reverence for what they fear. Do you not think so?

Euth. I do.

Socr. But I think that where there is reverence there also is fear. Does any man feel reverence and a sense of shame about anything, without at the same time dreading and fearing the reputation of wickedness?

Euth. No, certainly not.

Socr. Then, though there is fear wherever there is reverence, it is not correct to say that where there is fear there also is reverence. Reverence does not always accompany fear; for fear, I take it, is wider than reverence. It is a part of fear, just as the odd is a part of number, so that where you have the odd you must also have number, though where you have number you do not necessarily

57

have the odd. Now I think you follow me?

Euth. I do.

Socr. Well, then, this is what I meant by the question which I asked you. Is there always piety where there is justice? Or, though there is always justice where there is piety, yet there is not always piety where there is justice, because piety is only a part of justice? Shall we say this, or do you differ?

Euth. No, I agree. I think that you are right.

Socr. Now observe the next point. If piety is a part of justice, we must find out, I suppose, what part of justice it is? Now, if you had asked me just now, for instance, what part of number is the odd, and what number is an odd number, I should have said that whatever number is not even is an odd number. Is it not so?

Euth. Yes.

Socr. Then see if you can explain to me what part of justice is piety, that I may tell Meletus that now that I have been adequately instructed by you as to what actions are righteous and pious, and what are not, he must give up prosecuting me unjustly for impiety.

Euth. Well, then, Socrates, I should say that righteousness and piety are the part of justice which has to do with the careful attention which ought to be paid to the gods; and that what has to do with the careful attention which ought to be paid to men is the remaining part of justice.

Socr. And I think that your answer is a good one. Euthyphro. But there is one little point about which I still want to hear more. I do not yet understand what the careful attention is to which you refer. I suppose you do not mean that the attention which we pay to the gods is like the attention which we pay to other things. We say, for instance, do we not, that not everyone knows how to take care of horses, but only the trainer of horses?

Euth. Certainly.

Socr. For I suppose that the skill that is concerned with horses is the art of taking care of horses.

Euth. Yes.

Socr. And not everyone understands the care of dogs, but only the huntsman.

Euth. True.

Socr. For I suppose that the huntsman's skill is the art of taking care of dogs.

Euth. Yes.

Socr. And the herdsman's skill is the art of taking care of cattle.

Euth. Certainly.

Socr. And you say that piety and righteousness are taking care of the gods, Euthyphro?

Euth. I do.

Socr. Well, then, has not all care the same object? Is it not for the good and benefit of that on which it is bestowed? For instance, you see that horses are benefited and improved when they are cared for by the art which is concerned with them. Is it not so?

Euth. Yes, I think so.

Socr. And dogs are benefited and improved by the huntsman's art, and cattle by the herdsman's, are they not? And the same is always true. Or do you think care is ever meant to harm that which is cared for?

Euth. No, indeed; certainly not.

Socr. But to benefit it?

Euth. Of course.

Socr. Then is piety, which is our care for
the gods, intended to benefit the gods, or to improve them? Should you allow that you make any of
the gods better when you do a pious action?

Euth. No indeed; certainly not.

Socr. No, I am quite sure that that is not
your meaning, Euthyphro. It was for that reason
that I asked you what you meant by the careful attention which ought to be paid to the gods. I
thought that you did not mean that.

Euth. You were right, Socrates. I do not
mean that.

Socr. Good. Then what sort of attention to
the gods will piety be?

Euth. The sort of attention, Socrates, slaves
pay to their masters.

Socr. I understand; then it is a kind of
service to the gods?

Euth. Certainly.

Socr. Can you tell me what result the art
which serves a doctor serves to produce? Is it
not health?

Euth. Yes.

Socr. And what result does the art which
serves a shipwright serve to produce?

Euth. A ship, of course, Socrates.

Socr. The result of the art which serves a

builder is a house, is it not?

Euth. Yes.

Socr. Then tell me, my good friend: What result will the art which serves the gods serve to produce? You must know, seeing that you say that you know more about divine things than any other man.

Euth. Well, that is true, Socrates.

Socr. Then tell me, I beg you, what is that grand result which the gods use our services to produce?

Euth. There are many notable results, Socrates.

Socr. So are those, my friend, which a general produces. Yet it is easy to see that the crowning result of them all is victory in war, is it not?

Euth. Of course.

Socr. And, I take it, the farmer produces many notable results; yet the principal result of them all is that he makes the earth produce food.

Euth. Certainly.

Socr. Well, then, what is the principal result of the many notable results which the gods produce?

Euth. I told you just now, Socrates, that accurate knowledge of all these matters is not easily obtained. However, broadly I say this: if any man knows that his words and actions in prayer and sacrifice are acceptable to the gods, that is what is pious; and it preserves the state, as it does private families. But the opposite of what is acceptable to the gods is sacrilegious, and this it is that undermines and destroys everything.

61

Socr. Certainly, Euthyphro, if you had wished, you could have answered my main question in far fewer words. But you are evidently not anxious to teach me. Just now, when you were on the very point of telling me what I want to know, you stopped short. If you had gone on then, I should have learned from you clearly enough by this time what piety is. But now I am asking you questions, and must follow wherever you lead me; so tell me, what is it that you mean by piety and impiety? Do you not mean a science of prayer and sacrifice?

Euth. I do.

Socr. To sacrifice is to give to the gods, and to pray is to ask of them, is it not?

Euth. It is, Socrates.

Socr. Then you say that piety is the science of asking of the gods and giving to them?

Euth. You understand my meaning exactly, Socrates.

Socr. Yes, for I am eager to share your wisdom, Euthyphro, and so I am all attention; nothing that you say will fall to the ground. But tell me, what is this service of the gods? You say it is to ask of them, and to give to them?

Euth. I do.

Socr. Then, to ask rightly will be to ask of them what we stand in need of from them, will it not?

Euth. Naturally.

Socr. And to give rightly will be to give back to them what they stand in need of from us? It would not be very skillful to make a present to a man of something that he has no need of.

Euth. True, Socrates.

Socr. Then piety, Euthyphro, will be the art of carrying on business between gods and men?

Euth. Yes, if you like to call it so.

Socr. But I like nothing except what is true. But tell me, how are the gods benefited by the gifts which they receive from us? What they give is plain enough. Every good thing that we have is their gift. But how are they benefited by what we give them? Have we the advantage over them in these business transactions to such an extent that we receive from them all the good things we possess, and give them nothing in return?

Euth. But do you suppose, Socrates, that the gods are benefited by the gifts which they receive from us?

Socr. But what *are* these gifts, Euthyphro, that we give the gods?

Euth. What do you think but honor and praise, and, as I have said, what is acceptable to them.

Socr. Then piety, Euthyphro, is acceptable to the gods, but it is not profitable to them nor loved by them?

Euth. I think that nothing is more loved by them.

Socr. Then I see that piety means that which is loved by the gods.

Euth. Most certainly.

Socr. After that, shall you be surprised to find that your statements move about instead of staying where you put them? Shall you accuse me of being the Daedalus that makes them move, when you yourself are far more skillful than Daedalus was, and make them go round in a circle? Do you not see that our statement has come round to where it was before? Surely you remember that we have already

63

seen that piety and what is pleasing to the gods are quite different things. Do you not remember?

Euth. I do.

Socr. And now do you not see that you say that what the gods love is pious? But does not what the gods love come to the same thing as what is pleasing to the gods?

Euth. Certainly.

Socr. Then either our former conclusion was wrong or, if it was right, we are wrong now.

Euth. So it seems.

Socr. Then we must begin again and inquire what piety is. I do not mean to give in until I have found out. Do not regard me as unworthy; give your whole mind to the question, and this time tell me the truth. For if anyone knows it, it is you; and you are a Proteus whom I must not let go until you have told me. It cannot be that you would ever have undertaken to prosecute your aged father for the murder of a laboring man unless you had known exactly what piety and impiety are. You would have feared to risk the anger of the gods, in case you should be doing wrong, and you would have been afraid of what men would say. But now I am sure that you think that you know exactly what is pious and what is not; so tell me, my good Euthyphro, and do not conceal from me what you think.

Euth. Another time, then, Socrates, I am in a hurry now, and it is time for me to be off.

Socr. What are you doing, my friend! Will you go away and destroy all my hopes of learning from you what is pious and what is not, and so of escaping Meletus? I meant to explain to him that now Euthyphro has made me wise about divine things, and that I no longer in my ignorance speak carelessly about them or introduce reforms. And then I was going to promise him to live a better life

64

for the future.

Notes

[1]The anachronistic title "king" was retained by the magistrate who had jurisdiction over crimes affecting the state religion.—Ed.

[2]Daedalus' statues were reputed to have been so lifelike that they came alive.—Ed.

[3]Stasinus.

Adulthood: <u>The</u> <u>Problem</u>

Searching for Adulthood in America*
Winthrop D. Jordan

It is an interesting commentary on our culture
that we find ourselves asking: What does adulthood
mean? As with so many human affairs, the meaning
lies in the question. From a historian's vantage
point, what is arresting is that we should be asking a question that would have made so little sense
to our forebears.

A word of caution is in order: my present
assignment is to trace the history of the concept
of adulthood in one country—the United States. It
is immediately obvious that there are difficulties
in treating the concept within a single national
unit, particularly the United States, where one is
dealing with a multiplicity of cultural traditions.
One could argue that the United States is merely
one segment of Western culture or, today, of technological world culture. On the other hand, one
could stress the diversity of the nation and discuss concepts that have prevailed among various
American ethnic and religious groups. To do so
would entail entering a fascinating arena, but one
thicketed with complexities as to require a very
lengthy disquisition. We would have to deal, for
example, with such phenomena as ten-year-old black
youths calling each other "man," as well as with
their fathers who are called—or at least used to
be—"boys." We would have to deal, too, with Irish
Catholic families in which sons become "Fathers"
to their parents. There are myriad similar problems. Rather than plunge into this briarpatch, I
will confine myself to prevailing ideas in

*Reprinted by permission of the author and
American Academy of Arts and Sciences from
<u>Daedalus</u>, Fall, 1976, pp. 1-11.

America—most evident and predominant in the non-ethnic middle class—trusting that it will be borne in mind that many of these ideas were not, and are not, confined to this country and, indeed, that the concept of adulthood constitutes a most inappropriate vehicle for any attempt to define America's uniqueness. Indeed "adulthood," as we ordinarily think of it today, is largely an artifact of twentieth-century American culture. Historically that concept emerged by a process of exclusion, as a final product resulting from prior definitions of other stages in the human life cycle.

I

If one ransacks the cultural baggage of the early English settlers of this nation, one searches in vain for any well defined concept of adulthood. Perhaps one might at least expect to find some vague outlines of such a concept in the extensive Puritan literature on the family, but one does not. In early seventeenth-century England, the Reverend William Gouge's Of Domestical Duties managed to offer more than six hundred pages on the family without saying anything about the life cycle of families or of individuals.[1] Gouge's approach was typical of the day: he discussed the duties of the husband, of the wife, of children, and of servants. The roles played by each are entirely static; growth and even change are totally absent.

It would be a mistake to see Gouge's portrayal as a reflection of an entirely static society. His England was just the opposite: dynamic and in the throes of social and economic change—a restless, voyaging, trafficking, discovering nation whose accomplishments were so eloquently trumpeted by Richard Hakluyt. Rather, it makes much more sense to view the rigidities of Gouge's description as reflecting concern about increasing fluidity in the social and perhaps even familial structures of Tudor-Stuart England. While Hakluyt called upon the English to plant themselves in America, Gouge cautioned the godly to perform their domestic

67

duties—each according to his appointed familial station. The duties—not the development—of the roles were what counted.

If one turns to the theology of the early English settlers in America, which was predominantly Puritan or at least Low-Church Protestant, one finds an analogous situation. A predestinarian theology, no matter how much modified by covenants that restrained God's arbitrary power, was scarcely the body of thought to encourage notions of personal growth, maturing, or becoming psychologically adult. No matter how dynamic in the long run, Puritanism spoke for stasis, for striving to know one's existing condition rather than becoming something one was not. To some extent the conversion experience implied change, but it was a limited one since no matter how diligently the individual nurtured the seed of grace, in the end God did all. It is striking that the prevailing imagery of conversion was not one of maturation (despite the seed) but of rebirth. In the long run, indeed, the Arminianization of this theology was required before a fully developed psychological concept of adulthood could emerge. I use the ungainly term "Arminianization" as shorthand for that lengthy process by which Calvinist predestinarianism gave way to a theology that emphasized the individual's ability to gain salvation by means of his own efforts, often aided by revivalistic preaching. Only when the individual's own struggles were given far greater weight in the process of conversion would there be room for a process of reaching psychological maturity. In mid-nineteenth-century America, creeping Arminianization had rusted the bolts of the one-hoss shay pretty badly; it was then that one of the most popular religious books on the family could be entitled <u>Christian Nurture</u>.

It would be absurd to contend that our forebears in the nineteenth century—or in the seventeenth century—had absolutely no realization that human beings are born pretty helpless and irresponsible and that their capacities for dealing with the world gradually enlarge. They knew perfectly well that some people were grown-ups and others were children. Though they were not inclined to articulate their recognition of biological and psychological maturity, at times they were forced to draw distinctions based on the reality of human maturation.

In this connection it is instructive to turn to the realm of the law, which embodies a society's ground rules for social rights and responsibilities. Given the rigidities and formalism of Anglo-American written law, one would expect to find some chronological definition of when infant irresponsibility was judged to have ended and adult rights and duties were said to have been acquired. For centuries the common law, and until very recently American statutory and constitutional law, placed that age at 21. Twenty-one has traditionally been the end of nonage. This is not to say, however, that the law has been decisive and unambiguous in plumping for 21 (or 18), since there have always been considerable confusion and inconsistency on the matter. Indeed, the law has reflected a strong sense that individuals acquire capacities gradually, as well as the fact that, in this culture at least, males and females acquire them at different ages. In the seventeen-sixties, for example, Blackstone, the English common-law jurist who was so influential in America, summarized the situation as follows:

> The ages of male and female are different for different purposes. A male at <u>twelve</u> years old may take the oath of allegiance; at <u>fourteen</u> is at years of discretion, and therefore may consent or disagree to marriage, may choose his guardian, and, if his discretion be actually proved, may make his testament of his personal estate; at <u>seventeen</u> may be an executor; and at <u>twenty-one</u> is at his own disposal, and may alien his lands, goods, and chattels. A female also at <u>seven</u> years of age may be betrothed or given in marriage; at <u>nine</u> is entitled to dower; at <u>twelve</u> is at years of maturity, and therefore may consent or disagree to marriage, and, if proved to have sufficient discretion, may

bequeath her personal estate; at _fourteen_ is at years of legal discretion, and may choose a guardian; at _seventeen_ may be executrix; and at _twenty-one_ may dispose of herself and her lands.

Still more revealing of uncertainty concerning chronological age was Blackstone's discussion of the ages of criminal responsibility. From age 14 a person could be punished capitally; under the age of 7, he could not. But, Blackstone wrote, "the period between _seven_ and _fourteen_ is subject of much uncertainty," and he went on to cite "two instances, one of a girl thirteen, who was burned for killing her mistress; another of a boy still younger, that had killed his companion, and hid himself, who was hanged; for it appeared by his hiding that he knew he had done wrong, and could discern between good and evil."[2] A similar lack of certainty has prevailed in this country to this day, exacerbated by a federal system of government. Not only have the various states set various ages at various times for various purposes, but the national government has wavered on the matter. In general, marriage has tended to confer certain rights regardless of age, which is one reason why the states have regulated the age of marriage, with what consistency may be judged from the following:

MINIMUM AGE FOR MARRIAGE,
SELECTED STATES, 1971[3]

	WITH PARENTAL CONSENT		WITHOUT PARENTAL CONSENT	
	Male	Female	Male	Female
Alabama	17	14	21	18
Florida	18	16	21	21
Maine	16	16	20	18
Michigan	No provision	16	18	18
North Dakota	18	15	21	18
Texas	16	14	19	18

That females have earlier rights probably reflects assumptions about their customary subordination in

70

marriage rather than about their earlier maturation. As for males, their age of suitability for military service has been judged at various times to be as low as 16 years or as high as 21, with no clear trend through time nor correlation with wartime exigencies.[4]

And the relationship of these data with the concept of adulthood? It would be possible, of course, to argue that these various ages reflect a consciousness of maturation as a process, of adulthood as something people grow into. On the other hand, it may well be that the real importance of these figures lies in their imprecision, especially in a society so given to quantitative preciseness. Indeed, if there had existed a clearer concept of adulthood, there might well have been greater consistency regarding the age at which the society's members were deemed to have attained that status. It is in this light, perhaps, that we may view the very recent tendency to settle upon the single age of 18 for legal maturity for most or all purposes and for—the point is of some importance—both men and women. It is only in the nineteen-seventies that we are approaching a consensus as to the proper legal age of majority.

As another means of assessing the early shape of the concept of adulthood, one can turn to the term itself. If the <u>Oxford English Dictionary</u> is correct, the word "adulthood" came into use only a century ago; the <u>OED</u> gives 1870, though "adultness" appears a century earlier. The term "adult" itself is, of course, considerably older, but nonetheless a relatively recent acquisition. It derives from the past participle of the Latin <u>adolescere</u>, "to grow up," but it may have been adopted directly from the French <u>adulte</u>, itself a sixteenth-century adaptation of the Latin. It was used in English once in 1531 but, says the <u>OED</u>, was "not really naturalized till the middle of the seventeenth century." Even then it seems not to have firmly acquired its modern meaning(s), for in 1726 one author announced that "an adult Age is above the age of Puberty and under that of twenty-five years."

71

At least in my experience, the word was not frequently used in eighteenth- or even nineteenth-century America. And of course it has only been in recent years that the term has taken on the burden of freight it carries in such phrases as "adult education and "adult films" for "adults only."

II

All this is to argue the negative proposition that, to put the matter baldly, the concept of adulthood, in the psychological sense we ordinarily use today, did not appear in America at all until after the Civil War and not really until the early twentieth century. One reason for this absence, already suggested, was theological: American Christianity had to be Arminianized. Another necessary precondition for the emergence of a concept of adulthood was, once again to state the case bluntly, that the family had to be de-politicized— that is to say, notions about maturity and immaturity, mastery and dependence originally had pronouncedly political overtones in which we can detect the potentiality of a shift toward emphasizing these qualities in individuals.

The analogy between the family and the state has its own long history. It was very commonly drawn in seventeenth-century England and America. The family was, as the equation went, "a little commonwealth" whose head was its "governor." And of course familial imagery was very commonly used to describe the state. Amid all the contractualism of the seventeenth and eighteenth centuries, the king remained the "father" of his people. John Locke's instinct was perfectly sound when he advanced his political contract in the form of an attack upon Sir Robert Filmer's patriarchal theory of monarchy.

Although historians have not chosen to pay much attention to it, there was a crescendo of familial-political imagery at the time of the American Revolution. As he was so repeatedly denominated, George III was the "father" of his people and they properly owed him "filial" obedience and respect until he transformed that "natural" relationship be becoming a "tyrant." While George III was the "father," Great Britain was the "parent" or the "mother" country of the Colonies. It was precisely these natural relationships that Thomas Paine so successfully assailed in Common Sense when he denounced the king as "the royal brute of Great-Britain" (i.e., standing in an unnatural relationship to the colonists) and declared that Europe, not England, was the "parent" of America.

These terms were common currency, and it is scarcely any wonder that many writers extended the analogy by incorporating an image of maturation to describe what was happening. It was not a new image. In the seventeenth century, James Harrington had described the colonies in America as being "yet Babes that cannot live without sucking the Breasts of their Mother Citys," but they will "wean themselves," he warned, "when they come of age."5 In August, 1776, one English friend of the American cause, Richard Price, undertook to refute the common assertion that the "infant" colonies owed obedience to the "parent state":

Children having no property, and being incapable of guiding themselves, the author of nature has committed the care of them to their parents, and subjected them to their absolute authority. But there is a period when having acquired property, and a capacity of judging for themselves, they become independent agents; and when, for this reason, the authority of their parents ceases, and becomes nothing but the respect and influence due to benefactors. Supposing, therefore, that the order of nature in establishing the relation between parents and children, ought to have been the rule of our conduct to the Colonies, we should have been gradually relaxing our authority as they grew up. But like mad parents, we have done the contrary; and, at the very time when our authority should have been most relaxed, we have carried it to the greatest extent, and exercised it with the greatest rigour. No wonder then, that they have turned upon us; and obliged us to remember that they are not children.[6]

More pithily than Price, Thomas Paine announced airily, "To know whether it be the interest of the continent to be independent, we need only ask this easy, simple question: Is it the interest of a man to be a boy all his life?"[7]

This mode of political discourse became less common after the Revolution, but it did not dissipate entirely until after the Civil War. In the antebellum era, Americans declaimed on the virtues of "the founding fathers" and made George Washington "the Father of his country." At the time of the War of 1812, it was still possible to utilize (and to mix) the metaphor of maturation: We can watch them better than our fathers were able to do. In 1776, the vessel of state was launched into an unknown sea . . . and we were as children. . . . In 1812, we have a stable and solid government . . . we are abundantly supplied with weapons of defence, we are in a state of comparative manhood. . . ."[8] At the time of the "fratricidal" Civil War, after Lincoln refused to let the "erring sisters depart in peace," he was hailed as "Father Abra'am."[9] But the first president to be assassinated was the last to be assigned such paternity. We have only to try "Father Woodrow" or "Father Franklin" for sound to realize the inappropriateness of the concept in the twentieth century.

A major reason for the demise of this imagery in the political arena was growing concern about actual parents and children. Very briefly, that concern seems to have arisen almost immediately after the American Revolution. At first it manifested itself in discussions about what sort of education would be most proper for the new "infant" Republic and in attempts to produce a suitable literature for the little republicans who would all be becoming "citizens." By 1830, Americans were more than concerned about their children; they were downright worried. At the same time, in the eighteen-thirties, Americans began to worry about adults in a novel way, but not, emphatically, as adults. Rather, the concern was with men and women, with sex roles. This was, of course, the period of the beginnings of the women's rights movement—and of very widespread opposition to it. Much more energy, however, went into concern with parental roles, especially as to their proper sexual differentiation. American Victorians placed the woman on a pedestal, but that pillar was located specifically at the hearthside of the home. The wife was now more the mother, the husband the father. When he was not busy at the counting house he, too, belonged at home. The famous temperance poem caught the spirit exactly: "Father, dear father, come home with me now. . . ."

What this meant was that the antebellum process of depoliticization of the family was _pari passu_ the development of an ideology of domesticity. Antebellum America was not concerned with any bimodality between childhood and maturity, but rather with proper roles within the home. As is well known, this ideology was at least in some measure a response to rapidly changing social and economic conditions. In a commercializing, urbanizing, expanding economy, more and more men and women were working, traveling, and buying and selling away from home, and it is scarcely any wonder that the family home came to be a focus of concern.

This concern for domesticity interacted in a novel way with political discourse. A defensive South attempted to transform its commercial slavery into a domestic institution—domestic in the sense of being "peculiar" to the South, but domestic also in the sense that the plantation was increasingly thought of as a family. The master became a patriarch and his slaves, children. Northern critics cried out that the master was frequently the literal father of his slaves and that slavery was a brothel house—an anti-home. Southerners retorted that it was Northern wage slavery which threatened the family and that Northern women were "unsexing" themselves by leaving their hearthsides in order to

75

attend the "promiscuous assemblies" so characteristic of Northern "fanaticism."

At the same time, the egalitarianism of the Jacksonian era was helping to lay the groundwork for later changes in the way in which domestic roles would be conceived. Partly, the homogenizing of ranks and stations in life tended to reduce the citizenry to an undifferentiated mass. The widening of the suffrage, which was accomplished easily and noiselessly compared to the analogous process in Europe, produced a novel situation.

It is perhaps more profitable to think of the suffrage as being limited along new lines. If almost all white adult males could vote (as they could by the time of the Civil War) the suffrage was, in effect, no longer defined by property but by three other criteria—race, age, and sex.[10] In one sense, then, political democracy made the distinction between the political adult and the political child more important. At the same time, however, the sexual criterion effectively countered this tendency by drawing together members of each sex. Tocqueville was describing this process when he wrote that, as the laws and manners become more intimate and more egalitarian in America, "the realm of father and son become more intimate and more affectionate; rules and authority are less talked of; confidence and tenderness are oftentimes increased."[11] It was no accident that Tocqueville picked the male "realm of father and son."

The Jacksonian concern with proper sex roles was so strong as virtually to preclude, in and of itself, any interest in a concept of adulthood as such. A pronounced emphasis on the distinction between women and men tended to override any perception of commonality; manhood and womanhood perceptually overrode adulthood. What room was there for adulthood when a physician could write that after menopause a woman was "degraded to the level of a being who has no further duty to perform in this world"?[12] What mattered was the distinction between the male and the female parent. "The father may instruct," declared another writer, "but the mother instils; the father may command our reason, but the mother compels our instinct; the father may finish, but the mother must begin. The empire of the father is over the head; of the mother, over the heart."[13]

That such remarks were part of a very basic social change is suggested by the fact that in the mid nineteenth century there seems to have been less premarital sexual intercourse in America than at any time before or since. Even sex was only for parents (not to mention only for men and women). The modern "sexual revolution" (including more premarital pregnancies) seems to have begun in the United States in the very early twentieth century.[14] This was also the approximate time of two other demographic developments which may well have helped engender the development of an explicitly articulated concept of adulthood. Throughout the nineteenth century the fertility rate in the United States fell quite markedly. At the same time, particularly at the end of the century, the mortality rate declined. The combined result was that grown persons no longer spent such a large portion of their lives in the parental role; the "empty nest" syndrome is a relatively recent one.[15] What was to be done with this new period in the life cycle?

This development was accompanied, not by the discovery of adulthood, but by the discovery of adolescence and of old age. Both the term and the concept of "adolescence" were first widely popularized by G. Stanley Hall's book of that title in 1904, though the term itself is much older—considerably older, indeed, than the term "adult." There had been discussion of "youth," as distinct from "childhood," in the nineteenth century, but Hall's work placed "adolescence" firmly as a distinct phase of life and as a description of inner and outer behavior. It is suggestive that Hall placed considerable emphasis on adolescence as that period of life when religious conversion was most likely to be expected; in doing so he was drawing upon an emphasis which in the nineteenth century had accompanied the Arminianization of American Protestantism.

It is less well known that Hall later wrote another book entitled——not "Adulthood"——but Senescence (1922). In that book, Hall described "adolescence" as lasting until age 25 or 30, "maturity" from 25 or 30 to 40 or 45 (which left ten or, at best, twenty years for adulthood): "senescence," which he lumped with "old age," was, as announced by the subtitle, "The Last Half of Life." The difficulty that the concept of adulthood was having in getting off the ground is suggested by Hall's conclusion in a previous article (1921) that "leaving out of consideration here the initial prepubertal stage and the terminal one of the postclimacteric or old age proper, all the rest of life which lies between these is divided into two parts, adolescence and senescence, that the latter begins where the former ends [at about forty-five years of age], and that all we have thought characteristic of middle life consists of only the phenomena which are connected with the turn of the tide."[16]

Hall's work on adolescence was heavily influenced by post-Darwinian evolutionary biology. Mankind (particularly the much esteemed Teutonic and Anglo-Saxon portion thereof) was seen as evolving through stages into higher and higher forms. Hall himself thought individual development recapitulated the development of the species. Evolutionary biology worked to pave the way for various developmental psychologies. It was no accident that Hall was attracted by a far more powerful developmental model then being shaped in Europe; his interest and admiration were evident at the famous psychological conference at Clark University in 1909 at which he hosted Dr. Sigmund Freud.

The general tendency in various schools of psychology in the early twentieth century was to segment the life cycle into increasingly discrete and well defined units. An accompanying tendency was fully as important: the various segments of the life cycle were seen not merely as temporal stages but as <u>descriptions</u> of inner life and external behavior. Thus the "oral stage" was not merely a temporal segment of the life cycle but a psychological syndrome. Thus, too, "adolescence" was far more descriptive of a mode of behavior than was "youth" in the nineteenth century. The earlier, less content-laden segmenting of the life cycle in the nineteenth century was best typified by the popular prints showing "the stages of man," usually four or six stages such as childhood, youth, maturity, and old age.

A parallel process occurred in American schools and colleges. It was not merely the slow demise of the one-room schoolhouse which caused increasingly precise age-grading in the schools; it was a growing sense that age differences among young people really mattered. This same sense somewhat later permitted the development of the concept of "mental age" in connection with the I.Q. test. To speak of "the college years" as typifying any sort of behavior would have been difficult in the nineteenth century when those years ran from the early teens to the late twenties. In the nineteenth century, grown-ups attended lyceums; in the twentieth, they undertook "adult education."

Finally (and there is scarcely need to belabor the point) this same first quarter of the twentieth century saw the gradual extension of the suffrage to (mostly white) adult women. The body politic was no longer defined in sexual terms: only race and age remained. Politically, only adulthood mattered. Even within the family a parallel process occurred: by the nineteen-twenties, the Victorian mother and father were becoming good modern <u>parents</u>, self-consciously "raising" their children according to certain diffuse notions indirectly derived from Dr. Freud. The new medical specialty of pediatrics was by now respectably established. The twin streams were shortly to be united in one of the most popular books ever written for American adults—<u>Baby and Child Care</u> by Dr. Benjamin Spock. Despite the Doctor's emphasis on parenting, there

remained in his book strong traces of sex differentiation in the parental roles. But it is also true
that the book signaled which way the wind was blow-
ing. Spock has, in the nineteen-seventies, been
self-consciously revising his text with an eye to
meeting, even eliminating, sex differences in
parental duties.

III

Given these developments, the concept of
adulthood was bound to flower. What is surprising,
perhaps, is that it took until 1975 for a symposium
on adulthood to materialize, and that as of 1968,
the International Encyclopedia of the Social Sciences
has articles on "Aging" and "Adolescence," but none
on adulthood. The concept was fully evident in
popular magazines in the nineteen-twenties. By
1952, the bellwether magazine of popular taste was
offering a quiz, "condensed from McCall's," entitled "So You Think You're Grown Up!" "How old,"
the introduction asks, "do you have to be before
you're an adult? By psychological standards you
can be grown-up at 20 or a child at 50." After
fifteen questions ("1. Would you ever, by choice,
spend an evening alone?"), "to see how 'mature'
you are, turn to page 91."[17] From this sort of
thing it has been no step at all to the spate of
selfhood books of the nineteen-sixties and seventies. Since 1930 there have, of course, been interesting changes in the concept: Dale Carnegie
could scarcely have written a book entitled I'm
O.K.—You're O.K.

Americans had discovered in "adulthood" a
novel and ambiguous guide to the maze of an unu-
sually fluid, mobile society which offered a daz-
zling array of career lines. They were no longer
told to labor diligently in an appointed worldly
calling. As a guide to life they were now enjoined,
as one magazine put it, to "Act Your Age."[18]
William Gouge would have greeted such an injunction
with towering incomprehension.

Always the current emphasis is on growth and

change. At the popular level the approach is to provide a smorgasbord of "psychologies." A new magazine entitled Personal Growth offers as "some of the areas we cover": "Self-Actualization Techniques"; "Gestalt Therapy"; "Encounter Groups"; "Meditation"; "Bio-Energetic Analysis"; "Hypnotherapy"; "Relaxation Techniques"; "Self-Analysis"; "Transpersonal Psychology"; "Peak Experiences"; "Creativity Training"; "Depth Imagery & Dream Work"; "Primal Therapy"; "Psychoanalysis"; "Biofeedback Training"; "Transactional Analysis"; "Psychosynthesis"; and "Altered States of Consciousness."[19] One wants instantly to reach for the Alka-Selzer. At a slightly more serious level, the New York Times offers such articles as (in characteristic voice): "Three Phases of Adulthood: Transitions Termed as Difficult as Adolescence."[20]

What we seem to be involved in now is a synergistic interaction between a newly dynamic concept and a new social reality. Take, for example, the opening paragraph of a recent newspaper article entitled "Transition: How Adults Cope with Change":

> Adults don't stay put the way they used to. Everywhere you look, people are moving around, changing jobs, going back to school, getting divorced. Starting over, in short. At age 30, 40, 50, 60—there's no end to it.[21]

In such remarks we sense not only a description of real events but an endorsement of them. We also sense that without such endorsements the events would not be taking place.

What we are up against here is a very traditional problem in historical causation—the relationship between social and ideological change. We can see the two factors dynamically interacting in the case of legislation concerning children during the early years of the twentieth century. During the nineteenth century, a large proportion of children went to school until age 12 or 13, and then went to work. About 1900, as part of the process of industrialization, new machinery began displacing children in many jobs in agriculture, factories, and commercial establishments. What has been called "the first stringent" child-labor law was passed by Illinois in 1903.[22] Child-labor laws went hand in hand with compulsory-schooling laws which raised the age at which children were allowed to leave school. Increasingly, extended schooling was seen as necessary preparation for a life of work in a highly complex society. At the same time, women were coming to constitute a rapidly growing proportion of the total labor force. In other words, work, or "career," began to lose its linkage with sex just at the time when the age of "getting a job" was rising considerably. There was an increasingly solid social base for thinking of the late teens as an age when people of both sexes entered a distinct new phase of their lives, one which would last until it came to an abrupt halt, not so frequently as before by death, but by mandatory retirement. The junior citizens of the young Republic, trained by the schools for their adult careers, would eventually become "senior citizens," drawing retirement benefits with a number that had been assigned them when they first entered the work force. Accompanying these changes was widespread discussion of childhood and adolescence as periods of growth, learning, expanding horizons and capacities. There was much talk about chilren's play, no longer seen as reprehensible "idle pastimes," but as necessary to an expanding, exploring personality. Schooling and play became preparative for— and the moral equivalent of—work, the "business" of adults.

If one had to plump for any single factor as being of central importance in this process, it might well be the actuality and expectation of rapid social change—not limited to the United Sates, of course, but probably of longer standing there than in most other countries. Technology, geographical and social mobility, and social pluralism have worked to speed up life so that we not only expect our children to lead different lives from ourselves, but we expect our own lives to change, perhaps drastically, through time. In the more static world of our ancestors it would scarcely have been possible to conceive of time in the way which permitted Henri Bergson to write, at about the turn of the twentieth century, "To exist is to change; to change is to mature; to mature is to create oneself endlessly."[23] We have moved, over the years, from condition to process. In our culture, adulthood as a condition used to be simply assumed; as a process, it now seems to demand explanation.

Notes

[1]William Gouge, Of Domestical Duties (London, 1622).

[2]William Blackstone, Commentaries on the Laws of England, book 1, chap. 17, sec. 629-630.

[3]Virginia G. Cook, The Age of Majority (Lexington, Kentucky, 1972), p. 19.

[4]Commonwealth of Massachusetts, Report of the Legislative Research Council Relative to Lowering the Age of Majority ([Boston], 1971), pp. 25-30.

[5]Quoted in Christopher Hill, Puritanism and Revolution (New York, 1964), p. 311.

[6]Richard Price, "Observations on the Nature of Civil Liberty, etc.," section 1, quoted in Connecticut Courant, August 19, 1776.

[7]Philip S. Foner, ed., The Complete Works of Thomas Paine, 2 vols. (New York, 1945), I, p. 79.

[8]Niles' Weekly Register, II (July 27, 1812), pp. 284-85.

[9]Benjamin P. Thomas, Abraham Lincoln (London, 1953), pp. 325-40; David Donald, Lincoln Reconsidered (New York, 1959), p. 153; Willard A. and Porter W. Heaps, The Singing Sixties: The Spirit of Civil War Days Drawn from the Music of the Times (Norman, Oklahoma, 1960), pp. 89-90.

[10]In many Northern states, conventions which broadened white male suffrage at the same time specifically disfranchised black voters.

[11]Alexis de Tocqueville, Democracy in America, 2 vols. (New York, 1961), II, p. 233.

[12]Augustus Kinsley Gardiner, Conjugal Sins (New York, 1870), p. 150.

[13]Artemus Bowers Muzzey, The Fireside: An Aid to Parents (Boston, 1854), p. 9.

[14]Daniel Scott Smith, "The Dating of the American Sexual Revolution: Evidence and Interpretation," in Michael Gordon, ed., The American Family in Social-Historical Perspective (New York, 1973), pp. 321-35.

[15]Robert V. Wells, "Demographic Change and the Life Cycle of American Families," in Theodore K. Rabb and Robert I. Rotberg, eds., The Family in History: Interdisciplinary Essays (New York, 1971), pp. 85-94.

[16]Quoted in Dorothy Ross, G. Stanley Hall: The Psychologist as Prophet (Chicago and London, 1972), p. 431. The bracketed interpolation is Ross's.

[17]Reader's Digest, LXI (July, 1952), pp. 78, 92.

[18]Vital Speeches of the Day, XIV (Sept. 15, 1948), pp. 731-34.

[19]Advertising flyer for Personal Growth magazine received by the author, May, 1975.

[20]New York Times, July 11, 1971, p. 41.

[21]San Francisco Chronicle, June 4, 1975, p. 36.

[22]Ross M. Robertson, History of the American Economy, (3rd ed., New York, 1973), pp. 382-83. On the matter of child labor and schooling, I have greatly benefited from the counsel of Stuart Bruchey and David Tyack at the Center for Advanced Study in the Behavioral Sciences.

[23]Quoted in Sylvia Anthony, The Discovery of Death in Childhood and After (New York, 1972), p. 182.

The Adult Life Cycle

Stages of Adult Life*
Erik H. Erikson

Intimacy vs. Isolation

The strength acquired at any stage is tested by the necessity to transcend it in such a way that the individual can take chances in the next stage with what was most vulnerably precious in the previous one. Thus, the young adult, emerging from the search for and the insistence on identity, is eager and willing to fuse his identity with that of others. He is ready for intimacy, that is, the capacity to commit himself to concrete affiliations and partnerships and to develop the ethical strength to abide by such commitments, even though they may call for significant sacrifices and compromises. Body and ego must now be masters of the organ modes and of the nuclear conflicts, in order to be able to face the fear of ego loss in situations which call for self-abandon: in the solidarity of close affiliations, in orgasms and sexual unions, in close friendships and in physical combat, in experiences of inspiration by teachers and of intuition from the recesses of the self. The avoidance of such experiences because of a fear of ego loss may lead to a deep sense of isolation and consequent self-absorption.

The counterpart of intimacy is distantiation: the readiness to isolate and, if necessary, to destroy those forces and people whose essence seems dangerous to one's own, and whose "territory" seems to encroach on the extent of one's intimate

*Reprinted by permission of the author and W. W. Norton and Co., Inc. from <u>Childhood and Society</u>, 2nd edition, revised and enlarged, pp. 263-269. Copyright © 1964 by W. W. Norton and Co.

relations. Prejudices thus developed (and utilized and exploited in politics and in war) are a more mature outgrowth of the blinder repudiations which during the struggle for identity differentiate sharply and cruelly between the familiar and the foreign. The danger of this stage is that intimate, competitive, and combative relations are experienced with and against the selfsame people. But as the areas of adult duty are delineated, and as the competitive encounter, and the sexual embrace, are differentiated, they eventually become subject to that <u>ethical sense</u> which is the mark of the adult.

Strictly speaking, it is only now that <u>true genitality</u> can fully develop; for much of the sex life preceding these commitments is of the identity-searching kind, or is dominated by phallic or vaginal strivings which make of sex-life a kind of genital combat. On the other hand, genitality is all too often described as a permanent state of reciprocal sexual bliss. This then, may be the place to complete our discussion of genitality.

For a basic orientation in the matter I shall quote what has come to me as Freud's shortest saying. It has often been claimed, and bad habits of conversation seem to sustain the claim, that psychoanalysis as a treatment attempts to convince the patient that before God and man he has only one obligation: to have good orgasms, with a fitting "object," and that regularly. This, of course, is not true. Freud was once asked what he thought a normal person should be able to do well. The questioner probably expected a complicated answer. But Freud, in the curt way of his old days, is reported to have said: "Lieben und arbeiten" (to love and to work). It pays to ponder on this simple formula; it gets deeper as you think about it. For when Freud said "love" he meant <u>genital</u> love, and genital <u>love</u>; when he said love <u>and</u> work, he meant a general work-productiveness which would not preoccupy the individual to the extent that he loses his right or capacity to be a genital and a loving being. Thus we may ponder, but we cannot improve on "the professor's" formula.

86

Genitality, then, consists in the unobstructed capacity to develop an orgastic potency so free of pregenital interferences that genital libido (not just the sex products discharge in Kinsey's "outlets") is expressed in heterosexual mutuality, with full sensitivity of both penis and vagina, and with a convulsion-like discharge of tension from the whole body. This is a rather concrete way of saying something about a process which we really do not understand. To put it more situationally: the total fact of finding, via the climactic turmoil of the orgasm, a supreme experience of the mutual regulation of two beings in some way takes the edge off the hostilities and potential rages caused by the oppositeness of male and female, of fact and fancy, of love and hate. Satisfactory sex relations thus make sex less obsessive, overcompensation less necessary, sadistic controls superfluous.

Preoccupied as it was with curative aspects, psychoanalysis often failed to formulate the matter of genitality in a way significant for the processes of society in all classes, nations, and levels of culture. The kind of mutuality in orgasm which psychoanalysis has in mind is apparently easily obtained in classes and cultures which happen to make a leisurely institution of it. In more complex societies this mutuality is interfered with by so many factors of health, of tradition, of opportunity, and of temperament, that the proper formulation of sexual health would be rather this: A human being should be potentially able to accomplish mutuality of genital orgasm, but he should also be so constituted as to bear a certain amount of frustration in the matter without undue regression wherever emotional preference or considerations of duty and loyalty call for it.

While psychoanalysis has on occasion gone too far in its emphasis on genitality as a universal cure for society and has thus provided a new addiction and a new commodity for many who wished to so interpret its teachings, it has not always indicated all the goals that genitality actually should and must imply. In order to be of lasting

social significance, the utopia of genitality
should include:

1. mutuality of orgasm
2. with a loved partner
3. of the other sex
4. with whom one is able and willing to share
   a mutual trust
5. and with whom one is able and willing to
   regulate the cycles of
   a. work
   b. procreation
   c. recreation
6. so as to secure to the offspring, too, all
   the stages of a satisfactory development.

It is apparent that such utopian accomplishment on
a large scale cannot be an individual or, indeed,
a therapeutic task. Nor is it a purely sexual
matter by any means. It is integral to a culture's
style of sexual selection, cooperation, and competition.

The danger of this stage is isolation, that is
the avoidance of contracts which commit to intimacy.
In psychopathology, this disturbance can lead to
severe "character-problems." On the other hand,
there are partnerships which amount to an isolation
à deux, protecting both partners from the necessity
to face the next critical development—that of
generativity.

Generativity vs. Stagnation

In this book the emphasis is on the childhood
stages, otherwise the section on generativity would
of necessity be the central one, for this term en-
compasses the evolutionary development which has
made man the teaching and instituting as well as
the learning animal. The fashionable insistence
on dramatizing the dependence of children on adults
often blinds us to the dependence of the older generation on the younger one. Mature man needs to be
needed, and maturity needs guidance as well as encouragement from what has been produced and must

be taken care of.

Generativity, then, is primarily the concern in establishing and guiding the next generation, although there are individuals who, through misfortune or because of special and genuine gifts in other directions, do not apply this drive to their own offspring. And indeed, the concept generativity is meant to include such more popular synonyms as _productivity_ and _creativity_, which, however, cannot replace it.

It has taken psychoanalysis some time to realize that the ability to lose oneself in the meeting of bodies and minds leads to a gradual expansion of ego-interests and to a libidinal investment in that which is being generated. Generativity thus is an essential stage on the psychosexual as well as on the psychosocial schedule. Where such enrichment fails altogether, regression to an obsessive need for pseudo-intimacy takes place, often with a pervading sense of stagnation and personal impoverishment. Individuals, then, often begin to indulge themselves as if they were their own—or one another's—one and only child; and where conditions favor it, early invalidism, physical or psychological, becomes the vehicle of self-concern. The mere fact of having or even wanting children, however, does not "achieve" generativity. In fact, some young parents suffer, it seems, from the retardation of the ability to develop this stage. The reasons are often to be found in early childhood impressions; in excessive self-love based on a too strenuously self-made personality; and finally (and here we return to the beginnings) in the lack of some faith, some "belief in the species," which would make a child appear to be a welcome trust of the community.

As to the institutions which safeguard and reinforce generativity, one can only say that all institutions codify the ethics of generative succession. Even where philosophical and spiritual tradition suggests the renunciation of the right to procreate or to produce, such early turn to

89

"ultimate concerns," wherever instituted in monastic movements, strives to settle at the same time the matter of its relationship to the Care for the creatures of this world and to the Charity which is felt to transcend it.

If this were a book on adulthood, it would be indispensable and profitable at this point to compare economic and psychological theories (beginning with the strange convergencies and divergencies of Marx and Freud) and to proceed to a discussion of man's relationship to his production as well as to his progeny.

Ego Integrity vs. Despair

Only in him who in some way has taken care of things and people and has adapted himself to the triumphs and disappointments adherent to being, the originator of others or the generator of products and ideas—only in him may gradually ripen the fruit of these seven stages. I know no better word for it than ego integrity. Lacking a clear definition, I shall point to a few constituents of this state of mind. It is the ego's accrued assurance of its proclivity for order and meaning. It is a post-narcissistic love of the human ego—not of the self—as an experience which conveys some world order and spiritual sense, no matter how dearly paid for. It is the acceptance of one's one and only life cycle as something that had to be and that, by necessity, permitted of no substitutions: it thus means a new, a different love of one's parents. It is a comradeship with the ordering ways of distant times and different pursuits, as expressed in the simple products and sayings of such times and pursuits. Although aware of the relativity of all the various life styles which have given meaning to human striving, the possessor of integrity is ready to defend the dignity of his own life style against all physical and economic threats. For he knows that an individual life is the accidental coincidence of but one life cycle with but one segment of history; and that for him all human integrity stands or falls with the one

90

style of integrity of which he partakes. The style of integrity developed by his culture or civilization thus becomes the "patrimony of his soul," the seal of his moral paternity of himself (". . . pero el honor/Es patrimonio del alma": Calderón). In such final consolidation, death loses its sting.

The lack or loss of this accrued ego integration is signified by fear of death: the one and only life cycle is not accepted as the ultimate of life. Despair expresses the feeling that the time is now short, too short for the attempt to start another life and to try out alternate roads to integrity. Disgust hides despair, if often only in the form of "a thousand little disgusts" which do not add up to one big remorse: "mille petits dégoûts de soi, dont le total ne fait pas un remords, mais un gêne obscure." (Rostand)

Each individual, to become a mature adult, must to a sufficient degree develop all the ego qualities mentioned, so that a wise Indian, a true gentleman, and a mature peasant share and recognize in one another the final stage of integrity. But each cultural entity, to develop the particular style of integrity suggested by its historical place, utilizes a particular combination of these conflicts, along with specific provocations and prohibitions of infantile sexuality. Infantile conflicts become creative only if sustained by the firm support of cultural institutions and of the special leader classes representing them. In order to approach or experience integrity, the individual must know how to be a follower of image bearers in religion and in politics, in the economic order and in technology, in aristocratic living and in the arts and sciences. Ego integrity, therefore, implies an emotional integration which permits participation by followership as well as acceptance of the responsibility of leadership.

Webster's Dictionary is kind enough to help us complete this outline in a circular fashion. Trust (the first of our ego values) is here defined as "the assured reliance on another's integrity," the last of our values. I suspect that Webster had business in mind rather than babies, credit rather than faith. But the formulation stands. And it seems posible to further paraphrase the relation of adult integrity and infantile trust by saying that healthy children will not fear life if their elders have integrity enough not to fear death.

The Evolution of the Individual Life Structure*
Daniel J. Levinson

The sequence of eras . . . forms the gross scaffolding of the life cycle. Within this framework we can pursue the fundamental question of this inquiry: Is there a normal process of individual development in early and middle adulthood? As our study progressed, our findings led us from the idea of a steady, continuous process of development to the idea of qualitatively different periods in development. We began to identify a sequence of periods, from the end of adolescence to the middle forties, through which all of our subjects passed.

Some clues as to the nature of the periods have been noted in the discussion of the eras. As I have said, the shift from one era to the next is a major developmental change. It does not occur easily or quickly. Rather, there is a cross-era transition, a developmental period that normally lasts four or five years. In the Early Adult Transition (age 17 to 22) we conclude pre-adulthood and begin our entry into early adulthood. The Midlife Transition (age 40 to 45) enables a man to terminate early adulthood and to initiate middle adulthood. The discovery of these periods led us to ask whether there are not additional developmental periods in each era.

We found too that the eras are distinguished by changes in the overall character of living. The eras do not necessarily show themselves when one focuses on a single aspect of living, as most investigators have. To grasp the nature of adult development, we had to begin with the individual life in its patterning at a given time, and trace its evolution over the years. When we looked at each man's life from this vantage point, we first observed in broad outline the eras and cross-era transitions. Then, examining the life course more closely, we found within each era a series of developmental periods, similar in their basic nature to the cross-era transitions.

Many concepts and techniques are available for studying specific aspects of living. But how do we study the character of a man's life and its evolution over a span of years? Many will say that this is too difficult a task, that it includes "too many variables" and takes us beyond the limits of a single discipline. My answer: yes, the study of an individual life is beyond the scope of any single discipline, and it is very difficult to do well—but it can be done! In the present study we have, I believe, made a significant start, though it is only a start and there is a great deal left to do.

The concept we have created for this purpose—and it is the pivotal concept in our entire work—is the individual life structure. By "life structure" we mean the underlying pattern or design of a person's life at a given time. Here we are studying the lives of men. A man's life has many components: his occupation, his love relationships, his marriage and family, his relation to himself, his use of solitude, his roles in various social contexts—all the relationships with individuals, groups and institutions that have significance for him. His personality influences and is influenced by his involvement in each of them. We must start, however, with the overall life structure. Once the character of the individual's life has been identified, we can study in more detail the changes

93

occurring in personality, in the marital and occupational careers, and in other components of life.

We have found that, over the years, the life structure evolves through a standard sequence of periods. The developmental periods I shall soon describe are thus periods in the evolution of the life structure. I want to emphasize and re-emphasize this point, as it is frequently misunderstood. I am not talking about stages in ego development or occupational development or development in any single aspect of living. I am talking about periods in the evolution of the individual life structure. The periods, and the eras of which they are a part, constitute a basic source of order in the life cycle. The order exists at an underlying level. At the more immediate day-to-day level of concrete action, events and experience, our lives are often rapidly changing and fragmented.

We are now prepared to maintain that everyone lives through the same developmental periods in adulthood, just as in childhood, though people go through them in radically different ways. Each individual life has its own unique character. A valid theory of development is not a mold or blueprint specifying a single, "normal" course that everyone must follow. Its function, instead, is to indicate the developmental tasks that everyone must work on in successive periods, and the infinitely varied forms that such work can take in different individuals living under different conditions. Such a theory increases our sense of human potentialities and of the variousness of individual lives; it does not impose a template for conformity.

The Individual Life Structure

The concept of life structure—the basic pattern or design of a person's life at a given time—gives us a way of looking at the engagement of the individual in society. It requires us to consider both self and world, and the relationships between them. Our study has shown that the life structure goes through a process of development in adulthood.

94

It is the primary focus of our analysis. When I speak of adult development, I mean the evolution of the life structure during the adult years.

The concept of life structure provides a tool for analyzing what is sometimes called "the fabric of one's life." Through it we may examine the interrelations of self and world—to see how the self is in the world, and how the world is in the self. When an external event has a decisive impact, we consider how processes in the self may have helped to bring it about and to mediate its effects. When an inner conflict leads to dramatic action, we consider how external influences may have touched off the conflict and decided how it would be played out. We try to determine how various aspects of self and world influence the formation of a life structure and shape its change over time.

The life structure may be considered in terms of three perspectives:

a. The individual's <u>sociocultural world</u> as it impinges upon him has meaning and consequences for him. To understand a man's life, therefore, we must take into account the society in which he lives. We must place him within various social contexts—class, religion, ethnicity, family, political system, occupational structure—and understand their relevance for him. His life is modified by changes in the surrounding culture, in social movements and institutions, in the economy and the political climate. He is affected by massive events such as war and depression, and by more particular conditions in his own work, family and community life.

b. Some <u>aspects of his self</u> are lived out; other aspects are inhibited or neglected. The self includes a complex patterning of wishes, conflicts, anxieties and ways of resolving or controlling them. It includes fantasies, moral values and ideals, talents and skills, character traits, modes of feeling, thought and action. Part of the self is conscious; much is unconscious; and we must consider both parts. Important aspects of the self, initially formed in the pre-adult era, continue to influence a man's life in adulthood. We have to see how the person draws upon the self, or ignores it, in his everyday life. The self is an intrinsic element of the life structure and not a separate entity.

    c. We need to examine the man's <u>participation in the world</u>. The external world provides a landscape, a cast of characters, a variety of resources and constraints out of which a man fashions his own life. A man selectively uses and is used by his world, through his evolving relationships and roles as citizen, lover, worker, boss, friend, husband, father, member of diverse groups and enterprises. Participation involves transactions between self and world. The transactions take obvious forms, but subtle meanings and feelings play an important part in them.

    When studying the evolution of life structure, we are being biographical in the most fundamental sense: we start with the concrete life course as it evolves over time. The task of the biographer is to present a full picture of his subject's life. He tries to arrive at an interpretive construction that is factually accurate and that "makes sense" of the nature and sequence of this life. He places his subject in his social and historical context, and at the same time probes into the self, attempting to grasp the most private aspirations, qualities of character, torments and fulfillments. He tries to show how the person is both a reflection of his society and a creative agent making his unique contribution, large or small, to the continuity and change of his world. The term "biography" thus refers to a complex enterprise including a task, a method of work, a theoretical conception and a product. The biographer is, as it were, a hybrid: he is a historian-psychologist-sociologist-man-of-letters. While bringing together various theoretical approaches and sources of information, he must maintain his fidelity to the unique, idiosyncratic life of his subject. We are engaged here in one form of biography.

96

How shall we go about describing and analyzing the life structure? The most useful starting point, I believe, is to consider the <u>choices</u> a person makes and how he deals with their consequences. The important choices in adult life have to do with work, family, friendships and love relationships of various kinds, where to live, leisure, involvement in religious, political and community life, immediate and long-term goals.

Making a significant life choice is a complex matter. Choosing to enter an occupation is not like choosing a dessert or a brand of soap (though many models of decision-making treat them as if they were the same). The decision to marry grows out of a premarital relationship and is the starting point for an evolving marital relationship. A man's self and world are heavily involved in the character of the initial relationship, in the decision to marry, and in the further vicissitudes of the marriage.

So in describing the important choices in a man's life at a given time it is not enough to deal with the "choice" in isolation. It is not enough, in other words, simply to say that he is married to a particular woman, that he is a member of occupation X and employed at work place Y, or that he belongs to religion A, political party B and fraternal order C. It is necessary to go beyond a mere listing of items. We have to consider the meanings and functions of each choice within the individual life structure. As a component of the life structure, every choice is saturated by both self and world. To choose something means to have a <u>relationship</u> with it. The relationship becomes a vehicle for living out certain aspects of the self and for engaging in certain modes of participation in the world.

The primary components of the life structure are choices, in the sense I have just described. The components are not features of the self, such as motives and abilities, nor are they features of the world, such as institutions, groups and objects.

In characterizing each choice, however, it is necessary to understand the nature of the man's relationship with it, to place it within the life structure, and to see how it is connected to both self and world.

The components of the life structure are not a random set of items, like pebbles washed up at the seashore. Rather, like threads in a tapestry, they are woven into an encompassing design. Recurring themes in various sectors help to unify the overall pattern of the tapestry. Lives differ widely in the nature and patterning of the components.

One or two components (rarely as many as three) have a central place in the structure. Others, though important, are more peripheral, and still others are quite marginal or detached from the center. The central components have the greatest significance for the self and for the evolving life course. They receive the largest share of one's time and energy, and they strongly influence the choices made in other aspects of life. The peripheral components are easier to detach and change; they involve less investment of the self and are less crucial to the fabric of one's life.

The life structure may change in various ways. A component may shift from center to periphery or vice versa, as when a man who has been totally committed to work starts detaching himself from it and involves himself more in family life. A formerly important component may be eliminated altogether. The character of a man's relationships within a given component may change moderately or drastically For example, a man may remain in the existing marriage but enrich and deepen the marital relationship; he may modify the nature and meaning of his work, without changing occupations; or he may make a new choice of wife or occupation that leads to a qualitative change in the character of his life.

The components most likely to be central in a man's life are occupation, marriage-family, friendship and peer relationships, ethnicity and religion.

Leisure may also have a central place, when it serves important functions for the self and is more than a casual activity. Playing sports after work, or watching sports on TV, is a serious matter for many men.

We found that occupation and marriage-family are usually the most central components, though there are significant variations in their relative weight and in the importance of other components. Work and family are universal features of human life. Let's consider these components more closely.

· OCCUPATION. In all societies, work is a major part of individual life and of the social structure. Every man is required to contribute his labor in some form of work deemed useful for the tribe. A man's occupation is one of the primary factors determining his income, his prestige and his place in society. Universally, work is organized into a number of socially defined occupations that are taught, accorded differential value and reward, and integrated into simple or complex economic structures.

Over a span of years, a man chooses and forms an occupation. All men make one or more changes, some of them quite marked, within the original occupation or from one occupation to another. A man's occupation places him within a particular socioeconomic level and work world. It exerts a powerful influence upon the options available to him, the choices he makes among them, and his possibilities for advancement and satisfaction. His work world also influences the choices he makes in other spheres of life.

Occupation has important sources within the self and important consequences for the self. It is often the primary medium in which a young man's dreams for the future are defined, and the vehicle he uses to pursue those dreams. At best, his occupation permits the fulfillment of basic values and life goals. At worst, a man's work life over the years is oppressive and corrupting, and contributes to a growing alienation from self, work and society. In studying a man's life, we need to understand the meaning of work and the multiple ways in which it may serve to fulfill, to barely sustain or to destroy the self.

· MARRIAGE AND FAMILY. In all societies, a man is expected to marry and to take certain responsibilities within a familial system. There is, of course, great variation in the culturally defined roles of husband and father and in the structure of the family. A man usually wants to marry and to make his family a central component in his life structure.

Marriage ordinarily creates a new home base for the young man. It is a center on which he establishes his place in the community and his changing relationships with friends, parents and extended family. It provides a vehicle for traveling a particular path in early adulthood. His marital choice reflects some of his emerging values but violates others. It links him to certain social contexts while separating him from others.

If he marries "the girl next door," the marriage may make for stability and continuity in his life. In this case, he is more likely to live in the same neighborhood, to have an occupation and life style consistent with parental values, and to integrate his life within the ethnic and religious patterns of his forebears. On the other hand, marriage to a woman of different background and aspirations is likely to be part of a major shift in his life. Many of the meanings and functions of a marriage are implicit or even unconscious: they play themselves out over time in changing and often unanticipated ways.

A man's family life usually has a major effect on his ongoing life as a whole. His immediate family connects him to various other components of life, such as his original family, ethnicity and occupation. It places him within a larger world and provides a vehicle that is well designed for certain life journeys and poorly designed for others. It enables him to live out certain parts of the self and to leave others dormant or repressed.

The various professions and scientific disciplines often focus on one component of life to the relative exclusion of the others. For example, a good deal of research and counseling has been devoted to occupational careers. Investigators acknowledge that a man's work career is influenced by other factors, such as personality, family life and ethnic context. In general, however, they tend to ignore the non-occupational components or to consider them in only a cursory fashion. They have had no theoretical framework within which to interrelate the various components. Likewise, a good deal of research and counseling has been devoted to marriage and family. However, family and occupation have rarely been brought together in our understanding of adult life.

In the fields of personality research and clinical practice, the primary focus is usually on the self, to the neglect of the actualities of work, marriage, ethnicity and class in a man's life. Personality theory and psychotherapy will be strengthened when they take more account of the adult self as it is engaged with social institutions and with the fragmentation, destructiveness and creative possibilities which are the stuff of adult life in society.

The Self Is in the World, The World Is in the Self

In the scientific study of humanity, there has been a powerful tendency in each discipline to focus on a few aspects of human life and to neglect the others. One of the primary divisions is that between individual and society. Psychology and psychiatry focus chiefly upon the individual. Social sciences, such as sociology, social anthropology and political science, focus primarily upon society and collective life. They tend to ignore the individual altogether or to regard him as a

101

simple product of the shaping forces in society. Although the study of the individual life cycle is generally considered an appropriate field of inquiry in the social sciences, nevertheless it remains virtually untouched.

It is necessary to take a broader approach. We need to encompass both self and society, without making one primary and the other secondary or derivative. We need to take seriously the idea of adult development—that there is some underlying order in the life cycle—and the idea of adult socialization—that the self exists within a world and its evolution is intimately bound together with that world. The concept of life structure provides a starting point for this approach.

The individual life structure is a patterning of self and world. However, self and world are not two separate entities. They are not like billiard balls that, colliding, affect each other's course but not each other's nature. An essential feature of human life is the interpenetration of self and world. Each is inside the other. Our thinking about one must take account of the other.

The interpenetration of self and world has been beautifully portrayed by Arthur Miller in his plays and essays. His social-psychological view of drama parallels closely our view of adult development:

. . .society is inside of man and man is inside society, and you cannot even create a truthfully drawn psychological entity on the stage until you understand his social relations and their power to make him what he is and to prevent him from being what he is not. The fish is in the water and the water is in the fish.

Miller criticizes the "social realism" that prevailed in the American theater during the 1930s. Plays of this period depict the conflicts and contradictions in society but their characters are

102

lacking in individuality. He also critizes many plays of the 1950s, which **depict** the subjective experience of adolescents but have little to say about the adult self dealing with the responsibilities and potentialities of living in a complex society. Miller writes:

In my opinion, if our stage does not come to pierce through affects to an evaluation of the world it will contract to a lesser psychiatry and an inexpert one at that. We shall be confined to writing an "Oedipus" without the pestilence, an "Oedipus" whose catastrophe is private and unrelated to the survival of his people, an "Oedipus" who cannot tear out his eyes because there will be no standard by which he can judge himself; an "Oedipus," in a word, who on learning of his incestuous marriage, instead of tearing out his eyes, will merely wipe away his tears thus to declare his loneliness.

If we are to have a more truly adult theater, says Miller—and a more adequate basis for studying adult development, say I—we must recognize this interpenetration of self and world. The self is an intrinsic part of the external world. We cannot adequately grasp the nature of a man's world without seeing how it is colored and shaped by his self and the selves of others. And the external world is an intrinsic part of the self. We cannot grasp the full nature of the self without seeing how diverse aspects of the world are reflected and contained within it.

The structure of society is reflected in the self and the life structure. Every man's life gives evidence of his society's wisdom and integration as well as its conflicts, oppression and destructiveness. Society makes available to each of its members a limited range of individuals, groups, material resources, occupations and possibilities for social involvement and self-fulfillment. It influences his choices among these options, making some more attractive or more highly rewarded than others. Through its own structure, society brings about a patterning in the choices a man makes. A particular choice moves a man into a given world, or strengthens his position in that world; and at the same time it moves him away from other worlds he has been considering.

The external world also contributes to the substance of a man's changing attachments, aspirations, anxieties, identifications, creative productions. Every organization and social world has a culture, social structure and material conditions which affect the character of the relationships among the members. A man's particular external world presents significant meanings, feelings, identities and myths which he selectively uses and internalizes. It provides invitations to heroism, martyrdom, empty conformity, bitter or zestful struggle. It encourages the development of certain parts of the self, while hindering the development of others.

Although every man's life structure reflects the structure of society, it is also in some respects unique—a reflection of his specific self and circumstances. Out of the possibilities and constraints given in his environment, he makes his own choices and builds his own world. The self is a crucial factor in the formation and transformation of each individual's world.

To be truly engaged with his world, a man must invest important parts of his self in it and, equally, he must take the world into his self and be enriched, depleted and corrupted by it. In countless ways he puts himself into the world and takes the world into himself. Adult development is the story of the evolving process of mutual interpenetration. If we are to understand it we must learn how, in Miller's vivid imagery, the fish is in the water and the water is in the fish.

<u>Tasks and Periods in
the Evolution of the</u> Life Structure

When we used the concept of life structure in writing the biographies of our 40 men, we made a remarkable discovery: <u>the life structure evolves through a relatively orderly sequence during the adult years</u>. The essential character of the sequence is the same for <u>all</u> the men in our study and for the other men whose biographies we examined. It consists of a series of alternating stable (structure-building) periods and transitional (structure-changing) periods. These periods shape the course of adult psychosocial development.

The primary task of every stable period is to build a life structure: a man must make certain key choices, form a structure around them, and pursue his goals and values within this structure. To say that a period is stable in this sense is not necessarily to say that it is tranquil and without difficulty. The task of making major life choices and building a structure is often stressful indeed, and may involve many kinds of change.

Each stable period has additional tasks of its own which reflect its place in the life cycle and distinguish it from the other stable periods. No two periods in the life cycle are identical. They may have some common elements but they also differ in essential ways. Old age is not "merely" a second childhood, though it resembles childhood in certain aspects, and the Mid-life Transition is not "merely" a second adolescence, though developmental issues of adolescence (and other periods) are reactivated within it. A stable period ordinarily lasts six or seven years, ten at the most. For various reasons, internal and external, the life structure that has formed the basis for stability comes into question and must be modified.

A transitional period, as we have seen, terminates the existing life structure and creates the possibility for a new one. The primary tasks of every transitional period are to question and reappraise the existing structure, to explore various possibilities for change in self and world, and to move toward commitment to the crucial choices that form the basis for a new life structure in the ensuing stable period. Each transitional period has other, distinctive tasks reflecting its place in the life cycle. These periods ordinarily last four to five years.

Since the transitional periods play such a vital part in development, let me articulate their nature more fully. A transition is a bridge, or a boundary zone, between two states of greater stability. It involves a process of change, a shift from one structure to another.

The Mid-life Transition, for example, is a boundary zone between two great eras in the life cycle. As it starts, the person is primarily in the era of early adulthood. When it ends, middle adulthood is fully under way. During the Mid-life Transition itself, however, the person is truly "on the boundary": he is both in early adulthood and in middle adulthood. This transition separates the two eras, enabling one to end so that the next can begin. It serves also to connect them, bringing about interchange so that the past can be drawn upon and used selectively in building for the future. It is an intrinsic part of both eras and can be understood only from the conjoint perspective of both. Similarly, the Age Thirty Transition is a means of terminating the first adult life structure and of initiating a new structure for completing early adulthood, as we shall see.

A termination is an ending, a process of separation or loss. In some cases the separation is complete: I terminate a casual relationship, job, membership in a group or community, ownership of a house or book—and they pass entirely out of my life. I have no further contact with them, I rarely think about them, and only the most limited residue of their existence remains with me.

When the relationship with an object (person, group, setting, thing, symbol) has great meaning for me, however, termination does not mean a complete ending of the relationship. The relationship continues but in a changed and changing form. The most clear-cut and dramatic separations of this kind involve total loss of a significant object: someone I love dies; a quarrel leads to permanent parting from a friend or mentor; I move to a new locale and leave a world behind. I experience a profound loss and must come to terms with painful feelings of abandonment, grief and rage. Over time the lost object is more fully internalized and the relationship continues to evolve within my self and my life. Important aspects of the relationship are ended, but other aspects continue and new ones are created. I have lost the external object but I maintain the relationship with the now-internal object.

The separation is often partial rather than total. I continue to have some contact with the person or group, but a major change occurs in the nature of the relationship: a romantic love relationship becomes a modest friendship; an intense mentoring relationship becomes a more casual association in work; a marriage ends in divorce and the relationship goes on in new forms, such as friendly co-parenting or continuing hostility and recrimination. The relationship comes to a turning point and must be modified or transformed if it is to continue. A transitional period is required to terminate the past and start the future.

A good example is the young adult in the process of separating from parents. His developmental task is not to end the relationship altogether. Rather, he has to reject certain aspects (for instance, those in which he is the submissive or defiant child relating to all-controlling parents), to sustain other aspects, and to build in new qualities such as mutual respect between distinctive individuals who have separate as well as shared interests. Neither the young adult nor his parents find this an easy task.

As students of childhood development have shown, the processes of separation and individuation are closely linked. Drastic change and loss may be damaging, but under reasonably supportive conditions the process of separation leads to enrichment, differentiation and development of the self. This is as true of adulthood as of childhood.

The task of a developmental transition is to terminate a time in one's life: to accept the losses the termination entails; to review and evaluate the past; to decide which aspects of the past to keep and which to reject; and to consider one's wishes and possibilities for the future. One is suspended between past and future, and struggling to overcome the gap that separates them. Much from the past must be given up—separated from, cut out of one's life, rejected in anger, renounced in sadness or grief. And there is much that can be used as a basis for the future. Changes must be attempted in both self and world.

These tasks produce features common to all transitions. They are frequently times of crisis—of profound inner conflict, of feeling "in a state of suspended animation" as one of our men put it. After hearing a talk on the Mid-life Transition, a young man asked me, "How is it that I, at age 31, am having many of the experiences you ascribe to age 41—am I in a precocious Mid-life Transition?" The answer is, of course, no: he is going through a different transition appropriate to his place in the life cycle, but it is one that has many qualities in common with the other transitions such as those at mid-life and at puberty.

Along with the common features, certain developmental tasks and life issues are specific to each period and give it its distinctive character. The Age Thirty Transition, for example, is strongly colored by the imminence of Settling Down and the need to form a life structure through which one's youthful dreams and values can be realized. The Mid-life Transition brings new concerns with the loss of youth, the assumption of a more senior position in one's world, and the reworking of inner polarities. Some preoccupation with death—fearing it, being drawn to it, seeking to transcend it—is not uncommon in all transitions, since the process of termination-initiation evokes the imagery of death and rebirth. But the meanings of death and the kinds of developmental work to be done differ greatly from one transition to another.

As a transition comes to an end, it is time to make crucial choices, to give these choices meaning and commitment, and to start building a life structure around them. The choices mark the beginning of the next period. They are, in a sense, the major product of the transition. When all the efforts of the past several years are done—all the struggles to improve one's work or marriage, to explore alternative possibilities of living, to come more to terms with the self—a man must make his choices and place his bets. He must decide, "This I will settle for," and start creating a life structure that will serve as a vehicle for the next step in the journey.

A man may choose to reaffirm the commitment to an existing part of his life. He decides to remain in the marriage with the intention of making it work better. He gives up a serious extramarital relationship—or he embarks upon such a relationship in the hope that this will enrich his life while allowing the marriage and family to continue. Likewise, he may choose to remain in his present job rather than make a more drastic change entailing greater risks and discontinuity. If this is an active reaffirmation, he will make significant improvements in the character of the work even if the job title remains the same.

The decision to stay put is not always based on a reaffirmed commitment. It may stem more from resignation, inertia, passive acquiescence or controlled despair—a self-restriction in the context of severe external constraints. This kind of surface stability marks the beginning of a long-term decline unless new factors intervene (perhaps in the next transitional period) and enable him to form a more satisfactory life structure.

The choices made in a transitional period usually lead to moderate or drastic change in life structure. A man may divorce, remarry, change his job or occupation, make a geographical move, start new avocational pursuits that modify and enrich his life. A choice is often marked by an event that takes only a few days or weeks. The event is, however, embedded within a process of change that ordinarily extends over a span of several years. Thus, a divorce or a job change is the most conspicuous event within a complex transition that contains many other changes. In making the transition a man must de-structure his existing life pattern, work on a number of basic developmental tasks, and restructure a new life.

A transitional period comes to an end not when a particular event occurs or when a sequence is completed in one aspect of life. It ends when the tasks of questioning and exploring have lost their urgency, when a man makes his crucial commitments and is ready to start on the tasks of building, living within and enhancing a new life structure.

We did not begin this study with preformed hypotheses about developmental periods unfolding in an age-linked sequence. We were as surprised as everyone else by these discoveries. The findings with regard to <u>age</u> may be summarized briefly as follows. There is a single, most frequent age at which each period begins. There is a range of variation, usually about two years above and below the average. Thus, the Age Thirty Transition most often starts at age 28, the range being 26 to 29. The next period, Settling Down, usually starts at 33—and never before 30 or after 34, in our sample. The four occupational groups in our study showed only minor differences in the age at which every period began and ended. More specific data on age will be presented in the chapters on the successive periods.

The <u>developmental tasks</u> are crucial to the evolution of the periods. The specific character

of a period derives from the nature of its tasks.
A period begins when its major tasks become predominant in a man's life. A period ends when its
tasks lose their primacy and new tasks emerge to
initiate a new period. The orderly progression of
periods stems from the recurrent change in tasks.
The most fundamental tasks of a stable period are
to make firm choices, rebuild the life structure
and enhance one's life within it. Those of a transitional period are to question and reappraise the
existing structure, to search for new possibilities
in self and world, and to modify the present structure enough so that a new one can be formed.

Implicit in the concept of task is the idea
that it may be carried out well or poorly. When
a task is rather specific and concrete, it is
usually not difficult to evaluate how well it has
been performed. Evaluation of work on the developmental tasks is much more difficult. In some cases
it seems clear that the tasks of a period have been
met very poorly or very well, but in most cases the
picture is mixed. The assessment cannot be based
on a few criteria. It is important to understand
the developmental tasks and processes in their full
complexity, and to avoid making premature and oversimplified evaluations as to how well the tasks
have been handled.

We have made a small start, however, toward
dealing with the problem of evaluation. Since the
developmental tasks have so much to do with building, modifying and rebuilding the life structure,
it becomes important to define and evaluate the
"satisfactoriness" of a structure. During a stable
period, a man tries to build a structure that will
in some sense be satisfactory for him. During a
transitional period, he tries to reappraise (evaluate) the current structure and to move toward a new
and more satisfactory one. What meanings does
"satisfactory" have for him, and how shall we use
this term for our own purposes?

Broadly speaking, a life structure is satisfactory to the extent that it is <u>viable in society</u>

111

and _suitable for the self_. The perspectives of both society and self are needed here. A structure is viable to the extent that it works in the world. Within it, a man is able to adapt, to maintain his various roles and to receive sufficient rewards. A structure may be externally viable and yet not internally suitable if it does not allow him to live out crucially important aspects of his self. On the other hand, a structure may be suitable in terms of his inner dreams and values, and yet not be workable in the world. Often, a man's life structure is "fairly satisfactory": it works pretty well in the world, though it does not bring all the rewards the man had hoped for, and is moderately suitable for the self, though it does not permit him to live out some important wishes and values.

Every life structure provides diverse gains and costs for the man himself, for others and for society. The elements that constitute its great strengths are also sources of weakness and take their toll. A structure is never all of a piece. It contains some mixture of order and disorder, unity and diversity, integration and fragmentation. It is always flawed in some respects. It contains contradictions and gaps which can be modified only by basic changes in the structure itself. The contradictions often have painful consequences, but they may also enrich the process of living and provide an intrinsic basis for change and development.

No matter how satisfactory a structure is, in time its utility declines and its flaws generate conflict that leads to modification or transformation of the structure. It is as Marx said: every system contains within itself the seeds of its own destruction. The once-stable structure passes into a new transitional period. The seasons change. Developmental tasks are undertaken anew, and the lessons of growth are gathered and stockpiled against the new period coming. The pattern of adult development continues.

A period is defined in terms of its developmental tasks. It is not defined in terms of concrete events such as marriage or retirement. Many investigators have searched for significant events that might serve as signposts for developmental periods. This search has not been fruitful in generating a developmental theory, though it has contributed to the study of problems in adult life. It is more fruitful, I believe, to conceive of development in terms of tasks and periods in the evolution of life structure. We can then use this developmental perspective in understanding the significance of particular events.

Our lives are punctuated by events such as marriage, divorce, illness, the birth or death of loved ones, unexpected trauma or good fortune, advancement or failure in work, retirement, war, flourishing times and "rock bottom" times. We use the term <u>marker event</u> to identify an occasion of this kind, which has a notable impact upon a person's life. Marker events are usually considered in terms of the <u>adaptation</u> they require. They change a man's life situation and he must cope with them in some way. The further changes in his relationships, roles and personality are then understood as part of his adaptation to the new situation.

Yet, we also need to regard marker events from the viewpoint of <u>development</u>. They can occur at various ages and do not in themselves cause the start or end of a period. However, the age at which an event occurs is important. The significance of a marker event for an individual depends partly upon its place in the sequence of developmental periods.

Getting married, for example, is a marker event in a man's life, whatever his age and circumstances. It makes a great difference, however, just where in the evolution of the periods it occurs. If a man marries at the start of the Early Adult Transition, say at age 18 or 19, the decision to marry and the character of the marital relationship will be highly colored by his current developmental tasks. He is engaged in the process of separating from parents and forming an initial adult identity. He wants to be more independent and "adult," but he also feels unprepared for adult life and tends to seek a dependent relationship with a protective-caring-controlling figure other than a parent. The hazard of marrying at this point in his development is that the marital relationship may perpetuate the struggles with his parents. The result, often, is that he retains the childish qualities he had consciously rejected and fails to attain a more genuinely adult identity. There are similar hazards for the woman at this time, and each partner is implicated in the other's developmental struggles.

Likewise, a marital relationship that takes shape early in the period of Entering the Adult World, say at age 23 or 24, will reflect the developmental tasks of that time: to explore the possibilities of the adult world and to form a provisional life structure. The choice of a mate influences, and is influenced by, the overall character of that structure. One man tries to build a structure in which he can pursue his special dream or vision; he marries a woman who shares that dream and wants to join him on the journey toward its realization. Another man betrays his dream: seeking to build a structure that is more acceptable to parents or is "safer" in some inner sense, he marries a woman who will value and support this conservatism. At some later time he may blame her, with much or little justification, for her part in leading him away from his dream. The meaning and further vicissitudes of the marital relationship will be markedly different in the two cases. The variations are endless.

If the marriage occurs at the start of a period, when the developmental process is just getting under way, the early character of the marital relationship will be intimately bound up with the struggles of entering a new period. In contrast, a marriage occurring toward the end of a period is likely to be a culmination or outcome of the developmental efforts of that period and an indication that a new period is emerging.

In many cases, the marker event is not the result of a man's voluntary effort or choice, but is a result of circumstances beyond his control (such as war, economic depression and the illness or death of others). His current developmental period does not influence the timing of this event, but it does shape his adaptation to it and the influence it has on his subsequent life.

Preview of the Periods
in Adult Development

The sequence of periods begins with the Early Adult Transition (age 17 to 22), which links adolescence and early adulthood. It is followed by a structure-building period, Entering the Adult World, which lasts from about 22 to 28; the primary task of this period is to create a first adult life structure. This structure is modified in the Age Thirty Transition. During the Settling Down period (33 to 40), a man builds a second structure and reaches the culmination of early adulthood. The Mid-life Transition, from about 40 to 45, links early and middle adulthood. It is followed by a more stable period, during the middle and late forties, when a man builds a first life structure for middle adulthood.

The sequence of periods is pictured on page 116. In later chapters each period will be explored in detail. Here we shall briefly preview the periods and give an initial picture of their tasks and developmental sequence.

The Early Adult Transition: Moving from Pre-to Early Adulthood

The Early Adult Transition begins at age 17 and ends at 22, give or take two years. Its twin tasks are to terminate pre-adulthood and to begin early adulthood. The first task is to start moving out of the pre-adult world: to question the nature of that world and one's place in it; to modify or terminate existing relationships with important persons, groups, and institutions; to reappraise

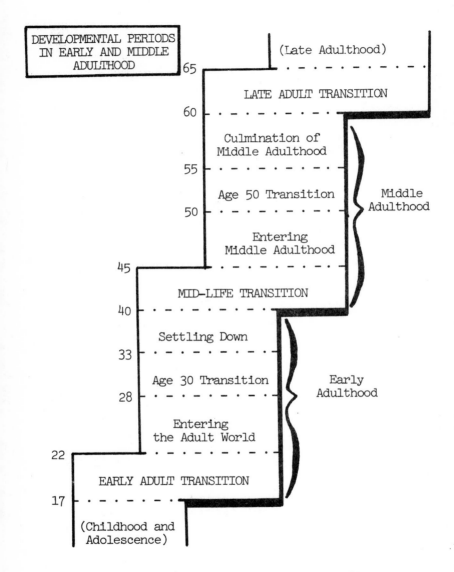

DEVELOPMENTAL PERIODS IN EARLY AND MIDDLE ADULTHOOD

and modify the self that formed in it. Various
kinds of separation, ending and transformation must
be made as one completes an entire season of life.

The second task is to make a preliminary step into the adult world: to explore its possibilities, to imagine oneself as a participant in it, to consolidate an initial adult identity, to make and test some preliminary choices for adult living. In this period a young man is on the boundary between adolescence and adulthood. The transition ends when he gets beyond the boundary and begins to create a life within the adult world.

The First Adult Life Structure: Entering the Adult World

This period extends from about 22 to 28. Its chief task is to fashion a provisional structure that provides a workable link between the valued self and the adult society. A young man must shift the center of gravity of his life; no longer a child in his family of origin, he must become a novice adult with a home base of his own. He makes and tests a variety of initial choices regarding occupation, love relationships (usually including marriage and family), peer relationships, values and life style.

The young man has two primary yet antithetical tasks: (a) He needs to explore the possibilities for adult living: to keep his options open, avoid strong commitments and maximize the alternatives. This task is reflected in a sense of adventure and wonderment, a wish to seek out all the treasures of the new world he is entering. (b) The contrasting task is to create a stable life structure: become more responsible and "make something of my life." Each task has sources and supports in the external world and in the self.

Finding a balance between these tasks is not an easy matter. If the first predominates, life has an extremely transient, rootless quality. If the second predominates, there is the danger of committing oneself prematurely to a structure, without sufficient exploration of alternatives. It is an exciting yet often confusing and painful process to explore the new adult world and, at the same

117

time, to try building a stable life within it. There is usually moderate or great discontinuity between the pre-adult world in which a man grew up and the adult world in which he forms his first life structure.

The Age Thirty Transition:
Changing the First Life Structure

This transition, which extends from roughly 28 to 33, provides an opportunity to work on the flaws and limitations of the first adult life structure, and to create the basis for a more satisfactory structure with which to complete the era of early adulthood. At about 28 the provisional quality of the twenties is ending and life is becoming more serious, more "for real." A voice within the self says: "If I am to change my life—if there are things in it I want to modify or exclude, or things missing I want to add—I must now make a start, for soon it will be too late."

Men differ in the kinds of changes they make, but the life structure is always different at the end of the Age Thirty Transition than it was at the beginning. Some men have a rather smooth transition, without overt disruption or sense of crisis. They modify their lives in certain respects, but they build directly upon the past and do not make fundamental changes. It is a time of reform, not revolution.

But for most men, our study reveals, this transition takes a more stressful form, the age thirty crisis. A developmental crisis occurs when a man has great difficulty with the developmental tasks of a period; he finds his present life structure intolerable, yet seems unable to form a better one. In a severe crisis he experiences a threat to life itself, the danger of chaos and dissolution, the loss of hope for the future. A moderate or severe crisis is very common during this period.

These first three periods—the Early Adult Transition, Entering the Adult World and the Age

118

Thirty Transition—generally last about fifteen years, from age 17 or 18 until 32 or 33. Together, they constitute the preparatory, "novice" phase of early adulthood.

The shift from the end of the Age Thirty Transition to the start of the next period is one of the crucial steps in adult development. At this time a man may make important new choices, or he may reaffirm old choices. If these choices are congruent with his dreams, talents and external possibilities, they provide the basis for a relatively satisfactory life structure. If the choices are poorly made and the new structure seriously flawed, he will pay a heavy price in the next period. Even the best structure has its contradictions and must in time be changed.

The Second Adult Life Structure:
Settling Down

The second life structure takes shape at the end of the Age Thirty Transition and persists until about age 40. This structure is the vehicle for the culmination of early adulthood. A man seeks to invest himself in the major components of the structure (work, family, friendships, leisure, community—whatever is most central to him), and to realize his youthful aspirations and goals.

In this period a man has two major tasks: (a) He tries to establish a niche in society: to anchor his life more firmly, develop competence in a chosen craft, become a valued member of a valued world. (b) He works at making it: striving to advance, to progress on a timetable. I use the term "making it" broadly to include all efforts to build a better life for oneself and to be affirmed by the tribe.

Until the early thirties, the young man has been a "novice" adult. He has been forming an adult life and working toward a more established place in adult society. His task in the Settling Down period is to become a full-fledged adult within his own world. He defines a personal enterprise, a direction in which to strive, a sense of the future, a

119

"project" as Jean-Paul Sartre has termed it. The enterprise may be precisely defined from the start or it may take shape only gradually over the course of this period.

The imagery of the <u>ladder</u> is central to the Settling Down enterprise. It reflects the interest in advancement and affirmation so central to this period. By "ladder" we refer to all dimensions of advancement—increases in social rank, income, power, fame, creativity, quality of family life, social contribution—as these are important for the man and his world. The ladder has both objective and subjective aspects: it reflects the realities of the external social world, but it is defined by the person in terms of his own meanings and strivings.

At the start of this period, a man is on the bottom rung of his ladder and is entering a world in which he is a <u>junior member</u>. His aims are to advance in the enterprise, to climb the ladder and become a <u>senior member</u> in that world. His sense of well-being during this period depends strongly on his own and others' evaluation of his progress toward these goals.

At the end of the Settling Down period, from about age 36 to 40, there is a distinctive phase that we call <u>Becoming One's Own Man</u>. The major developmental tasks of this phase are to accomplish the goals of the Settling Down enterprise, to become a senior member in one's world, to speak more strongly with one's own voice, and to have a greater measure of authority.

This is a fateful time in a man's life. Attaining seniority and approaching the top rung of his ladder are signs to him that he is becoming a man (not just a person, but a male adult). Although his progress brings new rewards, it also carries the burden of greater responsibilities and pressures. It means that he must give up even more of the little boy within himself—an internal figure who is never completely outgrown, and certainly not in early adulthood.

The Mid-Life Transition:
Moving from Early to Middle Adulthood

The late thirties mark the culmination of early adulthood. The Mid-life Transition, which lasts from roughly age 40 to 45, provides a bridge from early to middle adulthood. It brings a new set of developmental tasks. The life structure again comes into question. It becomes important to ask: "What have I done with my life? What do I really get from and give to my wife, children, friends, work, community—and self? What is it I truly want for myself and others?" A man yearns for a life in which his actual desires, values, talents and aspirations can be expressed.

Some men do very little questioning or searching during the Mid-life Transition. They are apparently untroubled by difficult questions regarding the meaning, value and direction of their lives. Other men realize that the character of their lives is changing, but the process is not a painful one. They are in a manageable transition, one without crisis. But for the great majority of men this is a period of great struggle within the self and with the external world. Their Mid-life Transition is a time of moderate or severe crisis. They question nearly every aspect of their lives and feel that they cannot go on as before. They will need several years to form a new path or to modify the old one.

We need developmental transitions in adulthood partly because no life structure can permit the living out of all aspects of the self. To create a life structure I must make choices and set priorities. Every choice I make involves the rejection of many other possibilities. Committing myself to a structure, I try over a span of time to enhance my life within it, to realize its potential, to bear the responsibilities and tolerate the costs it entails. During a transition period—and especially in the Mid-life Transition—the neglected parts of the self more urgently seek expression and stimulate the modification of the existing structure.

Entering Middle Adulthood:
Building a New Life Structure

The tasks of the Mid-life Transition must be given up by about age 45. A man has had his allotted time for reappraising, exploring, testing choices and creating the basis for a new life. The opportunity to question and search is present throughout middle adulthood and beyond, but at this point new tasks predominate. Now he must make his choices and begin forming a new life structure.

The end of the Mid-life Transition, like all shifts from one period to the next, is marked by a series of changes rather than one dramatic event. It may be evident only as a man looks back a few years later that he was in fact committing himself to the choices around which a new life structure took shape.

In some lives the shift is signaled by a crucial marker event—a drastic change in job or occupation, a divorce or love affair, a serious illness, the death of a loved one, a move to a new locale. Other lives show no conspicuous change: life at 45 seems to be just as it was at 39. If we look more closely, however, we discover seemingly minor changes that make a considerable difference. A man may still be married to the same woman, but the character of his familial relationships has changed appreciably for better or worse. Or the nature of his work life has altered: he is quietly marking time until retirement; his work has become oppressive and humiliating; or seemingly small changes in his mode of work have made his work life more satisfying and creative. A man's life structure, we have found, necessarily changes in certain crucial respects during the course of his Mid-life Transition.

The life structure that emerges in the middle forties varies greatly in its satisfactoriness, that is, its suitability for the self and its workability in the world. Some men have suffered such irreparable defeats in childhood or early adulthood, and have been so little able to work on the tasks of their Mid-life Transition, that they lack the inner and outer resources for creating a minimally adequate structure. They face a middle adulthood of constriction and decline. Other men form a life structure that is reasonably viable in the world but poorly connected to the self. Although they do their bit for themselves and others, their lives are lacking in inner excitement and meaning. Still other men have started a middle adulthood that will have its own special satisfactions and fulfillments. For these men, middle adulthood is often the fullest and most creative season in the live cycle. They are less tyrannized by the ambitions, passions and illusions of youth. They can be more deeply attached to others and yet more separate, more centered in the self. For them, the season passes in its best and most satisfying rhythm.

The Subsequent Periods in
Middle Adulthood

By his late forties, a man has formed an initial life structure for middle adulthood. Where does he go from here? Although we did not study men beyond this age, there is evidence that the sequence of stable and transitional periods continues over the entire life cycle. The developmental process of growth, decline and change continues. Here is a tentative view of the subsequent periods in middle adulthood.

There is an <u>Age Fifty Transition</u>, which normally lasts from about age 50 to 55. The functions of this period in middle adulthood are similar to those of the Age Thirty Transition in early adulthood. In it, a man can work further on the tasks of the Mid-life Transition and can modify the life structure formed in the mid-forties. It may be a time of crisis for men who changed too little in their Mid-life Transition and then built an unsatisfactory life structure. In our opinion, it is not possible to get through middle adulthood without having at least a moderate crisis in either the Mid-life Transition or the Age Fifty Transition.

From roughly age 55 to 60, a stable period is devoted to building a second middle adult structure, which provides a vehicle for completing middle adulthood. For men who are able to rejuvenate their selves and enrich their lives, the decade of the fifties can be a time of great fulfillment. This period is analogous to Settling Down in early adulthood. Finally, from about 60 to 65, the Late Adult Transition terminates middle adulthood and creates a basis for starting late adulthood. The tasks of this transition are to conclude the efforts of middle adulthood and to prepare oneself for the era to come. It is a period of significant development and represents a major turning point in the life cycle.

In every cross-era transition a new season is born and takes its initial shape. These transitions have a great effect on the future, but they never tell the whole story. Each new period makes its essential contribution to the life course. In every period we suffer because of the undone developmental work of previous periods—for ultimately these chickens do come home to roost—but we also have an opportunity to do further developmental work and to create a life more suitable to the self.

II

ALTERNATIVE LIFE-STYLES AND CHILDREN

Introduction

The often perplexing developmental task facing
young adults is developing a life style that is
meaningful and satisfying. In their late teens
and early twenties young adults find that they have
an identity. Sometimes it is difficult to determine how it came about. It may be consciously
chosen or vaguely adopted, or fallen into. Nevertheless, it is an identity developed in the context
of social and institutional relations created by
parents, teachers, ministers, and friends. Young
adults upon leaving school and home strike out on
their own and begin the exciting but demanding task
of creating a way of life of their own. This can
also be threatening; the comfort of an identity can
be lost when new and sometimes unexpected demands
are made by the employer, spouse, and close
friends. In this creative venture, the young adult
many continue the way of life experienced at home,
develop his own variation of what he knew in his
home, or opt for a new way. If married the partners attempt to create a way of life together that
is good. In each case, however, young adults are
at a choice point and they ask, "What kind of life-
style is best?" Life rarely settles to one such
issue. Rather, a broad issue of this type is
actually a congury of interrelated issues. Many
problems are faced; many choices are made; and a
pattern of life begins to evolve. While many
facets of this search for a personally satisfying
life could be discussed, a central issue is the
kind and quality of personal relations persons
ought to enter into and the responsibilities those

125

personal relations imply. It is at this juncture that the influence of individuals' identities come into play.

Each person has an identity forged in the context of home, school, church and peer groups. The young adult is ready to explore relations that new identity allows. Friendships are formed at work, or church, but these are limited in the depth of personal involvement they allow. The young adult seeks a relationship with a person of the opposite sex which is enduring, close, and intimate. Childhood friendships are left behind. They were valuable in performing an important role in self-discovery. But now the search is for an intimate relation with another person. This is an important dimension of the creation of a meaningful and satisfying adult way of life. While a plethora of alternative ways of living life are available to us, and many of them are clearly within the realistic bounds of the identity every young adult has established, the focal point of these alternatives is intimacy in all its dimensions: sex, marriage, male and female roles, and children. To create a significant intimacy means that young adults must work through issues in these and no doubt other areas. While these topics involve psychological, religious, and social questions, what philosophical questions must be faced?

Most young people assume that marriage is the proper context for a person to develop an intimate relation with a person of the opposite sex. This presupposition is supported by one's own home context, tradition, and social approval. The form marriage takes in the United States is monogamy, and it is usually supported on religious and social grounds as well as being the traditional thing to do. Recently, however, monogamy, as a legal, social institution, has come under attack. Some young adults choose to live together without going through the legal, religious aspects of marriage. They believe that what matters is the commitment the partners make to each other in the context of love; a piece of paper makes no difference to the quality of that commitment. To marry or not to marry must be decided on personal grounds alone. It is a matter of individual choice. In a day when some tend to appeal to some vulgar hedonistic ideal as a basis for thinking through this issue, it is important to consider the nature, function, and value of monogamy as a social institution. An important issue in the present debate over monogamy is whether or not it is more satisfactory than some other social arrangement for the development of intimacy. Some argue, including McMurtry, that monogamous marriage as an institution is damaging both to society and to the individuals involved. Monogamy must be abolished. It is important to recognize that McMurtry is attacking only monogamous marriage; other forms may be defensible. Others argue, including Bayles, that monogamy promotes interpersonal relationships and promotes the welfare of children. Since society has a legitimate interest in both of these dimensions of human life, it should defend monogamy. Closely related to the issue of monogamous marriage are the issues surrounding sex and the sexual relations.

The focal point of the relationship of intimacy is the sexual relation. Whatever the institutional form in which the sexual relation may be expressed, when the sexual relation is submitted to serious philosophical reflection some important issues arise. Two people who enter a sexual relation bring presuppositions to that relation. The structure and content of the relation will be significantly influenced by those presuppositions. When persons are interested in enhancing the quality of their lives, such as in the area of sexual relations, and it is clear that the beliefs they hold have a direct bearing on that quality, then it seems imperative to examine those beliefs. In the past few years the beliefs people hold about sex seem to have changed rapidly. This may be a reflection of the changing social, cultural conditions of their lives. Technological advances in contraceptive measures, sexual explicitness on television and in the cinema, the gay rights movement, sexually oriented magazines, and women's liberation have all played a part in changing cultural attitudes toward sex and sexual relations. In the search for a meaningful, valuable sexual relation contributory to living well as an adult, it is important to determine what characteristics the relation must have in order to be significant, life enriching, and valuable. Before this can be done, an important concept must be clarified. What is a normal sexual relation? This question must be answered before it makes sense to talk about those characteristics which make the normal sexual relation life enhancing. One way to approach the problem of clarification of the concept of a normal sexual relation is to determine what counts as sexual perversion. Through a process of conceptual analysis those values and beliefs which form the basis of the concept of a normal sexual relation can be brought out into the open and clarified and examined. If sexual perversion can be clarified then normal sexual relation will be clarified. This is the maneuver that Tom Nagel makes in his article on sexual perversion. However, in specifying the concepts of normal and abnormal sexual relations, it is important that more is done than examine the form of the relation. Otherwise, the beliefs about what is correct or incorrect, desirable or undesirable which give content to the form of the relation may be left unclarified and evaluated. Solomon focuses on the content of the relation. He discusses the weaknesses of the view that the sexual relation is simply communication. It is important to consider what is being communicated. Also, the expectations brought to the sexual encounter by the man and the woman will have significant implications for the quality of that relation. Important questions are raised by Nagel and Solomon. What is the sexual relation? What is its content? What ought to be communicated? Are there sexual relations which are perverse and morally reprehensible? Are there understandings of the sexual relation which when acted upon are damaging to the personhood of those involved? What understandings of the sexual relation are contributory to significant intimacy and to living life well as an adult? Another dimension to the search

128

for meaningful intimacy besides marriage and the sexual relation is the attitude toward children born within the intimacy.

The implications of the attempt to create the relation of intimacy go beyond the partners involved. It is within this relation that many people choose to have children. Children are born through two parents (cloning aside) and are traditionally nurtured by two parents. Erikson's view of intimacy is one in which all stages of satisfactory development are secured to the offspring of that intimacy. The presupposition held by most people is that children have not only obligations within the family but also rights. They believe that parents who mistreat a child are violating that child's rights. Furthermore, a child may be thought of as having the right to proper parenting. Yet the question can legitimately be asked whether or not children do have a right to the security Erikson discusses. Furthermore, do children albeit young and unable to care for themselves have inviolable rights by virtue of being members of society? Worsfield explores some alternative views of children's rights such as those held by Locke and Hobbes. However, he contends that within the theory of justice developed recently by John Rawls it is possible to argue cogently that children do have rights. Another issue related to the rights of children is whether or not infants and unborn children have the right to life? Is abortion morally justified? Is killing a newborn child ever right? Tooley contends that these issues resolve into the elemental issue of "what properties a thing must possess in order to have a serious right to life." He contends that the answer to this question turns on whether or not human fetuses and infants possess those properties.

While these and many other issues confront the young adult who is forging a life style with another person and for himself, the key problem is what kind of character should be created in the new relation of intimacy. The identity, values, and beliefs brought to the creation of this

129

character, this way of life, play a crucial role in the kind and quality of life developed. If the art of living is just that, an intelligent craftsmanship of the "materials" at ones disposal then these issues cannot be ignored. They demand the best of our philosophical capabilities.

Monogamy

Case

Despite their disagreement, Rachel and Jason cared for each other deeply. They had sensed when they first met that they were kindred souls, and their time together during these months had substantiated the fact. Jason had been with the company for a short time when Rachel joined the staff as head of her department. As they left the first executive staff meeting together, she had invited him out for a drink after which he invited her to dinner. They had since spent much of their free time together. Then came the disagreement which had made both of them uneasy for the last two weeks. Rachel's roommate had been transferred, leaving her with either full rent payment or the task of finding another roommate. She suggested to Jason that he move in with her. They enjoyed each other's company; in fact, they were becoming increasingly intimate. Jason was repulsed by the idea saying that if he moved in they would have to be married, and he wasn't ready to be married. Rachel argued that it was not only economically effective, it would be pleasurable to have him around. Besides, why worry about a piece of paper! Jason argued that the relationship would deteriorate and that he would eventually lose respect for himself as well as her. How could the disagreement be settled? It seemed so plain to each other that it would best be solved his (her) way.

Monogamy: A Critique*
John McMurtry

> Remove away that black'ning church
> Remove away that marriage hearse
> Remove away that man of blood
> You'll quite remove the ancient curse.
> —William Blake

I

Almost all of us have entered or will one day
enter a specifically standardized form of monogamous marriage. This cultural requirement is so
very basic to our existence that we accept it for
most part as a kind of intractable given—dictated
by the laws of God, Nature, Government, and Good
Sense all at once. Though it is perhaps unusual
for a social practice to be so promiscuously under-
written, we generally find comfort rather than
curiosity in this fact and seldom wonder how something could be divinely inspired, biologically
determined, coerced, and reasoned out all at the
same time. We simply take for granted.

Those in society who are officially charged
with the thinking function with regard to such
matters are no less responsible for this uncritical acceptance than is the man on the street. The
psychoanalyst traditionally regards our form of
marriage as a necessary restraint on the anarchic
id and not more to be queried than civilization
itself. The lawyer is as undisposed to questioning
the practice as he is to criticizing the principle
of private property (this is appropriate, as I
shall later point out). The churchman formally
perceives the relationship between man and wife to
be as inviolable and insusceptible to question as

*Reprinted from The Monist 56, no. 4 (1972), La
Salle, Illinois, with the permission of the author
and publisher.

the relationship between the institution he works for and the Christ. The sociologist standardly accepts the formalized bonding of heterosexual pairs as the indispensable basis of social order and perhaps a societal universal. The politician is as incapable of challenging it as he is the virtue of his own continued holding of office. And the philosopher (at least the English-speaking philosopher), as with most issues of socially controversial or sexual dimensions, ignores the question almost altogether.

Even those irreverent adulterers and unmarried couples who seem to be challenging the institution in the most basic possible way, in practice, tend merely to mimic its basic structure in unofficial form. The coverings of sanctities, taboos, and cultural habit continue to hold them with the grip of public clothes.

II

"Monogamy" means, literally, "one marriage." But it would be wrong to suppose that this phrase tells us much about our particular species of official wedlock. The greatest obstacle to the adequate understanding of our monogamy institution has been the failure to identify clearly and systematically the full complex of principles it involves. There are four such principles, each carrying enormous restrictive force and together constituting a massive social-control mechanism that has never, so far as I know, been fully schematized. To come straight to the point, the four principles in question are as follows:

1. <u>The partners are required to enter a formal contractual relation</u>: (a) whose establishment demands a specific official participant, certain conditions of the contractors (legal age, no blood ties, and so on), and a standard set of procedures; (b) whose governing terms are uniform for all and exactly prescribed by law; and (c) whose dissolution may only be legally effected by the decision of state representatives.

133

The ways in which this elaborate principle of contractual requirement is importantly restrictive are obvious. One may not enter into a marriage union without entering into a contract presided over by a state-investured official.[1] One may not set any of the terms of the contractual relationship by which one is bound for life. And one cannot dissolve the contract without legal action and costs, court proceedings, and in many places actual legislation. (This is the one and only contract in all English-speaking law that is not dissoluble by the consent of the contracting parties.) The extent of control here—over the most intimate and putatively "loving" relationships in all social intercourse—is so great as to be difficult to catalogue without exciting in oneself a sense of disbelief.

Lest it be thought there is always the real option of entering a common-law relationship free of such encumbrances, it should be noted that: (a) these relationships themselves are subject to state regulation, though of a less imposing sort; and (much more important) (b) there are very formidable selective pressures against common-law partnerships, such as employment and job discrimination, exclusion from housing and lodging facilities, special legal disablements,[2] loss of social and moral status (consider such phrases as "living in sin" and "make her an honest woman"), family shame and embarrassment, and so on.

2. <u>The number of partners involved in the marriage must be two and only two</u> (as opposed to three, four, five, or any of the almost countless possibilities of intimate union). This second principle of our specific form of monogamy (the concept of "one marriage," it should be pointed out, is consistent with any number of participating partners) is perhaps the most important and restrictive of the four principles we are considering. Not only does it confine us to just one possibility out of an enormous range, but it confines us to that single possibility that involves the least number of people, two. It is difficult to conceive of a more thoroughgoing mechanism for limiting

134

extended social union and intimacy. The fact that this monolithic restriction seems so "natural" to us (if it were truly "natural," of course, there would be no need for its rigorous cultural prescription by everything from severe criminal law[3] to ubiquitous housing regulations) simply indicates the extent to which its hold is implanted in our social structure. It is the institutional basis of what I will call the "binary frame of sexual consciousness," a frame through which all our heterosexual relationships are typically viewed ("two's company, three's a crowd") and in light of which all larger circles of intimacy seem almost inconceivable.[4]

   3. _No person may participate in more than one marriage at a time or during a lifetime_ (unless the previous marriage has been officially dissolved by, normally, one partner's death or a divorce). Violoation of this principle is, of course, a criminal offense (bigamy) that is punishable by a considerable term in prison. Of various general regulations of our marriage institution, it has experienced the most significant modification, not indeed in principle, but in the extent of flexibility of its "escape hatch" of divorce. The ease with which this escape hatch is opened has increased considerably in the past few years (the grounds for divorce being more permissive than previously) and it is in this regard most of all that the principles of our marriage institution have undergone formal alteration—that is, in plumbing rather than substance.

   4. _No married person may engage in any sexual relationship with any person other than the marriage partner._ Although a consummated sexual act with another person alone constitutes an act of adultery, lesser forms of sexual and erotic relationships[5] may also constitute grounds for divorce (for example, cruelty) and are generally proscribed as well by informal social convention and taboo. In other words, the fourth and final principle of marriage institution involves not only a prohibition of sexual intercourse per se outside one's wedlock (this term deserves pause) but a prohibition of all

135

one's erotic relations whatever outside this bond. The penalties for violation here are as various as they are severe, ranging from permanent loss of spouse, children, chattel, and income to job dismissal and social ostracism. In this way, possibly the most compelling natural force toward expanded intimate relations with others is strictly confined within the narrowest possible circle for (barring delinquency) the whole of adult life.[6] The sheer weight and totality of this restriction is surely one of the great wonders of all historical institutional control.

III

With all established institutions, apologetics for perpetuation are never wanting. Thus it is with our form of monogamous marriage.

Perhaps the most celebrated justification over the years has proceeded from the belief in a Supreme Deity, who secretly utters sexual and other commands to privileged human representatives. Almost as well known a line of defense has issued from a similarly confident conviction that the need for some social regulation of sexuality demonstrates the need for our specific type of two-person wedlock. Although these have been important justifications in the sense of being very widely supported, they are not—having other grounds than reason—susceptible to treatment here.

If we put aside such arguments, we are left, I think, with two major claims. The first is that our form of monogamous marriage promotes a profound affection between the partners that is not only of great worth in itself but invaluable as a sanctuary from the pressures of outside society. Since, however, there are no secure grounds whatever for supposing that such "profound affection" is not at least as easily achievable by any number of other marriage forms (that is, forms that differ in one or more of the four principles), this justification conspicuously fails to perform the task required of it.

136

The second major claim for the defense is that monogamy provides a specially loving context for child-upbringing. However, here again there are no grounds at all for concluding that it does so as, or any more, effectively than other possible forms of marriage. (The only alternative type of up-bringing to which it has apparently been shown to be superior is non-family institutional upbringing, which of course is not relevant to the present discussion.) Furthermore, the fact that at least half the span of a normal monogamous marriage involves no child-upbringing at all is overlooked here, as is the reinforcing fact that there is no reference to or mention of the quality of child-upbringing in any of the prescriptions connected with it.

In brief, the second major justification of our particular type of wedlock scents somewhat too strongly of red herring to pursue further.

There is, it seems, little to recommend the view that monogamy specially promotes "profound affection" between the partners or a "loving context" for child-upbringing. Such claims are simply without force. On the other hand, there are several aspects to the logic and operation of the four principles of this institution that suggest that it actually inhibits the achievement of these desiderata. Far from uniquely abetting the latter, it militates against them in these ways:

1. Centralized official control of marriage (which the Church gradually achieved through the mechanism of Canon Law after the fall of the Roman Empire[7] in one of the greatest seizures of social power of history) necessarily alienates the partners from full responsibility for and freedom in their relationship. "Profound closeness" between the partners—or at least an area of it—is thereby expropriated rather than promoted and "sanctuary" from the pressures of outside society prohibited rather than fostered.

2. Limitation of the marriage bond to two people necessarily restricts, in perhaps the most

unilateral way possible consistent with offspring survival, the number of adult sources of affection, interest, and material support and instruction for the young. The "loving context for child-upbringing" is thereby dessicated rather than nourished, providing the structural conditions for such notorious and far-reaching problems as sibling rivalry for scarce adult attention[8] and parental oppression through exclusive monopoly of the child's means of life.[9]

3. Formal exclusion of all others from erotic contact with the marriage partner systematically promotes conjugal insecurity, jealousy, and alienation in several ways. (a) It officially underwrites a literally totalitarian expectation of sexual confinement on the part of one's husband or wife: which expectation is, _ceteris paribus_, inevitably more subject to anxiety and disappointment than one less extreme in its demand and/or cultural-juridical backing.[10] (b) It requires so complete a sexual isolation of the marriage partners that should one violate the fidelity code the other is left alone and susceptible to a sense of fundamental deprivation and resentment. It stipulates such a strict restraint of sexual energies that there are habitual violations of the regulations, frequently if not always attended by willful deception and reciprocal suspicion about the occurence or quality of the extramarital relationship, anxiety and fear on both sides of permanent estrangement from partner and family, and overt and covert antagonism over the prohibited act in both offender (who feels "trapped") and offended (who feels "betrayed").

The disadvantages of the four principles of monogamous marriage do not, however, end with inhibiting the very effects they are said to promote. There are further shortcomings:

1. The restriction of marriage union to two partners necessarily prevents the strengths of larger groupings. Such advantages as the following are thereby usually ruled out: (a) the

138

security, range, and power of larger socioeconomic units; (b) the epistemological and emotional substance, variety, and scope of more pluralist interactions; (c) the possibility of extradomestic freedom founded on more adult providers and upbringers as well as more broadly based circles of intimacy.

2. The sexual containment and isolation that the four principles together require variously stimulates such social malaises as: (a) destructive aggression (which notoriously results from sexual frustration); (b) apathy, frustration, and dependence within the marriage bond; (c) lack of spontaneity, bad faith, and distance in relationships without the marriage bond; (d) sexual fantasizing, perversion, fetishism, prostitution, and pornography in the adult population as a whole.[11]

Taking such things into consideration, it seems difficult to lend credence to the view that the four principles of our form of monogamous marriage constitute a structure beneficial either to the marriage partners themselves or to their offspring (or indeed to anyone else). One is moved to seek for some other ground of the institution, some ground that lurks beneath the reach of our conventional apprehensions.

IV

The ground of our marriage institution, the essential principle that underwrites all four restrictions, is this: <u>the maintenance by one man or woman of the effective right to exclude indefinitely all others from erotic access to the conjugal partner</u>.

The first restriction creates, elaborates on, and provides for the enforcement of this right to exclude. And the second, third, and fourth restrictions together ensure that the right to exclude is—respectively—not cooperative, not simultaneously or sequentially distributed, and not permissive of even casual exception.

139

In other words, the four restrictions of our form of monogamous marriage together constitute a state-regulated, indefinite, and exclusive ownership by two individuals of one another's sexual powers. Marriage is simply a form of private property.[12]

That our form of monogamous marriage is, when the confusing layers of sanctity, apologetic, and taboo are cleared away, another species of private property should not surprise us.[13] The history of the institution is so full of suggestive indicators—dowries, inheritance, property alliances, daughter sales (of which women's wedding rings are a carry-over), bride exchanges, and legitimacy and illegitimacy—that it is difficult not to see some intimate connections between marital and ownership ties. We are better able still to apprehend the ownership essence of our marriage institution, when in addition we consider: (1) that until recently almost the only way to secure official dissolution of consummated marriage was to be able to demonstrate violation of one or both partner's sexual ownership, (that is, adultery); (2) that the imperative of premarital chastity is tantamount to a demand for retrospective sexual ownership by the eventual marriage partner; (3) that successful sexual involvement with a married person is prosecutable as an expropriation of ownership—"alienation of affections"—which is restituted by cash payment; (4) that the incest taboo is an iron mechanism that protects the conjugal ownership of sexual properties, both the husband's and wife's, from the access of affectionate offspring and the offsprings' (who themselves are future marriage partners) from access of siblings and parents;[14] (5) that the language of the marriage ceremony is the language of exclusive possession ("take," "to have and to hold," "forsaking all others and keeping you only unto him/her," and so on, not to mention the proprietary locutions associated with the marital relationship ("he's mine," "she belongs to him," "keep to your own husband," "wife stealer," "possessive husband," and so on).

Of course, it would be remarkable if marriage in our society was not a relationship akin to private property. In our socioeconomic system we relate to virtually everything of value by individual ownership: by, that is, the effective right to exclude others from the thing concerned.[15] That we do so as well with perhaps the most highly valued thing of all—the sexual partners' sexuality—is only to be expected. Indeed, it would probably be an intolerable strain on our entire social structure if we did otherwise.

This line of thought deserves pursuit. The real secret of our form of monogamous marriage is not that it functionally provides for the needs of adults who love one another or of the children they give birth to but that it serves the maintenance of our present social system. It is an institution that is indispensable to the persistence of the capitalist order[16] in the following ways:

1. A basic principle of current social relations is that some people legally acquire the use of other people's personal powers, from which they may exclude other members of society. This system operates in the work-place (owners and hirers of all types contractually acquire for their exclusive use workers' regular labor powers) and in the family (husbands and wives contractually acquire for their exclusive use their partner's sexual properties). A conflict between the structures of these primary relations—as would obtain were there a suspension of the restrictions governing our form of monogamous marriage—might well undermine the systemic coherence of present social intercourse.

2. The fundamental relation between individuals and things that satisfy their needs is, in our present society, that each individual has or does not have the effective right to exclude other people from the thing in question.[17] A rudimentary need is that for sexual relationship(s). Therefore the object of this need must be related to the one

141

who needs it as owned or not owned (that is, via marriage or not-marriage, or approximations thereof) if people's present relationship to what they need is to retain—again—systemic coherence.

3. A necessary condition for the continued existence of the present social formation is that its members feel a powerful motivation to gain favorable positions in it. But such social ambition is heavily dependent on the preservation of exclusive monogamy in that (a) the latter confines the discharge of primordial sexual energies to a single unalterable partner and thus typically compels those energies to seek alternative outlet,[18] such as business or professional success and (b) the exclusive marriage necessarily reduces the sexual relationships available to any one person to absolute (nonzero) minimum, a unilateral promotion of sexual shortage that in practice renders hierarchial achievement essential as an economic and "display" means for securing scarce partners.[19]

4. Because the exclusive marriage necessarily and dramatically reduces the possibilities of sexual-love relationships, it thereby promotes the existing economic system by: (a) rendering extreme economic self-interest—the motivational basis of the capitalistic process—less vulnerable to altruistic subversion; (b) disciplining society's members into the habitual repression of natural impulse required for long-term performance of repetitive and arduous work tasks; (c) developing a complex of suppressed sexual desires to which sales techniques may be effectively applied in creating those new consumer wants that provide indispensable outlets for ever increasing capital funds.

5. The present form of marriage is of fundamental importance to (a) the continued relative powerlessness of the individual family: which, with larger numbers would constitute a correspondingly increased command of social powers; (b) the continued high demand for homes, commodities, and services: which, with the considerable economies of scale that extended unions would permit, would

142

otherwise falter; (c) the continued strict necessity for adult males to sell their labor power and for adult women to remain at home (or vice
versa): which strict necessity would diminish
as the economic base of the family unit extended; (d) the continued immense pool of unsatisfied
sexual desires and energies in the population at
large: without which powerful interests and institutions would lose much of their conventional
appeal and force;[20] (e) the continued profitable
involvement of lawyers, priests, and state officials in the jurisdictions of marriage and divorce
and the myriad official practices and proceedings
connected thereto.[21]

VI

If our marriage institution is a linchpin of
our present social structure then a breakdown in
this institution would seem to indicate a breakdown in our social structure. On the face of it,
the marriage institution is breaking down—enormously increased divorce rates, nonmarital sexual
relationships, wife-swapping, the Playboy philosophy, and communes. Therefore one might be led
by the appearance of things to anticipate a profound alteration in the social system.

But it would be a mistake to underestimate
the tenacity of an established order or to over-
estimate the extent of change in our marriage institution. Increased divorce rates merely indicate the widening of a traditional escape hatch.
Nonmarital relationships imitate and culminate in
the marital mold. Wife-swapping presupposes ownership, as the phrase suggests. The Playboy philosophy is merely the view that if one has the money
one has the right to be titillated—the commercial
call to more fully exploit a dynamic sector of
capital investment. And communes—the most hope-
ful phenomenon—almost nowhere offer a praxis
challenge to private property in sexuality. It may
be changing. But history, as the old man puts it,
weighs like a nightmare on the brains of the living.

143

Notes

[1]Any person who presides over a marriage and is not authorized by law to do so is guilty of a criminal offense and is subject to several years imprisonment (for example, Canadian Criminal Code, Sec. 258.) Here and elsewhere, I draw examples from Canadian criminal law. There is no reason to suspect the Canadian code is eccentric in these instances.

[2]For example, offspring are illegitimate, neither the wife nor children are legal heirs, and the husband has no right of access or custody should separation occur.

[3]"Any kind of conjugal union with more than one person at the same time, whether or not it is by law recognized as a binding form of marriage—is guilty of an indictable offence and is liable to imprisonment for five years" (Canadian Criminal Code, Sec. 257, [1] [a] [ii]). Part 2 of the same section adds: "Where an accused is charged with an offence under this section, no averment or proof of the method by which the alleged relationship was entered into, agreed to or consented to is necessary in the indictment or upon the trial of the accused, nor is it necessary upon the trial to prove that the persons who are alleged to have entered into the relationship had or intended to have sexual intercourse."

[4]Even the sexual revolutionary Wilhelm Reich seems constrained within the limits of this "binary frame." Thus he says: "Nobody has the right to prohibit his or her partner from entering a temporary or lasting sexual relationship with someone else. He has only the right either to withdraw or to win the partner back" (Wilhelm Reich, The Sexual Revolution, trans. T. P. Wolfe [New York: Farrar, Straus & Giroux, 1970], p. 28. Emphasis added.) The possibility of sexual partners extending their union to include the other loved party (as opposed to one partner having either to "win" against this third party or to "withdraw" altogether) does not seem even to occur to Reich.

[5]I will be using "sexual" and "erotic" interchangeably throughout this paper.

[6]It is worth noting here that: (a) man has by nature the most "open" sexual instinct—year-round operativeness and response to a wide variety of stimuli—of all the species (except perhaps the dolphin); and (b) it is a principle of human needs in general that maximum satisfaction involves regular variation in the form of the need-object.

[7]"Roman law had no power of intervening in the formation of marriages and there was no legal form of marriage. . . . Marriage was a matter of simple private agreement and divorce was a private transaction" (Havelock Ellis, _Studies in the Psychology of Sex_ [New York: Random House, 1963], vol. 2, p. 429).

[8]The dramatic reduction of sibling rivalry through an increased number of adults in the house is a phenomenon that is well known in contemporary domestic communes.

[9]One of the few other historical social relationships I can think of in which one person holds thoroughly exclusive monopoly over another's means of life is slavery. Thus, as with another's slave, it is a criminal offense to "receive" or "harbor" another's child without "right of possession" (Canadian Criminal Code, Sec. 250).

[10]Certain cultures, for example, permit extramarital sexuality by married persons with friends, guests, or in-laws with no reported consequences of jealousy. From such evidence, one is led to speculate that the intensity and extent of jealousy at a partner's extramarital sexual involvement is in direct proportion to the severity of the accepted cultural regulations against such involvements. In short such regulations do not prevent jealousy so much as effectively engender it.

[11]It should not be forgotten that at the same time marriage excludes marital partners from sexual contact with others, it necessarily excludes those others from sexual contact with marital partners. Walls face two ways.

[12]Those aspects of marriage law that seem to fall outside the pale of sexual property holding—for example, provisions for divorce if the husband fails to provide or is convicted of a felony or is an alcoholic—may themselves be seen as simply

prescriptive characterizations of the sort of sexual property that the marriage partner must remain to retain satisfactory conjugal status; a kind of permanent warranty of the "good working order" of the sexual possession.

What constitutes the "good working order" of the conjugal possession is, of course, different in the case of the husband and in the case of the wife: an asymmetry within the marriage institution that, I gather, women's liberation movements are anxious to eradicate.

[13]It is instructive to think of even the non-legal aspects of marriage, for example, its sentiments, as essentially private-property structured. Thus the preoccupation of those experiencing conjugal sentiments with expressing how much "my very own," "my precious," the other is, with expressing, that is, how valuable and inviolable the ownership is and will remain.

[14]I think the secret to the long-mysterious incest taboo may well be the fact that in all its forms it protects sexual property: not only conjugal (as indicated above) but paternal and tribal as well. This crucial line of thought, however, requires extended separate treatment.

[15]Sometimes—as with political patronage, criminal possession, de facto privileges, and so forth—a power to exclude others exists with no corresponding "right" (just as sometimes a right to exclude exists with no corresponding power). Therefore, properly speaking, I should here use the phrase "power to exclude," which covers "effective right to exclude" as well as all nonjuridical enablements of this sort.

[16]It is no doubt indispensable as well—in some form or other—to any private-property order. Probably (if we take the history of Western society as our data base) the more thoroughgoing and developed the private-property formation is, the more total the sexual ownership prescribed by the marriage institution.

[17]Things in unlimited supply—like, presently, oxygen—are not of course related to people in this way.

[18]This is, of course, a Freudian or quasi-

Freudian claim. "Observation of daily life shows us," says Freud, "that most persons direct a very tangible part of their sexual motive powers to their professional or business activities" (Sigmund Freud, _Dictionary of Psychoanalysis_, ed. Nandor Fodor and Frank Gaynor [New York: Fawcett Publications, Premier Paperback, 1966], p. 139).

[19]It might be argued that exclusive marriage also protects those physically less attractive persons who—in an "open" situation—might be unable to secure any sexual partnership at all. The force of this claim depends, I think, on improperly continuing to posit the very principle of exclusiveness that the "open" situation rules out (for example, in the latter situation, X might be less attractive to Y than Z is and yet Z not be rejected, any more than at present an intimate friend is rejected who is less talented than another intimate friend).

[20]The sexual undercurrents of corporate advertisements, religious systems, racial propaganda, and so on, are too familiar to dwell on here.

[21]It is also possible that exclusive marriage protects the adult-youth power structure in the manner outlined on p. 138.

Marriage, Love, and Procreation*
    Michael D. Bayles

    The current era is one of that vulgar form of hedonism rejected by philosophical hedonists such as Epicurus and John Stuart Mill.[1] Apologists thinly disguise the tawdriness of a hedonism of biological pleasures by appeals to individual rights and autonomy. Far too frequently these appeals merely mask a refusal to accept responsibility. This failure to accept personal responsibility is

*Reprinted by permission of the author and Prometheus Books from _Philosophy and Sex_, ed. by Robert Baker and Frederick Elliston. Copyright © 1975 Michael Bayles.

periodically atoned for by ritualistic and ill-conceived attempts to help the poor and underprivileged people of the world.

One of the central focuses of the current vulgar hedonism has been sexual liberation. Premarital intercourse, gay liberation, no-fault divorce, open marriage (read, "open adultery"), polygamy, and orgies all have their advocates. About the only forms of sexual behavior yet to have strong advocates are pedophilia and bestiality. Any day now one may expect grade-school children to assert their right to happiness through pedophilia and animal lovers to argue that disapproval of bestiality is unfair to little lambs.

The result, especially in Western society, is an emphasis on sex that is out of all proportion to its significance for a eudaemonistic life—that is, a life worth living, including elements besides pleasure. The only ultimate test for the value of a life is whether at its end it is found to have been worth living. It is difficult to conceive of a person's thinking his life significant because it was a second-rate approximation to the sexual achievements of the notorious rabbit. However, many people seem to think such a life offers the highest ideal of a "truly human" existence, forgetting Aristotle's insight that reproduction is characteristic of all living things, not just humans.[2] Consequently, the institution of marriage has been attacked for hindering the achievement of this vulgar hedonistic ideal.

Attacks on Marriage

Not all attacks on the institution of marriage have been based solely on the vulgar hedonistic ideal. A more broad ranging, although no more plausible, attack has recently been made by John McMurtry. His attack is directed not against marriage per se but against that form of it found in Western society—monogamy. McMurtry does not merely find that monogamous marriage hinders the achieve-

ment of the vulgar hedonistic ideal. He also
claims it is at least one of the causes of the
following social ills: (1) Central official control
of marriage "<u>necessarily</u> alienates the partners from
full responsibility for and freedom in their relationship."[3] (2) Monogamy restricts the sources of
adult affection and support available to children.[4]
(3) It "systematically promotes conjugal insecurity,
jealousy, and alienation. . . ."[5] (4) It "prevents
the strengths of larger groupings."[6] (5) It stimulates aggression, apathy, frustration, lack of spontaneity, perversion, fetishism, prostitution, and
pornography.[7] (6) It serves to maintain the status
quo and capitalism.[8] (7) It supports the powerlessness of the individual family by keeping it small.[9]
(8) By promoting many small families it creates a
high demand for homes and consumer goods and services.[10] (9) It makes it necessary for many more
males to sell their labor than would be necessary if
monogamy were not practiced.[11] (10) By limiting
opportunities for sexual satisfaction it channels
unsatisfied desire into support for various institutions and interests.[12] (11) Finally, it promotes
financial profit for lawyers, priests, and so forth,
in marriage and divorce proceedings.[13] Such a cat-
alog of evils omits only a few social problems such
as political corruption and environmental deterioration, although even they are hinted at in numbers
8 and 11.

Many people have hoped that the simple-
mindedness that attributes all or most or even many
of society's ills to a single factor would disappear. At one time private ownership of the means
of production was the <u>bête noir</u> of society.[14] Recently is has been replaced in that role by unlimited population growth.[15] Both of these beasts
have been slain by the St. George of reasonableness.[16] McMurtry has called forth yet another
single-factor beast. There is no reason to suppose
this one to be any more powerful than its predecessors.

No attempt will be made in this essay to examine in detail McMurtry's criticisms of monogamous

marriage. In general they are characterized by a lack of historical and sociological perspective. It is unclear whether he is attacking the ideal of monogamous marriage as it perhaps existed a hundred years ago or as it exists today. Yet this difference is crucial. A century ago divorce was not widely recognized or accepted; today that is not true. When divorce was not recognized, concubinage and prostitution were quite prevalent, as was simply abandoning one's family. Such practices certainly mitigated the effect of the strict social rules that McMurtry discusses. Also, he criticizes monogamy for limiting the access of children to adult affection and support, since they must rely upon their parents alone for care. But in the extended family, which existed until the urbanization of society, that limitation was considerably less common than it may be at present.

McMurtry seems to be unaware of the social realities of modern society. He emphasizes the law as it is written rather than the law in action. It is generally recognized that despite the wording of statutes, marriages can in practice now be dissolved by mutual consent.[17] Nor is adultery usually prosecuted in those states in which it is still a crime. Nor does McMurtry present any sociological evidence for the various effects that he claims monogamous marriage has. Sometimes the evidence may well be against him. For example, he claims that monogamy supports the high demand for homes. Yet, for a century in Ireland monogamy coincided with a low demand for new homes. Couples simply postponed marriage until the male inherited the home of his parents, and those who did not inherit often did not marry.[18]

Underlying McMurtry's view of monogamous marriage is the Kantian conception of the marriage contract. According to Kant, marriage "is the Union of two Persons of different sex for life-long reciprocal possession of their sexual faculties."[19] McMurtry takes the following principle to be the essential ground of monogamous marriage: "the maintenance by one man or woman of the effective right to exclude indefinitely all others from erotic access to the conjugal partner."[20] Since by "possession" Kant meant legal ownership and the consequent right to exclude others, these two views come to the same thing. They both view marriage as chiefly concerned with private ownership of the means to sexual gratification, thus combining capitalism with vulgar hedonism (although Kant was not a hedonist).

Such a view of marriage is pure nonsense. However, it has more plausibility in today's era of vulgar hedonism than it did in Kant's time. Historically, the official aims of marriage, according to to the Catholic Church—which was the only church during the period of the establishment of monogamous marriage in Western society—were procreation and companionship. There was also a tendency to view it as a legitimate outlet for man's sinful nature.[21] It is this latter element that Kant and McMurtry have taken as the chief one.

In addition to the avowed purposes of marriage there were the actual social functions that it performed. The family unit was the basic social unit, not only for the education of children (that is, socialization, not formal schooling—which has only become widespread during the past century), but also for the production of necessities, including food and clothing, and for recreation. These historical functions of the extended-family unit based on monogamous marriage have been undermined by the development of industrial, urban society.[22] Consequently, the moral and legal status and functions of marriage require reexamination in the light of current social conditions.

Before undertaking such a reexamination it is necessary to distinguish between rules of marriage and attendant social rules. They are mixed together in the traditional social institution of monogamous marriage, but there is no necessity for this mix and it is probably unjustified. In particular one must distinguish between penal laws prohibiting various forms of sexual union—

homosexual, premarital, adulterous—and private arranging laws granting legal recognition to the marital relationship.[23] Private arranging laws do not prescribe punishment for offenses; instead, they enable people to carry out their desires. People are not punished for improperly made marriages; instead, the marriages are invalid and unenforceable. Laws against fornication, prostitution, cohabitation, and homosexuality are almost always penal. Objections to them cannot be transferred directly to the marriage relationship. All of these penal laws could be abolished and monogamous marriage could still be retained.

It may be claimed that despite their nonpenal form, marriage laws do in fact penalize those who prefer other forms of relationship. If homosexual and polygamous relationships are not legally recognized as "marriages," then persons desiring these forms of relationship are being deprived of some degree of freedom. When considering freedom one must be clear about what one is or is not free to do. Consider, for example, the case of gambling. One must distinguish between laws that forbid gambling and the absence of laws that recognize gambling debts. The latter does not deprive people of the freedom to contract gambling debts; it simply does not allow the use of legal enforcement to collect them. Similarly, the absence of laws recognizing polygamous and homosexual marriages does not deprive people of the freedom to enter polygamous and homosexual unions. Instead, it merely fails to provide legal recourse to enforce the agreements of the parties to such unions. The absence of laws recognizing such marriages does not deprive people of a freedom they previously had, for they were never able to have such agreements legally enforced. Nor have people been deprived of a freedom they would have if there were no legal system, for in the absence of a legal system no agreements can be legally enforced. If there is a ground for complaint, then, it must be one of inequality—that one type of relationship is legally recognized but others are not. However, a charge of inequality is warranted only if there are no relevant reasonable grounds for distinguishing between relationships. To settle that issue one must be clear about the state's or society's interests in marriage.

The rest of this essay is concerned with the purposes or functions of the marriage relationship in which society has a legitimate interest. It is not possible here to set out and to justify the purposes for which governments may legislate. It is assumed that the state may act to facilitate citizens' engaging in activities that they find desirable and to protect the welfare and equality of all citizens, including future ones. Government has an especially strong responsibility for the welfare of children. Of course, these legitimate governmental or social interests and responsibities must be balanced against other interests and values of citizens, including those of privacy and freedom from interference.

There is no attempt or intention to justify penal laws prohibiting forms of relationship other than monogamous marriage. Indeed, it is generally assumed that they ought not be prohibited and that more people will enter into them than has been the case. In such a context, monogamous marriage would become a more specialized form of relationship, entered into by a smaller proportion of the population than previously. Underlying this assumption are the general beliefs that many people are unqualified or unfit for a marital relationship and ought never to enter one and that many people marry for the wrong reasons. If true, these beliefs may explain why both marriage and divorce rates have been steadily rising in most Western countries during this century.[24]

Promoting Interpersonal Relationships

Alienation from others and loss of community are perceived by many to be among the most serious ills of modern, mass society. In such a situation it seems unlikely that many would deny the need for intimate interpersonal relationships of affection. The importance of such relationships for a good or eudaemonistic life have been recognized by philosophers as diverse as Aristotle and G. E. Moore.[25] In considering such interpersonal relationships to be among the most valuable elements of a good life, one must distinguish between the value of a good and the strength of the desire for it. Many people have a stronger desire for life than for such interpersonal relationships, but they may still recognize such relationships as more valuable than mere life. Life itself is of little value, but it is a necessary condition for most other things of value.

Among the most valuable forms of interpersonal relationship are love, friendship, and trust. These relationships are limited with respect to the number of persons with whom one can have them. Classically, there has been a distinction between agapeic and erotic love. Agapeic love is the love of all mankind—general benevolence. The concept of erotic love is more limited. In today's world erotic love is apt to be confused with sexual desire and intercourse. But there can be and always has been sex without love and love without sex. Personal love is more restricted than either agapeic love or sexual desire. It implies a concern for another that is greater than that for most people. Hence, it cannot be had for an unlimited number of other people.[26] Similar distinctions must be drawn between friendship and acquaintance, trust of a political candidate and trust of a friend.

Such interpersonal relationships require intimacy. Intimacy involves a sharing of information about one another that is not shared with others. Moreover, it often involves seclusion from others—being in private where others cannot observe.[27] In some societies where physical privacy is not possible, psychological privacy— shutting out the awareness of the presence of others—substitutes. Consequently, these valuable interpersonal relationships require intimacy and usually physical privacy from others, and at the

154

very least nonintrusion upon the relationship.

Moreover, these forms of interpersonal relationship require acts expressing the concern felt for the other person. In most societies acts of sexual intercourse have been such expressions of love and concern. It is not physically or psychologically necessary that sexual intercourse have this quasi-symbolic function, but it is a natural function of sexual intercourse. All that is here meant by "natural" is that in most societies sexual intercourse has this function, for which there is some psychological basis even though it is not contrary to scientific laws for it to be otherwise. Intercourse usually involves an element of giving of oneself, and one's sexual identity is frequently a central element of one's self-image. It is not, however, sexual intercourse that is intrinsically valuable but the feelings and attitudes, the underlying interpersonal relationship, that it expresses. Nonsexual acts also currently express such relationships, but sexual intercourse is still one of the most important ways of doing so. If sexual intercourse ceases to have this function in society, some other act will undoubtedly replace it in this function. Moreover, sexual intercourse will have lost much of its value.

If these interpersonal relationships of personal love and trust are of major value, it is reasonable for the state to seek to protect and foster them by according legal recognition to them in marriage. The specific forms of this recognition cannot be fully discussed. However, there is some basis for treating the partners to a marriage as one person. Historically, of course, the doctrine that the parties to a marriage are one person has supported the subjugation of women in all sorts of ways, for example, in their disability from owning property. But there is an underlying rationale for joint responsibility. Two people who, without a special reason such as taxes, keep separate accounts of income and expenditures do not have the love and trust of a couple who find such an accounting unnecessary. Moreover, in such

155

a joint economic venture there is no point to allowing one party to sue the other. Only the advent of insurance, whereby neither spouse, but a third party, pays, makes such suits seem profitable. Another recognition of these relationships—albeit one not frequently invoked—is that one is not forced to testify against his or her spouse. More important is that neither party is encouraged to violate the trust and intimacy of the relationship, for example, by encouraging one to inform authorities about bedroom comments of his or her spouse.[28]

The character of these valuable forms of interpersonal relationship provides an argument against according marriages of definite duration legal recognition equal to that accorded those that are intentionally of indefinite duration. For it to be "intentionally of indefinite duration," neither partner may, when entering the marriage, intend it to be for a specific period of time, for example, five years, nor may the marriage contract specify such a period. The following argument is not to show that marriages for a definite duration should not be recognized, but merely to show that they should not have equal standing with those intentionally of indefinite duration. The basic reason for unequal recognition is that interpersonal relationships that are not intentionally of indefinite duration are less valuable than those that are.

Suppose one were to form a friendship with a colleague, but the two mutually agree to be friends for only three years, with an option to renew the friendship at that time. Such an agreement would indicate a misunderstanding of friendship. Such agreements make sense for what Aristotle called friendships of utility, but in the modern world these friendships are business partnerships.[29] While there is nothing wrong with business friendships, they do not have the intrinsic value of personal friendships. In becoming close personal friends with someone, one establishes a concern and trust that would be seriously weakened or destroyed by setting a time limit to the friendship. It is sometimes claimed that time limits may be set because people will only be together for a while. But one need not see a person every day or even every year to remain friends. However, extended separation usually brings about a withering away of the friendship.

Similarly, the personal relationship of love and trust in marriage is of lesser value if it is intentionally for only a definite period of time. Moreover, the entering into a relationship that is intentionally of indefinite duration and legally recognized symbolizes a strength of commitment not found in other types of relationships. While two unmarried people may claim that there is no definite limit to their mutual commitment, their commitment is always questionable. Entering into a marital relationship assures the commitment more than does a mere verbal avowal.

There are two common objections to this argument. First, it is sometimes said that there may be special reasons for making marriages of short, definite duration, for example, if one partner will only live in the area for a while. But a personal love that is not strong enough to overcome difficulties of moving to another area and possible sacrifices of employment is not as close and strong as a love that can. Many married couples make such compromises and sacrifices. Second, it is sometimes claimed that commitment is in fact stronger when not legally reinforced, when one does not need the law to support the relationship. However, this claim overlooks the fact that when a married couple's relationship rests substantially upon their legal obligations, their relationship has already begun to deteriorate. The strength of commitment is established by the willingness to enter into a legal relationship that cannot be broken simply, without any difficulties. A person who is not willing to undertake the risk of the legal involvement in divorce should he desire to terminate the relationship is probably unsure of his commitment. Moreover, the legal relationship provides security against a sudden

and unexpected change in one's life—the breakup
of the social aspects will take some time, giving
one a chance to prepare for a new style of life.
Even then the change is often very difficult.

Hence, if marriage is for the purpose of providing legal recognition of some of the most valuable interpersonal relationships, it should grant
more protection and recognition to those intentionally of indefinite duration than to others.
Such a conclusion does not imply that divorce
should be impossible or exceedingly difficult.
Friendships frequently do not last forever despite
their not being intended for a limited period of
time. The same may happen to a marital relationship. So while this argument supports not according legal recognition to relationships intended to
be of definite duration equal to that accorded
those intended to be of indefinite duration, it
does not support restrictions on divorce in the
latter case. Moreover, the average length of time
of marriages has increased considerably since the
seventeenth century. When a couple married then,
one of them was likely to die within twenty years.
With today's increased life expectancy, both parties may live close to fifty years after they
marry.[30] Obviously, with such an increased possible length of marriage, there is a greater
chance for marital breakdown and divorce. One may
expect more divorces in marriages that have lasted
twenty to twenty-five years simply because there
are more such marriages. Nevertheless, such marriages are intentionally of indefinite duration—
for life.

Protecting the Welfare of Children

Another area of pervasive social interest that
has historically centered in marriage concerns the
procreation and raising of children. Society has
an interest not only in the number of children
born but their quality of life. This fact is in
deep conflict with the current emphasis on the
freedom of individuals to make reproductive decisions unfettered by social rules and restrictions.

Moreover, it is an area in which social control has traditionally been weak. Child abuse is widespread, and efforts to prevent it are mediocre at best. There are few general legal qualifications or tests for becoming a parent. Yet parenthood is one of the most potentially dangerous relationships that one person can have with another. If one is a poor college teacher, then at worst a few students do not receive a bit of education they might have. But as a parent one potentially can ruin completely the lives of one's children. At the least, they may develop into psychological misfits incapable of leading responsible and rewarding lives.

Essentially, there are three areas of social interest and responsibility with respect to procreation and the raising of children. First, there is a social interest in the sheer number of children born. The current emphasis on population control makes this interest abundantly clear.[31] Second, there is a social interest in the potentialities of children. This area includes concern for genetic and congenital birth defects and abnormalities. Over 5 percent of all children born have a genetic defect. The possibility of genetic control of those who are born will soon take on major significance. Already, approximately sixty genetic diseases as well as almost all chromosomal abnormalities can be detected in utero, and adult carriers of about eighty genetic defects can be identified.[32] Given the possibility of genetic control, society can no longer risk having genetically disadvantaged children by leaving the decision of whether to have children to the unregulated judgment of individual couples. Some social regulations with respect to genetic screening and, perhaps, eugenic sterilization are needed. While potential parents have interests of privacy and freedom in reproductive decisions, the social interests in preventing the suffering and inequality of possibly defective children may outweigh them in certain types of cases.

Third, the care and development of those who are born is a social interest and responsibility.

This interest has been recognized for some time in the form of children's homes and compulsory education. However, increasing knowledge about childhood development extends the area in which social interests and responsibility may be reasonably involved. To give an example at the most elementary level, the nutritional diet of children during their first three years is crucial for their future development. So also is their psychological support. The welfare of future generations is not a private but a social matter. It is a proper task of society, acting through its government, to ensure that the members of the next generation are not physical or psychological cripples due to the ignorance, negligence, or even indifference of parents.

Historically, society has attempted to control procreation through the institution of marriage. Society's means were primarily to stigmatize children born out of wedlock and to encourage the having of many children. It is now recognized that no useful purpose is served by stigmatizing children born out of wedlock as illegitimate. (However, some useful purpose may be served by not according children born out of wedlock all the rights of those born in wedlock, for example, inheritance without parental recognition.) The emphasis on having as many children as one can has also disappeared. It is not this historical concern with procreation that is misplaced in modern society but the forms that the concern has taken.

If society has the responsibility to protect the welfare of children, then some social regulation and control of human reproduction and development is justified. Such regulation and control need not be effected by penal laws. For example, social concern has traditionally been expressed in adoptions through regulations to ensure that those who adopt children are fit to care for them. That some regulations have been inappropriate and not reasonably related to the welfare of children is not in question. Rather, the point is that there has been regulation without penal laws, or

160

at lease without resorting primarily to penal laws. Nor can social regulation and control be solely by legislation. Legislation alone is usually ineffective; it must be supported by informal social rules and expectations.

Not only has modern biomedicine made sex possible without procreation; it has also made procreation possible without sex. The techniques of artificial insemination and fertilization, embryo transfer, ova donation, ectogenesis, and cloning now, or soon will, make it possible for people to reproduce without sexual intercourse.[33] Hence, not only may one have sex for pleasure, but one may reproduce for pleasure without sexual intercourse. Not only may people reproduce outside marriage; they are not even biologically required to have intercourse. Thus, sex and marriage may become dissociated from reproduction.

However, there are strong reasons for restricting procreation primarily to marriages of indefinite duration, which does not imply that such marriages should be restricted to procreation. Marriage has traditionally been the central social institution concerned with procreation. Consequently, if society is to exercise some control over procreation in the future, it would involve the least change in conditions to do so through marriage. Moreover, there is considerable evidence that the disruption of family life contributes to juvenile delinquency. Whether divorce or marital breakdown (with or without divorce) is a prime cause of such delinquency does not matter. The point is that the disruption of home life does seriously affect the development of children.[34] The chance of such disruption outside of a marriage that is intentionally of indefinite duration is higher than for that within. Moreover, there is some reason to believe that the presence of both mother and father is instrumental in the psychological development of children. In any case, the presence of two people rather than one provides the security that there will be someone to care for the children should one of the parents

die. Generally, children are better off being
with one parent than in a state orphanage, but
better off still with both parents. Hence, for
the welfare of children it seems best that procreation and child rearing primarily occur within
the context of marriages intentionally of indefinite duration.

While society has a responsibility for the
care and development of children, this general
responsibility is best carried out if specific
adults have obligations to care for specific children. In the past, the biological parent-child
relation has reinforced the allocation of responsibility for specific children and has been a
major factor in monogamy.[35] The separation of
reproduction and sexual intercourse threatens disruption of this assignment. For example, if ges-
tation occurs in an artificial womb in a labora-
tory, there may be no "parents," only a scientific
research group. More realistically, if a woman
has an embryo from ova and sperm donors transferred to her uterus, it is unclear who are the
child's parents. However, if there is to be
optimal care for children, specific adults must
have obligations for specific children. It cannot be left to somebody in general, for then nobody in particular is likely to do it. "Let
George do it" is too prevalent and careless an
attitude to allow with regard to children.

McMurtry's contention that monogamy restricts
the care for children is not well founded.[36]
First, if there are no specific adults responsible
for children, they may become "lost" in large
groups and victims of the "it's not my job" syndrome. Second, monogamy per se does not cut children off from the support and care of others. One
must distinguish the marital relationship from
living arrangements. It is the isolated situation
of the family that deprives children of such support. In many married-student housing complexes
children have access to other adults. Even in
general-residential neighborhoods with separate
family housing units, such support is available if

162

there is a sense of community in the neighborhood.

Given the social interests in and responsibility for the procreation and development of children, some more effective controls of parenthood appear desirable. If the primary locus of reproduction is to be within marriages of intentionally indefinite duration, then the easiest way to institute controls is to add requirements for people to enter such marriages. A few requirements such as blood tests are already generally prevalent. Alternatively, one might have a separate licensing procedure for procreation. Nonmarried couples and single people might also qualify for such licenses. Moreover, couples who want to marry but not have children would not have to meet requirements. However, the only requirements suggested below that might bar marriages are almost as important for those couples who do not have children as for those who do. If the requirements were tied to marriage they would be easier to administer. The only drawback is that unmarried people would not have to meet them. However, such requirements can and should be part of the medical practice of the "artificial" techniques of reproduction—artificial insemination and embryo transfer. And there are few if any effective methods, except generally accepted social rules, to control procreation outside of marriage.

One obvious requirement would be genetic screening. With modern medical techniques genetic problems do not imply that couples cannot become married, but they might be expected not to have children who are their genetic offspring. Artificial insemination and embryo transfer make it possible for almost everyone to have children, even though the children might not be genetically theirs. A general distinction between biological and social parenthood should be made, with legal emphasis on the latter.

More important, perhaps, is some general expectation of psychological fitness for family life and the raising of children. The difficulty with such an expectation is the absence of any clear criteria for fitness and reliable methods for determining who meets them. Perhaps, however, some formal instruction in family relations and child rearing would be appropriate. The Commission on Population Growth and the American Future has already called for an expansion of education for parenthood.[37] It is only a bit further to require some sort of minimal family education for marriage. Probably the easiest method for ensuring such education would be to make it a required subject in secondary schools. If that were done, few people would have difficulty meeting this requirement for marriage.

There should not be any financial or property qualifications for marriage.[38] Society's interest in and responsibility for the welfare of the population in general is such that governments should ensure an adequate standard of living for all persons. Were that to be done there would be no reason to impose any financial restrictions on marriage. Nonetheless, prospective parents should have more concern for their financial situation than is now frequently the case. The adequate care of children is an expensive task, financially as well as psychologically and temporally.

Conclusion

It may be objected that neither the argument from interpersonal relations nor that from the welfare of children specifically supports monogamous marriage. While loving relationships cannot extend to an indefinite number of people, they can extend to more than one other person. Also, a polygamous union may provide a reasonable environment for procreation. Hence, neither of the arguments supports monogamous marriage per se.

Logically, the objection is quite correct. But it is a misunderstanding of social philosophy to expect arguments showing that a certain arrangement is always best under all circumstances. The most that can be shown is that usually, or as a rule, one social arrangement is preferable to another. Practically, polygamous marriage patterns will probably never be prevalent.[39] For centuries they have been gradually disappearing throughout the world. If a disproportionate sex distribution of the population occurs in some areas or age groups (such as the elderly), then they may increase in significance. Unless that occurs, most people will probably continue to prefer marital monogamy.

More important, the burden of this paper has not been to defend the traditional ideal of marital union or even the current practice. Many of the traditional rules of marriage have been unjust, for example, the inequality between the sexes, both legally and in terms of social roles. Instead, it has been to defend social recognition of marriage of intentionally indefinite duration as a unique and socially valuable institution that society has interests in promoting and regulating. In particular, society has interests in and responsibility for promoting a certain form of valuable interpersonal relationship and protecting the welfare of children. Both of these purposes can be well served by monogamous marriage.

The image, then, is of a society with various forms of living together, but one in which marriage of intentionally indefinite duration would have a distinctive though lessened role as a special kind of socially and legally recognized relationship. There would not be laws prohibiting nonmarital forms of cohabitation. Divorce would be based on factual marital breakdown or mutual consent, with due regard for the welfare of children. Monogamous marriage would recognize a special form of personal relationship in which reproduction and child rearing primarily occur. Given the social interest in decreasing procreation, many people might marry but not have children, and others might not marry at all. Details of the legal marital relationship have not been specified, nor could they be in this brief essay

except with respect to the main social interests.
Questions of inheritance, legal residence and
name, social-security benefits, and so on, have
not been specified. Changes in laws with respect
to many of these matters can be made without affecting the arguments for the value of, social
responsibility for, and interest in marriage.
Above all, it is an image in which sexual intercourse plays a much smaller role in the conception of marriage and the good life in general, a
society in which vulgar hedonism has at least
been replaced by a broader-based eudaemonism.

Notes

[1]Epicurus, "Letter to Menoeceus," in The Stoic
and Epicurean Philosophers, ed. Whitney J. Oates
(New York: Modern Library, 1957), p. 31. Epicurus
even wrote, "Sexual intercourse has never done a
man good, and he is lucky if it has not harmed
him" (Fragment 8 in The Stoic and Epicurean Philosophers). John Stuart Mill, Utilitarianism,
chap. 2, especially paragraphs 1-9.

[2]De Anima 2. 4.

[3]"Monogamy: A Critique," The Monist 56 (1972);
reprinted herein, pp. 132-47. This quote appears
on page 137 of this volume (italics added). Subsequent references to McMurtry's essay are to
pages in this volume.

[4]Ibid., p. 138.

[5]Ibid.

[6]Ibid.

[7]Ibid., p. 139.

[8]Ibid., p. 141.

[9]Ibid., p. 142.

[10]Ibid.

[11]Ibid., p. 143.

[12]Ibid.

[13]Ibid.

[14]Karl Marx and Friedrich Engels, "Manifesto of
the Communist Party," Basic Writings on Politics
and Philosophy, ed. Lewis S. Feuer (Garden City,
N. Y.: Doubleday, Anchor Books, 1959), especially
p. 24.

[15]Paul R. Ehrlich, The Population Bomb (New York: Ballantine Books, 1968).

[16]Even new Marxists perceive other sources of problems. See Milovan Djilas, The New Class (New York: Praegaer, 1964); and, more generally, Richard T. DeGeorge, The New Marxism (New York: Pegasus, 1968), chap. 2. The importance of population for pollution, with which it is most frequently connected, has been contested by Barry Commoner, The Closing Circle (New York: Knopf, 1971), pp. 133-35. Ehrlich now clearly recognizes that various causal factors are important, although he still disagrees with Commoner on the importance of population growth; see Paul R. Ehrlich et al., Human Ecology (San Francisco: W. H. Freeman and Company, 1973), chap. 7, esp. pp. 206, 213-15, 221.

[17]Max Rheinstein, Marriage Stability, Divorce, and the Law (Chicago: University of Chicago Press, 1972), p. 251.

[18]Edwin D. Driver, "Population Policies of State Governments in the United States: Some Preliminary Observations," Villanova Law Review 15 (1970): 846-47.

[19]Immanuel Kant, The Philosophy of Law, trans. W. Hastie (Edinburgh: T. & T. Clark, 1887), p. 110.

[20]McMurtry, "Monogamy," p. 139; italics in original omitted.

[21]See John T. Noonan, Jr., Contraception (Cambridge, Mass.: Harvard University Press, 1966), pp. 312-14.

[22]Keith G. McWalter, "Marriage as Contract: Towards a Functional Redefinition of the Marital Status," Columbia Journal of Law and Social Problems 9 (1973): 615.

[23]Robert S. Summers, "The Technique Element of Law," California Law Review 59 (1971): 736-37, 741-45.

[24]Burton M. Leiser, Liberty, Justice and Morals (New York: Macmillan Co., 1973), p. 126; R[oland] Pressat, Population, trans. Robert and Danielle Atkinson (Baltimore: Penguin Books, 1970), pp. 84, 86; U. S. Commission on Population Growth and the American Future, Population and

the American Future (New York: Signet, New American Library, 1972), pp. 102-03.

[25]Aristotle, Nicomachean Ethics 9. 9-12; George Edward Moore, Principia Ethica (Cambridge: At the University Press, 1903), pp. 188, 203-05.

[26]It is thus misleading for McMurtry to write of monogamous marriage excluding "almost countless other possibilities of intimate union" with any number of persons (p. 134; my italics). On the limited nature of personal love or friendship see also Aristotle, Nicomachean Ethics 9. 10.

[27]For a discussion of these relationships and the need for privacy, see Charles Fried, "Privacy," in Law, Reason, and Justice, ed Graham Hughes (New York: New York University Press, 1969), pp. 45-69.

[28]See the discussion (in another context) of such a case in Nazi Germany by H. L. A. Hart, "Positivism and the Separation of Law and Morals," Harvard Law Review 71 (1958): 618-20; and Lon L. Fuller, "Positivism and Fidelity to Law—A Reply to Professor Hart," Harvard Law Review 71 (1958): 652-55.

[29]Nicomachean Ethics 8. 3. The vulgar hedonists treat marriage as a form of friendship for pleasure, but that is not the highest form of friendship.

[30]Pressat, Population, p. 52.

[31]For a more complete discussion see my "Limits to a Right to Procreate," in Ethics and Population, ed. Michael D. Bayles (Cambridge, Mass.: Schenkman Publishing Company, 1975).

[32]Daniel Callahan, The Tyranny of Survival (New York: Macmillan Co., 1973), p. 219.

[33]For a good general survey of these techniques and some suggestions for social controls, see George A. Hudock, "Gene Therapy and Genetic Engineering: Frankenstein Is Still a Myth, But It Should Be Reread Periodically," Indiana Law Journal 48 (1973): 533-58. Various ethical issues are discussed in Joseph Fletcher, The Ethics of Genetic Control (Garden City, N. Y.: Doubleday, Anchor Books, 1974). Successful human embryo implantation and growth to term after in vitro fertilization has been reported in Britain (see Time, July 29, 1974, pp. 58-59; and Newsweek, July

29, 1974, p. 70).

[34]President's Commission on Law Enforcement and Administration of Justice, The Challenge of Crime in a Free Society (New York: Avon Books, 1968), pp. 184-89.

[35]Daniel Callahan, "New Beginnings in Life: A Philosopher's Response," in The New Genetics and the Future of Man, ed. Michael P. Hamilton (Grand Rapids, Mich.: William B. Eerdmans Publishing Company, 1972), pp. 102-03.

[36]"Monogamy," p. 136.

[37]Population and the American Future, pp. 126-33, esp. 133.

[38]For some suggested financial requirements as well as others, see Jack Parsons, Population versus Liberty (Buffalo, N. Y.: Prometheus Books, 1971), p. 349.

[39]Even McMurtry appears to recognize this fact; see "Monogamy," p. 133.

Sex and Sexual Relations

Case

As they walked across the crowded restaurant eyes turned toward them, both strikingly attractive.

Loretta both enjoyed and was irritated by the attention; Howard's reaction was unabashed pride in his wife's good looks and their prosperous life-style.

After they were seated they began to peruse the menus before them. Loretta saw before her a long list of French words. She wondered why she could not muster a festive feeling for this tenth anniversary celebration. She was tired of trying to be the ideal mate, and for what? The French words before her made her think of the l'amour her husband would expect later. He said he loved her, but she didn't feel loved. Howard looked over his menu and was disturbed by the restlessness and dissatisfaction he saw on his wife's face. "What more could she want?" he thought. "She has a beautiful home, designer clothes, a good sex life." "What does she want anyway," he thought.

Sexual Perversion*
Thomas Nagel

There is something to be learned about sex
from the fact that we possess a concept of sexual
perversion. I wish to examine the concept, defending it against the charge of unintelligibility and
trying to say exactly what about human sexuality
qualifies it to admit of perversions. Let me make
some preliminary comments about the problem before
embarking on its solution.

Some people do not believe that the notion of
sexual perversion makes sense, and even those who
do disagree over its application. Nevertheless I
think it will be widely conceded that, if the concept is viable at all, it must meet certain general
conditions. First, if there are any sexual perversions, they will have to be sexual desires or practices that can be plausibly described as in some
sense unnatural, though the explanation of this
natural/unnatural distinction is of course the main
problem. Second, certain practices will be perversions if anything is, such as shoe fetishism, bestiality, and sadism; other practices, such as unadorned sexual intercourse, will not be; about
still others there is controversy. Third, if there
are perversions, they will be unnatural sexual
inclinations rather than merely unnatural practices
adopted not from inclination but for other reasons.
I realize that this is at variance with the view,
maintained by some Roman Catholics, that contraception is a sexual perversion. But although contraception may qualify as a deliberate perversion
of the sexual and reproductive functions, it cannot
be significantly described as a sexual perversion.
A sexual perversion must reveal itself in conduct
that expresses an unnatural sexual preference. And

*From Journal of Philosophy, vol. 66, no. 1
(January, 1969), pp. 5-17. Reprinted by permission
of the author and editor.

171

although there might be a form of fetishism focused on the employment of contraceptive devices, that is not the usual explanation for their use.

I wish to declare at the outset my belief that the connection between sex and reproduction has no bearing on sexual perversion. The latter is a concept of psychological, not physiological interest, and it is a concept that we do not apply to the lower animals, let alone to plants, all of which have reproductive functions that can go astray in various ways. (Think of seedless oranges.) Insofar as we are prepared to regard higher animals as perverted, it is because of their psychological, not their anatomical similarity to humans. Furthermore, we do not regard as a perversion every deviation from the reproductive function of sex in humans: sterility, miscarriage, contraception, abortion.

Another matter that I believe has no bearing on the concept of sexual perversion is social disapprobation or custom. Anyone inclined to think that in each society the perversions are those sexual practices of which the community disapproves, should consider all the societies that have frowned upon adultery and fornication. These have not been regarded as unnatural practices, but have been thought objectionable in other ways. What is regarded as unnatural admittedly varies from culture to culture, but the classification is not a pure expression of disapproval or distaste. In fact it is often regarded as a **ground** for disapproval, and that suggests that the classification has an independent content.

I am going to attempt a psychological account of sexual perversion, which will depend on a specific psychological theory of sexual desire and human sexual interactions. To approach this solution I wish first to consider a contrary position, one which provides a basis for skepticism about the existence of any sexual perversions at all, and perhaps about the very significance of the term. The skeptical argument runs as follows:

"Sexual desire is simply one of the appetites, like hunger and thirst. As such it may have various objects, some more common than others perhaps, but none in any sense 'natural.' An appetite is identified as sexual by means of the organs and erogenous zones in which its satisfaction can be to some extent localized, and the special sensory pleasures which form the core of that satisfaction. This enables us to recognize widely divergent goals, activities, and desires as sexual, since it is conceivable in principle that anything should produce sexual pleasure and that a nondeliberate, sexually charged desire for it should arise (as a result of conditioning, if nothing else). We may fail to empathize with some of these desires, and some of them, like sadism, may be objectionable on extraneous grounds, but once we have observed that they meet the criteria for being sexual, there is nothing more to be said on <u>that</u> score. Either they are sexual or they are not: sexuality does not admit of imperfection, or perversion, or any other such qualification—it is not that sort of affection."

This is probably the received radical position. It suggests that the cost of defending a psychological account may be to deny that sexual desire is an appetite. But insofar as that line of defense is plausible, it should make us suspicious of the simple picture of appetites on which the skepticism depends. Perhaps the standard appetites, like hunger, cannot be classed as pure appetites in that sense either, at least in their human versions.

Let us approach the matter by asking whether we can imagine anything that would qualify as a gastronomical perversion. Hunger and eating are importantly like sex in that they serve a biological function and also play a significant role in our inner lives. It is noteworthy that there is little temptation to describe as perverted an appetite for substances that are not nourishing. We should probably not consider someone's appetites as <u>perverted</u> if he liked to eat paper, sand, wood, or cotton. Those are merely rather odd and very unhealthy tastes: they lack the psychological

173

complexity that we expect of perversion. (Coprophilia, being already a sexual perversion, may be disregarded.) If on the other hand someone liked to eat cookbooks, or magazines with pictures of food in them, and preferred these to ordinary food—or if when hungry he sought satisfaction by fondling a napkin or ashtray from his favorite restaurant—then the concept of perversion might seem appropriate (in fact it would be natural to describe this as a case of gastronomical fetishism). It would be natural to describe as gastronomically perverted someone who could eat only by having food forced down his throat through a funnel, or only if the meal were a living animal. What helps in such cases is the peculiarity of the desire itself, rather than the inappropriateness of its object to the biological function that the desire serves. Even an appetite, it would seem, can have perversions if in addition to its biological function it has a significant psychological structure.

In the case of hunger, psychological complexity is provided by the activities that give it expression. Hunger is not merely a disturbing sensation that can be quelled by eating; it is an attitude toward edible portions of the external world, a desire to relate to them in rather special ways. The method of ingestion: chewing, savoring, swallowing, appreciating the texture and smell, all are important components of the relation, as is the passivity and controllability of the food (the only animals we eat live are helpless mollusks). Our relation to food depends also on our size: we do not live upon it or burrow into it like aphids or worms. Some of these features are more central than others, but any adequate phenomenology of eating would have to treat it as a relation to the external world and a way of appropriating bits of that world, with characteristic affection. Displacements or serious restrictions of the desire to eat could then be described as perversions, if they undermined that direct relation between man and food which is the natural expressions of hunger. This explains why it is easy to imagine gastronomical fetishism, voyeurism, exhibitionism, or

174

even gastronomical sadism and masochism. Indeed some of these perversions are fairly common.

If we can imagine perversions of an appetite like hunger, it should be possible to make sense of the concept of sexual perversion. I do not wish to imply that sexual desire is an appetite—only that being an appetite is no bar to admitting of perversions. Like hunger, sexual desire has as its characteristic object a certain relation with something in the external world; only in this case it is usually a person rather than an omelet, and the relation is considerably more complicated. This added complication allows scope for correspondingly complicated perversions.

The fact that sexual desire is a feeling about other persons may tempt us to take a pious view of psychological content. There are those who believe that sexual desire is properly the expression of some other attitude, like love, and that when it occurs by itself it is incomplete and unhealthy— or at any rate subhuman. (The extreme Platonic version of such a view is that sexual practices are all vain attempts to express something they cannot in principle achieve: this makes them all perversions, in a sense.) I do not believe that any such view is correct. Sexual desire is complicated enough without having to be linked to anything else as a condition for phenomenological analysis. It cannot be denied that sex may serve various functions—economic, social, altruistic—but it also has its own content as a relation between persons, and it is only by analyzing that relation that we can understand the conditions of sexual perversion.

I believe it is very important that the object of sexual attraction is a particular individual, who transcends the properties that make him attractive. When different persons are attracted to a single person for different reasons: eyes, hair, figure, laugh, intelligence—we feel that the object of their desire is nevertheless the same, namely that person. There is even an inclination to feel that this is so if the lovers have different sexual aims, if they include both men and women, for example. Different specific attractive characteristics seem to provide enabling conditions for the operation of a single basic feeling, and the different aims all provide expressions of it. We approach the sexual attitude toward the person through the features that we find attractive, but these features are not the objects of that attitude.

This is very different from the case of an omelet. Various people may desire it for different reasons, one for its fluffiness, another for its mushrooms, another for its unique combination of aroma and visual aspect; yet we do not enshrine the transcendental omelet as the true common object of their affections. Instead we might say that several desires have accidentally converged on the same object: any omelet with the crucial characteristics would do as well. It is not similarly true that any person with the same flesh distribution and way of smoking can be substituted as object for a particular sexual desire that has been elicited by those characteristics. It may be that they will arouse attraction whenever they recur, but it will be a new sexual attraction with a new particular object, not merely a transfer of the old desire to someone else. (I believe this is true even in cases where the new object is unconsciously identified with a former one.)

The importance of this point will emerge when we see how complex a psychological interchange constitutes the natural development of sexual attraction. This would be incomprehensible if its object were not a particular person, but rather a person of a certain kind. Attraction is only the beginning, and fulfillment does not consist merely of behavior and contact expressing this attraction, but involves much more.

The best discussion of these matters that I have seen appears in part III of Sartre's Being and Nothingness.[1] Since it has influenced my own

176

views, I shall say a few things about it now.
Sartre's treatment of sexual desire and of love,
hate, sadism, masochism, and further attitudes
toward others, depends on a general theory of consciousness and the body which we can neither expound nor assume here. He does not discuss perversion, and this is partly because he regards
sexual desire as one form of the perpetual attempt of an embodied consciousness to come to
terms with the existence of others, an attempt
that is as doomed to fail in this form as it is in
any of the others which include sadism and masochism (if not certain of the more impersonal deviations) as well as several nonsexual attitudes.
According to Sartre, all attempts to incorporate
the other into my world as another subject, i.e.,
to apprehend him at once as an object for me and
as a subject for whom I am an object, are unstable
and doomed to collapse into one or other of the
two aspects. Either I reduce him entirely to an
object, in which case his subjectivity escapes the
possession or appropriation I can extend to that
object; or I become merely an object for him, in
which case I am no longer in a position to appropriate his subjectivity. Moreover, neither of
these aspects is stable; each is continually in
danger of giving way to the other. This has the
consequence that there can be no such thing as a
successful sexual relation, since the deep aim of
sexual desire cannot in principle be accomplished.
It seems likely, therefore, that the view will not
permit a basic distinction between successful or
complete and unsuccessful or incomplete sex, and
therefore cannot admit the concept of perversion.

I do not adopt this aspect of the theory, nor
many of its metaphysical underpinnings. What interests me is Sartre's picture of the attempt. He
says that the type of possession that is the object of sexual desire is carried out by "a double
reciprocal incarnation" and that this is accomplished, typically in the form of a caress, in the
following way: "I make myself flesh in order to
impel the Other to realize for herself and for me
her own flesh, and my caresses cause my flesh to

177

be born for me in so far as it is for the Other _flesh causing her to be born as flesh_" (391; italics Sartre's). The incarnation in question is described variously as a clogging or troubling of consciousness, which is inundated by the flesh in which it is embodied.

The view I am going to suggest, I hope in less obscure language, is related to this one, but it differs from Sartre's in allowing sexuality to achieve its goal on occasion and thus in providing the concept of perversion with a foothold.

Sexual desire involves a kind of perception, but not merely a single perception of its object, for in the paradigm case of mutual desire there is a complex system of superimposed mutual perceptions—not only perceptions of the sexual object, but perceptions of oneself. Moreover, sexual awareness of another involves considerable self-awareness to begin with—more than is involved in ordinary sensory perception. The experience is felt as an assault on oneself by the view (or touch, or whatever) of the sexual object.

Let us consider a case in which the elements can be separated. For clarity we will restrict ourselves initially to the somewhat artificial case of desire at a distance. Suppose a man and a woman, whom we may call Romeo and Juliet, are at opposite ends of a cocktail lounge, with many mirrors on the walls which permit unobserved observation, and even mutual unobserved observation. Each of them is sipping a martini and studying other people in the mirrors. At some point Romeo notices Juliet. He is moved, somehow, by the softness of her hair and the diffidence with which she sips her martini, and this arouses him sexually. Let us say that X _senses_ Y whenever X regards Y with sexual desire. (Y need not be a person, and X's apprehension of Y can be visual, tactile, olfactory, etc., or purely imaginary; in the present example we shall concentrate on vision.) So Romeo senses Juliet, rather than merely noticing her. At this stage he is aroused by an unaroused object, so he is more in the sexual grip of his body than she of hers.

Let us suppose, however, that Juliet now senses Romeo in another mirror on the opposite wall, though neither of them yet knows that he is seen by the other (the mirror angles provide three-quarter views). Romeo then begins to notice in Juliet the subtle signs of sexual arousal: heavy-lidded stare, dilating pupils, faint flush, et cetera. This of course renders her much more bodily, and he not only notices but senses this as well. His arousal is nevertheless still solitary. But now, cleverly calculating the line of her stare without actually looking her in the eyes, he realizes that it is directed at him through the mirror on the opposite wall. That is, he notices, and moreover senses, Juliet sensing him. This is definitely a new development, for it gives him a sense of embodiment not only through his own reactions but through the eyes and reactions of another. Moreover, it is separable from the initial sensing of Juliet; for sexual arousal might begin with a person's sensing that he is sensed and being assailed by the perception of the other person's desire rather than merely by the perception of the person.

But there is a further step. Let us suppose that Juliet, who is a little slower than Romeo, now senses that he senses her. This puts Romeo in a position to notice, and be aroused by, her arousal at being sensed by him. He senses that she senses that he senses her. This is still another level of arousal, for he becomes conscious of his sexuality through his awareness of its effect on her and of her awareness that this effect is due to him. Once she takes the same step and senses that he senses her sensing him, it becomes difficult to state, let alone imagine, further iterations, though they may be logically distinct. If both are alone, they will presumably turn to look at each other directly, and the proceedings will continue on another plane. Physical contact and intercourse are perfectly natural extensions of

179

this complicated visual exchange, and mutual touch can involve all the complexities of awareness present in the visual case, but with a far greater range of subtlety and acuteness.

Ordinarily, of course, things happen in a less orderly fashion—sometimes in a great rush—but I believe that some version of this overlapping system of distinct sexual perceptions and interactions is the basic framework of any full-fledged sexual relation and that relations involving only part of the complex are significantly incomplete. The account is only schematic, as it must be to achieve generality. Every real sexual act will be psychologically far more specific and detailed, in ways that depend not only on the physical techniques employed and on anatomical details, but also on countless features of the participants' conceptions of themselves and of each other, which become embodied in the act. (It is a familiar enough fact, for example, that people often take their social roles and the social roles of their partners to bed with them.)

The general schema is important, however, and the proliferation of levels of mutual awareness it involves is an example of a type of complexity that typifies human interactions. Consider aggression, for example. If I am angry with someone, I want to make him feel it, either to produce self-reproach by getting him to see himself through the eyes of my anger, and to dislike what he sees—or else to produce reciprocal anger or fear, by getting him to perceive my anger as a threat or attack. What I want will depend on the details of my anger, but in either case it will involve a desire that the object of that anger be aroused. This accomplishment constitutes the fulfillment of my emotion, through domination of the object's feelings.

Another example of such reflexive mutual recognition is to be found in the phenomenon of meaning, which appears to involve an intention to produce a belief or other effect in another by bringing about his recognition of one's intention to produce that effect. (That result is due to H. P. Grice,[2] whose position I shall not attempt to reproduce in detail.) Sex has a related structure: it involves a desire that one's partner be aroused by the recognition of one's desire that he or she be aroused.

It is not easy to define the basic types of awareness and arousal of which these complexes are composed, and that remains a lacuna in this discussion. I believe that the object of awareness is the same in one's own case as it is in one's sexual awareness of another, although the two awarenesses will not be the same, the difference being as great as that between feeling angry and experiencing the anger of another. All stages of sexual perception are varieties of identification of a person with his body. What is perceived is one's own or another's <u>subjection</u> to or <u>immersion</u> in his body, a phenomenon which has been recognized with loathing by St. Paul and St. Augustine, both of whom regarded "the law of sin which is in my members" as a grave threat to the dominion of the holy will.[3] In sexual desire and its expression the blending of involuntary response with deliberate control is extremely important. For Augustine, the revolution launched against him by his body is symbolized by erection and the other involuntary physical components of arousal. Sartre too stresses the fact that the penis is not a prehensile organ. But mere involuntariness characterizes other bodily processes as well. In sexual desire the involuntary responses are combined with submission to spontaneous impulses: not only one's pulse and secretions but one's actions are taken over by the body; ideally, deliberate control is needed only to guide the expression of those impulses. This is to some extent also true of an appetite like hunger, but the takeover there is more localized, less pervasive, less extreme. One's whole body does not become saturated with hunger as it can with desire. But the most characteristic feature of a specifically sexual immersion in the body is its

ability to fit into the complex of mutual perceptions that we have described. Hunger leads to
spontaneous interactions with food; sexual desire
leads to spontaneous interactions with other persons, whose bodies are asserting their sovereignty
in the same way, producing involuntary reactions
and spontaneous impulses in them. These reactions
are perceived, and the perception of them is perceived, and that perception is in turn perceived;
at each step the domination of the person by his
body is reinforced, and the sexual partner becomes more possessible by physical contact, penetration, and envelopment.

Desire is therefore not merely the perception
of a preexisting embodiment of the other, but ideally a contribution to his further embodiment
which in turn enhances the original subject's
sense of himself. This explains why it is important that the partner be aroused, and not merely
aroused, but aroused by the awareness of one's
desire. It also explains the sense in which desire has unity and possession as its object:
physical possession must eventuate in creation of
the sexual object in the image of one's desire,
and not merely in the object's recognition of that
desire, or in his or her own private arousal.
(This may reveal a male bias: I shall say something about that later.)

To return, finally, to the topic of perversion: I believe that various familiar deviations
constitute truncated or incomplete versions of the
complete configuration, and may therefore be regarded as perversions of the central impulse.

In particular, narcissistic practices and
intercourse with animals, infants, and inanimate
objects seem to be stuck at some primitive version of the first stage. If the object is not
alive, the experience is reduced entirely to an
awareness of one's own sexual embodiment. Small
children and animals permit awareness of the embodiment of the other, but present obstacles to
reciprocity, to the recognition by the sexual

object of the subject's desire as the source of his (the object's) sexual self-awareness.

Sadism concentrates on the evocation of passive self-awareness in others, but the sadist's engagement is itself active and requires a retention of deliberate control which impedes awareness of himself as a bodily subject of passion in the required sense. The victim must recognize him as the source of his own sexual passivity, but only as the active source. De Sade claimed that the object of sexual desire was to evoke involuntary responses from one's partner, especially audible ones. The infliction of pain is no doubt the most efficient way to accomplish this, but it requires a certain abrogation of one's own exposed spontaneity. All this, incidentally, helps to explain why it is tempting to regard as sadistic an excessive preoccupation with sexual technique, which does not permit one to abandon the role of agent at any stage of the sexual act. Ideally one should be able to surmount one's technique at some point.

A masochist on the other hand imposes the same disability on his partner as the sadist imposes on himself. The masochist cannot find a satisfactory embodiment as the object of another's sexual desire, but only as the object of his control. He is passive not in relation to his partner's passion but in relation to his nonpassive agency. In addition, the subjection to one's body characteristic of pain and physical restraint is of a very different kind from that of sexual excitement: pain causes people to contract rather than dissolve.

Both of these disorders have to do with the second stage, which involves the awareness of oneself as an object of desire. In straightforward sadism and masochism other attentions are substituted for desire as a source of the object's self-awareness. But it is also possible for nothing of that sort to be substituted, as in the case of a masochist who is satisfied with self-inflicted pain or of a sadist who does not insist on playing a role in the suffering that arouses him. Greater difficulties of classification are presented by three other categories of sexual activity: elaborations of the sexual act; intercourse of more than two persons; and homosexuality.

If we apply our model to the various forms that may be taken by two-party heterosexual intercourse, none of them seem clearly to qualify as perversions. Hardly anyone can be found these days to inveigh against oral-genital contact, and the merits of buggery are urged by such respectable figures as D. H. Lawrence and Norman Mailer. There may be something vaguely sadistic about the latter technique (in Mailer's writings it seems to be a method of introducing an element of rape), but it [is] not obvious that this has to be so. In general, it would appear that any bodily contact between a man and a woman that gives them sexual pleasure, is a possible vehicle for the system of multi-level interpersonal awareness that I have claimed is the basic psychological content of sexual interaction. Thus a liberal platitude about sex is upheld.

About multiple combinations, the least that can be said is that they are bound to be complicated. If one considers how difficult it is to carry on two conversations simultaneously, one may appreciate the problems of multiple simultaneous interpersonal perception that can arise in even a small-scale orgy. It may be inevitable that some of the component relations should degenerate into mutual epidermal stimulation by participants otherwise isolated from each other. There may also be a tendency toward voyeurism and exhibitionism, both of which are incomplete relations. The exhibitionist wishes to display his desire without needing to be desired in return; he may even fear the sexual attentions of others. A voyeur, on the other hand, need not require any recognition by his object at all: certainly not a recognition of the voyeur's arousal.

It is not clear whether homosexuality is a
perversion if that is measured by the standard of
the described configuration, but it seems unlikely.
For such a classification would have to depend on
the possibility of extracting from the system a
distinction between male and female sexuality; and
much that has been said so far applies equally to
men and women. Moreover, it would have to be
maintained that there was a natural tie between
the type of sexuality and the sex of the body, and
also that two sexualities of the same type could
not interact properly.

Certainly there is much support for an ag-
gressive-passive distinction between male and female sexuality. In our culture the male's arousal
tends to initiate the perceptual exchange, he usually makes the sexual approach, largely controls
the course of the act, and of course penetrates
whereas the woman receives. When two men or two
women engage in intercourse they cannot both adhere to these sexual roles. The question is how
essential the roles are to an adequate sexual relation. One relevant observation is that a good
deal of deviation from these roles occurs in heterosexual intercourse. Women can be sexually aggressive and men passive, and temporary reversals
of role are not uncommon in heterosexual exchanges
of reasonable length. If such conditions are set
aside, it may be urged that there is something
irreducibly perverted in attraction to a body
anatomically like one's own. But alarming as some
people in our culture may find such attraction, it
remains psychologically unilluminating to class it
as perverted. Certainly if homosexuality is a
perversion, it is so in a very different sense
from that in which shoe fetishism is a perversion,
for some version of the full range of interpersonal perceptions seems perfectly possible between two persons of the same sex.

In any case, even if the proposed model is
correct, it remains implausible to describe as
perverted every deviation from it. For example,
if the partners in heterosexual intercourse

indulge in private heterosexual fantasies, that obscures the recognition of the real partner and so, on the theory, constitutes a defective sexual relation. It is not, however, generally regarded as a perversion. Such examples suggest that a simple dichotomy between perverted and unperverted sex is too crude to organize the phenomena adequately.

I should like to close with some remarks about the relation of perversion to good, bad, and morality. The concept of perversion can hardly fail to be evaluative in some sense, for it appears to involve the notion of an ideal or at least adequate sexuality which the perversions in some way fail to achieve. So, if the concept is viable, the judgment that a person or practice or desire is perverted will constitute a sexual evaluation, implying that better sex, or a better specimen of sex, is possible. This in itself is a very weak claim, since the evaluation might be in a dimension that is of little interest to us. (Though, if my account is correct, that will not be true.)

Whether it is a moral evaluation, however, is another question entirely—one whose answer would require more understanding of both morality and perversion than can be deployed here. Moral evaluation of acts and of persons is a rather special and very complicated matter, and by no means all our evaluations of persons and their activities are moral evaluations. We make judgments about people's beauty or health or intelligence which are evaluative without being moral. Assessments of their sexuality may be similar in that respect.

Futhermore, moral issues aside, it is not clear that unperverted sex is necessarily <u>preferable</u> to the perversions. It may be that sex which receives the highest marks for perfection <u>as sex</u> is less enjoyable than certain perversions; and if enjoyment is considered very important, that might outweigh considerations of sexual perfection in determining rational preference.

186

That raises the question of the relation between the evaluative content of judgments of perversion and the rather common general distinction between good and bad sex. The latter distinction is usually confined to sexual acts, and it would seem, within limits, to cut across the other: even someone who believed, for example, that homosexuality was a perversion could admit a distinction between better and worse homosexual sex, and might even allow that good homosexual sex could be better sex than not very good unperverted sex. If this is correct, it supports the position that, if judgments of perversion are viable at all, they represent only one aspect of the possible evaluation of sex, even qua sex. Moreover it is not the only important aspect: certainly sexual deficiencies that evidently do not constitute perversions can be the object of great concern.

Finally, even if perverted sex is to that extent not so good as it might be, bad sex is generally better than none at all. This should not be controversial: it seems to hold for other important matters, like food, music, literature, and society. In the end, one must choose from among the available alternatives, whether their availability depends on the environment or on one's own constitution. And the alternatives have to be fairly grim before it becomes rational to opt for nothing.

Notes

[1] Translated by Hazel E. Barnes (New York: Philosophical Library: 1956).
[2] "Meaning," Philosophical Review, LXVI, 3 (July 1957): 377-388.
[3] See Romans, VII, 23: and the Confessions, Book 8, V.

Sexual Paradigms[*]
Robert C. Solomon

It is a cocktail lounge, well-lit and mirror-
ed, not a bar, martinis and not beer, two strangers—a furtive glance from him, shy recognition
from her. It is 1950's American high comedy: boy
arouses girl, both are led through ninety minutes
of misunderstandings of identity and intention,
and, finally, by the end of the popcorn, boy kisses
girl with a clean-cut fade-out or panned clip of a
postcard horizon. It is one of the dangers of conceptual analysis that the philosopher's choice of
paradigms betrays a personal bias, but it is an
exceptional danger of sexual conceptual analysis
that one's choice of paradigms also betrays one's
private fantasies and personal obsessions.[1] No
doubt that is why, despite their extraprofessional
interest in the subject, most philosophers would
rather write about indirect discourse than intercourse, the philosophy of mind rather than the
philosophy of body.

In Tom Nagel's pioneering effort[2] there are
too many recognizable symptoms of liberal American
sexual mythology. His analysis is cautious and
competent, but absolutely sexless. His Romeo and
Juliet exemplify at most a romanticized version of
the initial phases of (hetero-)sexual attraction
in a casual and innocent pick-up. They "arouse"
each other, but there is no indication to what
end. They "incarnate each other as flesh," in
Sartre's awkward but precise terminology, but Nagel
gives us no clue as to why they should indulge in
such a peculiar activity. Presumably a pair of
dermatologists or fashion models might have a similar effect on each other, but without the slightest hint of sexual intention. What makes this

[*]From Journal of Philosophy, vol. 71, no. 11
(June 13, 1974), pp. 336-345. Reprinted by permission of the author and editor.

situation paradigmatically sexual? We may assume, as we would in a Doris Day comedy, that the object of this protracted arousal is sexual intercourse, but we are not told this. Sexuality without content. Liberal sexual mythology takes this Hollywood element of "leave it to the imagination" as its starting point and adds the equally inexplicit suggestion that whatever activities two consenting adults choose as the object of their arousal and its gratification is "their business." In a society with such secrets, pornography is bound to serve a radical end as a vulgar valve of reality. In a philosophical analysis that stops short of the very matter investigated, a bit of perverseness may be necessary just in order to refocus the question.

Sexual desire is distinguished, like all desires, by its aims and objects. What are these peculiarly sexual aims and objects? Notice that Nagel employs a fairly standard "paradigm case argument" in his analysis; he begins,

. . . certain practices will be perversions if anything is, such as shoe fetishism, bestiality and sadism; other practices, such as unadorned sexual intercourse will not be (5).

So we can assume that the end of Romeo and Juliet's tryst will be intercourse—we do not know whether "adorned" or not. But what is it that makes intercourse the paradigm of sexual activity—its biological role in conception, its heterosexuality, its convenience for mutual orgasm? Would Nagel's drama still serve as a sexual paradigm if Juliet turns out to be a virgin, or if Romeo and Juliet find that they are complementarily sado-masochistic, if Romeo is in drag, if they are both knee-fetishists? Why does Nagel choose two <u>strangers</u>? Why not, as in the days of sexual moralism, a happily married couple enjoying their seventh anniversary? Or is not the essence of sex, as Sartre so brutally argues, Romeo and Juliet's mutual attempts to possess each other, with each's own enjoyment only a secondary and essentially distracting effect? Are we expected to presume the most prominent paradigm, at least since Freud, the lusty ejaculation of Romeo into the submissive, if not passive, Juliet? Suppose Juliet is in fact a prostitute, skillfully mocking the signs of innocent arousal: is this a breach of the paradigm, or might not such subsequent "unadorned" intercourse be just the model that Nagel claims to defend?

To what end does Romeo arouse Juliet? And to what end does Juliet become affected and in turn excite Romeo? In this exemplary instance, I would think that "unadorned" intercourse would be perverse, or at least distasteful, in the extreme. It would be different, however, if the paradigm were our seven-year married couple, for in such cases "adorned" intercourse might well be something of a rarity. In homosexual encounters, in the frenzy of adolescent virginal petting, in cases in which intercourse is restricted for temporary medical or political reasons, arousal may be no different, even though intercourse cannot be the end. And it is only in the crudest cases of physiological need that the desire for intercourse is the sole or even the leading component in the convoluted motivation of sexuality. A nineteen-year-old sailor back after having discussed nothing but sex on a three-month cruise may be so aroused, but that surely is not the nature of Juliet's arousal. Romeo may remind her of her father, or of her favorite philosophy professor, and he may inspire respect, or fear, or curiosity. He may simply arouse self-consciousness or embarrassment. Any of these attitudes may be dominant, but none is particularly sexual.

Sexuality has an essential bodily dimension, and this might well be described as the "incarnation" or "submersion" of a person into his body. The end of this desire is interpersonal communication; but where Sartre gives a complex theory of the nature of this communication, Nagel gives us only an empty notion of "multi-level interpersonal awareness." Presumably the mutual arousal that is

the means to this awareness is enjoyable in itself.
But it is important that Nagel resists the current
(W.) Reichian-American fetish for the wonders of
the genital orgasm, for he does not leap to the
facile conclusion that the aim of sexual activity
is mutual or at least personal orgasm. It is here
that Nagel opens a breach with liberal sexual mythology, one that might at first appear absurd
because of his total neglect of the role of the
genitalia and orgasm in sexuality. But we have an
overgenitalized conception of sexuality, and, if
sexual satisfaction involves and even requires
orgasm, it does not follow that orgasm is the goal
of the convoluted sexual games we play with each
other. Orgasm is the "end" of sexual activity,
perhaps, but only in the sense that swallowing is
the "end" of tasting a Viennese torte.

There was a time, and it was not long ago
and may come soon again, when sexuality required
defending. It had to be argued that we had a
right to sex, not for any purpose other than our
personal enjoyment. But that defense has turned
stale, and sexual deprivation is no longer our
problem. The "swollen bladder" model of repressed
sexuality may have been convincing in sex-scared
bourgeois Vienna of 1905, but not today, where
the problem is not sexual deprivation but sexual
dissatisfaction. The fetishism of the orgasm,
now shared by women as well as men, threatens our
sex lives with becoming antipersonal and mechanical, anxiety-filled athletic arenas with mutual
multiple orgasm its goal. Behind much of this un-
happiness and anxiety, ironically, stands the liberal defense of sexuality as enjoyment. It is one
of the virtues of Nagel's essay that he begins to
overcome this oppressive liberal mythology. But
at the same time he relies upon it for his support
and becomes trapped in it, and the result is an
account which displays the emptiness we have
pointed out and the final note of despair with
which he ends his essay.

Liberal sexual mythology appears to stand
upon a tripod of mutually supporting platitudes:

(1) and foremost, that the essential aim (and even the sole aim) of sex is enjoyment; (2) that sexual activity is and ought to be essentially private activity, and (3) that any sexual activity is as valid as any other. The first platitude was once a radical proposition, a reaction to the conservative and pious belief that sexual activity was activity whose end was reproduction, the serving of God's will or natural law. Kant, for example, always good for a shocking opinion in the realm of normative ethics, suggests that sexual lust is an appetite with an end intended by nature, and that any sexual activity contrary to that end is "unnatural and revolting," by which one "makes himself an object of abomination and stands bereft of all reverence of any kind."[3] It was Sigmund Freud who destroyed this long-standing paradigm, in identifying sexuality as "discharge of tension" (physical and psychological), which he simply equated with "pleasure," regardless of the areas of the body or what activities or how many people happened to be involved. Sex was thus defined as self-serving, activity for its own sake, with pleasure as its only principle. If Freud is now accused of sexual conservatism, it is necessary to remind ourselves that he introduced the radical paradigm that is now used against him. Since Freud's classic efforts, the conception of sexuality as a means to other ends, whether procreation or pious love, has become bankrupt in terms of the currency of opinion. Even radical sexual ideology has confined its critique to the social and political abuses of this liberal platitude without openly rejecting it.

The second platitude is a hold-over from more conservative days, in which sexual activity, like defecation, menstruation, and the bodily reactions to illness, was considered distasteful, if not shameful and to be hidden from view. Yet this conservative platitude is as essential as the first, for the typically utilitarian argument in defense of sexuality as enjoyment is based on the idea that sex is private activity and, when confined to "consenting adults," should be left as a matter of taste. And sex is, we are reminded by liberals, a natural appetite, and therefore a matter of taste.

The platitude of privacy also bolsters the third principle, still considered a radical principle by many, that any sexual activity is as valid as any other. Again, the utilitarian argument prevails, that private and mutually consented activity between adults, no matter how distasteful it might be to others and no matter how we may think its enthusiasts to be depraved, is "their own business."

Nagel's analysis calls this tri-part ideology to his side, although he clearly attempts to go beyond it as well. The platitude of enjoyment functions only loosely in his essay, and at one point he makes it clear that sexuality need not aim at enjoyment. ("It may be that . . . perfection as sex is less enjoyable than certain perversions; and if enjoyment is considered very important, that might outweigh considerations of sexual perfection in determining rational preference" [16/17].) His central notion of "arousal," however, is equivocal. On the one hand, arousal is itself not necessarily enjoyable, particularly if it fails to be accompanied with expectations or release. But on the other hand, Nagel's "arousal" plays precisely the same role in his analysis that "tension" (or "cathexis") plays in Freud, and though the arousal itself is not enjoyable, its release is, and the impression we get from Nagel, which Freud makes explicit, is that sexual activity is the intentional arousal both of self and other in order to enjoy its release. On this interpretation, Nagel's analysis is perfectly in line with post-Freudian liberal theory.

Regarding the second platitude, Nagel's analysis does not mention it, but rather it appears to be presupposed throughout that sexuality is a private affair. One might repeat that the notion of privacy is more symptomatic of his analysis itself. One cannot imagine J. L. Austin spending a dozen pages describing the intentions and inclinations involved in a public performance of making a promise or christening a ship without mentioning the performance itself. Yet Nagel spends that much space giving us the preliminaries of sexuality without ever quite breaching the private sector in which sexual activity is to be found.

The third platitude emerges only slowly in Nagel's essay. He begins by chastising an approach to that same conclusion by a radical "skeptic," who argues of sexual desires, as "appetites,"

Either they are sexual or they are not; sexuality does not admit of imperfection, or perversion, or any other such qualification (7).

Nagel's analysis goes beyond this "skepticism" in important ways, yet he does conclude that "any bodily contact between a man and a woman that gives them sexual pleasure [italics mine], is a possible vehicle for the system of multi-level interpersonal awareness that I have claimed is the basic psychological content of sexual interaction" (15). Here the first platitude is partially employed to support the third, presumably with the second implied. Notice again that Nagel has given us no indication what distinguishes "sexual pleasure" from other pleasures, whether bodily pleasures or the enjoyment of conquest or domination, seduction or submission, sleeping with the president's daughter or earning thirty dollars.

To knock down a tripod, one need kick out only one of its supporting legs. I for one would not wish to advocate, along with several recent sexual pundits, an increased display of fornication and fellatio in public places, nor would I view the return of "sexual morality" as a desirable state of affairs. Surprisingly, it is the essential enjoyment of sex that is the least palatable of the liberal myths.

No one would deny that sex is enjoyable, but it does not follow that sexuality is the activity of "pure enjoyment" and that "gratification," or

"pure physical pleasure," that is, orgasm, is its
end. Sex is indeed pleasurable, but, as Aristotle
argued against the hedonists of his day, this enjoyment accompanies sexual activity and its ends,
but is not that activity or these ends. We enjoy
being sexually satisfied; we are not satisfied by
our enjoyment. In fact, one might reasonably hy-
pothesize that the performance of any activity,
pleasurable or not, which is as intensely promoted
and obsessively pursued as sex in America would
provide tremendous gratification. (One might further speculate on the fact that recent American
politics shows that "every (white, male Christian)
American boy's dream of becoming President" seems
to encourage the exploitation of all three sexual
platitudes of enjoyment, privacy, and "anything
goes." [Cf. H. Kissinger, "Power is the ultimate
aphrodisiac."])

If sexuality does not essentially aim at
pleasure, does it have any purpose? Jean-Paul
Sartre has given us an alternative to the liberal
theory in his Being and Nothingness, in which he
argues that our sexual relations with others, like
all our various relationships with others, are to
be construed as conflicts, modeled after Hegel's
parable of master and slave. Sexual desire is not
desire for pleasure, and pleasure is more likely
to distract us from sexuality than to deepen our
involvement. For Sartre, sexual desire is the
desire to possess, to gain recognition of one's
own freedom at the expense of the other. By "in-
carnating" and degrading him/her in flesh, one reduces him/her to an object. Sadism is but an extension of this domination over the other. Or one
allows himself to be "incarnated" as a devious
route to the same end, making the other his/her
sexual slave. Sexual activity concentrates its
attention on the least personal, most inert parts
of the body—breasts, thighs, stomach, and emphasizes awkward and immobile postures and activities.
On this model, degradation is the central activity
of sex, to convince the other that he/she is a
slave, to persuade the other of one's own power,
whether it be through the skills of sexual

technique or through the passive demands of being sexually served. Intercourse has no privileged position in this model, except that intercourse, particularly in these liberated times in which it has become a contest, is ideal for this competition for power and recognition. And no doubt Sartre, who, like Freud, adopts a paradigmatically male perspective, senses that intercourse is more likely to be degrading to the woman, who thus begins at a disadvantage.

Sartre's notion of sexuality, taken seriously, would be enough to keep us out of bed for a month. Surely, we must object, something has been left out of account, for example, the two-person Mitsein that Sartre himself suggests in the same book. It is impossible for us to delve into the complex ontology that leads Sartre into this pessimistic model, but its essential structure is precisely what we need to carry us beyond the liberal mythology. According to Sartre, sexuality is interpersonal communication with the body as its medium. Sartre's mistake, if we may be brief, is his narrow constriction of the message of that communication to mutual degradation and conflict. Nagel, who accepts Sartre's communication model but, in line with the liberal mythology, seeks to reject its pessimistic conclusions, makes a mistake in the opposite direction. He accepts the communication model, but leaves it utterly without content. What is communicated, he suggests, is arousal. But, as we have seen, arousal is too broad a notion; we must know arousal of what, for what, to what end. Nagel's notion of "arousal" and "interpersonal awareness" gives us an outline of the grammar of the communication model, but no semantics. One might add that sexaul activity in which what is aroused and intended are pleasurable sensations alone is a limiting and rare case. A sensation is only pleasurable or enjoyable, not in itself, but in the context of the meaning of the activity in which it is embedded. This is as true of orgasm as it is of a hard passion-bite on the shoulder.

This view of sexuality answers some strong questions which the liberal model leaves a mystery. If sex is pure physical enjoyment, why is sexual activity between persons far more satisfying than masturbation, where, if we accept recent physiology studies, orgasm is at its highest intensity and the post-coital period is cleansed of its interpersonal hassles and arguments? On the Freudian model, sex with other people ("objects") becomes a matter of "secondary process," with masturbation primary. On the communication model, masturbation is like talking to yourself; possible, even enjoyable, but clearly secondary to sexuality in its broader interpersonal context. (It is significant that even this carnal solipsism is typically accompanied by imaginings and pictures; "No masturbation without representation," perhaps.) If sex is physical pleasure, then the fetish of the genital orgasm is no doubt justifiable, but then why in our orgasm-cluttered sex lives are we so dissatisfied? Because orgasm is not the "end" of sex but its resolution, and obsessive concentration on reaching climax effectively overwhelms or distorts whatever else is being said sexually. It is this focus on orgasm that has made Sartre's model more persuasive; for the battle over the orgasm, whether in selfish or altruistic guise ("my orgasm first" or "I'll give you the best ever") has become an unavoidable medium for conflict and control. "Unadorned sexual intercourse," on this model, becomes the ultimate perversion, since it is the sexual equivalent of hanging up the telephone without saying anything. Even an obscene telephone caller has a message to convey.

Sexual activity consists in speaking what we might call "body language." It has its own grammar, delineated by the body, and its own phonetics of touch and movement. Its unit of meaningfulness, the body equivalent of a sentence, is the gesture. No doubt one could add considerably to its vocabulary, and perhaps it could be possible to discuss world politics or the mind-body problem by an appropriate set of invented gestures. But body language is essentially expressive, and its content is limited to interpersonal attitudes and feelings—shyness, domination, fear, submissiveness and dependence, love or hatred or indifference, lack of confidence and embarrassment, shame, jealousy, possessiveness. There is little value in stressing the overworked point that such expressions are "natural" expressions, as opposed to verbal expressions of the same attitudes and feelings. In our highly verbal society, it may well be that verbal expression, whether it be poetry or clumsy blurting, feels more natural than the use of our bodies. Yet it does seem true that some attitudes, e.g., tenderness and trust, domination and passivity, are best expressed sexually. Love, it seems, is not best expressed sexually, for its sexual expression is indistinguishable from the expressions of a number of other attitudes. Possessiveness, mutual recognition, "being-with," and conflict are expressed by body language almost essentially, virtually as its deep structure, and here Sartre's model obtains its plausibility.

According to Nagel, "perversion" is "truncated or incomplete versions of the complete configuration" (13). But again, his emphasis is entirely on the form of "interpersonal awareness" rather than its content. For example, he analyzes sadism as "the concentration on the evocation of passive self-awareness in others . . . which impedes awareness of himself as a bodily subject of passion in the required sense." But surely sadism is not so much a breakdown in communication (any more than the domination of a conversation by one speaker, with the agreement of his listener, is a breach of language) as an excessive expression of a particular content, namely the attitude of domination, perhaps mixed with hatred, fear, and other negative attitudes. Similarly, masochism is not simply the relinquishing of one's activity (an inability to speak, in a sense), for the masochist may well be active in inviting punishment from his sadistic partner. Masochism is excessive expression of an attitude of victimization, shame, or inferiority. Moreover, it is clear that there is

not the slightest taint of "perversion" in homosexuality, which need differ from heterosexuality
only in its mode of resolution. Fetishism and
bestiality certainly do constitute perversions,
since the first is the same as, for example, talking to someone else's shoes, and the second is
like discussing Spinoza with a moderately intelligent sheep.

This model also makes it evident why Nagel
chose as his example a couple of strangers; one has
far more to say, for one can freely express one's
fantasies as well as the truth, to a stranger. A
husband and wife of seven years have probably been
repeating the same messages for years, and their
sexual activity now is probably no more than an
abbreviated ritual incantation of the lengthy conversations they had years before. One can imagine
Romeo and Juliet climbing into bed together each
with a spectacular set of expectations and fantasies, trying to overwhelm each other with extravagant expressions and experiments. But it may be,
accordingly, that they won't understand each other,
or, as the weekend plods on, sex, like any extended conversation, tends to become either more
truthful or more incoherent.

Qua body language, sex admits of a least two
forms of perversion: one deviance of form, the
other deviance in content. There are the techniques of sexuality, overly celebrated in our society, and there are the attitudes that these
techniques allegedly express. Nagel and most
theorists have concentrated on perversions in
technique, deviations in the forms of sexual activity. But it seems to me that the more problematic perversions are the semantic deviations, of
which the most serious are those involving insincerity, the bodily equivalent of the lie. Enter-
taining private fantasies and neglecting one's
real sexual partner is thus an innocent semantic
perversion, while pretended tenderness and affection that reverses itself soon after orgasm is a
potentially vicious perversion. However, again
joining Nagel, I would argue that perverse sex is

not necessarily bad or immoral sex. Pretense is
the premise of imagination as well as of false-
hood, and sexual fantasies may enrich our lives
far more than sexual realities alone. Perhaps it
is an unfortunate comment on the poverty of contemporary life that our fantasies have become so
confined, that our sexuality has been forced to
serve needs which far exceed its expressive capacity. That is why the liberal mythology has been
so disastrous, for it has rendered unconscious
the expressive functions of sex in its stress on
enjoyment and, in its platitude of privacy, has
reduced sexuality to each man's/woman's private
language, first spoken clumsily and barely artic-
ulately on wedding nights and in the back seats
of Fords. It is thus understandable why sex is
so utterly important in our lives, and why it is
typically so unsatisfactory.

Notes

[1]I confess, for example, that certain male
biases infiltrate my own analysis. I thank
Janice Moulton for pointing this out to me.
[2]"Sexual Perversion," [Journal of Philosophy],
LXVI, 1, Jan. 16, 1969: 5-17.
[3]Metaphysics of Ethics, trans. Semple (Edinburgh: Clark, 1971) IV, pt. I, ch. 1, sec. 7.

Rights and Care of Children

Case

David was 15 years old, tall, angular, and a good kid. The psychologist told his parents that the only way for David to pull out of his present mental condition was to be hospitalized, to be "boxed" in so that he could receive the treatment he needed. David's parents had little success in getting David off to school each morning; and while he had earlier agreed to get some help, he stopped going to the psychologist. David's parents were highly educated people, very successful in their professions, and David never felt he could live up to the standard set in the family. His parents never put pressure on him; yet unless he made an A on every paper and test he thought he had failed. No amount of reassurance from his parents made a difference to the way he saw himself and his school work. But, David had stopped going to school, and that is against the law for someone his age. Late one night he begged and cried for help, and his parents turned to the psychologist again. So, there they were, standing in the parking lot of the doctor's office. David refused to go into the hospital. He promised he would go to school and do his work. His parents and the psychologist had heard that before. They told him he had to go right now, and he could either go standing up or he could go handicuffed and carried by the police; there were no other alternatives.

A Philosophical Justification
for Children's Rights*
Victor L. Worsfold

Historically, rights in society have been ascribed only to adults. Children have been treated
paternally; their conduct has been controlled by
parents or others in authority. Such control has
been justified, in the paternalist view, by the
need to protect children from themselves and
others. It is argued that children cannot be responsible for their own welfare because by their
nature they lack an adequate conception of their
own present and future interests.[1] They are said
to want instant gratification and to be incapable
of fully rational decisions.

Well-intentioned though this view may be, its
implicit claim that adults <u>do</u> have an adequate
conception of children's interests, and that they
are always willing to act upon this conception, is
open to serious question. In fact, parents often
do not know what is best for their children, and
children often can make sensible decisions for
themselves about their own lives. In addition,
the parents, however wise, may have interests and
preferences which do not coincide with those of
the child.

It will be the task of this article to challenge the paternalist view in its simplest and
most common variants, demonstrating that these do
not guarantee acceptable treatment of children.
I will maintain that although some of the tenets
of the paternalist view are unavoidable, they
should not commit us to a political or ethical
philosophy in which children have no rights of
their own. I will also argue that there is one

*From <u>Harvard Educational Review</u>, vol. 44, no. 1,
(February, 1974), pp. 142-157. Reprinted by
permission of the author and editor. Copyright ©
1974 by President & Fellows at Harvard College.

philosophical framework, John Rawls's theory of justice, which, while still paternalist, does provide a justification for according children rights to fair treatment. To assert rights to fair treatment, as Rawls does, is to assert an obligation on the part of adults to acknowledge the just claims of children. A claim which is just in Rawls's scheme is one which is consistent with the procedural principles of justice on which society should be founded, principles which should extend to children as well as adults. In Rawls's theory, the exercise of children's rights may not always be left to the children themselves, but children are presumed to be able to exercise their own rights unless all of society agrees that someone else should make decisions for them.

This article does not talk about which rights as a practical matter should be exercised by children themselves. It also does not discuss the ages at which the exercise of various rights should be permitted, or the realm of duties and obligations which should fall to children of various ages. What the article sets out to do is more basic: to challenge well-established philosophical preconceptions about a system of fair treatment for children, and to outline the basis for a new philosophical structure under which children can be regarded as full participants in society.

The Paternalism of Hobbes, Locke, and Mill

Thomas Hobbes, writing in the seventeenth century, offered one version of the paternalist view. Hobbes argued that children are cared for solely because they are capable of serving their fathers, and that the relationship between father and child must be founded on fear.[2] Children are assigned a position of complete dependence. Hobbes thought that "like the imbecile, the crazed and the beasts, over . . . children . . . there is no law."[3] Children have no natural rights and no rights by social contract because they lack the ability to make covenants with the other members of society and to understand the consequences of such contracts. Instead, children must acknowledge their fathers as sovereigns. Fathers have the power of life and death over children and "every man is supposed to promise obedience to him in whose power it is to save or destroy him."[4]

Hobbes's argument has an unfortunate flaw in that on the one hand it requires children to promise obedience, and on the other it assumes they are incapable of making such a promise and upholding its consequences. But the essence of the argument is clear. The relationship between father and child is seen as one of mutual benefit, in which in return for protection and livelihood the child must serve the father. Hobbes equates rights with powers. It follows that children cannot be granted rights, for the logic of the primary relationship between father and child does not permit it. Hobbes said, "There would be no reason why any man should desire to have children or to take care to nourish them if afterwards to have no other benefit from them than from other men."[5]

Writing later in the same century, John Locke took a somewhat different position. He asserted that children were to be under the jurisdiction of their parents "till they can be able to shift for themselves."[6] Until that time, the child lacks understanding, and therefore cannot exert his or her will. Locke compared this subjugation to wearing swaddling clothes, implying that children can cast off their dependency when they become adults and are rational enough to understand the principles by which they are governed. In Locke's view, there is an obligation for children to honor their parents. This obligation "ties up the child from anything that may ever injure or affront . . . the happiness or life of those from whom he has received his."[7] But in direct contradiction to Hobbes, Locke argues that this obligation is "far from giving parents a power of command over their children, or an authority to make laws and dispose as they please of their lives and liberties."[8] Introducing the notion of natural rights, he attributed rights to individuals as though these rights were intrinsic properties, which no other claim could preempt. Children, like adults, have natural rights which need to be protected. The development of the child's freedom is paramount, because that is God's will.

Locke did not address the objection that there might be conflicts between the natural rights of parents and children. Instead he espoused the doctrine that the child's good is the same as the parents'. Parental benevolence is sufficient to ensure the fulfillment of children's rights.

In both Hobbes's and Locke's views there is a clear demand that parents control the lives of children according to preconceived notions of the children's future welfare. In a Hobbesian society, this notion is that children are instruments, and must serve their parents in order to survive. In Locke's view, there is an emphasis on the emergent freedoms and responsibilities of the child. Locke, more than Hobbes, wants to constrain parental dominance of the child. But we must not sentimentalize Locke's thought, for well-meaning benevolence can be used to manage the affairs of children with the same effect as explicit force. Both involve the continued dependency of children on their parents. Each prevents children from making claims of their own and thereby hinders society from seeing them as worthy of respect as individuals.

In the nineteenth century, John Stuart Mill espoused another kind of paternalism. The libertarian persuasion usually associated with Mill does not extend to his thinking about children. In his discussion of the limits of society's authority over the individual, Mill declared that "the existing generation is master both of the training and the entire circumstances of the generation to come."[9] The power of society over children appears absolute. There is no sign of

Mill's principle of individual liberty, which
states that "(an individual) cannot rightfully be
compelled to do or forbear because it will be better for him to do so, because it will make him
happier, because in the opinions of others to do
so would be wise or even right."[10] Mill is explicit that this doctrine of the ultimate value of
personal choice does not extend to children: "We
are not speaking of children, or of young persons
below the age which the law may fix as that of
manhood or womanhood."[11]

Mill's justification for this position is
based in part on the need to protect children
against the possibility of injury from themselves
and others. He felt that freedom to make claims
had no place until the child was capable of self-
improvement as the result of rational discussion.[12]
Mill also argued the case against children's right
to free choice from a strictly utilitarian standpoint. The need to maximize overall goodness in
society dictates that childre, unlike adults,
should not be permitted the right to interpret
their own good, for fear they will not act in accordance with the public good. He realized that
the existing generation cannot make the next
"perfectly wise and good," but he insisted that
the existing generation is "well able to make the
rising generation as a whole as good and a little
better than itself."[13] In another passage, Mill
extended this view, saying that "the uncultivated
cannot be competent judges of cultivation. Those
who most need to be made wiser and better usually
desire it least, and if they desired it, would be
incapable of finding the way to it by their own
lights."[14] Paternalism, then, is acceptable in
the case of children because they are incapable
of deciding what is in their own and society's
best interest.

Taken together, these three philosophers
provide a coherent if somewhat negative attitude
toward children. As we progress from Hobbes's
thought through Locke's to Mill's, the strict
paternalism of Hobbes is replaced by an emphasis

on benevolence in the treatment of children.
Despite this, all three philosophers regard the
child as someone to be molded according to adult
preconceptions. None of these philosophers would
have considered seriously the perspective of children themselves in determining their own best interests. None accorded children rights of their
own.

Inadequacies of Certain Traditional
Justifications for Children's Rights

It is commonly thought that philosophers must
justify the rights of children by demonstrating
that children are part of a class of beings entitled to rights. The search for a philosophical
justification of children's rights might begin,
for instance, with the assertion that the right to
fair treatment is based on some element of <u>human
nature</u> which is common to both adults and children.
By this line of reasoning, children's rights may
be justified religiously, morally, or simply on
grounds of biological fact. Once a common element is accepted as the philosophical basis of
rights, then the rights of children become self-
evident.

This approach has the appeal of resolving in
a stroke what many would find problematic: that
in their fundamental rights children and adults
are the same. But it also raises problems, however. Even if we ignore the likely criticism
that this position begs important questions, we
must face the additional issues of precise definition of the shared attribute, on the one hand,
and class inclusion on the other. Any common element of human nature we select must be operation-
ally clear and must not err either by including
too many beings in the category of those deserv-
ing rights, or by excluding some important classes
of beings.

It has sometimes been argued that rationality
is the common element among all humans. We are
all human in that we are capable as rational

animals of understanding the reasons for our choice of personal ends. But this criterion can readily be challenged. One philosopher, Henry David Aiken, has doubts, for instance, about including in the category of rational beings "babies, fetuses, (and) people who are becoming senile."[15] Others maintain that those who lack exposure to education or so-called civilization should be added to Aiken's list. Various additional categories of humans, such as the mentally ill, also might have to be excluded. Surely all of these groups are worthy of certain rights.

As a prior question, of course, it is also extremely difficult to ascertain exactly what is meant by rationality, and whether we can operationalize it precisely enough to determine whether an individual possesses the capacity or does not. This, it would seem, is a major problem with the criterion as it relates to children. Rationality can be thought of in a number of ways, as the capacity for willful action, the capacity to infer the possible consequences of a choice, as an ability to use the moral precepts of a community, as the possession of a certain level of measured intelligence on some standardized IQ test, and so forth. The possible characterizations are numerous, and in general tend to be too narrow to include all those to whom we would wish to accord rights.

Those of a religious persuasion propose another possible common element for adults and children: both are members of a class of beings capable of suffering. But this view is too broad. Its application results in the inclusion of prisoners, invalids, and mental incompetents, for instance, and even animals. It is also difficult to know what should count as true suffering.

Even the argument that all humans are worthy of rights because they are members of the same species presents a dilemma. The category of "human" again raises problems of definition and class inclusion, as for instance in the case of unborn fetuses.

Aiken has an interesting response to the lack of a well-defined common element as a criterion for the ascription of rights to all persons. He construes human rights, and for our purposes children's rights, as belonging "normatively and ideally to persons to whom we, as moral beings, owe a certain kind of responsibility."[16] This shifts the argument for rights to a new position, making the ascription of one person's rights contingent on other people's moral obligations. But the position leads to a new set of difficulties. Consider a possible analogy between parents and colonialists. Imagine a developing country where a local political leader hopes he can convince the colonial authorities that, as moral persons, they have a responsibility to accord his countrymen respect, acknowledge their rights to fair treatment, and grant them nation status. Failure to do so, in the politicians' view, would indicate the failure of the colonialists to see the citizens of the developing country as their equals. The colonialists, on the other hand, might deny the developing country nationhood on the grounds of certain differences between themselves and the local people, like skin color, lack of maturity, and comparative poverty. Furthermore, they might insist that in recognizing the existence of these differences they were respecting the local people. By this familiar logic, if the developing country wants self-government later, then it is reasoned the country would be better under foreign rule now, since self-government demands a self-sufficiency and self-regulation the country presently could not sustain. This position, of course, ignores the possibility that the citizens of the developing country would in full cognizance prefer to be poor but independent now. Should their choice be respected, or should the colonialists continue to act as enlightened agents protecting their well-being?

Acting on Aiken's proposal, it may not be possible to address the developing country's point of view. His notion that we are to ascribe rights to persons because we ought to, that is, because such an ascription of rights is morally proper, will not provide a strong enough foundation against counter arguments. There are counter-vailing moral principles, and the colonialists need to be convinced of why they should yield control—that is, why self-governance is the developing country's right and why it is in the country's long-term self-interest. No argument can suffice which says that it is part of the colonialists' duty to accord nationhood. They might fervently believe that there are various classes of beings toward whom we have duties without owing them rights.

Children are in a situation analogous to that of the citizens of the developing country. The burden of proof is presently on them and on adults speaking in their behalf to demonstrate why they have a right to do what they prefer when it conflicts with what their parents or society prefer. Notions of morality which govern decisions of parents and society depend on how convincing their arguments can be. This example serves to illustrate why any entitlement to rights cannot be resolved without reference to some broader framework, a comprehensive theory of justice, to which all parties can agree. Without such a framework and such a consensus, moral claims will continue to be a matter of assertion and counter-assertion.

Necessary Features of Children's Rights

It is helpful to indicate briefly three features, first proposed by Maurice Cranston in justifying rights in general,[17] which are necessary in any scheme justifying children's rights. These will give a clear sense of why many previous attempts at justification have proved unsatisfactory, and why a rationale in the framework of a theory of justice may be more adequate.

Adopting the ideas of Cranston, the first necessary characteristic of children's rights is that they be practicable. By this Cranston means they must be theoretically possible, or acceptable within some larger conception of the good society. This meaning is grounded in statements prescribing or applying rules of fair treatment which are philosophically derived. Children's rights must cohere and be theoretically consistent within the society's conception of justice.

Children's rights can be theoretically possible or reasonable without being popular or practical to implement. In fact, it is hard to imagine any scheme which would significantly increase the domain of children's rights which would not raise objections in at least some small segment of the adult community. Moreover we need not expect children to exercise their rights well in society as we know it. Even if it is impossible in society as we know it to provide fair treatment for children, this does not make it wrong to claim fair treatment as a right. It only means that these rights must make sense within the framework of some reasonable conception of society.

A second necessary feature of children's rights is that they be genuinely universal, appropriate for all children everywhere. The idea, for instance, that only those who are white are to be accorded rights fails to take account of this feature. This criterion needs no great elaboration, except that there may be misunderstandings about its implications for different age groups. It might be objected, for instance, that preschoolers should not have rights while adolescents should, or that in any event the rights of the two groups should not be the same.

Our concern with including this criterion is much more a concern with establishing a philosophical doctrine of _capacity_, the groundwork for a presumption that children have rights, than it is a concern with the particular practical domain in which these rights are routinely exercies by children themselves. To establish the foundations for rights, making an adequate philosophical argument that they should be accorded, is not the same as spelling out the actual scope and nature of their exercise for every age group. This distinction is analogous to the distinction between capacity and exercise of rights which is made in the narrower context of the legal system. All persons do not enjoy the same legal rights, but all are presumed to have the same capacity for rights and enjoy the presumption that treatment will not be different for them than for others. In the law, this is called the doctrine of impartiality, or equal consideration. The meaning of capacity for rights is simply that no individual, whatever his or her age, should be <u>without</u> the rights accorded others in society.

This criterion obviously does not take us far toward determining those areas where children of various ages should be allowed to make practical decisions for themselves. It merely lays down one necessary precondition of any adequate philosophical argument for children's rights.

The third and last feature of chilren's rights is that they be <u>of paramount importance</u>. When fair treatment is accorded children as a right, it must override all other considerations in society's conduct toward children, for example, consideration of children's fun. This feature may be less clear than the others. It serves to override the utilitarian objection that when we do what is in children's best interest we should be concerned less with their rights and more with their pleasure or satisfaction, or the aggregate short-term and long-term good achieved for them and others. If the utilitarian principle were pre-eminent, then we can imagine many situations where adults could justify depriving children of rights simply on the grounds that there was a prior importance of children's satisfaction or well-being which required that certain rights not be allowed them; or, more comprehensively, it could be maintained that when the total good of society is taken into consideration children must be deprived of rights because this leads to more sensible decisions for the whole society, leading to the greatest good for the greatest number, children included. We can also

imagine many situations where a right to fair
treatment for children would require them to become involved in painstaking deliberations or
proceedings on their own behalf, which they might
prefer to avoid if their own pleasure were of
equal importance. Pleasure may be important in
the lives of children, and so may the aggregate
good of ends achieved for children, but neither
should have the same importance as children's
right to make just claims.

Children's Rights under John Rawls's Theory of Justice

An interesting and adequate framework for
children's rights can be established in the context of John Rawls's theory of justice. Rawls
bases his theory of the just society on a particular kind of social contract. A system of justice, for Rawls, requires that people "understand
the need for, and they are prepared to affirm, a
characteristic set of principles for assigning
basic rights and duties and for determining what
they take to be the proper distribution of the
benefits and burdens of social cooperation."[18]
His goal is to permit each individual to act according to a personal conception of his or her
own best interests, but not at the expense of
others.

In order to achieve Rawls's just society, individuals engage in a mutual process of evolving
principles of fair treatment for everyone, present and future. His central idea is that everyone
in the society must participate in choosing these
principles, and that the principles are to be
selected in a hypothetical state, or "original
position," in which the individuals are ignorant
of their own specific interests and circumstances
in real life. All participants in society are
self-interested in making their decisions. But
ignorance of their station in life and of the particular configuration of their society guarantees
for Rawls that the individuals will choose principles of justice impartially, with equality in

213

mind, so that no one is made to serve as an instrument of the interests of others.

In the Rawlsian scheme, the only constraints on selfishness in choosing the principles of justice are that the individuals make their choices behind the original "veil of ignorance," that they be rational in choosing, and that they understand roughly what might constitute an adequate theory of justice. Assuming these conditions are met, Rawls argues that only one set of principles of justice will emerge. They will be agreed upon by everyone, because all participants in society will see it in their own personal interest to come to the same general conclusions about adequate rules for the system of justice.

In their condition of ignorance and self-interest, the individuals will choose two fundamental principles of justice. The first is that each person should have a personal liberty compatible with a like liberty for all others; no one should be any freer than anyone else in society to pursue his or her own ends. The second is that societal inequalities are to be arranged such that all individuals must share whatever advantages and disadvantages the inequalities bring. This principle is intended to preclude discrimination against those who are born into poverty or natural deformity. Taken together, the two procedural principles provide the basis for the entire system of justice. Individuals agree to the principles because acting on them will best implement the individual's sense of his or her own good, as perceived in the original position of ignorance.

Rawls argues that in the original position, self-interested persons would want first to guarantee their own freedoms and would initially make the conservative assumption that others in society might want to curtail these freedoms. Thus their first motive would be to ensure that minimal guarantees of their own liberty were preserved. Rawls suggests that in everyone's case there is this kind of prior concern about preserving personal liberty. Assuming this minimal condition is met, individuals would then want to proceed with the fulfillment of other interests. Clearly the preservation of individual freedom is not without some cost to the individual, however, since in the initial state of ignorance it requires that an assurance of one's own freedom be made prior to knowledge of one's own practical identity and life circumstances. Thus, to ensure minimal personal freedom involves granting a like freedom to all others, and constraining one's own freedom as one would wish the freedom of others to be constrained.

Rawls also insists that when individuals engage in the mutually advantageous business of constructing a framework of justice, no individual would choose to submit to the restrictions of the society without expecting similar submission from others. And those who do submit to the restrictions would demand a just claim against all others in the society. Thus, all individuals would have a right to insist upon fair treatment at the hands of their fellows. The justification for this right does not depend on the moral convictions of the members of the society, or on any conditions of the individual, such as the capacity for suffering. Rather, the justification depends on the fact that all individuals in the society have freely agreed to make themselves subject to the claims of their fellow members. Each individual has rights against all others in the society.

In an interesting footnote, Rawls characterizes the rights granted under his scheme as "natural." By this Rawls means that the rights accorded to individuals "are assigned in the first instance to persons and that they are given special weight."[19] The principles of justice thus guarantee rights which are based on the nature of individuals. To violate rights is to that extent to violate the nature of the person. These thoughts are reminiscent of Cranston's remarks in reference to the rights of men, when he writes, "such rights are not given us by anybody; we have them already. The only thing needful is that they be acknowledged, recognized, and respected."[20]

What, then, about children and others whom society must treat paternally? Rawls is quite explicit about implications of his theory for these groups, and his point of view, while not radical, seems to contain major implications for children's rights.

In Rawls's theory, children are participants in the formation of the initial social contract to the extent they are capable. In order to participate fully in this process one must be rational, and this, for Rawls, means among other things that one must have attained the "age of reason."[21] But there is no attempt to rigidly define this age, or to link it with a particular conception of rationality or a particular notion of prerequisite skills and understanding. Instead, Rawls seems to imply that as children's competencies develop, their participation should increase.

Rawls points out that it is the capacity for accepting the principle of fairness which matters when deciding who is to count as a member of society. He writes that "a being that has this capacity, whether or not it is yet developed, is to receive the full protection of the principles of justice."[22] Children are pre-eminently such beings, and therefore qualify as members of the society, with just claims to fair treatment. Clearly some individuals in society will be better at applying the principles of justice than others. Any advantage those people receive from the exercise of these principles, however, will be regulated by the second principle of justice: people are not to enjoy a special advantage as a result of natural ability or social status. The characteristic which defines the just individual is the capacity for a sense of justice rather than the immediate realization of this capacity.

But skeptics may not yet be satisfied. They may argue that if children cannot participate fully in generating the principles necessary for the just society, they should not be accorded rights. In the Rawlsian view, however, it is more reasonable to assume that children _are_ competent to perform this initial task, at least in part, rather than risk the logical alternative to it; that they shall be denied the possibility of pursuing their own just ends. Rawls wants to take account of our intuitive sense that even quite young children often _do_ know what they want, and are capable of weighing alternatives and of acting on the decisions they make—precisely the kind of deliberation required of those choosing the original principles.

Consider, for instance, children participating in a family decision about where to live. To permit children to participate in making this kind of decision is to run the risk of allowing a wrong decision to emerge—a risk which our society is reluctant to take. But if children are to learn to make such decisions, then, as Aristotle pointed out, they must be allowed to act and to be responsible for the consequences of their actions. Adults may assist in making choices for children, even exert some influence. But there must be good reasons for children to accept the authority of the older generation. By analogy, as adults we sometimes relinquish personal exercise of rights because someone else's proven skills or special knowledge is sufficient to convince us we should allow that person to advise us and guide our actions. One example of this willingness is in our attitudes toward the expertise of the scientific community or the medical profession. But in such cases, authority is conditional on the way it promotes or inhibits the attainment of our goals, or the choice of wise goals. Likewise, for children the authority of adults depends upon the way it facilitates or prevents the achievement of personal ends.

For Rawls, lack of full participation by children in the original consensus does not lead to parental domination. In the hypothetical, original position of society, those choosing are choosing not merely for themselves but for all who are to come. This means that principles of fairness must be formulated in a temporal limbo as well as a spatial and social one. Participants must choose principles without knowing their age or generation, as well as not knowing their life situation. They must entertain the possibility of actually being children, or of not yet being born, and choices about principles of justice must be made with this contingency, among others, in mind.

Those selecting the principles of justice in the original position would probably consent to some form of paternalism. But they would be very reluctant to adopt any paternalism which did not protect them against abuses of authority by members of the older generation.

Others are authorized and sometimes required to act on our behalf and to do what we would do for ourselves if we were rational, this authorization coming into effect only when we cannot look after our own good. Paternalistic decisions are to be guided by the individual's own settled preferences and interests insofar as they are not irrational, or failing a knowledge of these, by the theory of primary goods. As we know less and less about a person, we act for him as we would act for ourselves from the standpoint of the original position. We try to get for him the things he presumably wants whatever else he wants. We must be able to argue that with the development or the recovery of his rational powers the individual in question will accept our decision on his behalf and agree with us that we did the best thing for him.[23]

The conception of children's interests implicit here is already more adequate than that of the classical paternalist schemes explored earlier. For Rawls, children are entitled to rights of their own. Also, the interests of the child are not necessarily synonymous with those of parents or protectors.

Even though the scheme is more libertarian than its predecessors, however, it still has one possible problem. Whenever adults act on behalf of a child, doing for the child what they would wish done for them if they were in the child's place, they do so without any mechanism available for children to question their judgment or dispute the correctness of their decisions. There may be no recourse for the child who feels that decisions are being made wrongly in his behalf. This objection is wholly analogous to objections raised to the "best interests of the child" standard as it is applied in legal proceedings, for instance, where adults often act according to their own conception of the child's best interests without sufficient chance for children themselves to take issues with this conception or to participate in the decision-making process.

Rawls anticipates this objection, and addresses the problem directly. First, he makes it clear that adults cannot claim after the fact that they have treated children fairly simply on the grounds that the children are finally persuaded of the correctness of their decision. To illustrate the danger of permitting such a rationalization, Rawls gives an example:

> . . . imagine two persons in full possession of their reason and will who affirm different religious or philosophical beliefs; and suppose that there is some psychological process that will convert each to the other's view, despite the fact that the process is imposed on them against their wishes. In due course, let us suppose, both will come to accept conscientiously their new beliefs. We are still not permitted to submit them to this treatment.[24]

The spectre of brainwashing raised here could readily be extended to various forms of socialization and education. The point of view of the child must be considered at the time any decision concerning his or her welfare is made, not later.

Rawls makes two additional stipulations. First, he states that "paternalistic intervention must be justified by the evident failure or absence of reason and will."[25] By this he means that there is a presumption of rationality, that is, of the full ability to decide for one's self. Only when it has been demonstrated that this presumption is unwarranted is it fair to act on another's behalf. This point has major implications for children's rights, shifting the burden of proof to those who would deny children the exercise of their own rights. Although there are no doubt many areas where children are justifiably denied the exercise of freedoms, the correctness of this denial is no longer taken for granted. On the contrary, it must be shown to be just.

Rawls also suggests that any paternalistic intervention must be "guided by the principles of justice and what is known about the subject's more permanent aims and preferences, or by the account of primary goods."[26] This suggests, at a minimum, that children should be consulted about their aims and preferences. While the information may not be perceived by the adult as pre-eminent in making decisions about the child's life, it should be weighed along with other information, and weighted more heavily to the extent the child is old enough to think rationally about the choices presented.

We can test the Rawlsian justification for children's rights against the three necessary characteristics outlined earlier: practicability, universality, and paramount importance. In general, all three features are taken into account by Rawls in setting out the principles of justice. In his procedural conception of justice, Rawls has provided a framework within which the granting of children's rights is practicable, that is, theoretically, sound. It is consistent with the theory that children be granted rights, and that these rights be exercised by children themselves wherever possible. The society must acknowledge the just claims of children, even if it is not always advantageous for adults to do so.

By his insistence on the need for impartiality in the original position, Rawls also allows for the universal aspect of children's rights. Those who must live with the chosen principles are the same people who decide on the principles. The notion of impartiality ensures that all shall be considered equally in the division of societal advantages and disadvantages. This view is in conflict with a classical utilitarian conception, which would have as its end the greatest happiness for the greatest number. The utilitarian approach could lead to policies benefiting some people at the expense of others, perhaps leading, for example, to enforced child labor on the grounds that such labor was most advantageous for society. To make a utilitarian argument of this sort is, as Rawls says, "to mistake impersonality for impartiality."[27] The utilitarian disregards the claims of those whose good is sacrificed.

The paramount importance of children's rights is also assured in Rawl's theory. The primacy of personal rights, as against some other conception of the highest good, is a central tenet of the theory. Children are individuals; hence this aspect of the framework extends to them as well as other members of society. To respect children by according them rights is to recognize that they possess "an inviolability"[28] which society cannot override.

The justification of chilren's rights under Rawls's theory has one major emphasis: children have a right to make just claims, and adults must be responsive to these claims. This conception of the just society, if widely accepted, would lead to a change in attitude on the part of adults. In according rights to children, the theory makes adults more accountable to children. They can no longer assume it is only at their pleasure that children are permitted to make claims and exercise freedoms. Adopting this new conception of children's rights would in itself be an important reform.

221

Notes

I wish to thank Robert W. O'Connor for his kind advice and encouragement in the course of my writing this paper.

[1] Gerald Dworkin, "Paternalism," in Morality and the Law, ed. R. A. Wasserstrom (Belmont, Cal.: Wadsworth, 1971), p. 119.

[2] This passage on Hobbes owes much to David P. Gauthier, The Logic of Leviathan (Oxford: Clarendon Press, 1965), p. 118.

[3] Thomas Hobbes, Leviathan (Molesworth ed., Vol. 3; London: J. Bohn, 1839-45), p. 257.

[4] Hobbes, p. 188.

[5] Hobbes, p. 329.

[6] John Locke, The Second Treatise of Government (New York: Bobbs Merrill, 1952), Sect. 60, p. 34.

[7] Locke, Sect. 66, p. 37.

[8] Locke, Sect. 66, p. 37.

[9] John Stuart Mill, On Liberty (New York: Washington Square Press, 1963), p. 207.

[10] Mill, p. 135.

[11] Mill, p. 136.

[12] Mill, p. 136.

[13] Mill, p. 207.

[14] Quoted by Dworkin, p. 116.

[15] Henry David Aiken, "Rights, Human and Otherwise," The Monist, 52 (October 1968), p. 513.

[16] Aiken, p. 514.

[17] Maurice Cranston, "Human Rights, Real and Supposed," in Political Theory and the Rights of Man, ed. David D. Raphael (Bloomington: Indiana University Press, 1967), pp. 55 ff.

[18] John Rawls, A Theory of Justice (Cambridge: Harvard University Press, 1972), p. 5.

[19] Rawls, p. 506.

[20] Maurice Cranston, "Human Rights: A Reply to Professor Raphael," in Raphael, p. 96.

[21] Rawls, p. 209.

[22] Rawls, p. 509.

[23] Rawls, p. 249.

[24] Rawls, pp. 249-250.

[25] Rawls, p. 250.

[26] Rawls, p. 250.

[27]Rawls, p. 190.
[28]Rawls, p. 586.

Abortion and Infanticide[1]*
Michael Tooley

This essay deals with the question of the morality of abortion and infanticide. The fundamental ethical objection traditionally advanced against these practices rests on the contention that human fetuses and infants have a right to life. It is this claim which will be the focus of attention here. The basic issue to be discussed, then, is what properties a thing must possess in order to have a serious right to life. My approach will be to set out and defend a basic moral principle specifying a condition an organism must satisfy if it is to have a serious right to life. It will be seen that this condition is not satisfied by human fetuses and infants, and thus that they do not have a right to life. So unless there are other substantial objections to abortion and infanticide, one is forced to conclude that these practices are morally acceptable ones. In contrast, it may turn out that our treatment of adult members of other species—cats, dogs, polar bears—is morally indefensible. For it is quite possible that such animals do possess properties that endow them with a right to life.

I. Abortion and Infanticide

One reason the question of the morality of infanticide is worth examining is that it seems very difficult to formulate a completely satisfactory liberal position on abortion without coming to grips with the infanticide issue. The

*From Philosophy and Public Affairs, vol. 2, no. 1 (Fall, 1972), pp. 37-65. Reprinted by permission of the author and Princeton University Press.

problem the liberal encounters is essentially that of specifying a cutoff point which is not arbitrary: at what stage in the development of a human being does it cease to be morally permissible to destroy it? It is important to be clear about the difficulty here. The conservative's objection is not that since there is a continuous line of development from a zygote to a newborn baby, one must conclude that if it is seriously wrong to destroy a newborn baby it is also seriously wrong to destroy a zygote or any intermediate stage in the development of a human being. His point is rather that if one says it is wrong to destroy a newborn baby but not a zygote or some intermediate stage in the development of a human being, one should be prepared to point to a <u>morally relevant</u> difference between a newborn baby and the earlier stage in the development of a human being.

Precisely the same difficulty can, of course, be raised for a person who holds that infanticide is morally permissible. The conservative will ask what morally relevant differences there are between an adult human being and a newborn baby. What makes it morally permissible to destroy a baby, but wrong to kill an adult? So the challenge remains. But I will argue that in this case there is an extremely plausible answer.

Reflecting on the morality of infanticide forces one to face up to this challenge. In the case of abortion a number of events—quickening or viability, for instance—might be taken as cutoff points, and it is easy to overlook the fact that none of these events involves any morally significant change in the developing human. In contrast, if one is going to defend infanticide, one has to get very clear about what make something a person, what gives something a right to life.

One of the interesting ways in which the abortion issue differs from most other moral issues is that the plausible positions on abortion appear to be extreme positions. For if a human fetus is a person, one is inclined to say that, in general, one would be justified in killing it only to save the life of the mother.[2] Such is the extreme conservative position.[3] On the other hand, if the fetus is not a person, how can it be seriously wrong to destroy it? Why would one need to point to special circumstances to justify such action? The upshot is that there is no room for a moderate position on the issue of abortion such as one finds, for example, in the Model Penal Code recommendations.[4]

Aside from the light it may shed on the abortion question, the issue of infanticide is both interesting and important in its own right. The theoretical interest has been mentioned: it forces one to face up to the question of what makes something a person. The practical importance need not be labored. Most people would prefer to raise children who do not suffer from gross deformities or from severe physical, emotional, or intellectual handicaps. If it could be shown that there is no moral objection to infanticide the happiness of society could be significantly and justifiably increased.

Infanticide is also of interest because of the strong emotions it arouses. The typical reaction to infanticide is like the reaction to incest or cannibalism, or the reaction of previous generations to masturbation or oral sex. The response, rather than appealing to carefully formulated moral principles, is primarily visceral. When philosophers themselves respond in this way, offering no arguments, and dismissing infanticide out of hand, it is reasonable to suspect that one is dealing with a taboo rather than with a rational prohibition.[5] I shall attempt to show that this is in fact the case.

II. Terminology: "Person" versus "Human Being"

How is the term "person" to be interpreted? I shall treat the concept of a person as a purely moral concept, free of all descriptive content.

Specifically, in my usage the sentence "X is a person" will be synonymous with the sentence "X has a (serious) moral right to life."

This usage diverges slightly from what is perhaps the more common way of interpreting the term "person" when it is employed as a purely moral term, where to say that X is a person is to say that X has rights. If everything that had rights had a right to life, these interpretations would be extensionally equivalent. But I am inclined to think that it does not follow from acceptable moral principles that whatever has any rights at all has a right to life. My reason is this. Given the choice between being killed and being tortured for an hour, most adult humans would surely choose the latter. So it seems plausible to say it is worse to kill an adult human being than it is to torture him for an hour. In contrast, it seems to me that while it is not seriously wrong to kill a newborn kitten, it is seriously wrong to torture one for an hour. This suggests that newborn kittens may have a right not to be tortured without having a serious right to life. For it seems to be true that an individual has a right to something whenever it is the case that, if he wants that thing, it would be wrong for others to deprive him of it. Then if it is wrong to inflict a certain sensation upon a kitten if it doesn't want to experience that sensation, it will follow that the kitten has a right not to have sensation inflicted upon it.[6] I shall return to this example later. My point here is merely that it provides some reason for holding that it does not follow from acceptable moral principles that if something has any rights at all, it has a serious right to life.

There has been a tendency in recent discussions of abortion to use expressions such as "person" and "human being" interchangeable. B. A. Brody, for example, refers to the difficulty of determining "whether destroying the foetus constitutes the taking of a human life," and suggests it is very plausible that "the taking of a human

life is an action that has bad consequences for
him whose life is being taken."[7] When Brody refers to something as a human life he apparently
construes this as entailing that the thing is a
person. For if every living organism belonging
to the species homo sapiens counted as a human
life, there would be no difficulty in determining
whether a fetus inside a human mother was a human
life.

The same tendency is found in Judith Jarvis
Thomson's article, which opens with the statement:
"Most opposition to abortion relies on the premise
that the fetus is a human being, a person, from
the moment of conception."[8] The same is true of
Roger Wertheimer, who explicitly says: "First off
I should note that the expressions 'a human life,'
'a human being,' 'a person' are virtually interchangeable in this context."[9]

The tendency to use expressions like "person"
and "human being" interchangeably is an unfortunate one. For one thing, it tends to lend covert
support to antiabortionist positions. Given such
usage, one who holds a liberal view of abortion
is put in the position of maintaining that fetuses, at least up to a certain point, are not human
beings. Even philosophers are led astray by this
usage. Thus Wertheimer says that "except for
monstrosities, every member of our species is indubitably a person, a human being, at the very
latest at birth."[10] Is it really <u>indubitable</u> that
newborn babies are persons? Surely this is a wild
contention. Wertheimer is falling prey to the
confusion naturally engendered by the practice of
using "person" and "human being" interchangeably.
Another example of this is provided by Thomson:
"I am inclined to think also that we shall probably have to agree that the fetus has already become a human person well before birth. Indeed, it
comes as a surprise when one first learns how
early in its life it begins to acquire human characteristics. By the tenth week, for example, it
already has a face, arms and legs, fingers and
toes; it has internal organs, and brain activity

is detectable."[11] But what do such physiological characteristics have to do with the question of whether the organism is a person? Thomson, partly, I think, because of the unfortunate use of terminology, does not even raise this question. As a result she virtually takes it for granted that there are some cases in which abortion is "positively indecent."[12]

There is a second reason why using "person" and "human being" interchangeably is unhappy philosophically. If one says that the dispute between pro- and anti-abortionists centers on whether the fetus is a human , it is natural to conclude that it is essentially a disagreement about certain facts, a disagreement about what properties a fetus possesses. Thus Wertheimer says that "if one insists on using the raggy fact-value distinction, then one ought to say that the dispute is over a matter of fact in the sense in which it is a fact that the Negro slaves were human beings."[13] I shall argue that the two cases are not parallel, and that in the case of abortion what is primarily at stake is what moral principles one should accept. If one says that the central issue between conservatives and liberals in the abortion question is whether the fetus is a person, it is clear that the dispute may be either about what properties a thing must have in order to be a person, in order to have a right to life—a moral question—or about whether a fetus at a given stage of development as a matter of fact possesses the properties in question. The temptation to suppose that the disagreement must be a factual one is removed.

It should now be clear why the common practice of using expressions such as "person" and "human being" interchangeably in discussions of abortion is unfortunate. It would perhaps be best to avoid the term "human" altogether, employing instead some expression that is more naturally interpreted as referring to a certain type of biological organism characterized in physiological terms, such as "member of the species Homo sapiens." My own approach will be to use the term "human" only in contexts where it is not philosophically dangerous.

III.   The Basic Issue: When is a Member of the Species Homo Sapiens a Person?

Settling the issue of the morality of abortion and infanticide will involve answering the following questions: What properties must something have to be a person, i.e., to have a serious right to life? At what point in the development of a member of the species Homo sapiens does the organism possess the properties that make it a person? The first question raises a moral issue. To answer it is to decide what basic[14] moral principles involving the ascription of a right to life one ought to accept. The second question raises a purely factual issue, since the properties in question are properties of a purely descriptive sort.

Some writers seem quite pessimistic about the possibility of resolving the question of the morality of abortion. Indeed, some have gone so far as to suggest that the question of whether the fetus is a person is in principle unanswerable: "we seem to be stuck with the indeterminateness of the fetus' humanity."[15] An understanding of some of the sources of this pessimism will, I think, help us to tackle the problem. Let us begin by considering the similarity a number of people have noted between the issue of abortion and the issue of Negro slavery. The question here is why it should be more difficult to decide whether abortion and infanticide are acceptable than it was to decide whether slavery was acceptable. The answer seems to be that in the case of slavery there are moral principles of a quite uncontroversial sort that settle the issue. Thus most people would agree to some such principle as the following: No organism that has experiences, that is capable of thought and of using language, and that has harmed no one, should be made a slave. In the case of abortion, on the other hand, conditions that are

generally agreed to be sufficient grounds for ascribing a right to life to something do not suffice to settle the issue. It is easy to specify
other, purportedly sufficient conditions that will
settle the issue, but no one has been successful
in putting forward considerations that will convince others to accept those additional moral
principles.

I do not share the general pessimism about
the possibility of resolving the issue of abortion
and infanticide because I believe it is possible
to point to a very plausible moral principle dealing with the question of necessary conditions for
something's having a right to life, where the conditions in question will provide an answer to the
question of the permissibility of abortion and
infanticide.

There is a second cause of pessimism that
should be noted before proceeding. It is tied up
with the fact that the development of an organism
is one of gradual and continuous change. Given
this continuity, how is one to draw a line at one
point and declare it permissible to destroy a member of Homo sapiens up to, but not beyond, that
point? Won't there be an arbitrariness about any
point that is chosen? I will return to this worry
shortly. It does not present a serious difficulty
once the basic moral principles relevant to the
ascription of a right to life to an individual
are established.

Let us turn now to the first and most fundamental question: What properties must something
have in order to be a person, i.e., to have a
serious right to life? The claim I wish to defend
is this: An organism possesses a serious right to
life only if it possesses the concept of a self as
a continuing subject of experiences and other mental states, and believes that it is itself such a
continuing entity.

My basic argument in support of this claim,
which I will call the self-consciousness require-

ment, will be clearest, I think, if I first offer a simplified version of the argument, and then consider a modification that seems desirable. The simplified version of my argument is this. To ascribe a right to an individual is to assert something about the prima facie obligations of other individuals to act, or to refrain from acting, in certain ways. However, the obligations in question are conditional ones, being dependent upon the existence of certain desires of the individual to whom the right is ascribed. Thus if an individual asks one to destroy something to which he has a right, one does not violate his right to that thing if one proceeds to destroy it. This suggests the following analysis: "A has a right to X" is roughly synonymous with "If A desires X, then others are under a prima facie obligation to refrain from actions that would deprive him of it."[16]

Although this analysis is initially plausible, there are reasons for thinking it not entirely correct. I will consider these later. Even here, however, some expansion is necessary, since there are features of the concept of a right that are important in the present context, and that ought to be dealt with more explicitly. In particular, it seems to be a conceptual truth that things that lack consciousness, such as ordinary machines, cannot have rights. Does this conceptual truth follow from the above analysis of the concept of a right? The answer depends on how the term "desire" is interpreted. If one adopts a completely behavioristic interpretation of "desire," so that a machine that searches for an electrical outlet in order to get its batteries recharged is described as having a desire to be recharged, then it will not follow from this analysis that objects that lack consciousness cannot have rights. On the other hand, if "desire" is interpreted in such a way that desires are states necessarily standing in some sort of relationship to states of consciousness, it will follow from the analysis that a machine that is not capable of being conscious, and consequently

231

of having desires, cannot have any rights. I
think those who defend analyses of the concept
of a right along the lines of this one do have
in mind an interpretation of the term "desire"
that involves reference to something more than
behavioral dispositions. However, rather than
relying on this, it seems preferable to make such
an interpretation explicit. The following analysis is a natural way of doing that: "A has a
right to X" is roughly synonymous with "A is the
sort of thing that is a subject of experiences
and other mental states, A is capable of desiring
X, and if A does desire X, then others are under
a prima facie obligation to refrain from actions
that would deprive him of it."

The next step in the argument is basically
a matter of applying this analysis to the concept
of a right to life. Unfortunately the expression
"right to life" is not entirely a happy one, since
it suggests that the right in question concerns
the continued existence of a biological organism.
That this is incorrect can be brought out by considering possible ways of violating an individual's right to life. Suppose, for example, that
by some technology of the future the brain of an
adult human were to be completely reprogrammed,
so that the organism wound up with memories (or
rather, apparent memories), beliefs, attitudes,
and personality traits completely different from
those associated with it before it was subjected
to reprogramming. In such a case one would surely say that an individual had been destroyed, that
an adult human's right to life had been violated,
even though no biological organism had been killed.
This example shows that the expression "right to
life" is misleading, since what one is really concerned about is not just the continued existence
of a biological organism, but the right of a subject of experiences and other mental states to
continue to exist.

Given this more precise description of the
right with which we are here concerned, we are now
in a position to apply the analysis of the concept

of a right stated above. When we do so we find that the statement "A has a right to continue to exist as a subject of experiences and other mental states" is roughly synonymous with the statement "A is a subject of experiences and other mental states, A is capable of desiring to continue to exist as a subject of experiences and other mental states, and if A does desire to continue to exist as such an entity, then others are under a prima facie obligation not to prevent him from doing so."

The final stage in the argument is simply a matter of asking what must be the case if something is to be capable of having a desire to continue existing as a subject of experiences and other mental states. The basic point here is that the desires a thing can have are limited by the concepts it possesses. For the fundamental way of describing a given desire is as a desire that a certain proposition be true.[17] Then, since one cannot desire that a certain proposition be true unless one understands it, and since one cannot understand it without possessing the concepts involved in it, it follows that the desires one can have are limited by the concepts one possesses. Applying this to the present case results in the conclusion that an entity cannot be the sort of thing that can desire that a subject of experiences and other mental states exist unless it possesses the concept of such a subject. Moreover, an entity cannot desire that it itself continue existing as a subject of experiences and other mental states unless it believes that it is now such a subject. This completes the justification of the claim that it is a necessary condition of something's having a serious right to life that it possess the concept of a self as a continuing subject of experiences, and that it believe that it is itself such an entity.

Let us now consider a modification in the above argument that seems desirable. This modification concerns the crucial conceptual claim advanced about the relationship between ascription of rights and ascription of the corresponding desires. Certain situations suggest that there may be exceptions to the claim that if a person doesn't desire something, one cannot violate his right to it. There are three types of situations that call this claim into question: (i) situations in which an individual's desires reflect a state of emotional disturbance; (ii) situations in which a previously conscious individual is temporarily unconscious; (iii) situations in which an individual's desires have been distorted by conditioning or by indoctrination.

As an example of the first, consider a case in which an adult human falls into a state of depression which his psychiatrist recognizes as temporary. While in the state he tells people he wishes he were dead. His psychiatrist, accepting the view that there can be no violation of an individual's right to life unless the individual has a desire to live, decides to let his patient have his way and kills him. Or consider a related case in which one person gives another a drug that produces a state of temporary depression; the recipient expresses a wish that he were dead. The person who administered the drug then kills him. Doesn't one want to say in both these cases that the agent did something seriously wrong in killing the other person? And isn't the reason the action was seriously wrong in each case the fact that it violated the individual's right to life? If so, the right to life cannot be linked with a desire to live in the way claimed above.

The second set of situations are ones in which an individual is unconscious for some reason—that is, he is sleeping, or drugged, or in a temporary coma. Does an individual in such a state have any desires? People do sometimes say that an unconscious individual wants something, but it might be argued that if such talk is not to be simply false it must be interpreted as actually referring to the desires the individual would have if he were now conscious. Consequently, if the analysis of the concept of a right proposed above were correct, it would follow that one does not violate an individual's right if one takes his car, or kills him, while he is asleep.

Finally, consider situations in which an individual's desires have been distorted, either by inculcation of irrational beliefs or by direct conditioning. Thus an individual may permit someone to kill him because he has been convinced that if he allows himself to be sacrificed to the gods he will be gloriously rewarded in a life to come. Or an individual may be enslaved after first having been conditioned to desire a life of slavery. Doesn't one want to say that in the former case an individual's right to life has been violated, and in the latter his right to freedom?

Situations such as these strongly suggest that even if an individual doesn't want something, it is still possible to violate his right to it. Some modification of the earlier account of the concept of a right thus seems in order. The analysis given covers, I believe, the paradigmatic cases of violation of an individual's rights, but there are other, secondary cases where one also wants to say that someone's right has been violated which are not included.

Precisely how the revised analysis should be formulated is unclear. Here it will be sufficient merely to say that, in view of the above, an individual's right to X can be violated not only when he desires X, but also when he would now desire X were it not for one of the following: (i) he is in an emotionally unbalanced state; (ii) he is temporarily unconscious; (iii) he has been conditioned to desire the absence of X.

The critical point now is that, even given this extension of the conditions under which an individual's right to something can be violated, it is still true that one's right to something can be violated only when one has the conceptual capability of desiring the thing in question. For example, an individual who would now desire not to be a slave if he weren't emotionally unbalanced, or if he weren't temporarily unconscious, or if he hadn't previously been conditioned to want to be a slave, must possess the concepts involved in the desire not to be a slave. Since it is really only the conceptual capability presupposed by the desire to continue existing as a subject of experiences and other mental states, and not the desire itself, that enters into the above argument, the modification required in the account of the conditions under which an individual's rights can be violated does not undercut my defense of the self-consciousness requirement.[18]

To sum up, my argument has been that having a right to life presupposes that one is capable of desiring to continue existing as a subject of experiences and other mental states. This in turn presupposes both that one has the concept of such a continuing entity and that one believes that one is oneself such an entity. So an entity that lacks such a consciousness of itself as a continuing subject of mental states does not have a right to life.

It would be natural to ask at this point whether satisfaction of this requirement is not only necessary but also sufficient to ensure that a thing has a right to life. I am inclined to an affirmative answer. However, the issue is not urgent in the present context, since as long as the requirement is in fact a necessary one we have the basis of an adequate defense of abortion and infanticide. If an organism must satisfy some other condition before it has a serious right to life, the result will merely be that the interval during which infanticide is morally permissible may be somewhat longer. Although the point at which an organism first achieves self-consciousness and hence the capacity of desiring to continue existing as a subject of experiences and other mental states may be a theoretically incorrect cutoff point, it is at least a morally safe one: any error it involves is on the side of caution.

IV. Some Critical Comments on Alternative
      Proposals

        I now want to compare the line of demarcation
I am proposing with the cutoff points traditionally
advanced in discussions of abortion. My fundamental claim will be that none of these cutoff points
can be defended by appeal to plausible, basic moral
principles. The main suggestions as to the point
past which it is seriously wrong to destroy something that will develop into an adult member of
the species Homo sapiens are these: (a) conception; (b) the attainment of human form; (c) the
achievement of the ability to move about spontaneously; (d) viability; (e) birth.[19] The corresponding moral principles suggested by these cutoff points are as follows: (1) It is seriously
wrong to kill an organism, from a zygote on, that
belongs to the species Homo sapiens. (2) It is
seriously wrong to kill an organism that belongs
to Homo sapiens and that has achieved human form.
(3) It is seriously wrong to kill an organism
that is a member of Homo sapiens and that is capable of spontaneous movement. (4) It is seriously wrong to kill an organism that belongs to Homo
sapiens and that is capable of existing outside
the womb. (5) It is seriously wrong to kill an
organism that is a member of Homo sapiens that is
no longer in the womb.

        My first comment is that it would not do
simply to omit the reference to membership in the
species Homo sapiens from the above principles,
with the exception of principle (2). For then
the principles would be applicable to animals in
general, and one would be forced to conclude that
it was seriously wrong to abort a cat fetus, or
that it was seriously wrong to abort a motile cat
fetus, and so on.

        The second and crucial comment is that none
of the five principles given above can plausibly
be viewed as a basic moral principle. To accept
any of them as such would be akin to accepting as
a basic moral principle the proposition that it is

237

morally permissible to enslave black members of the species Homo sapiens but not white members. Why should it be seriously wrong to kill an unborn member of the species Homo sapiens but not seriously wrong to kill an unborn kitten? Difference in species is not per se a morally relevant difference. If one holds that it is seriously wrong to kill an unborn member of the species Homo sapiens but not an unborn kitten, one should be prepared to point to some property that is morally significant and that is possessed by unborn members of Homo sapiens but not by unborn kittens. Similarly, such a property must be identified if one believes it seriously wrong to kill unborn members of Homo sapiens that have achieved viability but not seriously wrong to kill unborn kittens that have achieved that state.

What property might account for such a difference? That is to say, what <u>basic</u> moral principles might a person who accepts one of these five principles appeal to in support of his secondary moral judgment? Why should events such as the achievement of human form, or the achievement of the ability to move about, or the achievement of viability, or birth serve to endow something with a right to life? What the liberal must do is to show that these events involve changes, or are associated with changes, that are morally relevant.

Let us now consider reasons why the events involved in cutoff points (b) through (e) are not morally relevant, beginning with the last two: viability and birth. The fact that an organism is not physiologically dependent upon another organism, or is capable of such physiological independence, is surely irrelevant to whether the organism has a right to life. In defense of this contention, consider a speculative case where a fetus is able to learn a language while in the womb. One would surely not say that the fetus had no right to life until it emerged from the womb, or until it was capable of existing outside the womb. A less speculative example is the case of Siamese twins who have learned to speak. One doesn't want

238

to say that since one of the twins would die were the two to be separated, it therefore has no right to life. Consequently it seems difficult to disagree with the conservative's claim that an organism which lacks a right to life before birth or before becoming viable cannot acquire this right immediately upon birth or upon becoming viable.

This does not, however, completely rule out viability as a line of demarcation. For instead of defending viability as a cutoff point on the ground that only then does a fetus acquire a right to life, it is possible to argue rather that when one organism is physiologically dependent upon another, the former's right to life may conflict with the latter's right to use its body as it will, and moreover, that the latter's right to do what it wants with its body may often take precedence over the other organism's right to life. Thomson has defended this view: "I am arguing only that having a right to life does not guarantee having either a right to the use of or a right to be allowed continued use of another person's body—even if one needs it for life itself. So the right to life will not serve the opponents of abortion in the very simple and clear way in which they seem to have thought it would."[20] I believe that Thomson is right in contending that philosophers have been altogether too casual in assuming that if one grants the fetus a serious right to life, one must accept a conservative position on abortion.[21] I also think the only defense of viability as a cutoff point which has any hope of success at all is one based on the considerations she advances. I doubt very much, however, that this defense of abortion is ultimately tenable. I think that one can grant even stronger assumptions than those made by Thomson and still argue persuasively for a semiconservative view. What I have in mind is this. Let it be granted, for the sake of argument, that a woman's right to free her body of parasites which will inhibit her freedom of action and possibly impair her health is stronger than the parasite's right to life, and is so even if the parasite has as much right to

life as an adult human. One can still argue that
abortion ought not to be permitted. For if A's
right is stronger than B's, and it is impossible
to satisfy both, it does not follow that A's
should be satisfied rather than B's. It may be
possible to compensate A if his right isn't satisfied, but impossible to compensate B if his right
isn't satisfied. In such a case the best thing to
do may be to satisfy B's claim and to compensate
A. Abortion may be a case in point. If the fetus
has a right to life and the right is not satisfied, there is certainly no way the fetus can be
compensated. On the other hand, if the woman's
right to rid her body of harmful and annoying
parasites is not satisfied, she can be compensated. Thus it would seem that the just thing to do
would be to prohibit abortion, but to compensate
women for the burden of carrying a parasite to
term. Then, however, we are back at a (modified)
conservative position.[22] Our conclusion must be
that it appears unlikely there is any satisfactory
defense either of viability or of birth as cutoff
points.

Let us now consider the third suggested line
of demarcation, the achievement of the power to
move about spontaneously. It might be argued
that acquiring this power is a morally relevant
event on the grounds that there is a connection
between the concept of an agent and the concept
of a person, and being motile is an indication
that a thing is an agent.[23]

It is difficult to respond to this suggestion
unless it is made more specific. Given that one's
interest here is in defending a certain cutoff
point, it is natural to interpret the proposal as
suggesting that motility is a necessary condition
of an organism's having a right to life. But this
won't do, because one certainly wants to ascribe a
right to life to adult humans who are completely
paralyzed. Maybe the suggestion is rather that
motility is a sufficient condition of something's
having a right to life. However, it is clear that
motility alone is not sufficient, since this would

imply that all animals, and also certain machines, have a right to life. Perhaps, then, the most reasonable interpretation of the claim is that motility together with some other property is a sufficient condition of something's having a right to life, where the other property will have to be a property possessed by unborn members of the species Homo sapiens but not by unborn members of other familiar species.

The central question, then, is what this other property is. Until one is told, it is very difficult to evaluate either the moral claim that motility together with that property is a sufficient basis for ascribing to an organism a right to life or the factual claim that a motile human fetus possesses that property while a motile fetus belonging to some other species does not. A conservative would presumably reject motility as a cutoff point by arguing that whether an organism has a right to life depends only upon its potentialities, which are of course not changed by its becoming motile. If, on the other hand, one favors a liberal view of abortion, I think that one can attack this third suggested cutoff point, in its unspecified form, only by determining what properties are necessary, or what properties sufficient, for an individual to have a right to life. Thus I would base my rejection of motility as a cutoff point on my claim, defended above, that a necessary condition of an organism's possessing a right to life is that it conceive of itself as a continuing subject of experiences and other mental states.

The second suggested cutoff point—the development of a recognizably human form—can be dismissed fairly quickly. I have already remarked that membership in a particular species is not itself a morally relevant property. For it is obvious that if we encountered other "rational animals," such as Martians, the fact that their physiological makeup was very different from our own would not be grounds for denying them a right to life.[24] Similarly, it is clear that the

241

development of human form is not in itself a morally relevant event. Nor do there seem to be any grounds for holding that there is some other change, associated with this event, that is morally relevant. The appeal of this second cutoff point is, I think, purely emotional.

The overall conclusion seems to be that it is very difficult to defend the cutoff points traditionally advanced by those who advocate either a moderate or a liberal position on abortion. The reason is that there do not seem to be any basic moral principles one can appeal to in support of the cutoff points in question. We must now consider whether the conservative is any better off.

V. Refutation of the Conservative Position

Many have felt that the conservative's position is more defensible than the liberal's because the conservative can point to the gradual and continuous development of an organism as it changes from a zygote to an adult human being. He is then in a position to argue that it is morally arbitrary for the liberal to draw a line at some point in this continuous process and to say that abortion is permissible before, but not after, that particular point. The liberal's reply would presumably be that the emphasis upon the continuity of the process is misleading. What the conservative is really doing is simply challenging the liberal to specify the properties a thing must have in order to be a person, and to show that the developing organism does acquire the properties at the point selected by the liberal. The liberal may then reply that the difficulty he has meeting this challenge should not be taken as grounds for rejecting his position. For the conservative cannot meet this challenge either; the conservative is equally unable to say what properties something must have if it is to have a right to life.

Although this rejoinder does not dispose of the conservative's argument, it is not without bite. For defenders of the view that abortion is

242

always wrong have failed to face up to the question of the basic moral principles on which their position rests. They have been content to assert the wrongness of killing any organism, from a zygote on, if that organism is a member of the species Homo sapiens. But they have overlooked the point that this cannot be an acceptable basic moral principle, since difference in species is not in itself a morally relevant difference. The conservative can reply, however, that it is possible to defend his position—but not the liberal's —without getting clear about the properties a thing must possess if it is to have a right to life. The conservative's defense will rest upon the following two claims: first, that there is a property, even if one is unable to specify what it is, that (i) is possessed by adult humans, and (ii) endows any organism possessing it with a serious right to life. Second, that if there are properties which satisfy (i) and (ii) above, at least one of those properties will be such that any organism potentially possessing that property has a serious right to life even now, simply by virtue of that potentiality, where an organism possesses a property potentially if it will come to have that property in the normal course of its development. The second claim—which I shall refer to as the potentiality principle—is critical to the conservative's defense. Because of it he is able to defend his position without deciding what properties a thing must possess in order to have a right to life. It is enough to know that adult members of Homo sapiens do have such a right. For then one can conclude that any organism which belongs to the species Homo sapiens, from a zygote on, must also have a right to life by virtue of the potentiality principle.

The liberal, by contrast, cannot mount a comparable argument. He cannot defend his position without offering at least a partial answer to the question of what properties a thing must possess in order to have a right to life.

The importance of the potentiality principle,

243

however, goes beyond the fact that it provides support for the conservative's position. If the principle is unacceptable, then so is his position. For if the conservative cannot defend the view that an organism's having certain potentiality is sufficient grounds for ascribing to it a right to life, his claim that a fetus which is a member of Homo sapiens has a right to life can be attacked as follows. The reason an adult member of Homo sapiens has a right to life, but an infant ape does not, is that there are certain psychological properties which the former possesses and the latter lacks. Now, even if one is unsure exactly what these psychological properties are, it is clear that an organism in the early stages of development from a zygote into an adult member of Homo sapiens does not possess these properties. One need merely compare a human fetus with an ape fetus. What mental states does the former enjoy that the latter does not? Surely it is reasonable to hold that there are no significant differences in their respective mental lives—assuming that one wishes to ascribe any mental states at all to such organisms. (Does a zygote have a mental life? Does it have experiences? Or beliefs? Or desires?) There are, of course, physiological differences, but these are not in themselves morally significant. If one held that potentialities were relevant to the ascription of a right to life, one could argue that the physiological differences, though not morally significant in themselves, are morally significant by virtue of their causal consequences: they will lead to later psychological differences that are morally relevant, and for this reason the physiological differences are themselves morally significant. But if the potentiality principle is not available, this line of argument cannot be used, and there will then be no differences between a human fetus and an ape fetus that the conservative can use as grounds for ascribing a serious right to life to the former but not to the latter.

It is therefore tempting to conclude that the conservative view of abortion is acceptable if and

only if the potentiality principle is acceptable.
But to say that the conservative position can be
defended if the potentiality principle is acceptable is to assume that the argument is over once
it is granted that the fetus has a right to life,
and, as was noted above, Thomson has shown that
there are serious gorunds for questioning this
assumption. In any case, the important point here
is that the conservative position on abortion is
acceptable <u>only if</u> the potentiality principle is
sound.

One way to attack the potentiality principle
is simply to argue in support of the self-consciousness requirement—the claim that only an
organism that conceives of itself as a continuing
subject of experiences has a right to life. For
this requirement, when taken together with the
claim that there is at least one property, possessed by adult humans, such that any organism
possessing it has a serious right to life, entails the denial of the potentiality principle.
Or at least this is so if we add the uncontroversial empirical claim that an organism that
will in the normal course of events develop into
an adult human does not from the very beginning
of its existence possess a concept of a continuing subject of experiences together with a belief
that it is itself such an entity.

I think it best, however, to scrutinize the
potentiality principle itself, and not to base
one's case against it simply on the self-consciousness requirement. Perhaps the first point
to note is that the potentiality principle should
not be confused with principles such as the following: the value of an object is related to the
value of the things into which it can develop.
This "valuation principle" is rather vague. There
are ways of making it more precise, but we need
not consider these here. Suppose now that one
were to speak not of a right to life, but of the
value of life. It would then be easy to make the
mistake of thinking that the valuation principle
was relevant to the potentiality principle—

indeed, that it entailed it. But an individual's right to life is not based on the value of his life. To say that the world would be better off if it contained fewer people is not to say that it would be right to achieve such a better world by killing some of the present inhabitants. If having a right to life were a matter of a thing's value, then a thing's potentialities, being connected with its expected value, would clearly be relevant to the question of what rights it had. Conversely, once one realizes that a thing's rights are not a matter of its value, I think it becomes clear that an organism's potentialities are irrelevant to the question of whether it has a right to life.

But let us now turn to the task of finding a direct refutation of the potentiality principle. The basic issue is this. Is there any property J which satisfies the following conditions: (1) There is a property K such that any individual possessing property K has a right to life, and there is a scientific law L to the effect that any organism possessing property J will in the normal course of events come to possess property K at some later time. (2) Given the relationship between property J and property K just described, anything possessing property J has a right to life. (3) If property J were not related to property K in the way indicated, it would not be the case that anything possessing property J thereby had a right to life. In short, the question is whether there is a property J that bestows a right to life on an organism only because J stands in a certain causal relationship to a second property K, which is such that anything possessing that property ipso facto has a right to life.

My argument turns upon the following critical principle: Let C be a causal process that normally leads to outcome E. Let A be an action that initiates process C, and B be an action involving a minimal expenditure of energy that stops process C before outcome E occurs. Assume further that actions A and B do not have any other

246

consequences, and that E is the only morally significant outcome of process C. Then there is no moral difference between intentionally performing action B and intentionally refraining from performing action A, assuming identical motivation in both cases. This principle, which I shall refer to as the moral symmetry principle with respect to action and inaction, would be rejected by some philosophers. They would argue that there is an important distinction to be drawn between "what we owe people in the form of aid and what we owe them in the way of non-interference,"[25] and that the latter, "negative duties," are duties that it is more serious to neglect than the former, "positive" ones. This view arises from an intuitive response to examples such as the following. Even if it is wrong not to send food to starving people in other parts of the world, it is more wrong still to kill someone. And isn't the conclusion, then, that one's obligation to refrain from killing someone is a more serious obligation than one's obligation to save lives?

I want to argue that this is not the correct conclusion. I think it is tempting to draw this conclusion if one fails to consider the motivation that is likely to be associated with the respective actions. If someone performs an action he knows will kill someone else, this will usually be grounds for concluding that he wanted to kill the person in question. In contrast, failing to help someone may indicate only apathy, laziness, selfishness, or an amoral outlook: the fact that a person knowingly allows another to die will not normally be grounds for concluding that he desired that person's death. Someone who knowingly kills another is more likely to be seriously defective from a moral point of view than someone who fails to save another's life.

If we are not to be led to false conclusions by our intuitions about certain cases, we must explicitly assume identical motivations in the two situations. Compare, for example, the following: (1) Jones sees that Smith will be killed by a bomb unless he warns him. Jones's reaction is: "How lucky, it will save me the trouble of killing Smith myself." So Jones allows Smith to be killed by the bomb, even though he could easily have warned him. (2) Jones wants Smith dead, and therefore shoots him. Is one to say there is a significant difference between the wrongness of Jones's behavior in these two cases? Surely not. This shows the mistake of drawing a distinction between positive duties and negative duties and holding that the latter impose stricter obligations than the former. The difference in our intuitions about situations that involve giving aid to others and corresponding situations that involve not interfering with others is to be explained by reference to probable differences in the motivations operating in the two situations, and not by reference to a distinction between positive and negative duties. For once it is specified that the motivation is the same in the two situations, we realize that inaction is as wrong in the one case as action is in the other.

There is another point that may be relevant. Action involves effort, while inaction usually does not. It usually does not require any effort on my part to refrain from killing someone, but saving someone's life will require an expenditure of energy. One must then ask how large a sacrifice a person is morally required to make to save the life of another. If the sacrifice of time and energy is quite large it may be that one is not morally obliged to save the life of another in that situation. Superficial reflection upon such cases might easily lead us to introduce the distinction between positive and negative duties, but again it is clear that this would be a mistake. The point is not that one has a greater duty to refrain from killing others than to perform positive actions that will save them. It is rather that positive actions require effort, and this means that in deciding what to do a person has to take into account his own right to do what he wants with his life, and not only the other person's right to life. To avoid this confusion, we should confine ourselves to comparisons between situations in which the positive action involves minimal effort.

The moral symmetry principle, as formulated above, explicitly takes these two factors into account. It applies only to pairs of situations in which the motivations are identical and the positive action involves minimal effort. Without these restrictions, the principle would be open to serious objection; with them, it seems perfectly acceptable. For the central objection to it rests on the claim that we must distinguish positive from negative duties and recognize that negative duties impose stronger obligations than positive ones. I have tried to show how this claim derives from an unsound account of our moral intuitions about certain situations.

My argument against the potentiality principle can now be stated. Suppose at some future time a chemical were to be discovered which when injected into the brain of a kitten would cause the kitten to develop into a cat possessing a brain of the sort possessed by humans, and consequently into a cat having all the psychological capabilities characteristic of adult humans. Such cats would be able to think, to use language, and so on. Now it would surely be morally indefensible in such a situation to ascribe a serious right to life to members of the species Homo sapiens without also ascribing it to cats that have undergone such a process of development: there would be no morally significant differences.

Secondly, it would not be seriously wrong to refain from injecting a newborn kitten with the special chemical, and to kill it instead. The fact that one could initiate a causal process that would transform a kitten into an entity that would eventually possess properties such that anything possessing them ipso facto has a serious right to life does not mean that the kitten has a serious right to life even before it has been subjected to the process of injection and transformation.

The possibility of transforming kittens into persons will not make it any more wrong to kill newborn kittens than it is now.

Thirdly, in view of the symmetry principle, if it is not seriously wrong to refrain from initiating such a causal process, neither is it seriously wrong to interfere with such a process. Suppose a kitten is accidentally injected with the chemical. As long as it has not yet developed those properties that in themselves endow something with a right to life, there cannot be anything wrong with interfering with the causal process and preventing the development of the properties in question. Such interference might be accomplished either by injecting the kitten with some "neutralizing" chemical or simply by killing it.

But if it is not seriously wrong to destroy an injected kitten which will naturally develop the properties that bestow a right to life, neither can it be seriously wrong to destroy a member of Homo sapiens which lacks such properties, but will naturally come to have them. The potentialities are the same in both cases. The only difference is that in the case of a human fetus the potentialities have been present from the beginning of the organism's development, while in the case of the kitten they have been present only from the time it was injected with the special chemical. This difference in the time at which the potentialities were acquired is a morally irrelevant difference.

It should be emphasized that I am not here assuming that a human fetus does not possess properties which in themselves, and irrespective of their causal relationships to other properties, provide grounds for ascribing a right to life to whatever possesses them. The point is merely that if it is seriously wrong to kill something, the reason cannot be that the thing will later acquire properties that in themselves provide something with a right to life.

250

Finally, it is reasonable to believe that there are properties possessed by adult members of Homo sapiens which establish their right to life, and also that any normal human fetus will come to possess those properties shared by adult humans. But it has just been shown that if it is wrong to kill a human fetus, it cannot be because of its potentialities. One is therefore forced to conclude that the conservative's potentiality principle is false.

In short, anyone who wants to defend the potentiality principle must either argue against the moral symmetry principle or hold that in a world in which kittens could be transformed into "rational animals" it would be seriously wrong to kill newborn kittens. It is hard to believe there is much to be said for the latter moral claim. Consequently one expects the conservative's rejoinder to be directed against the symmetry principle. While I have not attempted to provide a thorough defense of that principle, I have tried to show that what seems to be the most important objection to it—the one that appeals to a distinction between positive and negative duties— is based on a superficial analysis of our moral intuitions. I believe that a more thorough examination of the symmetry principle would show it to be sound. If so, we should reject the potentiality principle, and the conservative position on abortion as well.

VI. Summary and Conclusions

Let us return now to my basic claim, the self-consciousness requirement: An organism possesses a serious right to life only if it possesses the concept of a self as a continuing subject of experiences and other mental states, and believes that it is itself such a continuing entity. My defense of this claim has been twofold. I have offered a direct argument in support of it, and I have tried to show that traditional conservative and liberal views on abortion and infanticide, which involve a rejection of it, are unsound. I

251

now want to mention one final reason why my claim
should be accepted. Consider the example mentioned in section II—that of killing, as opposed to
torturing, newborn kittens. I suggested there
that while in the case of adult humans most people
would consider it worse to kill an individual than
to torture him for an hour, we do not usually view
the killing of a newborn kitten as morally outra-
geous, although we would regard someone who tortured a newborn kitten for an hour as heinously
evil. I pointed out that a possible conclusion
that might be drawn from this is that newborn kittens have a right not to be tortured, but do not
have a serious right to life. If this is the correct conclusion, how is one to explain it? One
merit of the self-consciousness requirement is
that it provides an explanation of this situation.
The reason a newborn kitten does not have a right
to life is explained by the fact that it does not
possess the concept of a self. But how is one to
explain the kitten's having a right not to be tortured? The answer is that a desire not to suffer
pain can be ascribed to something without assuming
that it has any concept of a continuing self. For
while something that lacks the concept of a self
cannot desire that a self not suffer, it can desire that a given sensation not exist. The state
desired—the absence of a particular sensation, or
of sensations of a certain sort—can be described
in a purely phenomenalistic language, and hence
without the concept of a continuing self. So long
as the newborn kitten possesses the relevant phe-
nomenal concepts, it can truly be said to desire
that a certain sensation not exist. So we can
ascribe to it a right not to be tortured even
though, since it lacks the concept of a continuing
self, we cannot ascribe to it a right to life.

This completes my discussion of the basic
moral principles involved in the issue of abortion
and infanticide. But I want to comment upon an
important factual question, namely, at what point
an organism comes to possess the concept of a self
as a continuing subject of experiences and other
mental states, together with the belief that it is

itself such a continuing entity. This is obviously a matter for detailed psychological investigation, but everyday observation makes it perfectly clear, I believe, that a newborn baby does not possess the concept of a continuing self, any more than a newborn kitten possesses such a concept. If so, infanticide during a time interval shortly after birth must be morally acceptable.

But where is the line to be drawn? What is the cutoff point? If one maintained, as some philosophers have, that an individual possesses concepts only if he can express these concepts in language, it would be a matter of everyday observation whether or not a given organism possessed the concept of a continuing self. Infanticide would then be permissible up to the time an organism learned how to use certain expressions. However, I think the claim that acquisition of concepts is dependent on acquisition of language is mistaken. For example, one wants to ascribe mental states of a conceptual sort—such as beliefs and desires—to organisms that are incapable of learning a language. This issue of prelinguistic understanding is clearly outside the scope of this discussion. My point is simply that if an organism can acquire concepts without thereby acquiring a way of expressing those concepts linguistically, the question of whether a given organism possesses the concept of a self as a continuing subject of experiences and other mental states, together with the belief that it is itself such a continuing entity, may be a question that requires fairly subtle experimental techniques to answer.

If this view of the matter is roughly correct, there are two worries one is left with at the level of practical moral decisions, one of which may turn out to be deeply disturbing. The lesser worry is where the line is to be drawn in the case of infanticide. It is not troubling because there is no serious need to know the exact point at which a human infant acquires a right to life. For in the vast majority of cases in which infanticide is desirable, its desirability will be

253

apparent within a short time after birth. Since it is virtually certain that an infant at such a stage of its development does not possess the concept of a continuing self, and thus does not possess a serious right to life, there is excellent reason to believe that infanticide is morally permissible in most cases where it is otherwise desirable. The practical moral problem can thus be satisfactorily handled by choosing some period of time, such as a week after birth, as the interval during which infanticide will be permitted. This interval could then be modified once psychologists have established the point at which a human organism comes to believe that it is a continuing subject of experiences and other mental states.

The troubling worry is whether adult animals belonging to species other than Homo sapiens may not also possess a serious right to life. For once one says that an organism can possess the concept of a continuing self, together with the belief that it is itself such an entity, without having any way of expressing that concept and that belief linguistically, one has to face up to the question of whether animals may not possess properties that bestow a serious right to life upon them. The suggestion itself is a familiar one, and one that most of us are accustomed to dismiss very casually. The line of thought advanced here suggests that this attitude may turn out to be tragically mistaken. Once one reflects upon the question of the basic moral principles involved in the ascription of a right to life to organisms, one may find himself driven to conclude that our everyday treatment of animals is morally indefensible, and that we are in fact murdering innocent persons.

Notes

[1] I am grateful to a number of people, particularly the Editors of Philosophy & Public Affairs, Rodelia Hapke, and Walter Kaufmann, for their helpful comments. It should not, of course, be inferred that they share the views expressed in this paper.

[2]Judith Jarvis Thomson, in her article "A Defense of Abortion," <u>Philosophy & Public Affairs</u> I, no. I (Fall 1971): 47-66, has argued with great force and ingenuity that this conclusion is mistaken. I will comment on her argument later in this paper.

[3]While this is the position conservatives tend to hold, it is not clear that it is the position they ought to hold. For if the fetus is a person it is far from clear that it is permissible to destroy it to save the mother. Two moral principles lend support to the view that it is the fetus which should live. First, other things being equal, should not one give something to a person who has had less rather than to a person who has had more? The mother has had a chance to live, while the fetus has not. The choice is thus between giving the mother more of an opportunity to live while giving the fetus none at all and giving the fetus an opportunity to enjoy life while not giving the mother a further opportunity to do so. Surely fairness requires the latter. Secondly, since the fetus has a greater life expectancy than the mother, one is in effect distributing more goods by choosing the life of the fetus over the life of the mother.

The position I am here recommending to the conservative should not be confused with the offical Catholic position. The Catholic Church holds that it is seriously wrong to kill a fetus directly even if failure to do will result in the death of <u>both</u> the mother and the fetus. This perverse value judgment is not part of the conservative's position.

[4]Section 230.3 of the American Law Institute's <u>Model Penal Code</u> (Philadephia, 1962). There is some interesting, though at time confused, discussion of the proposed code in <u>Model Penal Code—Tentative Draft No. 9</u> (Philadelphia, 1959), pp. 146-162.

[5]A clear example of such an unwillingness to entertain seriously the possibility that moral judgments widely accepted in one's own society may nevertheless be incorrect is provided by Roger Wertheimer's superficial dismissal of infanticide

on pages 69-70 of his article "Understanding the Abortion Argument," Philosophy & Public Affairs I, no. I (Fall 1971): 67-95.

⁶Compare the discussion of the concept of a right offered by Richard B. Brandt in his Ethical Theory (Englewood Cliffs, N. J., 1959), pp. 434-441. As Brandt points out, some philosophers have maintained that only things that can claim rights can have rights. I agree with Brandt's view that "inability to claim does not destroy the right" (p. 440).

⁷B. A. Brody, "Abortion and the law," Journal of Philosophy, LXVIII, no. 12 (17 June 1971): 357-369. See pp. 357-358.

⁸Thomson, "A Defense of Abortion," p. 47.

⁹Wertheimer, "Understanding the Abortion Argument," p. 69.

¹⁰Ibid.

¹¹Thomson, "A Defense of Abortion," pp. 47-48.

¹²Ibid., p. 65.

¹³Wertheimer, "Understanding the Abortion Argument," p. 78.

¹⁴A moral principle accepted by a person is basic for him if and only if his acceptance of it is not dependent upon any of his (nonmoral) factual beliefs. That is, no change in his factual beliefs would cause him to abandon the principle in question.

¹⁵Wertheimer, "Understanding the Abortion Argument," p. 88.

¹⁶Again, compare the analysis defended by Brandt in Ethical Theory, pp. 434-441.

¹⁷In everyday life one often speaks of desiring things, such as an apple or a newspaper. Such talk is elliptical, the context together with one's ordinary beliefs serving to make it clear that one wants to eat the apple and read the newspaper. To say what one desires is that a certain proposition be true should not be construed as involving any particular ontological commitment. The point is merely that it is sentences such as "John wants it to be the case that he is eating an apple in the next few minutes" that provide a completely explicit description of a person's desires. If one fails to use such sentences one can be badly misled

about what concepts are presupposed by a particular desire.

[18]There are, however, situations other than
those discussed here which might seem to count
against the claim that a person cannot have a
right unless he is conceptually capable of having
the corresponding desire. Can't a young child,
for example, have a right to an estate, even
though he may not be conceptually capable of wanting the estate? It is clear that such situations
have to be carefully considered if one is to arrive at a satisfactory account of the concept of
a right. My inclination is to say that the correct description is not that the child now has a
right to the estate, but that he will come to have
such a right when he is mature, and that in the
meantime no one else has a right to the estate.
My reason for saying that the child does not now
have a right to the estate is that he cannot now
do things with the estate, such as selling it or
giving it away, that he will be able to do later
on.

[19]Another frequent suggestion as to the cutoff
point not listed here is quickening. I omit it
because it seems clear that if abortion after
quickening is wrong, its wrongness must be tied
up with the motility of the fetus, not with the
mother's awareness of the fetus' ability to move
about.

[20]Thomson, "A Defense of Abortion," p. 56.

[21]A good example of a failure to probe this
issue is provided by Brody's "Abortion and the
Law."

[22]Admittedly the modification is a substantial
one, since given a society that refused to compensate women, a woman who had an abortion would
not be doing anything wrong.

[23]Compare Wertheimer's remarks, "Understanding
the Abortion Argument," p. 79.

[24]This requires qualification. If their central nervous systems were radically different from
ours, it might be thought that one would not be
justified in ascribing to them mental states of an
experiential sort. And then, since it seems to be
a conceptual truth that only things having experi-

ential states can have rights, one would be forced to conclude that one was not justified in ascribing any rights to them.

25Philippa Foot, "The Problem of Abortion and the Doctrine of the Double Effect," The Oxford Review 5 (1967): 5-15. See the discussion on pp. 11ff.

III

SOCIAL RELATIONS

Introduction

A change occurs in adults around the age 38 to 42. They find themselves entering a time of life that is different from what they had known earlier. Sometimes the change is radical and quick and sometimes it is slow and almost imperceptible. However it occurs adults begin to recognize physical, emotional, and social differences. Men often notice a slight pouch around the middle that will not go away with dieting and exercise. They find that they are slowing down physically; their bodies will not perform with the ease and vigor of past years, and they do not recoup lost strength easily. At work young people are coming in and are being groomed as the new bright hopes for the company. No longer are they seen as the "young bucks" with a bright future; the future is now. What they will achieve with their business or profession is now being or has been achieved. They are at the end or near the end of the American success syndrome. Some begin looking around for a new source of motivation for working the long hours and giving the level of commitment they had given in the past. Unfortunately, they find little. The reasons for doing the job now seem to be different if they exist at all. At home the family is changing. The wife may be going through the empty nest syndrome; the children are leaving home to make their own way; a new type of relationship in the marriage seems to be needed. These physical, emotional, social, and business changes are called the mid-life crisis.

How the crisis of the middle years is worked through is largely dependent on how well developmental tasks of earlier stages have been accomplished. If intimacy has been established and isolation avoided, if one has been able to lose oneself in the creation of an intimate relation with another person, it is a natural move to caring not only for the children born of that relationship but also for those young adults attempting to make their way in the world. While it may be natural to care, it is not automatic. One can either face the tasks of this period and accomplish them successfully, or one can fail to face them and fail to grow as a person. Erikson calls this choice period Generativity vs. Stagnation. One is now no longer the young person making his way in the world and looking to others for help in doing so; he has made his way in the world and is now looked on for assistance in helping others make their way in the world. If he fails to do so he will be left out of the opportunities of this time in his life, left out of the only opportunities society presents him; he will probably stagnate. There will be nothing for him to do. He will be out of the main stream of society and will be left behind. The normal opportunities for growth will be missed.

To become generative and avoid stagnation, what are the major tasks to be performed? The Adult in mid-life has the responsibility for caring for a number of important areas of society: the economy, the educational system, the health delivery system, and the use of his own wealth. While there may be others these are clearly important areas in which he has legitimate interest. The Adult's relation to these important areas are both remote and immediate. They are remote in that he lives in a society with an economy, an educational system, a health delivery system, and wealth. With the overall pattern and movements in these areas he may have little impact except in so far as he votes or has the political or economic power to effect change. Yet each adult works in a business or a profession that has policies

affecting the economic lives of all those who work
in the organization. Usually he has input into
the organization; sometimes he has control over it.
Also, his children are oftentimes in school or his
employees are in school or their children are in
school and as a businessman, professional, or
worker he has an opportunity to express his opinion about the education of his children and of
those of other families. Health care in his community are also his concern. Again opportunities
to express views are present through the family
doctor, voting for hospital development, the local
newspaper, and the hospital board. The opportunities are present and he must undertake those
that present themselves. Finally he is concerned
with the wealth (however modest) he has accumulated and with that accumulated by society. He
uses it; he does something with it. Thus in these
major areas of concern the adult is faced with the
tasks of caring for and guiding his society as
best he can.

    As he faces the tasks of mid-life the adult
makes decisions in the areas that present themselves: health, education, economy , wealth.
The decisions he makes will be based on those presuppositions about what is true, valuable, and
real. His actions and decisions will manifest a
system of presuppositions, a system of beliefs.
At this point the philosophical issues arise.
What are the beliefs which underlie the decisions
and are those beliefs the most defensible ones?
The adult who faces the mid-life crisis must work
through a web of beliefs which are the glue of
the individual life structure. Those beliefs may
have been carried over from the stage of intimacy
or young adulthood or they may be new ones developed in the attempt to work successfully through
the tasks facing the adult who is attempting to
make this world a better place to live in. Whatever their origin, those beliefs are the basis
for the choices the adult makes and the pattern
of life that develops. The issue of the clarity
and tenability of ones beliefs is, thus, of overriding importance. While all beliefs in the areas

261

of the use of wealth, health care, education, and the economy cannot be discussed, some of the most important ones can be pointed out and investigated.

The economic system of any society is important. The goods and services needed by the society must be provided through society's own production or through imports. With the development of the capitalistic industrial economy in the West during the nineteenth century a major issue has recurred: should capitalism be allowed to function without interference or should the government or people step in to change it? Since the nineteenth century three answers have been given to this question: maintain capitalism without interference, maintain capitalism with interference from the government to mitigate capitalism's human liabilities, and overthrow capitalism and set up a socialist economy. These answers can be seen as beliefs which we can hold as we attempt to insure a stable system of production and of distribution of goods and services for our country. Which belief one holds makes a difference as to what he will chose and the relationships he will establish. Thus it is important to examine ones beliefs and determine their adequacy. Engels contends that the capitalistic economic system will be overthrown and the true socialistic nature of industry will manifest itself in a socialistic order. Popper contends that any type of holistic economic planning will fail to conform to the principles of scientific research. Only piecemeal economic planning can be scientifically accomplished. Thus, Engels addresses one issue: what belief about the nature of economic life is correct? Popper addresses another issue: assuming that the economy can be planned for our well-being, what kind of planning is most defensible?

A second area of interest for the adult in mid-life is how to handle the wealth he has accumulated or that society possesses. This issue is multifaceted. Not many of us have what we would

call wealth. We have assets in life insurance
policies, savings, and real estate, particularly
our homes. But most do not have great holdings.
It is a simple matter to leave the small amount
to our children or heirs. While individually we
may not have much wealth, as a nation we do have
great natural resources. At this point the issue
arises. The natural resources are limited. Oil
reserves will not last long at the present rate
of consumption; and coal reserves will not last
longer than three-hundred years. If we want our
children's children and their children and all
future generations to have adequate natural resources then some kind of conservation program
seems mandatory. Yet, we have the immediate responsibility of providing for the present generation. We will make choices as we face the tasks
of caring for the present society. An important
issue we must face in making those choices is
whether or not we have obligations to future generations in any area including natural resources.
How we act will evidence the beliefs we hold about
how we ought to handle our wealth, both natural
and accumulated. The philosophical issue is not
only what belief we do hold but also whether that
belief is defensible. Golding puts the philosophical issue in the form of a question: what
obligations, if any, do we have to future generations? The answer one gives to that question
will play a significant part in the decisions one
makes in handling his own wealth but also in the
way he uses the natural resources at his disposal—the way he drives his car or the set of the
thermostat at home.

Third, for most adults the educational system of their country has been a topic of concern
for many years. They formerly were interested in
education in the way a person who is going to
school would be or in the way a person who has
small children would be interested. But now they
assume the responsibility of the overall approach
their society takes to the education of its people. We will support some type of educational
system, and it is possibly true that we will

support a highly diverse system. Society needs not only public education, elementary through secondary, but also higher education, technical, liberal, and graduate education. Not all assumptions or beliefs can be examined here. Yet an important one is the belief that those who are capable and should assume responsible positions in society should be well educated. We believe they should be well educated if they are to be the leaders in society. But the issue is what kind of education should this leadership have? Whitehead contends that the best type of education is that which combines the theoretical and the practical. Human life is one of action and for that action to be the best it can be people need to temper the theoretical pursuits with the suggestiveness of the practical. Study mathematics but also study business, for example. Hutchins disagrees. He believes that the best kind of education for society's leaders is a theoretical education which prepares the mind to function well. If one can learn to think well, whatever practical problems arise one will be able to deal with them.

Finally, health care is a topic that becomes increasingly important for the adult in mid-life. Oftentimes his aging parents and friends require special care, and sometimes he experiences a deterioration of health that he did not expect. The medical profession is continually researching and developing new therapeutic techniques, and the public is expecting them. These rising expectations coupled with the technological advances have provided health care possibilities undreamed of years ago. We want to provide the best health care we can to all people in our country. This attitude, however, while admirable when acted upon forces us to face some difficult questions. We have the capability to resuscitate a person and keep their bodies alive. Under what conditions should this be done? Having the exotic saving therapy raises the moral issue as to under what conditions should the therapy be administered? Also, who should receive the limited resources when there are more people to be cared for than equipment to care for them? Thus our attitudes and technological advances raise some difficult moral problems. Reiser discusses the moral implications of medical technology. In our attempt to provide the best care for people we have and expect technological advances. However, providing care for some of the terminally ill who are in great pain becomes particularly difficult. Flew argues that we ought to believe that some persons be allowed to end their lives. He contends that some terminally ill persons ought to have the legal right not to be interferred with if they decide to take their own lives. He would contend that we are not giving them the best care if we interfer with their own taking of their lives.

Thus, the change from young adults to middle adulthood, while often difficult, brings with it the alternative of caring for the young not only those who are small and beginning their lives but also those who are being initiated to society, the young adults. The responsibility for making society a better place to live is accepted, and the tasks which accompany that decision are faced. These tasks include guiding and fostering development in education, health, economic life, and the use of natural and accumulated wealth. The way we respond to these challenges will reveal a network of beliefs about what ought to be done and how it ought to be done. These beliefs, basic to the life structure of the adult, require philosophical reflection. A failure to do so could bring about results that we would not want or expect.

The Free Enterprise System

Case

Spiraling inflation seemed to Joe and William beyond their control. They had voted for the presidential candidate they thought would bring the economy under control. But whatever the president did inflation seemed to get worse. Maybe, they thought, nothing can be done! The big politicians and big oil companies were not about to turn lose their enormous profits and pork barrel deals. Besides, why worry about what you cannot do anything about anyway. The only option to them seemed to be to pry more money out of the textile company they worked for. The Union had promised higher pay, better fringe benefits, and better working conditions. But as yet the Union had not been able to organize the people in the plant. The vote to unionize or not was coming up today. Joe argued that through the union pressure could be brought on the company for higher wages and benefits. This is the only way to move the textile company to giving the workers what they need to care for their families. William countered that his best interests lay in letting the law of supply and demand play freely in the marketplace. Union and government interference simply means higher prices and lower dollar value. It's best not to unionize.

Historical Materialism and Revolution*
Friedrich Engels

The materialist conception of history starts from the proposition that the production of the means to support human life and, next to production, the exchange of things produced, is the basis of all social structure; that in every society that has appeared in history, the manner in which wealth is distributed and society divided into classes or oders is dependent upon what is produced, how it is produced, and how the products are exchanged. From this point of view the final causes of all social changes and political revolutions are to be sought, not in men's brains, not in men's better insight into eternal truth and justice, but in changes in the modes of production and exchange. They are to be sought not in the <u>philosophy</u>, but in the <u>economics</u> of each particular epoch. The growing perception that existing social institutions are unreasonable and unjust, that reason has become unreason and right wrong,[1] is only proof that in the modes of production and exchange changes have silently taken place with which the social order, adapted to earlier economic conditions, is no longer in keeping. From this it also follows that the means of getting rid of the incongruities that have been brought to light must also be present, in a more or less developed condition, within the changed modes of production themselves. These means are not to be invented by deduction from fundamental principles, but are to be discovered in the stubborn facts of the existing system of production.

What is, then, the position of modern socialism in this connection?

*From <u>The Marx-Engel Reader</u> edited by Robert C. Tucker. W. W. Norton and Co., Inc. 1972. Reprinted by permission of the publisher.

The present structure of society—this is now pretty generally conceded—is the creation of the ruling class of today, of the bourgeoisie. The mode of production peculiar to the bourgeoisie, known, since Marx, as the capitalist mode of production, was incompatible with the feudal system, with the privileges it conferred upon individuals, entire social ranks and local corporations, as well as with the hereditary ties of subordination which constituted the framework of its social organisation. The bourgeoisie broke up the feudal system and built upon its ruins the capitalist order of society, the kingdom of free competition, of personal liberty, of the equality, before the law, of all commodity owners, of all the rest of the capitalist blessings. Thenceforward the capitalist mode of production could develop in freedom. Since steam, machinery, and the making of machines by machinery transformed the older manufacture into modern industry, the productive forces evolved under the guidance of the bourgeoisie developed with a rapidity and in a degree unheard of before. But just as the older manufacture, in its time, and handicraft, becoming more developed under its influence, had come into collision with the feudal trammels of the guilds, so now modern industry, in its more complete development, comes into collision with the bounds within which the capitalistic mode of production holds it confined. The new productive forces have already outgrown the capitalistic mode of using them. And this conflict between productive forces and modes of production is not a conflict engendered in the mind of man, like that between original sin and divine justice. It exists, in fact, objectively, outside us, independently of the will and actions even of the men that have brought it on. Modern socialism is nothing but the reflex, in thought, of this conflict in fact; its ideal reflection in the minds, first, of the class directly suffering under it, the working class.

Now, in what does this conflict consist?

Before capitalistic production, i.e., in the Middle Ages, the system of petty industry obtained generally, based upon the private property of the labourers in their means of production; in the country, the agriculture of the small peasant, freeman or serf; in the towns, the handicrafts organised in guilds. The instruments of labour—land, agricultural implements, the workshops, the tool—were the instruments of labour of single individuals, adapted for the use of one worker, and, therefore, of necessity, small, dwarfish, circumscribed. But, for this very reason they belonged, as a rule, to the producer himself. To concentrate these scattered, limited means of production, to enlarge them, to turn them into the powerful levers of production of the present day—this was precisely the historic role of capitalist production and of its upholder, the bourgeoisie. In the fourth section of _Capital_ Marx has explained in detail how since the fifteenth century this has been historically worked out through the three phases of simple cooperation, manufacture and modern industry. But the bourgeoisie, as is also shown there, could not transform these puny means of production into mighty productive forces without transforming them, at the same time, from means of production of the individual into _social_ means of production only workable by a collectivity of men. The spinning-wheel, the hand-loom, the blacksmith's hammer, were replaced by the spinning-machine, the power-loom, the steam-hammer; the individual workshop, by the factory implying the co-operation of hundreds and thousands of workmen. In like manner, production itself changed from a series of individual into a series of social acts, and the products from individual to social products. The yarn, the cloth, the metal articles that now came out of the factory, were the joint product of many workers, through whose hands they had successively to pass before they were ready. No one person could say of them; "I made that; this is _my_ product."

But where, in a given society, the funda-

269

mental form of production is that spontaneous division of labour which creeps in gradually and not upon any preconceived plan, there the products take on the form of <u>commodities</u>, whose mutual exchange, buying and selling, enable the individual producers to satisfy their manifold wants. And this was the case in the Middle Ages. The peasant, e.g., sold to the artisan agricultural products and bought from him the products of handicraft. Into this society of individual producers, of commodity producers, the new mode of production thrust itself. In the midst of the old division of labour, grown up spontaneously and upon <u>no definite plan</u>, which had governed the whole of society, now arose division of labour upon a <u>definite</u> plan, as organised in the factory; side by side with <u>individual</u> production appeared <u>social</u> production. The products of both were sold in the same market, and, therefore, at prices at least approximately equal. But organisation upon a definite plan was stronger than spontaneous division of labour. The factories working with the combined social forces of a collectivity of individuals produced their commodities far more cheaply than the individual small producers. Individual production succumbed in one department after another. Socialised production revolutionised all the old methods of production. But its revolutionary character was, at the same time, so little recognised that it was, on the contrary, introduced as a means of increasing and developing the production of commodities. When it arose, it found ready-made, and made liberal use of, certain machinery for the production and exchange of commodities: merchants' captial, handicraft, wage-labour. Socialised production thus introducing itself as a new form of the production of commodities, it was a matter of course that under it the old forms of appropriation remained in full swing, and were applied to its products as well.

In the mediaeval stage of evolution of the production of commodities, the question as to the owner of the product of labour could not arise. The individual producer, as a rule, had, from raw material belonging to himself, and generally his own handiwork, produced it with his own tools, by the labour of his own hands or of his family. There was no need for him to appropriate the new product. It belonged wholly to him, as a matter of course. His property in the product was, therefore, based <u>upon his own labour</u>. Even where external help was used, this was, as a rule, of little importance, and very generally was compensated by something other than wages. The apprentices and journeymen of the guilds worked less for board and wages than for education, in order that they might become master craftsmen themselves. .

Then came the concentration of the means of production and of the producers in large workshops and manufactories, their transformation into actual socialised means of production and socialised producers. But the socialised producers and means of production and their products were still treated, after this change, just as they had been before, i.e., as the means of production and the products of individuals. Hitherto, the owner of the instruments of labour had himself appropriated the product, because, as a rule, it was his own product and the assistance of others was the exception. Now the owner of the instruments of labour always appropriated to himself the product, although it was no longer <u>his</u> product but exclusively the product of the <u>labour of others</u>. Thus, the products now produced socially were not appropriated by those who had actually set in motion the means of production and actually produced the commodities, but by the <u>capitalists</u>. The means of production, and production itself, had become in essence socialised. But they were subjected to a form of appropriation which presupposes the private production of individuals, under which, therefore, everyone owns his own product and brings it to market. The mode of production is subjected to this form of appropriation, although it abolishes the conditions upon which the latter rests.[2]

This contradiction, which gives to the new

mode of production its capitalistic character, contains the germ of the whole of the social antagonisms of today. The greater the mastery obtained by the new mode of production over all important fields of production and in all manufacturing countries, the more it reduced individual production to an insignificant residuum, the more clearly was brought out the incompatibility of socialised production with capitalistic appropriation.

The first capitalists found, as we have said, alongside of other forms of labour, wage-labour ready-made for them on the market. But it was exceptional, complementary, accessory, transitory wage-labour. The agricultural labourer, though, upon occasion, he hired himself out by the day, had a few acres of his own land on which he could at all events live at a pinch. The guilds were so organized that the journeyman of today became the master of tomorrow. But all this changed as soon as the means of production became socialised and concentrated in the hands of capitalists. The means of production, as well as the product, of the individual producer became more and more worthless; there was nothing left for him but to turn wage-worker under the capitalist. Wage-labour, aforetime the exception and accessory, now became the rule and basis of all production; aforetime complementary, it now became the sole remaining function of the workers. The wage-worker for a time became a wage-worker for life. The number of these permanent wage-workers was further enormously increased by the breaking-up of the feudal system that occurred at the same time, by the disbanding of the retainers of the feudal lords, the eviction of the peasants from their homesteads, etc. The separation was made complete between the means of production concentrated in the hands of the capitalists, on the one side, and the producers, possessing nothing but their labour-power, on the other. The contradiction between socialised production and capitalistic appropriation manifested itself as the antagonism of proletariat and bourgeoisie.

We have seen that the capitalistic mode of production thrust its way into a society of commodity-producers, of individual producers, whose social bond was the exchange of their products. But every society based upon the production of commodities has this peculiarity: that the producers have lost control over their own social inter-relations. Each man produces for himself with such means of production as he may happen to have, and for such exchange as he may require to satisfy his remaining wants. No one knows how much of his particular article is coming on the market, nor how much of it will be wanted. No one knows whether his individual product will meet an actual demand, whether he will be able to make good his costs of production or even to sell his commodity at all. Anarchy reigns in socialised production.

But the production of commodities, like every other form of production, has its peculiar, inherent laws inseparable from it; and these laws work, despite anarchy, in and through anarchy. They reveal themselves in the only persistent form of social inter-relations, i.e., in exchange, and here they affect the individual producers as compulsory laws of competition. They are, at first, unknown to these producers themselves, and have to be discovered by them gradually and as the result of experience. They work themselves out, therefore, independently of the producers, and in antagonism to them, as inexorable natural laws of their particular form of production. The product governs the producers.

In mediaeval society, especially in the earlier centuries, production was essentially directed towards satisfying the wants of the individual. It satisfied, in the main, only the wants of the producer and his family. Where relations of personal dependence existed, as in the country, it also helped to satisfy the wants of the feudal lord. In all this there was, therefore, no exchange; the products, consequently, did not assume the character of commodities. The family of the peasant produced almost everything they

wanted: clothes and furniture, as well as means
of subsistence. Only when it began to produce
more than was sufficient to supply its own wants
and the payments in kind to the feudal lord, only
then did it also produce commodities. This surplus, thrown into socialised exchange and offered
for sale, became commodities.

The artisans of the towns, it is true, had
from the first to produce for exchange. But they,
also, themselves supplied the greatest part of
their own individual wants. They had gardens and
plots of land. They turned their cattle out into
the communal forest, which, also, yielded them
timber and firing. The women spun flax, wool,
and so forth. Production for the purpose of exchange, production of commodities, was only in
its infancy. Hence, exchange was restricted, the
market narrow, the methods of production stable;
there was local exclusiveness without, local unity within; the Mark in the country; in the town,
the guild.

But with the extension of the production of
commodities, and especially with the introduction
of the capitalist mode of production, the laws of
commodity production, hitherto latent, came into
action more openly and with greater force. The
old bonds were loosened, the old exclusive limits
broken through, the producers were more and more
turned into independent, isolated producers of
commodities. It became apparent that the production of society at large was ruled by absence of
plan, by accident, by anarchy; and this anarchy
grew to greater and greater height. But the chief
means by aid of which the capitalist mode of production intensified this anarchy of socialised
production was the exact opposite of anarchy. It
was the increasing organisation of production,
upon a social basis, in every individual productive establishment. By this, the old, peaceful,
stable condition of things was ended. Wherever
this organisation of production was introduced
into a branch of industry, it brooked no other
method of production by its side. The field of

labour became a battle-ground. The great geographical discoveries, and the colonisation following upon them, multiplied markets and quickened
the transformation of handicraft into manufacture.
The war did not simply break out between the individual producers of particular localities. The
local struggles begot in their turn national conflicts, the commercial wars of the seventeenth
and eighteenth centuries.

Finally, modern industry and the opening of
the world market made the struggle universal, and
at the same time gave it an unheard-of virulence.
Advantages in natural or artificial conditions of
production now decide the existence or non-exis-
tence of individual capitalists, as well as of
whole industries and countries. He that falls is
remorselessly cast aside. It is the Darwinian
struggle of the individual for existence transferred from Nature to society with intensified
violence. The conditions of existence natural to
the animal appear as the final term of human development. The contradiction between socialised
production and capitalistic appropriation now
presents itself as <u>an antagonism between the organisation of production in the individual workshop and the anarchy of production in society
generally</u>.

The capitalistic mode of production moves in
these two forms of the antagonism immanent to it
from its very origin. It is never able to get
out of that "vicious circle" which Fourier had
already discovered. What Fourier could not, indeed, see in his time is that this circle is
gradually narrowing; that the movement becomes
more and more a spiral, and must come to an end,
like the movement of the planets, by collision
with the centre. It is the compelling force of
anarchy in the production of society at large
that more and more completely turns the great
majority of men into proletarians; and it is the
masses of the proletariat again who will finally
put an end to anarchy in production. It is the
compelling force of anarchy in social production

that turns the limitless perfectibility of machinery under modern industry into a compulsory law by which every individual industrial capitalist must perfect his machinery more and more, under penalty of ruin.

But the perfecting of machinery is making human labour superfluous. If the introduction and increase of machinery means the displacement of millions of manual by a few machine-workers, improvement in machinery means the displacement of more and more of the machine-workers themselves. It means, in the last instance, the production of a number of available wage-workers in excess of the average needs of capital, the formation of a complete industrial reserve army, as I called it in 1845, available at the times when industry is working at high pressure, to be cast out upon the street when the inevitable crash comes, a constant dead weight upon the limbs of the working class in its struggle for existence with capital, a regulator for the keeping of wages down to the low level that suits the interests of capital. Thus it comes about, to quote Marx, that machinery becomes the most powerful weapon in the war of capital against the working class; that the instruments of labour constantly tear the means of subsistence out of the hands of the labourer; that the very product of the worker is turned into an instrument for his subjugation. Thus it comes about that the economising of the instruments of labour becomes at the same time, from the outset, the most reckless waste of labour power, and robbery based upon the normal conditions under which labour functions; that machinery, "the most powerful instrument for shortening labour time, becomes the most unfailing means for placing every moment of the labourer's time and that of his family at the disposal of the capitalist for the purpose of expanding the value of his capital." (Capital, English edition, p. 406.) Thus it comes about that the overwork of some becomes the preliminary condition for the idleness of others, and that modern industry, which hunts

276

after new consumers over the whole world, forces the consumption of the masses at home down to a starvation minimum, and in doing thus destroys its own home market. "The law that always equilibrates the relative surplus population, or industrial reserve army, to the extent and energy of accumulation, this law rivets the labourer to capital more firmly than the wedges of Vulcan did Prometheus to the rock. It establishes an accumulation of misery, corresponding with accumulation of capital. Accumulation of wealth at one pole is, therefore, at the same time, accumulation of misery, agony of toil, slavery, ignorance, brutality, mental degradation, at the opposite pole, i.e. on the side of the class that produces its own product in the form of capital." (Capital, p. 661.) And to expect any other division of the products from the capitalistic mode of production is the same as expecting the electrodes of a battery not to decompose acidulated water, not to liberate oxygen at the positive, hydrogen at the negative pole, so long as they are connected with the battery.

We have seen that the ever-increasing perfectibility of modern machinery is, by the anarchy of social production, turned into a compulsory law that forces the individual industrial capitalist always to improve his machinery, always to increase its productive force. The bare possibility of extending the field of production is transformed for him into a similar compulsory law. The enormous expansive force of modern industry, compared with which that of gases is mere child's play, appears to us now as a necessity for expansion, both qualitative and quantitative, that laughs at all resistance. Such resistance is offered by consumption, by sales, by the markets for the products of modern industry. But the capacity for extension, extensive and intensive, of the markets is primarily governed by quite different laws that work much less energetically. The extension of the markets cannot keep pace with the extension of production. The collision becomes inevitable, and as this cannot produce any real solution so long as it does not break in pieces the capitalist mode of production, the collisions become periodic. Capitalist production has begotten another "vicious circle."

As a matter of fact, since 1825, when the first general crisis broke out, the whole industrial and commercial world, production and exchange among all civilised peoples and their more or less barbaric hangers-on, are thrown out of joint about once every ten years. Commerce is at a standstill, the markets are glutted, products accumulate, as multitudinous as they are unsaleable, hard cash disappears, credit vanishes, factories are closed, the mass of the workers are in want of the means of subsistence, because they have produced too much of the means of subsistence; bankruptcy follows upon bankruptcy, execution upon execution. The stagnation lasts for years; productive forces and products are wasted and destroyed wholesale, until the accumulated mass of commodities finally filters off, more or less depreciated in value, until production and exchange gradually begin to move again. Little by little the pace quickens. It becomes a trot. The industrial trot breaks into a canter, the canter in turn grows into the headlong gallop of a perfect steeplechase of industry, commercial credit, and speculation which finally, after breakneck leaps, ends where it began—in the ditch of a crisis. And so over and over again. We have now, since the year 1825, gone through this five times, and at the present moment (1877) we are going through it for the sixth time. And the character of these crises is so clearly defined that Fourier hit all of them off when he described the first as "crise pléthorique," a crisis from plethora.

In these crises, the contradiction between socialised production and capitalist appropriation ends in a violent explosion. The circulation of commodities is, for the time being, stopped. Money, the means of circulation, becomes a hindrance

278

to circulation. All the laws of production and circulation of commodities are turned upside down. The economic collision has reached its apogee. <u>The mode of production is in rebellion against the mode of exchange</u>.

The fact that the socialised organisation of production within the factory has developed so far that it has become incompatible with the anarchy of production in society, which exists side by side with and dominates it, is brought home to the capitalists themselves by the violent concentration of capital that occurs during crises, through the ruin of many large, and a still greater number of small, capitalists. The whole mechanism of the capitalist mode of production breaks down under the pressure of the productive forces, its own creations. It is no longer able to turn all this mass of means of production into capital. They lie fallow, and for that very reason the industrial reserve army must also lie fallow. Means of production, means of subsistence, available labourers, all the elements of production and of general wealth, are present in abundance. But "abundance becomes the source of distress and want" (Fourier), because it is the very thing that prevents the transformation of the means of production and subsistence into capital. For in capitalistic society the means of production can only function when they have undergone a preliminary transformation into capital, into the means of exploiting human labour power. The necessity of this transformation into capital of the means of production and subsistence stands like a ghost between these and the workers. It alone prevents the coming together of the material and personal levers of production; it alone forbids the means of production to function, the workers to work and live. On the one hand, therefore, the capitalistic mode of production stands convicted of its own incapacity to further direct these productive forces. On the other, these productive forces themselves, with increasing energy, press forward to the removal of the existing contradiction to the abolition of their

quality as capital, to the <u>practical recognition</u>
<u>of their character as social productive forces</u>.

This rebellion of the productive forces, as
they grow more and more powerful, against their
quality as capital, this stronger and stronger
command that their social character shall be recognised, forces the capitalist class itself to
treat them more and more as social productive
forces, so far as this is possible under capitalist conditions. The period of industrial high
pressure, with its unbounded inflation of credit,
not less than the crash itself, by the collapse
of great capitalist establishments, tends to
bring about that form of the socialisation of
great masses of means of production which we meet
with in the different kinds of joint-stock companies. Many of these means of production and of
distribution are, from the outset, so colossal
that, like the railways, they exclude all other
forms of capitalistic exploitation. At a further stage of evolution this form also becomes
insufficient. The producers on a large scale in
a particular branch of industry in a particular
country unite in a trust, a union for the purpose
of regulating production. They determine the
total amount to be produced, parcel it out among
themselves, and thus enforce the selling price
fixed beforehand. But trusts of this kind, as
soon as business becomes bad, are generally liable to break up, and on this very account compel a yet greater concentration of association.
The whole of the particular industry is turned
into one gigantic joint-stock company; internal
competition gives place to the internal monopoloy
of this one company. This has happened in 1890
with the English alkali production, which is now,
after the fusion of 48 large works, in the hands
of one company, conducted upon a single plan,
and with a capital of £6,000,000.

In the trusts, freedom of competition changes
into its very opposite—into monopoly; and the
production without any definite plan of capitalistic society capitulates to the production upon

a definite plan of the invading socialistic society. Certainly this is so far still to the benefit and advantage of the capitalists. But in this case the exploitation is so palpable that it must break down. No nation will put up with production conducted by trusts, with so barefaced an exploitation of the community by a small band of dividend-mongers.

In any case, with trusts or without, the official representative of capitalist society—the state—will ultimately have to undertake the direction of production.[3] This necessity for conversion into state property is felt first in the great institutions for intercourse and communication—the post office, the telegraphs, the railways.

If the crises demonstrate the incapacity of the bourgeoisie for managing any longer modern productive forces, the transformation of the great establishments for production and distrubution into joint-stock companies, trusts and state property shows how unnecessary the bourgeoisie are for that purpose. All the social functions of the capitalist are now performed by salaried employees. The capitalist has no further social function than that of pocketing dividends, tearing off coupons, and gambling on the Stock Exchange, where the different capitalists despoil one another of their capital. At first the capitalistic mode of production forces out the workers. Now it forces out the capitalists, and reduces them, just as it reduced the workers, to the ranks of the surplus population, although not immediately into those of the industrial reserve army.

But the transformation, either into joint-stock companies and trusts, or into state ownership, does not do away with the capitalistic nature of the productive forces. In the joint-stock companies and trusts this is obvious. And the modern state, again, is only the organisation that bourgeois society takes on in order to support the external conditions of the capitalist mode of production against the encroachments as well of the workers as of individual capitalists. The modern state, no matter what its form, is essentially a capitalist machine, the state of the capitalists, the ideal personification of the total national capital. The more it proceeds to the taking over of productive forces, the more does it actually become the national capitalist, the more citizens does it exploit. The workers remain wage-workers—proletarians. The capitalist relation is not done away with. It is rather brought to a head. But, brought to a head, it topples over. State ownership of the productive forces is not the solution of the conflict, but concealed within it are the technical conditions that form the elements of that solution.

This solution can only consist in the practical recognition of the social nature of the modern forces of production, and therefore in the harmonising of the modes of production, appropriation, and exchange with the socialised character of the means of production. And this can only come about by society openly and directly taking possession of the productive forces which have outgrown all control except that of society as a whole. The social character of the means of production and of the products today reacts against the producers, periodically disrupts all production and exchange, acts only like a law of Nature working blindly, forcibly, destructively. But with the taking over by society of the productive forces, the social character of the means of production and of the products will be utilised by the producers with a perfect understanding of its nature, and instead of being a source of disturbance and periodical collapse, will become the most powerful lever of production itself.

Active social forces work exactly like natural forces: blindly, forcibly, destructively, so. long as we do not understand, and reckon with, them. But when once we understand them, when once we grasp their action, their direction, their effects, it depends only upon ourselves to sub- ject them more and more to our own will, and by means of them to reach our own ends. And this holds quite especially of the mighty productive forces of today. As long as we obstinately re- fuse to understand the nature and the character of these social means of action—and this under- standing goes against the grain of the capitalist mode of production and its defenders—so long these forces are at work in spite of us, in op- position to us, so long they master us, as we have shown above in detail.

But when once their nature is understood, they can, in the hands of the producers working together, be transformed from master demons into willing servants. The difference is as that be- tween the destructive force of electricity in the lightning of the storm, and electricity under command in the telegraph and the voltaic arc; the difference between a conflagration, and fire work- ing in the service of man. With this recognition, at last, of the real nature of the productive forces of today, the social anarchy of production gives place to a social regulation of production upon a definite plan, according to the needs of the community and of each individual. Then the capitalist mode of appropriation, in which the product enslaves first the producer and then the appropriator, is replaced by the mode of appro- priation of the products that is based upon the nature of the modern means of production; upon the one hand, direct social appropriation, as means to the maintenance and extension of pro- duction—on the other, direct individual appro- priation, as means of subsistence and of enjoy- ment.

Whilst the capitalist mode of production more and more completely transforms the great majority of the population into proletarians, it creates the power which, under penalty of its own destruction, is forced to accomplish this revolu- tion. Whilst it forces on more and more the

transformation of the vast means of production,
already socialised, into state property, it shows
itself the way to accomplishing this revolution.
The proletariat seizes political power and turns
the means of production into state property.

But, in doing this, it abolishes itself as
proletariat, abolishes all class distinctions and
class antagonisms, abolishes also the state as
state. Society thus far, based upon class antagonisms, had need of the state. That is, of an
organisation of the particular class which was
pro tempore the exploiting class, an organisation
for the purpose of preventing any interference
from without with the existing conditions of production, and, therefore, especially, for the purpose of forcibly keeping the exploited classes in
the condition of oppression corresponding with
the given mode of production (slavery, serfdom,
wage-labour). The state was the official representative of society as a whole; the gathering of
it together into a visible embodiment. But it
was this only in so far as it was the state of
that class which itself represented, for the time
being, society as a whole: in ancient times, the
state of slaveowning citizens; in the Middle Ages,
the feudal lords; in our own time, the bourgeoisie. When at last it becomes the real representative of the whole of society, it renders itself
unnecessary. As soon as there is no longer any
social class to be held in subjection; as soon as
class rule, and the individual struggle for existence based upon our present anarchy in production, with the collisions and excesses arising
from these, are removed nothing more remains to
be repressed, and a special repressive force, a
state, is no longer necessary. The first act by
virtue of which the state really constitutes itself the representative of the whole of society—
this is, at the same time, its last independent
act as a state. State interference in social
relations becomes, in one domain after another,
superfluous, and then dies out of itself; the
government of persons is replaced by the administration of things, and by the conduct of

processes of production. The state is not "abolished." It dies out. This gives the measure of the value of the phrase "a free state," both as to its justifiable use at times by agitators, and as to its ultimate scientific insufficiency; and also of the demands of the so-called anarchists for the abolition of the state out of hand.

Since the historical appearance of the capitalist mode of production, the appropriation by society of all the means of production has often been dreamed of, more or less vaguely, by individuals, as well as by sects, as the ideal of the future. But it could become possible, could become a historical necessity, only when the actual conditions for its realisation were there. Like every other social advance, it becomes practicable, not by men understanding that the existence of classes is in contradiction to justice, equality, etc., not by the mere willingness to abolish these classes, but by virtue of certain new economic conditions. The separation of society into an exploiting and an exploited class, a ruling and an oppressed class, was the necessary consequence of the deficient and restricted development of production in former times. So long as the total social labour only yields a product which but slightly exceeds that barely necessary for the existence of all; so long, therefore, as labour engages all or almost all the time of the great majority of the members of society—so long, of necessity, this society is divided into classes. Side by side with the great majority, exclusively bond slaves to labour, arises a class freed from directly productive labour, which looks after the general affairs of society: the direction of labour, state business, law, science, art, etc. It is, therefore, the law of division of labour that lies at the basis of the division into classes. But this does not prevent this division into classes from being carried out by means of violence and robbery, trickery and fraud. It does not prevent the ruling class, once having the upper hand, from consolidating its power at the expense of the working class, from turning its social leadership into an intensified exploitation of the masses.

But if, upon this showing, division into classes has a certain historical justification, it has this only for a given period, only under given social conditions. It was based upon the insufficiency of production. It will be swept away by the complete development of modern productive forces. And, in fact, the abolition of classes in society presupposes a degree of historical evolution at which the existence, not simply of this or that particular ruling class, but of any ruling class at all, and, therefore, the existence of class distinction itself has become an obsolete anachronism. It presupposes, therefore, the development of production carried out to a degree at which appropriation of the means of production and of the products, and, with this, of political domination, of the monopoly of culture, and of intellectual leadership by a particular class of society, has become not only superfluous but economically, politically, intellectually, a hindrance to development.

This point is now reached. Their political and intellectual bankruptcy is scarcely any longer a secret to the bourgeoisie themselves. Their economic bankruptcy recurs regularly every ten years. In every crisis, society is suffocated beneath the weight of its own productive forces and products, which it cannot use, and stands helpless, face to face with the absurd contradiction that the producers have nothing to consume, because consumers are wanting. The expansive force of the means of production bursts the bonds that the capitalist mode of production had imposed upon them. Their deliverance from these bonds is the one precondition for an unbroken, constantly accelerated development of the productive forces, and therewith for a practically unlimited increase of production itself. Nor is this all. The socialised appropriation of the means of production does away, not only with the present artificial restrictions upon production, but also with the positive waste and devastation of productive forces and products that are at the present time the inevitable concomitants of production, and that reach their height in the crises. Further, it sets free for the community at large a mass of means of production and of products, by doing away with the senseless extravagance of the ruling classes of today and their political representatives. The possibility of securing for every member of society, by means of socialised production, an existence not only fully sufficient materially, and becoming day by day more full, but an existence guaranteeing to all the free development and exercise of their physical and mental faculties—this possibility is now for the first time here, but <u>it is here</u>.[4]

With the seizing of the means of production by society, production of commodities is done away with, and, simultaneously, the mastery of the product over the producer. Anarchy in social production is replaced by systematic, definite organisation. The struggle for individual existence disappears. Then for the first time man, in a certain sense, is finally marked off from the rest of the animal kingdom, and emerges from mere animal conditions of existence into really human ones. The whole sphere of the conditions of life which environ man, and which have hitherto ruled man, now comes under the dominion and control of man, who for the first time becomes the real, conscious lord of Nature, because he has now become master of his own social organisation. The laws of his own social action, hitherto standing face to face with man as laws of Nature foreign to, and dominating him, will then be used with full understanding, and so mastered by him. Man's own social organisation, hitherto confronting him as a necessity imposed by Nature and history, now becomes the result of his own free action. The extraneous objective forces that have hitherto governed history pass under the control of man himself. Only from that time

will man himself, more and more consciously, make
his own history—only from that time will the
social causes set in movement by him have, in the
main and in a constantly growing measure, the results intended by him. It is the ascent of man
from the kingdom of necessity to the kingdom of
freedom.

Notes

[1]Mephistopheles, in Goethe's _Faust_.

[2]It is hardly necessary in this connection to
point out that, even if the _form_ of appropriation
remains the same, the _character_ of the appropriation is just as much revolutionised as production
is by the changes described above. It is, of
course, a very different matter whether I appropriate to myself my own product or that of another. Note in passing that wage-labour, which
contains the whole capitalistic mode of production in embryo, is very ancient; in a sporadic,
scattered form it existed for centuries alongside
of slave-labour. But the embryo could duly develop into the capitalistic mode of production
only when the necessary historical preconditions
had been furnished. (_Engels_)

[3]I say "have to." For only when the means of
production and distribution have _actually_ outgrown the form of management by joint-stock companies, and when, therefore, the taking them over
by the state has become _economically_ inevitable,
only then—even if it is the state of today that
effects this—is there an economic advance, the
attainment of another step preliminary to the
taking over of all productive forces by society
itself. But of late, since Bismarck went in for
state ownership of industrial establishments, a
kind of spurious socialism has arisen, degenerat-
ing, now and again, into something of flunkeyism,
that without more ado declares _all_ state ownership, even of the Bismarckian sort, to be socialistic. Certainly, if the taking over by the
state of the tobacco industry is socialistic,
then Napoleon and Metternich must be numbered
among the founders of socialism. If the Belgian

state, for quite ordinary political and financial reasons, itself constructed its chief railway lines; if Bismarck, not under any economic compulsion, took over for the state the chief Prussian lines, simply to be the better able to have them in hand in case of war, to bring up the railway employees as voting cattle for the government, and especailly to create for himself a new source of income independent of parliamentary votes—this was, in no sense, a socialistic measure, directly or indirectly, consciously or unconsciously. Otherwise, the Royal Maritime Company, the Royal porcelain manufacture, and even the regimental tailor shops of the Army would also be socialistic institutions, or even, as was seriously proposed by a sly dog in Frederick William III's reign, the taking over by the state of the brothels. (Engels)

[4]A few figures may serve to give an approximate idea of the enormous expansive force of the modern means of production, even under capitalist pressure. According to Mr. Giffen, the total wealth of Great Britain and Ireland amounted, in round numbers in

> 1814 to £2,200,000,000.
> 1865 to £6,100,000,000.
> 1875 to £8,500,000,000.

As an instance of the squandering of means of production and of products during a crisis, the total loss in the German iron industry alone, in the crisis 1873-78, was given at the second German Industrial Congress (Berlin, February 21, 1878) as £22,750,000. (Engels)

Piecemeal versus Utopian Engineering*
Karl Popper

Notwithstanding the objectionable associations which attach to the term 'engineering',[1] I shall use the term 'piecemeal social engineering' to describe the practical application of the results of piecemeal technology. The term is useful since there is need for a term covering social activities, private as well as public, which, in order to realize some aim or end, consciously utilize all available technological knowledge.[2] Piecemeal social engineering resembles physical engineering in regarding the ends as beyond the province of technology. (All that technology may say about ends is whether or not they are compatible with each other or realizable.) In this it differs from historicism, which regards the ends of human activities as dependent on historical forces and so within its province.

Just as the main task of the physical engineer is to design machines and to remodel and service them, the task of the piecemeal social engineer is to design social institutions, and to reconstruct and run those already in existence. The term 'social institution' is used here in a very wide sense, to include bodies of a private as well as of a public character. Thus I shall use it to describe a business, whether it is a small shop or an insurance company, and likewise a school, or an 'educational system', or a police force, or a Church, or a law court. The piecemeal technologist or engineer recognizes that

*From Karl Popper, The Poverty of Historicism, Harper Torchbooks (paperback), The Academy Library, Harper and Row, New York and Evanston, 1964; Basic books, New York, 1967; Routledge and Kegan Paul, London, 1967; 9th impression 1976. Reprinted by permission of the author and publisher.

only a minority of social institutions are consciously designed while the vast majority have
just 'grown', as the undesigned results of human actions.[3] But however strongly he may be
impressed by this important fact, as a technologist or engineer he will look upon them from a
'functional' or 'instrumental' point of view.[4]
He will see them as means to certain ends, or as
convertible to the service of certain ends; as
machines rather than as organisms. This does
not mean, of course, that he will overlook the
fundamental differences between institutions and
physical instruments. On the contrary, the technologist should study the differences as well as
the similarities, expressing his results in the
form of hypotheses. And indeed, it is not difficult to formulate hypotheses about institutions
in technological form as is shown by the following example: 'You cannot construct foolproof
institutions, that is to say, institutions whose
functioning does not very largely depend upon
persons: institutions, at best, can reduce the
uncertainty of the personal element, by assisting
those who work for the aims for which the institutions are designed, and on whose personal initiative and knowledge success largely depends.
(Institutions are like fortresses. They must be
well designed _and_ properly manned.)'[5]

The characteristic approach of the piecemeal
engineer is this. Even though he may perhaps
cherish some ideals which concern society 'as a
whole'—its general welfare, perhaps—he does not
believe in the method of re-designing it as a
whole. Whatever his ends, he tries to achieve
them by small adjustments and re-adjustments which
can be continually improved upon. His ends may
be of diverse kinds, for example, the accumulation of wealth or of power by certain individuals,
or by certain groups; or the distribution of
wealth and power; or the protection of certain
'rights' of individuals or groups, etc. Thus
public or political social engineering may have
the most diverse tendencies, totalitarian as well
as liberal. (Examples of far-reaching liberal

291

programmes for piecemeal reform have been given
by W. Lippmann, under the title "The Agenda of
Liberalism'.6) The piecemeal engineer knows,
like Socrates, how little he knows. He knows
that we can learn only from our mistakes. Accordingly, he will make his way, step by step,
carefully comparing the results expected with the
results achieved, and always on the look-out for
the unavoidable unwanted consequences of any reform; and he will avoid undertaking reforms of a
complexity and scope which make it impossible
for him to disentangle causes and effects, and
to know what he is really doing.

Such 'piecemeal tinkering' does not agree
with the political temperament of many 'activ-
ists'. Their programme, which too has been described as a programme of 'social engineering',
may be called 'holistic' or 'Utopian engineering'.

Holistic or Utopian social engineering, as
opposed to piecemeal social engineering, is never
of a 'private' but always of a 'public' character.
It aims at remodelling the 'whole of society' in
accordance with a definite plan or blueprint; it
aims at 'seizing the key positions'7 and at extending 'the power of the State . . . until the
State becomes nearly identical with society',8
and it aims, furthermore, at controlling from
these 'key positions' the historical forces that
mould the future of the developing society:
either by arresting this development, or else by
foreseeing its course and adjusting society to it.

It may be questioned, perhaps, whether the
piecemeal and the holistic approaches here described are fundamentally different, considering
that we have put no limits to the scope of a
piecemeal approach. As this approach is understood here, constitutional reforms, for example,
falls well within its scope; nor shall I exclude
the possibility that a series of piecemeal reforms
might be inspired by one general tendency, for example, a tendency towards a greater equalization
of incomes. In this way, piecemeal methods may lead

to changes in what is usually called the 'class structure of society'. Is there any difference, it may be asked, between these more ambitious kinds of piecemeal engineering and the holistic or Utopian approach? And this question may become even more pertinent if we consider that, when trying to assess the likely consequences of some proposed reform, the piecemeal technologist must do his best to estimate the effects of any measure upon the 'whole' of society.

In answering this question, I shall not attempt to draw a precise line of demarcation between the two methods, but I shall try to bring out the very different point of view from which the holist and the piecemeal technologist look upon the task of reforming society. The holists reject the piecemeal approach as being too modest. Their rejection of it, however, does not quite square with their practice; for in practice they always fall back on a somewhat haphazard and clumsy although ambitious and ruthless application of what is essentially a piecemeal method without its cautious and self-critical character. The reason is that, in practice, the holistic method turns out to be impossible; the greater the holistic changes attempted, the greater are their unintended and largely unexpected repercussions, forcing upon the holistic engineer the expedient of piecemeal improvization. In fact, this expedient is more characteristic of centralized or collectivistic planning than of the more modest and careful piecemeal intervention; and it continually leads the Utopian engineer to do things which he did not intend to do; that is to say, it leads to the notorious phenomenon of unplanned planning. Thus the difference between Utopian and piecemeal engineering turns out, in practice, to be a difference not so much in scale and scope as in caution and in preparedness for unavoidable surprises. One could also say that, in practice, the two methods differ in other ways than in scale and scope—in opposition to what we led to expect if we compare the two doctrines concerning the proper methods of rational social reform. Of these two doctrines, I hold that the one is true, while the other is false and liable to lead to mistakes which are both avoidable and grave. Of the two methods, I hold that one is possible, while the other simply does not exist: it is impossible.

One of the differences between the Utopian or holistic approach and the piecemeal approach may therefore be stated in this way: while the piecemeal engineer can attack his problem with an open mind as to the scope of the reform, the holist cannot do this; for he has decided beforehand that a complete reconstruction is possible and necessary. This fact has far-reaching consequences. It prejudices the Utopianist against certain sociological hypotheses which state limits to institutional control; for example, the one mentioned above in this section, expressing the uncertainty due to the personal element, the 'human factor'. By a rejection a priori of such hypotheses, the Utopian approach violates the principles of scientific method. On the other hand, problems connected with the uncertainty of the human factor must force the Utopianist, whether he likes it or not, to try to control the human factor by institutional means, and to extend his programme so as to embrace not only the transformation of society, according to plan, but also the transformation of man.[9] 'The political problem, therefore, is to organize human impulses in such a way that they will direct their energy to the right strategic points, and steer the total process of development in the desired direction.' It seems to escape the well-meaning Utopianist that this programme implies an admission of failure, even before he launches it. For it substitutes for his demand that we build a new society, fit for men and women to live in, the demand that we 'mould' these men and women to fit into his new society. This, clearly, removes any possibility of testing the success or failure of the new society. For those who do not like living in it only admit thereby that they are not yet fit to live in it; that their 'human

impulses' need further 'organizing'. But without
the possibility of tests, any claim that a 'scientific' method is being employed evaporates.
The holistic approach is incompatible with a
truly scientific attitude.

Notes

[1]Against the use of the term 'social engineering' (in the 'piecemeal' sense) it has been
objected by Professor Hayek that the typical engineering job involves the centralization of all
relevant knowledge in a single head, whereas it
is typical of all truly social problems that
knowledge has to be used which cannot be so
centralized. (See Hayek, Collectivist Economic
Planning, 1935, p. 210.) I admit that this fact
is of fundamental importance. It can be formulated by the technological hypothesis: 'You
cannot centralize within a planning authority
the knowledge relevant for such tasks as the
satisfaction of personal needs, or the utiliza-
tion of specialized skill and ability.' (A similar hypothesis may be proposed regarding the
impossibility of centralizing initiative in connection with similar tasks.) The use of the
term 'social engineering' may now be defended by
pointing out that the engineer must use the
technological knowledge embodied in these hypotheses which inform him of the limitations of
his own initiative as well as of his own knowledge.
[2]Including, if it can be obtained, knowledge
concerning the limitations of knowledge, as explained in the previous note.
[3]The two views—that social institutions are
either 'designed' or that they just 'grow'—correspond to those of the Social Contract theorists
and of their critics, for example, Hume. But
Hume does not give up the 'functional' or 'in-
strumentalist' view of social institutions, for
he says that men could not do without them. This
position might be elaborated into a Darwinian explanation of the instrumental character of undesigned institutions (such as language): if they

have no useful function, they have no chance of surviving. According to this view, undesigned social institutions may emerge as <u>unintended consequences of rational actions</u>: just as a road may be formed without any intention to do so by people who find it convenient to use a track already existing (as Descartes observes). It need hardly be stressed, however, that the technological approach is quite independent of all questions of 'origin'.

[4]For the 'functional' approach, see B. Malinowski, for example, 'Anthropology as the Basis of Social Science', in <u>Human Affairs</u> (ed. Cattell), especially pp. 206 ff. and 239 ff.

[5]This example, asserting that the efficiency of institutional 'machines' is limited, and that the functioning of institutions depends on their being supplied with proper personnel, may perhaps be compared with the principles of thermodynamics, such as the law of conservation of energy (in the form in which it excludes the possibility of a perpetual motion machine). As such, it may be contrasted with other 'scientistic' attempts to work out an analogy between the physical concept of energy and some sociological concepts such as power; see, for example, Bertrand Russell's <u>Power</u> (1938), p. 10 f., where this kind of scientistic attempt is made. I do not think that Russell's main point—that the various 'forms of power', such as wealth, propagandist power, naked power, may sometimes be 'converted' into one another—can be expressed in technological form.

[6]W. Lippmann, <u>The Good Society</u> (1937), ch. XI, pp. 203 ff. See also W. H. Hutt, <u>Plan for Reconstruction</u> (1943).

[7]The expression is often used by K. Mannheim in his <u>Man and Society in an Age of Reconstruction</u>; see his Index, and, for example, pp. 269, 295, 320, 381. This book is the most elaborate exposition of a holistic and historicist programme known to me and is therefore singled out here for criticism.

[8]See Mannheim, <u>ibid.</u>, 337. The passage is more fully quoted in section 23, where it is also criticized. (See note 2 above.)

[9]The Problem of Transforming Man' is the heading of a chapter of K. Mannheim's <u>Man and Society</u>. The following quotation is from that chapter, p. 199 f.

Wealth

Case

    Don and Doris had been improving their home little by little. Don wanted to put on a screened-in back porch. But when he looked at the cost of energy and the amount of gas and electricity he was using each year to heat and cool his home he began to have second thoughts about any changes until he had made the house energy efficient. While the cost was not out of reason for a person of his income, the amount of non-replacable energy being expended did bother him. What if we do not conserve our energy resources? What will our children's children and their children's children have to heat their homes and run the economy on? We simply must provide for those coming after us. Unfortunately, Doris had little patience with that attitude. Don's income had risen swiftly in the past few years, and had outpaced inflation; it was perfectly reasonable to have the back porch and pay the energy costs at the same time. Besides, she argued, what has kept America strong has been its technology. There is every reason to expect that with technological expertise the children of the future can take care of themselves. We have to live now and care for our children now. Each generation has to take care of itself.

Obligations to Future Generations[*]
M. P. Golding

The purpose of this note[1] is to examine the notion of obligations to future generations, a notion that finds increasing use in discussions of social policies and programs, particularly as concerns population distribution and control and environment control. Thus, it may be claimed, the solution of problems in these areas is not merely a matter of enhancing our own good, improving our own conditions of life, but is also a matter of discharging an obligation to future generations.

Before I turn to the question of the basis of such obligations—the necessity of the plural is actually doubtful—there are three general points to be considered: (1) Who are the individuals in whose regard it is maintained that we have such obligations, to whom do we owe such obligations? (2) What, essentially, do obligations to future generations oblige us to do, what are they aimed at? and (3) To what class of obligation do such obligations belong, what kind of obligation are they? Needless to say, in examining a notion of this sort, which is used in everyday discussion and polemic, one must be mindful of the danger of taking it—or making it out—to be more precise than it is in reality.

This cautionary remark seems especially appropriate in connection with the first of the above points. But the determination of the purview of obligations to future generations is both ethically and practically significant. It seems clear, at least, who does not come within their purview. Obligations to future generations

*Reprinted from The Monist, vol. 56, no. 1 (January, 1972), La Salle, Illinois, with permission of the author and publisher.

are distinct from the obligations we have to our presently living fellows, who are therefore excluded from the purview of the former, although it might well be the case that what we owe to future generations is identical with (or overlaps) what we owe to the present generation. However, I think we may go further than this and also exclude our most immediate descendants, our children, grandchildren and great-grandchildren, perhaps. What is distinctive about the notion of obligations to future generations is, I think, that it refers to generations with which the possessors of the obligations cannot expect in a literal sense to share a common life. (Of course, if we have obligations to future generations, understood in this way, we a fortiori have obligations to immediate posterity.) This, at any rate, is how I shall construe the reference of such obligations; neither our present fellows nor our immediate posterity come within their purview. What can be the basis of our obligations towards individuals with whom we cannot expect to share a common life is a question I shall consider shortly.

But if their inner boundary be drawn in this way, what can we say about their outer limits? Is there a cut-off point for the individuals in whose regard we have such obligations? Here, it seems, there are two alternatives. First, we can flatly say that there are no outer limits to their purview: all future generations come within their province. A second and more modest answer would be that we do not have such obligations towards any assignable future generation. In either case the referent is a broad and unspecified community of the future, and I think it can be shown that we run into difficulties unless certain qualifications are taken into account.

Our second point concerns the question of what it is that obligations to future generations oblige us to do. The short answer is that they oblige us to do many things. But an intervening step is required here, for obligations to future generations are distinct from general duties to perform acts which are in themselves intrinsically right, although such obligations give rise to duties to perform specific acts. Obligations to future generations are essentially an obligation to produce—or to attempt to produce—a desirable state of affairs _for_ the community of the future, to promote conditions of good living for future generations. The many things that we are obliged to do are founded upon this obligation (which is why I earlier questioned the necessity of the plural). If we think we have an obligation to transmit our cultural heritage to future generations it is because we think that our cultural heritage promotes, or perhaps even embodies, good living. In so doing we would hardly wish to falsify the records of our civilization, for future generations must also have, as a condition of good living, the opportunity to learn from the mistakes of the past. If, in addition, we believe lying to be intrinsically wrong we would also refrain from falsifying the records; but this would not be because we think we have any special duty to tell the truth to future generations.

To come closer to contemporary discussion, consider, for example, population control, which is often grounded upon an obligation to future generations. It is not maintained that population control is intrinsically right—although the rhetoric frequently seems to approach such a claim—but rather that it will contribute towards a better life for future generations, and perhaps immediate posterity as well. (If population control were intrinsically anything, I would incline to thinking it intrinsically wrong.) On the other hand, consider the elimination of water and air pollution. Here it might be maintained that we have a definite duty to cease polluting the environment on the grounds that such pollution is intrinsically bad[2] or that it violates a Divine command. Given the current mood of neo-paganism, even secularists speak of the despoilment of the environment as a sacrilege of sorts.

301

When the building of a new dam upsets the ecological balance and puts the wildlife under a threat, we react negatively and feel that something bad has resulted. And this is not because we necessarily believe that our own interests or those of future generations have been undermined. Both views, but especially the latter (Divine command), represent men as holding sovereignty over nature only as trustees to whom not everything is permitted. Nevertheless, these ways of grounding the duty to care for the environment are distinguishable from a grounding of the duty upon an obligation to future generations, although one who acknowledges such an obligation will also properly regard himself as a trustee to whom not everything is permitted. Caring for the environment is presumably among the many things that the obligation to future generations obliges us to do because we thereby presumably promote conditions of good living for the community of the future.

The obligation—dropping the plural again for a moment—to future generations, then, is not an immediate catalogue of specific duties. It is in this respect rather like the responsibility that a parent has to see to the welfare of his child. Discharging one's parental responsibility requires concern, seeking, and active effort to promote the good of the child, which is the central obligation of the parent and out of which grow the specific parental obligations and duties. The use of the term "responsibility" to characterize the parent's obligation connotes, in part, the element of discretion and flexibility which is requisite to the discharging of the obligation in a variety of antecedently unforeseeable situations. Determination of the specific duty is often quite problematic even—and sometimes especially—for the conscientious parent who is anxious to do what is good for his child. And, anticipating my later discussion, this also holds for obligatons to future generations. There are, of course, differences, too. Parental responsibility is enriched and reinforced by love, which can hardly obtain between us and future genera-

302

tions.[3] (Still, the very fact that the responsibility to promote the child's good is an obligation means that it is expected to operate even in the absence of love.) Secondly, the parental obligation is always towards assignable individuals, which is not the case with obligations to future generations. There is, however, an additional feature of likeness between the two obligations which I shall mention shortly.

The third point about obligations to future generations—to what class of obligation do they belong?—is that they are _owed_, albeit owed to an unspecified, and perhaps unspecifiable, community of the future. Obligations to future generations, therefore, are distinct from a general duty, when presented with alternatives for action, to choose the act which produces the greatest good. Such a duty is not owed to anyone, and the beneficiaries of my fulfilling a duty to promote the greatest good are not necessarily individuals to whom I stand in the moral relation of having an obligation that is owed. But when I owe it to someone to promote his good, he is never, to this extent, merely an incidental beneficiary of my effort to fulfill the obligation. He has a presumptive _right_ to it and can assert a claim against me for it. Obligations to future generations are of this kind. There is something which is due to the community of the future from us. The moral relation between us and future generations is one in which they have a claim against us to promote their good. Future generations are, thus, possessors of presumptive rights.

This conclusion is surely odd. How can future generations—the not-yet-born—_now_ have claims against us? This question serves to turn us finally to consider the basis of our obligations to future generations. I think it useful to begin by discussing and removing one source of the oddity.

It should first be noticed that there is no

oddity in investing present effort in order to promote a future state of affairs or in having an owed obligation to do so. The oddity arises only on a theory of obligations and claims (and, hence, of rights) that virtually identifies them with acts of willing, with the exercise of sovereignty of one over another, with the pressing of demands —in a word, with _making_ claims. But, clearly, future generations are not now engaged in acts of willing, are not now exercising sovereignty over us, and are not now pressing their demands. Future generations are not now making claims against us, nor will it be _possible_ for them to do so. (Our immediate posterity are in this last respect in a different case.) However, the identification of claims with making claims, demanding, is plausible within the field of rights and obligations because the content of a system of rights is historically conditioned by the making of claims. Individuals and groups put forward their claims to the goods of life, demand them as their right; and in this way the content is increasingly expanded towards the inclusion of more of these goods.

Nevertheless, as suggestive a clue as this fact is for the development of a theory of rights, there is a distinction to be drawn between _having_ claims and _making_ claims. The mere fact that someone claims something from me is not sufficient to establish it as his right, or that he has a claim relative to me. On the other hand, someone may have a claim relative to me whether or not he makes the claim, demands, or is even able to make a claim. (This is not to deny that claiming plays a role in the theory of rights.) Two points require attention here. First, some claims are frivolous. What is demanded cannot really be claimed as a matter of right. The crucial factor in determining this is the _social ideal_, which we may provisionally define as a conception of the good life for man. It serves as the yardstick by which demands, current and potential, are measured.[4] Secondly, whether someone's claim confers an entitlement upon him to receive what is claimed <u>from me</u> depends upon my moral relation to him, on whether he is a member of my <u>moral community</u>. It is these factors, rather than any actual demanding, which establish whether someone has a claim relative to me. (I should like to emphasize that I am not necessarily maintaining that the concepts of a social ideal and a moral community are involved in a theory of every kind of obligation, but, rather, that they are required by the kind of obligation being considered here.)

The concepts of a social ideal and a moral community are clearly in need of further explanation, yet as they stand the above considerations should serve to relieve a good deal of the oddity that is felt in the assertion that future generations now have claims against us and that they are possessors of presumptive rights. There is, however, a residual sense of peculiarity in the assertion because it still remains to be shown whether future generations are members of our moral community. A discussion of the question of membership in a moral community will, I think, shed light on these subjects.

Who are the members of my moral community? (Who is my neighbor?) The fact is that I am a member of more than one moral community, for I belong to a variety of groups whose members owe obligations to one another. And many of the particular obligations that are owed vary from group to group. As a result my obligations are often in conflict and I experience a fragmentation of energy and responsibility in attempting to meet my obligations. What I ought to desire for the members of one of these groups is frequently in opposition to what I ought to desire for the members of another of these groups. Moral communities are constituted, or generated, in a number of ways, one of which is especially relevant to our problem. Yet these ways are not mutually exclusive, and they can be mutually reenforcing. This is a large topic and I cannot go into its details here. It is sufficient for our purpose to take brief notice of two possible ways of generating a moral community so as to set in relief the particular kind of moral community that is requisite for obligations to future generations.

A moral community may be constituted by an explicit contract between its members. In this case the particular obligations which the members have towards each other are fixed by the terms of their bargain. Secondly, a moral community may be generated out of a social arrangement in which each member derives benefits from the efforts of other members. As a result a member acquires an obligation to share the burden of sustaining the social arrangement. Both of these are communities in which entrance and participation are fundamentally a matter of self-interest, and only rarely will there be an obligation of the sort that was discussed earlier, that is, a responsibility to secure the good of the members. In general the obligations will be of more specialized kinds. It is also apparent that obligations acquired in these ways can easily come into conflict with other obligations that one may have. Clearly, a moral community comprised of present and future generations cannot arise from either of these sources. We cannot enter into an explicit contract with the community of the future. And although future generations might derive benefits from us, these benefits cannot be reciprocated. (It is possible that the [biologically] dead do derive <u>some</u> benefits from the living, but I do not think that this possibility is crucial. Incidentally, just as the living could have obligations to the distant unborn, the living also have obligations to the dead. If obligation to the past is a superstition, then so is obligation to the future.)[5] Our immediate posterity, who will share a common life with us, are in a better position in this respect; so that obligations towards our children, born and unborn, conceivably <u>could</u> be generated from participation in a mutually beneficial social arrangement. This, however, would be misleading.

It seems, then, that communities in which entrance and participation are fundamentally matters of self-interest, do not fit our specifications. As an alternative let us consider communities based upon altruistic impulses and fellow-feeling. This, too, is in itself a large topic, and I refer to it only in order to develop a single point.

The question I began with was: Who are the members of my moral community? Now it is true that there are at least a few people towards whom I have the sentiments that are identified with altruism and sympathetic concern. But are these sentiments enough to establish for me the moral relationship of owing them an obligation? Are these enough to generate a moral community? The answer, I think, must be in the negative so long as these affections towards others remain at the level of animal feeling. The ancient distinction between mere affection, mere liking, and conscious desire is fundamental here. Genuine concern and interest in the well-being of another must be conscious concern. My desire for another's good must in this event be more than impulsive, and presupposes, rather, that I have a conception of his good. This conception, which cannot be a bare concept of what is incidentally a good but which is rather a conception of the good for him, further involves that he not be a mere blank to me but that he is characterized or described in some way in my consciousness. It is perhaps unnecessary to add that there is never any absolute guarantee that such a conceived good is not, in some sense, false or fragmentary. Nevertheless, an altruism that is literally mindless—if it can be called "altruism" at all—cannot be the basis of moral community.

But even if it be granted that I have a conception of another's good, I have not yet reached the stage of obligation towards him. We are all familiar with the kind of "taking an interest in the welfare of another" that is gracious and gift-like, a matter of noblesse oblige. It is

not so much that this type of interest-taking
tends to be casual, fleeting and fragmentary—
"cette charité froide qui on nomme altruisme"—
and stands in contrast to interest-taking that is
constant, penetrating and concerned with the
other's total good. It is, rather, a form of interest-taking, however "conceptual," that is a
manifestation of an unreadiness or even an unwillingness to recognize the other's claim (as
distinct, of course, from his claiming), the
other's entitlement, to receive his good from me.
An additional step is, therefore, required, and
I think it consists in this: that I acknowledge
this good as a good, that his good is good-to-
me. Once I have made this step, I cannot in conscious deny the pertinence of his demand, if he
makes one, although whether I should now act so
as to promote his good is of course dependent on
a host of factors. (Among these factors are
moral considerations that determine the permissibility of various courses of action and priorities of duty.) The basis of the obligation
is nevertheless secured.

This conclusion, it should be clear, does
not entail that I am required to concede the
status of an entitlement to every demand that is
made by someone in whose well-being I have an
interest. Some claims (claimings), as remarked
above, are frivolous. The test of this, in the
case we have been considering, is my conception
of the other's good. This conception is a model
in miniature of what I earlier called a social
ideal. However, the provisional definition of
it—a conception of the good life for man—was
unnecessarily broad. In using this term, I mean,
first of all, to contrast the ideal with a personal ideal of the good life. A personal ideal
of the good life is an ideal that is not necessarily maintained as desirable for others to
seek to achieve. It is what an individual, given
his unique interests and idiosyncrasies, sees as
the private end of his striving; while it does
not necessarily exclude elements of sociality, it
is not social in its purview. By the term

"social ideal," however, I mean primarily a conception of the good life for individuals under some general characterization and which can be maintained by them as good for them in virtue of this characterization. The term covers the possibility of a social ideal that is a conception of the good life for individuals characterized in the broadest terms, namely, as human. But a social ideal may be narrower in its scope. For example, one may have a conception of the good life for the city-dweller or for the outdoors type. Since it is possible for me to maintain as good-to-me a variety of ideals bearing upon groups of individuals characterized in different ways, it is possible for me to be a member of more than one moral community. It is in such circumstances, as mentioned earlier, that I will experience the conflicting pulls of obligation and competing claims upon my energy and effort.

(There is admittedly much more to be said in explanation of the nature of social ideals, for they need not be static. The implications of our ideals are not always immediately available, and they are enriched and clarified through experience. They are adaptable to new life-circumstances. And they can also become impoverished. Just as ideals are not static, neither are the characterizations of the individuals to whom the ideals are meant to apply. Another topic that requires further study is the "logic" of the ideal-claim relationship, a study of the ways in which ideals confer entitlements upon claims. Questions also arise concerning justice and reciprocity. This list could be extended; it is only meant to be suggestive. I make no pretence that I am able to solve these problems at this time.)

So far, in the above account of the generation of my moral community, the question of membership has been discussed solely in reference to those towards whom I initially have the sentiments that are identified with fellow-feeling. But we can go beyond this. Again we take our

clue from the history of the development of
rights. For just as the content of a system of
rights that are possessed by the members of a
moral community is enlarged over time by the
pressing of claims, demanding, so also is the
moral community enlarged by the pressing of
claims by individuals who have been hitherto excluded. The claiming is not only a claim for
something, but may also be an assertion: "Here
I am, I count too." The struggle for rights has
been a counter-struggle. The widening of moral
communities has been accompanied by attempts at
exclusion. It is important for us to take note
of one feature of this situation.

The structure of the situation is high-
lighted when a stranger puts forward his demand.
The question immediately arises, shall his claim
be recognized as a matter of right?[6] Initially
I have no affection for him. But is this crucial
in determining whether he ought to count as a
member of my moral community? The determination
depends, rather, on what he is like and what are
the conditions of his life. One's obligations to
a stranger are never immediately clear. If a
visitor from Mars or Venus were to appear, I
would not know what to desire for him. I would
not know whether my conception of the good life
is relevant to him and to his conditions of life.
The good that I acknowledge might not be good for
him. Humans, of course, are in a better case
than Martians or Venusians. Still, since the
stranger appears as strange, different, what I
maintain in my attempt to exclude him is that my
conception of the good is not relevant to him,
that "his kind" do not count. He, on the other
hand, is in effect saying to me: Given your
social ideal, you must acknowledge my claim, for
it is relevant to me given what I am; your good
is my good, also.[7] If I should finally come to
concede this, the full force of my obligation to
him will be manifest to me quite independently
of any fellow-feeling that might or might not be
aroused. The involuntary character of the obligation will be clear to me, as it probably never

is in the case of individuals who command one's
sympathy. And once I admit him as a member of my
moral community, I will also acknowledge my responsibility to secure this good for him even in
the absence of any future claiming on his part.

   With this we have completed the account of
the constitution of the type of moral community
that is required for obligations to future generations. I shall not recapitulate its elements.
The step that incorporates future generations into our moral community is small and obvious. Future generations are members of our moral community because, and insofar as, our social ideal
is relevant to them, given what they are and
their conditions of life. I believe that this
account applies also to obligations towards our
immediate posterity. However, the responsibility
that one has to see to the welfare of his children is in addition buttressed and qualified by
social understandings concerning the division of
moral labor and by natural affection. The basis
of the obligations is nevertheless the same in
both instances.[8] Underlying this account is the
important fact that such obligations fall into
the area of the moral life which is independent
of considerations of explicit contract and personal advantage. Moral duty and virtue also fall
into this area. But I should like to emphasize
again that I do not wish to be understood as
putting this account forward as an analysis of
moral virtue and duty in general.

   As we turn at long last specifically to our
obligations to future generations, it is worth
noticing that the term "contract" has been used
to cover the kind of moral community that I have
been discussing. It occurs in a famous passage in
Burke's Reflections on the Revolution in France:

   Society is indeed a contract. Subordinate contracts for objects of mere occasional interest
   may be dissolved at pleasure—but the state
   ought not to be considered as nothing better than
   a partnership agreement in a trade of pepper and

coffee, calico or tobacco, or some other such low concern, to be taken up for a little temporary interest, and to be dissolved by the fancy of the parties. It is to be looked upon with other reverence; because it is not a partnership in things subservient only to the gross animal existence of a temporary and perishable nature.

It is a partnership in all science; a partnership in all art; a partnership in every virtue, and in all perfection. As the ends of such a partnership cannot be obtained in many generations, it becomes a partnership not only between those who are living, but between those who are living, those who are dead and those who are to be born.

Each contract of each particular state is but a clause in the great primaeval contract of eternal society, linking the lower with the higher natures, connecting the visible and invisible world, according to a fixed compact sanctioned by the inviolable oath which holds all physical and all moral natures, each in their appointed place.

The contract Burke has in mind is hardly an explicit contract, for it is "between those who are living, those who are dead and those who are to be born." He implicitly affirms, I think, obligations to future generations. In speaking of the "ends of such a partnership," Burke intends a conception of the good life for man—a social ideal. And, if I do not misinterpret him, I think it also plain that Burke assumes that it is relatively the same conception of the good life whose realization is the object of the efforts of the living, the dead, and the unborn. They all revere the same social ideal. Moreover, he seems to assume that the conditions of life of the three groups are more or less the same. And, finally, he seems to assume that the same general characterization is true of these groups ("all physical and moral natures, each in their appointed place").

Now I think that Burke is correct in making assumptions of these sorts if we are to have obligations to future generations. However, it is precisely with such assumptions that the notion of obligation to future generations begins to run into difficulties. My discussion, until this point, has proceeded on the view that we <u>have</u> obligations to future generations. But do we? I am not sure that the question can be answered in the affirmative with any certainty. I shall conclude this note with a very brief discussion of some of the difficulties. They may be summed up in the question: Is our conception —"conceptions" might be a more accurate word— of the good life for man relevant[10] to future generations?

It will be recalled that I began by stressing the importance of fixing the purview of obligations to future generations. They comprise the community of the future, a community with which we cannot expect to share a common life. It appears to me that the more <u>remote</u> the members of this community are, the <u>more</u> problematic our obligations to them become. That they are members of our moral community is highly doubtful, for we probably do not know what to desire for them.

Let us consider a concrete example, namely, that of the maintenance of genetic quality. Sir Julian Huxley has stated:

> (I)f we don't do something about controlling our genetic inheritance, we are going to degenerate. Without selection, bad mutations inevitably tend to accumulate; <u>in the long run, perhaps 5,000 to 10,000 years from now,</u> we (sic) shall certainly have to do something about it. . . . Most mutations are deleterious, but we now keep many of them going that would otherwise have died out. If this continues indefinitely . . . then the whole genetic capacity of man will be much weakened.[11]

This statement, and others like it, raise many issues. As I have elsewhere (see footnote 1) discussed the problems connected with eugenic programs, positive and negative, I shall not go into details here. The point I would make is this: given that we do not know the conditions of life of the very distant future generations, we do not know what we ought to desire for them even on such matters as genic constitution. The chromosome is "deleterious" or "advantageous" only relative to given circumstances. And the same argument applies against those who would promote certain social traits by means of genetic engineering (assuming that social traits are heritable). Even such a trait as Intelligence does not escape immune. (There are also problems in eugenic programs having nothing to do with remoteness.) One might go so far as to say that if we have an obligation to distant future generations it is an obligation not to plan for them. Not only do we not know their conditions of life, we also do not know whether they will maintain the same (or a similar) conception of the good life for man as we do. Can we even be fairly sure that the same general characterization is true both of them and us?

The moral to be drawn from this rather extreme example is that the more distant the generation we focus upon, the less likely it is that we have an obligation to promote its good. We would be both ethically and practically well-advised to set our sights on more immediate generations and, perhaps, solely upon our immediate posterity. After all, even if we do have obligations to future generations, our obligations to immediate posterity are undoubtedly much clearer. The nearer the generations are to us, the more likely it is that our conception of the good life is relevant to them. There is certainly enough work for us to do in discharging our responsibility to promote a good life for them. But it would be unwise, both from an ethical and a practical perspective, to seek to promote the good of the very distant.

And it could also be _wrong_, if it be granted —as I think it must—that our obligations towards (and hence the rights relative to us of) near future generations and especially our immediate posterity are clearer than those of more distant generations. By "more distant" I do not necessarily mean "very distant." We shall have to be highly scrupulous in regard to anything we do for any future generation that also could adversely affect the rights of an intervening generation. Anything else would be "gambling in futures." We should, therefore, be hesitant to act on the dire predictions of certain extreme "crisis ecologists" and on the proposals of those who would have us plan for mere survival. In the main, we would be ethically well-advised to confine ourselves to removing the obstacles that stand in the way of immediate posterity's realizing the social ideal. This involves not only the active task of cleaning up the environment and making our cities more habitable, but also implies restraints upon us. Obviously, the specific obligations that we have cannot be determined in the abstract. This article is not the place for an evaluation of concrete proposals that have been made. I would only add that population limitation schemes seem rather dubious to me. I find it inherently paradoxical that we should have an obligation to future generations (near and distant) to determine in effect the very membership of those generations. [12]

A final point. If certain trends now apparent in our biological technology continue, it is doubtful that we should regard ourselves as being under an obligation to future generations. It seems likely that the man—humanoid(?)—of the future will be Programmed Man, fabricated to order, with his finger constantly on the Delgado button that stimulates the pleasure centers of the brain. I, for one, cannot see myself as regarding the good for Programmed Man as a good-to-me. That we should do so, however, is a necessary condition of his membership in our moral community, as I have argued above. The course of

315

these trends may very well be determined by whether we believe that we are, in the words of Burke, "but a clause in the great primaeval contract of eternal society, linking the lower with the higher natures, connecting the visible and invisible world, according to a fixed compact sanctioned by the inviolable oath which holds all physical and all moral natures, each in their appointed place." We cannot yet pretend to know the outcome of these trends. It appears that whether we have obligations to future generations in part depends on what we do for the present.

Notes

[1]This paper is highly speculative, and it is put forward with hesitation. It is an attempt to extend a position developed in my article "Towards a Theory of Human Rights," The Monist, 52, No. 4 (1968), 521-549, wherein I also discuss some of the classical and contemporary literature on Rights. See also my paper, "Ethical Issues in Biological Engineering," U.C.L.A. Law Review, 15 (1968), 443-479, esp. 451-463, wherein I discuss obligations to future generations and some of the problems they provoke. I know of no other explicit discussion of the topic. The author wishes to thank the Institute of Society, Ethics, and the Life Sciences (Hastings-on-Hudson, New York) for its support.

[2]See the remarks of Russell E. Train (Chairman of the Council on Environmental Quality), quoted in National Geographic, 138 (1970), 780: "If we're to be responsible we must accept the fact that we owe a massive debt to our environment. It won't be settled in a matter of months, and it won't be forgiven us."

[3]Cf. the discussion of Fernstenliebe (Love of the Remotest) in Nicolai Hartmann, Ethics, trans. by Coit, II (New York: The Macmillan Co., 1932), 317 ff.

[4]There is also another factor relevant to determining whether what is demanded can be claimed as a matter of right, namely, the availability of resources of goods. But I am suppressing this

for purposes of this discussion.

[5] Paraphrasing C. S. Lewis, The Abolition of Man (New York: The Macmillan Co., paperback ed. 1969), p. 56: "If my duty to my parents is a superstition, then so is my duty to posterity."

[6] When Sarah died, Abraham "approached the children of Heth, saying: I am a stranger and a sojourner with you; give me a possession of a burying-place with you, that I may bury my dead out of my sight" (Gen. 23:3,4). A classical commentary remarks that Abraham is saying: If I am a stranger, I will purchase it, but if I am a sojourner it is mine as a matter of right.

[7] Cf. T. H. Green, Lectures on the Principles of Political Obligation (New York and London: Longman's, 1959; Ann Arbor: University of Michigan Press, 1967), Sec. 140. I here acknowledge my debt to Green, in which acknowledgment I was remiss in my article on Human Rights.

[8] I think it an interesting commentary on our times that the rhetoric of obligation to future generations is so much used just when the family bond has become progressively tenuous.

[9] Reflections on the Revolution in France (London: Dent, 1910), pp. 93-94.

[10] The author at last begs pardon for having to use an abused word.

[11] In Evolution after Darwin, ed. by S. Tax, III (Chicago: University of Chicago Press, 1960), p. 61. Emphasis added.

[12] On this and other arguments relating to the problem, see Martin P. Golding and Naomi H. Golding, "Ethical and Value Issues in Population Limitation and Distribution in the United States," Vanderbilt Law Review, 24 (1971), 495-523.

Education

Case

The upcoming school board elections had been an occasional topic of conversation for Sue and Carolyn on their lunch breaks. Today Sue seemed agitated and more spirited in her attack on one of the candidates from her district. He had said in a speech the night before that if elected he would work for a work-study program in the high schools. Young people need to know math, history, English, and science, but these must be related to the world of work to be relevant. He also called for beefing up the fine arts program for the school district. The liberal arts are fine, but they need to be tempered with the reality of finding a job and making a living. Sue said that she could not believe her ears. Her experience in the liberal arts in high school and college convinced her that the best preparation for life was developing a sense of values and learning to think. There is enough time after completing school to worry about making a living. Instead of spending money for "relevance" spend it for smaller classes and better instruction.

Harvard: The Future*
Alfred North Whitehead

I

In the tercentenary celebrations of this
summer, Harvard marks the accomplishment of its
process of growth. About twenty-five years for
a man and about three hundred years for a university are the periods required for the attainment of mature stature. The history of Harvard
is no longer to be construed primarily in terms
of growth, but in terms of effectiveness.

I am talking of effectiveness in the wide
world, of impress on the course of events, without which civilized humanity would not be as in
fact it is. In the Cambridge of England, the
first college was founded in the year 1284, and
Emmanuel College in the year 1584. The English
university was then grown up. Within the next
one hundred and fifty years there occurred a
brilliant period—the brilliant period—of European civilization. It staged a decisive episode
in the drama of human life. In this episode the
English university played no mean part, from
Edmund Spenser and Francis Bacon at the outset to
Newton and Dryden at the close. Among other
things, Cambridge helped to contribute Milton,
Cromwell, and Harvard University.

The term 'European civilization' is now a
misnomer, for the centre of gravity has shifted.
Civilization haunts the borders of waterways.
The shores of the Mediterranean and the western
coasts of Europe are cases in point. But nowadays, relatively to our capacities, the dimensions

*From Atlantic Monthly, vol. 158, no. 3, (Septem-
ber, 1936), pp. 200-270. Copyright © by The
Atlantic Monthly Company, Boston, Mass. Reprinted by permission of the author and publisher.

of the world have shrunk, and the Atlantic Ocean plays the same rôle as the European seas in the former centuries. The total result is that the North American shores of the Atlantic are in the central position to influence the adventures of mankind, from East to West and from North to South. The static aspects of things are measured from the meridian of Greenwich; but the world will rotate around the long line of American shores.

What is the influence of Harvard to mean in the immediate future, originating thought and feeling during the next fifty years, or during the next one hundred and fifty years? Harvard is one of the outstanding universities in the very centre of human activity. At the present moment it is magnificiently equipped. It has enjoyed nigh seventy years of splendid management. A new epoch is opening in the world. There are new potentialities, new hopes, new fears. The old scales of relative quantitative importance have been inverted. New qualitative experiences are developing. And yet, beneath all the excitement of novelty, with its discard and rejection, the basic motives for human action remain, the old facts of human nature clothed in a novelty of detail. What is the task before Harvard?

It will be evident that in this summary presentation of the cultural problem the word 'Harvard' is to be taken partly in its precise designation of a particular institution and partly as a symbolic reference to the university system throughout the Eastern states of this country. A closely intertwined group of institutions, the outcome of analogous impulses, has in the last three hundred years gradually developed, from Charlottesville to Baltimore, from Baltimore to Boston, and from Boston to Chicago. Of these institutions some are larger and some are smaller, some are in cities and some are in country places, some are older and some are younger. But each of them has the age of the group, as moulded by this cultural impulse. The fate of the intellectual

civilization of the world is to-day in the hands
of this group—for such time as it can effectively retain the sceptre. And to-day there is no
rival. The Ægean coast line had its chance and
made use of it; Italy had its chance and made
use of it; France, England, Germany, had their
chance and made use of it. To-day the Eastern
American states have their chance. What use will
they make of it? The question has two answers.
Once Babylon had its chance, and produced the
Tower of Babel. The University of Paris fashioned the intellect of the Middle Ages. Will Harvard fashion the intellect of the twentieth
century?

II

We cannot usefully discuss the organization
of universities, considered as educational institutions, apart from a preliminary survey of the
general character of human knowledge, and of some
special features of modern life. Such a survey
elicits perplexities which have troubled learning
from the earliest days of the Greeks to the present moment. By introducing implicit assumptions
in respect to these problems, it is possible to
arrive at almost any doctrine respecting university organization.

In the first place, there is the division
into certainty and probability. Some items we
are certain about, others are matters of opinion.
There is an obvious common sense about this doctrine, and its enunciation goes back to Plato.
The class of certainties falls into two subdivi-
sions. In one subdivision are certain large general truths,—for example, the multiplication
table, axioms as to quantitative 'more or less,'
—and certain aesthetic and moral presuppositions.
In the other subdivision are momentary discrimi-
nations of one's own state of mind: for example,
a state of feeling—happiness at this moment; and
for another example, an item of sense perception
—that colored shape experienced at this moment.
But recollection and interpretation are both

deceitful. Thus this latter subdivision just touches certainty and then loses it. There is mere imitation of certainty.

In the class of probabilities there are to be found all our judgments as to the goings on of this world of temporal succession, except so far as these happenings are qualified by the certainties whenever they are relevant.

I repeat my affirmation that, in some sense or other, this characterization of human knowledge is indubitable. No one doubts the multiplication table; also everyone admits that a witness on the witness stand can only produce fallible evidence, which the judicial authorities endeavor to assess, again only fallibly.

The bearing of these doctrines on the procedures of education cannot be missed. In the first place: Develop intellectual activities by a knowledge of the certain truths, so far as they are largely applicable to human life. In the second place: Train the understanding of each student to assess probable knowledge in respect to those types of occurrences which for any reason will be of major importance in the exercise of his activities. In the third place: Give him adequate knowledge of the possibilities of aesthetic and moral satisfaction which are open to a human being, under conditions relevant to his future life.

So far there is no disagreement. Unfortunately, exactly at this point our difficulties commence. This is the reason why the prefatory analysis was necessary. These difficulties are best explained by a slight reference to the history of thought, stretching from Greece to William James.

Plato was a voluminous writer, and apparently all his works have come down to us. They constitute a discussion of the various types of certain knowledge, of probable knowledge, and of

aesthetic and moral ideals. This discussion,
viewed as elucidating the above-mentioned classification of knowledge which is to be the basis of
education, was a complete failure. He failed to
make clear what was certain; and where he was
certain, we disagree with him. He failed to make
clear the relationship of things certain to things
probable; and where he thought he was clear, we
disagree with him. He failed to make clear the
moral and aesthetic ends of life; and where he
thought he was clear, we disagree with him. No
two of his dialogues are completely consistent
with each other. No two modern scholars agree as
to what any one dialogue exactly means. This
failure of Plato is the great fact dominating the
history of European thought.

Also this failure was typical. It stretches
through every topic of human interest. Every
single generalization respecting mathematical
physics, which I was taught at the University of
Cambridge during my student period from the years
1880 to 1885, has now been abandoned in the sense
in which it was then held. The words are retained, but with different meanings.

The truth is that this beautiful subdivision
of human knowledge, whether you make it twofold
or threefold, goes up in smoke as soon as you try
to fasten upon it any exact meaning. As a vague
preliminary guide, it is useful. But when you
trust it without reserve, it violates the conditions of human experience. The history of thought
is largely concerned with the records of clear-
headed men insisting that they at last have discovered some clear, adequately expressed, indubitable truths. If clear-headed men throughout the
ages would only agree with each other, we might
cease to be puzzled. Alas, that is a comfort
denied to us.

III

The outcome of this brief survey is so fundamental in its relevance to education that it must

be elucidated further by considering it in reference to two topics—Mathematics, and the Abiding Importance of Plato.

The science of Mathematics is the very citadel of the doctrine of certainty. It is unnecessary to bring the large developments of the subject into this discussion. Let us consider the multiplication table. This table is concerned with simple interrelations of cardinal numbers, as for example, 'Twice three' is 'six.' Nothing can be more certain. But a little question arises: What are cardinal numbers? There is no universally accepted answer to this question. In fact, it is the battle ground of a controversy. The innocent suggestions which occur to us are traps which lead us into self-contradictions or into other puzzles. The notion of number is obviously concerned with the concept of a class, or a group, of many things. It expresses the special sort of many-ness in question. Unfortunately the notion of a class is beset with ambiguities leading to logical traps. We then have recourse to the fundamental notions of logic, and again encounter a contest of dissentient opinions. Logic is the chosen resort of clear-headed people, severally convinced of the complete adequacy of their doctrines. It is such a pity that they cannot agree with each other.

Analogous perplexities arise in respect to the fundamental notions of other mathematical topics: for example, the meaning of the notions of a point, of a line, and of a straight line. There is great confidence and no agreement.

Thus the palmary instances of human certainty, Logic and Mathematics, have given way under the scrutiny of two thousand years. To-day we have less apparent ground for certainty than had Plato and Aristotle. The natural rebound from this conclusion is skepticism. Trust your reflexes, says the skeptic, and do not seek to understand. Your reflexes are the outcome of routine. Your emotions are modes of reception of the process. There is no understanding, because there is nothing to understand.

Complete skepticism involves an aroma of self-destruction. It seems as the negation of experience. It craves for an elegy on the passing of rational knowledge—the beautiful youth drowned in the Sea of Vacuity.

The large practical effect of skepticism is gross acquiescence in what is immediate and obvious. Postponement, subtle interweaving, delicacies of adjustment, wide coördinations, moral restraint, the whole artistry of civilization, all presuppose understanding. And without understanding they are meaningless.

Thus, in practice, skepticism always means some knowledge, but not too much. It is indeed evident that our knowledge is limited. But the traditional skepticism is a reaction against an imperfect view of human knowledge.

It is in respect to this limitation of knowledge that the ancient division into certainties and probabilities is so misleading. It suggests that we have a perfectly clear indication of the items in question, and are either certain or uncertain as to the existence of some definite connection between them. For example, it presupposes that we have a perfectly clear indication of the numbers 2 and 3 and 6, and are either certain or uncertain as to whether twice three is six.

The fact is the other way round. We are very vague as to the meanings of 1, and 2, and 3, and 5, and 6. But we want to determine these meanings so as to preserve the relations, 'six is one more than five' and 'twice three is six.' In other words, we are more clear as to the interrelations of the numbers than as to their separate individual characters. We use the interrelations as a step toward the determinations of the things related.

This is an instance of the general truth, that our progress in clarity of knowledge is primarily from the composition to its ingredients. The very meaning of the notion of definition is the use of composition for the purpose of indication.

The important characterization of knowledge is in respect to clarity and vagueness.

The reason for this dominance of vagueness and clarity in respect to the problem of knowledge is that the world is not made up of independent things, each completely determinate in abstraction from all the rest. Contrast is of the essence of character. In its happy instances contrast is harmony; in its unhappy instances contrast is confusion. Our experience is dominated by composite wholes, more or less clear in the focus, and more or less vague in the penumbra, and with the whole shading off into umbral darkness which is ignorance. But throughout the whole, alike in the focal regions, the penumbral regions, and the umbral regions, there is baffling mixture of clarity and vagueness.

The primary weapon is analysis. And analysis is the evocation of insight by the hypothetical suggestions of thought, and the evocation of thought by the activities of direct insight. In this process the composite whole, the interrelations, and the things related, concurrently emerge into clarity.

One of the most interesting facts in the psychology of young students at the present time is the abiding interest of the platonic writings. From the point of view of displaying the sharp distinction between the certainties and the opinions involved in human knowledge, Plato failed. But he gave an unrivaled display of the human mind in action, with its ferment of vague obviousness, of hypothetical formulation, of renewed insight, of discovery of relevant detail, of partial understanding, of final conclusion,

with its disclosure of deeper problems as yet un-
solved. There we find exposed to our view the
problem of education as it should dominate a university. Knowledge is a process, adding content
and control to the flux of experience. It is the
function of a university to initiate its students
in the exercise of this process of knowledge.

IV

The problem before Harvard is set by the
termination of an epoch in European culture. For
three centuries European learning has employed
itself in a limited definite task. It was a
necessary task and an important task. Scholars,
in science and in literature, have been bril-
liantly successful. But they have finished that
task—at least for the time, although every task
is resumed after the lapse of some generations.
However, for the moment, the trivialization of
the traditional scholarship is the note of our
civilization.

The fundamental presupposition behind learning has been that of the possession of clear
ideas, as starting points for all expression and
all theory. The problem has been to weave these
ideas into compound structures, with the attributes either of truth, or of beauty, or of moral
elevation. There was preseumed to be no difficulty in framing sentences in which each word and
each phrase had an exact meaning. The only topics for discussion were whether the sentence when
framed was true or false, beautiful or ugly,
moral or shocking. European learning was founded
on the dictionary; and splendid dictionaries were
produced. With the culmination of the dictionaries the epoch has ended. For this reason, all
the dictionaries of all the languages have failed
to provide for the expression of the full human
experience.

The ultimate cause for this characteristic
of European learning was that from the close of
the dark ages civilization has been progressing

with the gradual recovery of the subtle, many-sided literature of the old classical civilization. Thought then had the character of a recovery of the wide variety of meanings embedded in Greek and Hellenistic written literature. The result was that everything that a modern scholar thought could have been immediately understood by Thucydides, or Democritus, or Plato, or Aristotle, or Archimedes. Any one of these men would have understood Newton's Laws of Motion at a glance. These laws were a new structure of old ideas. Perhaps Aristotle would have shied at Newton's first law. But he would have understood it. Any one of these men would have understood the American Declaration of Independence. There is nothing in the Constitution of the United States to puzzle them. Perhaps the addition of these five sages to an august tribunal might even facilitate the elucidation of its applications.

The conception of mind and matter, of motion in space, of individual rights, of the rights of social groups,—the world of tragedy, and of joy, and of heroism,—was thoroughly familiar to the ancients, and its obvious interrelations were expressed in language, and discussed, and rediscussed. Throughout the last three or four centuries the notion of learning was the discussion of the ways of the world with the linguistic tools derived from the past. This procedure of learning was the basis of progress from the simplicities of the dark ages to the modern civilization.

For this reason a narrow convention as to learning, and as to the procedures of institutions connected with it, has developed. Tidiness, simplicity, clarity, exactness, are conceived as characteristics of the nature of things, as in human experience. It is presupposed that a university is engaged in imparting exact, clear knowledge. Lawyers are apt to presuppose that legal documents have an exact meaning, even with the absence of commas.

328

Thus, to a really learned man, matter exists in test tubes, animals in cages, art in museums, religion in churches, knowledge in libraries.

It is easy to sneer. But there is a problem here—a very difficult problem; and the success of Harvard depends upon maintaining a proper interweaving of its intricacies. The development of learning, and the success of education, require selection. The human mind can only deal with limited topics, which exclude the vague immensity of nature. Thus the tradition of learning is the solid ground upon which the university must be founded, in respect to both sides of its activity—namely, the enlargement of knowledge and the training of youth.

The real problem is to adjust the activities of the learned institution so as to suffuse them with suggestiveness. Human nature loses its most precious quality when it is robbed of its sense of things beyond, unexplored and yet insistent. Mankind owes its progress beyond the iron limits of custom to the fact that, compared to the animals, men are amateurs. 'You Greeks are always children' is the taunt from Learning to Suggestiveness.

Learning is sensible, straightforward, and clear, if only you keep at bay the suggestiveness of things. This clarity is delusive, and is shot through and through with controversy. The traditional attitude of scholars is to choose a side, and to keep the enemy at bay by exposing their errors. Of course, in the clash of doctrine we must base thoughts and actions on those modes of statement which seem to express the larger truth. But it is fatal to dismiss antagonistic doctrines, supported by any body of evidence, as simply wrong. Inconsistent truths —that is, truths in the sense of conformity to some evidence—are seed beds of suggestiveness. The progress which they suggest lies at the very root of knowledge. It is concerned with the

recasting of the fundamental notions on which
the structure is built. The suggestion does not
primarily concern a new conclusion. Fundamental
progress has to do with the reinterpretation of
basic ideas.

At this point, the problem has only been
half stated. Experience does not occur in the
clothing of verbal phrases. It involves clashes
of emotion, and unspoken revelations of the nature of things. Revelation is the primary characterization of the process of knowing. The
traditional theory of education is to secure
youth and its teachers from revelation. It is
dangerous for youth, and confusing to teachers.
It upsets the accepted coördinations of doctrine.

Revelation is the enlargement of clarity. It
is not a deduction, though it may issue from a deduction. The dictionaries are very weak upon this
point.

V

Without doubt, in its preliminary stages
education is concerned with the introduction of
order into the mind of the young child. Experience starts as a 'blooming, buzzing confusion.' Order introduces enlargement, significance, importance, delicacies of perception.
For long years, the major aspect of education is
the reduction of confusion to order, and the
provision of weapons for this purpose.

And yet, even at the beginning of school
life, it has been found necessary to interfuse
the introduction of order with the enjoyment of
enterprise. The balance is difficult to hold.
But it is well known that education as mere imposed order of 'things known' is a failure. The
initial stages of reading, writing, and arith-
metic should be suffused with revelation.

At the other end of education, during the
university period, there is undoubtedly the excitement of novel knowledge—volumes of words.
But an inversion has entered upon the stage.
The child has to be taught the words that cor-

respond to the things; the senior at college has lost the things that correspond to the words. His mind is occupied by literary scenery; by doctrines derived from books; by experiments of a selected character, with selected materials, and such that irrelevancies are neglected. Even his games are organized. Novel impulse is frowned upon at the bridge table, on the football field, and on the river. No member of a crew is praised for the rugged individuality of his rowing.

The question is how to introduce the freedom of nature into the orderliness of knowledge. The ideal of universities, with staff and students shielded from the contemplation of the sporadic life around them, will produce a Byzantine civilization, surviving for a thousand years without producing any idea fundamentally new.

There is no one recipe. It is an obvious suggestion to collect an able, vigorous faculty and give it a free hand, with every encouragement. This principle of university management has been no news at Harvard since its foundation. Also the environment of New England facilitates its practice, by producing both the men and the requisite atmosphere. It is not as simple to follow this suggestion as it looks. For half a century, on both sides of the Atlantic, I have been concerned with appointments. Nothing is more difficult than to distinguish between a loud voice and vigor, or a flow of words and originality, or mental instability and genius; or a big book and fruitful learning. Also the work requires dependable men. But if you are swayed too heavily by this admirable excellence, you will gather a faculty which can be depended upon for being commonplace.

Curiously enough, the achievements of the faculty do not depend on the exact judiciousness of each appointment. In a vigorous society, ability, in the sense of capacity for high achievement, is fairly widespread. Undoubtedly it can only be ascribed to a minority; but this minority is larger than it is conventional to estimate. The real question is to transmute the potency for achievement into the actuality of achievement. The instrument for this purpose is the stimulus of the atmosphere. In other words, we come back to suggestiveness.

Knowledge should never be familiar. It should always be contemplated either under the aspect of novel application, or under the aspect of skepticism as to the extent of its application, or under the aspect of development of its consequences, or under the aspect of eliciting the fundamental meanings which it presupposes, or under the aspect of a guide in the adventures of life, or under the aspect of the aesthetic of its interwoven relationships, or under the aspect of the miraculous history of its discovery. But no one should remain blankly content with the mere knowledge that 'twice three is six'—apart from all suggestion of relevant activity.

What the faculty have to cultivate is activity in the presence of knowledge. What the students have to learn is activity in the presence of knowledge.

This discussion rejects the doctrine that students should first learn passively, and then, having learned, should apply knowledge. It is a psychological error. In the process of learning there should be present, in some sense or other, a subordinate activity of application. In fact, the applications are part of the knowledge. For the very meaning of the things known is wrapped up in their relationships beyond themselves. Thus unapplied knowledge is knowledge shorn of its meaning.

The careful shielding of a university from the activities of the world around is the best way to chill interest and to defeat progress. Celibacy does not suit a university. It must mate itself with action.

There again a problem arises. The mere
scattered happenings of daily affairs are veiled
from our analysis. So far as we can see, they
are chance issues. The real stimulation arises
from the discovery of coördinated theory illustrated in coördinated fact; and the further discovery that the fact stretches so far beyond the
theory, disclosing affiliations undreamed of by
learning.

VI

The picture of a university now forms itself before us. There is the central body of
faculty and students, engaged in learning, elab-
orating, criticizing, and appreciating the
varied structure of existing knowledge. This
structure is supported by the orthodox literature, by orthodox expositions of theory, by
orthodox speculation, and by orthodox experiments
disclosing orthodox novelty.

This prevailing orthodoxy is as it should
be. So far as this orthodox expression has been
systematized for the successful evocation of
types of aesthetic experience, and the successful indication of the structural interrelations
of experience, and the successful demonstration
of that structure—so far as this is accomplished, there is truth. We have argued that there
is an inherent vagueness in the meanings employed and in the conformities reached. Thus the
word 'orthodoxy' has been employed to denote the
vague, imperfect rightness of our formularized
knowledge at any moment. Our knowledge and our
skills are limited, and in the nature of things
there is infinitude ever pressing new details
into some clarity of discrimination.

Because of this imperfection, learned orthodoxy does well to ally itself where reason is
playing some part in determining the patterns of
occurrence. Orthodoxy can provide the controlled
experiment. But here we pass to that partial
control where some relevance is secured, but no

333

detail of happenings. Such contact is gained by the absorption into the university of those schools of vocational training for which systematized understanding has importance. These are the professional schools which should fuse closely with the more theoretical side of university work. At present, their chief examples are the schools of Law, Religion, Medicine, Business, Art, Education, Governmental Activities, Engineering. The essential character of these schools is that they study the control of the practice of life by the doctrines of orthodoxy.

The main advantage to a university of this fusion of vocational schools with the central core of theoretical consideration is the increase of suggestiveness. The orthodoxy of reigning theories is a constant menace. By fusion with the schools the area of useful suggestiveness is doubled. It now has two sources. There is the suggestiveness of the vagrant intellect as it comtemplates the orthodox expositions and the orthodox types of experiment. This is the suggestiveness of learning. But there is another suggestiveness derived from brute fact. Lawyers are faced with brute fact fitting into no existing legal classification. Religious experiences retain an insistent individuality. Each patient is a unique fact for a doctor. Business requires for its understanding the whole complexity of human motives, and as yet has only been studied from the narrow ledge of economics. Also Art, Education, and Governmental Activities are gold mines of suggestion. It is mid-summer madness on the part of universities to withdraw themselves from the closest contact with vocational practices.

Curiously, the withdrawal of universities from close association with the practice of life is modern. It culminated in the eighteenth and nineteenth centuries, and heralds the decay of a cultural epoch.

I am not talking of the theories that men

may have held at any time as to university functions. The point is as to the closeness of the relationship of the universities to the life around them—a closeness so natural as hardly to enter consciousness. In the first place, the universities arose out of nature, and were not exotic constructions imposed from above. The Papacy found universities; it did not devise them. Second, in studying the past we must distinquish between social barriers, trade secrets, and cultural doctrines.

In ancient Greece, whatever occupied a free citizen was worth study. That is why Socrates made himself a nuisance by cross-questioning people in the market place. He discovered the vagueness on which we have been insisting. Many things were done by slaves according to traditional methods. Nobody thought of lightening their labor; first, because it did not matter, and second, because there was no foreknowledge of the penetrating possibilities of modern science. Thus slave labor was a matter of course, without interest. But this is a social barrier, and not a doctrine of cultural activity. In the same way for the serfs of the Middle Ages. But here we must never forget the Benedictine monasteries and the variety of activities housed therein. Also the divine Plato was interested in drinking parties, and in the dances suitable for old gentlemen.

In a modern university the natural place for Aristotle would be somewhere between the Medical School, the Biological Departments, and the School of Education. But as life went on he would have looked in elsewhere. As to Plato, his two longest discourses are on political theory, the longer of the two being intensely practical. Also he made two long and dangerous journeys to give practical advice to governing people. His immediate pupils imitated his example. The Washington 'brain trust' is not an American invention.

In the many centuries between Greece and our own times, the direct interplay between universities and practical affairs has been continuous. Salerno, Bologna, Paris, Edinburgh, and the Oxford of Jowett at once come to mind. In fact, almost any university with any length of history before the eighteenth century tells the same tale. And as to men, it suffices to mention Erasmus, Locke, and Newton, among a thousand others.

The gross misunderstanding on this point arises from obliviousness of the part played by the great religious institutions, especially in the Middle Ages. They were concerned with action, emotion, and thought. They coördinated intimacies of human feeling. The men directing their activities permeated universities and active life, the same men passing from one to the other of the two spheres. The rapid penetration by the mendicant orders into universities illustrates this point. The survival power of the great religious confederations demonstrates some large conformity of their procedures to the structure of human experience.

For a thousand years the Catholic Church was the deepest influence in the seats of learning and in the social relations of mankind. The mediaeval universities were in touch with the life around them with a direct intimacy denied to their modern descendants. Of course, a large recasting of thought and doctrine was required. The first result was the brilliance of the seventeenth century. But household renovations are dangerous. For universities, the final result has been their seclusion from the variety of human feeling. To-day the activities of the mediaeval churchmen are best represented by the whole bundle of vocational activities, including those of the various churches. In modern life, men of science are the nearest analogues to the mediaeval clergy.

The mediaeval clergy and the cultural

humanism of the Hellenic world survive. Science
(the search for order realized in nature), Hellenism (the search for value realized in human
nature), Religion (the search for value basic for
all things), express three factors belonging to
the perfection of human nature. They can be
studied apart. But they must be lived together
in the one life of the individual. Thus there
is a tidal law in the emphasis of epochs. At
low tide factors are studied primarily in isolation. There is progress with manageable problems. The issue is trivialization; for meaning
evaporates.

Importance belongs to the one life of the
one individual. This is the doctrine of the
platonic soul. At the high tide, combinations
of factors dawn on consciousness with the importance of vivid shadows of this full unity of
experience. And the knowledge in the low tide
has required the high tide to provide composi-
tions as material for thought.

VII

A university should be, at one and the same
time, local, national, and world-wide. It is of
the essence of learning that it be world-wide,
and effectiveness requires local and national
adaptations. It is not easy to hold the balance.
But unless this difficult balance be held with
some genius, the university is to that extent
defective.

New England provides the near environment
for Harvard, and from that local environment the
institution derives its marked individuality,
which is its strength. Also the most direct
mission for Harvard is to serve the whole of
these United States. The maintenance of a great
civilization on this continent, from ocean to
ocean, is the first purpose of American university life.

But the ideal of the good life, which is

337

civilization,—the ideal of a university,—is the
discovery, the understanding, and the exposition,
of the possible harmony of diverse things, involving and exciting every mode of human experience. Thus it is the peculiar function of a
university to be an agent of unification. This
does not mean the suppression of all but one.
With the ideal before it, the notion of bare suppression sends a shiver through the academic
framework. It savors of treason. Even local
limitations are but means to the highest of all
ends. Even methods are limitations. The difficulty is to find a method for the transcendence of methods. The living spirit of a university should exhibit some approach to this transcendence of limits.

The pursuit of harmony has its difficulties, alike in the realm of action and in the
realm of understanding and in the realm of aesthetic enjoyment. The ideal of final harmony
lies beyond the reach of human beings. Thus any
civilized culture exhibits a mixture of harmony
and discord. The university is struggling with
discord in its journey toward harmony. It is
spreading the enjoyment of such harmonies as the
human tradition at that moment conveys, and it is
pioneering in the prairies of disordered experience.

When all has been said, the universe is
without bounds, learning is world-wide, and the
springs of emotion lie below conventionalities.
You cannot limit the sources of a great civilization; nor can you assign the stretch of its
influence.

To-day Harvard is the greatest of existing
cultural institutions. The opportunity is analogous to that of Greece after Marathon, to that
of Rome in the reign of Augustus, to that of
Christian institutions amid the decay of civilization. Each of these examples recalls tragic
failure. But in each there is success which has
secured enrichment of human life. If Greece had

338

never been, if Augustan Rome had never been, if
Institutional Christianity had never been, if
the University of Paris had never been, human
life would now be functioning on a lower level,
nearer to its animal origins. Will Harvard rise
to its opportunity, and in the modern world repeat the brilliant leadership of mediaeval Paris?

A Reply to Professor Whitehead*
   Robert M. Hutchins

                           I

     Professor Whitehead's article in the Sep-
tember _Atlantic_ on the future of Harvard deserves the study of everybody concerned with
higher education. It presents a vision of intellectual leadership. It does not deal with
athlectics, social life, building programmes,
or 'public relations.' It does not discuss the
size of classes, entrance examinations, or the
grading system. It takes for granted that the
task of the universities is intellectual leadership. It points out that this responsibility is
especially heavy in this country and at this
time; for we are entering a new cultural epoch,
and one which will be dominated by the American
universities. Mr. Whitehead begins and ends by
asking whether Harvard will fashion the intellect of the modern world as the University of
Paris fashioned that of the Middle Ages.

     The question, then, is how Harvard and her
sister universities can give intellectual leadership to the modern world. Mr. Whitehead finds
the answer principally in suggestiveness. The
tradition of learning is the solid ground upon

*From _Atlantic Monthly_, vol. 158, no. 5 (Novem-
ber, 1936), pp. 582-588. Copyright © by the
Atlantic Monthly Company, Boston, Mass. Reprinted by permission of the author and publisher.

which the university must be founded. But the
real problem is to suffuse the activities of
the learned with suggestiveness. A first-rate
faculty is, of course, indispensable, but it is
hard to get; and it is not enough. A faculty
does well because of the stimulus of the atmosphere, and the atmosphere results from suggestiveness.

From what does suggestiveness result? It
comes, even in mathematics, from action. Celibacy is not for a university; it must mate itself with action. This marriage is consummated
chiefly by the absorption into the university of
those schools of vocational training for which
systematized understanding has importance. Mr.
Whitehead reminds us that the mediaeval universities were intimately in touch with the life
around them. 'It is midsummer madness on the
part of universities to withdraw themselves from
the closest contact with vocational practices.'
The end that Mr. Whitehead proposes is intellectual leadership; the means he emphasizes are
vocational schools and association with practical affairs.

We may first ask whether this emphasis is
a timely one. It is something of a shock to
hear that the American universities should try
to be practical. The words of de Tocqueville
are in point: 'In the present age the human
mind must be coerced into theoretical studies;
it runs of its own accord to practical applications.' Under the pressure of the professions,
of occupations wanting to be professions, of
parents, donors, students, legislatures, and the
public, our institutions of higher learning have
absorbed schools of vocational training of in-
credible diversity and insignificance. For some
of them systematized understanding has importance. For others such understanding, if not
impossible, is at least improbable. Their subject matter is too frivolous to encourage it.

In those vocational schools for which

systematized understanding clearly has importance, such as those preparing for the learned professions, the communication of such understanding is now a negligible part of the course of study. Theology plays no great rôle in the education of a theological student; and the faculty of a well-known law school recently voted down the suggestion that a course in jurisprudence be introduced into the curriculum. The reason for this is that the demand for instruction in vocational practices is so urgent as to reduce instruction of any other kind to a peripheral status.

The pressure of the practical appears everywhere in our educational system. The result has been trivialization. Courses in how to drive an automobile have lately appeared in an excellent Middle-Western university. The newspapers report an effort to institute courses in bicycle riding in the public schools of South Bend, Indiana. These are simply two of the most recent instances of the general trend of American education. It is so full of action that thought seems fated to disappear from it. The danger of the American universities is not celibacy, but polygamy. They are mated to so many different kinds of action that nothing but a few divorces can save them from the consequences of their ardor.

II

Mr. Whitehead imposes no particular limitations upon the range of a university's interest. In ancient Greece, he says, whatever occupied a free citizen was worth study. In modern America, free citizens are occupied in killing one another with automobiles and in getting killed on bicycles. They are raising chickens and selling insurance and running typewriters. Are all these activities worth the study of a university? Apparently they are, for Mr. Whitehead reminds us that the divine Plato was interested in drinking parties, and in the

341

dances suitable for old men.

On the other hand, it may be said that Plato was interested in love and used a drinking party as the dramatic background for a discussion of it, and that he was trying to construct a good state and came upon the subject of the dances suitable to old men in the consideration of the activities of various groups in it. So the most light-hearted of the Socratic dialogues, the Ion, deals with the question whether the interpreter needs knowledge of the subject of his art. At any rate, we are concerned here with the curriculum; and I doubt if Plato would have made drinking parties or old men's dances a required course for the Athenian youth. The educational programme elaborated in the Republic, at least, contains no mention of either.

If Socrates, Plato, or, in modern times, Mr. Whitehead is the teacher, then truly bicycle riding and drinking parties may suffuse suggestiveness. In the hands of such masters as these no aspect of human activity is trivial, for it is never more than a few dialectical steps from any action to the discussion of the ideas in the light of which that action is intelligible; or, to express it in terms of Whitehead's doctrine of prehensions, no subject can be intrinsically trivial, because each actual occasion reflects all events in the universe, and may, properly treated, contribute to the knowledge of anything in the universe. But even on the supposition that no subject is intrinsically trivial, it would require a dialectician of the skill of Socrates to discover the significance of some of the themes now popular in the American classroom.

Teachers of such skill are so rare that a course of study cannot be constructed on the assumption that they will be in charge of it. With the majority of the teachers who are in charge of the curriculum the irrelevant detail must remain irrelevant. The philosophy of education that regards all things as potentially of

equal significance thus results in the presentation of miscellaneous dead facts. In vocational
schools it leads the teacher to emphasize technical routines at the expense of systematized
understanding. In the traditional realm of
scholarship it supports the practice of accumu-
lating items about the lives of authors, the influences to which they were exposed, and the
dates of their labors, without regard to the
contribution which such studies may make to the
understanding of their works.

This philosophy, which, when it is held by
the inspired few, suffuses suggestiveness and
illumination, is, when it is the doctrine of the
rest of us, dangerous, uncontrollable, and easily perverted. Far from summoning us to the
task of intellectual leadership, it may serve to
justify quite another view of a university: it
may be used to uphold the position that the university, instead of being 'an agent of unification,' should mirror the chaos of the world. I
fear that this is exactly the situation of the
American universities to-day. It is for that
reason that I doubt the timeliness of Mr. Whitehead's emphasis.

III

The goal which Mr. Whitehead sets before the
universities is the one they should strive to
reach. The road he has pointed out seems unlikely to take them there. What is the path by
which they may hope to come at last to the kind
of leadership exerted by their predecessors in
the Middle Ages? Mr. Whitehead invokes the example of the mediaeval universities, calling particular attention to some aspects of these institutions which, it seems to me, American universities do not need to be told about at present.
It is true, for example, that the mediaeval universities were in intimate touch with the life
around them. So are ours. But, as we have
seen, contact with daily life in itself is not a
guarantee of intellectual leadership, or even of

343

intellectual activity. Mr. Whitehead's historical model is striking; his analysis is suggestive. A consideration of either, however, makes
it apparent that the solution he offers would be
ineffective. It would be ideal in an ideal state
in which not only the rulers but the professors
were philosophers, and in which the citizens had
been educated to a point at which making dialec-
ticians drink hemlock would not seem the best
solution of their moral problems.

In looking for a path to Mr. Whitehead's
goal we notice, in the first place, that he
mentions two aspects of the contribution which a
university can make: it can perpetuate and advance knowledge, and it can stimulate, through
the suggestiveness of its manner of treating
knowledge, the use of knowledge in action, whether practical or speculative. 'Fundamental progress,' Mr. Whitehead says, 'has to do with the
reinterpretation of basic ideas.' For long ages,
during the Greek and Hellenistic periods, during
the Roman republic and empire, during the Middle
Ages and the Renaissance, indeed until only a
generation or two ago, men studied the master-
pieces of human thought as examples of excellence
and to familiarize themselves with the leading
ideas that have animated mankind. To be sure, in
different periods there have been important
changes in the list of works that were called
classics, but if one compares the classics esteemed by various ages, with due consideration of
the works made available by the state of learning
in each age, one is struck more by the constancy
displayed in the judgments of men of learning
than by the changes.

If the tradition of learning is the solid
ground upon which the universities must be
founded, then the American universities have a
difficult task ahead. The tradition of learning
is now fighting an uneven battle for continuation in the American educational system, and the
time seems to be approaching when only the last
remnants of that tradition will survive, and only

344

in the remoter corners of the graduate school.

Simply to advise the reinterpretation of basic ideas is not enough. Such reinterpretation requires a technique and a method. The Middle Ages and the Renaissance inherited such methods from antiquity and developed them further: the learned techniques of grammar, rhetoric, and logic for the interpretation of the writings of men, and the techniques of mathematics and the various branches of logic for the study of nature.

If the difference between certain and probable knowledge is as important as Mr. Whitehead says it is, and it seems to me difficult to overemphasize it, then it is important that men have the training to discover and assess that difference in the various subjects they study. If it is important to reinterpret basic ideas, it is important to have the training by which to understand the ideas expressed by other men and to express one's own version of those ideas or of the ideas alternative to them as clearly as they permit. What is important in any age, in fourth-century Athens, thirteenth-century Paris, or twentieth-century Cambridge, is not necessarily a common agreement on what ideas are basic, but a common acquaintance with the ideas which can seriously pretend to be basic, and a commensurate ability, derived from a common training, to appraise and understand those ideas.

A glance at the subject matter of the American course of study will show that the classics and the liberal arts have almost disappeared from it. A few students may still make the acquaintance of their fragmentary and isolated remains. The community produced by common training has vanished. The basic ideas that might have been recovered from the classics are unknown. Instead we are greeted daily with sensational discoveries which were old in the time of Erasmus and Leibniz and which are hailed as new to-day only because those who announce them and those to whom they

345

are announced have forgotten the tradition of learning.

Mathematics has survived, because its practical applications in the sciences are so apparent that it is permitted the idiosyncrasy of a difficult symbolic apparatus and an elaborate theoretical organization. But it has survived at the expense of becoming an item of technical or advanced study, suited only in its more elementary or popular forms to general education; hence the student of the arts is usually allowed to glory in the possession of an 'unmathematical' mind.

I do not insist on the classics, and still less on grammar, rhetoric, logic, or mathematics. It may be that we can find some better way of transmitting the accumulated wisdom of the race than having young people study what wise men have written. It may be that mathematics is too difficult for the bulk of our students, and that grammar, rhetoric, and logic are so dead that they cannot be resuscitated. I do insist that the ideal pursued in ancient Greece and mediaeval Paris is unattainable without a contemporary substitute for these disciplines and for the classics.

In the second place, Mr. Whitehead emphasizes the relationship of knowledge and action, and illustrates his point by the example of the mediaeval university. The fact that the mediaeval universities entered into the practical affairs of their time is less important for us than the manner of their entrance. Here we are concerned primarily with the nature of professional education in the Middle Ages. Not every vocation was a profession then. A profession was a body of men trained in a subject matter which had intellectual content in its own right. The aim of the group was the common good. These two requirements must have had something to do with limiting the professional disciplines to three: medicine, theology, and law.

If these standards were invoked to-day, there would not be many more professional disciplines now than there were in the Middle Ages. Only a Socrates could give intellectual content to some of the curricula now called professional. It is forty years since anyone would seriously ask the question put in 1896 by an old Wisconsin lawyer to a young one from the East: 'Is it really true that there are men in New York who are practising law for money?' A Chicago business man lately said in announcing an important deal, 'Our only motive is to make a profit.' Under these circumstances it may be doubtful whether business is yet a profession and whether the law has remained one.

Whatever effect the effort to achieve the mediaeval ideal proposed by Mr. Whitehead might have on the number and variety of a university's professional and vocational interests, certainly it would change the course of study and the attitude of teachers and students toward it in those professional schools that remained. The purpose for which any action was studied or taught would be to increase our understanding of that action and what it implies. The primary object of our course of study would be to give the student a grasp of the theory of the discipline. It would not be supposed, as it often is to-day, that the university should familiarize him with vocational practices. It would be supposed, as it too seldom is to-day, that he should learn the principles of the subject. Armed with these, he could familiarize himself, after leaving the university, with the practices of the vocation.

With these modifications I should be willing to accept the moral which Mr. Whitehead draws from the participation of the mediaeval universities in the life about them. There was then no 'university' which was presumably speculative, with professional schools that were presumably practical. The whole institution was both speculative and practical. The insight that produced

347

this organization was that everything speculative has significance in the practical dimension,
and everything practical, to be worth study, must
have a speculative basis. Our professional
schools are so definitely committed to familiar-
zing the student with vocational practices that
they have diffused themselves all over the realm
of the practical and have emphasized immediate
utility to the exclusion of their intellectual
tradition. One consequence of this is that a
student who does not enter the vocation after
graduating from a vocational school has largely
wasted his time. If such a student had studied
at Paris, or in the Academy, or even if he had
listened to Protagoras, he could at least feel
that he had had an education.

The course of study and the spirit in which
it was administered in our early universities
could lead to the consideration of law, medicine,
and theology as sciences. A university experience could be the guide either to a professional
career or to an enlightened life, or both. If
vocational schools are to contribute now to the
effort of the universities to fashion the intellect of the modern world as the University of
Paris fashioned that of the Middle Ages, it
would seem that such changes in them as would
make them almost unrecognizable to contemporary
eyes might be required.

IV

In the third place, Mr. Whitehead underlines
the unity of knowledge and the consequent unity
which should be aimed at in education. He says
that science, philosophy, and religion express
three factors belonging to the perfection of human nature; they can be studied apart, but must
be lived together. The great triumph of the
mediaeval university was precisely here: the
major disciplines were studied to a certain extent together. The three factors were studied
together because they must be lived together.
They were reconciled in the university and 'in

348

the one life of the individual.' The community
of learning begun with the classics and the liberal arts was extended to the highest levels of
the university. Within the American universities we have confusion, discord, and division.
Witness the fragmentary and scattered course of
study and the extremes to which the departmental
system has been carried. If the new epoch now
opening is to be anything but an epoch of collapse, if the universities are to exert intellectual leadership, they must repeat the triumph
of their forbears. It will be much more difficult now than it was then; for the great gains
we have made in science are matched by the losses
we have sustained in philosophy and religion.

It seems idle to hope that unity and harmony
can flow from a policy of treating all subjects
as of equal importance. The consequence of this
policy must be conflict and competition. Unity
and harmony involve organization. In any organization there must be order; and order involves
subordination. The mediaeval universities found
order through theology. I do not see that we
can do so. But unless we are willing first to
admit the necessity of some principle of order,
and second to seek for one, we cannot expect the
universities to be helpful in ushering in the
fourth European cultural epoch.

In seeking for a principle of order that
will serve contemporary needs we come at once
upon philosophy. Mr. Whitehead's philosophy, his
conception of an organic universe, which seems
to suggest to him the educational principle that
all things are potentially of equal significance,
will hardly be effective, as we have seen, in
making the American universities agents of unification and harmony. Let us try another approach, in terms of the distinction to which Mr.
Whitehead refers between certainty and probability, knowledge and opinion. We cannot abandon
this distinction because clear-headed men have
disagreed. To the extent that men are rational
they have found and will doubtless continue to

find that they can and should agree on matters of knowledge, though they may still disagree on matters of opinion. The object of a university is to increase the domain of knowledge and the extent to which men are rational. It is in this sense that a university acts as an agent of unification, struggling through discord to harmony.

Nor can we abandon what Mr. Whitehead first calls the indubitable distinction between knowledge and opinion because of his later remark that the important characterization of knowledge is in respect of clarity and vagueness. Mr. Whitehead does not abandon it himself. Even Hume could not hold to the bitter end the position that the only distinctions in cognition are in terms of degrees of clarity. He never questioned that there was a difference in kind between knowledge of the relations between ideas and knowledge of matters of fact.

Mr. Whitehead's condemnation of skepticism as self-destroying carries with it the insight that the skeptic must presuppose a distinction between knowledge and opinion. There must be some certain, clear knowledge. If there is knowledge, it should be taught as such, and it should be taught first. Let us then enumerate the disciplines in which there is certainty and let us place them at the beginning of our curriculum. Where we have no certainty, let us teach in accordance with the weight of the evidence, giving our doctrine such probability as can be found for it by appropriate arguments.

One result of this programme would be the reordering of the course of study. To-day most fields of learning are treated as matters of opinion, except mathematics; and in certain quarters even mathematics is regarded as arbitrary and postulational. Another result of this programme would be the reduction of the number of subjects; for when we realized how much opinion we were teaching as knowledge we should be compelled to eliminate some of it, or at least to

seek and teach a rational basis for it. A third
consequence of this approach would be the alteration of the content of courses: matters of fact,
which are probable, would be subordinate to and
illustrative of laws and the relations between
ideas, which are knowledge.

In order to obtain these results you must
have a faculty which can distinguish knowledge
from opinion because of having been trained in
the liberal arts or their modern equivalent,
whatever it may be. Such a faculty, for example,
would know what its own metaphysical presuppositions were, or would be able to eschew metaphysics. Its members would know that they were engaging in metaphysics when they enunciated metaphysical propositions; they would try on these
occasions to use a method appropriate to such
speculations; and they would be as conscientious
in acquiring proficiency in these methods before
announcing their conclusions as they would be to
practise the method of mathematics before coming
to a mathematical conclusion. Under such conditions we may have a unified university, not because an official dogma has been imposed upon it,
but because teachers and students can know what
they are talking about and can have some hope of
understanding one another. In this view the
ideal of a university is an understood diversity.

In such a university great teachers could
play their part; they would find no restrictions
placed upon their powers of suggestiveness and
revelation. Lesser souls, administrators and
competent teachers, would have some light to
guide their decisions and their instruction.
Methods would be rigorous, techniques would be
purified, the pieces of that puzzle which is the
curriculum would fall into place. Such a university might be an agent of harmony and unification
without suppressing the vagrant intellect or violating the claims of freedom. Such a university
might in the modern world repeat the brilliant
leadership of the University of Paris.

Case

The past twenty-four hours in the emergency room at General Hospital was not unusual except for the difficult decision in the Black case. Since his intern days Jim had wondered what he would do in such a situation, but until last night he had never faced it. Mr. Black, a victim of an automobile accident, was brought into the emergency room just before midnight. Although his heart continued to beat, his brain waves were not measurable. Jim's first reaction was to hook Mr. Black to life-sustaining machinery. The body was strong and only twenty-six years old. The man was married, had five small children, and according to his wife had no savings, medical insurance, or life insurance. Mrs. Black had spoken with Jim about her husband and had given Jim the card Black carried in his billfold. Black requested that in the event of death his organs be given to a needy recipient. When Jim questioned Mrs. Black she said that Black's brother had been on a dialysis machine for the past three years and was confident Black would want his organs to go to his brother. Tests indicated that there is good compatibility between the brothers' bodies. This was tough enough, but what put Jim in a quandry was the final statement on that card. Black indicated that under no circumstances should he be kept alive by machines. He had a right to die with dignity.

Therapeutic Choice and Moral Doubt in a Technological Age*
Stanley Joel Reiser, M.D.

The instruments and machines used by the contemporary physician are basically of two sorts: diagnostic—to perceive and evaluate the disturbances caused by illness—and therapeutic—to act to overcome these disturbances. This essay will focus on therapeutic technology, and particularly on the perplexing moral dilemmas its success has created for physicians and laymen. Certain contemporary episodes that delineate this problem and some of its roots in medical history will be examined.

In 1957, Pope Pius XII publicly discussed some questions that had been submitted to him by Dr. Bruno Haid, chief of anesthesia at the surgical clinic of the University of Innsbruck.[1] The questions concerned the morality of resuscitation, a term that was used for the techniques employed to forestall life-threatening episodes, particularly the threats posed by asphyxia, a severe lack of oxygen. Asphyxia generally causes death in several minutes unless the technology of resuscitation now available is promptly used. By the mid-nineteen-fifties the anesthesiologist no longer confined his work to the operating room, but practiced his art, more and more, during hospital emergencies that produced asphyxia, such as strangulation, open chest wounds, tetanus, poliomyelitis, poisoning by sedatives, and brain trauma.

The resuscitation of people who suffered from disorders such as these and who lapsed into a coma raised moral questions that seemed more

*Reprinted by permission of the author and American Academy of Arts and Sciences from Daedalus, Winter, 1977, pp. 47-56.

difficult to resolve than questions of resuscitative method. In some cases the anesthesiologist, using special instruments and manual techniques to maintain respiration and provide nourishment, could support a patient long enough for spontaneous breathing to resume. But if the damage suffered by the patient was so serious that death seemed certain, the anesthesiologist was driven to doubt the value and purpose of using resuscitative techniques. For, having initiated respiratory-assisting therapies on a patient in response to an emergency, what should the anesthesiologist do if after a slight improvement the patient's condition became static, and it was clear that only the automated artificial respiratory apparatus was sustaining his life?

Dr. Haid expressed the problems which arose from the modern practice of resuscitation as three questions. First, does one have the right or obligation to use resuscitation equipment on all patients, even those whose prognosis seems hopeless to the physician? Second, does one have the right or obligation to remove the resuscitation equipment if a patient's deep unconsciousness does not begin to abate in several days, knowing that its removal will result in his death? What does the physician do if the patient's family request that the physician remove the equipment? Third, should an unconscious patient whose body functions are maintained artificially, but who does not improve in several days, be considered de facto or de jure dead? Or must one wait for the heart to stop beating, the traditional criterion of death, despite the presence of the life-sustaining technology, before considering the patient dead?

Pope Pius began his answer to these questions with a statement of principle. He affirmed that natural reason and Christian morals imposed a duty on man to preserve health and life. But he maintained that in meeting this duty one was obliged to use only ordinary means (defined

354

according to the circumstances of person, place, time, and culture) that did not impose ponderous hardships on oneself or on others. A more stringent obligation, he held, would be too burdersome for most people, and would also endanger the attainment of the higher, more important spiritual ends of life. A person might take more than the basic steps to preserve life and health, but only so long as this act did not prevent him from performing these more serious spiritual duties.

With this as a preamble, the Pope responded specifically to Dr. Haid's questions. Was one obliged to use modern respiratory technology in cases judged hopeless by the physician, and even against the wishes of the family? Since such therapy exceeded the ordinary ministrations that physicians were bound to apply, they were under no obligation to use it. Further, in the case of unconscious patient, if resuscitation techniques imposed clear and substantial burdens on the patient's family, they could direct the physician to discontinue the use of his apparatus, and the physician could morally and lawfully comply. Should discontinuing the use of the life-sustaining apparatus cause the heart to stop beating, the act was to be considered only an indirect cause of death and not a direct assault on the life of the patient.

But if the resuscitative apparatus was left in place and a comatose patient showed no improvement after several days, when was he to be considered dead? This question perplexed the Pope. He thought that it did not truly fall within the competence of the Church to decide, but ventured a response: human life could be said to exist "as long as its vital functions— distinguished from the simple life of organs— manifest themselves spontaneously or even with the help of artificial processes."[2]

Almost a decade after the Pope delivered his statement, an ad hoc committee of Harvard faculty members, representing the disciplines of medicine, history, ethics, and law, convened to formulate new criteria of death.[3] Like the Pope, many physicians and laymen in this age of advanced resuscitative technology were troubled about the problem of determining when a person had died. This technology encouraged physicians to make greater efforts than they had in the past to sustain lives of critically injured people. But sometimes their efforts were only partially successful, and they led to situations where the heart beat continued while the brain was damaged irreversibly: the time-honored criterion of death—cessation of the heart beat—therefore seemed inadequate. The Harvard committee worked to develop criteria whose presence in such patients permitted physicians to declare that the patient had a permanently nonfunctioning brain and therefore had died. These criteria are essentially: (1) a total unawareness of externally applied stimuli; (2) the absence of spontaneous movement or breathing for at least an hour; (3) the absence of reflexes; and (4) the absence of electrical activity in the brain as detected by electroencephalograph readings during a twenty-four-hour period. If all these criteria were met, then the committee recommended that the patient be declared dead and that the artificial respirator be removed.

The issues considered by Pope Pius XII and the Harvard ad hoc committee were crystalized for the public, if not for many physicians, by the case of Karen Ann Quinlan. On the night of April 15, 1975, local police and an emergency squad were summoned to attend Karen who, for reasons yet unknown, had stopped breathing for at least two fifteen-minute periods. Friends administered mouth-to-mouth resuscitation during the first episode, and the police used a mechanical respirator during the second episode. She was taken to a local hospital in New Jersey, where attending physicians found, among other things, that the pupils of her eyes did not contract from the introduction of light and that she made no response when they administered ordinarily painful stimuli—both signs of serious brain damage probably caused by previous oxygen deprivation. She was immediately hooked up to a mechanical respirator.

When Dr. Robert Morse, a neurologist who subsequently became Karen's principal physician, examined her three days later, he found that her condition remained critical. She was still comatose and did not trigger the respirator, which meant that she was unable to breathe spontaneously or independently of it. She then was transferred to another hospital under the care of Dr. Morse. There more extensive tests were conducted, including an electroencephalogram. It was abnormal but indicated the presence of some brain activity. Dr. Morse, and several other physicians who examined her, portrayed Karen as a person whose brain had the capacity to maintain the "vegetative" aspects of neurological functioning—such as the regulation of blood pressure and swallowing—but had lost its "cognitive" capabilities—those that made possible talking, thinking, seeing, or feeling. By the yardstick of the criteria enumerated by the Harvard ad hoc committee, which had become a widely acknowledged standard in medicine, Karen was not "brain dead."

However, her physicians were unable to wean her from the respirator, and with the passage of time reached the conclusion that she could not live without it. Although attendants fed her through a tube inserted through the nose and down to the stomach. Karen became emaciated. Her posture was described as grotesque, arms and legs rigid and deformed. She was totally unaware of her surroundings and, according to her physicians, did not appear to suffer from a locked-in syndrome, a state in which a patient is conscious but totally paralyzed. Although Karen's principal physician, Dr. Morse, could not specifically foresee circumstances that would meliorate her condition, he was unwilling to declare that it was totally irreversible. Several other physicians who had examined her shared Dr. Morse's point of view and reemphasized with him that twenty-two-year-old Karen, for all her disability, did not meet the Harvard brain-death criteria.

From the outset of her illness, in the belief that she would recover, Karen's parents authorized her doctors to initiate all necessary life-preserving measures. Her parents were in constant attendance at the bedside and in close contact with Dr. Morse. But her deteriorating condition, the absence of any reasonable hope that she would get better, and Karen's own previous remarks to her parents that she never wanted to be kept alive by extraordinary measures prompted her parents to conclude, about three months after the onset of the affliction, that Karen should be removed from the respirator and nature allowed to take its course. They signed a release which freed Dr. Morse, the hospital, and the other people who attended Karen from all liability for the consequences of separating Karen from her machine. In making this decision, her parents received considerable support from their priest, who indicated that the request was permissible under the teachings of their faith, the Roman Catholic Church, a conclusion which the priest based principally upon the 1957 statement of Pope Pius XII.

Dr. Morse refused to remove Karen from the respirator. He based his decision on his concept of the moral standards of medical practice, which he believed did not allow him to disconnect the life-sustaining equipment from a patient who was not medically dead.

The impasse between Karen's parents and her physician prompted her parents to seek the help of the courts to have the apparatus removed. The first decision on the case came from the Superior Court of New Jersey. It ruled that decisions about medical care were the responsibility of the physician. Society had given him discretion over the nature, extent, and duration of care: "What justification is there to remove it from control

of the medical profession and place it in the
hands of the courts?," the presiding Judge Robert
Muir, Jr., asked.[4] He refused to grant the petition of Karen's father to become the sole
guardian of his daughter, because of his stated
intention to seek the discontinuance of what he
considered the extraordinary means which kept his
daughter alive. The parents appealed this decision to the Supreme Court of New Jersey. It
overruled the lower court, declaring on March 31,
1976, almost a year after Karen's illness began,
that no "interest of the State could compel Karen
to endure the unendurable, only to vegetate a
few measurable months with no realistic possibility of returning to any semblance of cognitive
or sapient life."[5] The Court was convinced that
Karen's parents acted as she would have acted if
she had the capacity to perceive her condition.
It declared that her parents could assert a right
to privacy for her and request cessation of the
life-sustaining technology. The Court saw an
analogy between Karen's situation and one in
which a competent and suffering terminally ill
patient would not be kept on a respirator against
his will, or resuscitated by most physicians
aware of his suffering and his grave prognosis.
It acknowledged the desirability, ordinarily, of
resolving such dilemmas within the privacy of the
physician-patient relationship. But it emphasized the benefit to society and to medicine resulting when courts introduce into the medical
decision-making process the values and common
moral judgments of the community at large: "The
law, equity and justice must not themselves quail
and be helpless in the face of modern technological marvels presenting questions hitherto un-
thought of."[6] The Court added that dilemmas of
this kind in medicine were augmented (in this era
of proliferating malpractice litigation) by the
hazard of legal action faced by physicians.

The Court appointed Karen's father as guardian with the power to choose new treating physicians. It ruled that, should these new physicians conclude that no reasonable possibility

359

existed of her emerging from coma and if a con-
sultative body of physicians at the hospital
serving as members of an ethics committee con-
curred, life-supporting technology could be removed without civil or criminal liability for any
participant.

Karen Quinlan was removed from her respirator and did not die. She now resides in a nurs-
ing facility and is still in a coma.

The fundamental purposes of medical therapy,
weighed by those who decided the issues in the
Quinlan case, have been considered intermittent-
ly in medical history. One of the earliest and,
for contemporary physicians, most valuable discussions of this subject took place in ancient
Greece between the fifth and fourth centuries
B.C., when medicine was dominated by the physician Hippocrates and his students and disciples.
Their instructive thoughts have been handed down
to us in a group of texts written by different
hands and known collectively as the Corpus Hip-
pocraticum. A problem that concerned physicians
at that time, and which is explored in the Corpus, is the relation of the medical art to the
natural processes of disease. How far can the
actions of the physician influence the healing
of the body? How far should the physician extend his medical techniques to fight nature?
The Hippocratic writings urge restraint. For
example, in one called The Art, the author asserts, in rejoinder to those who attributed the
physician's cures to luck or to the healing
power of nature, that there indeed is an art of
medicine. But the treatise emphasizes that the
natural forces which produce disease are powerful and that medical art has its limits: "I
will define what I conceive medicine to be. In
general terms, it is to do away with the sufferings of the sick, to lessen the violence of their
diseases, and to refuse to treat those who are
overmastered by their diseases, realizing that in
such cases medicine is powerless."[7]

The author of this treatise then defends
physicians against critics who censure them for
sometimes refusing to treat desperately ill persons: "For if a man demand from an art a power
over what does not belong to the art, or from
nature a power over what does not belong to nature, his ignorance is more allied to madness
than to lack of knowledge. For in cases where
we may have the mastery through the means af-
forded by a natural constitution or by an art,
there we may be craftsmen, but nowhere else.
Whenever therefore a man suffers from an ill
which is too strong for the means at the disposal of medicine, he surely must not even expect that it can be overcome by medicine."[8]

The Hippocratic physician was acutely
aware that his therapeutic powers were limited
by the forces of nature. The repetition and the
austere tone of the injunction to restrain one's
therapy in the face of the overwhelming power of
nature and not to exceed the possibilities of
the medical art elevate the counsel beyond a
suggestion about technique to a moral direction;
for the physician to have exceeded the possibilities of his art was to commit the sin of hubris.

Still, the reluctance of the Hippocratic
physician to offend nature and to stretch the
limits of his art was made easier by his knowledge that the patient had several alternatives
when medicine seemed powerless and the physician
could no longer help him: the patient could turn
to other resources for help. He could resort to
prayers and incantations. As Plutarch wrote:
"Those who are ill with chronic diseases and do
not succeed by the usual remedies and the customary diet turn to purifications and amulets and
dreams."[9] Patients could also resort to suicide,
a socially accepted escape from a life heavily
burdened by disease both among those with philosophical training and among average people.
Euripides wrote referring to people who patiently
endured long illness: "I hate men who would prolong their lives/By foods and drinks and charms

of magic art,/Perverting nature's course to keep
off death;/They ought, when they no longer serve
the land,/To quit this life, and clear the way
for youth."[10] Knowledge of the alternatives outside of medicine available to patients doubtless
helped to relieve the physician of responsibility
and to ease his conscience.

Prior to the twentieth century, physicians
treated disturbances of the physiological functions of the body mainly with diet, drugs, blood-
letting, and physical therapies such as bathing,
massage, and exercise. The principal use of
technology in medical therapy was in surgery,
which was generally employed to treat wounds, injuries to bones, and lesions on the outer surface
of the body such as ulcers and tumors. In the
Greco-Roman period, instruments for such purposes
were constructed, made of iron, steel, bronze,
even gold and silver. Over the centuries surgical
technologies grew in kind and number. For example, a 1674 treatise called The Chyrurgeons
Store-House describes fifteen sorts of forceps,
eleven sorts of knives, five sorts of needles; it
describes lancets designed to perforate tissue
and "pinchers" to extract teeth or draw out bones
sticking in the throat.[11] Such an armory of instruments often frightened the patient, and sur-
geons were advised to consider this problem in
preparing to operate. A French surgeon writing
in the early eighteenth century tells us:

'Tis customary to send to the Patient's
Chamber (some time before the Chirurgeon
comes) a Servant to dispose all things in
order; but frequently, by the quantity of
bits of Linnen which they cut, the heaps of
Lint which they make, and the spreading shew
of numerous Instruments, they strike Fear and
Terror into the Mind of the Patient, by giving him a cruel Idea of the Operation which
they are going about. I would that the
Chirurgeons would not shew themselves to
their Patients, 'till the Moment appointed
for the Operation; and that all things which

362

they want, were ready prepar'd at their own
Houses, or in a Chamber near the Patient, in
order to spare him the sight of those Prep-
aratives, which only inspire him with a Horror
for those who make them. . . . A Chirurgeon
must be naturally dextrous in Operation, and
that Address must be back'd with great Experience in his Profession; whence he should
learn how to place his Subject, to chuse the
most proper Instruments, to invent new ones
in particular Cases, and to make use of them
in such a manner as shall contribute as much
to the easing of the Patient, as the Satisfaction of the Spectators.[12]

In the nineteenth century, commercial firms
were founded to manufacture a large number of
surgical instruments. Before this time, they had
usually been produced by individuals, mostly instrument makers by trade. Yet not until the end
of the nineteenth century, when the problems of
pain, infection, and bleeding could be handled
effectively, was surgical technology widely employed to enter the interior of the body and
treat a large variety of medical problems.

Machines that sustain vital physiological
functions such as breathing (the mechanical respirator) or help to remove the waste products of
metabolism (the artificial kidney) are essentially inventions of the twentieth century and are
among the vanguard of its therapeutic technology.
The manual methods of artifical respiration used
in the early twentieth century were unsuited to
long-term administration. And the few machines
that existed to assist respiration, such as one
called a pulmotor, were ineffective and sometimes
injured patients. This created a need for a reliable mechanical device capable of steady work
over long periods of time, which would facilitate
breathing without harming the patient. The fore-
runners of such reliable machines, from which the
respirators that sustained Karen Quinlan evolved,
were the iron lungs built in the late nineteen-
twenties. One of the earliest iron lungs was

constructed in 1928 by the Americans Philip Drinker and Louis Shaw to alleviate the respiratory failure caused by poliomyelitis. In their first clinical test of the machine, the breathing of an eight-year-old girl afflicted with polio was maintained for 122 hours. But she succumbed to complications of her illness.[13]

A second machine that has become an important part of medical therapy is the artificial kidney, designed to cleanse the blood of waste products unexpelled when kidney function is seriously impaired. Experiments to develop an artificial kidney began in 1913. They failed for lack of a reliable drug to prevent the coagulation of the blood passed through the machine, lack of a good membrane through which the waste products could be filtered out of the blood, and the insufficient capacity of the early equipment. Willem Kolff, a Dutch physician, solved these problems and built the first clinically useful artificial kidney in Holland between 1940 and 1943. Kolff's machine could not be credited with preventing the death or producing the recovery of the first sixteen patients on which it was used. Success came only with the seventeenth patient, whose kidney function had temporarily failed as the result of an infection. After more than 11 hours on the artificial kidney, her condition improved dramatically. "The first understandable words she spoke that I remember," wrote Kolff, "were that she was going to divorce her husband, which indeed in time she did. Further recovery was uneventful."[14]

Since the nineteen-sixties, the growing availability of technological aids such as artificial respirators and artificial kidneys has engendered in both physicians and laymen a searching examination of the moral principles that should guide medical decisions. This examination, whose depth and intensity is unparalleled in medical history, has had as one of its underlying themes the notion of limits. A humility has been urged upon medicine to match the

considerable technological power it has created
to overcome the natural forces that produce illness. These cautionary observations are similar
to those of modern ecologists, who are urging us
to act with humility in dealing with the natural
world. The contemporary movement in medical
ethics in part asks physicians who control a
powerful technological store of therapy to consider, as the ancient Greeks did, the limits imposed on therapeutic undertakings by the biological make-up of man, and the moral and therapeutic consequences of accepting these limits.

The modern patient, disquieted by recent
developments, has also been prompted to consider
the problem of placing limits on the use of therapeutic technology. An example is the "living
will" that a number of people in the nineteen-
seventies have been making up. These wills are
documents in which a person can stipulate the
sort of care he wishes if afflicted by an irre-
mediable illness which might, at some stage, in-
capacitate and prevent him from expressing his
therapeutic preferences. The wills are intended
strongly to request, but not to compel, physicians to follow, if not the letter, then at least
the spirit of the wishes expressed in them. To
draw public attention to these documents and to
enhance their legal status, some lawmakers have
submitted them to state legislatures for certi-
fication. One such living will, considered but
not adopted by the Massachusetts legislature in
1974, reads in part:

> The availability of medical technology does
> not eliminate the need for human choices re-
> garding its use. This is especially true
> when a patient is irreversibly ill. The de-
> cision to cease employment of artificial means
> or heroic measures to prolong the life of the
> body belongs to the patient and/or the imme-
> diate family with the approval of the family
> physician. . . . In order that the rights of
> patients may be respected even after they are
> no longer able to participate actively in

decisions about themselves, they may choose
to indicate their wishes regarding refusal of
treatment in a written statement, as follows.
. . . "If there is no reasonable expectation
of my recovery from physical or mental disability, as certified by two physicians, I,
_____, request that I be allowed to
die and not be kept alive by artificial means
or heroic measures. I value life and the dignity of life, so that I am not asking that my
life be directly taken, but that my dying not
be unreasonably prolonged, nor the dignity of
life destroyed. . . ."[15]

The availability of therapeutic technology
has also prompted concern by society that touches
limits of another kind—financial. For example,
in the mid-nineteen-sixties, when the demand
grew for artificial-kidney machines among people
with chronic and potentially fatal kidney disease, a patient treated twice weekly with the
machine at the Veterans Hospital in Los Angeles
could run up a bill of twenty-eight thousand dollars a year.[16] Because of the high cost, and the
inadequate supply of artificial kidneys in relation to the demand for them, sometimes certain
patients were given preferences over other patients in allocating the scarce therapeutic resource. The distributive decisions made by an
advisory committee at the Seattle Artificial
Kidney Center, composed of physicians and laymen
who were supposed to represent the public interest, received wide publicity because the committee's decisions represented one of the first
modern peace-time efforts to allocate important
but scarce medical resources among specific individuals. The Center developed a set of admission criteria which it followed closely. They
were essentially: a slow deterioration of renal
function; an absence of longstanding hypertension
and its permanent complications; the patient's
emotional maturity and responsibility; his demonstrated willingness to cooperate; a "physiological" age of between 17 and 50; six months'
residence in the five-state area around Seattle;

366

the amount of his financial resources; his value to the community; potential for rehabilitation; and psychological and psychiatric status. In addition to this advisory committee on which laymen sat, all candidates for kidney machines were reviewed by a medical committee and the Center's medical director. A physician at the Center discussed some of the patients who were rejected in this selection process:

There was the beatnik—in his mid-twenties, doing poorly in college (in spite of considerable effort on the part of the faculty sponsor), poor job record, and apparently without funds or plans for the future. He just did not seem to fulfill the criteria of value to the community and rehabilitation potential. There was the lady of ill repute (a veritable Camille) and altho she had plenty of financial support, it was not felt that she could be considered a responsible citizen and her potential (interest) for rehabilitation seemed limited. A final example is the logger who seemed to qualify in every way, except that our staff and his employer simply were unable to put together any semblance of a financial package for his continued care. He expired the same day a letter of rejection and explanation went to his wife. . . . Rejection invariably has called forth lengthy soul-searching by the various deliberative bodies. In a sense rejection has made some of the staff feel they have failed the candidate. We have been accused of "playing God" by this process of selection, but with limited facilities and limited financial backing and nowhere else to turn for help, we experienced (many of us for the first time) the choice of taking patients on a first come, first served basis or by means of a super-triage system. We elected the latter course. Altho it may smack of smugness, we have been fairly well satisfied with our procedure. . . .[17]

The decision process used at the Seattle

Center evoked a variety of reactions. Many questioned the standards used to make these life and death determinations. The Center's emphasis on social and economic considerations in making their choices drew particular criticism. An article published in the UCLA Law Review in 1968 by a physician and an attorney characterized the selection process as a "disturbing picture of the bourgeoisie sparing the bourgeoisie."[18] A number of the decisions made by the Seatlle Center seemed to penalize non-conformity, and the authors commented that "the Pacific Northwest is no place for a Henry David Thoreau with bad kidneys."[19]

One ethicist strongly argued, in 1979, that when determinations which involve the sacrificing of life must be made, procedures which require human choices should yield to procedures which produce random choices, such as a lottery or a first-come, first-served method. If the value of human life transcends all other values, then it should not be subjected to a bartering strategy in which one person's worth is weighed against another's. Random selection seemed preferable, "because we have no way of knowing how really and truly to estimate a man's societal worth or his worth to others or to himself. . . . When tragically not all can be saved the rule of practice must be the equality of one life with every other life. . . ."[20] Popular literature discussed the Center's deliberations in articles often having provocative titles such as "They Decide Who Lives, Who Dies"[21] and "The Rest Are Simply Left to Die."[22]

Because many people were deeply disturbed by such allocative problems and some of the decisions they generated, the United States Congress, in 1972, passed legislation which required the federal government to assume financial responsibility for almost all patients who needed treatment with the artificial kidney, or who required a kidney transplantation.[23] By 1975, over 20,000 patients were receiving kidney dialysis. But its annual price, in excess of

$300 million, surpassed original estimates by approximately 50 per cent.[24] The cost overruns of the artificial kidney program, as well as of government programs, such as Medicare and Medicaid, that subsidize general health needs, have created a quandary for our society as we decide how to match almost limitless health-care needs with limited medical resources, and all in the context of a strongly held belief in the United States that health care is a social right. Interpretation of the meaning of this right is controversial. However, one can think of it not as a right to all the medical assistance that it is possible to receive (health care like all other things of value is limited), but rather a right of equal access to any national program of health benefits enacted, whatever its limits may be.[25]

Although technology has enabled the modern physician to advance beyond the therapeutic boundaries of his predecessors, he faces perplexing questions about the goals of its use. Moreover complicated and expensive apparatus and finding or training the experts needed to run it have created a problem of scarcity in relation to demand, and dilemmas of allocation and selection have become increasingly common features of medical care. These problems have helped to reveal that scientific and technological advances alone cannot produce optimum medical care. It is paradoxical, perhaps, that to apply the creations of our newest scientific disciplines, physicians must reexamine the moral principles by which they act, and turn to ethics, one of our oldest humanistic disciplines.

Notes

[1]Pope Pius XII, "The Prolongation of Life," The Pope Speaks, 4 (1958), pp. 393-98.
[2]Ibid., p. 398.
[3]"A Definition of Irreversible Coma: Report of the Ad Hoc Committee of the Harvard Medical School to Examine the Definition of Brain Death,"

Journal of the American Medical Association, 205 (1968), pp. 337-40.

[4]In the Matter of Karen Quinlan, An Alleged Incompetent, 348 A. 2d 801 at 818 (1976).

[5]In the Matter of Karen Quinlan, An Alleged Incompetent, 355 A. 2d 647 at 663 (1976).

[6]Ibid., 355 A. 2d at 665 (1976).

[7]W. H. S. Jones, Hippocrates, (Cambridge, Mass., 1923), p. 193.

[8]Ibid., pp. 203, 205.

[9]Ludwig Edelstein, "Greek Medicine in Its Relation to Religion and Magic," in Owsei Temkin and C. Lilian Temkin, eds., Ancient Medicine: Selected Papers of Ludwig Edelstein (Baltimore, 1967), p. 245. A valuable discussion of Greek medicine is also found in P. Lain Entralgo, Doctor and Patient (New York, 1969).

[10]Ludwig Edelstein, "The Distinctive Hellenism of Greek Medicine," in Temkin and Temkin, Ancient Medicine, p. 382.

[11]Johannes Scultetus, The Chyrurgeons Store-House (London, 1674).

[12]Pierre Dionis, A Course of Chirurgical Operations, Demonstrated in the Royal Garden At Paris (London, 1710), pp. 8-9.

[13]Philip Drinker and Charles F. McKhann, "The Use of a New Apparatus for the Prolonged Administration of Artificial Respiration," Journal of the American Medical Association, 92 (1929), pp. 1658-60.

[14]Willem J. Kolff, "First Clinical Experience with the Artificial Kidney," Annals of Internal Medicine, 62 (1963), p. 617.

[15]John S. Ames, III, "An Act RElating to Certain Medical Treatment," Legislative Proposal to Commonwealth of Massachusetts, 1974. Further discussion of the living will and a proposed new document is found in Sissela Bok. "Patient Directions for Care at the End of Life," New England Journal of Medicine, 295 (1976), pp. 367-69.

[16]David Sanders and Jesse Dukeminier, Jr., "Medical Advance and Legal Lag: Hemodialysis and Kidney Transplantation," UCLA Law Review, 15 (1968), p. 362.

[17]James W. Haviland, "Experiences in Estab-

lishing a Community Artificial Kidney Center,"
<u>Transactions of the American Clinical and Cli-
matological Association</u>, 77 (1966), pp. 133-34.
    [18]Sanders and Dukeminier, "Medical Advance and
Legal Lag," p. 378.
    [19]Ibid.
    [20]Paul Ramsey, <u>The Patient as Person</u> (New
Haven, 1970), pp. 256, 259.
    [21]Shana Alexander, "They Decide Who Lives, Who
Dies," <u>Life</u>, November 9, 1962, p. 102.
    [22]Jhan Robbins and June Robbins, "The Rest are
Simply Left to Die," <u>Redbook</u>, November, 1967,
p. 81.
    [23]U. S. Congress, <u>Social Security Amendments</u>,
Public Law 92-603, Sec. 299I, 92nd Cong., 1st
Sess., 1972.
    [24]<u>New York Times</u>, September 25, 1975, p. 24.
    [25]See, for an excellent analysis of this is-
sue, David Mechanic, "Rationing Health Care:
Public Policy and the Medical Market Place,"
<u>Hastings Center Report</u>, 6:1 (February, 1976), pp.
34-37; Charles Fried, "Equality and Rights in
Medical Care," <u>ibid</u>., pp. 29-34; and Eugene Outka,
"Social Justice and Equal Access to Health Care,"
<u>Journal of Religious Ethics</u>, 2:1 (1974), pp.
11-32.

The Principle of Euthanasia*
    Antony Flew

1

    My particular concern here is to deploy a
general moral case for the establishment of a
legal right to voluntary euthanasia. The first
point to emphasize is that the argument is about
<u>voluntary</u> euthanasia. Neither I nor any other

*From <u>Euthanasia and the Right to Die</u>, edited by
by A. B. Downing. Reproduced by permission of
the author and Humanities Press Inc., Atlantic
Highlands, N. J.

contributor to the present volume advocates the euthanasia of either the incurably sick or the miserably senile except in so far as this is the strong, constant, and unequivocally expressed wish of the afflicted candidates themselves. Anyone, therefore, who dismisses what is in fact being contended on the gratuitously irrelevant grounds that he could not tolerate compulsory euthanasia, may very reasonably be construed as thereby tacitly admitting inability to meet and to overcome the case actually presented.

Second, my argument is an argument for the establishment of legal right. What I am urging is that any patient whose condition is hopeless and painful, who secures that it is duly and professionally certified as such, and who himself clearly and continuously desires to die should be enabled to do so: and that he should be enabled to do so without his incurring, or his family incurring, or those who provide or administer the means of death incurring, any legal penalty or stigma whatsoever. To advocate the establishment of such a legal right is not thereby to be committed even to saying that it would always be morally justifiable, much less that it would always be morally obligatory, for any patient to exercise this right if he found himself in a position so to do. For a legal right is not as such necessarily and always a moral right; and hence, a fortiori, it is not necessarily and always a moral duty to exercise whatever legal rights you may happen to possess.

This is a vital point. It was—to refer first to an issue now at last happily resolved—crucial to the question of the relegalization in Great Britain of homosexual relations between consenting male adults. Only when it was at last widely grasped, and grasped in its relation to this particular question, could we find the large majorities in both Houses of Parliament by which a liberalizing bill was passed into law. For presumably most members of those majorities not only found the idea of homosexual relations repugnant

372

—as most of us do—but also believed such relations to be morally wrong—as I for one do not. Yet they brought themselves to recognize that neither the repugnance generally felt towards some practice, nor even its actual wrongness if it actually is wrong, by itself constitutes sufficient reason for making or keeping that practice illegal. By the same token it can in the present instance be entirely consistent to urge, both that there ought to be a legal right to voluntary euthanasia, and that it would sometimes or always be morally wrong to exercise that legal right.

Third, the case presented here is offered as a moral one. In developing and defending such a case I shall, of course, have to consider certain peculiarly religious claims. Such claims, however, become relevant here only in so far as they either constitute, or may be thought to constitute, or in so far as they warrant, or may be thought to warrant, conclusions incompatible with those which it is my primary and positive purpose to urge.

Fourth, and finally, this essay is concerned primarily with general principles, not with particular practicalities. I shall not here discuss or—except perhaps quite incidentally—touch upon any questions of comparative detail: questions, for instance, of how a Euthanasia Act ought to be drafted; of what safeguards would need to be incorporated to prevent abuse of the new legal possibilities by those with disreputable reasons for wanting someone else dead; of exactly what and how much should be taken as constituting an unequivocal expression of a clear and constant wish; of the circumstances, if any, in which we ought to take earlier calculated expressions of a patient's desires as constituting still adequate grounds for action when at some later time the patient has become himself unable any longer to provide sufficiently sober, balanced, constant and unequivocal expressions of his wishes; and so on.

I propose here as a matter of policy largely to ignore such particular and practical questions. This is not because I foolishly regard them as unimportant, or irresponsibly dismiss them as dull. Obviously they could become of the most urgent interest. Nor yet is it because I believe that my philosophical cloth disqualifies me from contributing helpfully to any down-to-earth discussions. On the contrary, I happen to be one of those numerous academics who are convinced, some of them correctly, that they are practical and businesslike men! The decisive reason for neglecting these vital questions of detail here in, and in favour of, a consideration of the general principle of the legalization of voluntary euthanasia is that they are all secondary to that primary issue. For no such subordinate question can properly arise as relevantly practical until and unless the general principle is conceded. Some of these practical considerations are in any event dealt with by other contributors to this volume.

2

So what can be said in favour of the principle? There are two main, and to my mind decisive, moral reasons. But before deploying these it is worth pausing for a moment to indicate why the onus of proof does not properly rest upon us. It may seem as if it does, because we are proposing a change in the present order of things; and it is up to the man who wants a change to produce the reasons for making whatever change he is proposing. This most rational principle of conservatism is in general sound. But here it comes into conflict with the overriding and fundamental liberal principle. It is up to any person and any institution wanting to prevent anyone from doing anything he wishes to do, or to compel anyone to do anything he does not wish to do, to provide positive good reason to justify interference. The question should therefore be: <u>not</u> "Why should people be given this new legal right?"; <u>but</u> "Why should people in this matter be restrained by law from doing what they want?"

Yet even if this liberal perspective is accepted, as it too often is not, and even if we are able to dispose of any reasons offered in defence of the present legal prohibitions, still the question would arise, whether the present state of the law represents a merely tiresome departure from sound liberal principles of legislation, or whether it constitutes a really substantial evil. It is here that we have to offer out two main positive arguments.

(1) First, there are, and for the foreseeable future will be, people afflicted with incurable and painful diseases who urgently and fixedly want to die quickly. The first argument is that a law which tries to prevent such sufferers from achieving this quick death, and usually thereby forces other people who care for them to watch their pointless pain helplessly, is a very cruel law. It is because of this legal cruelty that advocates of euthanasia sometimes speak of euthanasia as "mercy-killing." In such cases the sufferer may be reduced to an obscene parody of a human being, a lump of suffering flesh eased only by intervals of drugged stupor. This, as things now stand, must persist until at last every device of medical skill fails to prolong the horror.

(2) Second, a law which insists that there must be no end to this process—terminated only by the overdue relief of "death by natural causes"—is a very degrading law. In the present context the full force of this second reason may not be appreciated immediately, if at all. We are so used to meeting appeals to "the absolute value of human personality," offered as the would-be knock-down objection to any proposal to legalize voluntary euthanasia, that it has become hard to realize that, in so far as we can attach some tolerably precise meaning to the key phrase, this consideration would seem to bear in the

direction precisely opposite to that in which it is usually mistaken to point. For the agonies of prolonged terminal illness can be so terrible and so demoralizing that the person is blotted out in ungovernable nerve reactions. In such cases as this, to meet the patient's longing for death is a means of showing for human personality that respect which cannot tolerate any ghastly travesty of it. So our second main positive argument, attacking the present state of the law as degrading, derives from a respect for the wishes of the individual person, a concern for human dignity, an unwillingness to let the animal pain disintegrate the man.

Our first main positive argument opposes the present state of the law, and of the public opinion which tolerates it, as cruel. Often and appositely this argument is supported by contrasting the tenderness which rightly insists that on occasion dogs and horses must be put out of their misery, with the stubborn refusal in any circumstances to permit one person to assist another in cutting short his suffering. The cry is raised, "But people are not animals!" Indeed they are not. Yet this is precisely not a ground for treating people worse than brute animals. Animals are like people, in that they too can suffer. It is for this reason that both can have a claim on our pity and our mercy.[1]

But people are also more than brute animals. They can talk and think and wish and plan. It is this that makes it possible to insist, as we do, that there must be no euthanasia unless it is the firm considered wish of the person concerned. People also can, and should, have dignity as human beings. That is precisely why we are urging that they should be helped and not hindered when they wish to avoid or cut short the often degrading miseries of incurable disease or, I would myself add, of advanced senile decay.

3

In the first section I explained the scope
and limitations of the present chapter. In the
second I offered—although only after suggesting
that the onus of proof in this case does not
really rest on the proposition—my two main positive reasons in favour of euthanasia. It is
time now to begin to face, and to try to dispose
of, objections. This is the most important phase
in the whole exercise. For to anyone with any
width of experience and any capacity for compas-
sion the positive reasons must be both perfectly
obvious and strongly felt. The crucial issue is
whether or not there are decisive, overriding
objections to these most pressing reasons of the
heart.

(1) Many of the objections commonly advanced, which are often mistaken to be fundamental, are really objections only to a possible
specific manner of implementing the principle of
voluntary euthanasia. Thus it is suggested that
if the law permitted doctors on occasion to provide their patients with means of death, or where
necessary to do the actual killing, and they did
so, then the doctors who did either of these
things would be violating the Hippocratic Oath,
and the prestige of and public confidence in the
medical profession would be undermined.

As to the Hippocratic Oath, this makes two
demands which in the special circumstances we
have in mind may become mutually contradictory.
They cannot both be met at the same time. The
relevant section reads: "I will use treatments
to help the sick according to my ability and
judgment, but never with a view to injury and
wrong-doing. I will not give anyone a lethal
dose if asked to do so, nor will I suggest such
a course."[2] The fundamental undertaking "to help
the sick according to my ability and judgment"
may flatly conflict with the further promise not
to "give anyone a lethal dose if asked to do so."
To observe the basic undertaking a doctor may

have to break the further promise. The moral
would, therefore, appear to be: not that the
Hippocratic Oath categorically and unambiguously
demands that doctors must have no dealings with
voluntary euthanasia; but rather that the possible incompatibility in such cases of the different directives generated by two of its logically independent clauses constitutes a reason
for revising that Oath.

As to the supposed threat to the prestige of
and to our confidnece in the medical profession,
I am myself inclined to think that the fears expressed are—in more than one dimension—disproportionate to the realities. But whatever the
truth about this whole objection would bear only
against proposals which permitted or required
doctors to do, or directly to assist in, the
actual killing. This is not something which is
essential to the whole idea of voluntary euthanasia, and the British Euthanasia Society's
present draft bill is so formulated as altogether
to avoid this objection. It is precisely such
inessential objections as this which I have undertaken to eschew in this essay, in order to
consider simply the general principle.

(2) The first two objections which do really
bear on this form a pair. One consists in the
contention that there is no need to be concerned
about the issue, since in fact there are not any,
or not many, patients who when it comes to the
point want to die quickly. The other bases the
same complacent conclusion on the claim that in
fact, in the appropriate cases, doctors already
mercifully take the law into their own hands.
These two comfortable doctrines are, like many
other similarly reassuring bromides, both entirely wrong and rather shabby.

(a) To the first the full reply would probably have to be made by a doctor, for a medical
layman can scarcely be in a position to make an
estimate of the number of patients who would
apply and could qualify for euthanasia. But it

is quite sufficient for our immediate purposes to say two things. First, there can be few who have reached middle life, and who have not chosen to shield their sensibilities with some impenetrable carapace of dogma, who cannot recall at least one case of an eager candidate for euthanasia from their own experience—even from their own peacetime experience only. If this statement is correct, as my own inquiries suggest that it is, then the total number of such eager candidates must be substantial. Second, though the need for enabling legalization becomes progressively more urgent the greater the numbers of people personally concerned, I wish for myself to insist that it still matters very much indeed if but one person who would have decided for a quick death is forced to undergo a protracted one.

(b) To the second objection, which admits that there are many cases where euthanasia is indicated, but is content to leave it to the doctors to defy the law, the answer is equally simple. First, it is manifestly not true that all doctors are willing on the appropriate occasions either to provide the means of death or to do the killing. Many, as they are Roman Catholics, are on religious grounds absolutely opposed to doing so. Many others are similarly opposed for other reasons, or by force of training and habit. And there is no reason to believe that among the rest the proportion of potential martyrs is greater than it is in any other secular occupational group. Second, it is entirely wrong to expect the members of one profession as a regular matter of course to jeopardize their whole careers by breaking the criminal law in order to save the rest of us the labour and embarrassment of changing that law.

Here I repeat two points made to me more than once by doctor friends. First, if a doctor were convinced he ought to provide euthanasia in spite of the law, it would often be far harder for him to do so undetected than many laymen think, especially in our hospitals. Second, the present attitude of the medical establishment is such that if a doctor did take the chance, was caught and brought to trial, and even if the jury, as they well might, refused to convict, still he must expect to face complete professional disaster.

(3) The next two objections, which in effect bear on the principle, again form a pair. The first pair had in common the claim that the facts were such that the question of legislative action need not arise. The second pair are alike in that whereas both might appear to be making contentions of fact, in reality we may have in each a piece of exhortation or of metaphysics masquerading as an empirical proposition.

(a) Of this second relevant pair the first suggests that there is no such thing as an incurable disease. This implausible thesis becomes more intelligible, though no more true, when we recall how medical ideologues sometimes make proclamations: "Modern medicine cannot recognize any such thing as a disease which is incurable"; and the like. Such pronouncements may sound like reports on the present state of the art. It is from this resemblance that they derive their peculiar idiomatic point. But the advance of medicine has not reached a stage where all diseases are curable. And no one seriously thinks that it has. At most this continuing advance has suggested that we need never despair of finding cures some day. But this is not at all the same thing as saying, what is simply not true, that even now there is no condition which is at any stage incurable. This medical ideologue's slogan has to be construed as a piece of exhortation disguised for greater effect as a paradoxical statement of purported fact. It may as such be instructively compared with certain favourite educationalists' paradoxes: "We do not teach subjects, we teach children!"; or "There are no bad children, only bad teachers!"

(b) The second objection of this pair is

380

that on one can ever be certain that the condition of any particular patient is indeed hopeless. This is more tricky. For an objection of
this form might be given two radically different
sorts of content. Yet it would be easy and is
common to slide from one interpretation to the
other, and back again, entirely unwittingly.

Simply and straightforwardly, such an objection might be made by someone whose point was
that judgments of incurability are, as a matter
of purely contingent fact, so unreliable that no
one has any business to be certain, or to claim
to know, that anyone is suffering from an incurable affliction. This contention would relevantly be backed by appealing to the alleged fact
that judgments that "this case is hopeless,
period" are far more frequently proven to have
been mistaken than judgments that, for instance,
"this patient will recover fully, provided that
he undergoes the appropriate operation." This
naïve objector's point could be made out, or decisively refuted, only by reference to quantitative studies of the actual relative reliabilities
and unreliabilities of different sorts of medical
judgments. So unless and until such quantitative
empirical studies are actually made, and unless
and until their results are shown to bear upon
the question of euthanasia in the way suggested,
there is no grounded and categorical objection
here to be met.

But besides this first and straightforwardly
empirical interpretation there is a second interpretation of another quite different sort.
Suppose someone points to an instance, as they
certainly could and well might, where some patient whom all the doctors had pronounced to be
beyond hope nevertheless recovers, either as the
result of the application of new treatment derived from some swift and unforeseen advance in
medical science, or just through nature taking
its unexpected course. This happy but chastening
outcome would certainly demonstrate that the doctors concerned had on this occasion been mis-

381

taken; and hence that, though they had sincerely
claimed to know the patient's condition to have
been incurable, they had not really known this.
The temptation is to mistake it that such errors
show that no one ever really knows. It is this
perfectly general contention, applied to the particular present case of judgments of incurability, which constitutes the second objection in
its second interpretation. The objector seizes
upon the point that even the best medical opinion turns out sometimes to have been wrong (as
here). He then urges, simply because doctors
thus prove occasionally to have been mistaken
(as here) and because it is always—theoretically
if not practically—possible that they may be
mistaken again the next time, that therefore none
of them ever really knows (at least in such
cases). Hence, he concludes, there is after all
no purchase for the idea of voluntary euthanasia.
For this notion presupposes that there are patients recognizably suffering from conditions
known to be incurable.

The crux to grasp about this contention is
that, notwithstanding that it may be presented
and pressed as if it were somehow especially relevant to one particular class of judgments, in
truth it applies—if it applies at all—absolutely generally. The issue is thus revealed as not
medical but metaphysical. If it follows that if
someone is ever mistaken then he never really
knows, and still more if it follows that if it
is even logically possible that he may be mistaken then he never really knows, then, surely,
the consequence must be that none of us ever does
know—not really. (When a metaphysician says
that something is never really such and such, what
he really means is that it very often is, really.) For it is of the very essence of our cognitive predicament that we do all sometimes make
mistakes; while always it is at least theoretically possible that we may. Hence the argument,
if it hold at all, must show that knowledge, real
knowledge, is for all us mortal men forever unattainable.

What makes the second of the present pair of objections tricky to handle is that it is so easy to pass unwittingly from an empirical to a metaphysical interpretation. We may fail to notice, or noticing may fail convincingly to explain, how an empirical thesis has degenerated into metaphysics, or how metaphysical misconceptions have corrupted the medical judgment. Yet, once these utterly different interpretations have been adequately distinguished, two summary comments should be sufficient.

First, in so far as the objection is purely metaphysical, to the idea that real knowledge is possible, it applies absolutely generally; or not at all. It is arbitrary and irrational to restrict it to the examination of the principle of voluntary euthanasia. If doctors never really know, we presumably have no business to rely much upon any of their judgments. And if, for the same metaphysical reasons, there is no knowledge to be had anywhere, then we are all of us in the same case about everything. This may be as it may be, but it is nothing in particular to the practical business in hand.

Second, when the objection takes the form of a pretended refusal to take any decision in matters of life and death on the basis of a judgment which theoretically might turn out to have been mistaken, it is equally unrealistic and arbitrary. It is one thing to claim that judgments of incurability are peculiarly fallible: if that suggestion were to be proved to be correct. It is quite another to claim that it is improper to take vital decisions on the basis of sorts of judgment which either are in principle fallible, or even prove occasionally in fact to have been wrong. It is an inescapable feature of the human condition that no one is infallible about anything, and there is no sphere of life in which mistakes do not occur. Nevertheless we cannot as agents avoid, even in matters of life and death and more than life and death, making decisions to act or to abstain. It is only necessary and it is only possible to insist on ordinarily strict standards of warranted assertability, and on ordinarily exacting rather than obsessional criteria of what is beyond reasonable doubt.

Of course this means that mistakes will sometimes be made. This is in practice a corollary of the uncontested fact that infallibility is not an option. To try to ignore our fallibility is unrealistic, while to insist on remembering it only in the context of the question of voluntary euthanasia is arbitrary. Nor is it either realistic or honourable to attempt to offload the inescapable burdens of practical responsibility, by first claiming that we never really <u>know</u>, and then pretending that a decision not to <u>act</u> is somehow a decision which relieves us of all proper responsibility for the outcome.

(4) The two pairs of relevant objections so far considered have both been attempts in different ways to show that the issue does not, or at any rate need not, arise as a practical question. The next concedes that the question does arise and is important, but attempts to dispose of it with the argument that what we propose amounts to the legalization, in certain circumstances, of murder, or suicide, or both; and that this cannot be right because murder and suicide are both gravely wrong always. Now even if we were to concede all the rest it would still not follow, because something is gravely wrong in morals, that there ought to be a law against it; and that we are wrong to try to change the law as it now subsists. We have already urged that the onus of proof must always rest on the defenders of any restriction.

(a) In fact the <u>rest</u> will not do. In the first place, if the law were to be changed as we want, the present legal definition of "murder" would at the same time have to be so changed that it no longer covered the provision of euthanasia for a patient who had established that it

384

was his legal right. "Does this mean," someone may indignantly protest, "that right and wrong are created by Acts of Parliament?" Emphatically, yes: and equally emphatically, no. Yes indeed, if what is intended is legal right and legal offence. What is meant by the qualification "legal" if it is not that these rights are the rights established and sanctioned by the law? Certainly not, if what is intended is moral right and moral wrong. Some moral rights happen to be at the same time legal rights, and some moral wrongs similarly also constitute offences against the law. But, notoriously, legislatures may persist in denying moral rights; while, as I insisted earlier, not every moral wrong either is or ought to be forbidden and penalized by law.

Well then, if the legal definition of "murder" can be changed by Act of Parliament, would euthanasia nevertheless be murder, morally speaking? This amounts to asking whether administering euthanasia legally to someone who is incurably ill, and who has continually wanted it, is in all relevant respects similar to, so to speak, a standard case of murder; and whether therefore it is to be regarded morally as murder. Once the structure of the question is in this way clearly displayed it becomes obvious that the cases are different in at least three important respects. First, whereas the murder victim is (typically) killed against his will, a patient would be given or assisted in obtaining euthanasia only if he steadily and strongly desired to die. Second, whereas the murderer kills his victim, treating him usually as a mere object for disposal, in euthanasia the object of the exercise would be to save someone, at his own request, from needless suffering, to prevent the degradation of a human person. Third, whereas the murderer by his action defies the law, the man performing euthanasia would be acting according to law, helping another man to secure what the law allowed him.

It may sound as if that third clause goes

back on the earlier repudiation of the idea that moral right and wrong are created by Act of Parliament. That is not so. For we are not saying that this action would now be justifiable, or at least not murder morally, simply because it was now permitted by the law; but rather that the change in the law would remove one of possible reasons for moral objection. The point is this: that although the fact that something is enjoined, permitted, or forbidden by law does not necessarily make it right, justifiable, or wrong morally, nevertheless the fact that something is enjoyed or forbidden by a law laid down by established authority does constitute one moral reason for obedience. So a doctor who is convinced that the objects of the Euthanasia Society are absolutely right should at least hesitate to take the law into his own hands, not only for prudential but also for moral reasons. For to defy the law is, as it were, to cast your vote against constitutional procedures and the rule of law, and these are the foundations and framework of any tolerable civilized society. (Consider here the injunction posted by some enlightened municipal authorities upon their public litter bins: "Cast your vote here for a tidy New York!"—or wherever it may be.)

Returning to the main point, the three differences which we have just noticed are surely sufficient to require us to refuse to assimilate legalized voluntary euthanasia to the immoral category of murder. But to insist on making a distinction between legalized voluntary euthanasia and murder is not the same thing as, nor does it by itself warrant, a refusal to accept that both are equally immoral. What an appreciation of these three differences, but crucially of the first, should do is to suggest that we ought to think of such euthanasia as a special case not of murder but of suicide. Let us therefore examine the second member of our third pair of relevant objections.

(b) This objection was that to legalize

voluntary euthanasia would be to legalize, in
certain conditions, the act of assisting suicide.
The question therefore arises: "Is suicide always morally wrong?"

The purely secular considerations usually
advanced and accepted are not very impressive.
First, it is still sometimes urged that suicide
is unnatural, in conflict with instinct, a breach
of the putative law of self-preservation. All
arguments of this sort, which attempt directly to
deduce conclusions about what <u>ought</u> to be from
premises stating, or mis-stating, only what <u>is</u>
are—surely—unsound: they involve what philosophers label, appropriately, the "Naturalistic
Fallacy." There is also a peculiar viciousness
about appealing to what is supposed to be a descriptive law of nature to provide some justification for the prescription to obey that supposed
law. For if the law really obtained as a description of what always and unavoidably happens,
then there would be no point in prescribing that
it should; whereas if the descriptive law does
not in fact hold, then the basis of the supposed
justification does not exist. Furthermore, even
if an argument of this first sort could show that
suicide is always immoral, it could scarcely provide a reason for insisting that it ought also to
be illegal.

Second, it is urged that the suicide by his
act deprives other people of the services which
he might have rendered them had he lived longer.
This can be a strong argument, especially where
the suicide has a clear, positive family or public obligation. It is also an argument which,
even in a liberal perspective, can provide a
basis for legislation. But it is irrelevant to
the circumstances which advocates of the legalization of voluntary euthanasia have in mind. In
such circumstances as these, there is no longer
any chance of being any use to anyone, and if
there is any family or social obligation it must
be all the other way—to end your life when it
has become a hopeless burden both to yourself

and to others.

Third, it is still sometimes maintained that suicide is in effect murder—"self-murder." To this, offered in a purely secular context, the appropriate and apparently decisive reply would seem to be that by parity of reasoning marriage is really adultery—"own-wife-adultery." For, surely, the gravamen of both distinctions lies in the differences which such paradoxical assimilations override. It is precisely because suicide is the destruction of oneself (by one's own choice), while murder is the destruction of somebody else (against his wishes), that the former can be, and is, distinguished from the latter.

Yet there is a counter to this own-wife-adultery-move. It begins by insisting, rightly, that sexual relations—which are what is common to both marriage and adultery—are not in themselves wrong: the crucial question is, "Who with?" It then proceeds to claim that what is common to both murder and suicide is the killing of a human being; and here the questions of "Which one?" or "By whom?" are not, morally, similarly decisive. Finally appeal may be made, if the spokesman is a little old-fashioned, to the Sixth Commandment, or if he is in the contemporary swim, to the Principle of the Absolute Sanctity of Human Life.

The fundamental difficulty which confronts anyone making this counter move is that of finding a formulation for his chosen principle about the wrongness of all killing, which is both sufficiently general not to appear merely question-begging in its application to the cases in dispute, and which yet carries no consequences that the spokesman himself is not prepared to accept. Thus, suppose he tries to read the Sixth Commandment as constituting a veto on any killing of human beings. Let us waive here the immediate scholarly objections: that such a reading involves accepting the mistranslation "Thou shalt not kill" rather than the more faithful "Thou

388

shalt do no murder"; and that neither the children of Israel nor even their religious leaders construed this as a law forbidding all war and all capital punishment.3 The question remains whether our spokesman himself is really prepared to say that all killing, without any exception, is morally wrong.

It is a question which has to be pressed, and which can only be answered by each man for himself. Since I cannot give your answer, I can only say that I know few if any people who would sincerely say "Yes." But as soon as any exceptions or qualifications are admitted, it becomes excessively difficult to find any presentable principle upon which these can be admitted while still excluding suicide and assistance to suicide in a case of euthanasia. This is not just because, generally, once any exceptions or qualifications have been admitted to any rule it becomes hard or impossible not to allow others. It is because, particularly, the case for excluding suicide and assisting suicide from the scope of any embargo on killing people is so strong that only some absolutely universal rule admitting no exceptions of any sort whatever could have the force convincingly to override it.

Much the same applies to the appeal of the Principle of the Absolute Sanctity of Human Life. Such appeals were continually made by conservatives—many of them politically not Conservative but Socialist—in opposition to the recent efforts to liberalize the British abortion laws. Such conservatives should be, and repeatedly were, asked whether they are also opponents of all capital punishment and whether they think that it is always wrong to kill in a "just war." (In fact none of those in Parliament could honestly have answered "Yes" to both questions.) In the case of abortion their position could still be saved by inserting the qualification "innocent," a qualification traditionally made by cautious moralists who intend to rest on this sort of principle. But any such qualification,

389

however necessary, must make it almost impossible to employ the principle thus duly qualified to proscribe all suicide. It would be extraordinarily awkward and far-fetched to condemn suicide or assisting suicide as "taking an innocent life."

Eearlier in the present subsection I described the three arguments I have been examining as secular. This was perhaps misleading. For all three are regularly used by religious people; indeed versions of all three are to be found in St. Thomas Aquinas's Summa Theologica, the third being there explicitly linked with St. Augustine's laboured interpretation of the Sixth Commandment to cover suicide.[4] And perhaps the incongruity of trying to make the amended Principle of the Absolute Sanctity of Innocent Human Life yield a ban on suicide is partly to be understood as a result of attempting to derive from secularized premises conclusions which really depend upon a religious foundation. But the next two arguments are frankly and distinctively religious.

The first insists that human beings are God's property: "It is our duty to take care of God's property entrusted to our charge—our souls and bodies. They belong not to us but to God";[5] "Whoever takes his own life sins against God, even as he who kills another's slave sins against that slave's master";[6] and "Suicide is the destruction of the temple of God and a violation of the proptery rights of Jesus Christ."[7]

About this I restrict myself to three comments here. First, as it stands, unsupplemented by appeal to some other principle or principles, it must apply, if it applies at all, equally to all artificial and intentional shortening or lengthening of any human life, one's own or that of anyone else. Alone and unsupplemented it would commit one to complete quietism in all matters of life and death; for all interference would be interference with someone else's property. Otherwise one must find further particular moral revelations by which to justify capital punishment, war, medicine, and many other such at first flush impious practices. Second, it seems to presuppose that a correct model of the relation between man and God is that of slave and slave-master, and that respect for God's property ought to be the fundamental principle of morals. It is perhaps significant that it is to this image that St. Thomas and the pagan Plato, in attacking suicide, both appeal. This attempt to derive not only theological but all obligations from the putative theological fact of Creation is a common-place of at least one tradition of moral theology. In this derivation the implicit moral premise is usually that unconditional obedience to a Creator, often considered as a very special sort of owner, is the primary elemental obligation. Once this is made explicit it does not appear to be self-evidently true; nor is it easy to see how a creature in absolute ontological dependence could be the genuinely responsible subject of obligations to his infinite Creator. Third, this objection calls to mind one of the sounder sayings of the minister Tiberius: "If the gods are insulted let them see to it themselves." This remark is obviously relevant only to the question of legalization, not to that of the morality or the prudence of the action itself.

The second distinctively religious argument springs from the conviction that God does indeed see to it Himself, with a penalty of infinite severity. If you help someone to secure euthanasia, "You are sending him from the temporary and comparatively light suffering of this world to the eternal suffering of hell." Now if this appalling suggestion could be shown to be true it would provide the most powerful moral reason against helping euthanasia in any way, and for using any legislative means which might save people from suffering a penalty so inconceivably cruel. It would also be the strongest possible prudential reason against "suiciding oneself."[8] (Though surely anyone who knowingly incurred such a penalty would by that very action prove himself to be genuinely of unsound mind; and hence not justly punishable at all. Not that a Being contemplating such unspeakable horrors could be expected to be concerned with justice!)

About this second, peculiarly religious, argument there is, it would seem, little to be done except: either simply to concede that for anyone holding this belief it indeed is reasonable to oppose euthanasia, and to leave it at that; or, still surely conceding this, to attempt to mount a general offensive against the whole system of which it forms a part.

(5) The final objection is one raised, with appropriate modifications, by the opponents of every reform everywhere. It is that even granting that the principle of the reform is excellent it would, if adopted, lead inevitably to something worse; and so we had much better not make any change at all. Thus G. K. Chesterton pronounced that the proponents of euthanasia now seek only the death of those who are a nuisance to themselves, but soon it will be broadened to include those who are a nuisance to others. Such cosy arguments depend on two assumptions: that the supposedly inevitable consequences are indeed evil and substantially worse than the evil the reform would remove; and that the supposedly inevitable consequences really are inevitable consequences.

In the present case we certainly can grant the first assumptions if the consequence supposed is taken to be large-scaled legalized homicide in the Nazi manner. But whatever reason is there for saying that this would, much less inevitably must, follow? For there are the best of reasons for insisting that there is a world of difference between legalized voluntary euthanasia and such legalized mass-murder. Only if public opinion comes to appreciate their force will there be any chance of getting the reform we want. Then we should have no difficulty, in alliance doubtless with all our present opponents, in blocking any move to legalize murder which might conceivably arise from a misunderstanding of the case for voluntary euthanasia. Furthermore, it is to the point to remind such objectors that the Nazi atrocities they probably have in mind were in fact not the result of any such reform, but were the work of people who consciously repudiated the whole approach to ethics represented in the argument of the present essay. For this approach is at once human and humanitarian. It is concerned above all with the reduction of suffering; but concerned at the same time with other values too, such as human dignity and respect for the wishes of the individual person. And always it is insistent that morality should not be "left in the dominion of vague feeling or inexplicable internal convictions but should be . . . made a matter of reason and calculation."[9]

Notes

[1]Thus Jeremy Bentham, urging that the legislator must not neglect animal sufferings, insists that the "question is not 'Can they reason?' nor 'Can they talk?' but 'Can they suffer?'" (Principles of Morals and Legislation, Chap. XVII, n.)

[2]The Greek text is most easily found in Hippocrates and the Fragments of Heracleitus, ed. W. H. S. Jones and E. T. Withington for the Loeb series (Harvard Univ. Pr. and Heinemann), Vol. 1, p. 298. The translation in the present essay is mine.

[3]See, f.i., Joseph Fletcher, Morals and Medicine (1954; Gollancz, 1955), pp. 195-6. I recommend this excellent treatment by a liberal Protestant of a range of questions in moral theology too often left too far from liberal Roman Catholics.

[4]Part II: Q. 64, A5. The Augustine reference is to The City of God, 1, 20. It is worth comparing, for ancient Judaic attitudes, E. Westermarck's Origin and Development of the Moral Ideas. Vol. 1, pp. 246-7.

[5]See the Rev. G. J. MacGillivray, "Suicide and Euthanasia," p. 10; a widely distributed

393

Catholic Truth Society pamphlet.

[6] Aquinas, loc. cit.

[7] Koch-Preuss, Handbook of Moral Theology, vol. II, p. 76. This quotation has been taken from Fletcher, op. cit., p. 192.

[8] This rather affected-sounding gallicism is adopted deliberately: if you believe, as I do, that suicide is not always and as such wrong, it is inappropriate to speak of "committing suicide"; just as correspondingly if you believe, as I do not, that (private) profit is wrong, it becomes apt to talk to those who commit a profit."

[9] J. S. Mill's essay on Bentham quoted in F. R. Leavis, Mill on Bentham and Coleridge (Chatto & Windus, 1950), p. 92.

IV

PERSONHOOD AND MEANING
IN LIFE AND DEATH

Introduction

The last period of life is a time of sum-
ming up, rethinking the meaning of life and the
direction ones life has taken. It can be a time
of peace and tranquility brought about by a sense
of integrity or a time of heartache brought about
by despair about what might have happened but did
not. It is difficult to pinpoint the time this
occurs for most people. Oftentimes it occurs
when a person retires. Whenever it happens one
realizes that he is past the stage of carrying
the responsibility for establishing and caring
for the next generation. That obligation has
been relinquished to those in mid-life. What one
is able to accomplish at this stage of his life,
as with the others, is largely dependent on the
decisions made earlier. In a sense one is preparing for the end of life, and one does so by
becoming increasingly aware of the point or lack
of it that characterized his life. Either he can
find integrity in it or he can despair about it.

The integrity that he is searching for has,
according to Erikson, some identifiable characteristics. First, if his life has integrity it
has an identifiable order and purpose to it. One
can look back through life and see a leaning, a
direction amid the seeming chaos. Second, there
is a growing acceptance of the framework within
which ones life was lived. This framework is
part genetic and part the result of education and
training by society and parents. One can see

that his life took the direction that it did almost by necessity. While one believes that he was acting freely within this framework and at times even changed parts of the framework itself, yet there is the sense that he has only been an observer of the events of his life. Finally, one is ready to defend the dignity of his life-style against any charges. One's life, it is believed, has intrinsic worth. Such an understanding is an achievement on one's part; it will not happen automatically. In the search for integrity some important beliefs are carried into the creation of the new life structure. One may believe that he is a person, that he can find meaning in life, that his life is a result to some extent at least of his own efforts, and that there are better ways than others to regard death. Each of these beliefs will now be examined. The possibility of achieving integrity rests on the beliefs we hold.

First, the achievement of or the failure to achieve integrity is believed to be that of a person. It is also believed a person is in some sense the same person he was many years ago. And furthermore, whatever else I know I know that for sure. Yet, while we may have these beliefs about ourselves, are they defensible? Ernst Cassirer, after tracing the history of the views on the nature of man, contends that the nature of man at this point in the history of western civilization is problematic. In our attempt to know who we are we have many competing voices and there seems to be no basis for judging which voice is correct. Descartes states the view of man that has been dominant since the seventeenth century. While we may not be certain about other things, we can be sure that we exist and that we have to learn about ourselves and not be mistaken about what we learn. We persons are thinking beings. Hume, however, does not agree that we can be sure of what we learn about ourselves. He does not believe that we know our inner lives immediately and directly. Furthermore, it is questionable that our belief in our identify through time is justified. Bertocci, stating a view of

the person that is indebeted to Descartes, believes that persons are moral beings who are
complex time-binding entities. He believes we
are moral beings with identities through history
or time. We can achieve an integrity or meaning
in life.

Second, most people entering the last stage
of life believe it is reasonable to seek meaning
in their lives. It may not be found, but that
would be a failure on their part and not on the
possibility of its achievement. If it is believed that meaning can be achieved, where is it
to be found? How is it to be found? Today many
people turn to psychologists and psychoanalysts
to help them with their problems, particularly
those problems involved in finding some worth-
while point or direction to their lives. Social
scientists, particularly those with a clinical
orientation, have taught us that our emotions,
feelings, desires play a crucial role in our
lives. Often problems we face, including a sense
of directionlessness, are rooted in our emotional, conative lives. Persons are able to lead
happy lives again if they learn to accept their
emotions and redirect their desires into fruitful avenues. However, what may be overlooked in
an emotional, conative approach to finding meaning in life are the presuppositions about what
is true, real, and good. These are sometimes at
the base of our emotions and desires. Until
they have been articulated, clarified, and evaluated, it is unlikely that the emotional, conative dimensions of life can be worked through
successfully. Thus, a resource for finding
meaning in life that becomes important is philosophy. Aristotle believes that the life of persons gains meaning through their performing the
function proper to them, being fully human. Final
meaning, that about the nature of reality and how
humans fit into the whole scheme of things, is
achieved through the theoretical intellect. In
this area of study one can know for sure whether
his beliefs are correct or not. However, meaning which has to do with everyday life, with

action, is achieved through the practical intellect. Aristotle believed that knowledge cannot be achieved in this area; nevertheless, some reasonable suggestions can be made about being fully human in our everyday lives. Happy lives are the result of gathering relevant information about one's own situation and making the decision which keeps balance and proportion in one's life as one attempts to be fully human. Our failure to find meaning is a failure of gathering proper information and of sound practical thinking. If we are able to control our actions and maintain the balance needed to develop fully our potentialities we will be able to move to the final stage of the exercise of the theoretical intellect and the achievement of the knowledge of the nature and structure of reality. While philosophy has not recently been thought of as a resource for helping people find meaning in their lives, it has been rejected by those who follow another major tradition in Western culture, Christianity. Point and direction in life is not to be found either through psychology or philosophy; rather, it is found through faith in Jesus Christ. While many formulations can be made of what this means, Bouwsma develops his point through a contrast between manhood and adulthood. Meaning is not to be found where Aristotle thought it would be, in the well trained mind of the fully developed man. Fundamental to manhood is a belief that reason using information available to it is able to gain control over life so that it will move in the direction one believes to be best. The reason man does not find meaning in life is that he is ignorant and not in control of his life. The Christian, however, contends that man's problem is not ignorance and lack of control; it is sin, the attempt to be a god. Philosophy will not help man find meaning; only faith in God will. In accepting God as God and man as creature who is totally dependent on God, man finds his true nature and purpose. He is a creature. His purpose is to be fully a creature of God. The model he is to follow is Jesus of Nazareth. With that purpose and model

in mind he is to grow. Thus Bouwsma emphasizes
the root of adulthood, _adolescere_, to grow, as
the ideal for persons. Meaning can be found,
but it is not gained through psychoanalysis or
philosophy; it is found through the Christian
faith.

Third, in our search for integrity and to
avoid despair, we believe that the life we have
lived has been our own doing. No one else can
be held responsible for our lives. Yet, when we
look over the past, it seems that the events,
circumstances, and character of our lives was
largely not our doing. We seem to have been
caught in a web of time and place, and we simply
lived out what had been set for us. This raises
the issue of whether we were and are free to
change, modify, and redirect our lives or are
determined by forces both internal and external
to live the life we are and have lived. Campbell believes that persons are able to construct
and modify their characters and are able to act
contrary to their characters. Hospers, on the
contrary, contends that the character of persons
is made for them by the social and physical environment of their lives. A small child learns
habits, attitudes, and beliefs. These are reinforced through years of repetition, and they are
so ingrained that nothing can change them. The
whole of life is, then, an outworking of the
complex fabric of life instilled into the child
from birth. If meaning is found at the end of
life Campbell believes it is an achievement on
our part, and Hospers believes it is simply the
result of forces beyond our control.

Finally, if one has found integrity in life
one has also prepared himself for death. There
is a growing recognition of the worth of one's
life and an acceptance of that worth. Nothing
more can be done about one's life, and indeed,
nothing more needs to be done about it. The end
of life can be faced with calmness and peace.
But what is this "end of one's life," this death?
Gray examines the view of death held by Jaspers

and Heidegger. Heidegger attempted to capture the relation between human existence and death in his term, "being-toward-death." Death is not something that we will undergo at the end of our lives. It is a permanent possibility of our present existence. As finite creatures we are also carrying with us the immanent possibility of our death. This recognition produces anxiety. We attempt to overcome our anxiety by making death both a public event and also impersonal. Yet, these techniques are not adequate. The only way to deal with death is to face it head on. We must be consciously aware of the possibility and inevitability of our death. All we have for certain is the present moment. Therein must the fullness of life be found. Gray believes this view to be inadequate. Life is not only the present moment but also it is the past and the possibilities of the future. Even if he had achieved full meaning the moment before his death, it is tragic and defies understanding when a man of great talent dies in the midst of a rich and rewarding career. The demand for rationality, for some sense to this sort of thing, must give way to religious faith. Lewis, in his essay, "The Belief in Life after Death," contends that death and the after life is not to be understood through the teachings of the mind or of the heart. Rather, it is only through faith that death and life after death can be understood properly. Through faith in Jesus Christ one finds life in God. In so doing one finds the fullness of life, and that means now and forever more. The physical event of death is only another dimension of the Christian's life in God. Death is for the Christian a promise for a fullness of being only partially possessed in this life.

The last years of life are times for assessing the past and achieving a sense of integrity or falling into a feeling of despair. This major task is carried out on the basis of beliefs about the nature of personhood, the possibility of achieving meaning, our role in the pattern of our lives, and the meaning of death. While the tasks

of late adulthood are to some extent backward
looking they are also forward looking. The
achievement of integrity is the last great human act in preparation for the end of life. How
well this task is achieved is dependent on the
beliefs that are at the core of one's life structure.

The Nature of Persons

Case

Fred enjoyed his new surroundings. Since his wife, Mary, died last year he had been alone in that big house. The children came over occasionally, but he had no friends of his own to be with. When he moved to Scott Towers Linda, his granddaughter, began paying regular visits first to help him settle in and then just to visit. A new college graduate, she was beginning to make her way in a new job as a buyer in Jones' Department Store. When she arrived Fred was delighted to see her. Pleasantries soon passed and Fred asked the question that had been on his mind for a long time. Was she really happy? From what she had said in previous conversations he had wondered. He was surprised when she told him that she did not know how to answer that. She thought she knew herself pretty well while in college. Since graduation, moving into her own apartment, and working at the store her life had changed so much that she did not know who or what she was anymore. She could never go back to being the same person she was in college. The only thing clear to her now is that she has her work. The rest of her life was simply a cacophony of feelings, desires, emotions, and thoughts.

The Crisis in Man's Knowledge of Himself*
Ernst Cassirer

1 That self-knowledge is the highest aim of philosophical inquiry appears to be generally acknowledged. In all the conflicts between the different philosophical schools this objective remained invariable and unshaken: it proved to be the Archimedean point, the fixed and immovable center, of all thought. Nor did the most sceptical thinkers deny the possibility and necessity of self-knowledge. They distrusted all general principles concerning the nature of things, but this distrust was only meant to open a new and more reliable mode of investigation. In the history of philosophy scepticism has very often been simply the counterpart of a resolute <u>humanism</u>. By the denial and destruction of the <u>objective</u> certainty of the external world the sceptic hopes to throw all the thoughts of man back upon his own being. Self-knowledge—he declares—is the first prerequisite of self-realization. We must try to break the chain connecting us with the outer world in order to enjoy our true freedom. "La plus grande chose du monde c'est de scavoir être à soy," writes Montaigne.

Yet even this approach to the problem—the method of introspection—is not secure against sceptical doubts. Modern philosophy began with the principle that the evidence of our own being is impregnable and unassailable. But the advance of psychological knowledge has hardly confirmed this Cartesian principle. The general tendency of thought is nowadays again directed toward the opposite pole. Few modern psychologists would admit or recommend a mere method of introspection. In general they tell us that such a method

*Reprinted by permission of Yale University Press from <u>An Essay on Man</u> by Ernst Cassirer, pp. 1-22.

is very precarious. They are convinced that a
strictly objective behavioristic attitude is the
only possible approach to a scientific psychology. But a consistent and radical behaviorism
fails to attain its end. It can warn us against
possible methodological errors, but it cannot
solve all the problems of human psychology. We
may criticize or suspect the purely introspective
view, but we cannot suppress or eliminate it.
Without introspection, without an immediate awareness of feelings, emotions, perceptions, thoughts,
we could not even define the field of human psychology. Yet it must be admitted that by following this way alone we can never arrive at a comprehensive view of human nature. Introspection
reveals to us only that small sector of human
life which is accessible to our individual experience. It can never cover the whole field of
human phenomena. Even if we should succeed in
collecting and combining all the data, we should
still have a very meager and fragmentary picture
—a mere torso—of human nature.

Aristotle declares that all human knowledge
originates from a basic tendency of human nature
manifesting itself in man's most elementary actions and reactions. The whole extent of the
life of the senses is determined by and impreg-
nated with this tendency.

"All men by nature desire to know. An indication of this is the delight we take in our
senses; for even apart from their usefulness they
are loved for themselves; and above all others
the sense of sight. For not only with a view to
action, but even when we are not going to do anything we prefer seeing to everything else. The
reasons is that this, most of all senses, makes
us know and brings to light many differences between things."[1] This passage is highly characteristic of Aristotle's conception of knowledge
as distinguished from Plato's. Such a philosophical eulogy of man's sensuous life would be impossible in the work of Plato. He could never
compare the desire for knowledge with the delight

we take in our senses. In Plato the life of the senses is separated from the life of the intellect by a broad and insurmountable gulf. Knowledge and truth belong to a transcendental order —to the realm of pure and eternal ideas. Even Aristotle is convinced that scientific knowledge is not possible through the act of perception alone. But he speaks as a biologist when he denies this Platonic severance between the ideal and the empirical world. He attempts to explain the ideal world, the world of knowledge, in terms of life. In both realms, according to Aristotle, we find the same unbroken continuity. In nature as well as in human knowledge the higher forms develop from the lower forms. Sense perception, memory, experience, imagination, and reason are all linked together by a common bond; they are merely different stages and different expressions of one and the same fundamental activity, which attains its highest perfection in man, but which in a way is shared by the animals and all the forms of organic life.

If we were to adopt this biological view we should expect that the first stages of human knowledge would deal exclusively with the external world. For all his immediate needs and practical interests man is dependent on his physical environment. He cannot live without constantly adapting himself to the conditions of the surrounding world. The initial steps toward man's intellectual and cultural life may be described as acts which involve a sort of mental adjustment to the immediate environment. But as human culture progresses we very soon meet with an opposite tendency of human life. From the earliest glimmering of human consciousness we find an introvert view of life accompanying and complementing this extrovert view. The farther we trace the development of human culture from these beginnings the more this introvert view seems to come to the fore. Man's natural curiosity begins slowly to change its direction. We can study this growth in almost all the forms of the cultural life of man. In the first mythological

explanations of the universe we always find a
primitive anthropology side by side with a primitive cosmology. The question of the origin of
the world is inextricably interwoven with the
question of the origin of man. Religion does not
destroy these first mythological explanations.
On the contrary, it preserves the mythological
cosmology and anthropology by giving them new
shape and new depth. Henceforth self-knowledge
is not conceived as a merely theoretical interest. It is not simply a subject of curiosity or
speculation; it is declared to be the fundamental
obligation of man. The great religious thinkers
were the first to inculcate this moral requirement. In all the higher forms of religious life
the maxim "Know thyself" is regarded as a categorical imperative, as an ultimate moral and religious law. In this imperative we feel, as it
were, a sudden reversal of the first natural instinct to know—we perceive a transvaluation of
all values. In the histories of all the religions of the world—in Judaism, Buddhism, Confu-
cianism, and Christianity—we can observe the
individual steps of this development.

The same principle holds good in the general
evolution of philosophical thought. In its earliest stages Greek philosophy seems exclusively
concerned with the physical universe. Cosmology
clearly predominates over all the other branches
of philosophical investigation. It is, however,
characteristic of the depth and comprehensiveness
of the Greek mind that almost every individual
thinker represents at the same time a new general
type of thought. Beyond the physical philosophy
of the Milesian School the Pythagoreans discover
a mathematical philosophy, while the Eleatic
thinkers are the first to conceive the ideal of
a logical philosophy. Heraclitus stands on the
border line between cosmological and anthropological thought. Although he still speaks as a
natural philosopher, and he belongs to the "ancient physiologists," yet he is convinced that
it is impossible to penetrate into the secret of
nature without having studied the secret of man.

We must fulfil the demand of self-reflection if we wish to keep hold of reality and to understand its meaning. Hence it was possible for Heraclitus to characterize the whole of his philosophy by the two words edizêsamên emauton ("I have sought for myself").[2] But this new tendency of thought, although in a sense inherent in early Greek philosophy, did not come to its full maturity until the time of Socrates. Thus it is in the problem of man that we find the landmark separating Socratic from pre-Socratic thought. Socrates never attacks or criticizes the theories of his predecessors. He does not intend to introduce a new philosophical doctrine. Yet in him all the former problems are seen in a new light because they are referred to a new intellectual center. The problems of Greek natural philosophy and of Greek metaphysics are suddenly eclipsed by a new question which seems henceforth to absorb man's whole theoretical interest. In Socrates we no longer have an independent theory of nature or an independent logical theory. We do not even have a coherent and systematic ethical theory—in that sense in which it was developed in the later ethical systems. Only one question remains: What is man? Socrates always maintains and defends the ideal of an objective, absolute, universal truth. But the only universe he knows, and to which all his inquiries refer, is the universe of man. His philosophy—if he possesses a philosophy—is strictly anthropological. In one of the Platonic dialogues Socrates is described as being engaged in a conversation with his pupil Phaedrus. They are walking, and after a short time they come to a place outside the gates of Athens. Socrates bursts into admiration for the beauty of the spot. He is delighted with the landscape, which he praises highly. But Phaedrus interrupts. He is surprised that Socrates behaves like a stranger who is being shown about by a guide. "Do you ever cross the border?" he asks. Socrates puts symbolic meaning into his reply. "Very true, my good friend." he replies, "and I hope that you will excuse me when you hear the reason, which is, that I am a lover of knowledge, and the men who dwell in the city are my teachers, and not the trees, or the country."[3]

Yet when we study Plato's Socratic dialogues nowhere do we find a direct solution of the new problem. Socrates gives us a detailed and meticulous analysis of individual human qualities and virtues. He seeks to determine the nature of these qualities and to define them: goodness, justice, temperance, courage, and so on. But he never ventures a definition of man. How is this seeming deficiency to be accounted for? Did Socrates deliberately adopt a roundabout approach —one that allowed him only to scratch the surface of his problem without ever penetrating into its depth and its real core? But here, more than anywhere else, we should suspect Socratic irony. It is precisely the negative answer of Socrates which throws new and unexpected light on the question, and which gives us the positive insight into the Socratic conception of man. We cannot discover the nature of man in the same way that we can detect the nature of physical things. Physical things may be described in terms of their objective properties, but man may be described and defined only in terms of his consciousness. This fact poses an entirely new problem which cannot be solved by our usual modes of investigation. Empirical observation and logical analysis, in the sense in which these terms were used in pre-Socratic philosophy, here proved inefficient and inadequate. For it is only in our immediate intercourse with human beings that we have insight into the character of man. We must actually confront man, we must meet him squarely face to face, in order to understand him. Hence it is not a new objective content, but a new activity and function of thought which is the distinctive feature of the philosophy of Socrates. Philosophy, which had hitherto been conceived as an intellectual monologue, is transformed into a dialogue. Only by way of dialogical or dialectic thought can we approach the knowledge of human nature. Previously truth

408

might have been conceived to be a sort of ready-made thing which could be grasped by an effort of the individual thinker, and readily transferred and communicated to others. But Socrates could no longer subscribe to this view. It is as impossible—says Plato in the Republic—to implant truth in the soul of a man as it is to give the power of seeing to a man born blind. Truth is by nature the offspring of dialectic thought. It cannot be gained, therefore, except through a constant cooperation of the subjects in mutual interrogation and reply. It is not therefore like an empirical object; it must be understood as the outgrowth of a social act. Here we have the new, indirect answer to the question "What is man?" Man is declared to be that creature who is constantly in search of himself—a creature who in every moment of his existence must examine and scrutinize the conditions of his existence. In this scrutiny, in this critical attitude toward human life, consists the real value of human life. "A life which is unexamined," says Socrates in his Apology, "is not worth living."[4] We may epitomize the thought of Socrates by saying that man is defined by him as that being who, when asked a rational question, can give a rational answer. Both his knowledge and his morality are comprehended in this circle. It is by this fundamental faculty, by this faculty of giving a response to himself and to others, that man becomes a "responsible" being, a moral subject.

2 This first answer has, in a sense, always remained the classical answer. The Socratic problem and the Socratic method can never be forgotten or obliterated. Through the medium of Platonic thought it has left its mark[5] on the whole future development of human civilization. There is perhaps no surer or shorter way of convincing ourselves of the deep unity and perfect continuity of ancient philosophic thought than by comparing these first stages in Greek philosophy with one of the latest and noblest products of Graeco-Roman culture, the book To Himself written by the Emperor Marcus Aurelius Antoninus.

At first sight such a comparison may appear arbitrary; for Marcus Aurelius was not an original thinker, nor did he follow a strictly logical method. He himself thanks the gods that when he had set his heart on philosophy he did not become a writer of philosophy or a solver of syllogisms.[6] But Socrates and Marcus Aurelius have in common the conviction that in order to find the true nature or essence of man we must first of all remove from his being all external and incidental traits.

"Call none of those things a man's that do not fall to him as a man. They cannot be claimed of a man; the man's nature does not guarantee them; they are no consummations of that nature. Consequently neither is the end for which man lives placed in these things, nor yet that which is perfective of the end, namely the Good. Moreover, if any of these things did fall to a man, it would not fall to him to contemn them and set his face against them, . . . but as it is, the more a man can cut himself free, . . . from these and other such things with equanimity, by so much the more is he good."[7] All that which befalls man from without is null and void. His essence does not depend on external circumstances; it depends exclusively on the value he gives to himself. Riches, rank, social distinction, even health or intellectual gifts—all this becomes indifferent (adiaphoron). What matters alone is the tendency, the inner attitude of the soul; and this inner principle cannot be disturbed. "That which does not make a man himself worse than before cannot make his life worse either, nor injure it whether from without or within."[8]

The requirement of self-questioning appears, therefore, in Stoicism, as in the conception of Socrates, as man's privilege and his fundamental duty.[9] But this duty is now understood in a broader sense; it has not only a moral but also a universal and metaphysical background. "Never fail to ask thyself this question and to cross-examine thyself thus: What relation have I to this part of me which they call the ruling Reason (to hêgemonikon)?"10 He who lives in harmony with his own self, his demon, lives in harmony with the universe; for both the universal order and the personal order are nothing but different expressions and manifestations of a common underlying principle. Man proves his inherent power of criticism, of judgment and discernment, by conceiving that in this correlation the Self, not the Universe, has the leading part. Once the Self has won its inner form this form remains unalterable and imperturbable. "A sphere once formed continues round and true."11 That is, so to speak, the last word of Greek philosophy—a word that once more contains and explains the spirit in which it was originally conceived. This spirit was a spirit of judgment, of critical discernment between Being and Non-Being, between truth and illusion, between good and evil. Life in itself is changing and fluctuating, but the true value of life is to be sought in an eternal order that admits of no change. It is not in the world of our senses, it is only by the power of our judgment that we can grasp this order. Judgment is the central power in man, the common source of truth and morality. For it is the only thing in which man entirely depends on himself; it is free, autonomous, self-sufficing.12 "Distract not thyself," says Marcus Aurelius, "be not too eager, but be thine own master, and look upon life as a man, as a human being, as a citizen, as a mortal creature. . . . Things do not touch the soul, for they are external and remain immovable, but our disturbance comes only of that judgment that we form in ourselves. All these things, which thou seest, change immediately, and will no longer be; and constantly bear in mind how many of these changes thou hast already witnessed. The Universe—mutation, Life-affirmation."13

The greatest merit of this Stoic conception of man lies in the fact that this conception gives to man both a deep feeling of his harmony with nature and of his moral independence of nature. In the mind of the Stoic philosopher these assertions do not conflict; they are correlated with one another. Man finds himself in perfect equipoise with the universe, and he knows that this equipoise must not be disturbed by any external force. Such is the dual character of Stoic "imperturbability" (ataraxia). This Stoic theory proved to be one of the strongest formative powers of ancient culture. But it found itself suddenly in the presence of a new, and hitherto unknown, force. The conflict with this new force shook the classical ideal of man to its very foundations. The Stoic and the Christian theories of man are not necessarily hostile to one another. In the history of ideas they work in conjunction, and we often find them in close connection in one and the same individual thinker. Nevertheless, there always remains one point on which the antagonism between the Christian and the Stoic ideals proves irreconcilable. The asserted absolute independence of man, which in the Stoic theory was regarded as man's fundamental virtue, is turned in the Christian theory into his fundamental vice and error. As long as man perseveres in this error there is no possible road to salvation. The struggle between these two conflicting views has lasted for many centuries, and at the beginning of the modern era—at the time of the Renaissance and in the seventeenth century—we still feel its full strength.[14]

Here we can grasp one of the most characteristic features of anthropological philosophy. This philosophy is not, like other branches of philosophical investigation, a slow and continuous development of general ideas. Even in the history of logic, metaphysics, and natural philosophy we find the sharpest oppositions. This history may be described in Hegelian terms as a dialectic process in which each thesis is followed by its antithesis. Nevertheless there is an inner consistency, a clear logical order, connecting the different stages of this dialectic process. Anthropological philosophy, on the other hand, exhibits a quite different character. If we wish to grasp its real meaning and import, we must choose not the epic manner of description but the dramatic. For we are confronted, not with a peaceful development of concepts or theories, but with a clash between conflicting spiritual powers. The history of anthropological philosophy is fraught with the deepest human passions and emotions. It is not concerned with a single theoretical problem, however general its scope; here the whole destiny of man is at stake and clamoring for an ultimate decision.

This character of the problem has found its clearest expression in the work of Augustine. Augustine stands at the frontier of two ages. Living in the fourth century of the Christian era, he has grown up in the tradition of Greek philosophy, and it is especially the system of Neo-Platonism which has left its mark on his whole philosophy. But, on the other hand, he is the pioneer of medieval thought; he is the founder of medieval philosophy and of Christian dogmatics. In his <u>Confessions</u> we can follow every step of his way from Greek philosophy to Christian revelation. According to Augustine all philosophy prior to the appearance of Christ was liable to one fundamental error, and was infected with one and the same heresy. The power of reason was extolled as the highest power of man. But what man could never know until he was enlightened with a special divine revelation is that reason itself is one of the most questionable and ambiguous things in the world. Reason cannot show us the way to clarity, to truth and wisdom. For it is itself obscure in its meaning, and its origin is wrapped in mystery—in a mystery soluble only by Christian revelation. Reason for Augustine does not have a simple and unique but rather a double and divided nature. Man was created in the image of God; and in his original state, in which he went out from the hands of God, he was equal to his archetype. But all this has been lost through the fall of Adam. From that time on all the original power of reason has been obscured. And reason alone, when left to itself and its own faculties, never can

413

find the way back. It cannot reconstruct itself;
it cannot, by its own efforts, return to its
former pure essence. If such a reformation is
ever possible, it is only by supernatural aid,
by the power of divine grace. Such is the new
anthropology, as it is understood by Augustine,
and maintained in all the great systems of medieval thought. Even Thomas Aquinas, the disciple
of Aristotle, who goes back to the sources of
Greek philosophy, does not venture to deviate
from this fundamental dogma. He concedes to human reason a much higher power than Augustine
did; but he is convinced that reason cannot make
the right use of these powers unless it is guided
and illuminated by the grace of God. Here we
have come to a complete reversal of all the values upheld by Greek philosophy. What once seemed to be the highest privilege of man proves to
be his peril and his temptation; what appeared
as his pride becomes his deepest humiliation.
The Stoic precept that man has to obey and revere
his inner principle, the "demon" within himself,
is now regarded as dangerous idolatry.

It is not practicable here to describe further the character of this new anthropology, to
analyze its fundamental motives and to follow up
its development. But in order to understand its
purport we may choose a different and shorter
way. At the beginning of modern times there
appeared a thinker who gave to this anthropology
a new vigor and a new splendor. In the work of
Pascal it found its last and perhaps most impressive expression. Pascal was prepared for this
task as no other writer had been. He possessed
an incomparable gift for elucidating the most
obscure questions and condensing and concentrat-
ing complex and scattered systems of thought.
Nothing seems to be impermeable to the keenness
of his thought and the lucidity of his style. In
him are united all the advantages of modern literature and modern philosophy. But he uses them
as weapons against the modern spirit, the spirit
of Descartes and his philosophy. At first sight
Pascal seems to accept all the presuppositions

of Cartesianism and of modern science. There is nothing in nature that can resist the effort of scientific reason; for there is nothing that can resist geometry. It is a curious event in the history of ideas that it was one of the greatest and profoundest geometers who became the belated champion of the philosophical anthropology of the Middle Ages. When sixteen years old, Pascal wrote the treatise on conic sections that opened a new and a very rich and fertile field of geometrical thought. But he was not only a great geometer, he was a philosopher; and as a philosopher he was not merely absorbed in geometrical problems but he wished to understand the true use, the extent, and the limits of geometry. He was thus led to make that fundamental distinction between the "geometrical spirit" and the "acute or subtle spirit." The geometrical spirit excels in all these subjects that are capable of a perfect analysis—that may be divided into their first elements.[15] It starts with certain axioms and from them it draws inferences the truth of which can be demonstrated by universal logical rules. The advantage of this spirit consists in the clarity of its principles and in the necessity of its deductions. But not all objects are capable of such treatment. There are things which because of their subtlety and their infinite variety defy every attempt at logical analysis. And if there is anything in the world that we have to treat in this second way, it is the mind of man. What characterizes man is the richness and subtlety, the variety and versatility of his nature. Hence mathematics can never become the instrument of a true doctrine of man, of a philosophical anthropology. It is ridiculous to speak of man as if he were a geometrical proposition. A moral philosophy in terms of a system of geometry—an Ethica more geometrico demonstrata—is to the mind of Pascal an absurdity, a philosophical dream. Traditional logic and metaphysics are themselves in no better position to understand and solve the riddle of man. Their first and supreme law is the law of contradiction. Rational thought, logical and

415

metaphysical thought can comprehend only those objects which are free from contradiction, and which have a consistent nature and truth. It is, however, just this homogeneity which we never find in man. The philosopher is not permitted to construct an artificial man; he must describe a real one. All the so-called definitions of man are nothing but airy speculation so long as they are not based upon and confirmed by our experience of man. There is no other way to know man than to understand his life and conduct. But what we find here defies every attempt at inclusion within a single and simple formula. Contradiction is the very element of human existence. Man has no "nature"—no simple or homogeneous being. He is a strange mixture of being and nonbeing. His place is between these two opposite poles.

There is, therefore, only one approach to the secret of human nature: that of religion. Religion shows us that there is a double man— the man before and after the fall. Man was destined for the highest goal, but he forfeited his position. By the fall he lost his power, and his reason and will were perverted. The classical maxim, "Know thyself," when understood in its philosophic sense, in the sense of Socrates, Epictetus, or Marcus Aurelius, is therefore not only ineffectual, it is misleading and erroneous. Man cannot confide in himself and listen to himself. He has to silence himself in order to hear a higher and truer voice. "What shall become of you, then, O man! you who search out what is your true condition by your natural reason? . . . Know, then, haughty man, what a paradox you are to yourself. Humble yourself, impotent reason; be silent, imbecile nature; learn that man infinitely surpasses man, and hear from your master your true condition, which you are ignorant of. Listen to God."[16]

What is given here is not meant to be a theoretical solution of the problem of man. Religion cannot offer such a solution. By its

416

adversaries religion has always been accused of
darkness and incomprehensibility. But this
blame becomes the highest praise as soon as we
consider its true aim. Religion cannot be clear
and rational. What it relates is an obscure and
somber story: the story of the sin and the fall
of man. It reveals a fact of which no rational
explanation is possible. We cannot account for
the sin of man; for it is not produced or necessitated by any natural cause. Nor can we account
for man's salvation; for this salvation depends
on an inscrutable act of divine grace. It is
freely given and freely denied; there is no human action and no human merit that can deserve
it. Religion, therefore, never pretends to clarify the mystery of man. It confirms and deepens
this mystery. The God of whom it speaks is a
Deus absconditus, a hidden God. Hence even his
image, man, cannot be other than mysterious. Man
also remains a homo absconditus. Religion is no
"theory" of God and man and of their mutual relation. The only answer that we receive from
religion is that it is the will of God to conceal
himself. "Thus, God being concealed, every religion that does not say that God is concealed
is not true; and every religion which does not
render a reason for this, is not instructive.
Ours does all this: Vere tu es Deus absconditus.[17] . . . For nature is such, that it everywhere indicates a God lost, both in man and out
of man."[18] Religion is, therefore, so to speak,
a logic of absurdity; for only thus can it grasp
the absurdity, the inner contradiction, the chi-
merical being of man. "Certainly, nothing
strikes us more rudely than this doctrine, and
yet, without this mystery, the most incomprehensible of all, we are incomprehensible to ourselves. The knot of our condition takes its
twists and turns in this abyss; so that man is
more inconceivable without this mystery, than
this mystery is inconceivable to man."[19]

    3 What we learn from Pascal's example is that
at the beginning of modern times the old problem
was still felt in its full strength. Even after

417

the appearance of Descartes' Discours de la méthode the modern mind was still wrestling with the same difficulties. It was divided between two entirely incompatible solutions. But at the same time there begins a slow intellectual development by which the question What is man? is transformed and, so to speak, raised to a higher level. The important thing here is not so much the discovery of new facts as the discovery of a new instrument of thought. Now for the first time the scientific spirit, in the modern sense of the word, enters the lists. The quest now is for a general theory of man based on empirical observations and on general logical principles. The first postulate of this new and scientific spirit was the removal of all the artificial barriers that had hitherto separated the human world from the rest of nature. In order to understand the order of human things we must begin with a study of the cosmic order. And this cosmic order now appears in a wholly new light. The new cosmology, the heliocentric system introduced in the work of Copernicus, is the only sound and scientific basis for a new anthropology.

Neither classical metaphysics nor medieval religion and theology were prepared for this task. Both of these bodies of doctrine, however different in their methods and aims, are grounded in a common principle. They both conceive the universe as a hierarchic order in which man occupies the highest place. In Stoic philosophy and in Christian theology man was described as the end of the universe. Both doctrines are convinced that there is a general providence ruling over the world and the destiny of man. This concept is one of the basic presuppositions of Stoic and Christian thought.[20] All this is suddenly called into question by the new cosmology. Man's claim to being the center of the universe has lost its foundation. Man is placed in an infinite space in which his being seems to be a single and vanishing point. He is surrounded by a mute universe, by a world that is silent to his religious feelings and to his deepest moral

418

demands.

It is understandable, and it was indeed necessary, that the first reaction to this new conception of the world could only be a negative one —a reaction of doubt and fear. Even the greatest thinkers could not free themselves from this feeling. "Le silence éternel de ces espaces infinis m'effraye," says Pascal.[21] The Copernican system became one of the strongest instruments of that philosophical agnosticism and scepticism which developed in the sexteenth century. In his criticism of human reason Montaigne uses all the well-known traditional arguments of the systems of Greek scepticism. But he adds a new weapon which in his hands proves to be of the greatest strength and of paramount importance. Nothing is more apt to humiliate us and to break the pride of human reason than an unprejudiced view of the physical universe. Let man, he says in a famous passage of his Apologie de Raimond Sebond, "make me understand by the force of his reason, upon what foundations he has built those great advantages he thinks he has over other creatures. Who has made him believe that this admirable motion of the celestial arch, the eternal light of those luminaries that roll so high over his head, the wondrous and fearful motions of that infinite ocean, should be established and continue so many ages for his service and convenience? Can anything be imagined so ridiculous, that this miserable and wretched creature, who is not so much as master of himself, but subject to the injuries of all things, should call himself master and emperor of the world, of which he has not power to know the least part, much less to command the whole?"[22] Man is always inclined to regard the small circle in which he lives as the center of the world and to make his particular, private life the standard of the universe. But he must give up this vain pretense, this petty provincial way of thinking and judging. "When the vines of our village are nipped with frost, the parish-priest presently concludes that the indignation of God is gone out against all the human race . .

. Who is it that, seeing these civil wars of
ours, does not cry out, That the machine of the
whole world is upsetting, and that the day of
judgment is at hand! . . . But whoever shall
represent to his fancy, as in a picture, the
great image of our mother nature, pourtrayed in
her full majesty and lustre; whoever in her face
shall read so general and so constant a variety,
whoever shall observe himself in that figure, and
not himself but a whole kingdom, no bigger than
the least touch of a pencil, in comparison of the
whole, that man alone is able to value things
according to their true estimate and grandeur."23

Montaigne's words give us the clue to the
whole subsequent development of the modern theory
of man. Modern philosophy and modern science had
to accept the challenge contained in these words.
They had to prove that the new cosmology, far
from enfeebling or obstructing the power of human reason, establishes and confirms this power.
Such was the task of the combined efforts of the
metaphysical systems of the sixteenth and seventeenth centuries. These systems go different
ways, but they are all directed toward one and
the same end. They strive, so to speak, to turn
the apparent curse of the new cosmology into a
blessing. Giordano Bruno was the first thinker
to enter upon this path, which in a sense became
the path of all modern metaphysics. What is
characteristic of the philosophy of Giordano
Bruno is that here the term "infinity" changes
its meaning. In Greek classical thought infinity
is a negative concept. The infinite is the
boundless or indeterminate. It has no limit and
no form, and it is, therefore, inaccessible to
human reason, which lives in the realm of form
and can understand nothing but forms. In this
sense the finite and infinite, peras and hapeiron,
are declared by Plato in the Philebus to be the
two fundamental principles which are necessarily
opposed to one another. In Bruno's doctrine infinity no longer means a mere negation or limitation. On the contrary, it means the immeasurable
and inexhaustible abundance of reality and the

unrestricted power of the human intellect. It is in this sense that Bruno understands and interprets the Copernican doctrine. This doctrine, according to Bruno, was the first and decisive step toward man's self-liberation. Man no longer lives in the world as a prisoner enclosed within the narrow walls of a finite physical universe. He can traverse the air and break through all the imaginary boundaries of the celestial spheres which have been erected by a false metaphysics and cosmology.[24] The infinite universe sets no limits to human reason; on the contrary, it is the great incentive of human reason. The human intellect becomes aware of its own infinity through measuring its powers by the infinite universe.

All this is expressed in the work of Bruno in a poetical, not in a scientific language. The new world of modern science, the mathematical theory of nature, was still unknown to Bruno. He could not, therefore, pursue his way to its logical conclusion. It took the combined efforts of all the metaphysicians and scientists of the seventeenth century to overcome the intellectual crisis brought about by the discovery of the Copernican system. Every great thinker—Galileo, Descartes, Leibniz, Spinoza—has his special share in the solution of this problem. Galileo asserts that in the field of mathematics man reaches the climax of all possible knowledge—a knowledge which is not inferior to that of the divine intellect. Of course the divine intellect knows and conceives an infinitely greater number of mathematical truths than we do, but with regard to objective certainty the few verities known by the human mind are known as perfectly by man as they are by God.[25] Descartes begins with his universal doubt which seems to enclose man within the limits of his own consciousness. There seems to be no way out of this magic circle—no approach to reality. But even here the idea of the infinite turns out to be the only instrument for the overthrow of universal doubt. By means of this concept alone we can demonstrate the reality of God and, in an indirect way, the reality of the material world. Leibniz combines this metaphysical proof with a new scientific proof. He discovers a new instrument of mathematical thought—the infinitesimal calculus. By the rules of this calculus the physical universe becomes intelligible; the laws of nature are seen to be nothing but special cases of the general laws of reason. It is Spinoza who ventures to make the last and decisive step in this mathematical theory of the world and of the human mind. Spinoza constructs a new ethics, a theory of the passions and affections, a mathematical theory of the moral world. By this theory alone, he is convinced, can we attain our end: the goal of a "philosophy of man," of an anthropological philosophy, which is free from the errors and prejudices of a merely anthropocentric system. This is the topic, the general theme, which in its various forms permeates all the great metaphysical systems of the seventeenth century. It is the rationalistic solution of the problem of man. Mathematical reason is the bond between man and the universe; it permits us to pass freely from the one to the other. Mathematical reason is the key to a true understanding of the cosmic and the moral order.

4 In 1754 Denis Diderot published a series of aphorisms entitled Pensées sur l'interprétation de la nature. In this essay he declared that the superiority of mathematics in the realm of science is no longer uncontested. Mathematics, he asserted, has reached such a high degree of perfection that no further progress is possible; henceforth mathematics will remain stationary. "Nous touchons au moment d'une grande révolution dans les sciences. Au penchant que les esprits me paroissent avoir à la morale, aux belles lettres, à l'histoire de la nature et à la physique expérimentale j'oserois presque assurer qu'avant qu'il soit cent ans on ne comptera pas trois grands géomètres en Europe. Cette science s'arrêtera tout court où l'auront laissé les Bernoulli, les Euler, les Maupertuis et les d'Alem-

bert. Ils auront posés les colonnes d'Hercule,
on n'ira point au delà."26

Diderot is one of the great representatives
of the philosophy of the Enlightenment. As the
editor of the Encyclopédie he stands at the very
center of all the great intellectual movements
of his time. No one had a clearer perspective of
the general development of scientific thought; no
one had a keener feeling for all the tendencies
of the eighteenth century. It is all the more
characteristic and remarkable of Diderot that,
representing all the ideals of the Enlightenment,
he began to doubt the absolute right of these
ideals. He expects the rise of a new form of
science—a science of a more concrete character,
based rather on the observation of facts than on
the assumption of general principles. According
to Diderot, we have highly overrated our logical
and rational methods. We know how to compare,
to organize, and systematize the known facts; but
we have not cultivated those methods by which
alone it would be possible to discover new facts.
We are under the delusion that the man who does
not know how to count his fortune is in no better
position than the man who has no fortune at all.
But the time is near when we shall overcome this
prejudice, and then we shall have reached a new
and culminating point in the history of natural
science.

Has Diderot's prophecy been fulfilled? Did
the development of scientific ideas in the nineteenth century confirm his view? On one point,
to be sure, his error is obvious. His expectation that mathematical thought would come to a
standstill, that the great mathematicians of the
eighteenth century had reached the Pillars of
Hercules, proved to be entirely untrue. To that
eighteenth-century galaxy we must now add the
names of Gauss, of Riemann, of Weierstrass, of
Poincaré. Everywhere in the science of the nineteenth century we meet with the triumphal march
of new mathematical ideas and concepts. Nevertheless, Diderot's prediction contained an ele-

ment of truth. For the innovation of the intellectual structure of the nineteenth century lies in the place that mathematical thought occupies in the scientific hierarchy. A new force begins to appear. Biological thought takes precedence over mathematical thought. In the first half of the nineteenth century there are still some metaphysicians, such as Herbart, or some psychologists, such as G. Th. Fechner, who cherish the hope of founding a mathematical psychology. But these projects rapidly disappear after the publication of Darwin's work On the Origin of Species. Henceforth the true character of anthropological philosophy appears to be fixed once and for all. After innumerable fruitless attempts the philosophy of man stands at last on firm ground. We no longer need indulge in airy speculations, for we are not in search of a general definition of the nature or essence of man. Our problem is simply to collect the empirical evidence which the general theory of evolution has put at our disposal in a rich and abundant measure.

Such was the conviction shared by the scientists and philosophers of the nineteenth century. But what became more important for the general history of ideas and for the development of philosophical thought was not the empirical facts of evolution but the theoretical interpretation of these facts. This interpretation was not determined, in an unambiguous sense, by the empirical evidence itself, but rather by certain fundamental principles which had a definite metaphysical character. Though rarely acknowledged, this metaphysical cast of evolutionary thinking was a latent motivating force. The theory of evolution in a general philosophical sense was by no means a recent achievement. It had received its classical expression in Aristotle's psychology and in his general view of organic life. The characteristic and fundamental distinction between the Aristotelean and the modern version of evolution consisted in the fact that Aristotle gave a formal interpretation whereas the moderns attempted a material interpretation. Aristotle was convinced that in order to understand the general plan of nature, the origins of life, the lower forms must be interpreted in the light of the higher forms. In his metaphysics, in his definition of the soul as "the first actualization of a natural body potentially having life," organic life is conceived and interpreted in terms of human life. The teleological character of human life is projected upon the whole realm of natural phenomena. In modern theory this order is reversed. Aristotle's final causes are characterized as a mere "asylum ignorantiae." One of the principal aims of Darwin's work was to free modern thought from this illusion of final causes. We must seek to understand the structure of organic nature by material causes alone, or we cannot understand it at all. But material causes are in Aristotle's terminology "accidental" causes. Aristotle had emphatically asserted the impossibility of understanding the phenomenon of life by such accidental causes. Modern theory takes up this challenge. Modern thinkers have held that, after the innumerable fruitless attempts of former times, they have definitely succeeded in accounting for organic life as a mere product of chance. The accidental changes that take place in the life of every organism are sufficient to explain the gradual transformation that leads us from the simplest forms of life in a protozoon to the highest and most complicated forms. We find one of the most striking expressions of this view in Darwin himself, who is usually so very reticent with regard to his philosophical conceptions. "Not only the various domestic races," observes Darwin at the end of his book, The Variation of Animals and Plants under Domestication, "but the most distinct genera and orders within the same great class—for instance, mammals, birds, reptiles, and fishes—are all the descendants of one common progenitor, and we must admit that the whole vast amount of difference between these forms has primarily arisen from simple variability. To consider the subject under this point of view is enough to strike one dumb with amazement. But our amazement ought to be lessened when we reflect that beings almost infinite in number, during an almost infinite lapse of time, have often had their whole organization rendered in some degree plastic, and that each slight modification of structure which was in any way beneficial under excessively complex conditions of life has been preserved, whilst each which was in any way injurious has been rigorously destroyed. And the long-continued accumulation of beneficial variations will infallibly have led to structures as diversified, as beautifully adapted for various purposes and as excellently co-ordinated as we see in the plants and animals around us. Hence I have spoken of selection as the paramount power, whether applied by man to the formation of domestic breeds, or by nature to the production of species . . . If an architect were to rear a noble and commodious edifice, without the use of cut stone, by selecting from the fragments at the base of a precipice wedge-formed stones for his arches, elongated stones for his lintels, and flat stones for his roof, we should admire his skill and regard him as the paramount power. Now, the fragments of stone, thought indispensalbe to the architect, bear to the edifice built by him the same relation which the fluctuating variations of organic beings bear to the varied and admirable structures ultimately acquired by their modified descendents."[27]

But still another, and perhaps the most important, step had to be taken before a real anthropological philosophy could develop. The theory of evolution had destroyed the arbitrary limits between the different forms of organic life. There are no separate species; there is just one continuous and uninterrupted stream of life. But can we apply the same principle to human life and human culture? Is the cultural world, like the organic world, made up of accidental changes?—Does it not possess a definite and undeniable teleological structure? Herewith a new problem presented itself to all philosophers whose starting point was the general theory of evolution. They had to prove that the cultural world, the world of human civilization, is reducible to a few general causes which are the same for the physical as for the so-called spiritual phenomena. Such was the new type of philosophy of culture introduced by Hippolyte Taine in his Philosophy of Art and in his History of English Literature. "Here as elsewhere," said Taine, "we have but a mechanical problem; the total effect is a result, depending entirely on magnitude and direction of the producing causes . . . Though the means of notation are not the same in the moral and physical sciences, yet as in both the matter is the same, equally made up of forces, magnitudes, and directions, we may say that in both the final result is produced after the same method."[28] It is the same iron ring of necessity that encloses both our physical and our cultural life. In his feelings, his inclinations, his ideas, his thoughts, and in his production of works of art, man never breaks out of this magic circle. We may consider man as an animal of superior species which produces philosophies and poems in the same way as silkworms produce their cocoons or bees build their cells. In the preface to his great work, Les origines de la France contemporaine, Taine states that he is going to study the transformation of France as a result of the French Revolution as he would the "metamorphosis of an insect."

But here another question arises. Can we be content with counting up in a merely empirical manner the different impulses that we find in human nature? For a really scientific insight these impulses would have to be classified and systematized. Obviously, not all of them are on the same level. We must suppose them to have a definite structure—and one of the first and most important tasks of our psychology and theory of culture is to discover this structure. In the complicated wheelwork of human life we must find the hidden driving force which sets the whole mechanism of our thought and will in motion. The

427

principal aim of all these theories was to prove
the unity and homogeneity of human nature. But
if we examine the explanations which these theories were designed to give, the unity of human
nature appears extremely doubtful. Every philosopher believes he has found the mainspring and
master-faculty—l'idée maîtresse, as it was called by Taine. But as to the character of this
master-faculty all the explanations differ widely
from, and contradict, one another. Each individual thinker gives us his own picture of human nature. All these philosophers are determined em-
piricists: they would show us the facts and
nothing but the facts. But their interpretation
of the empirical evidence contains from the very
outset an arbitrary assumption—and this arbitrariness becomes more and more obvious as the
theory proceeds and takes on a more elaborate
and sophisticated aspect. Nietzsche proclaims
the will to power, Freud signalizes the sexual
instinct, Marx enthrones the economic instinct.
Each theory becomes a Procrustean bed on which
the empirical facts are stretched to fit a preconceived pattern.

Owing to this development our modern theory
of man lost its intellectual center. We acquired
instead a complete anarchy of thought. Even in
the former times to be sure there was a great
discrepancy of opinions and theories relating to
this problem. But there remained at least a general orientation, a frame of reference, to which
all individual differences might be referred.
Metaphysics, theology, mathematics, and biology
successively assumed the guidance for thought on
the problem of man and determined the line of investigation. The real crisis of this problem
manifested itself when such a central power capable of directing all individual efforts ceased
to exist. The paramount importance of the problem was still felt in all the different branches
of knowledge and inquiry. But an established
authority to which one might appeal no longer
existed. Theologians, scientists, politicians,
sociologists, biologists, psychologists, ethnol-

ogists, economists all approached the problem from their own viewpoints. To combine or unify all these particular aspects and perspectives was impossible. And even within the special fields there was no generally accepted scientific principle. The personal factor became more and more prevalent, and the temperament of the individual writer tended to play a decisive role. _Trahit sua quemque voluptas_: every author seems in the last count to be led by his own conception and evaluation of human life.

That this antagonism of ideas is not merely a grave theoretical problem but an imminent threat to the whole extent of our ethical and cultural life admits of no doubt. In recent philosophical thought Max Scheler was one of the first to become aware of and to signalize this danger. "In no other period of human knowledge," declares Scheler, "has man ever become more problematic to himself than in our own days. We have a scientific, a philosophical, and a theological anthropology that know nothing of each other. Therefore we no longer possess any clear and consistent idea of man. The evergrowing multiplicity of the particular sciences that are engaged in the study of men has much more confused and obscured than elucidated our concept of man."[29]

Such is the strange situation in which modern philosophy finds itself. No former age was ever in such a favorable position with regard to the sources of our knowledge of human nature. Psychology, ethnology, anthropology, and history have amassed an astoundingly rich and constantly increasing body of facts. Our technical instruments for observation and experimentation have been immensely improved, and our analyses have become sharper and more penetrating. We appear, nevertheless, not yet to have found a method for the mastery and organization of this material. When compared with our own abundance the past may seem very poor. But our wealth of facts is not necessarily a wealth of thoughts. Unless we succeed in finding a clue of Ariadne to lead us out

429

of this labyrinth, we can have no real insight
into the general character of human culture; we
shall remain lost in a mass of disconnected and
disintegrated data which seem to lack all conceptual unity.

Notes

[1]Aristotle, Metaphysics, Book A. 1 980   21.
English trans. by W. D. Ross, The Works of Aristotle (Oxford, Clarendon Press, 1924), Vol. VIII.
   [2]Fragment 101, in Diels, Die Fragmente der
Vorsokratiker, ed. by W. Krantz (5th ed. Berlin,
1934), I, 173.
   [3]Plato, Phaedrus 230A (Jowett trans.).
   [4]Plato, Apology 37E (Jowett trans.).
   [5]In the following pages I shall not attempt
to give a survey of the historical development of
anthropological philosophy. I shall merely select a few typical stages in order to illustrate
the general line of thought. The history of the
philosophy of man is still a desideratum. Whereas the history of metaphysics, of natural philosophy, of ethical and scientific thought has been
studied in all detail, we are here still at the
beginning. During the last century the importance of this problem has been felt more and more
vividly. Wilhelm Dilthey has concentrated all
his efforts upon its solution. But Dilthey's
work, however rich and suggestive, remained incomplete. One of the pupils of Dilthey, Bernhard
Groethuysen, has given an excellent description
of the general development of anthropological
philosophy. But unfortunately even this description stops short of the last and decisive step—
that of our modern era. See Bernhard Groethuysen, "Philosophische Anthropologie," Handbuch der
Philosophie (Munich and Berlin, 1931), III, 1-207.
See also Groethuysen's article, "Towards An Anthropological Philosophy," Philosophy and History, Essays Presented to Ernst Cassirer (Oxford,
Clarendon Press, 1936), pp. 77-89.
   [6]Marcus Aurelius Antoninus, Ad se ipsum (eis
heauton), Bk. I, par. 8. In most of the following passages I quote the English version of C. R.

Haines, The Communings with Himself of Marcus Aurelius Antoninus (Cambridge, Mass., Harvard University Press, 1916), Loeb Classical Library.

[7] Marcus Aurelius, op. cit., Bk. V, par. 15.

[8] Idem, Bk. IV, par. 8.

[9] Idem, Bk. III, par. 6.

[10] Idem, Bk. V, par. 11.

[11] Idem, Bk. VIII, par. 41.

[12] Cf. idem, Bk. V, par. 14. Ho logos kai hē logikē technē dynameis eisin heautais arkoumenal kai tois kath' heautas ergois.

[13] Ho Kosmos alloiōsis ● ho bios hypolēpsis Bk. IV, par. 3. The term "affirmation" or "judgment" seems to me a much more adequate expression of the thought of Marcus Aurelius than "opinion," which I find in all the English versions I have consulted. "Opinion" (the Platonic doxa) contains an element of change and uncertainty which is not intended by Marcus Aurelius. As equivalent terms for hypolēpsis we find in Marcus Aurelius krisis, krima, diakrisis. Cf. Bk. III, par. 2; VI, par. 52; VIII, pars. 28, 47.

[14] For a detailed account see Cassirer, Descartes (Stockholm, 1939), pp. 215 ff.

[15] For the distinction between l'esprit géométrique and l'esprit de finesse compare Pascal's treatise "De l'esprit géométrique" and Pascal's Pensées, ed. by Charles Louandre (Paris, 1858), chap. ix. p. 231. In the passages which follow I quote the English translation of O. W. Wight (New York, 1861).

[16] Pensées, chap. x, sec. 1.

[17] Idem, chap. xii, sec. 5.

[18] Idem, chap. xiii, sec. 3.

[19] Idem, chap. x, sec. 1.

[20] For the Stoic concept of providence (pronoia) see, for instance, Marcus Aurelius, op. cit., Bk. II, par. 3.

[21] Pascal, op. cit., chap. xxv, sec. 18.

[22] Montaigne, Essais, II, chap. xii. English trans. by William Hazlitt, The Works of Michael de Montaigne (2d ed. London, 1845), p. 205.

[23] Idem, I, chap. xxv. English trans., pp. 65 f.

[24] For further details see Cassirer, Individuum und Kosmos in der Philosophie der Renaissance

431

(Leipzig, 1927), pp. 197 ff.

[25]Galileo, Dialogo dei due massimi sistemi del mondo, I (Edizione nazionale), VII, 129.

[26]Diderot, Pensées sur l'interprétation de la nature, sec. 4; cf. secs. 17, 21.

[27]Darwin, The Variation of Animals and Plants under Domestication (New York, D. Appleton & Co., 1897), II, chap. xxviii, 425 f.

[28]Taine, Histoire de la littérature anglaise, Intro. English trans. by H. van Laun (New York, Holt & Co., 1872), I, 12 ff.

[29]Max Scheler, Die Stellung des Menschen im Kosmos (Darmstadt, Reichl, 1928), pp. 13 f.

Of The Nature Of The Human Mind*
René Descartes

Yesterday's Meditation has filled my mind with so many doubts that it is no longer in my power to forget them. Nor do I yet see how I will be able to resolve them. I feel as though (24) I were suddenly thrown into deep water, being so disconcerted that I can neither plant my feet on the bottom nor swim on the surface. I shall nevertheless make every effort to conform precisely to the plan commenced yesterday and put aside every belief in which I could imagine the least doubt, just as though I knew that it was absolutely [19] false. And I shall continue in this manner until I have found something certain, or at least, if I can do nothing else, until I have learned with certainty that there is nothing certain in this world. Archimedes, to move the earth from its orbit and place it in a new position, demanded nothing more than a fixed and immovable fulcrum: in a similar manner I shall have the right to entertain high hopes if I am

fortunate enough to find a single truth which is
certain and indubitable.

I suppose accordingly, that everything that
I see is false; I convince myself that nothing
has ever existed of all that my deceitful memory
recalls to me. I think that I have no senses;
and I believe that body, shape, extension, motion, and location are merely inventions of my
mind. What then could still be thought true?
Perhaps nothing else, unless it is that there is
nothing certain in the world.

But how do I know that there is not some
entity, of a different nature from what I have
just judged uncertain, of which there cannot be
the least doubt? Is there not some God or some
other power who gives me these thoughts? But I
need not think this to be true, for possibly I
am able to produce them myself. Then, at the
very least, am I not an entity myself? But I
have already denied that I had any senses or any
body. However, at this point I hesitate, for
what (25) follows from that? Am I so dependent
upon the body and the senses that I could not
exist without them? I have just convinced myself
that nothing whatsoever existed in the world,
that there was no sky, no earth, no minds, and no
bodies; have I not thereby convinced myself that
I did not exist? Not at all; without doubt I existed if I was convinced ⌈or even if I thought
anything⌉. Even though there may be a deceiver
of some sort, very powerful and very tricky, who
bends all his efforts to keep me perpetually deceived, there can be no slightest doubt that I
exist, since he deceives me; and let him deceive
me as much as he will, he can never make me be
nothing as long as I think that I am something.
Thus, after having thought well on this matter,
and after examining all things with care, I must
finally conclude and maintain that this proposition: <u>I am, I exist</u>, is necessarily true every
time that I pronounce it or conceive it in my
mind.

433

But I do not yet know sufficiently clearly what I am, I who am sure that I exist. So I must henceforth take very great care that I do not incautiously mistake [20] some other thing for myself, and so make an error even in that knowledge which I maintain to be more certain and more evident than all other knowledge ⌜that I previously had⌝. That is why I shall now consider once more what I thought myself to be before I began these last deliberations. Of my former opinions I shall reject all that are rendered even slightly doubtful by the arguments that I have just now offered, so that there will remain just that part alone which is entirely certain and indubitable.

What then have I previously believed myself to be? Clearly, I believed that I was a man. But what is a man? Shall I say a rational animal? Certainly not, for I would have to determine what an "animal" is and what is meant by "rational"; and so, from a single question, I would find myself gradually enmeshed in an infinity of others more difficult ⌜and more inconvenient⌝, and I would not care to waste the little time and leisure remaining to me in disentangling such difficulties. I shall rather pause here to consider the ideas which previously arose naturally and of themselves (26) in my mind whenever I considered what I was. I thought of myself first as having a face, hands, arms, and all this mechanism composed of ⌜bone and flesh ⌐and⌐ members⌐, just as it appears in a corpse, and which I designated by the name of "body." In addition, I thought of the fact that I consumed nourishment, that I walked, that I perceived and thought, and I ascribed all these actions to the soul. But either I did not stop to consider what this soul was or else, if I did, I imagined that it was something very rarefied and subtle, such as a wind, a flame, or a very much expanded air which ⌜penetrated into and⌝ was infused thoughout my grosser components. As for what body was, I did not realize that there could be any doubt about it, for I thought that I recognized its nature very distinctly. If I had wished to explain

it according to the notions that I then entertained, I would have described it somewhat in
this way: By "body" I understand all that can
be bounded by some figure: that can be located
in some place and occupy space in such a way that
every other body is excluded from it; that can be
perceived by touch or sight or hearing or taste
or smell; that can be moved in various ways, not
by itself but by some other object by which it is
touched ⌈and from which it receives an impulse⌉.
For to possess the power to move itself, and also
to feel or to think, I did not believe at all
that these are attributes of corporeal nature; on
the contrary, rather, I was astonished [21] to
see a few bodies possessing such abilities.

But I, what am I, on the basis of the present hypothesis that there is a certain spirit
who is extremely powerful and, if I may dare to
say so, malicious ⌈and tricky⌉, and who uses all
his abilities and efforts in order to deceive me?
Can I be sure that I possess the smallest fraction of all those characteristics which I have
just now said belonged to the nature of body?
(27) I pause to consider this attentively. I
pass and repass in review in my mind each one of
all these things—it is not necessary to pause
to take the time to list them—and I do not find
any one of them which I can pronounce to be part
of me. Is it characteristic of me to consume
nourishment and to walk? But if it is true that
I do not have a body, these also are nothing but
figments of the imagination. To perceive?[1] But
once more, I cannot perceive without the body,
except in the sense that I have thought I perceived various things during sleep, which I recognized upon waking not to have been really perceived. To think?[2] Here I find the answer.
Thought is an attribute that belongs to me; it
alone is inseparable from my nature.

I am, I exist—that is certain; but for how
long do I exist? For as long as I think; for it
might perhaps happen, if I totally ceased thinking, that I would at the same time completely

435

cease to be. I am now admitting nothing except
what is necessarily true. I am therefore, to
speak precisely, only a thinking being, that is
to say, a mind, an understanding,[3] or a reasoning
being, which are terms whose meaning was previously unknown to me.

I am something real and really existing, but
what thing am I? I have already given the answer: a thing which thinks. And what more? I
will stimulate my imagination ⌜to see if I am not
something else beyond this⌝. I am not this as-
semblage of members which is called a human body;
I am not a rarefied and penetrating air spread
throughout all these members; I am not a wind,
⌜a flame,⌝ a breath, a vapor, or anything at all
that I can imagine and picture to myself—since
I have supposed that all that was nothing, and
since, without abandoning this supposition, I
find that I do not cease to be certain that I am
something.

But perhaps it is true that those same
things which I suppose not to exist because I do
not know them are really no different from the
self which I do know. As to that I cannot decide; I am not discussing that question at the
moment, since I can pass judgment only upon those
things which are known to me: I know that I exist and I am seeking to discover what I am, that
"I" that I know to be. Now it is very [22] certain that this notion ⌜and knowledge of my be-
ing⌝, thus precisely understood, does not depend
on things whose existence (28) is not yet known
to me; and consequently ⌜and even more certain-
ly⌝, it does not depend on any of those things
that I ⌜'can'⌝ picture in my imagination. And
even these terms, "picture" and "imagine," warn
me of my error. For I would be imagining falsely
indeed were I to picture myself as something;
since to imagine is nothing else than to contemplate the shape or image of a bodily entity, and
I already know both that I certainly exist and
that it is altogether possible that all these
images, and everything in general which is in-

436

volved in the nature of body, are only dreams
⌐and illusions⌐. From this I see clearly that
there was no more sense in saying that I would
stimulate my imagination to learn more distinctly what I am than if I should say: I am now
awake, and I see something real and true; but
because I do not yet perceive it sufficiently
clearly, I will go to sleep on purpose, in order
that my dreams will show it to me with more
truth and evidence. And thus I know manifestly
that nothing of all that I can understand by
means of the imagination is pertinent to the
knowledge which I have of myself, and that I
must remember this and prevent my mind from
thinking in this fashion, in order that it may
clearly perceive its own nature.

But what then am I? A thinking being.[4]
What is a thinking being? It is a being which
doubts, which understands, ⌐which conceives,⌐
which affirms, which denies, which wills, which
rejects, which imagines also, and which perceives. It is certainly not a trivial matter if
all these things belong to my nature. But why
should they not belong to it? Am I not that
same person who now doubts almost everything,
who nevertheless understands ⌐and conceives⌐
certain things, who ⌐is sure of and⌐ affirms the
truth of this one thing alone, who denies all
the others, who wills and desires to know more
about them, who rejects error, who imagines many
things, sometimes even against my will, and who
also perceives many things, as through the medium of 'the senses ⌐or` the organs of the body⌐?
Is there anything in all that which is not just
as true as it is certain that I am and that I exist, even though I were always asleep (29) and
though the one who created me directed all his
efforts to deluding me? And is there any one of
these attributes which can be distinguished from
my thinking or which can be said to be separable
from my nature? For it is so obvious that it is
I who doubt, understand, and desire, that nothing
could be added to make it more evident. And I
am also certainly the same on who imagines; [23]

437

for once more, even though it could happen that
the things I imagine are not true, nevertheless
this power of imagining cannot fail to be real,
and it is part of my thinking. Finally I am the
same being which perceives—that is, which observes certain objects as though by means of the
sense organs, because I do really see light, hear
noises, feel heat. Will it be said that these
appearances are false and that I am sleeping?
⌜Let it be so; yet at the very least⌝ it is certain that it seems to me that I see light, hear
noises, and feel heat. This much cannot be
false, and it is this, properly considered, which
in my nature is called perceiving, and that,
again speaking precisely, is nothing else but
thinking.

    As a result of these considerations, I be-
gin to recognize what I am ⸢somewhat better
⌜and⸣ with a little more clarity and distinct-
ness⌝ than heretofore. But nevertheless ⸢it
still seems to me, and⸣ I cannot keep myself
from believing that corporeal things, images of
which are formed by thought and which the senses
themselves examine, are ⸢much⸣ more distinctly
known than that indescribable part of myself
which cannot be pictured by the imagination. Yet
it would truly be very strange to say that I know
and comprehend more distinctly things whose existence seems doubtful to me, that are unknown to
me and do not belong to me, than those of whose
truth I am persuaded, which are known to me, and
which belong to my real nature ⸢—to say, in a
word, that I know them better than myself⸣. But
I see well what is the trouble: my mind ⸢is a
vagabond who⸣ likes to wander and is not yet able
to stay within the strict bounds of truth. Therefore, let us ⌜give it the rein once more ⸢and⌝
allow it every kind of liberty, (30) ⌜permitting
it to consider the objects which appear to be external,⌝ so that when a little later we come to
restrain it ⌜gently and⌝ at the right time ⸢and
force it to the consideration of its own nature
and of the things that it finds in itself⸣, it
will more readily permit itself to be ruled and

guided.

Let us now consider the ⌜commonest⌝ things, which are commonly believed to be the most distinctly known ⌜⸌and the easiest of all to know⸍⌝, namely, the bodies which we touch and see. I do not intend to speak of bodies in general, for general notions are usually somewhat more confused; let us rather consider one body in particular. Let us take, for example, this bit of wax which has just been taken from the hive. It has not yet completely lost the sweetness of the honey it contained; it still retains something of the odor of the flowers from which it was collected; its color, shape, and size are apparent; it is hard and cold; it can easily be touched; and, if you knock on it, it will give out some sound. Thus everything which can make a body distinctly known are found in this example.

But now while I am talking I bring it close to the fire. What remains of the taste evaporates; the odor vanishes; its color changes; its shape is lost; its size increases; it becomes liquid; it grows hot; one can hardly touch it; and although it is knocked upon, it [24] will give out no sound. Does the same wax remain after this change? We must admit that it does; no one denies it ⸌, no one judges otherwise⸍. What is it then in this bit of wax that we recognize with so much distinctness? Certainly it cannot be anything that I observed by means of the senses, since everything in the field of taste, smell, sight, touch, and hearing are changed, and since the same wax nevertheless remains.

The truth of the matter perhaps, as I now suspect, is that this wax was neither that sweetness of honey, nor that ⌜pleasant⌝ odor of flowers, nor that whiteness, nor that shape, nor that sound, but only a body which a little while ago appeared to my senses under these forms and which now makes itself felt under others. But what is it, to speak precisely, that I imagine

439

⌜when I conceive it⌝ in this fashion? Let us consider it attentively (31) and, rejecting everything that does not belong to the wax, see what remains. Certainly nothing is left but something extended, flexible, and movable. But what is meant by flexible and movable? Does it consist in my picturing that this wax, being round, is capable of becoming square and of passing from the square into a triangular shape? Certainly not; ⌜it is not that,⌝ since I conceive it capable of undergoing an infinity of similar changes, and I could not compass this infinity in my imagination. Consequently this conception that I have of the wax is not achieved by the faculty of imagination.

Now what is this extension? Is it not also unknown? For it becomes greater in the melting wax, still greater when it is completely melted, and much greater again when the heat increases still more. And I would not conceive ⌜clearly and⌝ truthfully what wax was if I did not think that even this bit of wax is capable of receiving more variations in extension than I have ever imagined. We must therefore agree that I cannot even conceive what this bit of wax is by means of the imagination, and there is nothing but my understanding[5] alone which does conceive it. I say this bit of wax in particular, for as to wax in general, it is still more evident. But what is this bit of wax which cannot be comprehended except by ⌜the understanding, or by⌝ the mind? Certainly it is the same as the one that I see, that I touch, that I imagine; and finally it is the same as I always believed it to be from the beginning. But what is here important to notice is that perception[6] ⌜, or the action by which we perceive,⌝ is not a vision, a touch, nor an imagination, and has never been that, even though it formerly appeared so; [25] but is solely an inspection by the mind, which can be imperfect and confused as it was formerly, or clear and distinct as it is at present, as I attend more or less to the things ⌜which are in it and⌝ of which it is composed.

Now I am truly astonished when I consider
⌐how weak my mind is and⌐ how apt I am to fall
into error. For even though I consider all this
in my mind without speaking, (32) still words
impede me, and I am nearly deceived by the terms
of ordinary language. For we say that we see
the same wax if it is present, and not that we
judge that it is the same from the fact that it
has the same color or shape. Thus I might be
tempted to conclude that one knows the wax by
means of eyesight, and not uniquely by the perception of the mind. So I may by chance look
out of a window and notice some men passing in
the street, at the sight of whom I do not fail
to say that I see men, just as I say that I see
wax; and nevertheless what do I see from this
window except hats and cloaks which might cover
⌐ghosts, or⌐ automata ⌐which move only by
springs⌐? But I judge that they are men, and
thus I comprehend, solely by the faculty of
judgment which resides in my mind, that which I
believed I saw with my eyes.

A person who attempts to improve his understanding beyond the ordinary ought to be ashamed
to go out of his way to criticize the forms of
speech used by ordinary men. I prefer to pass
over this matter and to consider whether I understood what wax was more evidently and more
perfectly when I frist noticed it and when I
thought I knew it by means of the external
senses, or at the very least by common sense, as
it is called, or the imaginative faculty; or
whether I conceive it better at present, after
having more carefully examined what it is and how
it can be known. Certainly it would be ridiculous to doubt the superiority of the latter method of knowing. For what was there in that first
perception which was distinct ⌐and evident⌐?
What was there which might not occur similarly to
the senses of the lowest of the animals? But
when I distinguished the real wax from its superficial appearances, and when, just as though I
had removed its garments, I consider it all naked, it is certain that although there might

still be some error in my judgment, I could not conceive it in this fashion without a human mind. (33)

And now what shall I say of the mind, that is to say, of myself? For so far I do not admit in myself anything other than the mind. Can it be that I, who seem to perceive this bit of wax [26] so ⌐clearly and¬ distinctly, do not know my own self, not only with much more truth and certainty, but also much more distinctly and evidently? For if I judge that the wax exists because I see it, certainly it follows much more evidently that I exist myself because I see it. For it might happen that what I see is not really wax; it might also happen that I do not even possess eyes to see anything; but it could not happen that, when I see, or what amounts to the same thing, when I think I see, I who think am not something. For a similar reason, if I judge that the wax exists because I touch it, the same conclusion follows once more, namely, that I am. And if I hold to this judgment because my imagination, or whatever other entity it might be, persuades me of it, I will still reach the same conclusion. And what I have said here about the wax can be applied to all other things which are external to me.

Furthermore, if the idea or knowledge of the wax seems clearer and more distinct to me after I have investigated it, not only by sight or touch, but also in many other ways, with how much more ⌐evidence,¬ distinctness ⌐and clarity¬ must it be admitted that I now know myself; since all the reasons which help me to know and conceive the nature of the wax, or of any other body whatsoever, serve much better to show the nature of my mind! And we also find so many other things in the mind itself which can contribute to the clarification of its nature, that those which depend on the body, such as the ones I have just mentioned, hardly deserve to be taken into account.

And at last here I am, having insensibly

returned to where (34) I wished to be; for since
it is at present manifest to me that even bodies
are not properly known by the senses nor by the
faculty of imagination, but by the understanding
alone; and since they are not known in so far as
they are seen or touched, but only in so far as
they are understood by thinking, I see clearly
that there is nothing easier for me to understand
than my mind. But since it is almost impossible
to rid oneself so soon of an opinion of long
standing, it would be wise to stop a while at this
point, in order that, by the length of my meditation, I may impress this new knowledge more deeply upon my memory. [27]

Notes

1 [L. sentire; F. sentir.]
2 [L. cogitare; F. penser.]
3 [L. intellectus; F. entendement.]
4 [L. res cogitans; F. une chose qui pense.]
5 [L. mens; F. entendement.]
6 [L. perceptio; F. perception.]

Of Personal Identity*
David Hume

There are some philosophers, who imagine we
are every moment intimately conscious of what we
call our Self; that we feel its existence and its
continuance in existence; and are certain, beyond
the evidence of a demonstration, both of its perfect identity and simplicity. The strongest sensation, the most violent passion, say they, instead of distracting us from this view, only fix
it the more intensely, and make us consider their
influence on self either by their pain or pleas-

*From A Treatise of Human Nature by David Hume
edited by L. A. Selby-Bigge. Reprinted by permission of Oxford University Press. Copyright
© Oxford University Press, 1978.

ure. To attempt a farther proof of this were to
weaken its evidence; since no proof can be deriv'd from any fact, of which we are so intimately conscious; nor is there any thing, of which
we can be certain, if we doubt of this.

Unluckily all these positive assertions are
contrary to that very experience, which is plead-
ed for them, nor have we any idea of self, after
the manner it is here explain'd. For from what
impression cou'd this idea be deriv'd? This
question 'tis impossible to answer without a manifest contradiction and absurdity; and yet 'tis
a question, which must necessarily be answer'd,
if we wou'd have the idea of self pass for clear
and intelligible. It must be some one impression, that gives rise to every real idea. But
self or person is not any one impression, but
that to which our several impressions and ideas
are suppos'd to have a reference. If any impression gives rise to the idea of self, that
impression must continue invariably the same,
thro' the whole course of our lives; since self
is suppos'd to exist after that manner. But
there is no impression constant and invariable.
Pain and pleasure, grief and joy, passions and
sensations succeed each other, and never all exist at the same time. It cannot, therefore, be
from any of these impressions, or from any other,
that the idea of self is deriv'd; and consequently there is no such idea.

But farther, what must become of all our
particular perceptions upon this hypothesis? All
these are different, and distinguishable, and
separable from each other, and may be separately
consider'd, and may exist separately, and have no
need of any thing to support their existence.
After what manner, therefore, do they belong to
self; and how are they connected with it? For my
part, when I enter most intimately into what I
call myself, I always stumble on some particular
perception or other, of heat or cold, light or
shade, love or hatred, pain or pleasure. I never
can catch myself at any time without a perception,

and never can observe any thing but the perception. When my perceptions are remov'd for any
time, as by sound sleep; so long am I insensible
of myself, and may truly be said not to exist.
And were all my perceptions remov'd by death, and
cou'd I neither think, nor feel, nor see, nor
love, nor hate after the dissolution of my body,
I shou'd be entirely annihilated, nor do I conceive what is farther requisite to make me a perfect non-entity. If any one upon serious and un-
prejudic'd reflexion, thinks he has a different
notion of himself, I must confess I can reason no
longer with him. All I can allow him is, that he
may be in the right as well as I, and that we are
essentially different in this particular. He may,
perhaps, perceive something simple and continu'd,
which he calls himself; tho' I am certain there
is no such principle in me.

But setting aside some metaphysicians of this
kind, I may venture to affirm of the rest of mankind, that they are nothing but a bundle or col-
lection of different perceptions, which succeed
each other with an inconceivable rapidity, and
are in a perpetual flux and movement. Our eyes
cannot turn in their sockets without varying our
perceptions. Our thought is still more variable
than our sight; and all our other senses and faculties contribute to this change; nor is there
any single power of the soul, which remains un-
alterably the same, perhaps for one moment. The
mind is a kind of theatre, where several perceptions successively make their appearance; pass,
re-pass, glide away, and mingle in an infinite
variety of postures and situations. There is
properly no simplicity in it at one time, nor
identity in different; whatever natural propension we may have to imagine that simplicity and
identity. The comparison of the theatre must not
mislead us. They are the successive perceptions
only, that constitute the mind; nor have we the
most distant notion of the place, where these
scenes are represented, or of the materials, of
which it is compos'd.

What then gives us so great a propension to ascribe an identity to these successive perceptions, and to suppose ourselves possest of an invariable and uninterrupted existence thro' the whole course of our lives? In order to answer this question, we must distinguish betwixt personal identity, as it regards our thought or imagination, and as it regards our passions or the concern we take in ourselves. The first is our present subject; and to explain it perfectly we must take the matter pretty deep, and account for that identity, which we attribute to plants and animals: there being a great analogy betwixt it, and the identity of a self or person.

We have a distinct idea of an object, that remains invariable and uninterrupted thro' a suppos'd variation of time; and this idea we call that of identity or sameness. We have also a distinct idea of several different objects existing in succession, and connected together by a close relation; and this to an accurate view affords as perfect a notion of diversity, as if there was no manner of relation among the objects. But tho' these two ideas of identity, and a succession of related objects be in themselves perfectly distinct, and even contrary, yet 'tis certain, that in our common way of thinking they are generally confounded with each other. That action of the imagination, by which we consider the uninterrupted and invariable object, and that by which we reflect on the succession of related objects, are almost the same to the feeling, nor is there much more effort of thought requir'd in the latter case than in the former. The relation facilitates the transition of the mind from one object to another, and renders its passage as smooth as if it contemplated one continu'd object. This resemblance is the cause of the confusion and mistake, and makes us substitute the notion of identity, instead of that of related objects. However at one instant we may consider the related succession as variable or interrupted, we are sure the next to ascribe to it a perfect identity, and regard it as invariable and uninterrupted. Our propensity to this mistake is so great from the resemblance above-mention'd, that we fall into it before we are aware; and tho' we incessantly correct ourselves by reflexion, and return to a more accurate method of thinking, yet we cannot long sustain our philosophy, or take off this biass from the imagination. Our last resource is to yield to it, and boldly assert that these different related objects are in effect the same, however interrupted and variable. In order to justify to ourselves this absurdity, we often feign some new and unintelligible principle, that connects the objects together, and prevents their interruption or variation. Thus we feign the continu'd existence of the perceptions of our senses, to remove the interruption; and run into the notion of a soul, and self, and substance, to disguise the variation. But we may farther observe, that where we do not give rise to such a fiction, our propension to confound identity with relation is so great, that we are apt to imagine[1] something unknown and mysterious, connecting the parts, beside their relation; and this I take to be the case with regard to the identity we ascribe to plants and vegetables. And even when this does not take place, we still feel a propensity to confound these ideas, tho' we are not able fully to satisfy ourselves in that particular, nor find any thing invariable and uninterrupted to justify our notion of identity.

Thus the controversy concerning identity is not merely a dispute of words. For when we attribute identity, in an improper sense, to variable or interrupted objects, our mistake is not confin'd to the expression, but is commonly attended with a fiction, either of something invariable and uninterrupted, or of something mysterious and inexplicable, or at least with a propensity to such fictions. What will suffice to prove this hypothesis to the satisfaction of every fair enquirer, is to shew from daily experience and observation, that the objects, which are variable or interrupted, and yet are suppos'd

to continue the same, are such only as consist of
a succession of parts, connected together by resemblance, contiguity, or causation. For as such
a succession answers evidently to our notion of
diversity, it can only be by mistake we ascribe
to it an identity; and as the relation of parts,
which leads us into this mistake, is really nothing but a quality, which produces an association
of ideas, and an easy transition of the imagination from one to another, it can only be from the
resemblance, which this act of the mind bears to
that, by which we contemplate one continu'd object, that the error arises. Our chief business,
then, must be to prove, that all objects, to
which we ascribe identity, without observing
their invariableness and uninterruptedness, are
such as consist of a succession of related objects.

In order to this, suppose any mass of matter, of which the parts are contiguous and connected, to be plac'd before us; 'tis plain we
must attribute a perfect identity to this mass,
provided all the parts continue uninterruptedly
and invariably the same, whatever motion or
change of place we may observe either in the
whole or in any of the parts. But supposing some
very _small_ or _inconsiderable_ part to be added to
the mass, or substracted from it; tho' this absolutely destroys the identity of the whole,
strictly speaking; yet as we seldom think so accurately, we scruple not to pronounce a mass of
matter the same, where we find so trivial an alteration. The passage of the thought from the
object before the change to the object after it,
is so smooth and easy, that we scarce perceive
the transition, and are apt to imagine, that 'tis
nothing but a continu'd survey of the same object.

There is a very remarkable circumstance,
that attends this experiment; which is, that tho'
the change of any considerable part in a mass of
matter destroys the identity of the whole, yet
we must measure the greatness of the part, not
absolutely, but by its _proportion_ to the whole.

448

The addition or diminution of a mountain wou'd not be sufficient to produce a diversity in a planet; tho' the change of a very few inches wou'd be able to destroy the identity of some bodies. 'Twill be impossible to account for this, but by reflecting that objects operate upon the mind, and break or interrupt the continuity of its actions not according to their real greatness, but according to their proportion to each other: And therefore, since this interruption makes an object cease to appear the same, it must be the uninterrupted progress of the thought, which constitutes the imperfect identity.

This may be confirm'd by another phaenomenon. A change in any considerable part of a body destroys its identity; but 'tis remarkable, that where the change is produc'd <u>gradually</u> and <u>insensibly</u> we are less apt to ascribe to it the same effect. The reason can plainly be no other, than that the mind, in following the successive changes of the body, feels an easy passage from the surveying its condition in one moment to the viewing of it in another, and at no particular time perceives any interruption in its actions. From which continu'd perception, it ascribes a continu'd existence and identity to the object.

But whatever precaution we may use in introducing the changes gradually, and making them proportionable to the whole, 'tis certain, that where the changes are at last observ'd to become considerable, we make a scruple of ascribing identity to such different objects. There is, however, another artifice, by which we may induce the imagination to advance a step farther; and that is, by producing a reference of the parts to each other, and a combination to some <u>common end</u> or purpose. A ship, of which a considerable part has been chang'd by frequent reparations, is still consider'd as the same; nor does the difference of the materials hinder us from ascribing an identity to it. The common end, in which the parts conspire, is the same under all their variations, and affords an easy transition of the

imagination from one situation of the body to
another.

But this is still more remarkable, when we
add a sympathy of parts to their common end, and
suppose that they bear to each other, the reciprocal relation of cause and effect in all their
actions and operations. This is the case with
all animals and vegetables; where not only the
several parts have a reference to some general
purpose, but also a mutual dependance on, and
connexion with each other. The effect of so
strong a relation is, that tho' every one must
allow, that in a very few years both vegetables
and animals endure a total change, yet we still
attribute identity to them, while their form,
size, and substance are entirely alter'd. An
oak, that grows from a small plant to a large
tree, is still the same oak; tho' there be not
one particle of matter, or figure of its parts
the same. An infant becomes a man, and is sometimes fat, sometimes lean, without any change in
his identity.

We may also consider the two following
phaenomena, which are remarkable in their kind.
The first is, that tho' we commonly be able to
distinguish pretty exactly betwixt numerical and
specific identity, yet it sometimes happens, that
we confound them, and in our thinking and reasoning employ the one for the other. Thus a man,
who hears a noise, that is frequently interrupted
and renew'd, says, it is still the same noise;
tho' 'tis evident the sounds have only a specific
identity or resemblance, and there is nothing
numerically the same, but the cause, which produc'd them. In like manner it may be said without breach of the propriety of language, that
such a church, which was formerly of brick, fell
to ruin, and that the parish rebuilt the same
church of free-stone, and according to modern
architecture. Here neither the form nor materials are the same, nor is there any thing common to the two objects, but their relation to
the inhabitants of the parish; and yet this alone

is sufficient to make us denominate them the same. But we must observe, that in these cases the first object is in a manner annihilated before the second comes into existence; by which means, we are never presented in any one point of time with the idea of difference and multiplicity; and for that reason are less scrupulous in calling them the same.

Secondly, We may remark, that tho' in a succession of related objects, it be in a manner requisite, that the change of parts be not sudden nor entire, in order to preserve the identity, yet where the objects are in their nature changeable and inconstant, we admit of a more sudden transition, than wou'd otherwise be consistent with that relation. Thus as the nature of a river consists in the motion and change of parts; tho' in less than four and twenty hours these be totally alter'd; this hinders not the river from continuing the same during several ages. What is natural and essential to any thing is, in a manner, expected; and what is expected makes less impression, and appears of less moment, than what is unusual and extraordinary. A considerable change of the former kind seems really less to the imagination, than the most trivial alteration of the latter; and by breaking less the continuity of the thought, has less influence in destroying the identity.

We now proceed to explain the nature of personal identity, which has become so great a question in philosophy, especially of late years in England, where all the abstruser sciences are study'd with a peculiar ardour and application. And here 'tis evident, the same method of reasoning must be continu'd, which has so successfully explain'd the identity of plants, and animals, and ships, and houses, and of all the compounded and changeable productions either of art or nature. The identity, which we ascribe to the mind of man, is only a fictitious one, and of a like kind with that which we ascribe to vegetables and animal bodies. It cannot, therefore, have a different origin, but must proceed from a like operation of the imagination upon like objects.

But lest this argument shou'd not convince the reader; tho' in my opinion perfectly decisive; let him weigh the following reasoning, which is still closer and more immediate. 'Tis evident, that the identity, which we attribute to the human mind, however perfect we may imagine it to be, is not able to run the several different perceptions into one, and make them lose their characters of distinction and difference, which are essential to them. 'Tis still true, that every distinct perception, which enters into the composition of the mind, is a distinct existence, and is different, and distinguishable, and separable from every other perception, either contemporary or successive. But, as, notwithstanding this distinction and separability, we suppose the whole train of perceptions to be united by identity, a question naturally arises concerning this relation of identity; whether it be something that really binds our several perceptions together, or only associates their ideas in the imagination. That is, in other words, whether in pronouncing concerning the identity of a person, we observe some real bond among his perceptions, or only feel one among the ideas we form of them. This question we might easily decide, if we wou'd recollect what has been already prov'd at large, that the understanding never observes any real connexion among objects, and that even the union of cause and effect, when strictly examin'd, resolves itself into a customary association of ideas. For from thence it evidently follows, that identity is nothing really belonging to these different perceptions, and uniting them together; but is merely a quality, which we attribute to them, because of the union of their ideas in the imagination, when we reflect upon them. Now the only qualities, which can give ideas an union in the imagination, are these three relations above-mention'd. These are the uniting principles in the ideal world, and with-

452

out them every distinct object is separable by
the mind, and may be separately consider'd, and
appears not to have any more connexion with any
other object, than if disjoin'd by the greatest
difference and remoteness. 'Tis, therefore, on
some of these three relations of resemblance,
contiguity and causation, that identity depends;
and as the very essence of these relations consists in their producing an easy transition of
ideas; it follows, that our notions of personal
identity, proceed entirely from the smooth and
uninterrupted progress of the thought along a
train of connected ideas, according to the principles above-explain'd.

The only question, therefore, which remains,
is, by what relations this uninterrupted progress
of our thought is produc'd, when we consider the
successive existence of a mind or thinking person. And here 'tis evident we must confine ourselves to resemblance and causation, and must
drop contiguity, which has little or no influence
in the present case.

To begin with resemblance; suppose we cou'd
see clearly into the breast of another, and observe that succession of perceptions, which constitutes his mind or thinking principle, and suppose that he always preserves the memory of a
considerable part of past perceptions; 'tis evident that nothing cou'd more contribute to the
bestowing a relation on this succession amidst
all its variations. For what is the memory but
a faculty, by which we raise up the images of
past perceptions? And as an image necessarily
resembles its object, must not the frequent placing of these resembling perceptions in the chain
of thought, convey the imagination more easily
from one link to another, and make the whole seem
like the continuance of one object? In this particular, then, the memory not only discovers the
identity, but also contributes to its production,
by producing the relation of resemblance among
the perceptions. The case is the same whether
we consider ourselves or others.

As to <u>causation</u>; we may observe, that the
true idea of the human mind, is to consider it
as a system of different perceptions or different
existences, which are link'd together by the relation of cause and effect, and mutually produce,
destroy, influence, and modify each other. Our
impressions give rise to their correspondent
ideas; and these ideas in their turn produce other impressions. One thought chaces another, and
draws after it a third, by which it is expell'd
in its turn. In this respect, I cannot compare
the soul more properly to any thing than to a republic or commonwealth, in which the several members are united by the reciprocal ties of government and subordination, and give rise to other persons, who propagate the same republic in
the incessant changes of its parts. And as the
same individual republic may not only change its
members, but also its laws and constitutions; in
like manner the same person may vary his character and disposition, as well as his impressions
and ideas, without losing his identity. Whatever
changes he endures, his several parts are still
connected by the relation of causation. And in
this view our identity with regard to the passions serves to corroborate that with regard to
the imagination, by the making our distant perceptions influence each other, and by giving us
a present concern for our past or future pains
or pleasures.

As memory alone acquaints us with the continuance and extent of this succession of perceptions, 'tis to be consider'd, upon that account chiefly, as the source of personal identity.
Had we no memory, we never shou'd have any notion
of causation, nor consequently of that chain of
causes and effects, which constitute our self or
person. But having once acquir'd this notion of
causation from the memory, we can extend the same
chain of causes, and consequently the identity of
our persons beyond our memory, and can comprehend
times, and circumstances, and actions, which we
have entirely forgot, but suppose in general to
have existed. For how few of our past actions

are there, of which we have any memory? Who can
tell me, for instance, what were his thoughts
and actions on the first of January 1715, the
11th of March 1719, and the 3d of August 1733?
Or will he affirm, because he has entirely forgot
the incidents of these days, that the present
self is not the same person with the self of that
time; and by that means overturn all the most
establish'd notions of personal identity? In
this view, therefore, memory does not so much
produce as discover personal identity, by shewing
us the relation of cause and effect among our different perceptions. 'Twill be incumbent on those,
who affirm that memory produces entirely our personal identity, to give a reason why we can thus
extend our identity beyond our memory.

The whole of this doctrine leads us to a
conclusion, which is of great importance in the
present affair, viz. that all the nice and sub-
tile questions concerning personal identity can
never possibly be decided, and are to be regarded
rather as grammatical than as philosophical difficulties. Identity depends on the relations of
ideas; and these relations produce identity, by
means of that easy transition they occasion. But
as the relations, and the easiness of the transition may diminish by insensible degrees, we
have no just standard, by which we can decide any
dispute concerning the time, when they acquire or
lose a title to the name of identity. All the
disputes concerning the identity of connected objects are merely verbal, except so far as the relation of parts gives rise to some fiction or imaginary principle of union, as we have already
observ'd.

What I have said concerning the first origin
and uncertainty of our notion of identity, as
apply'd to the human mind, may be extended with
little or no variation to that of simplicity. An
object, whose different co-existent parts are
bound together by a close relation, operates upon
the imagination after much the same manner as one
perfectly simple and indivisible, and requires

455

not a much greater stretch of thought in order
to its conception. From this similarity of operation we attribute a simplicity to it, and
feign a principle of union as the support of this
simplicity, and the center of all the different
parts and qualities of the object.

Thus we have finish'd our examination of the
several systems of philosophy, both of the intellectual and moral world; and in our miscellaneous
way of reasoning have been led into several topics; which will either illustrate and confirm
some preceding part of this discourse, or prepare
the way for our following opinions. 'Tis now
time to return to a more close examination of our
subject, and to proceed in the accurate anatomy
of human nature, having fully explain'd the nature of our judgment and understanding.

Notes

[1]If the reader is desirous to see how a great
genius may be influenc'd by these seemingly trivial principles of the imagination, as well as the
mere vulgar, let him read my Lord <u>Shaftsbury's</u>
reasonings concerning the uniting principle of
the universe, and the identity of plants and animals. See his <u>Moralists</u>' or, <u>Philosophical
rhapsody</u>.

The Essence of a Person*
    Peter A. Bertocci

"Know thyself!" This distum in the Upani-
shads (800 B.C.) is also that of the Greeks. But
what is meant by "know" and by "self" is different. The Biblical counsel, "Know thyself as
created in the image of God," also reminds us that
man's conception of himself is influenced by his

*Reprinted from <u>The Monist</u>, Vol. 62, No. 1, with
the permission of the author and the publisher.

conception of his relation to his ultimate environment (hereafter, Environment). In fundamental terms, there is no East and West when reflective men ask: What is the essence of man? I cannot in this paper pay adequate respect to certain historic approaches to the answer, but they are in mind as I develop a personalistic, temporalistic view of man.[1]

1. The awareness that human beings have of themselves, their capacity for self-consciousness, distinguishes them from all other living beings including those that are most like them biologically. Whatever the scope and limitations of consciousness and self-consciousness may be, only the self-conscious being can know them as he inspects his activities, differentiates them, and relates them to each other and to any set of beings-events.

2. There is nothing in this statement that precludes any specific view of Environment or any specific view of whatever, beyond self-conscious awareness, is essential to its essence. Assuming, as I shall, that what the self-conscious person experiences and judges is necessary to any full account of himself and of Environment, it is critical to know by what criterion the person assigns priority to experiences (and judgments based upon them).

No experiences are to be given priority until the claim made thereupon comes before competing claims in the court of self-conscious reasoning. Reasoning is the activity whereby the person weaves together the different dimensions of experience with a view to discovering which hypothesis about them as a whole is more inclusively systematic. The truth-seeker who guides himself by this criterion of experiential coherence never suspends the demands of logical consistency. But neither does he allow them to bar the way of any experiential truth-claim to the court of experience as a whole, reason-ably interpreted. And this criterion of truth applies to the ideals by which the self-conscious being guides his action and his interpretation of other value-experiences.

3. We may now explicitly define a _person_ as that quality of self-conscious being who is capable of guiding himself by reason-able ideals of truth and value. Obviously, there can be no injunction against substituting for _person_ such words as _self_, _soul_, _spirit_, _mind_, _psyche_, provided it is clear that we have in mind, minimally, a self-conscious being capable of criticizing his experiences and actions by reason-able ideals. Such qualifications as male, female, and homosexual are important to the understanding of much in a person's life-history. But when _person_ dominates our reference it is the capacity to govern oneself by reasoned ideals that is of the essence. (In this context I may add that a conception of the _total_ person would include an account of a person's body and of his unconscious. Yet such accounts are not reasonable unless they enable us to understand at least what we find in self-conscious experience—to which we confine ourselves here.)

4. What is comprehended in _self-conscious-ness_? I am assuming that consciousness is an ultimate; there is no going beyond it to explain it. Nor can we go looking for something, consciousness, independent of the activities that distinguish us whenever we are conscious in any manner. It is these activities and their potential that define consciousness. Without assuming that these differentiations are final, a person is aware of himself as the complex unity of activity-potentials: sensing, remembering, imagining, thinking, feeling, emoting, wanting, willing, oughting, and activities of aesthetic and religious appreciation. These activities—however finally interpreted—are better conceived of as dimensions, not levels, of person-al being; they constitute the experiential phases of a person's self-consciousness.

5. But the question that keeps arising is: What is meant by _self_ (and particularly a per-son-al self)? Even those who in the end deny that their self can be understood as an intrinsic unity agree that consciousness is 'owned,' as James said. That is, the experienceing and experiences by which _I_ define 'myself,' however rapidly they 'stream by,' are, for all their complexity, mine. For me to be conscious at all, and certainly for me to be self-conscious, is to be the unity of these experiencings and ex-periences. Leibniz was correct: there is no state or activity of consciousness independent of the complex unity. _I_ am never, at least _as_ "I experience myself," a compound of 'states,' 'ex-periencings,' or phases.'

Why, then, doubt that I am intrinsic unity of my activities? Because there is no straight path from my complex unity as experienced to an undeniable interpretation of it. To begin with, it is not enough to say that I am a unity. I must go on to say that I am a unity in continu-ity.

Baffling as it seems to hold that I am one and complex in any moment, it is more baffling to understand how I can be the same person, con-tinuing from moment to moment, day to day, when I am also aware of myself as different. Inter-mittent intervals between conscious experiencing accentuate the problem: I awaken as myself, re-freshed, different, yet the same I; the change is mine. Yet the change is so persistent, so uninvited in many of its occurrences, that one understands why the unity and continuity are held to be not intrinsic but products of changing circumstances. Yet these views, whether held by Hume or Buddhist thinkers[2] are more impressive as negations of particular views of unity than as the convincing denial of the unity-in-continuity, sameness-in-change that characterizes persons. Change as change, flux as flux, without _logos_, as Heraclitus taught us once and for all, is unin-telligible. If a succession of experiences is to be known as a succession there must be an experient of succession; succession has no meaning otherwise.3 And to adapt C. A. Campbell's example: If I am to be not only the hearer of the ninth successive stroke of Big Ben, I must be present to hear the first as well as the ninth. I cannot be aware of them or my own successive states if I am not "the same" at the beginning and at the end.

There is no gain-saying this basic thesis, and we return to the contention that a person is an intrinsic unity-in-continuity. However, sobered by the impressive resistance to this view, we shall work toward a conception of this unity that will profit from the objections to an unchanging soul-substance or person. The objection that is not impressive against it is that, did such a soul exist, we should be able to know it as we know sensory objects or other entities. No, we shall not find ourselves, as subject or as agent, modelled after other sorts of entities, or known as they are known. We shall return to ourselves, elusive4 indeed in contrast to "entitative" existence, and find our unity and continuity in the activities we experience as ours (though our actual knowledge of our limitations will be learned). Our conscious activities are not unified by a soul that is in any way other than these activities in their unique, complex unity.

It is tempting to hold that I have my activities. Since I am never exhausted by any one of them, and since I identify myself despite changes in them and their 'contexts,' it is also tempting to hold to my self-identity. But while maintaining that I am this unity of activities, I shall suggest that I am a self-identifying unity in change, a self-identifying being-becoming. For any substantive view of the person does fall before the objection that the soul cannot be itself, the same, and be involved in the activities that are said to depend upon its unchanging unity. It is this objection that rides hard against a substantive-soul and pervades my attempt to reconstrue the inescapable unity and the inescapable change that characterize the self-conscious unity-in-continuity of a person.[5]

5. The unity that is undeniable is the complex now of self-experience, a present that is no mathematical point but a saddle-back span, a telic moment erlebt with its own changing activity, that is no sooner experienced than it gives way to another moment. This datum-person[6] is no monad without windows, yet, were this I, as datum-person, nothing more than an additive focus of forces in an ambient, there would be no accounting for the qualitative experience each of us has of himself. The task, then, is to understand the continuity of nows with the past and the anticipated future. Any attempt to explain this continuity by an unchanging person-substance (or a pure-ego) that unifies successive pasts, presents, and futures, fails to do justice to the actual duree of any moment and to the changes from moment to moment. Yet, as we have seen, to say that moments follow moments is unintelligible without a unity that is not lost in the succession of states or moments of consciousness.

6. On what grounds can we justify the claim that a datum-person, a now-I, is continuous with a past (that is no longer) and with a future (that is not yet)? An experientially coherent answer finds them within the matrix of now-activities. Were there no reasoning "in" the datum-person there would be no hope of connecting any datum-person with other nows. But reasoning by itself does not itself provide the other erlebt data that ground the conviction of the continuity of the datum-person with its past. The experiential base, to adapt a theme of H. H. Price[7] for my purpose here, is what each of us experiences in his present recognition, the experience of "again." This experience is given— as indubitably as are sensory or emotive experiences. The experient may be wrong about what is

referred to in the again-context; that is, those again-features are not those of my friend, as I assumed at first flush; but I cannot deny the 'again-ness' as such.

It is customary in this situation to invoke "memory" to save the continuity. But, after all, memory—besides involving recall as well as recognition—labels the fact to be explained. We postulate retention in order to understand the recognition and recall. But retention would be a blank mystery without any experiential root in indubitable experience, "again," that the reasoning datum-person seeks to explain. I would not, I suggest, know that I had a past (that is no longer existent) did I not experience myself "again" (I-again). What I come to decide about the total nature of myself as past, and about my prospects for the future, is, insofar as we can trust our conclusion, the most coherent interpretation of what can be held before us as actually experienced.

But does this not mean that each of us is shut up in a solipsism of the present moment, to use Santayana's phrase? I have been urging that an epistemic ground for the conviction of unity-in-continuity or continuity-in-unity is an experience, 'again,' that has not received enough attention in this connection. I shall move on to an ontological hypothesis for understanding unity-in-continuity, but only after referring to an equally important ground for affirming the person's unity-in-continuity.

Any person finds that many of his cognitive claims about indubitable experiences—such as "again"—can be mistaken. But how is error possible to begin with? What kind of being can be in error (or in truth)? Only a being, I suggest, who can undergo the experience of referring beyond itself what he undeniably experiences. Thus, the experienced situation, "red disc," is referred "objectively" to what is beyond the situation, "the red light." But the cognitive agent discovers that this "objective reference" does not "characterize" the object referred to—in this case, the red light. At the moment of referring he had no doubt that what he experienced as "there" is, as he experiences it, there! But to his surprise he now discovers that it is not where he refers it; he is in error.

I am not concerned here with how error occurs or how we overcome it, but only with the condition presupposed by its occurrence. What is the locus of the objectively referred experience during the period that the cognitive agent is in error? That he was conscious of it (the red disc) cannot be denied; that he referred it cannot be denied. But if, as is plain, it cannot be identical with what it is refered to, then it could only exist in his consciousness. My conclusion: only a being who can be aware of x, continue to be and become as he refers the x experienced beyond itself, and thus be the "locus" of x whether or not his reference is correct— only such a unity-in-continuity, on such a being-becoming, can render the very occurrence of error intelligible.

I draw another conclusion that is not irrelevant to defining the essence of the person. I cannot explain the fact of error (and, of course, of truth-claims) by identifying my conscious unity with my brain, as defined in any proferred physico-chemical-biological account. For what can it possibly mean for a brain-cell to refer an experienced x beyond itself? This road is a dead end, and I return to the further description and interpretation of self-conscious unity-in-continuity. I am far from denying relationships that are discovered and discoverable between conscious and unconscious and biological and physical realms. I am arguing only that the essence of personal unity-in-continuity cannot be identical with extended or spatial being and movements in cells.

8. I must forego reinforcing this brief

study of remembering and of objective reference by analysis of the affective-conative aspects of the datum-person; they cannot be cut away from the other dimensions in the matrix of the datum and continuing person. To be, as Plato said, is to act and be acted upon; for a person to be is to act, be acted upon, and thus to become as his activities with their potential interact with environments and Environments. I have already referred to a person, therefore, as a cognitive-agent, telescoping the dimensional activities referred to above. An adequate theory would need to define the qualities of emotion, feeling and wanting that are fundamental to the telic agency of persons. The omission of such analysis must not keep us from drawing the conclusion that our study so far justifies. To be a person as a continuing unity of activity-potentials is to be neither a substance nor a series. To be a person is to be a being-becoming telic agent.

Some will immediately identify this view with the process-philosophy of A. N. Whitehead and its impressive development by Charles Hartshorne. But the personalistic temporalism I am presenting here finds it difficult to see how recent process-philosophy, and Hartshorne[8] in particular, can keep from slipping into sheer succession, whatever that might be. It is easy to picture a datum-person moving out of a past and into a future. But if the past is indeed 'no longer' and the future indeed 'not-yet,' there is, in more than a manner of speaking, nothing to come from and nothing to go to. Yet in his attempt to account for the continuity of the person, Hartshorne seems to suggest that the person is in the last analysis the product of a series, or route, of momentary experients. When we ask how the members of the series become or are linked, we are told that every now prehends its past (and its contemporary world) selectively and that the route is what defines the (composite) person.

I agree that the experience of every person

is intrinsically selective, that some telic aim
is regnant and guides his own relatively passive
receptivity and his active response. But what
can it mean to say that a person in the present
grasps the past if the past is no longer? Within
any erlebt crescent and concrescent datum-person,
there is, to be sure, waxing and waning. But
since no present cannot reach back and grasp
what is no longer, what does it mean to say that
a present matrix prehends a (gone) past? The
problem of unity-continuity is not solved by affirming a present that is even causally linked,
presumably, with a past that is no longer. Another conception of unity-in-continuity may be
truer to what persons actually experience in
their being-becoming agency.

9. Assume, then, a telic, active, datum-
person. He experiences, we have said, objective
reference, and he can be mistaken. He anticipates a future that may not occur as imagined.
He also undergoes the indubitable "again" as
aspects of many of his experiences, and he may
be incorrect about his interpretation. Reasoning about these and other experiences, the
datum-person grounds his belief in his past and
builds his understanding of himself as a being
who is capable of retaining (and forgetting) his
past (selectively and unselectively). However,
it is always in a present matrix that remembering and other cognitive activities occur as aspects of the erlebt Gestalt. In any now the
person is the being-becoming of his activity-
potentials as he expresses himself in, and re-
sponds to environments—without which there is no
understanding of the actual development and
changes in his experience.

To repeat, on this view it is always a selective being-becoming, a datum-person, who expresses and adjusts himself in the varied dimensions of his being that are the crucible of his
existence. There is no reaching back to grasp a
past, for the past must be a factor in the now
that is expressing-adjusting its activity-poten-

465

tials in accordance with its regnant aim. The
new now, guided by this regnant aim, is able to
identify this now, pregnant with its selected
past, with itself as past. The mystery of this
unity of person-al being-becoming is that the
person can maintain his given unity as he ex-
presses-adjusts himself and thus changes in interaction with his environments. He cannot ac-
commodate all environments and all desires and
plans; his existence at any stage is a qualitative response, good or bad, but crescent because
it, including that selected past, accommodates as
it interacts with environments and thus maintains
its own unity-in-continuity.

If any diagram were even to suggest my meaning it would be a spiral, with unity to begin
with, a spiral enlarging itself as a consequence
of its selective openness to the press it re-
sponds to. The image of rings of growth in a
tree would be helpful if they did not suggest
more or less even growth <u>around</u> a center, when in
fact concrescence witnesses to its uneven career
in the environment. Thus, the ground for affirming continuity of the datum-person as now
(a) with the subsequent now (b) is that (b) is a
unity that is datum-person (a) with (b) as its
new change-growth. The route or series of successive experiences is possible because each
moment in the succession <u>is</u> the original and
creative unity that is able to maintain its essential activity-potentials as it interacts with
its ambient.

Accordingly, the person is no self-<u>identical</u>
homunculus, no unchanging soul-substance, immanent in but transcending change. Indeed, what
we experience ourselves to be is self-<u>identifying</u>
beings—never the same in any logical or mathematical sense, and always able to identify ourselves as what we are and become. It is at this
point—self-identifying unity-in-continuity—
that I would locate the mystery of being, and not
in terms of any logical identity or mechanical
conception of accretion. (And it is this kind of

466

active-being-becoming that serves as analogical base for what is meant to be and become at any sub-human and divine level.)

10. We must now focus on another dimension of the telic, self-conscious person, one that along with reason, makes it possible to speak of him as capable of guiding himself by ideals. I am referring to will-agency, or free-will. The quality of purpos*ive* activity that a person undergoes as an affective-conative agent must be differentiated from the quality of purpose*ful* experience whereby he unifies his wants in view of some goal. In many situations the person allows the strongest affective-conative complex to "resolve" the conflicts among wants. But in many other situations, when, say, the unapproved desire would predominate if the situation were left to resolve itself, the person experiences himself as free to exert himself in favor of his approved alternative. This _fiat_, to borrow William James' term, as experienced, is undeniable; it too is as given as red, or as anger. This is not to say that this _fiat_ requires no interpretation, but it does mean that interpretation of this experience should not be imposed on it from other realms that neglect the quality of the experience itself.

It is, however, one thing to say that the person wills a goal, but another to say that his willing can achieve the goal. I have elsewhere[9], therefore, distinguished will-agency from the actual power of the willing (will-power). This distinction is tied to the fact that the willing person, given the impediments in the situation within and beyond him, may be less effective than he anticipated. He does not deny that he experiences agency, but he becomes aware that he misjudged his actual power. Thus, while willing is a constitutive activity, will-power derives from the actual interplay of the factors involved at choice-point. Some opponents of will-agency fear the horrendous result they (needlessly) anticipate were free will asserted, namely, that a person could then capriciously create chaos in his experience. But this opposition neglects the fact that will-agency does not occur within a vacuum, that the person at choice-point confronts habits, attitudes, traits within his acquired nature as well as the constitutive factors in his nature as he interacts with environments and Environment.

Even were this distinction of will-agency and will-power completely erroneous, the hypothesis that the person in fact has no freedom to will among alternatives does have consequences even more horrendous than the alleged caprice that free-will would introduce into human experience. For if, despite his erlebt willing, a person's experience and behavior is always the outcome of events that converge upon, and within, him at any moment, the pursuit and achievement of true conclusions becomes impossible. For once we hold that true conclusions are outcomes of the dominant factors at work in a person at a given point, the truth-outcome is no different from the outcome of the play of any other complex of convergent factors. But a person's claim that a certain conclusion is true rests on the assumption that he has been able to guide his search by his ideal of truth. For example, as I interpret the evidence, presumably I have been able to resist the clamor of desire and the press of factors within me and beyond me as I try to draw the conclusion justified by the evidence. Note: if I have no will-agency at all, even to will the continuance of thinking (when my desire favors giving up), if I have no will-agency to forego a conclusion, or to postpone it until I am convinced that it is the one best related to the evidence at hand, then what can I possibly mean to say that my conclusion is true (and not the sheer outcome of events that left me no choice)?

Hence, to the indubitalbe awareness of will-agency, I have added a theoretical consideration without which it means nothing to say that a conclusion is true. The consequences of this thesis

are far-reaching. For what happens in and to a
person is one thing, but what he chooses to do as
far as he can is his own unique province. A person is a shaper and creator within the scope of
his activity-potentials and the psychological
situation that has resulted from his cirtical and
uncritical selectivity in the past. It should be
clear that to affirm the autonomy of the person
is not to affirm his isolation from environments
but to affirm that within limits he can control
and direct his own activities. He can no more
lose his will-agency than he can his wanting or
his sensing or his reasoning; but the power of
his agency enjoys no carte blanche. He is responsible within the limits of his responsivity
(which in turn has been affected by the situations in which his telic agency has been present,
in different ways and degrees in the past).

A person, then, is a unique responsive-
responsible being; he is a co-creator with other
persons, and, in most theistic views, with God.
To create is not necessarily to choose the good
—Socrates, Moses, Jesus, Galileo, Gandhi, Herod,
Hitler, were creator-persons. What such persons
chose to create and the actual power to realize
their goals depended not only on the quality of
choice within the scope of their inner constitutive and acquired natures but also on the external environments with which they interacted.

11. This view of the person as a wanting-
willing-reasoning agent is the ground for resistance to interpretations of the person, advanced in the name of "depth" religious experience (particularly the mystical), and of some
rationalistic visions of Environment. In the
latter the intrinsic unity and freedom of the
person is lost to a network of relations that
connect all there is in a systematic whole—so
that whatever individuality there seems to be is
a mode of the One or a focus of the System. The
personalistic objection to such a rationalistic
vision is that it not only undermines the experienced unity of the person but also the faith of

the rationalist who, as thinking agent, still
needs to persist in thinking at difficult junc-
tures. Moreover, the failure to recognize agency
also undermines such experience of moral good and
evil undergone as persons participate in the creation of aesthetic, religious, and other values.
On the other hand, there simply is no adequate
justification for the view that a personalistic
view of the person "atomizes" ethical responsibility. For the person interacts with complex
environments and decides what quality of relationship will be most creatively-responsive-
responsible. At the same time, the unity that is
open to him is no web of relationships in which
his freedom and individuality is lost; the unity
is the kind of harmony open to purposers as they
relate to each other in interactive response to
Environment.

The personalistic rejoinder to those mystics[10] who appeal to a union that transcends plu-
rality and temporality, or to a union that loses
"self" assumes this same line of argument. But
the personalist also adds: the qualitative
uniqueness of the experience of "loss of self" in
union with the Ultimate is not itself interpreted
monistically by mystics within the great religions.[11] Nevertheless, what may be said about
those views of religious enlightenment or salvation that stresses the loss of self, the rising
above self, "bliss-fully", or the realizing of
the real Self or the One that one's sense of individuality obscures? The personalist agrees
that the disciplined effort can and should put
aside self-absorbed and selfish desires with
which persons can so readily—and disastrously—
identify their good. But he questions the assumption that all the sensory and the desiring
dimensions of self-experience are selfish and
"world"-bound.[12] In any case, he asks: Must we
not recognize the agent who, knowing that he is
trapped in "self," controls his body, his
thoughts, and his feelings so that he can "unite,"
and who, returning to the realm of existence or
appearance, can sustain his enlightenment and

create better foci for his living? In short, without neglecting or minimizing the experience of union, without "reducing" the experience of the holy "moralistically," or "rationalistically," the variety of religious experience itself requires that its interpretation be related, be reasonably interwoven, with the ethical dimensions of the person's experience and with other relevant epistemic and metaphysical issues.

12. As I have already suggested, a more complete estimate of the essence of the person would expound constitutive motive-emotions unique to the person (such as wonder, tenderness, sympathy, respect), and the essentially personal activity-potentials of oughting and of aesthetic and religious appreciation. Until these activities are allowed to speak for themselves, their voice will not be heard by those who approach them from possibly (at least) alien perspectives —for example, their place in biological and social organization and from preconceived notions of Divinity and Environment. I now draw together here considerations from our partial analysis that would form the background for further study in the light of other dimensions.

a. To say that every person is autonomous (within limits) is not to deny that his arrival, survival, and quality of fulfillment depends on factors beyond himself. There is no reasonable ground, I would argue, for supposing that the family of values that persons discover as essential to their quality of survival are alien to their conception of Environment. But it is unreasonable to deny that these values are joint-products of the interplay of wanting-knowing persons with environments and Environment that sustain, threaten, and destroy some organizations of value more than others. For the fact remains that whatever the dimensions of Environment may be, persons have appeared, and they can discipline their constitutive natures so that they can express and adapt themselves to realms beyond themselves and can discover new ways of critical,

471

active, and appreciation response. Herein lies
the ground for the faith that the person is no
alien in the Environment; although the question
of nature of the kinship is open for further
study. What is not to be reasonably denied is
that science, art, morality, religion, and philosophy are the products of persons in an Environment whose own varied regularities are the
context for the realms of value—theoretical,
aesthetic, ethical, and religious—that make for
quality in the environments person co-create.

b. A caution is still in order. Persons
cannot acquire information and evaluate their
value-experience without organizing the affective-conative as well as the sensory-memorial-
imaginative dimensions of their experience. And,
as I have hinted, much of the error-and-truth and
good-and-evil they undergo depends on the use
they make of their will-agency as they realize
ideals. Persons are the only beings who have so
much latitude in shaping the quality of their
own future as they build their environments in
relation to Environment. Persons, indeed, pushed
by their unique affective-conative givens, can so
exert their reflective activities as to orches-
trate their prior responses into organized meanings and values that they also "substain" by
their resolves (personal, conventional, legal).
In so doing, they themselves contribute, for better and for worse, new orders of value-disvalue
in relation to the environment. Persons and
their value-realms cannot therefore be said to
be forms or modes of the Environment alone. The
efforts of individuals and of their social organizations can no more be ontically identified, as
such, than can the individuals with Environment.
Their agency as persons, their reflection as persons, will always be involved in creating personal, social, political, aesthetic, and religious structures that may not encourage individual
positive creativity; instead of building mansions
for the soul they build hospitals and prisions.

c. However, this quality, his freedom, as

472

judged by some standard of goodness, should not be substituted for a person's free agency (as affirmed above). The quality of individual freedom dependent as it is on the social order and on other conditions in which the person is born and struggles for fulfillment must not be substituted for the will-agency of persons. For the agency of a reliable-capable person, since it never lives in a vacuum, is neither an idle luxury nor destined to favor specific social systems, individualistic or authoritarian. At this point the personalist, in Kantian fashion, stresses that to minimize will-agency is to forfeit the quintessential quality in all person-al experience, the pearl of great price that though not the only pearl, still enhances every other value among the values and ideals open for personal fulfillment. To be sure, from this reflective will-agency may stem the desolation and despair rooted in one's awareness that he has himself contributed to suffering and evil, that he himself has wasted his substance; but from this self-critical will-agency there also comes the priceless awareness that he is no pawn, no thing among other things; he is something in and for himself. But this is never the last word!

It is not the last word because persons as reason-capable agents cannot escape the fact that other persons, as _persons_, have the right, even when they do not have the power, to be respected as they too express-adjust themselves in relation to environments and Environment. The burden of proof for treating persons, in themselves and others, without regard to their sensitivities, capacities, and achievements can never be determined unilaterally among reason-capable persons. However, this means that while each person is the crucible of growth, his creativity as a person consists qualitatively in his contribution to establishing the conditions for a community of persons who can increase their potential for creativity in value-realization. The tensive harmony, the "creative insecurity," involved in the positive compromises that originate in mutual

473

concern for mutual growth is the goal of the responsive-responsible community.

In this kind of communitarian organization persons "share" goals as they respond to each other's needs and remain sensitive to the varied dimensions of Environment. But they never "participate" as "parts" of a larger Whole.[13] For they are co-creators whose qualitative (not ontic) individuality is compossibly enhanced insofar as they guide their thoughts, sensitivities, and actions in response to environments and the Environment.

It may be noted—in closing an essay that has not begun to do justice to moral aesthetic, and religious dimensions of personal consciousness—that at no point has it been contended that persons are monads without windows, or that persons can develop their activity-potentials without the aid especially of other persons, or that the physico-chemical-biological environment is not the necessary condition of much of their existence and survival, or that in their aesthetic and religious responsiveness, as in their moral sensitivities and imperatives, there are no clues to their own complete nature in relation to Environment. But a personalist may suggest that even in the flight of the alone to the Alone, without the self-conscious connective reasoning of a free person, we cannot lose the self-identifying agent who makes the flight, and who returns with a sense of the unified horizons for himself and others.

Accordingly, persons as persons need to care for community; they need to respect critically each other's horizons, not only because they realize that they are limited and err, but because they know that in every dimension of their being-becoming they will create with insight only as they can trust each other and Environment to conserve and increase the value of what is worth preserving. The community of persons-in-care is the community that only persons

474

can create—persons I should want to add, who are co-creators with the cosmic Person. But, in any case, the religious experience, however ecstatic, once seen in relation to other dimensions of self-consciousness, will deepen and broaden the cre-activity of the person only as he accepts those risks of his responsiveness and agency that char-acterize him as a person among persons.

Notes

[1]This paper stands in the tradition of Amer-ican personalistic idealism as developed by Borden Parker Bowne (1847-1910) and of Edgar S. Brightman (1814-1953). But it is strongly influ-enced by the work of Frederick R. Tennant (1866-1957), William James (1842-1910), Henri Bergson (1859-1941), Alfred North Whitehead (1861-1947), Charles Hartshorne and H. D. Lweis, as well as Ramanuja (1017-1137) and Iqbal (1877-1938).

[2]See K. Venkata Ramanan, Nagarjuna's Philos-ophy (Rutland, Vermont: Charles E. Tuttle Co., 1966), especially Chapters 3 and 10, for an ex-position of the Buddhist Middle Way.

[3]This Kantian theme is central to the per-sonalism of Bowne. See his Metaphysics (Harper, 1892, revised 1989) and Theory of Thought and Knowledge (New York: Harper, 1897).

[4]See the masterly analysis of opposing recent views in H. D. Lewis, The Elusive Mind (London: Allen and Unwin; New York: Humanities, 1969), especially Chapters 11-15.

[5]The thesis to be developed is further ex-pounded in my The Person God Is (London: Allen and Unwin; New York: Humanities, 1970), Chapters 2-6.

[6]See Edgar S. Brightman, Person and Reality, edited by Peter A. Bertocci in collaboration with J. E. Newhall and R. S. Brightman (New York: Ronald Press, 1958), especially Chapters 3, 4, 10, 11, 18, for more systematic exposition of this temporalistic view of personal identity (that differs from the 'substantive' view of his teacher, B. P. Bowne).

[7]H. H. Price, Thinking and Experience (Cam-

bridge: Harvard University Press, 1953), Chapter 2 and 3.

[8]See Charles Hartshorne, The Logic of Perfection and Other Essays in Neoclassical Metaphysics (La Salle, Illinois: Open Court, 1962), especially Chapters 6, 7, and 8. See also my essay, "Hartshorne on Personal Identity: A Personalistic Critique," Process Studies 2 (Fall 1972): 216-221.

[9]Peter A. Bertocci and Richard M. Millard, Personality and the Good: Psychological and Ethical Perspectives (New York: McKay, 1963), Chapter 8.

[10]See P. N. Srinivasachari, The Philosophy of Visistadvaita for an excellent statement of the contrasting arguments of Advaita thought (Sankara and followers) and the more personalistic thrust of Ramanuja. For further learned analysis of such contrasts the works of P. T. Raju are always helpful, not the least Introduction to Comparative Philosophy (Lincoln: University of Nebraska Press, 1962).

[11]See, for example, the interpretation of the Islamic tradition including Sufism, in the volume Iqbal: Poet-Philosopher of Pakistan, edited by Hafeez Malik (New York: Columbia University Press, 1971), especially Chapters 10-15. A distinguished analysis of the differences (although biased in favor of Monistic interpretation) is to be found in W. T. Stace, Mysticism and Philosophy (New York: Lippincott, 1960).

[12]In this connection Susil Kumal Maitra's The Ethics of the Hindus (Calcutta: University of Calcutta, 1956) should not be neglected especially in its contrast of Hindu, Buddhist, and Visistadyaita perspectives.

[13]The contrasting themes here are developed by Paul Tillich in the three volumes of Systematic Theology (Chicago: Chicago University Press, 1951, 1957, 1963), and in Chapters 9, 12-14 of my The Person God Is (note 5 above); and in my Religion As Creative Insecurity (Westport, Conn.: Greenwood Press, reprint 1973).

Finding Meaning in Life

Case

Larry had been in difficult situations before when he was trying to decide about entering Law School or go into business and when he wondered about asking Suzanne to marry him. But no crisis seemed as deep seated and intense as this one. The job he had enjoyed as chief counsel for Anabasco Oil was no longer challenging; his marriage was in the first stages of breaking up; his children were leaving home for school. The life he had under control was coming apart. Maybe he was going through what some of his friends had gone through: a mid-life crisis. What he wanted was direction, meaning. He felt like Dante must have felt—lost in a dark wood. But what, if anything, would be his own Virgil?

A Philosophical Approach

The Good Life*
   Aristotle

Book I

1. The good as the aim of action

Every art or applied science[1] and every systematic investigation, and similarly every action
and choice,[2] seem to aim at some good; the good,
therefore, has been well defined as that at which
all things aim.[3] But it is clear that there is a
difference in the ends at which they aim: in
some cases the activity[4] is the end, in others
the end is some product[5] beyond the activity. In
cases where the end lies beyond the action the
product is naturally superior to the activity.

Since there are many activities, arts, and
sciences,[6] the number of ends is correspondingly
large: of medicine the end is health, of ship-
building a vessel, of strategy, victory, and of
household management, wealth. In many instances
several such pursuits are grouped together under
a single capacity:[7] the art of bridle-making,
for example, and everything else pertaining to
the equipment of a horse are grouped together under horsemanship; horsemanship in turn, along
with every other military action, is grouped together under strategy; and other pursuits are
grouped together under other capacities. In all
these cases the ends of the master sciences are
preferable to the ends of the subordinate sciences, since the latter are pursued for the sake

of the former. This is true whether the ends of
the actions lie in the activities themselves or,
as is the case in the disciplines just mentioned,
in something beyond the activities.

2. Politics as the master science of the good

Now, if there exists an end in the realm of
action which we desire for its own sake, an end
which determines all our other desires; if, in
other words, we do not make all our choices for the
sake of something else—for in this way the process will go on infinitely so that our desire
would be futile and pointless—then obviously this
end will be the good, that is, the highest good.
Will not the knowledge of this good, consequently,
be very important to our lives?   Would it not
better equip us, like archers who have a target to
aim at, to hit the proper mark? If so, we must
try to comprehend in outline at least what this
good is and to which branch of knowledge or to
which capacity it belongs.

This good, one should think, belongs to the
most sovereign and most comprehensive master science, and politics[8] clearly fits this description.
For it determines which sciences ought to exist
in states, what kind of sciences each group of
citizens must learn, and what degree of proficiency each must attain. We observe further that
the most honored capacities, such as strategy,
household management, and oratory, are contained
in politics. Since this science uses the rest of
the sciences, and since, moreover, it legislates
what people are to do and what they are not to do,
its end seems to embrace the ends of the other
sciences. Thus it follows that the end of politics is the good for man. For even if the good is
the same for the individual and the state, the
good of the state clearly is the greater and more
perfect thing to attain and to safeguard. The attainment of the good for one man alone is, to be
sure, a source of satisfaction; yet to secure it
for a nation and for states is nobler and more
divine. In short, these are the aims of our in-

vestigation, which is in a sense an investigation of social and political matters.

3. The limitations of ethics and politics

Our discussion will be adequate if it achieves clarity within the limits of the subject matter. For precision cannot be expected in the treatment of all subjects alike, any more than it can be expected in all manufactured articles. Problems of what is noble and just, which politics examines, present so much variety and irregularity that some people believe that they exist only by convention and not by nature. The problem of the good, too, presents a similar kind of irregularity, because in many cases good things bring harmful results. There are instances of men ruined by wealth, and others by courage. Therefore, in a discussion of such subjects, which has to start from a basis of this kind, we must be satisfied to indicate the truth with a rough and general sketch: when the subject and the basis of a discussion consist of matters that hold good only as a general rule, but not always, the conclusions reached must be of the same order. The various points that are made must be received in the same spirit, For a well-schooled man is one who searches for that degree of precision in each kind of study which the nature of the subject at hand admits: it is obviously just as foolish to accept arguments of probability from a mathematician as to demand strict demonstrations from an orator.

Each man can judge competently the things he knows, and of these he is a good judge. Accordingly, a good judge in each particular field is one who has been trained in it, and a good judge in general, a man who has received an all-round schooling. For that reason, a young man is not equipped to be a student of politics; for he has no experience in the actions which life demands of him, and these actions form the basis and subject matter of the discussion. Moreover, since he follows his emotions,[9] his study will be pointless and unprofitable, for the end of this kind of

480

study is not knowledge but action. Whether he is young in years or immature in character makes no difference; for his deficiency is not a matter of time but of living and of pursuing all his interests under the influence of his emotions. Knowledge brings no benefit to this kind of person, just as it brings none to the morally weak. But those who regulate their desires and actions by a rational principle[10] will greatly benefit from a knowledge of this subject. So much by way of a preface about the student, the limitations which have to be accepted, and the objective before us.

4. <u>Happiness is the good, but many views are held about it</u>

To resume the discussion: since all knowledge and every choice is directed toward some good, let us discuss what is in our view the aim of politics, i.e., the highest good attainable by action. As far as its name is concerned, most people would probably agree: for both the common run of people and cultivated men call it happiness, and understand by "being happy" the same as "living well" and "doing well." But when it comes to defining what happiness is, they disagree, and the account given by the common run differs from that of the philosophers. The former say it is some clear and obvious good, such as pleasure, wealth, or honor; some say it is one thing and others another, and often the very same person identifies it with different things at different times: when he is sick he thinks it is health, and when he is poor he says it is wealth; and when people are conscious of their own ignorance, they admire those who talk above their heads in accents of greatness. Some thinkers used to believe that there exists over and above these many goods another good, good in itself and by itself, which also is the cause of good in all these things. An examination of all the different opinions would perhaps be a little pointless, and it is sufficient to concentrate on those which are most in evidence or which seem to make some sort of sense.

Nor must we overlook the fact that arguments which proceed from fundamental principles[11] are different from arguments that lead up to them. Plato, too, rightly recognized this as a problem and used to ask whether the discussion was proceeding from or leading up to fundamental principles, just as in a race course there is a difference between running from the judges to the far end of the track and running back again.[12] Now, we must start with the known. But this term has two connotations: "what is known to us" and "what is known" pure and simple. Therefore, we should start perhaps from what is known to us. For that reason, to be a competent student of what is right and just, and of politics generally, one must first have received a proper upbringing in moral conduct. The acceptance of a fact as a fact is the starting point, and if this is sufficiently clear, there will be no further need to ask why it is so. A man with this kind of background has or can easily acquire the foundations from which he must start. But if he neither has nor can acquire them, let him lend an ear to Hesiod's words:

> That man is all-best who himself works
>   out every problem. . . .
> That man, too, is admirable who follows
>   one who speaks well.
> He who cannot see the truth for himself,
>   nor, hearing it from others,
> store it away in his mind, that man
>   is utterly useless.[13]

*   *   *

7. <u>The good is final and self-sufficient;
   happiness is defined</u>

Let us return again to our investigation into the nature of the good which we are seeking. It is evidently something different in different actions and in each art: it is one thing in medicine, another in strategy, and another again in each of the other arts. What, then, is the good of each? Is it not that for the sake of which everything else is done? That means it is health

in the case of medicine, victory in the case of
strategy, a house in the case of building, a different thing in the case of different arts, and
in all actions and choices it is the end. For it
is for the sake of the end that all else is done.
Thus, if there is some one end for all that we do,
this would be the good attainable by action; if
there are several ends, they will be the goods
attainable by action.

Our argument has gradually progressed to the
same point at which we were before,[14] and we must
try to clarify it still further. Since there are
evidently several ends, and since we choose some
of these—e.g., wealth, flutes, and instruments
generally—as a means to something else, it is
obvious that not all ends are final. The highest
good,[15] on the other hand, must be something final. Thus, if there is only one final end, this
will be the good we are seeking; if there are several, it will be the most final and perfect of
them. We call that which is pursued as an end in
itself more final than an end which is pursued for
the sake of something else; and what is never
chosen as a means to something else we call more
final than that which is chosen both as an end in
itself and as a means to something else. What is
always chosen as an end in itself and never as a
means to something else is called final in an unqualified sense. This description seems to apply
to happiness above all else: for we always choose
happiness as an end in itself and never for the
sake of something else. Honor, pleasure, intelligence, and all virtue we choose partly for themselves—for we would choose each of them even if
no further advantage would accrue from them—but
we also choose them partly for the sake of happiness, because we assume that it is through them
that we will be happy. On the other hand, no one
chooses happiness for the sake of honor, pleasure,
and the like, nor as a means to anything at all.

We arrive at the same conclusion if we approach the question from the standpoint of self-
sufficiency. For the final and perfect good seems

to be self-sufficient. However, we define something as self-sufficient not by reference to the "self" alone. We do not mean a man who lives his life in isolation, but a man who also lives with parents, children, a wife, and friends and fellow citizens generally, since man is by nature a social and political being.[16] But some limit must be set to these relationships; for if they are extended to include ancestors, descendants, and friends of friends, they will go on to infinity. However, this point must be reserved for investigation later. For the present we define as "self-sufficient" that which taken by itself makes life something desirable and deficient in nothing. It is happiness, in our opinion, which fits this description. Moreover, happiness is of all things the one most desirable, and it is not counted as one good thing among many others. But if it were counted as one among many others, it is obvious that the addition of even the least of the goods, would make it more desirable; for the addition would produce an extra amount of good, and the greater amount of good is always more desirable than the lesser. We see then that happiness is something final and self-sufficient and the end of our actions.

To call happiness the highest good is perhaps a little trite, and a clearer account of what it is, is still required. Perhaps this is best done by first ascertaining the proper function[17] of man. For just as the goodness and performance of a flute player, a sculptor, or any kind of expert, and generally of anyone who fulfills some function or performs some action, are thought to reside in his proper function, so the goodness and performance of man would seem to reside in whatever is his proper function. Is it then possible that while a carpenter and a shoemaker have their own proper functions and spheres of action, man as man has none, but was left by nature a good-for-nothing without a function?[18] Should we not assume that just as the eye, the hand, the foot, and in general each part of the body clearly has its own proper function, so man too has some function over and above the functions of his parts? What can this function possibly be? Simply living? He shares that even with plants, but we are now looking for something peculiar to man. Accordingly, the life of nutrition and growth must be excluded.[19] Next in line there is a life of sense perception. But this, too, man has in common with the horse, the ox, and every animal. There remains then an active life of the rational element. The rational element has two parts: one is rational in that it obeys the rule of reason, the other in that it possesses and conceives rational rules. Since the expression "life of the rational element" also can be used in two senses, we must make it clear that we mean a life determined by the activity,[20] as opposed to the mere possession, of the rational element. For the activity, it seems, has a greater claim to be the function of man.

The proper function of man, then, consists in an activity of the soul in conformity with a rational principle or, at least, not without it. In speaking of the proper function of a given individual we mean that it is the same in kind as the function of an individual who sets high standards for himself:[21] the proper function of a harpist, for example, is the same as the function of a harpist who has set high standards for himself. The same applies to any and every group of individuals: the full attainment of excellence must be added to the mere function. In other words, the function of the harpist is to play the harp; the function of the harpist who has high standards is to play it well. On these assumptions, if we take the proper function of man to be a certain kind of life, and if this kind of life is an activity of the soul and consists in actions performed in conjunction with the rational element, and if a man of high standards is he who performs these actions well and properly, and if a function is well performed when it is performed in accordance with the excellence appropriate to it; we reach the conclusion that[22] the good of man is an activity of the soul in conformity with excellence or virtue, and if there are several virtues, in conformity with the best and most complete.

But we must add "in a complete life." For one swallow does not make a spring, nor does one sunny day; similarly, one day or a short time does not make a man blessed[23] and happy.

This will suffice as an outline of the good: for perhaps one ought to make a general sketch first and fill in the details afterwards. Once a good outline has been made, anyone, it seems, is capable of developing and completing it in detail, and time is a good inventor or collaborator in such an effort. Advances in the arts,[24] too, have come about in this way, for anyone can fill in gaps. We must also bear in mind what has been said above, namely that one should not require precision in all pursuits alike, but in each field precision varies with the matter under discussion and should be required only to the extent to which it is appropriate to the investigation. A carpenter and a geometrician both want to find a right angle, but they do not want to find it in the same sense: the former wants to find it to the extent to which it is useful for his work, the latter, wanting to see truth, (tries to ascertain) what it is and what sort of thing it is. We must, likewise, approach other subjects in the same spirit, in order to prevent minor points from assuming a greater importance than the major tasks. Nor should we demand to know a causal explanation in all matters alike; in some instances, e.g., when dealing with fundamental principles, it is sufficient to point out convincingly that such-and-such is in fact the case. The fact here is the primary thing and the fundamental principle. Some fundamental principles can be apprehended by induction, others by sense perception, others again by some sort of habituation,[25] and others by still other means. We must try to get at each of them in a way naturally appropriate to it, and must be scrupulous in defining it correctly, because it is of great importance for the subsequent course of the discussion. Surely, a good beginning is more than half the whole, and as it comes to light, it sheds light on many problems.

*   *   *

9. How happiness is acquired

This also explains why there is a problem whether happiness is acquired by learning, by discipline, or by some other kind of training, or whether we attain it by reason of some divine dispensation or even by chance. Now, if there is anything at all which comes to men as a gift from the gods, it is reasonable to suppose that happiness above all else is god-given; and of all things human it is the most likely to be god-given, inasmuch as it is the best. But although this subject is perhaps more appropriate to a different field of study, it is clear that happiness is one of the most divine things, even if it is not god-sent but attained through virtue and some kind of learning or training. For the prize and end of excellence and virtue is the best thing of all, and it is something divine and blessed. Moreover, if happiness depends on excellence, it will be shared by many people; for study and effort will make it accessible to anyone whose capacity for virtue is unimpaired. And if it is better that happiness is acquired in this way rather than by chance, it is reasonable to assume that this is the way in which it is acquired. For, in the realm of nature, things are naturally arranged in the best way possible—and the same is also true of the products of art and of any kind of causation, especially the highest. To leave the greatest and noblest of things to chance would hardly be right.

A solution of this question is also suggested by our earlier definition, according to which the good of man, happiness, is some kind of activity of the soul in conformity with virtue. All the other goods are either necessary prerequisites for happiness, or are by nature co-workers with it and useful instruments for attaining it. Our results also tally with what we said at the outset: for we stated that the end of politics is the best of ends; and the main concern of politics is to engender a certain character in the citizens and to make them good and disposed to perform noble actions.

We are right, then, when we call neither a horse nor an ox nor any other animal happy, for none of them is capable of participating in an activity of this kind. For the same reason, a child is not happy, either; for, because of his age, he cannot yet perform such actions. When we do call a child happy, we do so by reason of the hopes we have for his future. Happiness, as we have said, requires completeness in virtue as well as a complete lifetime. Many changes and all kinds of contingencies befall a man in the course of his life, and it is possible that the most prosperous man will encounter great misfortune in his old age, as the Trojan legends tell about Priam. When a man has met a fate such as his and has come to a wretched end, no one calls him happy.

10. Can a man be called "happy" during his lifetime?

Must we, then, apply the term "happy" to no man at all as long as he is alive? Must we, as Solon would have us do, wait to see his end?[26] And, on this assumption, is it also true that a man is actually happy after he is dead? Is this not simply absurd, especially for us who define happiness as a kind of activity? Suppose we do not call a dead man happy, and interpret Solon's words to mean that only when a man is dead can we safely say that he has been happy, since he is now beyond the reach of evil and misfortune—this view, too, is open to objection. For it seems that to some extent good and evil really exist for a dead man, just as they may exist for a man who lives without being conscious of them, for example, honors and disgraces, and generally the successes and failures of his children and descendants.[27] This presents a further problem. A man who has lived happily to his old age and has died as happily as he lived may have many vicissitudes befall his descendants: some of them may be good and may be granted the kind of life which they deserve, and others may not. It is, further, obvious that the descendants may conceivably be removed from their ancestors by various degrees. Under such circumstances, it would be odd if the dead man would share in the vicissitudes of his descendants and be happy at one time and wretched at another. But it would also be odd if the fortunes of their descendants did not affect the ancestors at all, not even for a short time.

But we must return to the problem raised earlier, for through it our present problem perhaps may be solved. If one must look to the end and praise a man not as being happy but as having been happy in the past, is it not paradoxical that at a time when a man actually is happy this attribute, though true, cannot be applied to him? We are unwilling to call the living happy because changes may befall them and because we believe that happiness has permanence and is not amenable to changes under any circumstances, whereas fortunes revolve many times in one person's lifetime. For obviously, if we are to keep pace with a man's fortune, we shall frequently have to call the same man happy at one time and wretched at another and demonstrate that the happy man is a kind of chameleon, and that the foundations (of his life) are unsure. Or is it quite wrong to make our judgment depend on fortune? Yes, it is wrong, for fortune does not determine whether we fare well or ill, but is, as we said, merely an accessory to human life; activities in conformity with virtue constitute happiness, and the opposite activities constitute its opposite.

The question which we have just discussed further confirms our definition. For no function of man possesses as much stability as do activities in conformity with virtue: these seem to be even more durable than scientific knowledge. And the higher the virtuous activities, the more durable they are, because men who are supremely happy spend their lives in these activities most intensely and most continuously, and this seems to be the reason why such activities cannot be forgotten.

The happy man will have the attribute of permanence which we are discussing, and he will remain happy throughout his life. For he will always or to the highest degree both do and contemplate what is in conformity with virtue; he will bear the vicissitudes of fortune most nobly and with perfect decorum under all circumstances, inasmuch as he is truly good and "four-square beyond reproach."[28]

But fortune brings many things to pass, some great and some small. Minor instances of good and likewise of bad luck obviously do not decisively tip the scales of life, but a number of major successes will make life more perfectly happy; for, in the first place, by their very nature they help to make life attractive, and secondly, they afford the opportunity for noble and good actions. On the other hand, frequent reverses can crush and mar supreme happiness in that they inflict pain and thwart many activities. Still, nobility shines through even in such circumstances, when a man bears many great misfortunes with good grace not because he is insensitive to pain but because he is noble and highminded.

If, as we said, the activities determine a man's life, no supremely happy man can ever become miserable, for he will never do what is hateful and base. For in our opinion, the man who is truly good and wise will bear with dignity whatever fortune may bring, and will always act as nobly as circumstances permit, just as a good general makes the most strategic use of the troops at his disposal, and a good shoemaker makes the best shoe he can from the leather available, and so on with experts in all other fields. If this is true, a happy man will never become miserable; but even so, supreme happiness will not be his if a fate such as Priam's befalls him. And yet, he will not be fickly and changeable; he will not be dislodged from his happiness easily by any misfortune that comes along, but only by great and numerous disasters such as will make it impossible for him to become happy again in a short time; if he recovers his happiness at all, it will be only after a long period of time, in which he has won great distinctions.

Is there anything to prevent us, then, from defining the happy man as one whose activities are an expression of complete virtue¹, and who is sufficiently equipped with external goods, not simply at a given moment but to the end of his life? Or should we add that he must die as well as live in the manner which we have defined? For we cannot foresee the future, and happiness, we maintain, is an end which is absolutely final and complete in every respect. If this be granted, we shall define as "supremely happy" those living men who fulfill and continue to fulfill these requirements, but blissful only as human beings. So much for this question.

*   *   *

Notes

¹Technē.
²Proairesis.
³We do not know who first gave this definition of the good. It is certainly implied in the Platonic dialogues, especially in <u>Republic</u> IV; but the most likely candidate for the formulation here is Eudoxus, for whom see below, X. 2, 1172b9-15. But it is clear from this passage, from X. 2, 1172b35-36, and from <u>Rhetoric</u> I. 6, 1362a23 that Aristotle himself subscribed to this definition.
⁴Energeia.
⁵Ergon.
⁶Epistēmē.
⁷Dynamis.

491

[8]Politikē is the science of the city-state, the polis, and its members, not merely in our narrow 'political' sense of the word but also in the sense that a civilized human existence is, according to Plato and Aristotle, only possible in the polis. Thus politikē involves not only the science of the state, 'politics,' but of our concept of 'society' as well.

[9]Pathos.

[10]The fundamental meaning of logos is 'speech,' 'statement,' in the sense of a coherent and rational arrangement of words; but it can apply to a rational principle underlying many things, and may be translated in different contexts by 'rational account,' 'explanation,' 'argument,' 'treatise,' or 'discussion.' In chap. 7 below, logos is used in a normative sense, describing the human faculty which comprehends and formulates rational principles and thus guides the conduct of a good and reasonable man.

[11]Archē.

[12]A Greek race course was U-shaped with the starting line at the open end, which is also where the judges would have their place. The race was run around a marker set up toward the opposite end of the U, and back again to the starting line.

[13]Hesiod, Works and Days 293, 295-297, as translated by Richmond Lattimore in Hesiod: The Works and Days; Theogony; The Shield of Herakles (Ann Arobr: University of Michigan Press, 1959.)

[14]The reference is to the beginning of chap. 2 above.

[15]Teleios.

[16]Cf. Politics I. 2, 1253a3; politikē.

[17]Ergon.

[18]The translation here has to be more explicit than the Greek: argon is a double-entendre, which means literally 'without function' or 'doing no work' but was also used colloquially to denote a 'loafer.'

[19]Cf. Aristotle's later work, the De Anima II. 2, 413a20 ff., where the different kinds of life are elaborated to include the life of nutrition,

of sense perception, of thought, and of movement,
to which desire is added in II. 3, 414a31.

[20]Energeia.

[21]This is the first occurrence in the Nic. Eth.
of the spoudaios (literally, 'serious man'), whom
Aristotle frequently invokes for purposes similar
to those which make modern laws invoke the "reasonable man." However, Aristotle's stress is
less on the reasonableness of a man under particular circumstances than on a person who has a
sense of the importance of living his life well
and of fulfilling his function in society in accordance with the highest standards.

[22]There is no good reason to follow Bywater in
bracketing lines 12-16 ("if we take the proper
function of man . . .we reach the conclusion
that") on the grounds that they merely repeat the
preceding argument. On the contrary, they provide an excellent summary and should be retained.

[23]The distinction Aristotle seems to observe
between makarios, 'blessed' or 'supremely happy,'
and eudaimōn, 'happy,' is that the former describes happiness insofar as it is god-given,
while the latter describes happiness as attained
by man through his own efforts.

[24]Technē.

[25]This, according to Aristotle, is the way in
which the fundamental principles of ethics are
learned, and for that reason a person must be mature in order to be able to study ethics properly.
It is most important for the modern reader to note
that Aristotle is not trying to persuade his listener of the truth of these principles, but takes
it for granted that he has learned them at home.
Cf. also above, chap. 3, 1095a2-11, and II. 1.

[26]This is one of the main points made by Solon,
Athenian statesman and poet of the early sixth
century B.C., in his conversation with the Lydian
king, Croesus, in Herodotus I. 32.

[27]The comment on this passage by J. Burnet,
The Ethics of Aristotle (London, 1900), p. 49, is
worth quoting:

> There is no question here as to the departed
> being aware of what goes on in this world. On
> the contrary, the point is that what happens

after a man's death may affect our estimate of
his life in just the same way as what happens
in his lifetime without his being aware of it.
Neither makes any difference to the man himself, but the popular belief is ...that it
must affect our estimate of it. We cannot call
that life a success which leads to failure,
even though the man himself may never know of
his failure, or may die in time to escape it.
So with the fortunes of children. Even now we
say 'what would his father think, if he were
alive?'

It should be added, however, that the Greeks had
a much stronger feeling for the cohesion of the
family than we do; cf. G. Glotz, <u>La Solidarité de
la famille dans le droit criminel en Grèce</u> (Paris,
1904).

[28] A quotation from a poem of Simonides (<u>ca.</u>
556-468 B.C.), which is discussed by Socrates and
Protagoras in Plato's <u>Protagoras</u> 338e-348a.

Book II

1. Moral virtue as the result of habits

Virtue, as we have seen, consists of two
kinds, intellectual virtue and moral virtue. Intellectual virtue or excellence owes its origin
and development chiefly to teaching, and for that
reason requires experience and time. Moral virtue, on the other hand, is formed by habit, <u>ethos</u>,
and its name <u>ēthikē</u>, is therefore derived, by a
slight variation, from <u>ethos</u>. This shows, too,
that none of the moral virtues is implanted in us
by nature, for nothing which exists by nature can
be changed by habit. For example, it is impossible for a stone, which has a natural downward
movement, to become habituated to moving upward,
even if one should try ten thousand times to inculcate the habit by throwing it in the air; nor
can fire be made to move downward, nor can the
direction of any nature-given tendency be changed
by habituation. Thus, the virtues are implanted
in us neither by nature nor contrary to nature:

we are by nature equipped with the ability to receive them, and habit brings this ability to completion and fulfillment.[1]

Furthermore, of all the qualities with which we are endowed by nature, we are provided with the capacity first, and display the activity afterward.[2] That this is true is shown by the senses: it is not by frequent seeing or frequent hearing that we acquired our senses, but on the contrary we first possess and then use them; we do not acquire them by use. The virtues, on the other hand, we acquire by first having put them into action, and the same is also true of the arts.[3] For the things which we have to learn before we can do them we learn by doing: men become builders by building houses, and harpists by playing the harp. Similarly, we become just by the practice of just actions, self-controlled by exercising self-control, and courageous by performing acts of courage.

This is corroborated by what happens in states. Lawgivers make the citizens good by inculcating (good) habits in them, and this is the aim of every lawgiver; if he does not succeed in doing that, his legislation is a failure. It is in this that a good constitution differs from a bad one.

Moreover, the same causes and the same means that produce any excellence or virtue can also destroy it, and this is also true of every art. It is by playing the harp that men become both good and bad harpists, and correspondingly with builders and all the other craftsmen: a man who builds well will be a good builder, one who builds badly a bad one. For if this were not so, there would be no need for an instructor, but everybody would be born as a good or a bad craftsman. The same holds true of the virtues: in our transactions with other men it is by action that some become just and others unjust, and it is by acting in the face of danger and by developing the habit of feeling fear or confidence that some become brave men and others cowards. The same applies to the appetites and feelings of anger: by reacting in one way or in another to given circumstances some people become self-controlled and gentle, and others self-indulgent and short-tempered. In a word, characteristics[4] develop from corresponding activities. For that reason, we must see to it that our activities are of a certain kind, since any variations in them will be reflected in our characteristics. Hence it is no small matter whether one habit or another is inculcated in us from early childhood; on the contrary, it makes a considerable difference, or rather, all the difference.

2. Method in the practical sciences

The purpose of the present study is not, as it is in other inquiries, the attainment of theoretical knowledge:[5] we are not conducting this inquiry in order to know what virtue is, but in order to become good, else there would be no advantage in studying it. For that reason, it becomes necessary to examine the problem of actions, and to ask how they are to be performed. For, as we have said, the actions determine what kind of characteristics are developed.

That we must act according to right reason is generally conceded and may be assumed as the basis of our discussion. We shall speak about it later[6] and discuss what right reason is and examine its relation to the other virtues. But let us first agree that any discussion on matters of action cannot be more than an outline and is bound to lack precision; for as we stated at the outset,[7] one can demand of a discussion only what the subject matter permits, and there are no fixed data in matters concerning action and questions of what is beneficial, any more than there are in matters of health. And if this is true of our general discussion, our treatment of particular problems will be even less precise, since these do not come under the head of any art which can be transmitted by percept, but the agent must consider on each different occasion what the situation demands, just as in medicine and in navigation. But although such is the kind of discussion in which we are engaged, we must do our best.

First of all, it must be observed that the nature of moral qualities is such that they are destroyed by defect and by excess. We see the same thing happen in the case of strength and of health, to illustrate, as we must, the invisible by means of visible examples:[8] excess as well as deficiency of physical exercise destroys our strength, and similarly, too much and too little food and drink destroys our health; the proportionate amount, however, produces, increases, and preserves it. The same applies to self-control, courage, and the other virtues: the man who shuns and fears everything and never stands his ground becomes a coward, whereas a man who knows no fear at all and goes to meet every danger becomes reckless. Similarly, a man who revels in every pleasure and abstains from none becomes self-indulgent, while he who avoids every pleasure like a boor becomes what might be called insensitive. Thus we see that self-control and courage are destroyed by excess and by deficiency and are preserved by the mean.

Not only are the same actions which are responsible for and instrumental in the origin and development of the virtues also the causes and means of their destruction, but they will also be manifested in the active exercise of the virtues. We can see the truth of this in the case of other more visible qualities, e.g., strength. Strength is produced by consuming plenty of food and by enduring much hard work, and it is the strong man who is best able to do these things. The same is also true of the virtues: by abstaining from pleasures we become self-controlled, and once we are self-controlled we are best able to abstain from pleasures. So also with courage: by becoming habituated to despise and to endure terrors we become courageous, and once we have become courageous we will best be able to endure terror.

3. Pleasure and pain as the test of virtue

An index to our characteristics is provided by the pleasure or pain which follows upon the tasks we have achieved. A man who abstains from bodily pleasures and enjoys doing so is self-controlled; if he finds abstinence troublesome, he is self-indulgent; a man who endures danger with joy, or at least without pain, is courageous; if he endures it with pain, he is a coward. For moral excellence is concerned with pleasure and pain; it is pleasure that makes us do base actions and pain that prevents us from doing noble actions. For that reason, as Plato says,[9] men must be brought up from childhood to feel pleasure and pain at the proper things; for this is correct education.

Furthermore, since the virtues have to do with actions and emotions, and since pleasure and pain are a consequence of every emotion and of every action, it follows from this point of view, too, that virtue has to do with pleasure and pain. This is further indicated by the fact that punishment is inflicted by means of pain. For punishment is a kind of medical treatment and it is the nature of medical treatments to take effect through the introduction of the opposite of the disease.[10] Again, as we said just now,[11] every characteristic of the soul shows its true nature in its relation to and its concern with those factors which naturally make it better or worse. But it is through pleasures and pains that men are corrupted, i.e., through pursuing and avoiding pleasures and pains either of the wrong kind or at the wrong time or in the wrong manner, or by going wrong in some other definable respect. For that reason some people[12] define the virtues as states of freedom from emotion and of quietude. However, they make the mistake of using these terms absolutely and without adding such qualifications as "in the right manner," "at the right or wrong time," and so forth. We may, therefore, assume as the basis of our discussion that virtue, being concerned with pleasure and pain in the way we have described, makes us act in the best way in matters involving pleasure and pain, and that vice does the opposite.

The following considerations may further illustrate that virtue is concerned with pleasure and pain. There are three factors that determine choice and three that determine avoidance: the noble, the beneficial, and the pleasurable, on the one hand, and on the other their opposites: the base, the harmful, and the painful. Now a good man will go right and a bad man will go wrong when any of these, and especially when pleasure is involved. For pleasure is not only common to man and the animals, but also accompanies all objects of choice: in fact, the noble and the beneficial seem pleasant to us. Moreover, a love of pleasure has grown up with all of us from infancy. Therefore, this emotion has come to be ingrained in our lives and is difficult to erase. Even in our actions we use, to a greater or smaller extent, pleasure and pain as a criterion. For this reason, this entire study is necessarily concerned with pleasure and pain; for it is not unimportant for our actions whether we feel joy and pain in the right or the wrong way. Again, it is harder to fight against pleasure than against anger, as Heraclitus says;[13] and both virtue and art are always concerned with what is harder, for success is better when it is hard to achieve. Thus, for this reason also, every study both of virtue and of politics must deal with pleasures and pains, for if a man has the right attitude to them, he will be good; if the wrong attitude, he will be bad.

We have now established that virtue or excellence is concerned with pleasures and pains; that the actions which produce it also develop it and, if differently performed, destroy it; and that it actualizes itself fully in those activities to which it owes its origin.

4. Virtuous action and virtue

However, the question may be raised what we mean by saying that men become just by performing just actions and self-controlled by practicing self-control. For if they perform just actions and exercise self-control, they are already just and self-controlled, in the same way as they are literate and musical if they write correctly and practice music.[14]

But is this objection really valid, even as regards the arts? No, for it is possible for a man to write a piece correctly by chance or at the prompting of another: but he will be literate only if he produces a piece of writing in a literate way, and that means doing it in accordance with the skill of literate composition which he has in himself.

Moreover, the factors involved in the arts and in the virtues are not the same. In the arts, excellence lies in the result itself, so that it is sufficient if it is of a certain kind. But in the case of the virtues an act is not performed justly or with self-control if the act itself is of a certain kind, but only if in addition the agent has certain characteristics as he performs it: first of all, he must know what he is doing; secondly, he must choose to act the way he does, and he must choose it for its own sake; and in the third place, the act must spring from a firm and unchangeable character. With the exception of knowing what one is about, these considerations do not enter into the mastery of the arts; for the mastery of the virtues, however, knowledge is of little or no importance, whereas the other two conditions count not for a little but are all-decisive, since repeated acts of justice and self-control result in the possession of these virtues. In other words, acts are called just and self-controlled when they are the kind of acts which a just or self-controlled man would perform; but the just and self-controlled man is not he who performs these acts, but he who also performs them in the way just and self-controlled men do.

Thus our assertion that a man becomes just by performing just acts and self-controlled by performing acts of self-control is correct; without performing them, nobody could even be on the way to becoming good. Yet most men do not perform such acts, but by taking refuge in argument they think that they are engaged in philosophy and that they will become good in this way. In so doing, they act like sick men who listen attentively to what the doctor says, but fail to do any of the things he prescribes. That kind of philosophical activity will not bring health to the soul any more than this sort of treatment will produce a healthy body.

5. Virtue defined: the genus

The next point to consider is the definition of virtue or excellence. As there are three kinds of things found in the soul: (1) emotions, (2) capacities, and (3) characteristics, virtue must be one of these. By "emotions" I mean appetite, anger, fear, confidence, envy, joy, affection, hatred, longing, emulation, pity, and in general anything that is followed by pleasure or pain; by "capacities" I mean that by virtue of which we are said to be affected by these emotions, for example, the capacity which enables us to feel anger, pain, or pity; and by "characteristics" I mean the condition, either good or bad, in which we are, in relation to the emotions: for example, our condition in relation to anger is bad, if our anger is too violent or not violent enough, but if it is moderate, our condition is good; and similarly with our condition in relation to the other emotions.

Now the virtues and vices cannot be emotions, because we are not called good or bad on the basis of our emotions, but on the basis of our virtues and vices. Also, we are neither praised nor blamed for our emotions: a man does not receive praise for being frightened or angry, nor blame for being angry pure and simple, but for being angry in a certain way. Yet we are praised or blamed for our virtues and vices. Furthermore, no choice is involved when we experience anger or fear, while the virtues are some kind of choice or at least involve choice. Moreover, with regard to our emotions we are said to be "moved," but with regard to our virtues and vices we are not said to be "moved" but to be "disposed" in a certain way.

For the same reason, the virtues cannot be capacities, either, for we are neither called good or bad nor praised or blamed simply because we are capable of being affected. Further, our capacities have been given to us by nature, but we do not by nature develop into good or bad men. We have discussed this subject before.[15] Thus, if the virtues are neither emotions nor capacities, the only remaining alternative is that they are characteristics.[16] So much for the genus of virtue.

6. Virtue defined: the differentia

It is not sufficient, however, merely to define virtue in general terms as a characteristic: we must also specify what kind of characteristic it is. It must, then, be remarked that every virtue or excellence (1) renders good the thing itself of which it is the excellence, and (2) causes it to perform its function well. For example, the excellence of the eye makes both the eye and its function good, for good sight is due to the excellence of the eye. Likewise, the excellence of a horse makes it both good as a horse and good at running, at carrying its rider, and at facing the enemy. Now, if this is true of all things, the virtue or excellence of man, too, will be a characteristic which makes him a good man, and which causes him to perform his own function well. To some extent we have already stated how this will be true;[17] the rest will become clear if we study what the nature of virtue is.

Of every continuous entity that is divisible
into parts it is possible to take the larger, the
smaller, or an equal part, and these parts may be
larger, smaller, or equal[18] either in relation to
the entity itself, or in relation to us. The
"equal" part is something median between excess
and deficiency. By the median of an entity I understand a point equidistant from both extremes,
and this point is one and the same for everybody.
By the median relative to us I understand an
amount neither too large nor too small, and this
is neither one nor the same for everybody. To
take an example: if ten is many and two is few,
six is taken as the median in relation to the entity, for it exceeds and is exceeded by the same
amount, and is thus the median in terms of arith-
metical proportion. But the median relative to
us cannot be determined in this manner: if ten
pounds of food is much for a man to eat and two
pounds little, it does not follow that the trainer
will prescribe six pounds, for this may in turn
be much or little for him to eat; it may be little
for Milo[19] and much for someone who has just begun to take up athletics. The same applies to
running and wrestling. Thus we see that an expert in any field avoids excess and deficiency,
but seeks the median and chooses it—not the median of the object but the median relative to us.

If this, then, is the way in which every
science perfects its work, by looking to the median and by bringing its work up to that point—
and this is the reason why it is usually said of
a successful piece of work that it is impossible
to detract from it or to add to it, the implication being that excess and deficiency destroy
success while the mean safeguards it (good craftsmen, we say, look toward this standard in the performance of their work)—and if virtue, like nature, is more precise and better than any art, we
must conclude that virtue aims at the median. I
am referring to moral virtue: for it is moral
virtue that is concerned with emotions and actions, and it is in emotions and actions that excess, deficiency, and the median are found. Thus

we can experience fear, confidence, desire, anger, pity, and generally any kind of pleasure and pain either too much or too little, and in either case not properly. But to experience all this at the right time, toward the right objects, toward the right people, for the right reason, and in the right manner—that is the median and the best course, the course that is a mark of virtue.

Similarly, excess, deficiency, and the median can also be found in actions. Now virtue is concerned with emotions and actions; and in emotions and actions excess and deficiency miss the mark, whereas the median is praised and constitutes success. But both praise and success are signs of virtue or excellence. Consequently, virtue is a mean in the sense that it aims at the median. This is corroborated by the fact that there are many ways of going wrong, but only one way which is right—for evil belongs to the indeterminate, as the Pythagoreans imagined, but good to the determinate. This, by the way, is also the reason why the one is easy and the other hard: it is easy to miss the target but hard to hit it. Here, then, is an additional proof that excess and deficiency characterize vice, while the mean characterizes virtue: for "bad men have many ways, good men but one."[20]

We may thus conclude that virtue or excellence is a characteristic involving choice, and that it consists in observing the mean relative to us, a mean which is defined by a rational principle, such as a man of practical wisdom[21] would use to determine it. It is the mean by reference to two vices: the one of excess and the other of deficiency. It is, moreover, a mean because some vices exceed and others fall short of what is required in emotion and in action, whereas virtue finds and chooses the median. Hence, in respect of its essence and the definition of its essential nature virtue is a mean, but in regard to goodness and excellence it is an extreme.

Not every action nor every emotion admits of

a mean. There are some actions and emotions
whose very names connote baseness, e.g., spite,
shamelessness, envy; and among actions, adultery,
theft, and murder. These and similar emotions
and actions imply by their very names that they
are bad; it is not their excess nor their deficiency which is called bad. It is, therefore,
impossible ever to do right in performing them:
to perform them is always to do wrong. In cases
of this sort, let us say adultery, rightness and
wrongness do not depend on committing it with the
right woman at the right time and in the right
manner, but the mere fact of committing such action at all is to do wrong. It would be just as
absurd to suppose that there is a mean, an excess, and a deficiency in an unjust or a cowardly or a self-indulgent act. For if there were,
we would have a mean of excess and a mean of deficiency, and an excess of excess and a deficiency of deficiency. Just as there cannot be
an excess and a deficiency of self-control and
courage—because the intermediate is, in a sense,
an extreme—so there cannot be a mean, excess,
and deficiency in their respective opposites:
their opposites are wrong regardless of how they
are performed; for, in general, there is no such
thing as the mean of an excess or a deficiency,
or the excess and deficiency of a mean.

*   *   *

8. The relation between the mean and its
    extremes

There are, then, three kinds of disposition:
two are vices (one marked by excess and one by
deficiency), and one, virtue, the mean. Now,
each of these dispositions is, in a sense, opposed to both the others: the extremes are opposites to the middle as well as to one another,
and the middle is opposed to the extremes. Just
as an equal amount is larger in relation to a
smaller and smaller in relation to a larger
amount, so, in the case both of emotions and of
actions, the middle characteristics exceed in relation to the deficiencies and are deficient in

relation to the excess. For example, a brave man seems reckless in relation to a coward, but in relation to a reckless man he seems cowardly. Similarly, a self-controlled man seems self-indulgent in relation to an insensitive man and insensitive in relation to a self-indulgent man, and a generous man extravagant in relation to a stingy man and stingy in relation to an extravagant man. This is the reason why people at the extremes each push the man in the middle over to the other extreme: a coward calls a brave man reckless and a reckless man calls a brave man a coward, and similarly with the other qualities.

However, while these three dispositions are thus opposed to one another, the extremes are more opposed to one another than each is to the median; for they are further apart from one another than each is from the median, just as the large is further removed from the small and the small from the large than either one is from the equal. Moreover, there appears to be a certain similarity between some extremes and their median, e.g., recklessness resembles courage and extravagance generosity; but there is a very great dissimilarity between the extremes. But things that are furthest removed from one another are defined as opposites, and that means that the further things are removed from one another the more opposite they are.

In some cases it is the deficiency and in others the excess that is more opposed to the median. For example, it is not the excess, recklessness, which is more opposed to courage, but the deficiency, cowardice; while in the case of self-control it is not the defect, insensitivity, but the excess, self-indulgence which is more opposite. There are two causes for this. One arises from the nature of the thing itself: when one of the extremes is closer and more similar to the median, we do not treat it but rather the other extreme as the opposite of the median. For instance, since recklessness is believed to be more similar and closer to courage, and cowardice less similar, it is cowardice rather than recklessness which we treat as the opposite of courage. For what is further removed from the middle is regarded as being more opposite. So much for the first cause which arises from the thing itself. The second reason is found in ourselves: the more we are naturally attracted to anything, the more opposed to the median does this thing appear to be. For example, since we are naturally more attracted to pleasure we incline more easily to self-indulgence than to a disciplined kind of life. We describe as more opposed to the mean those things toward which our tendency is stronger; and for that reason the excess, self-indulgence, is more opposed to self-control than is its corresponding deficiency.

9. How to attain the mean

Our discussion has sufficiently established (1) that moral virtue is a mean and in what sense it is a mean; (2) that it is a mean between two vices, one of which is marked by excess and the other by deficiency; and (3) that it is a mean in the sense that it aims at the median in the emotions and in actions. That is why it is a hard task to be good; in every case it is a task to find the median: for instance, not everyone can find the middle of a circle, but only a man who has the proper knowledge. Similarly, anyone can get angry—that is easy—or can give away money or spend it; but to do all this to the right person, to the right extent, at the right time, for the right reason, and in the right way is no longer something easy that anyone can do. It is for this reason that good conduct is rare, praiseworthy, and noble.

The first concern of a man who aims at the median should, therefore, be to avoid the extreme which is more opposed to it, as Calypso advises: "Keep clear your ship of yonder spray and surf."[22] For one of the two extremes is more in error than the other, and since it is extremely difficult to hit the mean, we must, as the saying has it, sail

507

in the second best way and take the lesser evil; and we can best do that in the manner we have described.

Moreover, we must watch the errors which have the greatest attraction for us personally. For the natural inclination of one man differs from that of another, and we each come to recognize our own by observing the pleasure and pain produced in us (by the different extremes). We must then draw ourselves away in the opposite direction, for by pulling away from error we shall reach the middle, as men do when they straighten warped timber. In every case we must be especially on our guard against pleasure and what is pleasant, for when it comes to pleasure we cannot act as unbiased judges. Our attitude toward pleasure should be the same as that of the Trojan elders was toward Helen, and we should repeat on every occasion the words they addressed to her.[23] For if we dismiss pleasure as they dismissed her, we shall make fewer mistakes.

In summary, then, it is by acting in this way that we shall best be able to hit the median. But this is no doubt difficult, especially when particular cases are concerned. For it is not easy to determine in what manner, with what person, on what occasion, and for how long a time one ought to be angry. There are times when we praise those who are deficient in anger and call them gentle, and other times when we praise violently angry persons and call them manly. However, we do not blame a man for slightly deviating from the course of goodness, whether he strays toward excess or toward deficiency, but we do blame him if his deviation is great and cannot pass unnoticed. It is not easy to determine by a formula at what point and for how great a divergence a man deserves blame; but this difficulty is, after all, true of all objects of sense perception: determinations of this kind depend upon particular circumstances, and the decision rests with our (moral) sense.

This much, at any rate, is clear: that the median characteristic is in all fields the one that deserves praise, and that it is sometimes necessary to incline toward the excess and sometimes toward the deficiency. For it is in this way that we will most easily hit upon the median, which is the point of excellence.

Notes

[1] What we get in this paragraph is Aristotle's answer to the problem raised at the opening of Plato's _Meno_ (70a) whether excellence is acquired by teaching, by practice, or by nature. This problem, also hinted at by Aristotle at the beginning of I. 3 above, is fully articulated in _Eudemian Ethics_ I. 1, 1214a14 ff.

[2] _Energeia_ and _dynamis_. For Aristotle, the _dynamis_ ('capacity,' 'ability,' 'potentiality') remains latent until it is developed into an _energeia_ ('actuality,' 'activity'), i.e., into an actual result or achievement.

[3] _Techne_.

[4] _Hexis_.

[5] _Theoria_.

[6] See VI. 13.

[7] See I. 3.

[8] This looks like a direct reference to Anaxagoras' statement (frg. B 21a DK[6]): "Appearances are a glimpse of the unseen."

[9] See Plato, _Republic_ III. 12, 401e–402a; _Laws_ II. 653a–654d.

[10] The idea here evidently is that the pleasure of wrongdoing must be cured by applying its opposite, i.e., pain.

[11] At the end of chap. 2, 1104a27–29.

[12] Probably Speusippus is meant here.

[13] Heraclitus, frg. B 85 DK[6]: "To fight against anger is hard; for it buys what it wants at the price of the soul."

[14] It is difficult to find an exact English equivalent for _mousike_. For although the concept includes music, its meaning is wide enough to encompass all those artistic and intellectual activities over which the Muses preside. Accordingly,

it ranges from the writing and reciting of poetry to dancing, astronomy, etc.

[15]See above, chap. 1.

[16]For this peculiar argument, which defines virtue as a characteristic by a process of elimination of alternatives, see the discussion of quality in Categories 8, 8b25-11a38, where Aristotle distinguishes four types of quality: (a) characteristic and disposition (hexis, diathesis), (b) capacity and incapacity (dynamis, adynamia), (c) affective quality and emotion (pathetike poiotes, pathos), and (d) shape and form (schema, morphe). These and none other are the only possible types of quality, and since (d) shape and form obviously have nothing to do with the qualities (i.e., virtues) of the soul, only the first three are dealt with here. For a fuller treatment, see H. H. Joachim, pp. 81-85. Cf. hexis.

[17]See above, chap. 2.

[18]It is impossible to capture in English the overtone these three words carry. They can also mean "too large," "too small," and "fair."

[19]Milo of Croton, said to have lived in the second half of the sixth century B.C., was a wrestler famous for his remarkable strength.

[20]The author of this verse is unknown.

[21]Phronesis. The concept is discussed more fully in VI. 5.

[22]Homer, Odyssey XII. 219-220. The advice was actually given not by Calypso but by Circe (XII. 108-110), and in the lines quoted here Odysseus is the speaker, relaying the advice to his helmsman. Aristotle's quotations from Homer are apparently made from memory, and are rarely exact.

[23]The reference is to Homer, Iliad III. 156-160, tr. Richmond Lattimore (Chicago: University of Chicago Press, 1951):

'Surely there is no blame on Trojans and strong-greaved Achaians if for long time they suffer hardship for a woman like this one. Terrible is the likeness of her fact to immortal goddesses. Still, though she be such, let her go away in the ships, lest she be left behind, a grief to us and our children.'

A Religious Approach

Christian Adulthood*
William J. Bouwsma

The elasticity of Christianity, as it has accommodated itself to two thousand years of cultural change, is well known; and it poses special problems for the identification of a peculiarly "Christian" conception of what it means to be an adult. It is also likely to make any attempt at such definition seem arbitrary. I shall nevertheless try to show in this essay that Christianity does contain a characteristic conception of healthy human maturity, but to do so it will be necessary to distinguish between what I shall call <u>historical</u> and <u>normative</u> Christianity. Historical Christianity reflects the composite of those cultural impulses that make up what is commonly thought of as Christian civilization; much of it is not specifically Christian, although it constitutes a large part of what has been believed by Christians. Its conception of "adulthood" is often an eclectic mixture of somewhat contrary impulses, and it is likely to be unstable. But normative Christianity is an ideal type. It is normative in the sense that it builds on and is consistent with those biblical norms about human nature and human destiny that give to Christianity whatever precise identity it may possess. It is also, therefore, heavily indebted to Judaism. It is not ahistorical, but it can rarely be found in a pure form. Its conception of adulthood can be stated with come coherence.

The conception of maturity in historical Christianity can be further described as a mix-

*Reprinted by permission of the author and American Academy of Arts and Sciences from <u>Daedalus</u>, Spring 1976.

ture of two quite different notions, which I shall call the idea of <u>manhood</u> and the idea of <u>adulthood</u>. The significance of this second distinction may be suggested by the differing etymologies of the two terms. The Germanic <u>man</u> is considered by most linguists to be derived from an Indo-European verb meaning "to think" (cf. the Latin <u>mens</u>); it thus refers to a supposedly qualitive difference between human beings and other animals, and "manhood" would thus imply entrance into a fully rational existence. But <u>adult</u> comes from the Latin <u>adolescere</u>, "to grow up." It is (or can be) neutral about the nature of growth; it implies a process rather than the possession of a particular status or specific faculty. The two terms, which are often confused in our culture, can also be taken to represent the two major but contrasting impulses in the Western tradition. <u>Adulthood</u>, as I will use it here, is related to the anthropology of the Bible; and its suggestion of process hints at the distinctively dynamic qualities of the Hebrew language.[1] But <u>manhood</u> is a creation of classical antiquity, and it reflects the need of classical culture to organize all experience in terms of adsolute, static, and qualitative categories.

The idea of manhood is elaborated in the classical formulations of <u>paideia</u> or <u>humanitas</u>, which pointed, for the Greek and Latin educational traditions, to the peculiar excellence of the human species. Unlike adulthood, manhood tends, with rare exceptions, to be sexually specific, and thus it is one source of the tendency to deny full maturity to women.[2] It also differs from adulthood in its rejection of individuality, and it is oriented to the goal rather than the processes of human development. We can see this in the relative indifference of classical humanism to the psychology of the child and its significance for the formation of the man.[3] Childhood, in this conception, was conceived not as the positive foundation of maturity but as formlessness or chaos, and manhood was the result of the imposition on this refractory matter, by education, of an ideal form. With the achievement of manhood, childhood was decisively and happily left behind.

Embedded in this conception were both the metaphysical distinction between form and substance, with its hints of anthropological dualism, and a characteristic distinction, within man, among the several elements of the human personality; soul and body, or reason, will, and passion. These were seen not merely as analytical devices but as real, qualitative distinctions corresponding to distinctions in the structure of all reality. Similarly, childhood and manhood had to be qualitatively distinct; they could not coincide, for insofar as a human being was still a child he could not be a man. Here we may discern the characteristic resistance of ancient rationalism to ambiguity and paradox.

In this view, some of man's faculties were also ontologically superior and sovereign, others inferior, dangerous except in subordination, and thus demanding suppression. Manhood was specifically associated with the rule of reason, which was at once the spark of divinity in man, his access to the higher rationality of the divinely animated cosmos, and the controlling principle of human behavior; the function of reason was to order the personality into conformity with the larger order of the universe as it was apprehended by the mind. The principles of reason thus come from "above," and the ideal man is therefore a fully rational being who pits his reason against the chaotic forces both within himself and in the world.

The assimilation of this conception into historical Christianity has been responsible for its tendencies to an idealism in which the religious quest is understood as a commitment to higher things, with a corresponding contempt for lower. Anthropologically, this has often pitted the soul (more or less associated with reason) against the passions and the body; it has also been responsi-

513

ble for the doubtful association of Christianity
with the notion of the immortality of a disembod-
ied soul. And certain conclusions have followed
for the ideal of human maturity often encountered
in historical Christianity. This conception is
the source of a Christian ethics of repression,
directed (like the pagan ethics of the Hellenistic
world) chiefly against sexuality as the most im-
perious of the bodily passions; of Christian distrust of spontaneity, a quality especially associated with childhood; and of the notion of the
mature Christian—this might be called the Christian ideal of manhood—as a person who has so
successfully cultivated his own bad conscience,
his guilt for his persistent attraction to lower
things, that he can only come to terms with his
existence by a deliberate and rigorous program of
self-discipline and self-denial in the interest
of saving his soul. The Christian man, in this
conception, has consciously separated himself as
far as possible from his childhood, in obedience
to a higher wisdom that is readily distinguishable from folly.[4]

We can encounter this conception of Christianity in many places, notably among its modern
critics. Nietzsche's morbid caricature of Christianity owed a good deal to the conception,[5]
though Nietzsche also understood the significance
of biblical Christianity better than many of his
Christian contemporaries.[6] And of course this
kind of Christianity is now peculiarly vulnerable
to attack. A case in point is a recent work by a
British psychologist, whose position will both
help to bring out the human implications of the
classical strand in historical Christianity and
throw into relief what I will present as normative Christianity. This writer addressed herself
especially to the historical impact of Christianity on human development. Noting Jesus' association of childhood with the kingdom of heaven, she
remarked:

Socrates encouraged his young followers to develop towards maturity; Jesus tried to reduce

514

his to the level of children. The Gospels contain numerous statements in which the attitudes of children are compared favorably with those of adults. . . . These statements are so often quoted with approval that probably few pause to consider whether it is really a good thing for adults to think and behave like children. What attracted Jesus towards "little children," obviously, was their unquestioning trust in adults, and his ideal was to be surrounded by adults who had a similar trust in him.

This writer's somewhat uncritical commitment to the classical ideal of a manhood that leaves childhood behind seems reasonably clear, though her sense of the implications of that ideal and of the historical roots of the kind of Christianity she indicts is somewhat confused. But her attitude is not uncommon, and her depiction of one prominent strand in historical Christianity is not unfounded. She discerns in Christianity an authoritarian impulse that, rejecting true adulthood, aims to reduce adults to a childish malleability, and so proves also destructive of the positive qualities of childhood. Christianity, in her view, is a "harsh, joyless, guilt-obsessed religion that makes happiness suspect and virtue unattractive." It is, in essence, an "ascetic, otherworldly religion which for centuries has served to stifle the free intelligence and to limit disastrously the range of human sympathies." It is dominated by "a self-centred preoccupation with one's own virtue and one's own salvation," and accordingly the Christian has a "negative, passive, masochistic character and (an) obsession with suffering and sacrifice."[7]

But this indictment neglects to notice that similar charges against historical Christianity have been periodically made from within the Christian community, a fact which suggests that we may find in Christianity itself a very different understanding of the Christian position. Thus it has not escaped the attention of Christians that the authority claimed for Christian belief has at

times tended to degenerate into an authoritarianism that contradicts the central meaning of Christianity. It is undeniable, for example, and certainly by Christians, that the Christian clergy
have in some periods claimed, as Christ's succes-
sors, to be "fathers" with a more than legitimate
paternal authority over the laity, their "children." In 1301, for example, Boniface VIII
brought a long tradition of such paternalism to a
climax in a stern letter to the king of France.
"Hearken, dearest son," he wrote, "to the precepts
of thy father and bend the ear of thy heart to the
teaching of the master who, here on earth, stands
in place of Him who alone is master and lord."[8]
But the practical authoritarianism in Christian
history is easily exaggerated; the claims of ec-
clesiastical authority have rarely gone unchal-
lenged. Those of Pope Boniface, indeed, resulted
in a major disaster for the papacy at the hands of
men who also considered themselves Christians.
Some Christians have also rejected in principle
the attitudes he represented. Calvin, for example, placed a highly unfavorable construction on
clerical paternalism. "Hence it appears," he
declared, "what kind of Christianity there is under the Papacy, when the pastors labor to the ut-
most of their power to keep the people in absolute
infancy."[9] Indeed, the papacy itself has shown
recent indications of sympathy for Calvin's position. The aggiornamento of John XXIII has been
widely interpreted as an admission of the coming-
of-age of the laity, and Pope John himself suggested a new understanding of adulthood in his
transparent inability to take seriously his own
status and dignity as an adult. Paradoxically,
this was somehow interpreted by many of those who
observed him as the most persuasive evidence of
his maturity.

The paradox of Pope John takes us to the
heart of the conception of adulthood in normative
Christianity, which I shall now approach directly
through a text in the Pauline letter to the
Ephesians:[10]

> So shall we all at last attain to the unity in-
> herent in our faith and our knowledge of the
> Son of God—to mature manhood, measured by
> nothing less than the full stature of Christ.
> We are no longer to be children, tossed by the
> waves and whirled about by every fresh gust of
> teaching. . . . No, let us speak the truth in
> love; so shall we fully grow up in Christ. He
> is the head, and on him the whole body depends.
> Bonded and knit together by every constituent
> joint, the whole frame grows through the due ac-
> tivity of each part, and builds itself up in love.

Here we are immediately introduced to several important themes. One is the strictly metaphorical
meaning of "childhood," whose characteristics may
be encountered in men of all ages; another is the
association of maturity with personal stability.
Still another is the identification of full adulthood with the loving solidarity of mankind, and
this will concern us later. But it is of particular importance for our immediate purposes that
the measure of true adulthood is finally "the full
stature of Christ," for this is an absolute standard, in relation to which no man, whatever his
age, can claim to be fully an adult. This peculiarity of Christian adulthood especially struck
Calvin, who emphasized it in commenting on the
text:[11]

> As (the apostle) had spoken of that full-grown
> age toward which we proceed throughout the
> whole course of our life, so now he tells us
> that, during such a progress, we ought not to
> be like children. He thus sets an intervening
> period between childhood and maturity. Those
> are children who have not yet taken a step in
> the way of the Lord, but still hesitate, who
> have not yet determined what road they ought
> to choose, but move sometimes in one direction,
> and sometimes in another, always doubtful, al-
> ways wavering. But those are thoroughly found-
> ed in the doctrine of Christ, who, although not
> yet perfect, have so much wisdom and vigor as
> to choose what is best, and proceed steadily in
> the right course. Thus the life of believers,

longing constantly for their appointed status, is like adolescence. So when I said that in this life we are never men, this ought not to be pressed to the other extreme, as they say, as if there were no progress beyond childhood. After being born in Christ, we ought to grow, so as not to be children in understanding . . . although we have not arrived at man's estate, we are at any rate older boys.

Here the paradox is fully stated: that the Christian, however ripe in years, cannot think of himself as a completed man. Christianity has, then, a conception of full adulthood; the goal of human development is total conformity to the manhood of Christ. But since this is a transcendent goal, the practical emphasis in Christian adulthood is on the process rather than its end. Since it is impossible to achieve perfect maturity in this life, the duty of the Christian is simply to develop constantly toward it. The essential element in the Christian idea of adulthood is, accordingly, the capacity for growth, which is assumed to be a potentiality of any age of life. It is in this sense that the Christian life is like adolescence, that stage in which the adult seems, however ambiguously, trembling to be born.

But adolescence also suggests the coexistence, within the personality, of the child and whatever it is that he promises to become, and this points to another peculiarity of the Christian view: its insistence on the continuity, rather than the absolute qualitative difference, between the child and the man. The developing adult is assumed to incorporate positively the individual and (in fact) irrepressible character of the child. Adulthood assumes that the child cannot be left behind, but is the basis of the more mature personality. Thus the child lives on in the man, so that child and man are somehow identical, a conclusion, from the standpoint of classical manhood, that is paradoxical and absurd. It is evident also that the idea of adulthood is related to various other Christian paradoxes:

that the last shall be first, that foolishness is
wisdom, and that God, who is himself "highest,"
should lower himself to become a corporeal man—
and indeed, as though this metaphysical confusion
were not sufficiently degrading, that he should
come not as a hero or a king but as a humble figure who is put to death for others. The paradox
of adulthood points to the folly of the cross.

Similarly adulthood does not recognize real
qualitative and hierarchical distinctions within
the personality; it sees man, whether child or
adult, as a living whole. It may sometimes use
such terms as "spirit," "soul," "mind," or
"flesh"; but this vocabulary (which also reflects
the difficulties of translating the thought of
one culture into the language of another) is intended to describe various modes of activity of
what is, in itself, an undifferentiated unity.
The anthropology of normative Christianity can
only be pictured, not as a hierarchy of discrete
faculties, but as a circle organized around a
vital center, the core of human being (cf. Latin
cor, "heart"), whose qualities, for good or evil,
permeate the whole.[12] Thus, where classical anthropology sought to understand man by identifying the several faculties of the personality and
ranking them according to their objective value,
normative Christianity has been inclined to accept and even to celebrate the mysteries of the
total personality.[13]

This conception of Christian adulthood is,
of course, not only normative; it has also found
concrete historical expression, though I think it
has rarely been dominant in the history of Christianity.[14] Nevertheless, the availability to
Christians in all subsequent ages of the canonical
Scriptures and the constant effort to penetrate to
their meaning have meant that, however obscured by
misunderstandings arising out of the cultural limitations of their readers, a biblical conception
of adulthood has always played at least a counter-
point to the classical conception of manhood. It
has never altogether disappeared from later West-

ern culture, however muted it may have become; it has regularly helped to block radical intrusions of the classical idea of manhood into Christianity (I suspect that both Arianism and Pelagianism are linked to that conception); and occasionally, though usually only briefly, it has swelled out unmistakably as a major theme. It is prominent in the mature Augustine, in the more Pauline manifestations of the Catholic and Protestant Reformations, and in twentieth-century neo-orthodoxy and biblical theology, with their heightened cultural relativism and their enhanced sensitivity to history.

This conception of adulthood is in fact so inextricably linked to normative Christianity as a whole that we can trace it through a series of basic and specifically Jewish and Christian doctrines and, in this way, explore its implications more deeply. Its foundations can be discerned in the biblical account of the creation, which incorporates a number of insights basic to Christian thought. This is not, as in the creation myths of surrounding peoples, the culmination of a primordial struggle between a creator and the forces of chaos, coeternal with, perhaps even anterior to, him; it is a true beginning. This has various implications. God created the universe; and, as this was eventually understood, he created it out of nothing,[15] a doctrine that establishes both the absolute transcendence of God and his full sovereignty over every aspect of creation.[16] And since the creation specifically included the heavens as well as the earth, the story subverts the classical distinctions between high things and low.[17] If hierarchies of any kind are admissible in the biblical universe, they cannot, at any rate, have any sacred basis. They possess only relative value; all created things are, in the only relationship of absolute significance, on the same level, as creatures.[18] For man this means not only that he must recognize his creatureliness but that he must see it in every aspect of his being. No part of him is divine, and therefore none can claim to rule by divine right over the others.[19] Among its other implications, this precludes the possibility of repression as a way of ordering the personality. Because man was created as a whole, indeed in God's own image, every aspect of man is good and worthy of development, for "God saw all that he had made, and it was very good" (Gen. 1:31).[20]

In addition, this good creation is depicted as a work of time, and, as the sequel reveals, God has built into it the dimension of process and change. Time and change, so dimly regarded in the classical world of thought, are therefore also necessarily good; the biblical God underlined their positive significance by presenting himself, after the fall, as the Lord of history who encounters and reveals himself to man in temporal experience.[21] The Old Testament is fundamentally historical, and the New is based on a further series of historical events in which God uniquely enters and sanctifies time.[22] In this conception the past acquires peculiar significance. It is that aspect of time which man can know through memory, which indeed he must ponder deeply because it gives meaning to the present and promise to the future.[23] The past demonstrates God's care and will for man and therefore it cannot be ignored or repudiated. This explains why the Scriptures so frequently summon man to remember the past, for in an important sense it is contemporaneous with all subsequent time.

The significance of the past also points to the indelible importance of all human experience. It gives meaning to the particular temporal experiences that have shaped each individual during the whole course of his life, so that the biblical idea of time is the foundation for the conception of the worth of the individual personality.[24] But it also gives meaning to the collective experiences of mankind into which all individual experience is ultimately submerged, a conception basic to the discovery of the great historical forces that transcend individual experience.[25] Fundamental to the Christian view of man is, therefore, an insistence on a process of growth in which the past is not left behind but survives, shapes, and is absorbed into the present.[26] The unalterable past provides a stable base for the identity alike of each individual and of every society. St. Augustine's Confessions, with its vivid delineation of a personality changing yet continuous with its past, is a product of this conception.[27] The absence of genuine biography in the classical world has often been remarked.[28] By the same token, the great classical histories sought to reveal the changeless principles governing all change, while the biblical histories were concerned with change itself as God's work and with its shaping impact on men.

The Christian life, then, is conceived as indefinite growth, itself the product of a full engagement with temporal experience involving the whole personality. The Christian is not to evade the challenges, the struggles, the difficulties and dangers of life, but to accept, make his way through, and grow in them. He must be willing to disregard his vulnerability and to venture out, even at the risk of making mistakes, for the sake of growth.[29] This understanding of life finds expression in the figure of the Christian as wayfarer (viator) or pilgrim; Christian conversion is thus not, as in the mystery religions, an immediate entrance into a safe harbor but rather, though its direction has been established, the beginning of a voyage into the unknown.[30] As movement in a direction, it also implies progress, but a progress that remains incomplete in this life.[31] The "other-worldliness" of Christianity is significant, in this context, as the basis of the open-endedness of both personal and social development.

From this standpoint, just as the essential condition of Christian adulthood is the capacity for growth, the worst state of man is not so much his sinfulness (for sins can be forgiven) as the cessation of growth, arrested development, remaining fixed at any point in life. In these terms, just as adulthood requires growth, its opposite—what might be called the Christian conception of immaturity—is the refusal to grow, the inability to cope with an open and indeterminate future (that is, the future itself), in effect the rejection of life as a process.

There is, however, a close connection between the rejection of growth and the problem of sin; the refusal to grow is, in an important sense, the source of all particular sins. The story of the fall reveals the connection, and may also be taken as the biblical analysis of the causes and the consequence of human immaturity. It contrasts essential man, as God created him, with actual man, man as he appears in history, who is fearful of the future and afraid of growth. The story explains this as a result of man's faithlessness. For the fall is caused not by a breach of the moral law but by man's violation of the relationship fundamental to his existence; it belongs to religious rather than to ethical experience. Primordial man, whose goodness stems from his dependence on God, is depicted as rejecting the creatureliness basic to his perfection and claiming independent value and even divinity for himself. He seeks to become "like gods," and implicit in this pretension is the rejection of his own further development. By complacently making himself as he is the divine center of his universe, he rejects the possibility of change and learns to fear all experience. Thus he loses his openness to the future and his capacity for growth; in short he repudiates his capacity for adulthood.[32] The claim to divinity, therefore, paradoxically results in a pervasive anxiety. And out of this anxiety man commits a whole range of particular ethical sins, the end products of his faithlessness. Thus, too, he begins to suffer particular sensations of guilt.[33]

A further symptom of his immaturity may be seen in man's perennial tendency, implicit in his claim to divinity, to absolutize his understanding of the universe in a frantic effort to hold his anxiety in check. This, I take it, would be

the Christian explanation for the relatively
small influence of a biblical understanding of
the human situation in Christendom itself. Man
solemnly invests his culture, which is in fact
always contingent on his own limited and self-
centered vision and need, with ultimate meaning,
thereby imprisoning himself within a man-made,
rigidly bounded, and internally defined universe
that further destroys the possibility for growth.
He philosophizes, claims access to the real truth
of things, to being-in-itself. This is the significance normative Christianity would assign to
the absolute qualitative distinctions of classical culture, a man-made substitute for biblical
faith. Harvey Cox has described such constructions as a "play-pen," a nice image in its implications for human development.[34] Their power to
inhibit human sympathy, with its special value
for personal growth, is suggested by the need of
the Greek (in an impulse with which we are all
quite familiar) to see the man who differed from
himself as a barbarian. Without faith—what Tillich has called the courage to be, which is also
the courage to become—the only escape from man's
intolerable fear of chaos is the idolatry of cultural absolutism. So, without faith, man tends
to bigotry, for any grasp of the universe other
than his own is too dangerous for him to contemplate. It is in this light that we can understand the full implications of the pagan charge
that the early Christians were enemies of culture. In a sense this was true then, and it remains true; for normative Christianity all culture is a human artifact, and no absolute validity can be attached to its insights. Such a position is always likely to be disturbing, as
every social scientist has discovered.

Yet normative Christianity does not deny the
practical values of culture. It simply insists
that, just as man is a creature of God, so culture is a creature of man, not his master. Secularized in this way, culture can serve many useful human purposes, and it can even become a vehicle of Christian purposes when men fully recog-

nize their dependence on God.[35] But culture can never be ultimately serious. Indeed, there are tensions in the Scriptures that suggest that some dimensions of biblical religion itself may be understood as products of culture, or at any rate set in a larger context within which, like culture, they can be seen to possess only relative authority. Job discovered this in his confrontation with an inscrutable but infinitely holy God, and we can also sense something of this in the tension in the Old Testament between prophetic religion and the law. The law is like culture in the sense that it defines and particularizes sins, and the prophets do not deny the validity of such definition. But prophetic religion also insists, not simply that there is more to be said about man's situation before God than this, but, in addition, that definition is significant only in relation to the indefinite and open.[36]

If the Christian analysis of the evils in historical existence can be understood as a diagnosis of immaturity, the Christian conception of salvation can be similarly construed as a description of the only way to recover that capacity for growth in which true adulthood consists. The basic problem here is to replace anxiety with faith, so that man can enter an open future with confidence and grow through his experience. But here he encounters a problem he cannot solve. Faith is a function of man's dependence on God, but it is precisely this relationship that man in historical existence has repudiated. In effect he has destroyed the "true self" God made, and he must therefore be remade. And as Augustine asked, "If you could not make yourself, how could you remake yourself?"[37] Described psychologically, the predicament in which man finds himself is one of entrapment and bondage—in short, of total helplessness.[38] Furthermore, because man was created a living whole and repudiated his creatureliness as a whole, there is no area of his personality left untouched by his alienation from God and thus from his true self. This is the precise meaning of the often misunderstood doctrine of total depravity:

525

it signifies that man has no resources by which he can save himself.

Yet exactly here, in the recognition that this is the case, lies the first step toward the resumption of growth. Once man sees himself as he is, acknowledges his limits, perceives the contingency of all his own constructions, and admits that they have their sources only in himself, he is well on the way to accepting his creaturehood and open to the possibility of faith. Faith begins, then, not in illusion but in an absolute and terrifying realism; its first impulse is paradoxically the perception that faith itself is beyond man's own control, that there is no help in him, that his only resource is the grace of a loving God. The Christian, as Barth remarked, is "moved by a grim horror of illusion." "What is pleasing to God comes into being when all human righteousness is gone, irretrievably gone, when men are uncertain and lost, when they have abandoned all ethical and religious illusions, and when they have renounced every hope in this world and in this heaven. . . . Religion is the possibility of the removal of every ground of confidence except confidence in God alone. Piety is the possibility of the removal of the last traces of a firm foundation upon which we can erect a system of thought."[39] Salvation thus begins with confession, the admission of sin and ultimately of faithlessness, which is therapeutic in the sense that it demands total honesty and is directed to the removal of every false basis for human development. Augustine's Confessions might be described as the Christian form of psychoanalysis, the retracing, in God's presence and with his help, of the whole course of a life, which aims to recover the health of faith.[40]

By confession and repentance, themselves a response to faith, man recognizes his helplessness and thus becomes open to help. This help is revealed and made available by God himself through the saving work of Christ, in which God again demonstrates his infinite concern with history. The

526

response to Christ in faith expresses man's full acceptance of that creatureliness which is the essential condition of his authentic existence and growth; the answer to sin is not virtue but faith. By faith man is dramatically relieved of his false maturity, his claims to a self-defined "manhood," and enabled to being again to grow. This is why conversion can be described as a "rebirth," which resembles birth also in that it is not subject to the control of him who is reborn; baptism, the ritual of rebirth, is an initiation into true existence. Freed from the anxieties of self-sufficiency by faith, man can grow, both individually and collectively. Indeed, only now has he the strength to face directly the contingency, the inadequacy, the slavery and sinfulness of all merely human culture. He can risk seeing it clearly because, with faith, he has also received the gift of hope. From this standpoint the Gospel is the good news because it frees man for adulthood.

But this is an adulthood that involves, always, the whole man; thus its goal is symbolized not by the immortaility of the soul but by the resurrection of the body as representing the total self that must be made whole. As Augustine exclaimed in old age, "I want to be healed completely, for I am a complete whole."[41] Christian maturity is manifested, therefore, not only in the understanding but more profoundly in the affective life and in the loving actions that are rooted in the feelings. Christ is above all the model of absolute love. Conformity to this loving Christ is the goal of human development; in Augustine's words, "he is our native country." But he is also the key to Christian adulthood, for "he made himself also the way to that country."[42] The Christian grows both in Christ and to Christ.

Again we encounter a set of paradoxes, the first of which is that man's full acceptance of his creatureliness, the admission of his absolute dependence on God in Christ, proves to be the essential condition of human freedom. For the only

alternative to the life of faith is bondage to
the self, to the anxieties and the false abso-
lutisms embedded in human culture, by which man
is otherwise imprisoned. Faith, in these terms,
is the necessary condition of true autonomy, of
freedom not from the constraints of experience—
the Stoic ideal—but freedom to grow in and
through them that is essential to adulthood. The
Pauline injunction to work out one's own salvation in fear and trembling suggests this freedom,
and suggests also the strains attendant on growth,
but it would be impossible to fulfill without the
faith that "it is God which worketh in you both
to will and to do of his pleasure" (Phil. 2:13).
This kind of freedom supplies the strength to
challenge authority maturely, without the rebel-
liousness, arrogance, and destructiveness symptomatic of insecurity, or to criticize the definition of one's own life and to examine the dubious
sources of one's own actions.[43]

At the same time, obedience to God paradoxically proves a far lighter burden than obedience
to human ordinances or the requirements of culture, even though—another paradox—it is, in any
final sense, impossible. For Christian righteousness consists not in a moral quality that must be
maintained at all costs but in a relationship of
favor and peace with God that is the source (rather than the consequence) of moral effort. If the
Christian is in some sense virtuous, his virtue
arises from love rather than duty, and if he
fails, he can count on forgiveness. Thus, though
he must recognize and confess his guilt as part
of his more general realism, he is not to nourish
or cling to it, for this would amount to the rejection of God's love. Repentance means allowing
our guilt to be God's concern, and all guilt,
otherwise so paralyzing for the moral life, must
be swallowed up in love and gratitude. Christian
adulthood is a growth away from, not toward guilt.

By the same token it cannot be repressive,
not only because no power in the human personality is entitled to excise or even control any

other (this is the happy implication of total depravity), but above all because such an effort,
since it cannot touch the quality of the heart,
would be superficial and in the end futile.
Christian thinkers have sometimes displayed great
insight into the nature of self-imposed control.
Calvin's description of the process implies some
acquaintance with its physiological consequences,
as well as realism about the social necessity for
restraint in a world in which those, too, who are
growing in Christ must recognize that they are not
fully and dependably adult: "the more (men) restrain themselves, the more violently they are in-
flamed within; they ferment, they boil, ready to
break out into external acts, if they were not
prevented by this dread of the law. . . . But yet
this constrained and extorted righteousness is
necessary to the community. . . ."[44] But the
ideal of Christian adulthood is not control but
spontaneity; it is, in Augustine's words, to "love
and do what you will."[45]

The spontaneity in the Christian ideal of
adulthood points to still another paradox: its
deliberate cultivation of, and delight in, the
qualities of the child, now understood less meta-
phorically.[46] Childhood, after all, assumes
growth, and it is in this respect fundamentally
different from childishness, which rejects it; in
this sense childhood is a model for adulthood.
Indeed, childhood welcomes the years, unaware that
they bring decay and death, and the deep and fear-
less interest of the child in his experience permits him to ask simple but profound questions
that, later, may seem wearisome or too dangerous
to be entertained. The child is not afraid to express wonder and astonishment.[47] Thus the confident trust in life of a healthy child, so different from the wariness that develops with age, has
often been taken in Christian thought as a natural
prototype of faith; in this sense, the adult
Christian life is something like a return to
childhood. As Kierkegaard remarked, it seems to
reverse the natural order: "Therefore one does
not begin by being a child and then becoming pro-

gressively more intimate (with God) as he grows older; no, one becomes more and more a child."[48] But there is, in this reversal, realism about the actual results of maturation, which ordinarily destroys the openness and wonder of childhood and replaces it with disguises and suspicion, with sophistication and a "knowingness" that chiefly serve to exclude a profounder knowledge. For the man, a return to the values of childhood is only possible when the inadequacies of his pretended manhood have been recognized in repentance and confession and he can take the way of faith. Then the growth of the man can again be like that of the child.[49]

This suggests a further peculiarity in the Christian view of adulthood: its lack of interest in chronological disparity. All Christians, insofar as they are growing in Christ, are equally becoming adults—or equally children.[50] Baptism is no respecter of age. An important consequence of this is to limit the authority and influence of parents, for where parent and child are both growing up in Christ,[51] the parent cannot be the only, or even the primary, pattern of maturity.[52] The Christian parent has failed unless his child achieves sufficient autonomy to establish his own direct relation to Christ. Nor is there sexual differentiation in the Christian conception: girls and boys, women and men are equally growing up in Christ.

But there is still another respect in which Christian adulthood merges with childhood: in its appreciation for play. This may be related to Paul's contrast between the wisdom of this world and the divine foolishness by which its hollowness is revealed.[53] The recurrent figure of the Christian fool, both child and saint, has sought to embody this conception. But it also has lighter, if equally serious, implications. The security of dependence on a loving God makes it unnecessary to confront life with a Stoic solemnity; the Christian can relax, even (again paradoxically) when he is most profoundly and actively confronting the sinfulness of the world. He can enjoy playfully (which also means to delight in, for itself, not to exploit instrumentally, for himself) the goodness of the creation. His culture can be an unbounded playground for free and joyous activity. He can risk the little adventures on which play depends. The loving human relationships of the Christian life can find expression in mutual play, through which we give pleasure to one another. Play is a natural expression of the joy of faith, which makes it possible to engage in life, even the hard work of life, as a game that has its own seriousness (for without their special kind of seriousness games could scarcely interest us), and that yet can be enjoyed precisely because the ultimate seriousness of existence lies elsewhere, with God.54 But play is also related to that seriousness. Bushnell saw play as "the symbol and interpreter" of Christian liberty and pointed to its place in the eschatological vision of Zechariah 8:5: "And the streets of the city shall be full of boys and girls, playing in the streets."55

I have treated these various elements in the Christian conception of adulthood as aspects of an ideal for individual development, but to leave the matter at this would be to neglect an essential dimension of the Christian position. Like Judaism, Christianity has usually seen the individual in close and organic community with others. The Pauline description of growing up in Christ, though it has obvious implications for the individual, is primarily concerned with the growth of the Christian community; it is finally the church as one body, and perhaps ultimately all mankind, that must reach "mature manhood." The primary experiences through which the Christian grows are social experiences. One encounters Christ and the opportunity to serve him in others; the maturity of the individual is realized only in loving unity with others.56 The power of growth is thus finally a function of community, and, at the same time, maturity finds expression in identification with other men; Christ, the model of human

531

adulthood, was supremely "the man for others."[57] Through this identification of the individual with the body of Christ, the Christian conception of adulthood merges finally into history and eschatology.

Notes

[1] Cf. Thorlief Boman, Hebrew Thought Compared with Greek, tr. Jules L. Moreau (New York, 1970), esp. pp. 28-33, 45-69.

[2] An exception can be found in Seneca's letter to his mother, known as the Consolation to Helvia, in which he recommends a standard program of literary and philosophical studies to console her for his exile.

[3] Cf. H. I. Marrou, A History of Education in Antiquity, tr. George Lamb (New York, 1964), pp. 297-98.

[4] A good example of this ideal is John Chrysostom's address to Christian parents on the upbringing of children, translated by M. L. W. Laistner in his Christianity and Pagan Culture in the Later Roman Empire (Ithaca, 1951), pp. 85-122. "Thou art raising up a philosopher and athlete and citizen of heaven," Chrysostom declared; for this he recognized "wisdom" as "the master principle which keeps everything under control," the height of which is "refusal to be excited at childish things." The purpose of education for him is to make the Christian boy "sagacious and to banish all folly": that is, to make him a precocious little Stoic sage. He is to "know the meaning of human desires, wealth, reputation, power" that he "may disdain these and strive after the highest." And the fruit of his maturity consists in the ability to control his passions: if he can only learn "to refrain from anger, he has displayed already all the marks of a philosophic mind."

[5] Cf. The Antichrist, no. 51, tr. Walter Kaufmann: "We others who have the courage to be healthy and also to despise—how we may despise a religion which taught men to misunderstand the body! which does not want to get rid of supersti-

tious belief in souls! which turns insufficient
nourishment into something 'meritorious'! which
fights health as a kind of enemy, devil, temptation! which fancies that one can carry around a
'perfect soul' in a cadaver of a body, and which
therefore found it necessary to concoct a new
conception of 'perfection'—a pale, sickly, idi-
otic-enthusiastic character, so-called 'holiness.'
Holiness—merely a series of symptoms of an impoverished, unnerved, incurably corrupted body."
From the standpoint of normative Christianity,
this seems fair enough as a characterization of
much that has professed to represent Christianity. Wagner's Parsifal is a familiar and particularly morbid expression of this conception.

[6]For a perceptive essay on Nietzsche's relation to Christianity, see Karl Barth, Church Dogmatics, III:2 (Edinburgh, 1960), pp. 231-42.
[7]Margaret Knight, Honest to Man (London,
1974), pp. 41-42, 193, viii, 21, 196. The popular character of this work by no means reduces
its value for our purposes.
[8]Quoted by John Mundy, Europe in the High
Middle Ages (London, 1973), p. 323.
[9]Calvin's New Testament Commentaries, XI, tr.
T. H. L. Parker (Grand Rapids, 1972), p. 183 (on
Ephesians 4:14.
[10]Ephesians 4:13-16. I use the translation in
The New English Bible. The precise authorship of
this epistle is a matter of dispute, but there
seems to be little doubt about its Pauline inspiration.
[11]New Testament Commentaries, XI, pp. 182-84.
On Paul's metaphorical use of childhood, see
Paul Ricoeur, The Symbolism of Evil, tr. Emerson
Buchanan (Boston, 1969), p. 149.
[12]For biblical anthropology in general, see
Hans Walter Wolff, Anthropology of the Old Testament, tr. Margaret Kohl (Philadelphia, 1974),
esp. pp. 7-9. On Paul's anthropological terminology, so often misunderstood in historical Christianity, cf. Günther Bornkamm, Paul, tr. D. M. G.
Stalker (London, 1971), p. 131.
[13]Cf. Augustine, Confessions, tr. R. S. Pine-
Coffin (London, 1961), p. 224: "What, then, am

I, my God? What is my nature? A life that is
ever varying, full of change, and of immense power. . . . This is the great force of life in living man, mortal though he is." There is much of
this attitude also in Pascal's Pensées, for example, no. 434: "What a chimera then is man! What
a novelty! What a monster, what a chaos, what a
contradiction, what a prodigy! Judge of all
things, imbecile worm of the earth; depository of
truth, a sink of uncertainty and error; the pride
and refuse of the universe!" Barth, Church Dogmatics, III:2, pp. 110-11, has this "[Man's] existence is he himself, who in his very subjectivity, in his very undefinability, is seeking
after the mystery of himself. . . ."

[14]The common notion of the "infinite elasticity
of Christianity" (in Hegel's phrase) is somewhat
misleading; this quality might, with approximately equal justice, be called the infinite elasticity of Hellenism.

[15]There is a useful survey of this idea in the
early church in Barth, Church Dogmatics, III:2,
pp. 152-53. I do not mean to suggest that creation ex nibilo is clear in the Genesis account;
cf. E. A. Speiser, Genesis [The Anchor Bible]
(Garden City, 1964), pp. 13-14. But Job 26:7 suggests it, and it is clearly spelled out in 2
Macc. 7:28.

[16]Cf. Reinhold Niebuhr, The Nature and Destiny
of Man (New York, 1941), I, pp. 133-34.

[17]Cf. Barth, Church Dogmatics, III:2, pp.
350-51.

[18]Wolff, Anthropology, p. 162.

[19]Augustine appears to be struggling toward
this conception in De natura et gratis, ch. 38:
"I am of the opinion that the creature will never
become equal with God, even when so perfect a holiness is accomplished within us as that it shall be
quite incapable of receiving an addition. No, all
who maintain that our progress is to be so complete
that we shall be changed into the substance of God,
and that we shall thus become what He is should
look well to it how they build up their opinion;
upon myself I must confess that it produces no
conviction." But there is a tentativeness here

that suggests the difficulty of the idea of man's creatureliness for the Hellenistic Christian.

[20]Niebuhr, I. p. 167, suggests that "sometimes the authority of this simple dictum . . .was all that prevented Christian faith from succumbing to dualistic and acosmic doctrines which pressed in upon the Christian church."

[21]Augustine's Confessions is, of course, a kind of extended essay on this theme; cf. his On Christian Doctrine, tr. D. W. Robertson, Jr. (Indianapolis, 1958), p. 64: ". . . the order of time, whose creator and administrator is God. . . ."

[22]Cf. Emil Brunner, "The Problem of Time," in Creation: The Impact of an Idea, ed. Daniel O'Connor and Francis Oakley (New York, 1969), p. 124.

[23]Cf. Augustine, Confessions, 222-23: "Who is to carry the research beyond this point? Who can understand the truth of the matter? O Lord, I am working hard in this field, and the field of my labors is my own self. I have become a problem to myself, like land which a farmer works only with difficulty and at the cost of much sweat. For I am not now investigating the tracts of the heavens, or measuring the distance of the stars, or trying to discover how the earth hangs in space. I am investigating myself, my memory, my mind." See also Rudolf Bultmann, Primitive Christianity in its Contemporary Setting, tr. R. H. Fuller (Cleveland, 1956), pp. 144-45.

[24]On this point, cf. Charles Norris Cochrane, Christianity and Classical Culture (New York, 1957), p. 456; Niebuhr, I, p. 69; Bultmann, p. 180; and Kierkegaard, The Concept of Dread, tr. Walter Lowrie (Princeton, 1957), p. 26: ". . . the essential characteristic of human existence, that man is an individual and as such is at once himself and the whole race, in such wise that the whole race has part in the individual, and the individual has part in the whole race."

[25]Eric Auerbach, Mimesis, tr. Willard Trask (Garden City, 1957), chs. 1-3, is especially perceptive on this characteristic of biblical, as opposed to classical, literature.

[26]Kiekegaard's conception of the stages on

life's way may perhaps be taken as a reflection of
this tendency in Christian thought; Kierkegaard's
three stages do not simply replace each other,
but the later stages absorb the earlier.

[27]Cochrane, pp. 386ff.; Peter Brown, Augustine
of Hippo: A Biography (Berkeley, 1967), p. 173.

[28]As in Bultmann, p. 130.

[29]This seems to be implied in the Divine Comedy, in which the way to Paradise begins with the
full moral experience of the Inferno.

[30]Cf. Brown, p. 177, on Augustine's understanding of conversion as a beginning. As Augustine
remarks in Christian Doctrine, p. 13, the Christian life is "a journey or voyage home." The notion of life as movement was also important for
Luther: "For it is not sufficient to have done
something, and now to rest . . . this present life
is a kind of movement and passage, or transition
. . . a pilgrimage from this world into the world
to come, which is eternal rest" (quoted by Ger-
hard Ebeling, Luther: An Introduction to His
Thought, tr. R. A. Wilson [Philadelphia, 1970],
pp. 161-62). Calvin devoted particular attention
to this theme (Institutes, III. vi, p. 5): "But
no one . . . has sufficient strength to press on
with due eagerness, and weakness so weighs down
the greater number that, with wavering and limp-
ing and even creeping along the ground, they move
at a feeble rate. Let each one of us, then, proceed according to the measure of his puny capacity
and set out upon the journey we have begun. No
one shall set out so inauspiciously as not daily
to make some headway, though it be slight. Therefore, let us not cease so to act that we may make
some unceasing progress in the way of the Lord.
And let us not despair at the slightness of our
success; for even though attainment may not correspond to desire, when today outstrips yesterday the effort is not lost. Only let us look toward our mark with sincere simplicity and aspire
to our goal; not fondly flattering ourselves, nor
excusing our own evil deeds, but with continuous
effort striving toward this end: that we may sur-
pass ourselves in goodness until we attain to
goodness itself. It is this, indeed, which

through the whole course of life we seek and follow. But we shall attain it only when we have cast off the weakness of the body, and are received into full fellowship with him" (Battles tr.). Bunyan's Pilgrim's Progress vividly dramatizes the conception.

[31]Ricoeur, pp. 272-74, is instructive on the conception of progress implicit in Paul's understanding of the transition from the law to the grace of Christ: "the fall is turned into growth and progress; the curse of paradise lost becomes a test and a medicine." Augustine interpreted his own life as a progression in understanding: "I am the sort of man who writes because he has made progress, and who makes progress—by writing" (quoted by Brown, 353). For Thomas à Kempis, the Christian life is marked by a concern "to conquer self, and by daily growing stronger than self, to advance in holiness" (Imitation of Christ, tr. Leo Sherley-Price [London, 1952], p. 31). For Luther, progress was a condition of all existence, for "progress is nothing other than constantly beginning. And to begin without progress is extinction. This is clearly the case with every movement and every act of every creature." Thus one must "constantly progress, and anyone who supposes he has already apprended does not realize that he is only beginning. For we are always travelling, and must leave behind us what we know and possess, and seek for that which we do not yet know and possess" (quoted by Ebeling, pp. 161-62.

[32]Bultmann, esp. p. 184.

[33]This interpretation of the fall owes a good deal to Ricoeur. For the transition from anxiety to sin, see Niebuhr, I. pp. 168, 182-86.

[34]The Secular City (New York, 1965), p. 119.

[35]For a survey of Christian attitudes to culture, see H. Richard Niebuhr, Christ and Culture (New York, 1951).

[36]Ricoeur, pp. 58-59, 144-45, 321.

[37]Quoted by Gerhart B. Ladner, The Idea of Reform: Its Impact on Christian Thought and Action in the Age of the Fathers (Cambridge, Mass., 1959), p. 406.

[38]Ricoeur, p. 93.
[39]The Epistle to the Romans, tr. Edwyn C. Hoskyns (London, 1933), pp. 68, 87-88.
[40]Cf. Brown, p. 175.
[41]Quoted by Brown, p. 366.
[42]Christian Doctrine, p. 13.
[43]Cf. Paul Tillich, The Eternal Now (New York, 1956), p. 158.
[44]Institutes, II. vii, p. 10. Melanchthon was particularly subtle about human behavior that does not correspond to the impulses of the "heart"; the result is not, in fact, rationality, but, to follow Lionel Trilling's distinction, both insincerity and inauthenticity: "Therefore it can well happen that something is chosen which is entirely contrary to all affections. When this happens, insincerity takes over, as when, for example, someone treats graciously, amicably, and politely a person whom he hates and wishes ill to from the bottom of his heart, and he does this perhaps with no definite reason" (Loci communes theologici, tr. Lowell J. Satre, in Melanchthon and Bucer, ed. Wilhelm Pauck [London, 1969] , p. 28).
[45]Quoted by Anders Nygren, Agape and Eros, tr. Philip S. Watson (New York, 1969), p. 454.
[46]On the virtues of a childlike spontaneity, cf. Horace Bushnell, Christian Nurture (New Haven, 1916; first ed., 1888), p. 5: "A child acts out his present feelings, the feelings of the moment, without qualification or disguise."
[47]Cf. Niebuhr, Beyond Tragedy (New York, 1937), pp. 143-48.
[48]Journals and Papers, tr. Howard V. and Edna H. Hong (Bloomington, 1967), I, p. 122, no. 272.
[49]Niebuhr, Beyond Tragedy, pp. 148-52. At the same time Augustine's portrayal of infancy in the Confessions should warn us, in its realism, that Christianity is not merely sentimental about childhood, in which it can also detect the flaws of maturity. But this is again to suggest their identity.
[50]Bushnell noted, p. 136, that the apostolic church included children and observed, pp. 139-40, that "just so children are all men and women; and,

if there is any law of futurition in them to justify it, may be fitly classed as believing men and women."

[51]Cf. Bushnell, 10: ". . . since it is the distinction of Christian parents that they are themselves in the nurture of the Lord, since Christ and the Divine Love, communicated through him, are become the food of their life, what will they so naturally seek as to have their children partakers with them, heirs together with them, in the grace of life?"

[52]Barth emphasizes this, Church Dogmatics, III:4, p. 248. It is a significant feature of the Christian conception, indeed in a patriarchal society a revolutionary feature, that the Son, rather than the Father, is the model of adulthood. Lest this peculiarity seem to invite too simple an interpretation, however, the paradoxical unity of Father and Son in the Trinity must also be kept in mind.

[53]Cf. Tillich, Eternal Now, pp. 155-57.

[54]For Christianity and play, I have been stimulated by Lewis B. Smedes, "Theology and the Playful Life," in God and the Good: Essays in Honor of Henry Stob, ed. Clifton Orlebeke and Lewis B. Smedes (Grand Rapids, 1975), pp. 46-62. In view of common misunderstandings about the normative Christian attitude to sexuality, it is worth quoting Smedes—who certainly represents the normative position—on the playfulness of sex, p. 59: "The sexual component of our nature testifies that man was meant to find the most meaningful human communion in a playful relationship. In mutual trust and loving commitment, sexual activity is to be a playful festivity. It attests that human being is closest to fulfilling itself in a game. To be in God's image, then, includes being sexual, and sexuality is a profound call to play." Smedes also has useful comments on recent theologies of play.

[55]Bushnell, pp. 290-92.

[56]Cf. Augustine, City of God, XIX, v: "For how could the city of God . . . either take a beginning or be developed, or attain its proper destiny, if the life of the saints were not a social

539

life?" Luther was emphatic: "We ought not to
isolate ourselves but enter into companionship
with our neighbor. Likewise it . . . is contrary to the life of Christ, who didn't choose
solitude. Christ's life was very turbulent, for
people were always moving about him. He was
never alone, except when he prayed. Away with
those who say, 'Be gald to be alone and your
heart will be pure'" ("Table Talk," no. 1329).
    [57]Cf. Barth, <u>Church Dogmatics</u>, III:2, pp.
222ff.

Free Will and Determinism

Case

The jury room was too warm, and the agitation of the jurors added to the general discomfort. The judge had given his instructions, and, now the decision of guilt or innocence lay with the jury. The man on trial, Bill Williams, is accused of murdering his girl friend. They had recently broken off their relationship, and friends claimed Williams was deeply jealous and upset. Two state witnesses definitely implicated Williams in the murder. The defense attorney claimed that the couple had taken "trips" on L.S.D. and that the girl's death occurred while his client was under the drug's influence and unable to control or recall his actions.

Has the Self 'Free Will'?*
C. A. Campbell

It is something of a truism that in philosophic enquiry the exact formulation of a problem
often takes one a long way on the road to its
solution. In the case of the Free Will problem I
think there is a rather special need of careful
formulation. For there are many sorts of human
freedom; and it can easily happen that one wastes
a great deal of labor in proving or disproving a
freedom which has almost nothing to do with the
freedom which is at issue in the traditional problem of Free Will. The abortiveness of so much of
the argument for and against Free Will in contemporary philosophical literature seems to me due
in the main to insufficient pains being taken
over the preliminary definition of the problem.
. . .

Fortunately we can at least make a beginning
with a certain amount of confidence. It is not
seriously disputable that the kind of freedom in
question is the freedom which is commonly recognized to be in some sense a precondition of
moral responsibility. Clearly, it is on account
of this integral connection with moral responsibility that such exceptional importance has always been felt to attach to the Free Will problem.
But in what precise sense is free will a precondition of moral responsibility, and thus a postulate of the moral life in general? This is an
exceedingly troublesome question; but until we
have satisfied ourselves about the answer to it,
we are not in a position to state, let alone decide, the question whether 'Free Will' in its
traditional, ethical, significance is a reality.

Our first business, then, is to ask, exactly

*From <u>On Selfhood and Godhood</u> by C. A. Campbell.
Reprinted by permission of the publisher George
Allen and Unwin Ltd.

what kind of freedom is it which is required for
moral responsibility? And as to method of procedure in this inquiry, there seems to me to be no
real choice. I know of only one method that carries with it any hope of success; viz. (namely)
the critical comparison of those acts for which,
on due reflection, we deem it proper to attribute
moral praise or blame to the agents, with those
acts for which, on due reflection, we deem such
judgments to be improper. The ultimate touch-
stone, as I see it, can only be our moral consciousness as it manifests itself in our more
critical and considered moral judgments. The
'linguistic' approach by way of the analysis of
moral <u>sentences</u> seems to me, despite its present
popularity, to be an almost infallible method for
reaching wrong results in the moral field. . . .

The first point to note is that the freedom
at issue (as indeed the very name 'Free <u>Will</u>
Problem' indicates) pertains primarily not to
overt acts but to inner acts. The nature of
things has decreed that, save in the case of
one's self, it is only overt acts which one can
directly observe. But a very little reflection
serves to show that in our moral judgments upon
others their overt acts are regarded as significant only in so far as they are the expression of
inner acts. We do not consider the acts of a robot to be morally responsible acts; nor do we
consider the acts of a man to be so save (except)
in so far as they are distinguishable from those
of a robot by reflecting an inner life of choice.
Similarly, from the other side, if we are satisfied (as we may on occasion be, at least in the
case of ourselves) that a person has definitely
elected to follow a course which he believes to
be wrong, but has been prevented by external circumstances from translating his inner choice into
an overt act, we still regard him as morally
blameworthy. Moral freedom, then, pertains to
<u>inner</u> acts.

The next point seems at first sight equally
obvious and uncontroversial; but, as we shall see,

it has awkward implications if we are in real earnest with it (as almost nobody is). It is the
simple point that the act must be one of which
the person judged can be regarded as the <u>sole</u> author. It seems plain enough that if there are
any <u>other</u> determinants of the act, external to
the <u>self</u>, to that extent the act is not an act
which the <u>self</u> determines, and to that extent not
an act for which the self can be held morally responsible. The self is only part-author of the
act, and his moral responsibility can logically
extend only to those elements with the act (assuming for the moment that these can be isolated)
of which he is the <u>sole</u> author.

The awkward implications of this apparent
truism will be readily appreciated. For, if we
are mindful of the influence exerted by heredity
and environment, we may well feel some doubt
whether there is any act of will at all of which
one can truly say that the self is sole author,
sole determinant. No man has a voice in determining the raw material of impulses and capacities that constitute his hereditary endowment,
and no man has more than a very partial control
of the material and social environment in which
he is destined to live his life. Yet it would be
manifestly absurd to deny that these two factors
do constantly and profoundly affect the nature of
a man's choices. That this is so we all of us
recognize in our moral judgments when we "make
allowances," as we say, for a bad heredity or a
vicious environment, and acknowledge in the victim of them a diminished moral responsibility for
evil courses. Evidently we do <u>try</u>, in our moral
judgments, however crudely, to praise or blame a
man only in respect of that of which we can regard him as <u>wholly</u> the author. And evidently we
do recognize that, for a man to be the author of
an act in the full sense required for moral responsibility, it is not enough merely that he
'wills' or 'chooses' the act; since even the most
unfortunate victim of heredity or environment
does, as a rule, 'will' what he does. It is significant, however, that the ordinary man, though

well enough aware of the influence upon choices of heredity and environment, does not feel obliged thereby to give up his assumption that moral predicates <u>are</u> somehow applicable. Plainly he still believes that there is <u>something</u> for which a man is morally responsible, something of which we can fairly say that he is the sole author. <u>What is this something</u>? To that question common-sense is not ready with an explicit answer—though an answer is, I think, implicit in the line which its moral judgments take. I shall do what I can to give an explicit answer later in this lecture. Meantime it must suffice to observe that, if we are to be true to the deliverances of our moral consciousness, it is very difficult to deny that <u>sole</u> authorship is a necessary condition of the morally responsible act.

Thirdly we come to a point over which much recent controversy has raged. We may approach it by raising the following question. Granted an act of which the agent is sole author, does this 'sole authorship' suffice to make the act a morally free act? We may be inclined to think that it does, until we contemplate the possibility that an act of which the agent is sole author might conceivably occur as a necessary expression of the agent's nature; the way in which, e.g. some philosophers have supposed the Divine act of creation to occur. This consideration excites a legitimate doubt; for it is far from easy to see how a person can be regarded as a proper subject for moral praise or blame in respect of an act which he <u>cannot help</u> performing—even if it be his own 'nature' which necessitates it. Must we not recognize it as a condition of the morally free act that the agent "could have acted otherwise" than he in fact did? It is true, indeed, that we sometimes praise or blame a man for an act about which we are prepared to say, in the light of our knowledge of his established character, that he "could no other." But I think that a little reflection shows that in such cases we are not praising or blaming the man strictly for what he does <u>now</u> (or at any rate we ought not to be), rather for those past acts of his which have generated the firm habit of mind from which his _present_ act follows 'necessarily'. In other words, our praise and blame, so far as justified, are really retrospective, being directed not to the agent _qua_ (in the function or capacity of) performing _this_ act, but to the agent _qua_ performing those past acts which have built up his present character, and in respect to which we presume that he _could_ have acted otherwise, that there really _were_ open possibilities before him. These cases, therefore, seem to me to constitute no valid exception tö what I must take to be the rule, viz. that a man can be morally praised or blamed for an act only if he could have acted otherwise.

Now philosophers today are fairly well agreed that it is a postulate of the morally responsible act that the agent "could have acted otherwise" in _some_ sense of that phrase. But sharp differences of opinion have arisen over the way in which the phrase ought to be interpreted. There is a strong disposition to water down its apparent meaning by insisting that it is not (as a postulate of moral responsibility) to be understood as a straightforward categorical proposition, but rather as a disguised hypothetical proposition. All that we really require to be assured of, in order to justify our holding X morally responsible for an act, is, we are told, that X could have acted otherwise _if_ he had _chosen_ otherwise (Moore, Stevenson); or perhaps that X could have acted otherwise _if_ he had had a different character, or _if_ he had been placed in different circumstances.

I think it is easy to understand, and even, in a measure, to sympathize with, the motives which induce philosophers to offer these counterinterpretations. It is not just the fact that "X could have acted otherwise," as a bald categorical statement, is incompatible with the universal sway of causal law—though this is, to some philosophers, a serious stone of stumbling. The more widespread objection is that it at least looks as though it were incompatible with that causal continuity of an agent's character with his conduct which is implied when we believe (surely with justice) that we can often tell the sort of thing a man will do from our knowledge of the sort of man he is.

We shall have to make our accounts with that particular difficulty later. At this stage I wish merely to show that neither of the hypothetical propositions suggested—and I think the same could be shown for _any_ hypothetical alternative —is an acceptable substitute for the categorical proposition "X could have acted otherwise" as the presupposition of moral responsibility.

Let us look first at the earlier suggestion —"X could have acted otherwise _if_ he had chosen otherwise." Now clearly there are a great many acts with regard to which we are entirely satisfied that the agent is thus situated. We are often perfectly sure that—for this is all it amounts to—if X had chosen otherwise, the circumstances presented no external obstacle to the translation of that choice into action. For example, we often have no doubt at all that X, who in point of fact told a lie, could have told the truth _if_ he had so chosen. But does our confidence on this score allay all legitimate doubts about whether X is really blameworthy? Does it entail that X is free in the sense required for moral responsibility? Surely not. The obvious question immediately arises: "But _could_ X have _chosen_ otherwise than he did?" It _is_ doubt about the true answer to _that_ question which leads most people to doubt the reality of moral responsibility. Yet on this crucial question the hypothetical proposition which is offered as a sufficient statement of the condition justifying the ascription of moral responsibility gives us no information whatsoever.

Indeed this hypothetical substitute for the

categorical "X could have acted otherwise" seems to me to lack all plausibility unless one contrives to forget why it is, after all, that we ever come to feel fundamental doubts about man's moral responsibility. Such doubts are born, surely, when one becomes aware of certain reputable world-views in religion or philosophy, or of certain reputable scientific beliefs, which in their several ways imply that man's actions are necessitated, and thus could not be otherwise than they in fact are. But clearly a doubt so based is not even touched by the recognition that a man could very often act otherwise if he so chose. That proposition is entirely compatible with the necessitarian theories which generate our doubt: indeed it is this very compatibility that has recommended it to some philosophers, who are reluctant to give up either moral responsibility or Determinism. The proposition which we must be able to affirm if moral praise or blame of X is to be justified is the categorical proposition that X could have acted otherwise because—not if—he could have chosen otherwise; or, since it is essentially the inner side of the act that matters, the proposition simply that X could have chosen otherwise.

For the second of the alternative formulae suggested we cannot spare more than a few moments. But its inability to meet the demands it is required to meet is almost transparent. "X could have acted otherwise," as a statement of a precondition of X's moral responsibility, really means (we are told) "X could have acted otherwise if he were differently constituted, or if he had been placed in different circumstances." It seems a sufficient reply to this to point out that the person whose moral responsibility is at issue is X; a specific individual, in a specific set of circumstances. It is totally irrelevant to X's moral responsibility that we should be able to say that some person differently constituted from X, or X in a different set of circumstances, could have done something different from what X did.

Let me, then, briefly sum up the answer at which we have arrived to our question about the kind of freedom required to justify moral responsibility. It is that a man can be said to exercise free will in a morally significant sense only insofar as his chosen act is one of which he is the sole cause or author, and only if—in the straightforward, categorical sense of the phrase —he "could have chosen otherwise."

I confess that this answer is in some ways a disconcerting one, disconcerting, because most of us, however objective we are in the actual conduct of our thinking, would <u>like</u> to be able to believe that moral responsibility is real: whereas the freedom required for moral responsibility, on the analysis we have given, is certainly far more difficult to establish than the freedom required on the analyses we found ourselves obliged to reject. If, e.g. moral freedom entails only that I could have acted otherwise <u>if</u> I had chosen otherwise, there is no real 'problem' about it all. I am 'free' in the normal case where there is no external obstacle to prevent my translating the alternative choice into action, and not free in other cases. Still less is there a problem if all that moral freedom entails is that I could have acted otherwise <u>if</u> I had been a differently constituted person, or been in different circumstances. Clearly I am <u>always</u> free in <u>this</u> sense of freedom. But, as I have argued, these so-called 'freedoms' fail to give us the preconditions of moral responsibility, and hence leave the freedom of the traditional free-will problem, the freedom that people are really concerned about, precisely where it was.

* * *

That brings me to the second, and more constructive, part of this lecture. From now on I shall be considering whether it is reasonable to believe that man does in fact possess a free will of the kind specified in the first part of the lecture. If so, just how and where within the

complex fabric of the volitional life are we to
locate it?—for although free will must presumably belong (if anywhere) to the volitional side
of human experience, it is pretty clear from the
way in which we have been forced to define it
that it does not pertain simply to volition as
such; not even to all volitions that are commonly
dignified with the name of 'choices.' It has
been, I think, one of the more serious impediments to profitable discussion of the Free Will
problem that Libertarians and Determinists alike
have so often failed to appreciate the comparatively narrow area within which the free will
that is necessary to save morality is required to
operate. It goes without saying that this failure has been gravely prejudicial to the case for
Libertarianism. I attach a good deal of importance, therefore, to the problem of locating free
will correctly within the volitional orbit. Its
solution forestalls and annuls, I believe, some
of the more tiresome clichés of Determinist
criticism.

We saw earlier that Common Sense's practice
of 'making allowances' in its moral judgments for
the influence of heredity and environment indicates Common Sense's conviction, both that a just
moral judgment must discount determinants of
choice over which the agent has no control, and
also (since it still accepts moral judgments as
legitimate) that something of moral relevance
survives which can be regarded as genuinely self-
originated. We are now to try to discover what
this 'something' is. And I think we may still
usefully take Common Sense as our guide. Suppose
one asks the ordinary intelligent citizen why he
deems it proper to make allowances for X, whose
heredity and/or environment are unfortunate. He
will tend to reply, I think, in some such terms
as these: that X has more and stronger tempta-
tions to deviate from what is right than Y or Z,
who are normally circumstanced, so that he must
put forth a stronger moral effort if he is to
achieve the same level of external conduct. The
intended implication seems to be that X is just

as morally praiseworthy as Y or Z _if_ he exerts an equivalent moral effort, even though he may not thereby achieve an equal success in conforming his will to the 'concrete' demands of duty. And this implies, again, Common Sense's belief that _in moral effort_ we have something for which a man is responsible _without qualification_, something that is _not_ affected by heredity and environment but depends _solely_ upon the self itself.

Now in my opinion Common Sense has here, in principle, hit upon the one and only defensible answer. Here, and here alone, so far as I can see, in the act of deciding whether to put forth or withhold the moral effort required to resist temptation and rise to duty, is to be found an act which is free in the sense required for moral responsibility; an act of which the self is sole author, and of which it is true to say that "it could be" (or, after the event, "could have been") "otherwise." Such is the thesis which we shall now try to establish.

The species of argument appropraite to the establishment of a thesis of this sort should fall, I think, into two phases. First, there should be a consideration of the evidence of the moral agent's own inner experience. What _is_ the act of moral decision, and what does it imply, from the standpoint of the actual participant? Since there is no way of knowing the act of moral decision—or for that matter any other form of activity—except by actual participation in it, the evidence of the subject, or agent, is on an issue of this kind of palmary importance. It can hardly, however, be taken as in itself conclusive. For even if that evidence should be overwhelming-ly to the effect that moral decision does have the characteristics required by moral freedom, the question is bound to be raised—and in view of considerations from other quarters pointing in a contrary direction is _rightly_ raised—Can we _trust_ the evidence of inner experience? That brings us to what will be the second phase of the argument. We shall have to go on to show, if we are to make good our case, that the extraneous considerations so often supposed to be fatal to the belief in moral freedom are in fact innocuous to it.

In the light of what was said in the last lecture about the self's experience of moral decision as a creative activity, we may perhaps be absolved from developing the first phase of the argument at any great length. The appeal is throughout to one's own experience in the actual taking of the moral decision in the situation of moral temptation. "Is it possible," we must ask, "for anyone so circumstanced to disbelieve that he could be deciding otherwise?" The answer is surely not in doubt. When we decide to exert moral effort to resist a temptation, we feel quite certain that we could withhold the effort; just as, if we decide to withhold the effort and yield to our desires, we feel quite certain that we could exert it—otherwise we should not blame ourselves afterwards for having succumbed. It may be, indeed, that this conviction is mere self-delusion. But that is not at the moment our concern. It is enough at present to establish that the act of deciding to exert or to withhold moral effort, as we know it from the inside in actual moral living, belongs to the category of acts which "could have been otherwise."

Mutatis mutandis (with the necessary changes), the same reply is forthcoming if we ask, "Is it possible for the moral agent in the taking of his decision to disbelieve that he is the sole author of that decision?" Clearly he cannot disbelieve that it is he who takes the decision. That, however, is not in itself sufficient to enable him, on reflection, to regard himself as solely responsible for the act. For his "character" as so far formed might conceivably be a factor in determining it, and no one can suppose that the constitution of his "character" is uninfluenced by circumstances of heredity and environment with which he has nothing to do. But as we pointed out in the last lecture, the very essence of the moral decision as it is experienced is that it is a decision whether or not to <u>combat</u> our strongest desire, and our strongest desire <u>is</u> the expression in the situation of our character as so far formed. Now clearly our character cannot be a factor in determing the decision whether or not to <u>oppose</u> our character. I think we are entitled to say, therefore, that the act of moral decision is one in which the self is for itself not merely 'author' but 'sole author.'

We may pass on, then, to the second phase of our constructive argument; and this will demand more elaborate treatment. Even if a moral agent <u>qua</u> making a moral decision in the situation of 'temptation' cannot help believing that he has free will in the sense at issue, a moral freedom between real alternatives, between genuinely open possibilities—are there, nevertheless, objections to a freedom of this kind so cogent that we are bound to distrust the evidence of 'inner experience?'

I begin by drawing attention to a simple point whose significance tends, I think, to be under-estimated. If the phenomenological analysis we have offered is substantially correct, no one while functioning as a moral agent can help believing that he enjoys free will. Theoretically he may be completely convinced by Determinist arguments, but when actually confronted with a personal situation of conflict between duty and desire he is quite certain that it lies with him here and now whether or not he will rise to duty. It follows that if Determinists could produce convincing theoretical arguments against a free will of this kind, the awkward predicament would ensue that man has to deny as a theoretical being what he has to assert as a practical being. Now I think the Determinist ought to be a good deal more worried about this than he usually is. He seems to imagine that a strong case on general theoretical grounds is enough to prove that the 'practical' belief in free will, even if inescapable for us as practical beings, is mere illusion. But in fact it proves nothing of the sort. There is no reason whatever why a belief that we find ourselves obliged to hold _qua_ practical beings should be required to give way before a belief which we find ourselves obliged to hold _qua_ theoretical beings; or, for that matter, _vice versa_. All that the theoretical arguments of Determinism can prove, unless they are reinforced by a refutation of the phenomenological analysis that supports Libertarianism, is that there is a radical conflict between the theoretical and the practical sides of man's nature, an antimony at the very heart of the self. And this is a state of affairs with which no one can easily rest satisfied. I think therefore that the Determinist ought to concern himself a great deal more than he does with phenomenological analysis, in order to show, if he can, that the assurance of free will is not really an inexpugnable element in man's practical consciousness. There is just as much obligation upon him, convinced though he may be of the soundness of his theoretical arguments, to expose the errors of the Libertarian's phenomenological analysis, as there is upon us, convinced though we may be of the soundness of the Libertarian's phenomenological analysis, to expose the errors of the Determinist's theoretical arguments.

However, we must at once begin the discharge of our own obligation. The rest of this lecture will be devoted to trying to show that the arguments which seem to carry most weight with Determinists are, to say the least of it, very far from compulsive.

*   *   *

These arguments can, I think, be reduced in principle to no more than two: first, the argument from 'predictability;' second, the argument from the alleged meaninglessness of an act supposed to be the self's act and yet not an expression of the self's character. Contemporary criticism of free will seems to me to consist almost exclusively of variations on these two themes. I shall deal with each in turn.

On the first we touched in passing at an
earlier stage. Surely it is beyond question (the
critic urges) that when we know a person intimately we can foretell with a high degree of ac-
curacy how he will respond to at least a large
number of practical situations. One feels safe
in predicting that one's dog-loving friend will
not use his boot to repel the little mongrel that
comes yapping at his heels; or again that one's
wife will not pass with incurious eyes (or indeed pass at all) the new hat-shop in the city.
So to behave would not be (as we say) 'in character.' But, so the criticism runs, you with
your doctrine of 'genuinely open possibilities,'
of a free will by which the self can diverge from
its own character, remove all rational basis from
such prediction. You require us to make the absurd supposition that the success of countless
predictions of the sort in the past has been mere
matter of chance. If you <u>really</u> believed in your
theory, you would not be surprised if tomorrow
your friend with the notorious horror of strong
drink should suddenly exhibit a passion for
whisky and soda, or if your friend whose taste
for reading has hitherto been satisfied with the
sporting columns of the newspapers should be discovered on a fine Saturday afternoon poring over
the works of Hegel. But of course you <u>would</u> be
surprised. Social life would be sheer chaos if
there were not well-grounded social expectations;
and social life is not sheer chaos. Your theory
is hopelessly wrecked upon obvious facts.

Now whether or not this criticism holds good
against some versions of Libertarian theory I
need not here discuss. It is sufficient if I can
make it clear that against the version advanced
in this lecture, according to which free will is
localized in a relatively narrow field of operation, the criticism has no relevance whatsoever.

Let us remind ourselves briefly of the setting within which, on our view, free will func-

tions. There is X, the course which we believe we ought to follow, and Y, the course towards which we feel our desire is strongest. The freedom which we ascribe to the agent is the freedom to put forth or refrain from putting forth the moral effort required to resist the pressure of desire and do what he thinks he ought to do.

But then there is surely an immense range of practical situations—covering by far the greater part of life—in which there is no question of a conflict within the self between what he most desires to do and what he thinks he ought to do? Indeed such conflict is a comparatively rare phenomenon for the majority of men. Yet over that whole vast range there is nothing whatever in our version of Libertarianism to prevent our agreeing that character determines conduct. In the absence, real or supposed, of any 'moral' issue, what a man chooses will be simply that course which, after such reflection as seems called for, he deems most likely to bring him what he most strongly desires; and that is the same as to say the course to which his present character inclines him.

Over by far the greater area of human choices, then, our theory offers no more barrier to successful prediction on the basis of character than any other theory. For where there is no clash of strongest desire with duty, the free will we are defending has no business. There is just nothing for it to do.

But what about the situations—rare enough though they may be—in which there is this clash and in which free will does therefore operate? Does our theory entail that there at any rate, as the critic seems to suppose, 'anything may happen?'

Not by any manner of means. In the first place, and by the very nature of the case, the range of the agent's possible choices is bounded by what he thinks he ought to do on the one hand,

and what he most strongly desires on the other. The freedom claimed for him is a freedom of decision to make or withhold the effort required to do what he thinks he ought to do. There is no question of a freedom to act in some 'wild' fashion, out of all relation to his characteristic beliefs and desires. This so-called 'freedom of caprice,' we often charged against the Libertarian, is, to put it bluntly, a sheer figment of the critic's imagination, with no <u>habitat</u> (place) in serious Libertarian theory. Even in situations where free will does come into play it is perfectly possible, on a view like ours, given the appropriate knowledge of a man's character, to predict within certain limits how he will respond.

But 'probable' prediction in such situations can, I think, go further than this. It is obvious that where desire and duty are at odds, the felt 'gap' (as it were) between the two may vary enormously in breadth in different cases. The moderate drinker and the chronic tippler may each want another glass, and each deem it his duty to abstain, but the felt gap between desire and duty in the case of the former is trivial beside the great gulf which is felt to separate them in the case of the latter. Hence it will take a far harder moral effort for the tippler than for the moderate drinker to achieve the same external result of abstention. So much is matter of common agreement. And we are entitled, I think, to take it into account in prediction, on the simple principle that the harder the moral effort required to resist desire the less likely it is to occur. Thus in the example taken, most people would predict that the tippler will very probably succumb to his desires, whereas there is a reasonable likelihood that the moderate drinker will make the comparatively slight effort needed to resist them. So long as the prediction does not pretend to more than a measure of probability, there is nothing in our theory which would disallow it.

I claim, therefore, that the view of free will I have been putting forward is consistent with predictability of conduct on the basis of character over a very wide field indeed. And I make the further claim that the field will cover all the situations in life concerning which there is any empirical evidence that successful prediction is possible.

Let us pass on to consider the second main line of criticism. This is, I think, much the more illuminating of the two, if only because it compels the Libertarian to make explicit certain concepts which are indispensable to him, but which, being desperately hard to state clearly, are apt not to be stated at all. The critic's fundamental point might be stated somewhat as follows:

"Free will as you describe it is completely unintelligible. On your own showing no <u>reason</u> can be given, because there just <u>is</u> no reason, why a man decides to exert rather than to withhold moral effort, or <u>vice versa</u>. But such an act—or more properly, such an 'occurrence'—it is nonsense to speak of as an act of a <u>self</u>. If there is nothing in the self's character to which it is, even in principle, in any way traceable, the self has nothing to do with it. Your so-called 'freedom,' therefore, so far from supporting the self's moral responsibility, destroys it as surely as the crudest Determinism could do."

If we are to discuss this criticism usefully, it is important, I think, to begin by getting clear about two different senses of the word 'intelligible.'

If, in the first place, we mean by an 'intelligible' act one whose occurrence is in principle capable of being inferred, since it follows necessarily from something (though we may not know in fact from what), then it is certainly true that the Libertarian's free will is unintelligible. But that is only saying, is it not, that

the Libertarian's 'free' act is not an act which
follows necessarily from something! This can
hardly rank as a <u>criticism</u> of Libertarianism. It
is just a description of it. That there can be
nothing unintelligible in <u>this</u> sense is precisely
what the Determinist has got to <u>prove</u>.

Yet it is surprising how often the critic of
Libertarianism involves himself in this circular
mode of argument. Repeatedly it is urged against
the Libertarian, with a great air of triumph, that
on his view he can't say <u>why</u> I now decide to rise
to duty, or now decide to follow my strongest desire in defiance of duty. Of course he can't. If
he could he wouldn't <u>be</u> a Libertarian. To 'account for' a 'free' act is a contradiction in
terms. A free will is <u>ex hypothesi</u> (by hypothesis) the sort of thing of which the request for
an <u>explanation</u> is absurd. The assumption that an
explanation must be in principle possible for the
act of moral decision deserves to rank as a classic example of the ancient fallacy of 'begging
the question.'

But the critic usually has in mind another
sense of the word 'unintelligible.' He is apt to
take it for granted that an act which is unintelligible in the <u>above</u> sense (as the morally free
act of the Libertarian undoubtedly is) is unintelligible in the <u>further</u> sense that we can attach no meaning to it. And this is an altogether
more serious matter. If it could really be shown
that the Libertarian's 'free will' were unintelligible in this sense of being meaningless, that,
for myself at any rate, would be the end of the
affair. Libertarianism would have been conclu-
sively refuted.

But it seems to me manifest that this can
<u>not</u> be shown. The critic has allowed himself, I
submit, to become the victim of a widely accepted but fundamentally vicious assumption. He has
assumed that whatever is meaningful must exhibit
its meaningfulness to those who view it from the
standpoint of external observation. Now if one

chooses thus to limit one's self to the rôle of
external observer, it is, I think, perfectly
true that one can attach no meaning to an act
which is the act of something we call a 'self'
and yet follows from nothing in that self's character. But then why should we so limit ourselves, when what is under consideration is a subjective activity? For the apprehension of subjective acts there is another standpoint available, that of inner experience, of the practical
consciousness in its actual functioning. If our
free will should turn out to be something to
which we can attach a meaning from this standpoint, no more is required. And no more ought to
be expected. For I must repeat that only from
the inner standpoint of living experience could
anything of the nature of 'activity' be directly
grasped. Observation from without is in the nature of the case impotent to apprehend the active
qua (as) active. We can from without observe se-
quences of states. If into these we read activity (as we sometimes do), this can only be on
the basis of what we discern in ourselves from
the inner standpoint. It follows that if anyone
insists upon taking his criterion of the meaningful simply from the standpoint of external observation, he is really deciding in advance of the
evidence that the notion of activity, and a
fortiori (even more so) the notion of a free will,
is 'meaningless.' He looks for the free act
through a medium which is in the nature of the
case incapable of revealing it, and then, because
inevitably he doesn't find it, he declares that
it doesn't exist!

But if, as we surely ought in this context,
we adopt the inner standpoint, then (I am suggesting) things appear in a totally different light.
From the inner standpoint, it seems to me plain,
there is no difficulty whatever in attaching meaning to an act which is the slef's act and which
nevertheless does not follow from the self's character. So much I claim has been established by
the phenomenological analysis, in this and the
previous lecture, of the act of moral decision in

560

face of moral temptation. It is thrown into particularly clear relief where the moral decision is to make the moral effort required to rise to duty. For the very function of moral effort, as it appears to the agent engaged in the act, is to enable the self to act against the line of least resistance, against the line to which his character as so far formed most strongly inclines him. But if the self is thus conscious here of combating his formed character, he surely cannot possibly suppose that the act, although his own act, issues from his formed character? I submit, therefore, that the self knows very well indeed—from the inner standpoint—what is meant by an act which is the self's act and which nevertheless does not follow from the self's character.

What this implies—and it seems to me to be an implication of cardinal importance for any theory of the self that aims at being more than superficial—is that the nature of the self is for itself something more than just its character as so far formed. The 'nature' of the self and what we commonly call the 'character' of the self are by no means the same thing, and it is utterly vital that they should not be confused. The 'nature' of the self comprehends, but is not without remainder reducible to, its 'character;' it must, if we are to be true to the testimony of our experience of it, be taken as including also the authentic creative power of fashioning and refashioning 'character.'

The misguided, and as a rule quite uncritical, belittlement, of the evidence offered by inner experience has, I am convinced, been responsible for more bad argument by the opponents of Free Will than has any other single factor. How often, for example, do we find the Determinist critic saying, in effect, "Either the act follows necessarily upon precedent states, or it is a mere matter of chance and accordingly of no moral significance." The disjunction is invalid, for it does not exhaust the possible alternatives. It

seems to the critic to do so only because he <u>will</u>
limit himself to the standpoint which is proper,
and indeed alone possible, in dealing with the
physical world, the standpoint of the external
observer. If only he would allow himself to assume the standpoint which is not merely proper
for, but necessary to, the apprehension of subjective activity, the inner standpoint of the
practical consciousness in its actual functioning, he would find himself obliged to recognize
the falsity of his disjunction. Reflection upon
the act of moral decision as apprehended from the
inner standpoint would force him to recognize a
<u>third</u> possibility, as remote from chance as from
necessity, that, namely, of <u>creative activity</u>, in
which (as I have ventured to express it) nothing
determines the act save the agent's doing of it.

There we must leave the matter. But as this
lecture has been, I know, somewhat densely packed, it may be helpful if I conclude by reminding
you, in bald summary, of the main things I have
been trying to say. Let me set them out in so
many successive theses.

1. The freedom which is at issue in the
traditional Free Will problem is the freedom
which is presupposed in moral responsibility.
2. Critical reflection upon carefully considered attributions of moral responsibility reveals that the only freedom that will do is a
freedom which pertains to inner acts of choice,
and that these acts must be acts (<u>a</u>) of which
the self is <u>sole</u> author, and (<u>b</u>) which the self
could have performed otherwise.
3. From phenomenological analysis of the
situation of moral temptation we find that the
self as engaged in this situation is inescapably
convinced that it possesses a freedom of precisely the specified kind, located in the decision to
exert or withhold the moral effort needed to rise
to duty where the pressure of its desiring nature
is felt to urge it in a contrary direction.
Passing to the question of the <u>reality</u> of
this moral freedom which the moral agent believes

himself to possess, we argued:

4. Of the two types of Determinist criticism which seem to have most influence today,
that based on the predictability of much human
behavior fails to touch a Libertarianism which
confines the area of free will as above indicated.
Libertarianism so understood is compatible with
all the predictability that the empirical facts
warrant. And:

5. The second main type of criticism, which
alleges the 'meaninglessness' of an act which is
the self's act and which is yet not determined by
the self's character, is based on a failure to
appreciate that the standpoint of inner experience is not only legitimate but indispensable
where what is at issue is the reality and nature
of a subjective activity. The creative act of
moral decision is inevitably meaningless to the
mere external observer; but from the inner standpoint it is as real, and as significant, as anything in human experience.

What Means This Freedom?*
    John Hospers

    I want to mention a factor that I think is
of enormous importance and relevance: namely,
unconscious motivation. There are many actions—
not those of an insane person (however the term
"insane" be defined), nor of a person ignorant of
of the effects of his action, nor ignorant of some
relevant fact about the situation, nor in any obvious way mentally deranged—for which human beings in general and the courts in particular are
inclined to hold the doer responsible, and for
which, I would say, he should not be held responsible. The deed may be planned, it may be carried

out in cold calculation, it may spring from the agent's character and be continuous with the rest of his behavior, and it may be perfectly true that he could have done differently <u>if</u> he had wanted to; nonetheless his behavior was brought about by unconscious conflicts developed in infancy, over which he had no control and of which (without training in psychiatry) he does not even have knowledge. He may even <u>think</u> he knows why he acted as he did, he may <u>think</u> he has conscious control over his actions, he may even <u>think</u> he is fully responsible for them; but he is not. Psychiatric casebooks provide hundreds of examples. The law and common sense, though puzzled sometimes by such cases, are gradually becoming aware that they exist; but at this early stage countless tragic blunders still occur because neither the law nor the public in general is aware of the genesis of criminal actions. The mother blames her daughter for choosing the wrong men as candidates for husbands; but though the daughter thinks she is choosing freely and spends a considerable amount of time "deciding" among them, the identification with her sick father, resulting from Oedipal fantasies in early childhood, prevents her from caring for any but sick men, twenty or thirty years older than herself. Blaming her is beside the point; she cannot help it, and she cannot change it. Countless criminal acts are thought out in great detail; yet the participants are (without their own knowledge) acting out fantasies, fears, and defenses from early childhood, over whose coming and going they have no conscious control.

Now, I am not saying that none of these persons should be in jails or asylums. Often society must be protected against them. Nor am I saying that people should cease the practices of blaming and praising, punishing and rewarding; in general these devices are justified by the results—although very often they have practically no effect; the deeds are done from inner compulsion, which is not lessened when the threat of punishment is great. I am only saying that fre-

quently persons we think responsible are not
properly to be called so; we mistakenly think
them responsible because we assume they are like
those in whom no unconscious drive (toward this
type of behavior) is present, and that their behavior can be changed by reasoning, exhorting,
or threatening.

I

I have said that these persons are not responsible. But what is the criterion for responsibility? Under precisely what conditions is a
person to be held morally responsible for an action? Disregarding here those conditions that
have to do with a person's ignorance of the situation or the effects of his action, let us concentrate on those having to do with his "inner
state." There are several criteria that might
be suggested:

1. The first idea that comes to mind is
that responsibility is determined by the presence
or absence of premeditation—the opposite of "premeditated" being, presumably, "unthinking" or
"impulsive." But this will not do—both because
some acts are not premeditated but responsible,
and because some are premeditated and not responsible.
Many acts we call responsible can be as unthinking or impulsive as you please. If you rush
across the street to help the victim of an automobile collison, you are (at least so we would
ordinarily say) acting responsibly, but you did
not do so out of premeditation; you saw the accident, you didn't think, you rushed to the scene
without hesitation. It was like a reflex action.
But you acted responsibly: unlike the knee jerk,
the act was the result of past training and past
thought about situations of this kind; that is
why you ran to help instead of ignoring the inci-
dent or running away. When something done originally from conviction or training becomes habitual, it becomes like a reflex action. As Aristotle said, virtue should become second nature

565

through habit: a virtuous act should be performed as if by instinct; this, far from detract-
ing from its moral worth, testifies to one's mastery of the desired type of behavior; one does
not have to make a moral effort each time it is
repeated.
There are also premeditated acts for which,
I would say, the person is not responsible. Premeditation, especially when it is so exaggerated
as to issue in no action at all, can be the result of neurotic disturbance or what we sometimes
call an emotional "block," which the person in-
herits from long-past situations. In Hamlet's
revenge on his uncle (I use this example because
it is familiar to all of us), there was no lack,
but rather a surfeit, of premeditation; his actions were so exquisitely premeditated as to make
Freud and Dr. Ernest Jones look more closely to
find out what lay behind them. The very premeditation camouflaged unconscious motives of which
Hamlet himself was not aware. I think this is an
important point, since it seems that the courts
often assume that premeditation is a criterion of
responsibility. If failure to kill his uncle had
been considered a crime, every court in the land
would have convicted Hamlet. Again: a woman's
decision to stay with her husband in spite of endless "mental cruelty" is, if she is the victim of
an unconscious masochistic "will to punishment,"
one for which she is not responsible; she is the
victim and not the agent, no matter how profound
her conviction that she is the agent; she is
caught in a masochistic web (of complicated genesis) dating back to babyhood, perhaps a repetition of a comparable situation involving her own
parents, a repetition-compulsion that, as Freud
said, goes "beyond the pleasure principle."
Again: a criminal whose crime was carefully planned step by step is usually considered responsible,
but as we shall see in later examples, the overwhelming impulse toward it, stemming from an un-
usually humiliating ego defeat in early childhood, was as compulsive as any can be.
2. Shall we say, then, that a person is not
responsible for his act unless he can defend it

with reasons? I am afraid that this criterion is no better than the previous one. First, intellectuals are usually better at giving reasons than nonintellectuals, and according to this criterion would be more responsible than persons acting from moral conviction not implemented by reasoning; yet it is very doubtful whether we should want to say that the latter are the more responsible. Second, the giving of reasons itself may be suspect. The reasons may be rationalizations camouflaging unconscious motives of which the agent knows nothing. Hamlet gave many reasons for not doing what he felt it was his duty to do: the time was not right, his uncle's soul might go to heaven, etc. His various "reasons" contradicted one another, and if an overpowering compulsion had not been present, the highly intellectual Hamlet would not have been taken in for a moment by these rationalizations. The real reason, the Oedipal conflict that made his uncle's crime the accomplishment of his own deepest desire, binding their fates into one and paralyzing him into inaction, was unconscious and of course unknown to him. One's intelligence and reasoning power do not enable one to escape from unconsciously motivated behavior; it only gives one greater facility in rationalizing that behavior; one's intelligence is simply used in the interests of the neurosis—it is pressed into service to justify with reasons what one does quite independently of the reasons.

If these two criteria are inadequate, let us seek others.

3. Shall we say that a person is responsible for his action unless it is the result of unconscious forces of which he knows nothing? Many psychoanalysts would probably accept this criterion. If it is not largely reflected in the language of responsibility as ordinarily used, this may be due to ignorance of fact: most people do not know that there are such things as unconscious motives and unconscious conflicts causing human beings to act. But it may be that if they did, perhaps they would refrain from holding persons responsible for certain actions.

I do not wish here to quarrel with this cri-

terion of responsibility. I only want to point
out the fact that if this criterion is employed
a far greater number of actions will be excluded
from the domain of responsibility than we might
at first suppose. Whether we are neat or untidy,
whether we are selfish or unselfish, whether we
provoke scenes or avoid them, even whether we can
exert our powers of will to change our behavior—
all these may, and often do, have their source in
our unconscious life.

4. Shall we say that a person is responsible for his act unless it is <u>compelled</u>? Here we
are reminded of Aristotle's assertion (<u>Nicoma-
chean Ethics</u>, Book III) that a person is responsible for his act except for reasons of either
ignorance or compulsion. Ignorance is not part
of our problem here (unless it is unconsciously
induced ignorance of facts previously remembered
and selectively forgotten—in which case the forgetting is again compulsive), but compulsion is.
How will compulsion do as a criterion? The difficulty is to state just what it means. When we
say an act is compelled in a psychological sense,
our language is metaphorical—which is not to say
that there is no point in it or that, properly
interpreted, it is not true. Our actions are compelled in a literal sense if someone has us in
chains or is controlling our bodily movements.
When we say that the storm compelled us to jet-
tison the cargo of the ship (Aristotle's example),
we have a less literal sense of compulsion, for at
least it is open to us to go down with the ship.
When psychoanalysts say that a man was compelled
by unconscious conflicts to wash his hands constantly, this is also not a literal use of "compel"; for nobody forced his hands under the tap.
Still, it is a typical example of what psychologists call <u>compulsive</u> behavior: it has unconscious causes inaccesible to introspection, and
moreover nothing can change it—it is as inevitable for him to do it as it would be if someone
were forcing his hands under the tap. In this it
is exactly like the action of a powerful external
force; it is just as little within one's conscious
control.

In its area of application this interpretation of responsibility comes to much the same as
the previous one. And this area is very great
indeed. For if we cannot be held responsible for
the infantile situations (in which we were after
all passive victims), then neither, it would seem,
can we be held responsible for compulsive actions
occurring in adulthood that are inevitable consequences of those infantile situations. And, psychiatrists and psychoanalysts tell us, actions
fulfilling this description are characteristic of
all people some of the time and some people most
of the time. Their occurrence, once the infantile
events have taken place, is inevitable, just as
the explosion is inevitable once the fuse has been
lighted; there is simply more "delayed action" in
the psychological explosions than there is in the
physical ones.

(I have not used the word "inevitable" here
to mean "causally determined," for according to
such a definition every event would be inevitable
if one accepted the causal principle in some form
or other; and probably nobody except certain philosophers uses "inevitable" in this sense. Rather,
I use "inevitable" in its ordinary sense of "cannot be avoided." To the extent, therefore, that
adult neurotic manifestations <u>can</u> be avoided, once
the infantile patterns have become set, the assertion that they are inevitable is not true.)
5. There is still another criterion, which
I prefer to the previous ones, by which a man's
responsibility for an act can be measured: the
degree to which that act can (or could have been)
<u>changed by the use of reasons</u>. Suppose that the
man who washes his hands constantly does so, he
says, for hygienic reasons, believing that if he
doesn't do so he will be poisoned by germs. We
now convince him, on the best medical authority,
that his belief is groundless. Now, the test of
his responsibility is whether the changed belief
will result in changed behavior. If it does not,
as with the compulsive hand washer, he is not
acting responsibly, but if it does, he is. It is
not the <u>use</u> of reasons, but their <u>efficacy in</u>

changing behavior, that is being made the criterion of responsibility. And clearly in neurotic
cases no such change occurs; in fact, this is often made the defining characteristic of neurotic
behavior: it is unchangeable by any rational
considerations.

II

I have suggested these criteria to distinguish actions for which we can call the agent responsible from those for which we cannot. Even
persons with extensive knowledge of psychiatry do
not, I think, use any one of these criteria to
the exclusion of the others; a conjunction of two
or more may be used at once. But however they
may be combined or selected in actual application, I believe we can make the distinction along
some such lines as we have suggested.

But is there not still another possible
meaning of "responsibility" that we have not yet
mentioned? Even after we have made all the above
distinctions, there remains a question in our
minds whether we are, in the final analysis, responsible for any of our actions at all. The
issue may be put this way: How can anyone be responsible for his actions, since they grow out of
his character, which is shaped and molded and
made what it is by influences—some hereditary,
but most of them stemming from early parental environment—that were not of his own making or
choosing? This question, I believe, still troub-
les many people who would agree to all the distinctions we have just made but still have the
feeling that "this isn't all." They have the uneasy suspicion that there is a more ultimate
sense, a "deeper" sense, in which we are not responsible for our actions, since we are not responsible for the character out of which those
actions spring. This, of course, is the sense
Professor Edwards was describing.

Let us take as an example a criminal who,
let us say, strangled several persons and is

himself now condemned to die in the electric chair. Jury and public alike hold him fully responsible (at least they utter the words "he is responsible"), for the murders were planned down to the minutest detail, and the defendant tells the jury exactly how he planned them. But now we find out how it all came about; we learn of parents who rejected him from babyhood, of the childhood spent in one foster home after another, where it was always plain to him that he was not wanted; of the constantly frustrated early desire for affection, the hard shell of nonchalance and bitterness that he assumed to cover the painful and humiliating fact of being unwanted, and his subsequent attempts to heal these wounds to his shattered ego through defensive aggression.

The criminal is the most passive person in this world, helpless as a baby in his motorically inexpressible fury. Not only does he try to wreak revenge on the mother of the earliest period of his babyhood; his criminality is based on the inner feeling of being incapable of making the mother even feel that the child seeks revenge on her. The situation is that of a dwarf trying to annoy a giant who superciliously refuses to see these attempts. . . . Because of his inner feeling of being a dwarf, the criminotic uses, so to speak, dynamite. Of that the giant must take cognizance. True, the "revenge" harms the avenger. He may be legally executed. However, the primary inner aim of forcing the giant to acknowledge the dwarf's fury is fulfilled.[1]

The poor victim is not conscious of the inner forces that exact from him this ghastly toll; he battles, he schemes, he revels in pseudoagression, he is miserable, but he does not know what works within him to produce these catastrophic acts of crime. His aggressive actions are the wriggling of a worm on a fisherman's hook. And if this is so, it seems difficult to say any longer, "He is responsible." Rather, we shall put him behind bars for the protection of society, but we

shall no longer flatter our feeling of moral superiority by calling him personally responsible
for what he did.

Let us suppose it were established that a
man commits murder only if, sometime during the
previous week, he has eaten a certain combination
of foods—say, tuna fish salad at a meal also including peas, mushroom soup, and blueberry pie.
What if we were to track down the factors common
to all murders committed in this country during
the last twenty years and found this factor present in all of them, and only in them? The example is of course empirically absurd; but may it
not be that there is some combination of factors
that regularly leads to homicide, factors such as
are described in general terms in the above quotation? (Indeed the situation in the quotation
is less fortunate than in our hypothetical example, for it is easy to avoid certain foods once
we have been warned about them, but the situation
of the infant is thrust on him; something has already happened to him once and for all, before he
knows it has happened.) When such specific factors are discovered, won't they make it clear
that it is foolish and pointless, as well as immoral, to hold human beings responsible for
crimes? Or, if one prefers biological to psychological factors, suppose a neurologist is
called in to testify at a murder trail and produces X-ray pictures of the brain of the criminal; anyone can see, he argues, that the cella
turcica was already calcified at the age of nine-
teen; it should be a flexible bone, growing, enabling the gland to grow.[2] All the defendant's
disorders might have resulted from this early
calcification. Now, this particular explanation
may be empirically false; but who can say that no
such factors, far more complex, to be sure, exist?

When we know such things as these, we no
longer feel so much tempted to say that the criminal is responsible for his crime; and we tend
also (do we not?) to excuse him—not legally (we
still confine him to prison) but morally; we no

longer call him a monster or hold him personally
responsible for what he did. Moreover, we do
this in general, not merely in the case of crime:
"You must excuse Grandmother for being irritable;
she's really quite ill and is suffering some pain
all the time." Or: "The dog always bites children after she's had a litter of pups; you can't
blame her for it: she's not feeling well, and
besides she naturally wants to defend them." Or:
"She's nervous and jumpy, but do excuse her: she
has a severe glandular disturbance."

Let us note that the more thoroughly and in
detail we know the causal factors leading a person to behave as he does, the more we tend to
exempt him from responsibility. When we know
nothing of the man except what we see him do, we
say he is an ungrateful cad who expects much of
other people and does nothing in return, and we
are usually indignant. When we learn that his
parents were the same way and, having no guilt
feelings about this mode of behavior themselves,
brought him up to be greedy and avaricious, we
see that we could hardly expect him to have developed moral feelings in this direction. When
we learn, in addition, that he is not aware of
being ungrateful or selfish, but unconsciously
represses the memory of events unfavorable to
himself, we feel that the situation is unfortunate but "not really his fault." When we know
that this behavior of his, which makes others
angry, occurs more constantly when he feels tense
or insecure, and that he now feels tense and insecure, and that relief from pressure will diminish it, then we tend to "feel sorry for the poor
guy" and say he's more to be pitied than censured.
We no longer want to say that he is personally
responsible; we might rather blame nature or his
parents for having given him an unfortunate constitution or temperament.

In recent years a new form of punishment has
been imposed on middle-aged and elderly parents. Their children, now in their twenties,
thirties or even forties, present them with a

573

modern grievance: "My analysis proves that you are responsible for my neurosis." Over-awed by these authoritative statements, the poor tired parents fall easy victims to the newest variations on the scapegoat theory.

In my opinion, this senseless cruelty—which disinters educational sins which had been buried for decades, and uses them as the basis for accusations which the victims cannot answer—is unjustified. Yes, "the truth loves to be centrally located" (Melville), and few parents—since they are human—have been perfect. But granting their mistakes, they acted as their neurotic difficulties forced them to act. To turn the tables and declare the children not guilty because of the impersonal nature of their own neuroses, while at the same time the parents are personally blamed, is worse than illogical; it is profoundly unjust.[3]

And so, it would now appear, neither of the parties is responsible: "they acted as their neurotic difficulties forced them to act." The patients are not responsible for their neurotic manifestations, but then neither are the parents responsible for theirs; and so, of course, for their parents in turn, and theirs before them. It is the twentieth-century version of the family curse, the curse on the House of Atreus.

"But," a critic complains, "it's immoral to exonerate people indiscriminately in this way. I might have thought it fit to excuse somebody because he was born on the other side of the tracks, if I didn't know so many bank presidents who were also born on the other side of the tracks." Now, I submit that the most immoral thing in this situation is the critic's caricature of the conditions of the excuse. Nobody is excused merely because he was born on the other side of the tracks. But if he was born on the other side of the tracks and was a highly narcissistic infant to begin with and was repudiated or neglected by his parents and . . . (here we list a finite number of conditions), and if this complex of factors is _regularly_ followed by certain behavior traits in adulthood, and moreover _unavoidably_ so—that is, they occur no matter what he or anyone else tries to do—then we excuse him morally and say he is not responsible for his deed. If he is not responsible for A̲, a series of events occurring in his babyhood, then neither is he responsible for B̲, a series of things he does in adulthood, provided that B̲ inevitably—that is, unavoidably —follows upon the occurrence of A̲. And according to psychiatrists and psychoanalysts, this often happens.

But one may still object that so far we have talked only about neurotic behavior. Isn't non-neurotic or normal or not unconsciously motivated (or whatever you want to call it) behavior still within the area of responsibility? There are reasons for answering "No" even here, for the normal person no more than the neurotic one has caused his own character, which makes him what he is. Granted that neurotics are not responsible for their behavior (that part of it which we call neurotic) because it stems from undigested infantile conflicts that they had no part in bringing about, and that are external to them just as surely as if their behavior had been forced on them by a malevolent deity (which is indeed one theory on the subject); but the so-called normal person is equally the product of causes in which his volition took no part. And if, unlike the neurotic's, his behavior is changeable by rational considerations, and if he has the will power to overcome the effects of an unfortunate early environment, this again is no credit to him; he is just lucky. If energy is available to him in a form in which it can be mobilized for constructive purposes, this is no credit to him, for this too is part of his psychic legacy. Those of us who can discipline ourselves and develop habits of concentration of purpose tend to blame those who cannot, and call them lazy and weak-willed; but what we fail to see is that they literally cannot do what we expect; if their psyches were structured like ours, they could, but as they are burdened with a tyrannical superego (to use psychoanalytic jargon for the moment), and a weak defenseless ego whose energies are constantly consumed in fighting endless charges of the superego, they simply cannot do it, and it is irrational to expect it of them. We cannot with justification blame them for their inability, any more than we can congratulate ourselves for our ability. This lesson is hard to learn, for we constantly and naïvely assume that other people are constructed as we ourselves are.

For example: A child raised under slum conditions, whose parents are socially ambitious and envy families with money, but who nevertheless squander the little they have on drink, may simply be unable in later life to mobilize a drive sufficient to overcome these early conditions. Common sense would expect that he would develop the virtue of thrift; he would make quite sure that he would never again endure the grinding poverty he had experienced as a child. But in fact it is not so: The exact conditions are too complex to be specified in detail here, but when certain conditions are fulfilled (concerning the subject's early life), he will always thereafter be a spendthrift, and no rational considerations will be able to change this. He will listen to the rational considerations and see the force of these, but they will not be able to change him, even if he tries; he cannot change his wasteful habits any more than he can lift the Empire State Building with his bare hands. We moralize and plead with him to be thrifty, but we do not see how strong, how utterly overpowering, and how constantly with him, is the opposite drive, which is so easily manageable with us. But he is possessed by the all-consuming, all-encompassing urge to make the world see that he belongs, that he has arrived, that he is just as well off as anyone else, that the awful humiliations were not real, that they never actually occurred, for isn't he now able to spend and spend? The humiliation must be blotted out; and conspicuous, flashy, expensive, and wasteful buying will do this; it shows the world what the world must know! True, it is only for the moment; true, it is in the end self-defeating, for wasteful consumption is the best way to bring poverty back again; but the person with an overpowering drive to mend a lesion to his narcissism cannot resist the avalanche of that drive with this puny rational consideration. A man with his back against the wall and a gun at his throat doesn't think of what may happen ten years hence. (Consciously, of course, he knows nothing of this drive; all that appears to consciousness is its shattering effects; he knows only that he must keep on spending—not why —and that he is unable to resist.) He hasn't in him the psychic capacity, the energy to stem the tide of a drive that at that moment is all-powerful. We, seated comfortably away from this flood, sit in judgment on him and blame him and exhort him and criticize him; but he, carried along by the flood, cannot do otherwise than he does. He may fight with all the strength of which he is capable, but it is not enough. And we, who are rational enough at least to exonerate a man in a situation of "overpowering impulse" when we recognize it to be one, do not even recognize this as an example of it; and so, in addition to being swept away in the flood that childhood conditions rendered inevitable, he must also endure our lectures, our criticisms, and our moral excoriation.

But, one will say, he could have overcome his spendthrift tendencies; some people do. Quite true: some people do. They are lucky. They have it in them to overcome early deficiencies by exerting great effort, and they are capable of exerting the effort. Some of us, luckier still, can overcome them with but little effort; and a few, the luckiest, haven't the deficiencies to overcome. It's all a matter of luck. The least lucky are those who can't overcome them, even with great effort, and those who haven't the ability to exert the effort.

But, one persists, it isn't a matter simply of luck; it _is_ a matter of effort. Very well then, it's a matter of effort; without exerting the effort you may not overcome the deficiency. But whether or not you are the kind of person who has it in him to exert the effort is a matter of luck.

All this is well known to psychoanalysts. They can predict, from minimal clues that most of us don't notice, whether a person is going to turn out to be lucky or not. "The analyst," they say, "must be able to use the residue of the patient's unconscious guilt so as to remove the symptom or character trait that creates the guilt. The guilt must not only be present, but <u>available</u> for use, <u>mobilizable</u>. If it is used up (absorbed) in criminal activity, or in an excessive amount of self-damaging tendencies, then it cannot be used for therapeutic purposes, and the prognosis is negative." Not all philosophers will relish the analyst's way of putting the matter, but at least as a physician he can soon detect whether the patient is lucky or unlucky—and he knows that whichever it is, it <u>isn't the patient's fault</u>. The patient's conscious volition cannot remedy the deficiency. Even whether he will co-operate with the analyst is really out of the patient's hands: if he continually projects the denying-mother fantasy on the analyst and unconsciously identifies him always with the cruel, harsh forbidder of the nursery, thus frustrating any attempt at impersonal observation, the sessions are useless; yet if it happens that way, he can't help that either. That fatal projection is not under his control; whether it occurs or not depends on how his unconscious identifications have developed since his infancy. He can try, yes—but the ability to try enough for the therapy to have effect is also beyond his control; the capacity to try more than just so much is either there or it isn't—and either way "it's in the lap of the gods."

The position, then, is this: if we <u>can</u> overcome the effects of early environment, the ability to do so is itself a product of the early

environment. We did not give ourselves this
ability; and if we lack it we cannot be blamed
for not having it. Sometimes, to be sure, moral exhortation brings out an ability that is
there but not being used, and in this lies its
occasional utility; but very often its use is
pointless, because the ability is not there.
The only thing that can overcome a desire, as
Spinoza said, is a stronger contrary desire; and
many times there simply is no wherewithal for
producing a stronger contrary desire. Those of
us who do have the wherewithal are lucky.

There is one possible practical advantage
in remembering this. It may prevent us (unless
we are compulsive blamers) from indulging in
righteous indignation and committing the sin of
spiritual pride, thanking God that we are not as
this publican here. And it will protect from
our useless moralizings those who are least
equipped by nature for enduring them.

As with responsibility, so with deserts.
Someone commits a crime and is punished by the
state; "he deserved it," we say self-righteously
—as if we were moral and he immoral, when in
fact we are lucky and he is unlucky—forgetting
that there, but for the grace of God and a fortunate early environment, go we. Or, as Clarence
Darrow said in his speech for the defense in the
Loeb-Leopold case:

I do not believe that people are in jail because they deserve to be. . . . I know what
causes the emotional life. . . . I know it is
practically left out of some. Without it they
cannot act with the rest. They cannot feel
the moral shocks which safeguard others. Is
(this man) to blame that his machine is imperfect? Who is to blame? I do not know. I
have never in my life been interested so much
in fixing blame as I have in relieving people
from blame. I am not wise enough to fix it.[4]

Notes

[1]Edmund Bergler, The Basic Neurosis (New York: Grune and Stratton, 1949), p. 305.

[2]Meyer Levin, Compulsion (New York: Simon and Schuster, 1956), p. 403.

[3]Edmund Bergler, The Superego (New York: Grune and Stratton, 1952), p. 320.

[4]Levin, op. cit., pp. 439-40, 469.

<u>Death</u> <u>and</u> <u>Life</u> After <u>Death</u>

Case

     Phyllis had known the death of her friends
and had been able to take it in stride. After
all when one gets older it is expected. But
somehow she had believed that she and Schaeffer
would go on forever. But Schaeffer had passed
away in his sleep quite unexpectedly. And now
the pain of the grief was deeper and more consuming than she thought possible. How many times
she had thought that if she could just understand
it and maybe believe that she would see Schaeffer
again then she could bear the wrenching surges of
grief that pass uncontrollably through her.

The Problem of Death in Modern Philosophy*
J. Glenn Gray

"A free man thinks of nothing less than of
death, and his wisdom is not a meditation upon
death but upon life." This sentence, Proposition 67, Part IV, of Spinoza's Ethics is a remarkable proposition, I think, and is predicated
upon a no less remarkable metaphysics. In Spinoza's eyes, our universe is a vast mechanical
order, marked by perfection of function and fullness of being. There are no abysses in it, nothing unintelligible or impenetrable by reason.
God or Nature is an all-upholding, necessary power which prevents any loss of anything ever possessing real existence. If we could ask Spinoza:
"Why should we not upon occasion meditate upon
death?" he would no doubt answer: "Because death
has no reality and you should meditate only upon
essentials, upon eternal things. For by so doing
you will become like the eternal: calm, self-
sufficient, happy, indestructible, free. You will
be directed in everything by reason, which can
not pass away. Thus death is of no consequence to
the free man and no fit problem for philosophical
meditation!"

Spinoza, who is notable for having lived his
philosophy, accordingly dismissed the subject,
and, apart from the quoted proposition and a short
demonstration under it, there is hardly a mention
of death in his considerable writings. Though
Spinoza and Spinozism met great opposition in the
seventeenth, eighteenth, and nineteenth centuries,
this particular proposition seems to have enjoyed
nearly universal assent among thinkers. For the
question of death has occupied modern thought
astonishingly little. Socrates once defined phi-

*From The Modern Vision of Death, Nathan A. Scott
editor, John Knox Press, 1967, pp. 45-67. Copyright © by J. Glenn Gray. Reprinted by permission of the publisher and deceased author's wife.

losophy as "the pursuit of death" and he became
immortal by his teaching and example of how a
philosopher should conduct himself in the face of
death. In many Greek and Roman thinkers, Socrates' definition of philosophy met with intellectual approval as complete as the moral fervor
stimulated by his death. The writers of the
Renaissance were also largely preoccupied with
the awareness of death and the problems posed by
this awareness. But the theme largely disappeared in the post-Renaissance epochs from both philosophy and art, and I think that its disappear-
ance has not been enough noticed. The ground
swell of the Enlightenment with its hope for human improvement, its anti-historical bias, and
its trust in mathematical science may have contributed something toward eclipsing the concern
with human mortality. Other problems claimed
attention. Though death, as an unpleasant occurrence, could not be denied, it did not lend
itself easily to scientific analysis. Morally it
harmonized ill with faith in progress, perfectibility, and the concept of rationality of the
world order.

In the twentieth century, death has been
rediscovered as a philosophical idea and problem.
It is in fact with the contemporary German existentialists, Karl Jaspers and Martin Heidegger,
near the center of their interpretation of reality and human existence. They assert emphatically that a proper understanding of, and right attitude toward, death, one's own death, is not
only a sine qua non of genuine experience, but
also of gaining any illumination about the nature
of the world. They could not be further removed
from the precept of Spinoza which we have already
quoted, nor more out of line with dominant em-
phases of modern thought. I want to examine this
present-day formulation of the idea of death and
attempt to evaluate it. In what follows I shall
be dealing chiefly with the two German existentialists because they have emphasized this theme
much more than have Kierkegaard, Sartre, and the
minor figures of this school of thought. Some-

thing of what is said in general on this topic
will be applicable, to be sure, to all the existentialists, but for the more specific analysis
Jaspers and Heidegger are necessarily the major
sources.

What meaning and significance can be attached to the fact that man must die? How should I
regard my own death as a future event? What
values are to be derived from regarding it at all
as contrasted with forgetting about it and living
as though death were not real? If we are to find
intelligible the answers existentialists give to
these questions, we must first gain some appreciation of what I shall call the philosophic mood of
existentialism, and review a little of the metaphysics. Existentialism consists chiefly, I think,
of a pervasive mood and a metaphysics and the two
are, curiously enough, related to the point where
they mutually determine each other.

The mood can perhaps best be identified as a
feeling of the homelessness of man. This world
into which we come or are thrown as human creatures is radically insufficient to the claims and
the requirements of the spirit. Our natural and
social environment oppresses us with its foreign-
ness, its unsuitability as a home for all that is
specifically human about us as individuals. If
we are genuine persons, sensitive to the human
situation, we can gain no hold or support in nature or society. They are not our element. We
are in the world, as Christians are wont to say,
but not of it. All attempts to find a home for
the spirit in this temporal, spatial realm are
foredoomed. And this because the course of events
is essentially unintelligible, not above reason as
the Romantics thought, nor hidden from reason as
in the Kantian philosophy. No, man's reason, like
his soul, is a stranger in a world, impenetrable
and unknowable, which cares not for him. Any
order and meaning, if there are to be any, must be
created by individual effort and resolve, and created anew by each individual all the time.

This deep-rooted conviction of homelessness places the existentialists at once in sharp contrast to idealistic and naturalistic philosophies in the Western heritage. The great idealists have always stressed coming to be at home in the world as the goal of all striving. Since Hegel particularly, idealism has been imbued with a sense of the intimate relationships existing between the individual and society, the individual and Nature, the individual and God or the Absolute. The true individual, for idealism, is not isolated but implicated in the whole world, in all its variegated relationships. Existential homelessness is, on the other hand, in equal contrast with the mood of the various naturalistic philosophies of our day. Naturalists always find the locus of human values and the source of social and individual aspirations in the world of material nature. Nature is always maternal and any estrangement from her is an arbitrary, irrational, even sinful act on the part of the individual. But the existentialists take no joy in Nature, and derive no metaphysical principles from her.

It is, in truth, difficult to find any good analogies in the Western tradition with the existentialist mood. It is tempting, but unprofitable, to liken this mood with Romanticism, particularly the pessimistic Romanticism of Schopenhauer and his followers. There are, of course, affinities, but the existentialists can hardly be said to share the hopelessness, the cynical detachment, and the consolatory aestheticism of Romantic pessimism. They vigorously protest against the critical charges of nihilism and despair as the outcome of their point of view, and on the whole, I think, rightly so. Bertrand Russell's famous little essay "A Free Man's Worship" voices an attitude toward Nature somewhat similar to existentialism, and the consolation Russell offers of comradeship with the few like-minded in "the long march through the night of life" is not unlike Jaspers' conviction that communication between single individuals is of timeless validity. Yet there is, on closer glance, a great difference. For Russell's mood, short-lived as most of his are, was evidently derived from his acquaintance with natural science and represented a heroic attitude of revolt against the facts which science teaches. Like that of so many Englishmen of the nineteenth century, his pathos derives from reaction to a science whose truths are no longer disputable but are at the same time an offense to the human spirit. Existentialism's mood is not so defiant and heroic. With Jaspers and Heidegger, at least, this "disenchantment of the world" brought about by science is assumed as a matter of course, and is not a cause for heroics. The sense of strangeness and estrangement between the individual and his world in existentialism is engendered, I think, though hardly explained by, the experiences of everyday living in a radically unstable social world. Not the revelations of science, but the applied technology of science is a chief source of existentialist sadness, in contrast to that of Russell. If space permitted, one might more profitably search for analogues to the existential mood among ancient writers in Greco-Roman or Jewish history.

For this philosophical mood is involved in a metaphysics which has not been at all prevalent in Western thought, and is in fact in sharp contradiction to the great systems. The German term unheimlich, which literally translates as "unhome-like," has in fact the denotation of the "uncanny." When you feel in German unheimlich zu Mute, you are seized with a nameless fear. You are out of your element, but more than that you have an intuition of abysses hidden from normal moods. These rare experiences of the uncanny, the existentialists hold, are revelatory of the innermost nature of reality. At such times we feel a sense of deep unease; we are threatened and oppressed by everything in general and nothing in particular. We are filled with dread or anguish, a psychological state which has for the existentialists metaphysical origins.[1] If someone asks us what is troubling us when we are oppressed with this feeling of the uncanny, we are

586

likely to answer: "It is nothing." These words
are truer than we know. For what has oppressed
us is the primary intuition that we are not sustained by infinite power and plenitude of being,
as so many philosophers have taught. On the contrary, we, human creatures, perceive dimly in the
experience of the uncanny that the world rests on
nothing. It has no basis or ground. Human existence, as one form of Being, is suspended over the
abyss of Non-being. As Heidegger puts it: "To
exist as a human being means to be exposed to
Nothingness."[2] The concept of Non-being or Nothingness is not merely a legitimate category of
this metaphysics, it becomes the one which determines all other categories. Nothingness precedes,
envelops, and conditions all Being. In the experience of Dread we are confronted with the hidden truth that there is no ultimate consolation,
that the end of all striving is shipwreck, the
abyss of Non-being. It is hard to discover this
truth, harder still to face it and live by it.
Weak natures never know this mood of Dread at all,
Kierkegaard insisted. And the German existentialists hold that even the strongest of us know
it rarely, because we are chiefly creatures of
comfort, not seekers of truth. Nevertheless, the
experience of Dread is not something genuine persons want to avoid; it is, on the contrary, something to be sought and endured. These men believe
strongly in the conviction of Goethe that "Das
Schaudern ist der Menschheit bestes Teil" (The
chill of dread is man's best quality). Only
through the convulsion of our normal state of
being can we reach the salvation of Existenz and
overcome the original sin of merely vegetating in
the everyday world. Of course, for Kierkegaard
and the religious branch of existentialism, the
experience of Dread is only preliminary to salvation in a fundamental sense: it precedes the leap
of faith. And faith is defined as absolute trust
in the Christian God of love, in whom eternal life
is possible for man. To Jaspers, Heidegger, and
Sartre, on the other hand, the salvation that can
come by way of Dread is this-worldly; it lies in
the quality of experience that issues from living

in the truth. Dread does not precede anything; it reveals the truth of Nothingness and conditions our perception of all other truths. As Jaspers puts it: "The bottomless character of the world must become revealed to us, if we are to win through to the truth of the world."

There is, say the existentialists, a true and a false way of evaluating the human situation. Of primary importance for the true way is the denudation of the spirit, the stripping away of all subterfuges, comforts, and evasions. Our true condition is one of exposure: in reality, we are defenseless, naked to the winds of chance and blind accident. There is an expressive German participle, geborgen, which translates into English as "secure" or "safe," but connotes the delightful feeling of protectedness, the comfort of being hidden away or concealed from lurking dangers. The little bird is geborgen in the nest, the infant in the womb, the beloved in the arms of a strong and tender lover. By exposure is meant just the opposite of this. Though the desire for protection and security, for Geborgenheit, is a characteristic and primary impulse of human creatures, it is also a profound illusion. Spiritually, we are all exposed to the yawning abyss, the primal night which originates all and to which we all return. Only a small fraction of mankind ever recognizes this to be their real state, but it is no less true because of that.

Perhaps Karl Jaspers has made clearest the meaning of exposure in his description of the so-called "boundary situations." Every individual lives at every moment in a situation, one that is, to be sure, constantly changing and never totally grasped or understood. Boundary situations are situations involving a limit or an end, and, unlike the ordinary ones, they do not change in essence. These situations which reveal the limits of our being to us, and which are inescapable and constitutive of genuine life, are experiences of guilt, of suffering, conflict, chance, and death. Such experiences are not to

be understood in conceptual terms; their implications are hidden from our ordinary logic. But
by entering open-eyed into these boundary experiences, resolved to know them by direct acquaintance, we expose ourselves to that kind of
vital experience which existentialists call
truth.

The most extreme spiritual exposure is the
exposure to death, and it is the most impenetrable of the boundary situations. It is the one
which makes shipwreck of all·human life inevitable. Death belongs to the human situation as
such and to the situation of each individual.
"Shipwreck is the ultimate," writes Jaspers,
meaning thereby that hopes for immortality are
vain. Our frail crafts are afloat on an unending
sea around which there are no ports. To recognize this fact, the painful fact of human fini-
tude, the inevitability of death, can alone make
living meaningful and significant. This way is
the path of liberation through truth. For "the
deepest intimacy with actuality is at the same
time the readiness to true shipwreck."3

What, then, is the fruitful way to regard
death? How can we make of our own death an event
of great import? Jaspers and Heidegger answer in
effect: You must gain a vivid realization of
death as a constitutive part of life, not as a
mere end of life. Death is a phenomenon within
life. If it is taken into life in a personal
way, it will effect a revolution in our behavior.
The fact of our mortality can properly be regarded
as a fountain of possibility and potentiality.
Indeed, in Heidegger's terms, death is at once
"the most personal, the most detached, unrelated,
and unsurpassable potentiality."5 Once we learn
to grasp the reality of death as life's greatest
possibility, we shall not simply await it passively as a passing away of a biological sort, nor
brood over it, nor desire to hasten its coming.
Death will be regarded neither as a friend nor
as a stranger.

The first requirement in becoming aware of death as a possibility of increase of Being is to recognize that death is always and ever my own, something that belongs to my very essence, as Nothingness belongs to Being. No one can take my place in death, nor can I, in this sense, ever die for another. I always die alone and the very meaning of death to me, according to Heidegger, is attained only in contemplation of my own death.

It is true that Jaspers makes a significant distinction between the death of a dearest friend and one's own death. The death of a friend can be "the deepest wound" in life. The friend dies alone, as everyone must, and seemingly the separation is absolute and forever. Yet for the one who remains behind, continuation of the communication the two friends have enjoyed is in a real, if mystical, sense possible. Communication, being nonphysical and not really confined in language, does not necessarily require the actual presence of the communicants. But to expound what Jaspers understands by communication and by the closely related concept of transcendence would require a separate essay. As far as I can see these ideas stand in rather sharp contradiction with his teachings on death and inevitable shipwreck, and place him religiously somewhere between the fervent Protestantism of Kierkegaard and the atheism of Sartre. In this respect his philosophy as a whole is to the last degree equivocal and ambivalent.

Nevertheless, for Jaspers as for Heidegger the decisive fact about death is that each person must regard his own death as the paramount reality. It is unsharable, the most isolated, separate, unrelated of life's possibilities, and for that reason the most significant. The individual who has achieved genuineness welcomes an event and a situation where everything depends on himself, unaided and unconsoled. Such an individual will also face the realization that, though our death is certain, the hour of its coming is indefinite and indeterminable. We must be certain <u>that</u> we shall die, and we can never know when we shall die. As a consequence of this seemingly common-place truth, we must learn to live always in the face of death.

Before following out the implications of this conclusion, we must explain what Jaspers and Hei-degger regard as the ordinary, which are, in their view, the perverse and false, ways of regarding death. The all but universal practice, they hold, is to refuse to accept the reality of death. For Jaspers the usual ways of escape are those of "positivism" and "mysticism." The positivist com-monly follows the dubious wisdom of Epicurus, and repeats the formula: "While I am, death is not, and when death is, I am not. Therefore, death is of no concern to me." Now, it is true enough that I can not actually experience my death, and the consolation the positivists offer would be real enough if it were the fear of physical death that troubled us. But, as Jaspers rightly insists, I think, the thing about death which we fear is chiefly the prospect of no longer being, of van-ishing into nullity. It is an "existential dread" at the prospect which grips the thoughtful person, and this feeling has little biological import. Against this dread, this shudder at Non-being, the positivist has no weapons. He knows only "help-less despair." No better is the other classic escape which Jaspers calls "worldless mysticism." Mystics, of whatever sort, refuse to believe in the reality of death because they do not accept the world of our experience as being real. They set up an unbridgeable dualism between an alleged real world and the experienced world of phenomena. Their faith is in immortality or metempsychosis, and death is only a moment of transition, a phy-sical change, often an object of longing. It loses for the mystics, illegitimately, its true character as boundary situation. The mystics com-mit the opposite error from that of positivism in not accepting the organic aspect of all human ex-istence, the union of spirit and flesh.

Heidegger's analysis of the common way of

591

escape from facing death is perhaps more subtle.
We rob ourselves, he maintains, of the sense of
death's reality by making of it a public event,
something that happens to everybody indiscriminately, and hence to no one in particular. We
strive to make death just another event, among
many, happening every day to somebody, and presumably someday to me, but it doesn't concern me
at this time. Death is certain, we are wont to
say, but hasn't happened to me yet. By our very
manner of speaking we betray our desire to evade
this most private, isolated, and unsurpassable
possibility. In the end there comes to be a
tacit agreement not to speak of death. The subject is tactless; the event itself an imperti-
nence. Undue concern about it is a certain mark
of cowardice. Heidegger's analysis of the impersonal pronoun in German, das Man (the one),
as expressive of the fallen state of mankind in
general and of the unwillingness to face death in
particular, has become well known. In English we
use, more commonly, the third person plural in an
impersonal sense: "they say," "they do it," etc.
When the pronoun is used thus impersonally we exclude this person and that person, and ourselves,
of course, and frequently designate no one at all.
Like our use of words such as "the public" or
"the masses" as large categories with no individual members, so we speak of "one," "they," "the
others," and mean really no one in particular.
This escape into impersonality is for existentialism the original sin. It signifies a blunt-
ing of all intense feeling, an escape from personal responsibility, a refusal to regard death
as something of profoundest concern to the individual personality. For I unconsciously identify
myself with the impersonal "one." So we live in
everyday banality, fallen creatures who shield
ourselves from that which could make us genuine
persons. We prefer forgetfulness to awareness
and death overtakes us, as it overtook Ilya Ilitch
in Tolstoi's famous short story, horrible to the
last degree because life was vacuous and without
authenticity.

To overcome this inveterate drive to unreal-
ity—this fallen, lost state—it is imperative to
recognize that we live hourly in the face of death
and to learn to act on that awareness. I must
take as literally true and applicable to me the
fact that my death is certain and can take place
any instant. I have no claim on any but the present moment. On it, however, I have an absolute
claim. It can be wholly mine. And mine is the
responsibility of making the moment intense and
full. I have the responsibility of separating at
every moment in my life the essential from the
inessential, the genuine from the false. Such
responsibility can only really be assumed if one
has learned to live in the face of death. "What
in the face of death remains essential is done
existentially; what falls away is mere <u>Dasein</u>"[5]
(literally, "being there").

What does this mean practically to anyone
who is concerned about becoming a wholly genuine
person? The answer of the existentialists is that
it means, for one thing, that we can not plan our
lives as a whole or even as a significant part of
a whole. We can not think of genuineness in terms
of fulfillment. Life has nothing whatever to do
with fulfillment. Some people fulfill themselves,
at least in a superficial sense, and live on; many
more die with potentialities unrealized; the majority, indeed, die after wasted lives which have
been merely used up, having never really "come to
themselves." Jaspers writes:

In life everything attained is like death.
Nothing completed can live. In so far as we
strive for completeness, we are striving toward
the finished, the dead. . . . As a drama for
others a life can appear to be complete; in
reality it does not possess this character.
Life is tension and goal, inadequacy and un-
fulfillment.[6]

Living in the face of death then means living in
such fashion that life can be broken off at any
moment and not be rendered meaningless by such

accident. We do not as genuine persons put the goals of our life somewhere in the future and make their attainment the measure of life's meaning. Meaningful living, for the existentialists, requires to be conceived not in terms of completion or in terms of duration, but rather in terms of an intensification and clarification of life's possibilities from moment to moment.

Heidegger's analysis of the nature of time helps to clarify and deepen this central doctrine of existentialism. Though his treatment in Sein und Zeit is complex and involved, it may be possible to suggest briefly the part relevant to our theme. For us as human creatures, says Heidegger, time is not truly conceived as a smooth passage from a past to a future through a present, just as death is not rightly conceived as a mere snipping of life spun out on a thread. Time does not flow, does not carry us along; it is not at all what Bergson held it to be. We must consider that the present moment is all we ever experience and inhabit. The present moment contains the whole richness of the world and the whole potentiality of experience. The past and the future are contained in our consciousness in the present, and, in a real sense, only there. The past, the "has been," acts as a restraining weight on our present; the future, the "not yet," as a liberating, releasing force. That is, the future can be liberating if it is conceived as part of the present, as experienced time and not as external calendar or clock time. Heidegger does not deny the reality of objective time, as some of his American critics seem to think. But he does hold that to gain genuine experience we must internalize time, learn to regard it as personal and private, our time as opposed to that of clocks and calendars. If we so regard it, time as linear progression will disappear from our thinking, and the future will be seen to belong to the present in a fundamental way. Though more is involved, Heidegger's chief emphasis in his treatment of time is that the future must be regarded in a new way, as part of the existential moment. As he sums it up in a sentence, difficult to translate:

"Future" means, in the sense used here, not a
Now that has not yet really become present,
some time that will be, but on the contrary
the coming (<u>Kunft</u>) in which existence in its
most personal potentiality of Being approaches
itself. The "running ahead" (<u>Vorlaufen</u>) in
the present makes existence genuinely future.[7]

The future is thus for experienced, inner
time always a realm of present possibility. The
"not yet" is experienced as a "running forward"
in thought into what might or can be. As genuine human beings we are open, uncompleted, "un-
fulfillable"; Heidegger seems at times to think
that our potentiality, the "not yet," is all that
genuinely <u>is</u>. The external future can bring us
nothing we do not already possess, provided we
are genuine persons. Potentiality is thus uncon-
nected with teleology of an organic sort. Though
life is always directed toward the future, as existentialists say, this expression is likely to
be misleading unless we understand the term "future" as a dimension of the present.

How then is death related to this "not yet"
which forms so great a part of our inner present?
Heidegger proposes two interesting analogies, only
to reject them. First, of the moon, when we say
it is not yet full we mean that we do not perceive, say, the quarter that is not visible. But
this is only a matter of perception, not of being.
The invisible quarter is there all the time. The
reverse is true of the human "not yet." With us
it is a question of actual growth of being, not
so with the moon. Secondly, of fruit, we say that
it is becoming ripe but is not yet ripe. This
analogy is much more adequate than the moon analogy because we are dealing with an actual change
of being here, not with mere perception. Moreover, the condition of ripeness toward which the
unripe fruit grows is not something external,
brought about by others, or merely added as a sum,
but is a constitutive part of the fruit. The "not

yet" in this case belongs, as in human life, to the internal being of the fruit.

Nevertheless, the analogy is radically imperfect, as all analogies drawn from the organic world will be for the existentialists. Existentialism is emphatically not a "process philosophy" of either a naturalistic or idealistic sort. The ripeness of the fruit signifies its perfection or completion, its telos, whereas death can not be so conceived. Death is not the fulfillment of the "not yet," as ripeness is of the fruit requiring a definite time. On the contrary it is a Bevorstand, an imminence, something always directly before you. Being unto death, a phrase Heidegger borrows from Kierkegaard, is a way of life that looks at the possibility of death as an intimate part of life; it isolates man, it throws him back upon himself, it offers him the possibility of becoming a personality. As a way of life, this being unto death recognizes that life is delivered up to death at every instant—"a man is old enough to die as soon as he is born"—and at the same time affirms this fact as a great privilege and the most difficult challenge.

Once the full reality of personal death is accepted, the moment is informed with a sense of urgency and mission. The individual is liberated from the banality of existence in society, the fallen state of the mass of mankind. Genuine personality, painful and even tragic, will be achieved by the exceptional person through resoluteness, a key Heideggerian term. The genuine person gains resoluteness in realizing that existence must be given meaning; it does not as such possess it. He will be committed to an exploration of the dimensions of the present moment, to make his life in some way distinctive and unique. He will no longer avoid exposure nor the shudder of dread before Nothingness. On the contrary these will be his meat and drink.

Moreover, exposure to the most intimate and

extreme experience of all, that of death, will develop a love of openness, or overt behavior, which is what Jaspers and Heidegger call truth. Like other philosophers, they lay claim to the discovery of important truth as the raison d'être of their philosophy. Truth for them is not something caught in the bonds of logic or concepts. It is a way of behaving or being. To be existentially is to be in the truth. Human existence is in the truth when Being is unveiled, opened, bared to the light. But concealment, obscurity, hiddenness, are in the very nature of things. Truth as an act is the uncovering of Being; it is a clarification, the lightening of Being, Erhellung des Seins. The clarified, enlightened individual portrays Being as it is to the extent that he exposes himself to the most extreme openness there is: the openness toward death. Here the existentialists' ultimate claim is plainly that the individual who lives in the face of death will not only gain insight into the truth of Being, but he will be that truth, at least a substantial part of it. And he will have gained freedom, which is identified in Heidegger with truth, and which has, with Sartre, become a theme of greater import than the theme of death. But the further analysis of truth and of freedom, as the existentialists see them, belongs to another paper. Let us turn to a brief evaluation of this idea of death and ask ourselves how much of the reasoning we can accept.

As Americans we are nearly certain to find something perverse in this European point of view. As a philosophy it is too bleak, too extreme, above all, too individualistic for us. Our normal response to this claim that life can gain authenticity only if pointed toward death is to assert that there are other and better ways. If you want your life to be genuine, meaningful, and intense, we rejoin, why not devote yourself wholeheartedly to social ideals? This means for us, I think, getting ourselves involved in important and urgent projects to the extent that our yearning for love and devotion is effectively satisfied. We

597

realize our true selves by submerging them in such suprapersonal goals as world peace, racial equality, political and economic democracy, and the like. Personal life can be rescued from emptiness and futility, we think, only by recourse to the social or the political. My help is not in me. If I do not catch the vision of service in a great social cause I am lost. Salvation, like almost everything else, has for us become social salvation.

This overwhelming emphasis on the social is, of course, not simply an American phenomenon. It forms a large part of the current spirit of our Western civilization, and as such it is so intimately part of us that any deepgoing criticism is likely to sound quixotic in the extreme. Like all of the critics of existentialism I have read, I think that this philosophy is one-sided and unbalanced in its neglect, not to say repudiation, of the social dimensions of existence. At the same time, I am convinced that our very preoccupation with the social in this century has generated a deep dissatisfaction which makes existentialism darkly appealing. One need not renounce his faith in democracy in order to feel in his marrow that, expand the concept how he will, it is still insufficient spiritual nourishment. The same is surely true of communism, and our other purely social and secular religions. They are not enough to live by, and the suspicion grows that we all use these social faiths at times to escape the discipline of self-examination and self-knowledge. It is, in one sense, so easy to give oneself to a social and socially-approved goal, and, conversely, so difficult, as Kierkegaard knew, to attain to true selfhood or, as he put it, "subjectivity." We have today a great many convinced democrats and we have many communists who stake their all on communism as a way of life, but we have far fewer individuals with real depth and range to their personality. Whatever strictures we can and must bring against existentialism as a whole, it is hard to resist the point of Heidegger's analysis of the flight into impersonality, hard to deny that we have too often sought mere warmth in the crowd, preferring the protection and bliss of social anonymity to the opportunity for genuine personal growth. The hard tasks of self-examination and self-evaluation are certainly as vital in this age as in any preceding, and it may be existentialism's mission to make this evident. Few things are calculated, I think, to aid that task more than the courageous recognition that we are as individuals subject at every moment to death and that on one can spare us from it. If that recognition does not shake us into honesty and into seriousness, it can confidently be affirmed that nothing else will.

Nevertheless, an insistent question arises to challenge the existentialist doctrine at this point. Can we really conduct our lives in such fashion that an untimely death will not destroy the meaning and the purpose we have built into our existence? Or put more pointedly: Can a meaningful life be constructed out of existential moments? It seems to me to be hightly doubtful, without modifying severely some of their premises. The existentialist analysis of time, involving as it does a sweeping denial of objective process and development, is hard to accept. Spiritual living, like organic life in this at least, seems to require time of the more conventional sort to realize values and to create meanings. It is doubtless illusory to think that a life can be a whole, an artistic unit, whatever ripeness and maturity we attain. But, clearly, there are varying degrees of wholeness and these are to some extent dependent on the number of calendar years attained. The achievement of genuine selfhood appears to me to be almost as much a process in time as, let us say, is the gaining of adequate understanding of a philosophical proposition about genuine selfhood. Authenticity is not attained at once by any of us and is probably never entirely pure, and unalloyed with its opposite. Inner, private time is, to be sure, more relevant as a measure of this growth than is chronological age. But, first, it is a growth,

not an instantaneous state of being, and, second,
this inner, private time is not to be disassoci-
ated, save in thought, from objective, public
time.

The difficulty here is that the existentialists do not go far enough. They are not so much
wrong as they are inadequate. The future is what
Heidegger recognizes it to be—and more. If I am
to achieve the resoluteness Heidegger desires,
the calmness (Gefasst sein) Jaspers cherishes, I
require goals not only future in present thought,
but cumulative progress in calendar time toward
their attainment. I know that they like to speak
of resoluteness as such and commitment without an
object, but their critics have pointed out with
great unanimity the difficulty of being resolute
about resoluteness and committed to commitment.
It is hard to escape the conviction that spiritual growth and relative fulfillment make up a
large part of whatever point our human lives
possess.

If this be granted against the existentialists, we are left, of course, with the problem of
the unrealized, the undeveloped life which is cut
off by an untimely end. Recognizing untimeliness,
as the existentialists do not, we seem to leave
the fact of death as uninterpreted and irrational
as it is in other philosophies. Death seems to
make a mockery of all human potentialities and
dreams. In so far as it is more than a biological
end, it stands before us as a blind, irreconcilable surd. On the one hand, we find it impossible
to resist the existentialists' warning that we
should be ready to die at any moment and hence
should try to make sense of life, independent of
duration. Yet, on the other hand, it is next to
impossible to do this, so arbitrary and ambivalent
is the end of life in full career. The awareness
of death may well be, for many of us, a deep
fountain of possibility, stirring us into full
realization of the preciousness of living. But as
an untimely occurrence, it can be also an unmitigated calamity, defying all efforts at under-

standing. I can only conclude that the yearning for rationality must here make place for religious faith in larger meanings. Though belief in immortality should not tempt us, as it did Spinoza, to deny the reality of death or to avoid facing its great threat, still there must be some deep-seated faith that we are not suspended over an abyss. We can grant the existentialists that awareness of personal death brings greater intensity and clarification to life, but at the same time we need not renounce our conviction that death as an occurrence holds, also, the promise of a greater fullness of Being.

Notes

[1]All the existentialists have treated this concept at length, but the best critical treatment of it I find in Otto Friedrich Bollnow's Existenz Philosophie, Kohlmann Verlag, Stuttgart. I am indebted to this brief, excellent treatise at several points in this essay.
[2]Martin Heidegger, Was ist Metaphysik?, p. 32.
[3]Karl Jaspers, Von der Wahrheit, p. 529.
[4]Martin Heidegger, Sein und Zeit, p. 250.
[5]Karl Jaspers, Philosophie, p. 486.
[6]Ibid., p. 490
[7]Martin Heidegger, Sein und Zeit, p. 325.

The Belief in Life after Death[1]*
    Hywel D. Lewis

There can be little doubt that the greater part of mankind has believed, in some way or at some level, that they have a destiny beyond the fleeting transitory existence we have in the

*From Contemporary Studies in Philosophical Idealism, Thomas O. Buford and John Howie editors, Claude Stark and Co. publishers, 1975, pp. 149-160. Reprinted by permission of the author and publisher.

persent life. This belief is deeply rooted in
most of the great religions, and most persons in
the past have subscribed to some kind of religion.
Even Shinto, although a very secular religion in
some respect, makes much of the worship of ancestors who are thought to be still "around" in some
form. Theravada Buddhism, in spite of its skepticism, at least leaves the matter open and,
while presenting special difficulties for any
view of personal survival, has drifted into forms
of belief and practice which involve at least some
notion of a round of various existences; Mahayana
Buddism makes it very explicit. The so-called
primitive religions seem also to center on the
expectation of some kind of further existence.
How profoundly religious allegiances have affected people's attitudes and how firmly religious
persons have adhered to their professed beliefs
is a more debatable matter. But few things have
affected the general life and culture of people
in the past more than religion: it has been a
main determinant of attitudes, a shaper of major
presuppositions; and it would not be incautious
in the least to affirm on this basis that, at
some level, by far the greater part of mankind
has committed itself to the expectation of a life
besides the present one and has shaped its activities accordingly.

Could the same be said today? There can be
little doubt that most communities today have
become much more secular than at any previous
time. How deep or permanent is this change may
not be easy to settle. Some, like myself, regard
it as a phase in the profounder and more intelligent recovery of religion, although this by no
means involves commendation of secular attitudes
or the canonizing of them as inevitable stages in
some dialectic of religious progress. But without
going further into this particular question, I
would hazard fairly confidently the guess that,
where the question of belief in life after death
is concerned, most persons, if a poll of some kind
were taken, would still return a fairly firm positive answer, even in countries where vast material

changes have brought about considerable seculari-
zation. What importance we should ascribe to that
I leave unanswered for the moment.

Beliefs can be held in a variety of ways and
at different levels. There are at least two main
ways in which this is true in respect to the present theme. A belief can be held at one level only
when we adhere to it in spite of the fact that the
evidence for it (or other reasons for holding it)
is not very strong. There are some beliefs which
we can hold with much more confidence than others.
They need not be the most important beliefs. If
I believe that it is fine and sunny at the moment,
I have only to look up from my desk or step out
into the garden to be sure of this, and anyone
who calls will confirm it. I am equally certain
that I have a pencil in my hand and am writing
with it. I see and hold it, and that is about
the greatest certainty we could have. Philosophical questions could be asked about the status of
things like pencils or the nature of perception.
But for all normal purposes I am as certain as
anyone could wish to be that I am holding a pencil and that the sun is shining. I am not so
certain that the point of this pencil will not
suddenly break or that the weather will hold for
my walk this evening. But the pencil looks firm
enough and the weather seems set for a glorious
day. I make plans accordingly. I am not quite
so certain of what falls outside my immediate
purview, though in many cases as certain as makes
no difference. I am quite certain that King's
College still stands in the Strand. In principle
there could have been some weakness in the structure causing it to collapse this morning, but having heard no hint or rumor of this, I do not give
the possibility serious thought. But there are a
host of other matters, ascertainable in perception, of which I am less certain. A road near my
home in North Wales was closed recently, but I
only learned of this when I go there.

In more serious matters we are often a good
deal more certain of some things than of others.

Some of my acquaintances I trust absolutely, but I am cautious about others. Confidence is sometimes misplaced, and we must go on the strength of the evidence at the time. We likewise adhere with varying degrees of firmness to certain principles, socialism or pacifism for instance, and some are swayed more than others by evidence and rational reflection. But clearly, when a strong case can be made out for something and objections met, we are normally disposed to think favorably of it and try to put prejudice aside. One reason therefore for the weakness of a belief and oscillation in the firmness of our adherence to it is the difficulty of making out a simple overwhelming case, as I can for my belief that it is not raining in my garden at the moment. The belief in a future life cannot be established with that kind of conclusiveness. If it could only idiots would doubt it.

This is what has set many persons searching for some foolproof way of ascertaining that the dead do in fact live again. The most obvious approach here is parapsychology and mediumistic evidence. Some religious people are very contemptuous of this. It will not, so they say, prove the resurrection but only the survival or immortality of the soul, of which some religious people take a curiously dim view. But this is, in my view, a very great mistake. The evidence may not give us all that we want to establish in a religious context—it certainly cannot provide all that the Christian means by "the life eternal." But if it did the trick it would certainly give us a great deal. It might not prove that we live for ever; but if some kind of mediumistic or kindred evidence could be found which made it tolerably certain (as certain as we are about conditions in some of the planets we can more easily study, for example) that someone whose lifeless corpse we had seen put in its coffin and buried or cremated was now all the same unmistakably in communication with us, in whatever trivial a way, this would be momentous.

I can in fact think of nothing that would
startle people more, or have greater news value.
A journalist who failed to report it would obviously be falling down on his job. The trouble is
that there is much to dispute about mediumistic
evidence, and most people take the line that,
while "there may be something in it," it is all
too uncertain to be taken seriously—and in the
meantime there is much to tell against it, including the lifeless corpse. I repeat therefore
that if confidence could be established in the
psychical approach to the question of survival,
it would be a matter of enormous importance. The
issue is not, of course, the straightforward one
of finding conclusive or very impressive evidence;
there are peculiar difficulties about the interpretation of the evidence available, as critics
are not slow to point out. Some views about the
nature of persons would rule out from the start
the interpretation of any evidence in terms of
actual survival, and those who defend the possibility of survival must reckon with such views as
a vital part of their undertaking. But apart from
this, and even allowing for some psychical phenomena, there are differing ways in which it is proposed to interpret the available evidence. Clair-
voyance and telepathy among the living might cover
much of it. I myself find much of the evidence
impressive, and I am even more impressed by the
fact that very clearsighted investigators with the
highest philosophical competence like C. D. Broad
and H. H. Price have thought it worth taking very
seriously, the latter being fully convinced of its
adequacy to establish at least some form of survival.

There are, admittedly, some people who would
prefer the evidence to be negative, and Broad is
perhaps the most notable example. There are indeed disconcerting aspects to the possibility of
another life. It may not by any means be all that
we expect now; but even so, and allowing fully for
the somber side of those possibilities, my own expectation would be that most people would be immensely relieved and excited if they had firm

assurance comparable to that which we may have about ordinary matters of fact that the friends they had lost were alive "somewhere" and might even be contacted, and that their own existence would not come finally to its end at the close of their earthly life. This assurance could in fact make a vast difference to the way we think of ourselves and our lives at present. We do not have to think of morality in terms of rewards and punishments to appreciate what a change it would make to our present attitudes and restlessness if we were certain that this life is "not all."

For these reasons I do not think that religious people should be as contemptuous or suspicious as many seem to be of the investigation of the alleged paranormal evidence for survival. They are indeed entitled to insist that this will not give them any of the essentials of a Christian faith or the reasons for holding it, and we need thus to be warned not to confuse major issues or draw attention away from the sort of assurance on which the Christian faith depends. All the same, an assurance that men do live after they are dead (even if it extends to only a limited period) would make a very considerable breach in the hard wall of skepticism which confronts us now and open men's minds to further possibilities which come closer to the profounder and more exhilarating insights which the Christian claims. It has been said in a classical context that philosophy can "make room for faith." This has sometimes been understood in a way that implies that philosophy has no place in faith as such, and it is, alas, this travesty that appeals most to those who invoke the distinction most often today, thus maintaining an unholy alliance between religious dogmatism or uncritical relativism and philosophical skepticism. This was certainly not Kant's idea, and without pretending to follow him further in how he thought of faith, we can insist that there are rational ingredients capable of philosophical refinement at the center of a religious faith. Nonetheless, philosophical and other secular assurances which do not affect the core of

606

a Christian commitment can help to open men's minds to possibilities which prepare the way for a deeper religious understanding.

There are a great many ways in which this holds today, and there are many important and exciting tasks for religious philosophers who rightly understand their prospects and have the energy and courage to persist. But I cannot investigate these now; I must content myself with the insistence that philosophical and scientific investigation of the religious implications and possibilities of psychical research is a respectable and important part of seeking a better understanding and acceptance of Christian beliefs. The pitfalls are many, but that is no reason for avoiding the subject as many religious thinkers do today. If the results prove negative no harm is done, for this is not what faith turns upon; if positive, a great deal is gained. In any case, our first concern is with the truth, disconcerting or otherwise.

I come now to the second main way in which a belief may be held "at one level" of our minds only, namely when we believe, as it is sometimes put, with "one side of our minds" or "one part of us." To some extent, this is true of all of us, and it needs to be reckoned with more than is commonly the case in matters of belief. In extreme cases we have the situation memorably described by Plato in his account of what he called "the democratic man:"

> Day after day he gratifies the pleasures as they come—now fluting down the primrose path of wine, now given over to teetotalism and banting; one day in hard training, the next slacking and idling, and the third playing the philosopher. Often he will take to politics, leap to his feet and do or say whatever comes into his head; or he conceives an admiration for a general, and his interests are in war; or for a man of business, and straightway that is his line. He knows no order or

necessity in life; but he calls life as he conceives it pleasant and free and divinely blessed, and is ever faithful to it.

This is not, in the main at least, a case of insincerity or hypocrisy. In certain moods men genuinely do believe what they do not believe at all at other times. This is how some well-known public figures leave the impression of a deep insincerity of which they may not really be guilty. They really do believe, perhaps quite fervently at times, what they also seem to reject or disregard, though there may be insincerity as well. We are, all of us, more of a mixture than we care to admit.

There has, on occasion, been serious commendation of this frame of mind, as in some doctrines of a dual standard or in the nineteenth century notion of a "truth of the heart" which could ease the intellectual strain for us by being entertained alongside an incompatible "truth of the mind." I hope no one today encourages this kind of intellectual schizophrenia. But we must all be on our guard against the insidiousness of our temptation to lapse into it in subtle ways.

It is here also that we may find the element of truth in John Baillie's famous account of believing something "at the bottom of our hearts" which we deny "at the top of our minds." Baillie's mistake was to suppose that this must be true of all unbelief. That is certainly not the way to take the measure of unbelief or the magnitude of our task in resisting it. But it may well cover many cases; and even notable atheists, like Bertrand Russell, come sometimes very close to the substance of what we profess.

The sum of this, for our purpose (it is a theme of great importance which needs to be treated more fully on its own account), is that our beliefs need to be cultivated. That is not a commendation of wishful thinking or of naive refusal to look serious difficulties in the face. But profound and precious beliefs about spiritual matters can neither be achieved nor maintained in a casual way. This is again what we learn from Plato, who spoke eloquently about "the long and toilsome route" out of the cave and how easy it is to lose a true belief or to substitute for it a merely superficial opinion. We have to be like athletes, a comparison to which St. Paul was also very prone, resisting "the softer influence of pleasure" and "the sterner influence of fear."

The saints have indeed been well aware of this: they are constantly wrestling with doubt and despair; the pilgrim sinks deep in the Slough of Despond; our hymns are full of varieties of mood, from triumphant certainties to deep despair, from the hilltops to the valleys and the shadows; and this is as it should be—we have to win our way through doubt to firm belief and the renewal of belief. But this is no mere intellectual matter; it is more a maintaining of the set of our thoughts and dispositions, of living with the evidence which leads to spiritual discernment; and for this reason we should welcome the importance that is accorded today to contemplation. Meditation has its discipline, and there are those who can guide us. This is often travestied and sometimes almost equated with physical exercises or mechanical stimuli. We need to understand much better what contemplation means, for it is in the fullness of meditation, which extends to thought and practice alike, that faith is renewed. This will have rational ingredients among which philosophical thought has a prominent place.

The belief in life after death is not an easy one. There is much to induce us to identify ourselves with our bodies, and philosophers today find it hard to avoid that. This is not the place to put the case against them—I have tried to do that elsewhere. But we all know what will happen soon to our bodies. They will rot or be burned. To believe seriously that we can survive this needs some very clear thinking, and I do not discount in this context the oddity we all feel, I imagine, of the notion of our own total extinction. But what I most wish to stress at the moment is the strenuousness at the intellectual level, and at the level of committed religious living, of maintaining a genuine belief. Belief in life after death is a momentous one, and the burden of our witness to it has come to be taken too lightly.

In the sophisticated thinking relevant to a belief in afterlife, there is one item of exceptional importance to which I wish to draw attention and which will be my chief concern for the remainder of this discussion. It is at this point that I find myself sharply at odds with Plato and with the vast range of philosophical thinking for which he has been largely responsible. Plato, you will recall, maintained that genuine reality consisted of certain general principles, the ideas or the forms, as we call them. These are not concepts, though the best way for us to begin to understand them is in terms of universals; they are in his view real, indeed the only true reality. They are also closely interrelated, and in the progress of Plato's own thought there is a deepening insistence on the essential interrelatedness of the forms. At the center and transcending all is the form of the Good; and it is in our glimpse or vision of this at the end of our toilsome route that we find our clue to the ultimate necessity of all the rest.

Particular things, it is thus affirmed, "the choir of heaven and the furniture of earth" (in the words of a kindred but more down-to-earth spirit), in the rush and travail of our own lives derive such reality as they have from the forms themselves; they have a questionable borrowed reality. The wise man will seek to draw away from the insubstantial fleeting world of particulars and center his thought not on "shadows" but on the only true realities, the forms. He will in this sense seek what is "above." It is significant that, in spite of this denigration of the particular and the seeming exclusiveness of the bifurcation into the world of particulars and the

world of forms, Plato continues to think of the
soul as essentially individual. Exactly where it
fits is not clear but it is certain that Plato
never wavers on this—the soul is the individual,
now and always; and it is also for Plato immortal
because it is essentially indestructible, and it
is indestructible because it has an essential affinity with the forms; the eternal world of forms
is its home.

It is this affinity with the world of forms
that Plato stresses most of all in claiming the
immortality of the soul. The inadequacy of his
other argumentation has often been exposed, but
his main considerations provide a not unimpres-
sive view of the immortality of the soul. It has
many of the ingredients we would also stress:
the sense of the inevitable transitoriness of our
present existence, the urgency with which we are
pressed to look to the things "above" (almost as
the Bible tells us to "lay up treasures for yourselves in heaven, where neither moth nor rust
doth corrupt"), the abiding conviction that at
the heart of all is the absolute transcendent
Good, the source of our being and our home. We
must not despise this understanding; it is never
monistic, "soul is soul" whatever else we say,
and it has helped extensively to shape Christian
understanding at various times. But it has one
radical weakness. It does not take proper account of the here and now. This is not because
Plato adopts an unmitigated otherworldly view as
in extreme monism. He set the course, on the
contrary, for the effective rebuttal of the arguments of Parmenides, whose force he well appreciated. The philosopher, in some ways like the
avatar, has to return to succor and provide for
others. In the world of forms there is an essential variety. Nonetheless the particular, whether
in the world of nature or in our own lives, tends
to count solely as a reflection of the true reality of eternal verities. The persistence of
this view is the source of the main points of disagreement one would have with Plato.

611

This is seen to good advantage in Plato's treatment of the family and personal relations. He did not think physical enjoyment in any form an evil thing, but he rated it very lowly, not appreciating how physical enjoyment enters into a fuller experience to make it more meaningful. The intimacy of full personal encounter and a rounded friendship seems to give way before the idea of the blueprint and the pattern laid up in heaven (which is surprising in view of Plato's own enjoyment of excellent friendships and his great regard for Socrates). Appetite tends to remain brute appetite; it does not become an ingredient in a richer experience. For the same reasons, the morally or physically handicapped receive very harsh treatment. If they do not play their proper part in the fulfillment of "the pattern," they are dispensable. The same clues yield us the secret of Plato"s famous perversity about poetry and the arts. A very great literary artist himself, and very consciously attracted to poetry, he would have none of it officially. This is because he understood well that poetry does not deal in essences or universal notions—a point about which our late and gifted friend Dr. Austin Farrer was peculiarly confused.[2] Art is some illumination of the particular, even in its rarefied and abstract forms, and it is for this reason that literature, music, painting and all the other arts are accorded such a very lowly place in a scheme of things which puts all its premium on the impersonal and eternal aspect of things.[3]

This is where true religion provides its corrective, and that is why Plato can never set the model for a truly religious philosophy. For religion, as I understand it, has always an element of revelation at the core of it; and in revelation the transcendent discloses and shapes itself for our illumination in a peculiar involvement of itself with a particular situation, a time and place at which the revelation happens notwithstanding that it may not always be precisely specifiable. The disclosure is to someone, and may well include some transmutation of what is presented immediately in his environment. It speaks of the "beyond," but it is also altogether of the here and now. Others may appropriate it, and it takes its place in the exchanges of committed religious living as the gradual refinement of our understanding of God and the sense of his presence.

This puts immeasurable worth on particular things, on an essentially created world in which the divine splendor shines, and on the lives of all. All the earth is holy, a "sacramental universe" as it has been boldly put, and personal existence as the peculiar center of divine involvement acquires a significance which nothing can efface, a place at the heart of the life of God. This is what the mystic perceives and this is why he speaks of an absorption in which God is all in all. This is a travesty if, as often happens, it is taken neat. God is God, but the point of true religion is the discovery of our place in the life of God himself, and as the disclosure deepens and the essentially self-giving character of it reveals itself, as the bond tightens, we know that we are "of God" and have no home but God. The inestimable worth that is placed on each, even "weak things" and "things that are despised," puts the question of the elimination of anything out of the question. This is in some ways a terrible truth for us to realize, for whatever is evil in our lives or persons is present there in this holy relationship. It is no wonder, therefore, that outstandingly saintly persons have been so peculiarly tormented by the sense of sin as to seem to others obsessed and unbalanced. We may much resent the words "sinners in the hands of an angry God," and indeed few things have been more travestied and misdirected, in theory or experience, than the sense of sin and the fear of God. But there is a certain horror, and an abysmal consuming wretchedness—the worm that does not die—in the spectacle of one's own life aglow in all its forms in the life of God. That is where the costliness of redeeming love begins to be seen.

In the peculiar claims of the Christian religion, the unfolding of divine love in history
and the manifold experiences of men is alleged to
come to a finality of fulfillment in Christ.
Here God himself comes as a man to put the seal of
his redeeming activity on the indissoluble bond
of our own lives in his. Of the way we must understand this, and of the infinite sadness of the
many travesties of it, we cannot speak here. But
the Christian should have no doubt about "the
price that was paid." Christianity without sacrifice does not begin to get off the ground, and
it is in the sacrifice we celebrate in a holy communion that we find the ultimate seal on our own
abiding destiny as sons of God. There can be no
elimination of what is so completely of God himself.

These assurances in no way dispense with the
need for thought; they have thought at the core of
them. The wise Christian will come to terms with
this, most of all in a developing culture. Insight is not random, and faith is not blind. Both
are at the opposite poles to unreason. There is
much work also in preparing the ground: in dealing, for example, with problems about the nature
of persons, as indicated earlier, in sifting the
evidence of psychical research, and in hard
thought about the peculiarly tantalizing problem
presented by extensive evil in a world governed by
divine love. The latter problem does in fact find
some easement in the present case in the very substance of what faith affirms; for, in the affirmation of a life beyond, we do have a broader can-
vas on which to view the various ills men endure
now. Compensation in after life could afford a
partial solution at least to the problem of evil,
and some of the most impressive writers on the
subject of late, such as C. A. Campbell, A. C.
Ewing and John Hick, give it particular prominence. I go more cautiously with it, as indeed do
Campbell and Ewing, because I wish to stand firmly
on our present assurances. In these the feeling

we have that it would be strange for personal existence to be eclipsed for reasons incidental to what our natures properly are and what we do deserves more prominence than is often accorded to it; and here the study of other religions could be very relevant. But the main weight has still to be placed on the peculiar assurance of faith through divine disclosure.

This lends particular urgency at the present time to the proclamation of Christian truth and our witness to it. This should include at center the affirmation of a life beyond, and if we fail in this we shall place a serious limitation on any renewal of faith in our time. The relevance of our proclamation to present ills will be much weakened. This is not because the new problems of today spring directly from irreligion; they come about largely through the complexities of a changed situation and marked advances in our understanding of ourselves and our environment. At the same time the limiting of our horizons to the here and now is not without profound effect, and, on the positive side, the transformation in attitude and expectation which could be induced by a detached and objective sense of illimitable possibilities of richer experience would be hard to calculate. The palliatives and substitutes would easily dwindle beside it.

It is in the context of this expectation and the renewal of faith in its fullness that the Christian should consider the question of a life after death. The hope we have in this precise sense is not a luxury, a secondary consideration to be investigated on its own account; it belongs to the essence of a Christian commitment. To tie that to some isolated doctrine of the Resurrection, or make the Resurrection stories pivotal on their own account, is a bad mistake. The work and person of Christ must be taken in its fullness, but it seems to be unthinkable that it should not be thought to include, in explicit word and in implication, the affirmation of our abiding place at the heart of God's love. We can form little con-

615

ception of what this will be; the new dimensions of it go far beyond our present limitations and boldest speculation, involving transformations of the quality of life as much as its formal scope. It does not yet "appear what we shall be" but we shall be "like him," and that, to any who consider the matter seriously, is about as remarkable an expectation as that we shall exist without our present bodies. Indeed, it is in many ways the most bewildering item of our faith, as sober realistic theologians appreciated earlier in this century, however muddled in other ways. This is nonetheless the bold truth the Christian must proclaim, and in the long run we do better with the daunting character of the full Christian assurance than with half-hearted humanist travesties of it. That is one reason why narrowly dogmatic Christians succeed better, for a time at least, then the rest of us. Other reasons are less estimable. An enduring faith must be open and reflective. But it must be _faith_ and the fullness of it, and that unmistakably includes our own conservation, sancitified beyond our dimmest understanding and renewed in the knowledge of the price that was paid, at the heart of the life of God. "For God so loved the world, that he gave his only begotten Son, that whosoever believeth in him, should not perish but have everlasting life." There is no Christian faith without "everlasting life," and it is in the fullness of faith, as a rounded personal apprehension, that this life of "the world to come" becomes also our proper possession "in this time now." In essentials it is all a matter of the right kind of faith.

Notes

[1] The Drew Lecture delivered at the Whitefield Memorial Church on October 20, 1973, and printed by permission of the Trustees, New College, London.
[2] See The Glass of Vision (Westminster: Dacre Press, 1948), chap. 7, pp. 113-131, and my comment in Our Experience of God, chap. 7, pp. 131-

145.

³Cf. my paper "On Poetic Truth," in <u>Morals and Revelation</u> (London: Allen & Unwin, 1951), chap. 10, pp. 232-255.